MODERN WEED MANAGEMENT

WITH SPECIAL REFERENCE TO AGRICULTURE IN THE TROPICS AND SUBTROPICS

THIRD FULLY UPDATED AND ENLARGED EDITION

O. P. Gupta
Ex-Director of Research
Rajasthan Agricultural University,
Bikaner

AGROBIOS (INDIA)

Published by:
AGROBIOS (INDIA)
Agro House, Behind Nasrani Cinema
Chopasani Road, Jodhpur 342 002
Phone: 91-0291-2642319, Fax: 2643993
E. mail: agrobios@sify.com

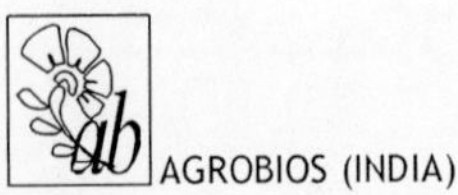
AGROBIOS (INDIA)

First Edition 1998
Second Edition 2004
Third Edition 2007

ISBN No.: 978-81-7754-413-8

Published by: Dr. Updesh Purohit for Agrobios (India), Jodhpur ***Lasertypeset at:*** Yashee Computers, Jodhpur
Cover Design by: Reena
Printed at: AGROBIOS DIGITALS, Jodhpur

We have to choose
between feeding:
the weeds
or
the crops

Dedicated to all concerned
with Weed Management

PREFACE TO THE THIRD EDITION

Weed science is perhaps one agricultural science that is making advances by leaps and bounds; both in terms of identification of the new problems and inventing their new solutions. Weed species are not only changing their dominance patterns worldwide, but these are also bringing forth several new herbicide resistant races. New alien weeds are invading our land (and water) time and again, and, thus, disturbing the native biodiversity of the region under attack. Herbicides developed to tackle such ever growing weed problems are posing concerns about their possible residues in our food and water. Hundreds of research papers are being published every year round the world to resolve these and many more weed management related problems in order to ensure sustainable agriculture and food security. Keeping all such aspects of the progress of weed science in view, the author strongly felt need to religiously update and enlarge the previous edition of Modern Weed Management, which is now in your hands.

A unique feature of the progress of weed science research is that the past findings never become inapposite or behind the times, bar a very few basic physiological elements of the herbicide behaviour. The fast accumulating new research information actually advances the past valuable findings, without acting as replacements to these. *Consequently, in the present edition of the book while the past findings of even 1966 have been retained, there is a thematic updating of the chapters with the current most research results reported up to the year 2007*. Further, the completely new topics created in the subject have been discussed in the book by supplementing it with two new chapters. The intense updating of the old chapters and addition of the new ones collectively reflect the exciting developments in weed science in this third edition of Modern Weed Management. I hope the readers shall enjoy reading it as much as I did working on it for them.

Suggestions are welcome from the readers for their possible use in future editions of the book.

O. P. G.

CONTENTS

12 IMPORTANT HERBICIDE FAMILIES AND MOLECULES 177

13 THE FUNCTIONAL FEATURES OF COMMON HERBICIDES........203

APPENDICES

Chapter 1

THE WEED MENACE

Plants are man's most valuable assets without which he could not have survived on earth. But we cannot afford to let them grow indiscriminately all over the land and water-bodies, else a place for us and our activities will be difficult to find. Of the more than 300,000 species of plants known in the world, hardly 3,000 are of economic value to us. When one grows any of these economic species of plants, invariably, a variety of volunteer vegetation comes up simultaneously which is competitive and undesirable. Besides, several plants are unwanted because either these are responsible for many a human and animal health hazard, or they hamper the activities of man in some other ways. Human concerns regarding such plants - the weeds - are described in this first chapter.

1.1 WEEDS DEFINED

A weed is a plant growing where it is not desired. This definition of weed, as one would note, does not identify a particular portion of plant kingdom as weedy. Rather, it tags the weedy nature of a plant to the situation in which it occurs and the human attitude towards it. Thus, a plant could be undesirable at one place and desirable, or of little concern, at the other. Bermudagrass (*Cynodon dactylon)*, foxtail (*Cenchrus ciliaris*) and goosegrass (*Eleusine indica*), for instance, are valuable plants in pastures, but in crop fields these are well known inapposite troublesome weeds. Likewise, quackgrass (*Agropyron repens*) forms a very good soil binding plant on certain erodable lands, but it is a serious weed in arable crop fields and orchards. Pricklypear (*Opuntia* spp.) is an effective biological fence plant, as well as a valuable plant in deserts to hold the sand. But in pastures and rangelands of many countries, including India, it has become a very aggressive weed on millions of hectares of otherwise productive land. Waterlily (*Nymphaea* sp.), lotus (*Nelumbo* sp.), and waternut (*Trapa natans*) are amongst the most troublesome aquatic weeds, yet these are cultivated in specific water-bodies as ornamental or edible root/fruit plants. Not only this, even the self-sown crop plants like sorghum, pearlmillet, and soybean growing in patches in some other crops, say cotton or sugarcane, are to be considered as weeds. Petunia, an attractive floricultural plant, likewise may become a weed on agricultural lands.

Fig. 1.1: Weeds, with their numerous species and land races, are time-tested plants adapted to grow under severe biotic and abiotic stresses in a wide range of agroclimatic conditions. *Top* = A sugarcane plant badly chocked with weeds, largely *Trianthema* sp. *Bottom* = A bean crop; the *right* half infested severely with weeds, particularly the grasses, and the *left* half herbicide-treated, weedfree crop rows.

Further, there are numerous plants which grow on roadsides without any concern to man beyond a green looking vegetation. But when these very plants hinder the proper vision of the curves on the roads, these form weedy vegetation for the motorists. *To conclude, basically it is the situation involving space and time, as well as the individual's interest in it, which class a particular component of vegetation as weedy, and that there is no part of the flora classified as weeds by either the nature or the scientists.*

A corollary to the discussion on above definition of weeds, is that these are ***plants growing in places and at times when we wanted either some other plants to grow or no plant to grow at all.*** So long as a plant is growing at a place and time without interfering with man's interests, it is not looked upon as a weed. In other words, while all weeds are unwanted plants, all unwanted plants may not be weeds. In this sense it is very important that plants listed as weeds are qualified by the situation in which they adversely affect man's affairs. This situation may be a crop field, roadside, utility rights-of-way, air field, water-body, woodland, garden, orchard, *etc.*

Despite the good intentions of the above accepted definitions of weed, for all intents and purposes, about 30,000 plant species have been identified as weedy in the world infesting various crop and non-crop land situations, including the aquatic environment. (see later Chapter -3 and Appendix-1).

Fig. 1.2: The choice is between harvesting the weeds and the crop. *Left* = A weedy crop of wheat. *Right* = A weedfree crop of wheat. The major weed in the field was *Chenopodium album*.

Fig. 1.3: Crops fail to express their full genetic yield potential in the presence of weeds. *Top* = A maize crop almost completely overpowered with variety of weeds, prominently *Ipomoea* sp. *Bottom* = A weedfree crop of maize with healthy cobs. Don't let your grains be stolen by weeds.

1.2 WEED MENACE IN AGRICULTURE

Weeds are ubiquitous and insidious tyrants on earth. Their presence in and around agricultural land inflicts enormous losses which must be borne by all of us. Still, their menace is often ignored because they lack the drama and publicity of sudden outbreaks; so very commonly exhibited by several plant diseases and insect pests. Weed scientists know this, but others, unfortunately, do not. The sight of an uniformly suppressed growth of a weedy crop often does not distract a passer-by till it comes to harvesting. Even then there is tendency to ascribe the low crop yields to causes other than the weeds. But the fact remains that directly the weeds reduce the crop yields and, indirectly, they elevate farm production costs through energy spent in controlling them.

Further, the negative values of weeds are depicted during harvesting, marketing, storage, and dockage of the weedy crops. Add to this the increased pests and diseases in different crops in the succeeding years and menace to our irrigation systems. Recent estimates by an Indian industry chamber, Assocham, placed the collective crop losses due to weeds, insect pests, and plant pathogens in 2006-07 in India at Rs 14 lac million. The weeds are notorious in being responsible for major part of this loss.

1.2.1 Reduction in Crop Yields and Production Efficiency

Exhaustive scientific data are available on the losses caused by uncontrolled growth of weeds in the productivity of different crops. Some of these experimental data are summarised in Table 1.1 which show yield reductions of 34.3% to 89.8%. On country basis such losses in crop yields have been estimated at 15-30% in wheat, 30-35% in rice, and 18-85% each in maize, sorghum, pulses, and oilseeds (Mukhopadhyay, 1991-92). But as the farmers adopt some kind of weeding in their fields, it still leaves us with a conservative estimate of at least 10% reduction in crop yields*. Unfortunately, such estimates on yield losses caused by weeds in orchard and plantation crops in India are presently unavailable.

Besides the direct reductions in crop yields inflicted due to the presence of weeds, there are many indirect ways by which the weeds may be troublesome in agriculture. For example, in weedy fields farm operations like application of fertilizers, insecticides, and irrigation become cumbersome. Even when a crop is made despite the presence of weeds, it may be difficult to harvest it, particularly when prickly weeds like wild safflower (*Carthamus oxyacantha*), Canada thistle (*Cirsium arvense*), and cocklebur (*Xanthium strumarium*) invade the fields. Cowage (*Mucuna pruriens*) riles the harvest labour by causing itching. Bindweed (*Convolvulus arvensis*) and morningglories (*Ipomoea* spp.) bind the crop plants together so well that their harvesting becomes almost impossible. The weeds at harvest time also bring about excessive wear and tear of the farm machines. Add to this the cost of separating weed seeds (and fruits) from the grain and other farm produce. There is yet another way the weeds limit our annual agricultural production. This is by permanently occupying the thousands of hectares of otherwise productive land and taking these out of cultivation.

**It has been estimated that losses in crop yields due to weeds in advanced countries are 5%, and in the least developed countries, about 25%.*

Fig. 1.4: In the early stages of growth of a crop like cotton, the weeds often hide the crop plants. Note the alternate strips of weedfree (*front*) and weedy crop (*middle*).

Table 1.1: Losses in Crop Yields Caused by Uncontrolled Growth of Weeds

Crop	Yield in q/ha			Source
	Weedfree	Weedy	loss (%)	
Food Crops				
Wheat (*Triticum aestivum*)	27.7	18.2	34.3	Tiwari & Parihar (1993)
Barley (*Hordeum vulgare*)	41.6	25.2	39.4	Balyan & Malik (1994)
Rice (*Oryza sativa*)	68.9	21.1	69.4	Singh *et al.* 1991)
Sorghum (*Sorghum vulgare*)	53.0	36.8	30.6	Satao & Nalamwar (1992)
Pearlmillet (*Pennisetum glaucum*)	34.6	19.6	43.4	Kumar & Shaik (1993)
Maize (*Zea mays*)	31.8	13.1	58.8	Sharma & Natiyal (1993)
Chickpea (*Cicer arietinum*)	20.6	10.4	49.5	Singh & Singh (1992)
Blackgram (*Vigna mungo*)	13.5	9.4	30.4	Rita *et al.* (1995)
Greengram (*Vigna radiata*)	11.2	5.8	48.2	Sandhu *et al.* (1993)
Lentil (*Lens culinaris*)	23.6	13.5	42.8	Parmar *et al.* (1994)
Peas (*Pisum sativum*)	19.0	11.9	37.4	Kundra *et al.* (1993)
Redgram (*Cajanus cajan*)	16.5	10.8	34.5	Vaishya (1993)
Fatty Oil Crops				
Groundnut (*Arachis hypogaea*)	28.6	10.5	63.3	Yadav *et al.*(1986)
Mustard (*Brassica juncea*)	18.5	12.3	33.5	Yadav *et al* (1995)
Soybean (*Glycine max*)	20.8	12.7	38.	Singh & Kolar (1994)
Sunflower (*Helianthus annus*)	15.4	11.4	26.0	Patel *et al* (1994)
Fibre Crops				
Cotton (*Gossypium* spp.)	23.4	12.3	47.4	Panwar *et al.* (1995)
Jute (*Corchorus capsularis*)	21.5	11.1	48.4	Singh *et al.* (1994)
Sugar Crops				
Sugarcane (*Saccharum spontaneum*)	763.0	467.0	38.8	Chauhan & Singh (1993)
Sugarbeet (*Beta vulgaris*)	802.0	238.0	70.3	Srivastava & Singh (1979)
Vegetable Crops				
Cauliflower (*Brassica oleracea*)	80.8	41.6	48.5	Porwal & Singh (1993)
Okra (*Hibiscus esculentus*)	106.8	10.9	89.8	Singh *et al.* (1993)
Carrot (*Daucus carota*)	134.2	35.6	73.5	Singh & Malik (1983)
Onion (*Allium cepa*)	230.97	21.57	90.7	Singh & Singh (1994)
Potato (*Solanum tuberosum*)	188.0	135.0	28.2	Singh & Lal (1994)
Other Crops				
Fodder maize (*Z. mays*)	374.3	119.0	68.2	Singh & Prasad (1994)
Mint (*Mentha arvensis*) (herbage)	257.0	41.0	84.0	Jaidev *et al.* (1993)
Tobacco (*Nicotiana tabacum*) (cured leaf)	1373.0	293.0	78.7	Raghuvanshi & Sannibabu (1991)

The yield and quality of crops may be hampered by weeds in yet another way. Growing within and outside the fields these frequently provide shelter to insect pests and disease organisms of crops and act as alternate hosts to these, both during the crop season and off season. Later, the specific insect pests and disease organisms migrate to the main crops where they inflict high intensity damage. Some such observations are tabulated in Table 1.2.

Fig. 1.5: A weedy (*Top*) and weedfree (*Bottom*) crop of beans (Courtesy: NRCWS, Jabalpur).

Table 1.2: Some Examples of Weeds Acting as Alternate Hosts of Crop Pests and Diseases for Providing Either Feed, Shelter, or Reproductive Sites* (*From: Doederlein and Sites (1993); Du Rant et al. (1994), Ellis (1992); Hu & Nie (1989); Jaidev et al. (1993) Larson (1994); Shanower et al. (1993), Suhardi (1993); Yang et al. (1994), and others*

Host Weed	Insect-pest/disease organism hosted	Crop affected
Weeds Hosting Insect-pests		
Aeschynomene sp.	Grasshoppers (vectors of *Colletotrichum*)	Rice
Achyranthus sp.	leaf eating caterpillars	Lucerne and maize
Brassica kaber	Aphids	Brassica crops and brinjal
B. kaber, *Ipomoea* spp., and *Plantago* spp.	Melon aphis	Melons, cucumbers, and squashes
Chenopodium album and *Amaranthus* and *Datura* spp.	Gram caterpillar	Redgram, cotton, okra, pea, tomato and brinjal
C. album	Stalk borer	Tomato, maize, lilies, and asters
Crotolaria sp.	Hairy caterpillar	Castor
Digera arvensis and *Amaranthus* spp.	Caterpillars	Tobacco and cruciferous crops
Echinochloa, *Panicum,* and *Zizania* spp.	Stem borer	Rice
Kochia, *Amaranthus,* and *Salvia* spp.	Thrips	Onion
Solanum spp.	Weevils	Bell pepper
Tinospora cordifolia	Fruit sucking moth	Citrus
Trianthema, *Solanum,* and *Chenopodium* spp.	Greasy cutworm	potato, chickpea and pea.
Weeds Hosting Plant Pathogens		
Agropyron, *Verticillum*, and *Portulaca* spp.	Wilt	Tomato
C. album, *Polygonum* spp., *Senecio* sp., and *Stelaria* sp.	*Aphanomyces* spp.	Spinach
Cynodon dactylon and *Digitaria* sp.	Sting nematode	Several vegetables
Cenchrus ciliaris	Ergot	Pearlmillet
Commelina spp.	Certain viral diseases and parasitic nematodes	Banana
Daucus carota	Blight	Carrot
Euphorbia hypercifolia	Anthracnose	Shallot (*Allium cepa* group)
Leersia oryzoides	Bacterial blight	Rice
Melothria pendula	Mosaic vectors	Watermelon
Plantago and *Veronica* spp.	T. M. Virus	Tobacco and tomato
Salsola kali	Curly top virus vectors	Sugarbeet
Saccharum spontaneum	Downy mildew	Maize
Solanum and *Physalis* spp.	Mosaic and cyst nematode	Solanaceous vegetables, tobacco, and cocoa.

Fig. 1.6: *Top* = A wheat field badly infested with littleseed canarygrass (*Phalaris minor*). Note its inflorescence as distinctly different from the wheat ears, although at their seedling stages the two plants apparently look alike. *Bottom* = A wheat field kept free of canarygrass with postemergent isoporturon.

1.2.2 Erosion of Crop Quality

Weeds mar the quality of farm produce in many ways. Contamination of food grains with weed seeds, particularly of poisonous nature, fetches low price. The weedy grains produce flour with bad odour. In warehouses the weed seeds and weed fragments continue respiration and thus cause the grain to heat and rot. In tea the presence of loranthus (*Dendrophthoe falcata*) impairs its quality. In cotton the dry weed fragments adhered to its lint hinder its spinning process. In dryland agriculture weeds cause severe moisture stress and force the food grains to shrivel. The vegetables and fruits are discoloured and deshaped in the presence of weeds. *Cirsium arvense,* a common weed of mint plantations, when crushed with the mint leaves weakens its oil quality.

Fig. 1.7: Orchards too require weedfree environment for their healthy tree growth. Note the weedy area in the background and the herbicide-treated area in the foreground

1.3 WEED MENACE IN ANIMAL HUSBANDRY

Growing with the forage crops, weeds often help to fill the carts and silos but it is in the milk and meat returns that their damage becomes apparent. The chemical analyses of the weedy and weedfree forages may sometimes not show differing nutritive values, particularly when there are leguminous weeds in the mixture, but it is in the feeding tests that the animals exhibit clear preference for the weedfree forages. When some hungry animals are forced to feed upon a weedy forage, their meat and milk get odd-flavoured and tainted. Weeds like *Cichorium intybus, Allium* spp., *Argemone mexicana, Brassica kaber, Anthemis cotula, Thalapsi sp., Ambrosia sp., Helenium sp.,* and *Oxalis acetosella* are particularly notorious in this respect.

Certain weeds cause sickness in farm animals while others may prove fatal due to high levels of specific alkaloids, tannins, oxalates, glucosides, or nitrates. Halogeton (*H. glomeratus*) a weed of arid and semiarid regions, has brought death to herds of sheep with its high oxalate content. Johnsongrass (*Sorghum halepense*) at its tillering stage and *Xanthium pungens* at its cotyledon stage are poisonous to animals due to their high prussic acid contents. Corncockle (*Agrostemma githago*) seeds have been found poisonous to horses, cattle, and poultry. Their toxic principle is githagin (or agrostemine). Puncturevine (*Tribullus terrestris*), a weed of drylands, induces in sheep extrasensitivity to light. Also, its thorny fruits cause sores in the hooves of the grazing farm animals. The spiny fruits of *Xanthium strumarium, Achyranthus aspera, Cenchrus settigerous, Cirsium arvense,* and *Cenchrus incertus* stick on to the mouth, tail, and body of animals which annoys or irks them badly.

The leaves of lantana (*Lantana camara*) induce acute photosensitivity and jaundice in animals due to their toxic principle 'Lantradene- A'. Carrotgrass (*Parthenium hysterophorus*) causes contact dermatitis in livestock and it is reported to be poisonous to sheep. *Ageratum* spp. growing in abundance in Himalayas and Nilgiris are often found hazardous to livestock. In Rajasthan there is growing concern about rapid spread of the weed golden crownbeard (*Verbesina enceliodes*) since it is poisonous to sheep and goat. Locoweeds (*Astragalus* and *Oxytropis* spp.) inflict abortive and tetratogenic effects on sheep and cattle. Such weeds possess a toxic alkaloid 'swainsonine'. *Lupinus sericeus* induces crooked calf disease in cattle. *Rhododendron* sp. has been found responsible for causing diarrhoea in the grazing milch animals in Kashmir. It also stains the milk of the affected animals with blood.

Leafy spurge (*Euphorbia esula*) causes scours and weakness in cattle, and it is fatal to sheep. *Crotolaria* sp. is fatal to chick. Sweetclover (*Melitotus alba*) contains a dicumarin which acts as an antiblood – coagulant in animals. *Heliotropium amplexicaule, Helenium* spp., and *Datura stramonium* are other sickening weeds for the farm animals.

Under drought conditions weeds like *Chenopodium, Amaranthus, Cirsium,* and *Polygonum* spp. develop nitrate levels as high as 1000 ppm or more, which causes asphyxia in animals. Spines of *Tribullus terrestris* can puncture animal skin. When ingested these can also injure the stomach. The hair of neetle (*Urtica urens*) can cause severe itching and inflammation in animals.

1.4 WEED MENACE TO HUMAN HEALTH

Health, comfort, and work efficiency of man are adversely affected by weeds. Numerous people are plagued year after year with hay fever and asthma aggravated by pollens of *Ambrosia artemissifolia* and *Franseria* sp. The airborne pollens and other biotic particles of several other weeds belonging to diverse families are known to cause rhinitis and conjuctivitis. Carrotgrass (*Parthenium hysterophorus*), poison ivy (*Rhus* spp.), common regweed (*Ambrosia artemesiifolia*), and sneezeweed (*Helenium* spp.) are held responsible for different kinds of dermal allergies in humans.

Weeds provide food, protection, and habitat for the reproduction of vectors of fatal human diseases. Aquatic weeds like waterlettuce (*Pistia lanceolata*), salvinia (*Salvinia auriculata*) and alligatorweed (*Alternanthera* sp.) shelter the alternate hosts and vectors of malaria, yellow fever, encephalitis, dengue fever, and filariasis. Tsetse fly, which transmits African sleeping sickness (trypanosomiasis) causing protozoan, flourishes under the cover of brush weeds. Eyegnats, serving as vectors of mastitis and tropical ulcer, also breed on certain weeds.

Then there are weeds which cause direct food poisoning. Wheat flour contaminated with the seeds of corncockle (*Agrostemma githago*) gives bread a bitter taste and irritates the gastric-tract of the consumer. Mexican poppy (*Agremone mexicana*) seeds crushed with mustard seeds have brought death and blindness to thousands of people in India. Milk from animals feeding upon this weed can cause glaucoma in humans. The *Argemone* toxicity is due to alkaloids sanguinarine and 11-Oxotriacontanoic acid. Some other poisonous weed seeds are from darnel (*Lolium temulentum*), wildmustard (*Brassica kaber*), saponaria (*Saponaria vaccaria*), and wildgarlic (*Allium vineale*). Their seeds often contaminate our food grains.

1.5 WEED MENACE TO AQUATIC ECOSYSTEMS

Not only on land, weeds are a nuisance also in and around water-bodies. Aquatic weeds make their appearance repulsive and decline their recreational values. In other water-bodies they hinder navigation and fishing. Water-flow in irrigation canals and channels is slowed. The potable and drinking water-bodies are fouled by the presence of decomposing aquatic weeds (Gupta, 2001).

1.6 WEED MENACE TO INDUSTRY AND PUBLIC UTILITIES

Weeds growing on industrial sites and air fields are potential source of fire hazards, besides being unseemly. They hide industrial pipelines and valves and contribute to deterioration of stores, equipment, and material. Weeds force the fence lines to corrode and obstruct road signs and curves on highways. The working road widths are reduced by weeds, thus making these prone to accidents, particularly at the turns. Some weeds penetrate through even asphaltic surfaces which get weakened. Weeds growing around electric poles prevent their ready access to the work crews. Weeds also weaken the rail tracks and airstrips.

1.7 WEED MENACE TO FORESTS AND PASTURES

In forests and pastures the weeds are great impedance to the regeneration of natural vegetation. In outer Himalayas, lantana (*Lanatana camara*) has made large areas of forests and pastures useless. Now carrotgrass (*Parthenium hysterophorus*) has also entered these areas in a big way. In Maharashtra, many forest nurseries, and in Karnataka and Andhra Pradesh large forest areas have come under the grip of this weed. In high altitude forests of Assam and West Bengal, another weed *Chromolena odorata* has suppressed the native forest plant species. Its impact is noticed in the thin pine stands of the hilly regions of N-E India too. In West Bengal, about 11% of high forest area and 38% of plantation area have been affected by *Mikania micrantha*. With the world's wood needs increasing every year by 64 million cu m, there is need to manage the weeds in our forests in a better way to allow natural regeneration of the desired forest floral species and increase the productivity of the existing trees. Also, the weedfree buffer strips are essential in forests for preventing fire hazards.

1.8 CREATIVITY WITH WEEDS AND THEIR UTILIZATION

Those plants that we call 'weeds' can often have many useful functions. Of these, their medicinal use is perhaps the most ancient one in India. Most *Ayurvedic* medicines used by us comprise either dry powder or extracts of many well known weeds. It shall be interesting to go through the label information given on the container of any such medicine and confirm the fact. It can be further witnessed from any book entitled 'medicinal plants' which comprise largely weeds of our crop and non-crop lands (and water-bodies) (Jain & Fillip, 1991; Duke, 2002; Sala, 2003). Even several homeopathic medicines carry super-purified extracts of plants, better known to our agriculturists as weeds.

Typha and *Saccharum* spp. are used in cottage industry for making ropes and thatch boards. *Cyperus tegedum* and *Clinogyne dichotoma* dry shoots are used on large scale to make mats. In Mandla District of Madhya Pradesh (India), Lantana is being turned into eye-catching furniture, baskets, pen stands, and even flowerpots (www.exploreruralindia.org). In Bolvia, South America, tall reeds growing on river banks are tansformed by the natives with architectural wonders, including homes floating islands and strong boats. In Egypt, Papyrus is used for making efficient boats for use in the river Nile. *Cichorium intybus* roots are used for adding flavour to the coffee powder. Weeds like *Chenopodium album, Amaranthus viridis, and Portulaca* sp., form good leafy vegetables.

Certain weeds have been used to donate specific genes to our crop plants, for instance, *Saccharum spontaneum* has been widely exploited for developing the present noble canes for North India. Fruits and rhizomes of certain weeds are used as vegetable and food material. Attempts are underway to convert weedy vegetation into useful manure, animal feed, paper-pulp, biogas, and edible proteins on commercial basis to make physical control of weeds more attractive (Gupta, 2001).

More recently, certain weeds have exhibited nematicidal properties. Their incorporation into the soil has been found to result in greatly reduced rootknot nematode population (Subramaniyam and Vadivelu, 1991 and Malik *et al.*, 1987). Some promising weeds in this respect are *Crotolaria, Parthenium, Calotropis*, and *Eichhornia* spp.

Several entomologists have observed that parasites and predators of certain crop pests also survive on insect pests of certain weeds. Thus, such weeds help in maintaining the continuity of life cycle of certain useful parasites. *Trichogramma chilonis* is one such parasite found feeding upon the eggs of *Catopsilla* sp. which infests the weed *Cassia occidentalis,* as well as upon the eggs of castor semi-looper which damages the castor plants.

Certain plants, often listed as weeds, have proved useful indicators of metals in the geological substrata and the environment (Lakshmanan, 1995). Such plants concentrate in their tissues specific metals in excess of their concentrations present in the environment. Now satellite imaging has become a powerful tool in locating distribution of such plants, and the subject has come to be known as **indicator geobotany**. Some examples of the so called weedy plants holding good possibility of helping the geologists in indicating the presence of diverse metals in earth (or water) are: *Salsola nitrata* (for boron), *Crotolaria cobaltica* (for cobalt), *Aclypha* and *Commelina* spp.(for copper), *Acacia patens* (for iron), *Crotolaria florida* (for manganese), *Artemisa tridentata* (for gold, cadmium, and uranium), and *Eichhornia crassipes* (for copper, lead, zinc, and cadmium in waterbodies). The presence of *Equisetum arvensis* indicates waterlogging and that of *Urtica diocia,* a fertile soil.

Enlightened with economic potential of certain weeds, some authors tend to define weeds as *"plants for which economic uses and virtues are yet to be discovered"*. But this, in no way, lowers the undersirable nature of weeds in agriculture or reduce our concern towards them as harmful plants. As a matter of compromise someone suggested yet another, rather less specific definition of weed, namely, a plant not intentionally sown and whose undesirable qualities outweigh its good points. However, all this can not dissuade a farmer from fighting weeds on and around his farm. **The cultivation of certain weedy plants as medicinal plants, greens, and forage is a completely different issue; not to be confused with their occurrence on our farm lands where they incur whooping yield and quality losses.**

1.9 MISUTILIZATION OF WEEDS

Certain weeds have been used for purposeful adulteration of food in peace time, and for toxicating mankind in war time. A common example of adulteration of crop seeds with weed seeds is of mustard seeds mixed with Mexicanpoppy seeds, already described. The resulting oil is very harmful to humans. Growing chicory plants with lucerne and berseem to increase the forage yields, likewise, is an unhealthy adulteration of these forage crops.

The history reveals that during war time the rootstocks of false hellebore (*Veratum* sp.) were used to poison the drinking water of the enemy. Another weed, henbane was used to extract 'truth serum' in the Korean war. It forced the prisoners to reveal truth, unknowingly (Fulweiler, 1984). But now it is all behind the times. In recent years the narcotic drug 'cannabis' prepared from the foliage of hemp (*Cannabis sativa*) has been misused by some law-breaking athletes and players for improving their performance at the international meets and games popularly called 'doping'. It attracts severe punishments though. The dense growths of weeds like *Cannabis sativa* and *Phragmites karka,* provide good hiding places for terrorists in several countries. *In agriculture the major misuse of weeds in India today is allowing these to grow in agricultural fields and feed these later to cattle as forage, which has its repercussions, both in terms of lowered crop productivity and cattle ill health.*

SUMMARY

Weeds are plants growing where, and when, they are not desired. The term is highly relative to a situation; for instance, plenty of grass is good in pastures but very undesirable in crop fields. In crop fields the weeds rob the farmer of his profits by reducing yields and lowering the quality of his crops on one hand and by wasting his investments in high quality seeds, fertilizers, irrigation, and labour on the other. Many a time the weeds wreak such havoc on the crop lands that the weedy crops are even complete failures. Many weeds harbour insect pests and crop diseases, and make farm operations cumbersome. The cost of removing weeds adds to the cost of production of crops. Indeed, weeds constitute a major problem in agriculture and the losses due to them are far greater than are usually realized. Farmers in India, as in many other countries of the world, spend a major part of their life fighting weeds and weed hazards.

In grasslands, upon ingestion several weeds are directly responsible for causing diseases and poisoning in the grazing animals. Indirectly these weeds are involved in human health problems of allergies and other sickness by way of harbouring their vectors. Besides all this, the aesthetic values of surroundings also suffer badly at the hands of weeds. In fact, in many advanced countries lowering of the aesthetic values is the primary objection to weeds. Their presence around living and working places makes the surroundings dull and insipid, which is considered as stigma in present age.

The aquatic weeds contaminate water-bodies and reduce the quantity and quality of water therein. The aquacultural production is adversely affected by them. On roadsides, railway tracks, woodlands, and various industrial sites, weeds are potent source of fire hazards, accidents, low work efficiency, and deterioration of stored equipment and other material.

Weeds are the oldest pollutants of our environment; a fact which man has ignored and lived with it for long. Therefore it is important that they are controlled in time to avoid unproductive use of the plant growth factors by them and enable the crop plants to fully utilize these and express their true productivity.

Some weeds have been utilized by man in developing countries for various purposes like medication, foraging, green-manuring, thatching, and making ropes. And their new uses *eg* making paper and fibre-pulp and extracting proteins are being developed. *But just because a weed is of some utility, it can not be allowed to grow in agricultural fields and compete with our crop plants there, if our aim was to harvest high, economic and quality produce.* In fact, any weed must be curbed on farmland at the earliest opportunity, preferably, before it had chance to germinate and compete with our crop plants, directly or indirectly. Any research effort on the utilization of weeds occurring in agricultural fields is thus unnecessary and not in line with the principles of good weed management. However, strong Research and Development (R&D) efforts are needed to utilize masses of aquatic and non-crop land weeds that were cut or uprooted by physical means at huge costs. This shall recover, at least partially, the expenditure made on their physical removal and thus indirectly help their management in water-bodies and varied non-crop situations. In this respect, so far, composting or vermicomposting of the harvested weeds has proved most feasible.

SELECTED BIBLIOGRAPHY

1. Balyan, R. S. and Malik, R. K. 1994. Chemical weed control studies in barley. Ind. J. Weed Sci. 26 (1 & 2) : 1-5
2. Biradar, A.P. and M.B. Patil, 2001. Studies on utilisation of prominent weeds for vermiculating. Ind. J. Weed Sci. 33:229-230.
3. Chauhan. R. S. and Singh, G. B. 1993. Chemical weed control in spring planted sugarcane. Ind. J. Weed Sci. 25 (1 & 2) : 47-50
4. Doederlein, T. A. and Sites, R. W. 1993. Host plant preferences of *F. occidentalis* and *T. tabaci* for onions and associated weeds. J. Eco. Ento. 86 (6) : 1706-1713
5. Duke, J. A. *et al.* 2002. Medicinal herbs, II Edition. CRC Press, Boca Raton, London. 870p.
6. Du Rant, J. A. *et al.* 1994. Early season incidence of thrips on wheat, cotton, and three wild host plant species in S. Carolina. J. Agri. Ento. 11 (11) : 61-71
7. Ellis, P. R. 1992. The influence of weed vegetation on population of aphids and their natural enemies. Phytoparasatica 20 (suppl.) : 71-75
8. Fulweiler, M. 1984. Green heroes. Weeds Today 15 (40) : 9-11
9. Gajalakshmi, S. *et al.* 2002. High rate composting - vermicomposting of waterhyacenth (*Eichhornia crassipes* Mart. Solms). Bioresource Technology 83(3):235-239. (Pondicherry, India)
10. Gajalakshmi, S. *et al.* 2002. Vermicomposting of different forms of waterhyacinth by the earthworm *Eudrilus eugemiae* kinberg, Bioresource Technology 82(2): 165-169. (India)
11. Gautam, K. *et al.* 2001. Antibacterial properties of some weeds of family Asteraceae against *Xanthonomas campestris* and *Erwinia chrysanthemi.* Ind. J. Weed Sci. 33:231-233.
12. Ghosh, B.C. and S. Palit 2003. Recycling of weed biomass into vermicompost for organic farming. Abst. Bienn. Conf. ISWS held 12-14 March 2003 at G.B.P. Univ. Agr. Technol. Pantnagar (India): 91.
13. Girija, T. *et al.* 2005. Vermicomposting of aquatic weeds. Ind. J. Weed Sci. 37(1 & 2): 155-157.
14. Gupta, O. P. 2001. Weedy Aquatic Plants: Their Menace and Management. Agrobios (India), Jodhpur, 273 p.
15. Hoque, M. M. and Olvide, J. L. 1986. Rodent activity and damage in clean and weedy crop fields. Philippine Agriculturist 69 (3) : 329-340
16. Jain S.K. and R.A.D. Fillip 1991. Medicinal Plant of India, Vol. 1 & 2. Reference Publications Inc., USA, 849 P.
17. Kumar, B. V. and Shaik, M. 1993. Efficacy of herbicide sprays as an alternative to manual weeding in pearlmillet. Ind. J. Agro. 38(2) : 218-222

18. Kundra, H. C. *et al.* 1993. Efficacy of weed management practices in pea. Ind. J. Weed Sci. 25(1 & 2) : 1-6
19. Lakshmanan, K. K. 1995. The use of plants in prospecting for metals. Everyman's Science XXX (5) : 145-146.
20. Lym, R. G. and Kirby, D. R. 1987. Cattle foraging behaviour in leafyspurge-infested rangeland. Weed Technol. 1: 314-318.
21. Malik, M. S. *et al.* 1987. Nematicidal activity of extracts of *Xanthium strumarium*. Pesticides 21 (10) : 19-20.
22. Masood Ali. 1992. Weeds are a great threat to *kharif* pulses. Ind. Fmg. 42 (5) : 27, 29-30.
23. Mukhopadhya, S.K. 1991-92. Emerging problems and advances in weed management. Ind. Sci. Cong., 79th session, Calcutta, India, 1-16.
24. Naidu, V.S.G.R. *et al.* 2005. Weeds That Heal. National Research Centre for Weed Science (ICAR), Jabalpur. 134 p.
25. Oudhia, P. 2001. Medicinal weeds in banana orchards: a boon for small farmers of Chhattisgarh (India). Agricultural Science Digest 21(4) : 267-268. (India)
26. Panwar, R. S. *et al.* 1995. Effect of application time and hoeing on efficiency of pendimethalin in cotton. Ind. J. Agro. 40.
27. Parihar, S. S. and Kanodia, K. C. 1987. Beware of the exotic weeds. Ind. Fmg. 37 (1) : 24-25, 27.
28. Parmar, J. S. *et al.* 1994. Weed control studies in lentil. Ind. J. Weed Sci. 26 (1 & 2) : 49-50.
29. Patal, Z. G. *et al.* 1994. Effect of weed control methods on yield and yield attributes of sunflower. Ind. J. Agro. 39(2) : 330-331.
30. Patel, B. B. and Upadhyay, P. N. 1989. Integrated weed management in chicory (*Cichorium intybus* L.). Ind. J. Agro. 34(4) : 474-475.
31. Pingale, S. V. *et al.* 1973. A study on weed seeds found in food grains. United Int. Press. Link House, New Delhi, 22 pp.
32. Porwal, M. K. and Gupta, O. P. 1993. Relationship between weed biomass and crude protein content in wheat as influenced by various methods of weed control. Crop Res. 6(3) : 377-82.
33. Porwal, M. K. and Singh, M. M. 1993. Efficacy of herbicides for weed control in cauliflower. Ind. J. Weed Sci. 25 (1 & 2): 55 - 60.
34. Qudhia, P.2001. Common rice weeds used for first aid by Chhattisgarh farmers. Agricultural Science Digest 21(4) : 273-274. (India)
35. Rao, M. J. V. *et al.* 1989. Estimates of grain yield losses caused in sorghum by *Striga asiatica* (L.) Kuntze obtained using the regression approach., Agri. Ecosystem and Envi., 25 (2-3). 139-149.
36. Rita, M. *et al.* 1995. Method of weed management on weed biomass, yield of blackgram, and nitrogen uptake. Ind. J. Agro 40 (1) : 114-115.
37. Sala, A.V. 2003. Indian Medicinal Plants Vol. 2. Orient Longman 416 p.
38. Sandhu, K. S. *et al.* 1993. Studies on weed control in mungbean (*Vigna radiata*). Ind. J. Weed Sci. 25 (1 & 2), 61-65.

39. Sandhu, P. S. and Walia, U. S. 1993. Weed management in spring planted sugarcane. Ind. J. Weed Sci. 25 (3 & 4): 92-96.

40. Satao, B. N. and Nalamwar, R. V. 1992. Integrated weed control in hybrid sorghum. Ind. J. Weed Sci. 24 (1 & 2) : 22-25.

41. Shanower, T. G. *et al.* 1993. A typical oviposition behaviour in *Helicoverpa armigera* (Hubner). Int. Chickpea Newsletter 28 : 16-17.

42. Sharma, J. and Nayital, S. C. 1993. Weed management in maize + blackgram intercropping in mid hills of H. P. Ind. J. Weed Sci. 25 (1 & 2) : 43-46.

43. Shivakumar, H. R. and Muniyappa, T. V. 1994. Effect of weed control methods on moisture and chlorophyll content in mulberry leaves. Ind. J. Weed Sci. 26 (1 & 2) : 99-100.

44. Singh, A. K. *et al.* 1993. Critical stage of weed-competition in pigeonpea + sesame intercropping under dryland conditions. Ind. J. Weed Sci. 25 (3 & 4) : 71 - 76.

45. Singh, C. M. *et al.*1993. Study on the weed management in okra. Ind. J. Weed Sci. 25 (1 & 2) : 92-95.

46. Singh, D. P. *et al.* 1994. Weed control in white jute. Ind. J. Agro. 39(3) : 437-441.

47. Singh, G. and Prasad, R. 1994. Studies on the control of *Trianthema portulacastrum* L. in fodder maize. Ind. J. Weed Sci. 26 (1 & 2) : 64-67.

48. Singh, G. and Singh, D. 1992. Weed-crop competition studies in chickpea (*Cicer arietinum* L.). Ind. J. Weed Sci. 24 (1 & 2) : 1-5.

49. Singh, H. and Kolar, J. S. 1994. Crop-weed competition studies in soybean (*Glycene max* L. Merrill). Ind. J. Weed Sci. 26 (1 & 2) : 83-86.

50. Singh, K. and Lal, S. S. 1994. Herbicidal weed control efficiency in potato under N. E. hill conditions. Ind. J. Agro. 39 (2) : 336-339.

51. Singh, K. P. and Malik, Y. S. 1983. Chemical weed control in carrot seed crop. Ind. J. Weed Sci. 15 (1) : 12-16.

52. Singh, M. P. and Singh, K. P. 1994. Effect of crop-weed competition on growth and yield of *kharif* onion. Ind. J. Weed Sci. 26 (3-4) : 18-21.

53. Singh, P. H. *et al.* (eds.) 2006. Handbook of Sustainable Weed Management. Food Products Press, 10 Alece Street, Binghamton, N.Y. (USA), 892p.

54. Singh, R. *et al.*1993. Crop-weed competition in Japanese mint under foot hill conditions of U. P. Ind. J. Agro. 38 (3) : 443-448.

55. Singh, S. J. *et al.* 1992. Studies on weed management in onion. Ind. J. Weed Sci. 24 (1 & 2) : 6-10.

56. Singh, T. *et al.* 1991. Critical period of competition between wrinklegrass and transplanted paddy. Ind. J. Weed Sci. 23 (1 & 2) : 1-5.

57. Sinha, S.P. *et al.* 2005. Nutrient utilization by winter maize and weeds as influenced by integrated weed management. Ind. J. Agro. 50(4) :303-304.

58. Srivastava, S. N. L. and Singh, O. P. 1979. Studies on the chemical control of weeds in sugarbeet. Ind. J. Agro. 23 (4) : 88-89.

59. Subramaniyan, S. and Vadivelu, S. 1991. Effects of *Crotolaria spectabilis* extracts on *Meloidogyne incognita*. Int. Nematology Network Newsletter, 8-10.

60. Suhardi, H. A. 1993. Anthracnose on shallot (*Allium cepa*) group *Aggregatum* in Java. Onion Newsletter for the Tropics 5 : 48-50.
61. Thakur, C. 1984. Weed Science, 2nd ed. Metropolitan (India), 495p.
62. Tiwari, R. B. and Parihar, S. S. 1993. Weed management studies in wheat. Ind. J. Weed Sci. 25 (394) : 88-90.
63. Vaishya, R. D. 1993. Efficacy of some herbicides for weed control in pigeonpea. Ind. J. Weed Sci. 25 (3 & 4) : 120-122.
64. Williams, M. C. 1984. Poisonous plants. Part VI, Introduced poisonous plants. Weeds Today 15 (2) : 1-2.
65. Xia, H. *et al.* 2001. Waterhyacinth accelerating the degradation of malathion in aqueous solution. China EnvironmentalScience 21(6): 553-555.(China)
66. Yadav, R. P. *et al.* 1995. Yield and economic analysis of weed control practices in Indian mustard. Ind. J. Agro. 40 (1) : 122-124.
67. Yadav, S. K. *et al.* 1986. Studies on removal of nutrients by weeds and their control in groundnut. Ind. J. Agro. 31 (2) : 177-180.
68. Zimdahl, R.L. 2002. The President Said. Weed Sci. 50(1): 14-25.(USA).

Chapter 2

WEED-CROP COMPETITION

Competition is the action of endeavouring to gain what another endeavours to gain at the same time. Among plant communities each plant is in a state of continuous competition with its neighbouring plants for various growth elements, both above and under the ground. Our concern here is with such a competition between the weeds and the crops growing on agricultural lands which tends to limit, or even extinct, the weaker competitor; invariably the crops. In fact, without the selfish interference by man, the weeds can easily wipe out the crop plants from earth in comparatively short period. By their nature the weedy plants are adapted to thrive at the expense of our "refined" field and plantation crops.

Volumes of research into the primary elements of weed-crop competition have drawn our concern to mineral nutrients, moisture, and light. Weed-crop competition for ground space is not usually upheld by the modern researchers. Generally the phrase implies to competition for elements contained there in the space, rather than for the space per se. Competition for CO_2 may occur but, probably, under extremely crowded plant community conditions because normally its atmospheric levels fail to approach the CO_2 compensation point. Besides all this, there is a growing view that plants indulge in some kind of chemical warfare in the soil, called allelopathy.

2.1 COMPETITION FOR NUTRIENTS

Competition for nutrients constitutes an important aspect of weed-crop competition. While N has been investigated extensively, and it may be the most important element in plant competition, but the competition may occur also for other nutrients required for plant growth. Weeds usually absorb mineral nutrients faster than many of our crop plants and accumulate them in their tissues in relatively larger amounts. Species of *Amaranthus*, for example, often accumulate over 3% N in their dry matter and fall into the category of nitrophills. *Digitaria* sp., on the other hand, is a phosphorus accumulator with a P_2O_5 content of over 3.36%. *Chenopodium* and *Portulaca* spp. are likewise potassium lovers, with over 4.0% K_2O in their dry matter. More interesting is the example of *Setaria lutescens* which accumulates zinc. The Zn concentration of this weed may be as high as 585 ppm of dry matter. At this level it amounts to removal of about three times more zinc by this weed than by an average cereal crop. In Bihar, maize fields were estimated to lose each year about 118 Zn, 45 Cu, 190 g Mn, and 4765 g Fe per ha in weeds. Some additional data on N, P_2O_5, and K_2O removal by some common weeds and certain crops are given in Table 2.1.

Table 2.1: Mineral Composition of Certain Common Weeds and Crop Plants on Dry Weight Basis

Plant species	N	P_2O_5	K_2O
Weeds			
Achyranthus aspera	2.21*	1.63*	1.32
Amaranthus viridis	3.16**	0.06	4.51**
Argemone mexicana	1.01	1.36*	1.33
Cassia occidentalis	3.08**	1.56*	2.31
Celosia argentea	2.41	0.39	3.50*
Chenopodium album	2.59*	0.37	4.34**
Cleome viscosa	1.96	1.53*	5.81**
Commelina benghalensis	2.02*	1.46*	1.86
Convolvulus arvensis	2.02*	1.01*	2.00
Corchorus acutangulus	1.87	0.90	2.53
Cynodon dactylon	1.72	0.25	1.75
Cyperus rotundus	2.17*	0.26	2.73
Dactyloctenium aegyptium	2.78*	0.24	1.65
Digitaria sanguinalis	2.00*	3.36**	3.48**
Echinochloa colonum	2.98**	0.40	2.96
Eclipta alba	1.61	1.49*	1.52
Euphorbia hirta	1.98	1.53*	1.96
Melilotus alba	2.45*	1.53*	1.85
Portulaca quadrifida	2.40*	0.09	4.57*
Solanum xanthocarpum	2.56*	1.63*	2.12
Sorghum halepense	0.69	0.26	0.83
Trianthema monogyna	2.34*	0.30	1.15
Xanthium strumarium	2.47*	0.64	2.54
Crops			
Oryza sativa	1.13	0.34	1.10
Saccharum officinarum	0.33	0.19	0.67
Triticum aestivum	1.33	0.59	1.44

*Compiled from different sources cited in the bibliography.

**Asterisks depict particularly high nutrient contents.

Further, the weeds possess not only capacity for heavy absorption and accumulation of plant nutrients but they also gather huge quantities of dry matter. A dry matter production of 1-10 t/ha in weeds is not uncommon, which amounts to undue removal of plant nutrients from the fields each crop season (Table 2.2). Gupta (1960) found that from a weedy sugarcane field at Delhi, weeds removed about 162 kg N, 24 Kg P_2O_5, and 203 kg K_2O per ha against only 28 kg N, 17 kg P_2O_5, and 62 kg K_2O per ha by the crop. Weeding the fleld elevated the nutrient removal by sugarcane to 111 kg N, 81 kg P_2O_5, and 253 kg K_2O per ha. In Gujarat, Patel (1983) found loss of 31 kg N, 19 kg P_2O_5, and 41 kg K_2O per ha through weeds from rice fields. In Tamil Nadu, such losses were estimated at 36.7 kg N, 4 kg P_2O_5, and 21 kg K_2O per ha. (Srinivasan and Palaniappan, 1994). Porwal and Gupta (1988-89) estimated the average nutrient removal by weeds from wheat field as 32.45 kg N/ha and 5.07 kg P_2O_5/ha during the crop season, The potato fields lost on an average 63 kg N, 11 kg P_2O_5, and 88 kg K_2O per ha through this pest (Mani, 1975). Singh and Kolar (1994) reported that a weedy crop of soybean could remove only 87.7 kg N/ha against a weed-free crop which removed 132.7 Kg N/ha. Shahi (1978) estimated a loss of 32 kg N/ha each year through *Chenopodium album* alone from dryland wheat fields in the country. In South India, Rajan and Sankaran (1974) estimated that the nutrient removal by weeds during the first thirty days of maize growth was 59 kg N, 10 kg P, and 59 kg K per ha, which was 7-10 times more than the nutrient removal by the crop. Such investigations showed at least two things in common, *viz.*, (i) the weeds removed large quantities of nutrients from the soil* and (ii) that the removal of weeds allowed the crops to accelerate their nutrient absorption, greatly. However, these studies leave several questions unanswered.

Table 2.2: Nutrient Removal by Weeds and Crop Under Weedy and Weed-Free Situations*

Treatment	Nutrient removal (Kg/ha)					
	By Weeds			By Crop		
	N	P_2O_5	K_2O	N	P_2O_5	K_2O
Wheat						
Unweeded	21.7	2.9	28.2	59.3	12.8	46.8
Weeded	1.2	0.2	1.6	75.9	15.6	69.2
Paddy (Transplated)						
Unweeded	74.0	6.0	108.0	60	5	9
Weeded	0	0	0	174	14	238
Maize						
Unweeded	46.7	7.1	61.6	46.4	6.3	82.5
Weeded	6.1	0.9	8.0	143.7	21.7	190.9
Groundnut						
Unweeded	163.0	21.9	142.0	55.2	21.2	27.2
Weeded	10.1	2.7	9.2	150.6	60.6	74.4
Sugarcane						
Unweeded	162.2	23.8	202.9	28.3	17.3	61.8
Weeded	49.7	7.7	110.6	110.6	80.7	253.1
Mentha (1st harvest)						
Unweeded	59.6	13.0	77	24.2	5.2	34.6
Weeded	0	0	0	100.0	13.0	104.0

*Compiled from different sources cited in the bibliography.

For example, can we eliminate weed-crop competition for nutrients by applying additional nutrients to satisfy the needs of both the weeds and the crop? What about weed-crop competition at very early stage of crop growth when the nutrient removal by both, the weeds and crops, is low? Are all essential nutrients competed for by the weed and crop plants with same intensity? Weed scientists have time and again been engaged in answering these questions in order to manage weeds more effectively.

Lastly, it is important at this stage to point out that numerous examples of nutrient losses through weeds should not give an impression that in a weed-free situation the quantity of nutrients removed by the crop shall always be similar to those removed by the weeds and the crop together in a weedy field. It will all depend upon the kind of weeds and the crop in question, time and extent of weed growth (particularly the root growth), and several other such factors.*

2.2 COMPETITION FOR MOISTURE

Research has established that weed-crop competition for moisture usually occurs along with other elements of competition. It becomes increasingly critical with increasing soil moisture stress, as occurring in the dry farming areas of the semi-arid and arid regions of the world. In general, for producing equal dry matter, weeds transpire more water than do most of our crop plants (Table 2.3). Therefore, in dryland agriculture the actual evapotranspiration from the weedy crop fields is much more than the evaporanspiration from a weedfree crop field. In such an agrisystem, during a dry spell the weedy crops exhibit wilting or other moisture stress symptoms much earlier than a weedfree crop. So much so, in a weedy field the soil moisture may be exhausted much before the crop reaches its fruiting stage, which is often the peak consumptive use period of the crop, causing significant cuts in crop yields. Shahi (1978) determined the consumptive use of water of a common weed *Chenopodium album* as 550 mm against 479 mm for wheat. It was further noted that the weeds removed moisture evenly from up to 90 cm soil depth, while the major uptake of moisture by wheat was limited to the top 15 cm of soil.

Further, in weedy fallow fields too, the weeds removed valuable, conserved soil moisture. At the Dry Farming Research Station at Rohtak (India), weeds growing in fallow fields were found to consume as much as 70-120 ha mm of soil moisture which was capable of producing 15-20 q/ha of food grain the following season. In another study, while a summer weedy fallow retained only about 50 ha mm water up to winter season, the clean fallow fields contained 100 ha mm of available soil moisture. Obviously, about half the stored soil moisture was lost to the atmosphere through weeds from the weedy fallows.

Similar observations were reported by Wiese and Vandiver (1970). In irrigated fields too, weeds grab lion's share of the applied water. Saini *et al.* (1993) found that in a *weedy*

***Footnote:** It may be useful to learn here that with weeds turned back into the soil there is no net loss of nutrients from the field. Rather the weeds standing in the fallow fields prevent excessive loss of nutrients through leaching and fixation. Some weed species may even help improve available nutrient status of surface soil, for instance, of Zn by Setaria lutescens. Still, the weeds cannot be allowed to multiply even on the fallow lands since later they infest crops heavily and compete for nutrients at a time when the crop needed these most.*

situation irrigation increased the sugarcane yields by less than 1t/ha in 1984, and by less than 3t/ha in 1985 against about 10 and 28t/ha increases in the *weedfree* plots in the two years, respectively (Table 2.5).

Table 2.3: Transpiration Coefficients of Certain Weeds and Crops (After Kanitkar *et al.*, 1960)

Plant species	Transpiration coefficient `Q'	Plant species	Transpiration coefficient `Q'
WEEDS		*Tephrosia purpurea*	1108
Amaranthus viridis	336	*Tribulus terrestris*	221
Cynodon dactylon	813	*Tridax procumbens*	1402
Digitaria sanguinalis	696	*Xanthium strumarium*	331
Echinochloa colonum	674	**CROPS**	
Ischaemum pilosum	556	*Zea mays*	352
Salsola kali var *tenuifoila*	542	*Sorghum vulgare*	394 (430)

Table 2.4: Rooting Depths of Some Common weeds (After Rao, I. M. 1961. paper presented at the 1st All India Weed Control Seminar held. Oct. 3-4, at Bombay, India)

Weeds species	Maximum observed rooting depth (m)	Weeds species	Maximum observed rooting depth (m)
Amaranthus paniculatus	0.5	*H. indica*	1.0
Cleome sp.	0.6	*Polygonum plebejum*	1.2
Convolvulus arvensis	2.4	*Portulaca oleracea*	0.8
Eclipta alba	0.9	*Trianthema monogyna*	1.2
Euphorbia prostrata	1.3	*Tribulus terrestris*	1.2
Heliotropium eichwaldii	1.0	*Voluterlla divaricata*	2.3

Table 2.5: Effect of Irrigation on Sugarcane Yield Under Variable Weedy Situations During 1984-85 and 1985-86 in Himachal Pradesh (India) (After Saini *et al.*, 1993)

Treatments (weed control)	Sugarcane Yield (t/ha)			
	1984-85		1985-86	
	Unirrigated	Irrigated	Unirrigated	Irrigated
Unweeded	23.85	24.70	24.93	27.59
Handweeded	37.45	47.16	38.42	66.89
Atrazine 2 kg/ha, PE	31.31	38.39	31.86	58.57
C. D. Interaction (P=0.05)	2.40	3.76		

Comments: *In the unweeded situation irrigation could not increase the cane yield, while in the weedfree situation it increased it, markedly.*

2.3 COMPETITION FOR LIGHT (SOLAR ENERGY)

Plant height and vertical leaf area distribution define effective components of the competitive struggle for light (Graf & Hill, 1992). It becomes most important element of weed-crop competition when moisture and nutrients in soil are plentiful, and weeds have an edge over crop plants in respect of their height. Light competition may commence very early in the crop season if a dense weed growth smothers the crop seedlings. Crops like cotton, potato, several vegetables, sugarcane, etc. are prone to heavy weed growths at their seedling stages and, consequently, suffer badly at the hands of shading effects of weeds. An important feature of competition for light in plant communities is that unlike competition for N and moisture, once the crop seedlings are shaded by weeds, later on providing additional solar energy cannot make up for the crop stunting caused earlier.

2.4 ALLELOPATHY

Green plants produce numerous secondary metabolites, many of which are capable of initiating chemical warfare among the neighbouring plants growing in a community. These chemicals have been designated as **allelo-chemicals** and the process as **allelopathy.** Both, crop and weedy plants may possess such allelopathic compounds, but, unfortunately, the weed species often possess much higher levels of these than our present day crop varieties which have lost such metabolites during their breeding by man for high yield and quality. This is now considered a very important mechanism available with most weeds to stunt the growth of crops. The allelopathic compounds may be released from plants into the soil as either root exudates or as decomposition products of their dead and worn-out tissues. Some weedy plants have also been found to release volatile allelopathic compounds from their foliage which prove unhealthy to the nearby crop plants. The allelopathic compounds studied so far are found to largely belong to two chemical groups *viz.*, the Phenolic compounds and the Terpenoids, which comprise molecules like benzoic acids, cinnamic acids, phenolic acids, cumarins, hydroquinones, benzoquinones, thiopenes, juglone, and cineoles *etc.* (Rizvi and Rizvi, 1992). Some authors prefer to call the harmful plant interactions of such chemicals as **teletoxy**, but the broader term **allelopathy** is still widely accepted. The allelopathic effects of several weeds on specific crop plants have been demonstrated by way of preparing their hydro-leachates and irrigating the test plants with these. A few, recent laboratory demonstrations of allelopathy include: inhibition of germination of certain small grains with *Cyperus rotundus* tuber leachates (Lella, 1995); inbibition of growth of many agronomic crops with *Parthenium* sp. extracts (Mersie and Singh, 1987); reduction in the germination of cabbage and egg plants with *Amaranthus retroflexus* extracts (Qasem, 1995), and reduction in the growth of wheat plants with exudates of *Avena fatua*, *Phalaris minor*, and *Chenopodium album* (Porwal and Gupta, 1986).

Further, sometimes a daughter plant hydroleachates may exhibit teletoxy to its parent plant itself. This process is called **autotoxy**. This phenomenon is exhibited by *Parthenium hysterophorus* (Kohli and Rani, 1992).

While one is concerned about the adverse allelopathic influence of weeds on the crop plants, there are several instances when such a phenomenon is observed amongst the weeds themselves, giving scientists opportunity to use it in Allelopathic Control of certain weeds using specific botanicals (Chapter 6). However, in this chapter our concern is with the deleterious effects of weed exudates on crop plants. But, despite numerous examples of laboratory demonstrations of such allelopathy, direct proof of the extent of existence of the phenomenon in field conditions is more difficult to obtain. It is so because under field conditions the secondary metabolites from weeds may be subjected in soil to biodegradation, adsorption, leaching, and like phenomena; leaving little amount, if at all, for damaging meaningfully the crop growth. Moreover, such weed exudates are usually crop specific, for example, Varshney and Saxena (1994) found allelopathic effects of nutsedge (*Cyperus rotundus*) on beans (*Vigna sativa*) and lentil (*Lens esculentus*), but not on pea (*Pisum sativium*) and chickpea (*Cicer arietinum*).

Allelopathy, in true sense, does not form any aspect of weed-crop competition, although it causes weed-crop interference. Therefore, the weed scientists now prefer to talk of *weed-crop interference* rather than weed-crop competition. The term weed-crop interference includes competition, as well as, the possible allelopathy. A comprehensive review on the subject is provided by Rizvi and Rizvi (1992).

More recently the term 'allelopathy' has been redefined by the International Alleloapthy Society, making it more accommodative than before. It now includes the secondary metabolites produced by both living and non-living tissues of green plants, micro-organisms, virus, and fungi that influence the growth and development of biological systems. Also, now the promotive effects of such metabolities on plants have been suggested for inclusion in the subject of allelopathy (Kathiresan Rm, 2002).

2.5 CRITICAL PERIOD OF WEED -CROP COMPETITION

The critical period of weed-crop competition is defined as that shortest time span in the ontogeny of crop when weeding will result in the highest economic returns. The crop yield levels obtained by managing the weeds during this period should provide crop yields sufficiently close to those obtained by the full season freedom from weeds.

Unfortunately, most farmers erroneously assume that removing weeds any time during the growing season was good enough for obtaining full benefits of weeding in terms of increased crop yields. But contrary to it substantial scientific evidences are now available which show beyond doubt that the time of weeding a crop is as important as the weeding itself. A fundamental principle of plant ecology is that early occupants of the ground tend to discourage or exclude the later ones. This holds good also in agriculture. The weeds that germinate either before or along the crop offer stronger competition to it than the later germinating ones. It has been observed that these early weeds accumulate dry matter faster than the crop seedlings. In maize, for instance, it has been found that during the initial period of 2-3 weeks after crop emergence, weeds complete about 15-18% of their full season growth, while the crop plants accomplish only 2-3% of it. Several such observations have favoured need of early season weeding in most of the annual crops. In general, there is hypothesis that for producing optimum yields the annual crops require a weedfree respite for the first 1/4 -1/3 of their growing period., (Fig. 2.1). Longer duration weed control usually did not give additional economic production. Gogoi *et al.* (1993) reported that the dryland wheat plots weeded up to first 45 days after sowing gave 24.26 q/ha grain yield, which was only 4.5% less than the maximum yield of 25.4 q/ha obtained from the all season weedfree plots (Table 2.6) Likewise, only little increases in yields of upland rice, soybean, chickpea, and pigeonpea-sesame intercrops, were obtained when these crops were kept weedfree longer than 30, 40, 60, and 45 days after sowing, respectively (Tables 2.7 to 2.10).

Singh *et al.* (1971) found that in cotton, good weed control was necessary for up to two weeks after crop emergence. Delay in weeding caused unrecoupable losses in the lint yield. Groundnut, a slow prostrate growing crop, required freedom from weeds almost up to 6-8 weeks after emergence to obtain optimum yields (Rethinam *et al.*, 1976). In sugarbeet, weeding could be delayed up to its four, true leaves stage. Thereafter, effective weed control must be maintained up to its 10-12, true leaves stage.

Table 2.6: Effect of Variable Period of Weed-Crop Competition in Dryland Wheat (After Gogoi *et al.*, 1993)

Treatment	Grain yield of wheat (q/ha)
Weedy up to first:	
15 d. a. s.	24.66
30 d. a. s.	23.50
45 d. a. s.	22.94
60 d. a. s.	21.19
Full crop season	15.44
Weedfree up to first:	
15 d. a. s.	16.03
30 d. a. s.	22.14
45 d. a. s.	24.26
60 d. a. s.	25.17
Full crop season	25.41
C. D. (P = 0.05)	1.90

Comments: *Weeding during the first 30 to 45 d. a. s. was critical requirement in dryland wheat.*

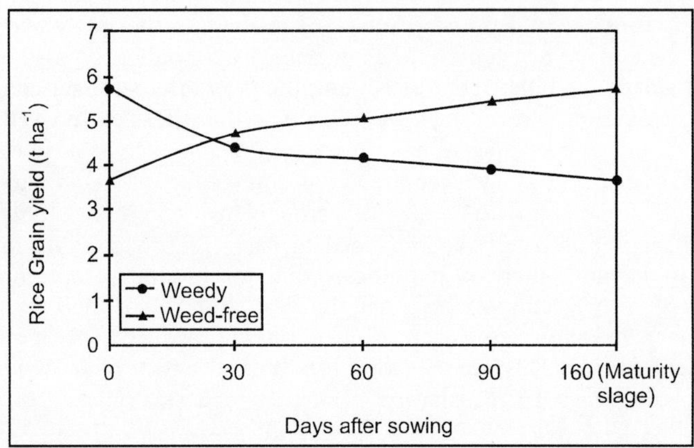

Fig. 2.1: Grain Yield of Rainfed, Direct-Seeded, Lowland Rice as Affected by Weedy and Weedfree Variable Durations at Cuttack (India). (After Moorthy and Saha, 2005).

***Comments:** In this field experiment a season-long weedy rice crop lost about 40% of its grain yield. Of this, almost 30% losses had occurred due to the presence of weeds in the initial 45 days of crop growth. Conversely, the full season freedom from weeds boosted the rice grain yield by about 40%, of which 25% yield gains were found associated with weedfree period of initial 45 days alone. Keeping a field crop weedfree for the entire crop period is now considered neither necessary nor economical and feasible. All weeding efforts should therefore be directed to ensure initial 30-45 days of weedfree crop growth.*

Table 2.7: Effect of Variable Period Weed-Crop Competition in Upland, Direct Seeded Rice During 1986 (After Tewari and Singh, 1991)

Treatment	Grain yield of rice (q/ha)
Weedy up to first:	
15 d. a. s.	8.91
30 d. a. s.	7.78
45 d. a. s.	6.50
Full crop season	5.10
Weedfree up to first:	
15 d. a. s.	6.50
30 d. a. s.	8.33
45 d. a. s.	7.93
Full crop season	9.26
C. D. (P = 0.05)	1.67

***Comments:** 1. Weeding during the initial 15 to 30 d.a.s. was most critical requirement in direct seeded rice.*

Table 2.8: Effect of Variable Period Weed-Crop Competition in Soybean in Hill Region of U.P., in 1986 (After Arya *et al.*, 1994)

Treatment	Grain yield of soybean (q/ha)
Weedy up to first:	
20 d. a. s.	26.85
40 d. a. s.	25.47
60 d. a. s.	23.79
Full crop season	19.49
Weedfree up to first:	
20 d. a. s.	24.07
40 d. a. s.	26.79
60 d. a. s.	29.72
Full crop season	29.07
C. D. (P = 0.05)	4.12

***Comments:** 1. Weeding during the initial 20 to 40 days after sowing was most critical requirement in soybean.*

In sugarcane Singh *et al.* (1980) found 4 to 16 weeks' period after planting critical for competition from weeds. But in potato only 2 to 4 weeks' period after planting was considered crucial for weeding. Delayed weeding caused considerable shrinkage in tuber yield, (Gupta *et al.*, 1979). A rapidly growing crop like mungbean responded most to weeding 35 days after sowing (Singh, *et al.*, 1978).

Table 2.9: Effect of Variable Period Weed-Crop Competition in Unirrigated Chickpea at Pant Nagar (India) (After Singh and Singh, 1992)

Treatment	Grain yield of chickpea (q/ha)			
	1981	1982	1983	Mean
Weedy up to first				
30 d. a. s.	18.0	15.0	18.2	17.1
60 d. a. s	13.8	9.9	14.0	12.6
90 d. a. s	14.3	7.6	12.1	11.3
120 d. a. s.	12.3	6.7	1.2	10.1
Full crop season	12.2	7.8	11.2	10.4
Weedfree up to first				
30. d. a. s.	15.3	14.5	16.4	15.4
60 d. a. s.	19.7	20.2	21.3	20.4
90 d. a. s.	19.2	20.3	21.2	20.2
120 d. a. s.	20.3	20.3	20.2	20.3
Full crop season	20.5	20.0	21.2	20.6
C. D. (P = 0.05)	2.32	1.32	2.12	-

Comments: *Weed-free condition during the initial 30 and 60 days after sowing was critical requirement in chickpea.*

Table 2.10: Effect of Variable Period Weed-Crop Competition in Pigeonpea-Sesame Intercropping System Under Dryland Conditions (After Singh *et al.*, 1993)

Treatment	Pigeonpea equivalent grain yield (q/ha) (Pooled data of 1989 and 1990)
Weedy up to first:	
15 d. a. s.	17.98
30 d. a. s	14.50
45 d. a. s.	11.87
60 d. a. s.	11.08
Full crop season	10.46
Weedfree up to first:	
15 d. a. s.	11.62
30 d. a. s.	14. 34
45 d. a. s.	17.33
60 d. a. s.	17.91
Full crop season	18.34
LSD (P=0.05)	1.02

Comments: *Weeding during 15 and 30 days after sowing was critical requirement in pigeonpea-sesame intercropping.*

Vegetables are highly susceptible to dense growth of weeds which they encounter from their emergence time. In onion, even an initial two weeks competition from weeds can throttle the bulk growth. In several other transplanted vegetables, an initial four weeks after planting period is considered critical in this respect. In okra, weeding must begin three weeks after sowing and the crop should be kept weedfree up to another three weeks. In cucumber, 12-36 days period after crop emergence was found critical for competition from weeds (Friesen, 1978). In irrigated sunflower, weeding was found essential up to four weeks after emergence of the crop.

While the above discussion support, in general, the need for early weeding in field crops, it should not be misinterpreted to advocate weeding as soon as the first weed appeared in the field. Moreover, the results on determination of critical period of weed-crop competition are whelmingly location specific. For instance, under dry farming situation of Maharashtra (India), even in an annual crop like hybrid sorghum, Satao and Nalamwar (1992) reported two, late weedings at 45 and 60 days after sowing as most productive. Likewise, in a perennial crop like mentha (*Mentha arvensis*), two critical periods of weed-crop competition were recorded; 30 to 75 days after planting in the first crop and 15 to 60 days after the first cut for the second crop (Singh *et al.*, 1993).

From the foregoing account, despite great variability in results, it can be concluded that for each crop situation there is a critical period of weed-crop competition, and that this period lies somewhere in the early period of crop growth (Fig. 2.1). The exact competition period, however, is highly crop specific and can vary with several weed factors, including the time of weed occurrence, weed density, etc. The perennial plantation and orchard crops shall behave differently than the annual field crops, in this respect.

2.6 WEED AND CROP DENSITY AND SPATIAL UNIFORMITY EFFECTS

Even a cursory review of a portion of weed competition literature leads to the conclusion that increasing the **weed density** decreases crop yield. However, this weed density-crop yield relationship diverges from linear. A few weeds usually do not affect the crop yield. Also, the maximum weed effect *ie* a total crop loss, obviously cannot be exceeded and usually the debacle occurs at less than the maximum weed density. Weed-competition and crop yield relationship is thus usually a sigmoidal relationship (Fig. 2.1) (Zimdahl, 1980). Frequently, in this relationship correlation coefficients of -0.9 are obtained. Equations based on the decay exponential curves are worked out to estimate crop losses per unit increase in weed density. When weed density variations among the weed control treatments fall within a short range of the middle of the above curve, often it appears as a linear function of crop yield. But then it should be neither intra-polated nor extra-polated. In some experiments the author observed that for each quintal dry matter gathered by the weeds, we lost 20-75 kg food grain or 72 q of potato tubers. More data of this kind should be generated to determine the quantum of efforts that must be put in for weeding different crops in different areas. In no case zero weed density is to be aimed at since it will be highly uneconomical to achieve; besides being unnecessary (Fig. 2.2).

The **crop density** also affects the weed biomass production. Experimenters have studied this relationship in terms of crop populations, seeding rates, and row widths. They found that, in general, a more dense crop population reduced the weed growth. Al-Hneidi and Mehta (1992) reportel that maintaining 2 plants of cotton per hill, the growths of mono- and dicot-weeds were reduced by 18.44% and 42.58%, respectively, over the crop population of 1 plant per hill (Table 2.11). Similarly, in wheat reducing the row spacing from 20 cm to 15 cm caused significant reduction of 11.87% and 18.30% in dry mattter yield of *Lolium* and *Phalaris* spp., respectively (Table 2.12). Further, often increasing the crop population and consequent suppression of weed growth may finally result in increased crop yields (Table 2.13). But this phenomenon remains operative only when the added crop population load did not become self-competitive for soil moisture and other nutrients, whence both, the weed and crop yield, might shrink and weeding may become a prime necessity.

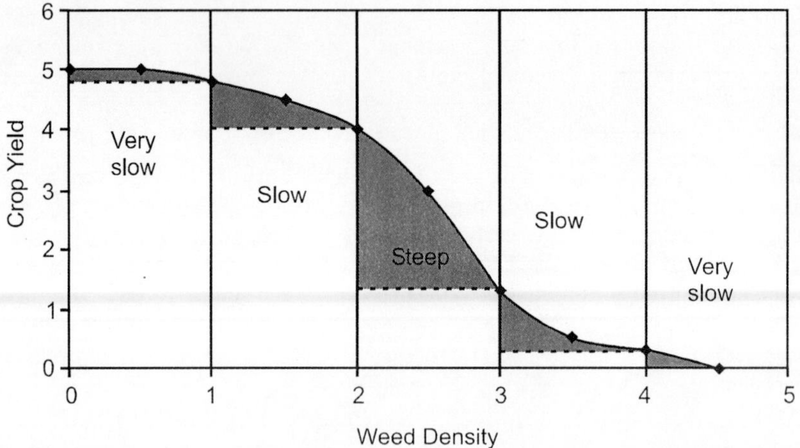

Fig. 2.2: Weed Density and Crop Yield Relationship During the Initial 45 days' Growth Period of an Annual Crop ----- A Theoretical Representation (Author).

Comments: *Progressive increase in the density of weeds in the crop field reduced the crop yields at variable rates. Initially, up to a certain weed density there was no crop loss at all, where after it (crop loss) increased slowly. Increasing the weed density further resulted in a steep reduction in the crop yield up to a certain level (of weed density) whence again the pace of crop yield losses slowed down in response to the increasing weed densities till, at least in some cases, the zero yield level was reached. In view of these universal observations on weed-crop relationships,* ***it is neither necessary nor feasible to remove every blade of weed from the crop fields.*** *For each crop situation, there is a critical weed density maxima beyond which it cannot be allowed to rise (A similar trend is noted in per unit dry matter production and crop performance relationships).*

Along with the crop density, the **spatial unifirmity** of the crop seedlings also affects the competition that the crops offer to the associated weeds. In the normal sowing of close row crops like the winter grains, the crop seedling distribution within the row is highly *clumped*, leading to considerable intra-row competition among them. When the spaces between the rows (inter-row spaces) are initially weedfree, the plasticity allows the crop plants to grow towards these spaces of high resource availability, diluting thus the intra-row competition and offering them considerable opportunity to compete with the later germinating weeds. But in the event of the crop and weed seedlings appearing simultaneously on the ground, the clumped crop plants can hardly suppress the weed seedlings. Reducing the crop row spacing shall obviously improve its spatial uniformity as well as competitiveness with weeds. The spatial uniformity in crops can be further advanced by its grid (cross) sowing which tends to equalize further the two dimensional distances. In row crops like maize and millets it is usually achieved by either mechanical dropping of the seeds at equi-distances within the row or later by thinning the crop seedlings at desired intervals.

Table 2.11: Effect of Number of Hybrid Cotton Plants Per Hill on the Growth of Associated Weeds (After Al-Hneidi and Mehta, 1992)

Treatments	**Dry weed biomass (q/ha)**					
	Monocot weeds			**Dicot weeds**		
Number of cotton plants per hill	**1 plant/hill**	**2 plants/hill**	**% drop over (1)**	**1 plant/hill**	**2 plants/hill**	**% drop over (4)**
	(1)	**(2)**	**(3)**	**(4)**	**(5)**	**(6)**
Weed control						
Unweeded check	13.45	10.97	18.44	6.27	3.60	42.58
Handweed four times	11.37	5.66	50.21	2.98	2.16	27.52
Fluchloralin at 1.0 kg/ha f. b. 2 intercultivations	5.80	3.42	41.03	1.26	1.09	13.49
C. D. Interaction (P = 0.05)		2.03			7.29	

Although most researches have demonstrated the benefits of increasing the crop density and crop spatial uniformity, usually a very high degree of uniformity may not be necessary to obtain a major increase in weed suppression. The goal can be achieved with only minor modifications in the prevailing sowing technology, keeping the economics and crop performance in view (Olsen *et al.*, 2005).

Table 2.12: Effect of Reduction in Row Spacing of Wheat on the Yield of Weeds at Palampur (India), during 1989 and 1990 (After Angiras and Sharma, 1993)

Row spacing	**Dry weed biomass (q/ha) (Pooled data of two years)**	
	***Lolium* sp.**	***Phalaris* sp.**
20 cm	8.84	6.94
15 cm	7.79	5.67
C. D. (P=0.05)	0.29	0.55

Table 2.13: Effect of Row Spacing in Wheat on Weed and Crop Yields in Maharashtra, India (After Jadhao and Nalamwar, 1993)

Row spacing	(Pooled data of 1986 and 1987)	
	Dry weed biomass (q/ha)	Grain yield of wheat (q/ha)
22.5 cm	6.68	26.9
15.0 cm	6.05	29.03
Cross sowing at 22.5 cm	5.47	30.35
C. D. (P=O.05)	0.44	0.55

2.7 PLANT SPECIES EFFECTS

2.7.1 Weed Species Effects

Weeds differ in their ability to compete with crops at similar density levels. This is primarily because of differences in their growth habits and to some extent in the allelopathic effects they may exert on the germination and growth of neighbouring crop plants. For example, at early stage of growth, cocklebur (*Xanthium strumarium)* and wild mustards (*Brassica* and *Sinapsis* spp). are better competitors of crops than many grass weeds because they possess fast growing leaves that shade the ground heavily. Also, three weeks after germination, *Brassica* spp. develop more extensive root system than the grasses. In dry areas, perennial weeds like *Cirsium arvense* and *Convolvulus arvensis* have been found more competitive than the annual weed species because of their deep roots and early, heavy shoot growths. Smith (1974) found that *Echinochloa crusgalli* and northern jointvetch (*Aeschynomene viginica)* in density of 10 plants m^{-2} each reduced rice yields by 20 and 11 q/ha, respectively. Because of such differential competitive abilities of different weed species, it has been further established that for similar weed densities, a composite stand of weed species is always more competitive to crops than solid stand of a single weed species.

2.7.2 Crop Species and Varietal Effects

Crops and their varieties differ in their competing abilities with weeds. Several researches are available to differentiate crop species and varieties in this respect. Among the winter grains, for example, the decreasing order of weed competing ability is: barley, rye, wheat, and oat. High tolerance of barley to competition from weeds is assigned to its ability to develop more extensive roots during its intitial three weeks' growth period than the other grains.

Fast canopy forming and tall crops generally suffer less from weed competition than the slow growing and short stature ones. For this reason the dwarf and semi-dwarf varieties of crops are usually more susceptible to competition from weeds than the tall varieties because initially they grow slowly. Also, their short stature shades the weeds less effectively. Sandhu *et al.* (1981) compared three varieties of wheat in respect of their competing ability with wildoat and found that the wildoat growth increased with increasing dwarfness of wheat plant (Table 2.14). In recent years, several new dwarf varieties of wheat have been brought under cultivation. No doubt these are less competitive to weeds than the tall cultivars, but because these are planted late the dwarf wheats (and barley) escape an initial flush of weeds. However, by the same token, they are more susceptible to the late germinating weeds like *Cirsium arvense, Carthamus oxyacantha, Phalaris minor,* and *Avena fatua*. Kolar and Mehra (1992) reported that in dwarf wheats the dry biomass of weeds (*Phalaris, Melilotus* and *Chenopodium* spp.) was almost double of that found in the tall genotypes. This was so because the early planted tall varieties of wheat were well up by the time weeds germinated.

Table 2.14: Effect of Three Wheat Genotypes on the Dry Matter Production of Associated Wildoat (*Avena fatua*) and Grain Yield of Wheat. Mean data of three years (After Sandhu *et al.*, 1981, Ind. J. Weed Sci. 13 (2) 146-49)

Wheat Genotype	Dry biomass of wildoat (q/ha)	Grain yield of wheat (q/ha)	
		Unweeded	Weeded
Tall genotype (C-306)	28.3	27.6	36.8
Two gene dwarf (WI-711)	40.1	22.6	46.6
Three gene dwarf (WL-903)	54.7	19.7	43.6

Weeds in small grain crops usually first tend to reduce their number of ear bearing shoots per unit area (ebt). But as the weed competition becomes more intense, the ear length and thousand grain weight of such crops are also adversely affected by the weeds.

Kulkarni *et al.* (1963) studied the weed-crop competition in two varieties of groundnut *viz*, TMV-2 (bunch type) and TMV-3 (spreading type). They found that whereas TMV-2 groundnut suffered a loss of over 30% in its pod yield under uncontrolled weed-crop competition, TMV-3 lost only about 15% of its yield. The spreading groundnut variety TMV-3, because of its smothering effect, was found infested with about half the weeds recorded with the bunch variety TMV-2. Likewise, longer duration cultivars of rice have been found more competitive to weeds than the short duration ones.

Since the crop species and varieties are found to differ in their competing ability with weeds, this trade is obviously a genetic one. Based on such observations, plant breeders are attempting to develop crop varieties tolerant to specific weeds, particularly to the parasitic ones. Some crop varieties found particularly competitive to weeds are:- Upland rice : Kalinga-III, RR-151-3; Chickpea : JG-16, JG-11, JG 315; Wheat : WH 147, Raj 3765, C 306; and Pea : JP 885.

2.8 SOIL AND CLIMATIC INFLUENCES

The role of soil fertility in manipulating weed-crop competition has been investigated extensively in the hope of reducing it to the advantage of the crop. But, unfortunately, most experimental results have not favoured this. The elevated soil fertility usually stimulated weeds more than the crop, reducing thus the crop yields. It then derives that improving soil fertility, without controlling the weeds, strengthened the competing ability of weeds for other plant growth elements like soil moisture and light although the competition for the applied nutrient may become less intensive. In fact, fertilization of weedy crop could increase crop yields to a much lower level than the yield increase obtained when a weedfrec crop was fertilised, simultaneously. Elevation of soil fertility of a weedy field resulted in an uneconomic and very low fertilizer use efficiency.

But variable results when fertilization improved the growth of a weedy crop and suppressed the weeds, are also available. Such results are obtained when the soil was acutely deficient in a particular nutrient, and the nutrient was applied selectively, both in time and space, so that it was largely available to the crop plants. Still, it may be pointed out that such benefits of fertilization to weedy crops in comparison to fertilisation of the weedfree crops are justified only in terms of respective percentages. The absolute yields are no doubt always the highest in plots weeded and fertilized, simultaneously.

The moisture variations in soil may also influence the course of weed-crop competition. Weeds are adapted to grow well and compete with the crops, both in moisture stress and ample moisture conditions. This is so because there are different species of weeds available suited to highly variable moisture conditions. Removal of an intense moisture stress by irrigation may thus benefit crops more than the weeds, leading to increased crop yields. However, it all depends upon the weed-crop situation at the time of irrigation. If the weeds were already present at the time of irrigation, they would often grow so luxuriantly as to completely over power the crop. But if the crop is irrigated after it has grown 15 cm or more tall in a weedfree environment, irrigation could hasten closing-in of crop rows, thus suppressing the weeds. In any case, amelioration of weed-crop competition by irrigation is no substitute to weeding.

In submergence conditions of paddy cultivation, weeds are put to a disadvantage to start with. But if there is a break in submergence, the weeds may germinate and grow more vigorously than the crop, even if fields were submerged later on. Our knowledge of weed-crop competition for moisture is very much limited. We need to study the responses of our major weeds to variable moisture regimes to get a real insight into the subject.

Abnormal soil reactions (very high or very low pH) often aggravate weed competition. It is beacause while specific weed species suited to different soil reactions exist with us, our crops grow best only in a specified range of soil pH. As such, weeds offer more intense competition to crops on abnormal pH soils than on the normal pH soils. No critical studies on this aspect of weed competition are, however, available on hand.

Climate influences the species composition and density of weeds. Therefore, it cannot be without its influence on weed-crop competition. Adverse weather conditions *eg.* drought, excessive rains, and extremes of temperature, will favour weeds since most of our crop plants are susceptible to climatic stresses. The weed competition is further intensified when crop cultivation is stretched to marginal lands and, too far from their optimum climatic requirements. All such stresses weaken crop's inherent capacity to fight weeds.

Further, the time of germination of weeds in relation to crop germination is a primary factor in weed-crop competition, which is governed by climate. And our knowledge of the exact germination requirements of weeds is so meagre that we are unable to anticipate their germination behaviour.

Scanty literature available on factors affecting the germination of weeds in field conditions shows that weed emergence in fields was more rapid on soils kept continuously wet by rainfall than those that dried three days after planting crops. The differences in germination of weeds narrowed as the temperature increased, because then the weed seeds absorbed enough moisture in the first three days wet period itself before the soil dried. For germination of seeds of *Amaranthus retroflexus* 'redroot pigweed' and *Echinochloa colomm* 'barnyardgrass' best temperature was 17°C for eight hours at night and 25°C for 16 hours in the day.

2.9 CROPPING PRACTICES EFFECTS

Cropping practices, such as time and method of planting crops, crop density and geometry, and crop species and varieties have pronounced effects on weed-crop interference. In general, when the time of germination of a crop coincides with the emergence of first flush of weeds, it leads to intense weed-crop interference. Usually, more the delay in the emergence of weeds, less is the weed-crop interference. Kolar and Mehra (1992) reported that October sown wheat attracted weed biomass of 22.0 q/ha, against the November and December planted crop which permitted weed yield of only 10-12q/ha.

The method of planting crops may also affect the course of weed-crop competition in crop fields. Weed seeds germinate most readily from the top 1.25 cm of soil, though it is considerable up to 2.5 cm depth (Yenish, *et. al.*, 1992). Only few weeds such as, *Avena, Centaurea, Fumaria, Galium, Vicia,* and *Xanthium spp.*, germinate from even 15 cm soil depth. Such weeds are classed as deep germinating weeds against the surface germinating (0.25 cm deep) and shallow germinating (up to 5 cm deep) ones. Therefore, a planting method that dries the top 3 to 5 cm of soil rapidly enough to deny weed seeds opportunity to absorb moisture for their successful germination, usually postpones weed emergence up untill the first irrigation. By this time the crop plants are well established to compete with the late germinating weeds. On the contrary, in a planting method that leaves the soil surface moist for considerable time after planting crops, the weed seeds absorb enough moisture to germinate readily. This induces severe weed-crop interference.

Crop density and rectangularity are very important in determining the quantum and quality of crop environment available for the growth of weeds. Wide row spacings with simultaneous high, intra-row crop plant populations may induce dense weed growth. In fact, in this situation there may develop additional, undesirable competition between the adjacent crop plants themselves. In this respect, square planting of crops in which there are equal row and plant spacings should be ideal in reducing within the crop plant competition. But in practice the density of crop plants seems to be more dominant than their rectangularity in deciding the course of weed-crop competition. It is so because competition among individuals of the same species of plants is comparatively weaker than competition among individuals of the different species.

SUMMARY

The weed-crop competition is critical in obtaining optimum crop yields because of the far greater competing ability of the former (weeds) than the latter (crops). Weeds deplete the crop fields of large quantities of mineral nutrients and moisture, shade the crop seedlings and vie for the space where the crop plants should grow their roots. Besides, the weeds inflict their *allelopathic effects* on crop plants which is largely through their depressive root exudates.

Important factors governing the course and intensity of weed-crop interference have been discussed with the objective of learning to manipulate the crop environment to the disadvantage of weeds. Among these factors are: (1) critical period of weed-crop interference, (2) intensity of weeds and crop performance, (3) weed species effects, (4) soil fertility status, (5) soil water regime (6) soil reaction, (7) climate, and (8) cropping practices *eg* method and time of planting of crops, crop population, crop species, and crop varieties.

SELECTED BIBLIOGRAPHY

1. Aegazy *et al.* 2001. Allelopathic effect of Nymphaea lotus L. on growth and yield of cultivated rice around lake Manzala (Nile Delta). Hydrobiologia 464: 133-142 (Egypt).
2. Afentouli, C.G. and Eleftherohorinos, I.G. 1999 Competition between wheat and canarygrass biotypes and their response to herbicides. Weed Sci. 47: 55-61.
3. Al-Hneidi, H. and Mehta, H. M. 1992. Study on integrated- weed management in hybrid cotton. Ind. J. weed Sci. 24 (1 & 2); 78-80.
4. Anand, K.B. and R.D. Vaishya 2002. Effect of weed control measures on weeds. N uptake by weeds and yield of mustard. Ind. J. Weed Sci. 34:305-306.
5. Angiras, N. M. and Sharma, V. 1993. Effect of cultural manipulations and weed control methods on crop-weed competition in wheat. Ind. J. Weed Sci. 23 (3 & 4) : 6-10.
6. Arya, M. P. S., *et al.* 1994. Crop-weed competition in soybean (*Glycine max*) with special reference to *Oxalis latifolio*. Ind. J. Agro. 39 (1) : 136-139.
7. Bhargava, K. and Reddy, T. Y. 1993. Growth pattern of weeds in semi-dry rice (*Oryza sativa*) under different weed management practices. Ind. J. Agro. 38(2) : 295-298.
8. Chandrasagar, G. 1983. Weed-Crop competition studies in maize. Ind. J. Weed Sci. 15 (2) : 137-142.
9. Chopra, N. and Chopra, N. K. 2006. Crop-weed competition and determination of critical period in onion under NW plain zone. Ind. J. Weed Sci. 38 (1&2): 89-91.
10. Dashora, G. K. *et al.* 1990. Weed-crop competition studies in mustard. Ind. J. Agro.35 (4) : 417-419.
11. Devendra, R., *et al.* 1986. Comparative growth pattern of *Echinochloa* sp. and rice in monocultures. Ind. J. Weed Sci. 18 : 71-78.
12. Friesen, G. H. 1978. Weed-interference in transplanted tomato. Weed Sci. 27 (1) : 11-13.
13. Gill, B. S. *et al.* 1986. Studies on the critical period of weed-crop competition in groundnut. J. of Res., P. A. U. 23 (3) : 394-397.
14. Gogoi, A. K., *et al.* 1993. Critical period of crop-weed competition in rainfed wheat. Ind. J. Weed Sci. 25 (3 & 4) : 90-91.

15. Graf, B. and Hill, J. E. 1992. Modelling the competition for light and nitrogen between rice and *Echinochloa crusgalli*. Agri. Systems 40 (94) : 345-359.

16. Gupta, O. P. *et al.* 1979. Evaluation of response of potato to chemical control of early weed infestation. IAAS. J. 1 (4): 139-143.

17. Harvey, R. G. and Wagner, C. R. 1994. Using estimates of weed pressure to establish crop yield loss equations. Weed Technol. 8 (1) : 114-118.

18. Inderjit, 2002. Allelopathic effect of *Pluchea lanceolata* on mustard. Weed Biology and Mgmt. 2: 200.

19. Jadhao, S. L. and Nalamwar, R. V. 1993. Studies on weed management in irrigated wheat as affected by plant geometry, genotype, and manual weeding. Ind. J. Weed Sci. 25 (3 & 4) : 18-21.

20. Jaya Kumar, R. 1985. Categorisation of some important weeds based on nutrient concentration. Mad. Agri. J. 72 (11) : 646-649.

21. Jaya Kumar, R. *et al.* 1987. Nutrient uptake by certain field crops and associated weeds and its effect on yield. Pesticides 21 (November) : 37-48.

22. Jaya kumar, R. *et al.* 1990. Interference periods of weeds with cotton. Pestology 14 (10) : 28-29.

23. Jaya Kumar, R., *et al* 1989. Allelopathic effect of *Cassia sericea* on *Parthenium hysterophorus*. Madras Agric. J. 76 (11) : 645-47.

24. Kanitkar, N. V. *et al.* 1960. Dry Farming in India. Pub. Ind. Council of Agri. Research, New Delhi (II ed.).

25. Kar, B. C. 1993. Crop-weed competition in rice bean (*Vigna umbellata*). Ind. J. Agro. 38 (3) : 511-512.

26. Kathiresan, Rm. 2002. Allelopathy – Optism to Realism. Bull. Annamalai University, Annamalainagar (T.N.), India.

27. Klingman, T. E. and Oliver, L. R. 1994. Influence of cotton and soybean planting date on weed interference. Weed Sci. 42 (1) : 61-65.

28. Kohli, R. K. and Rani, D. 1992. Exploitation of allelopathic phenomenon to the improvement of herbicidal action of glyphosate. Ind. J. Weed Sci. 24 (1 & 2) : 65-68.

29. Kolar, J. S. and Mehra, S. P. 1992. Changing scenario of weed flora in agroecosystems of Punjab. (IN) Changing Scenario of Our Environment. (Eds) Dhaliwal, G. S. *et al.*, P.A.U., Ludhiana (India) : 252-262.

30. Kulkarni, L. G. *et al.* 1963. Studies on weeding and interculture in relation to weed control on the yield of groundnuts. Ind. Oil Seeds J. 7 (1) : 126-129.

31. Kumari, A. and Kohli, R. K. 1987. Autotoxicity of ragweed parthenium (*Parthenium hysterophorus*). Weed Sci. 35 : 629-632.

32. Lella, D. 1995. Allelopathic effects of purple nutsedge (*Cyperus rotundus* L.) tubers on the growth of field crops. Allelopathy Journal 2 (1) : 89-92.

33. Mani, V. S. 1975. Nutrient drain by weed growth in crop fields. Fert. News 20 (3) : 21-27.

34. Mersie, W. and Singh, M. 1987. Allelopathic effect of parthenium (*Parthenium hysterophorus L.*) extract and residue on some agronomic crops and weeds. J. Chem. Ecol. 13 (7) : 1739 - 1747.

35. Mishra, J.S. *et al.* 2002. Interference of common dayflower (*Commelina communis*) in soybean. Ind. J. Weed Sci. 34:295-296.

36. Moorthy, B. T. S. and S. Shaha, 2005. Studies on crop-weed competition in rainfed, direct-seeded, lowland rice. Ind. J. Weed Sci. 37 (3&4): 267-268.

37. Mukhopadhyay, S. K. 1974. Increasing fertiliser efficiency through weed control. Fert. News 19 (12) : 56-58.

38. Nandanassababady, T. and O.S. Kandaswamy 2002. Effect of chemical and cultural weed control on nutrient removal by cotton and associated weeds. Ind. J. Weed Sci. 34:316-317.

39. Nandlal, T. R. and Pandia M. L. 1988. Effect of weed removal at various stages on nutrient uptake by weeds in brinjal (*Solanum melongena L.*). Ind. J. Weed Sci. 20 (4) : 12-15.

40. Narwal, S. S. and Tauro, P. 1994. Allelopathy in Agriculture and Forestry. (Ed) Scientific Publishers, Jodhpur (India).

41. Olsen, J. *et al.* 2005. Increased density and spatial uniformity increased weed suppression by spring wheat. Weed Research 45: 316-321.

42. Pandey, A.K. *et al.* 2002. Studies on crop-weed competition and weed dyanamics in maize under Ind-hill conditions of N-W Himalayas. Ind. J. Weed Sci. 34:63-67.

43. Pandey, J. and Thakur, K. N. 1988. Effect of herbicides and N on nutrient romoval by weeds in transplanted rice. Ind. J. Agro. 33 (4) : 359-363.

44. Panwar, L.S. *et al.* 2000. Population dyanamics of weed flora and their growth in tall and dwarf wheats as influenced by irrigation and nitrogen. Weed Sci. 32:164-168.

45. Patel, C. L. *et al.* 1983. Fertiliser use efficiency in relation to weed control in transplanted rice. Ind. J. Weed Sci. 15(2) : 199-202.

46. Petersen, J. 2005. Competition between weeds and spring wheat for ^{15}N – labelled nitrogen applied in pig slurry. Weed Res. 45(2): 103-113.

47. Porwal, M. K. and Gupta, O. P. 1986. Allelopathic influence of winter weeds on germination and growth of wheat. International J. Tropical Agriculture 4(3) : 276-279.

48. Porwal, M. K. and Gupta, O. P. 1988-89. Effect of weed control on the uptake of N and P by wheat and weeds. RAJAU Res. J. 11 (1-2) : 1-6.

49. Prakash, V. and Srivastva, A. K. 2006. Crop-weed competition studies in tomato under mid-hills of NW Himalayas. Ind. J. Weed Sci. 38 (1&2): 86-88.

50. Qasem, J. R. 1995. Allelopathic effects and *Amaranthus retroflexus* and *Chenopodium murale* on vegetable crops. Allelopathy Journal 2 (1) : 49-66.

51. Rajan, A. V. and Sankaran, S. 1974. Studies on crop-weed competition for nutrients and its effect on grain yield of maize (*vr.* Ganga-5). Mad. Agr. J. 61 (4): 413-416.

52. Ramamoorthy, K. 1991. Effect of integrated weed management on nutrient uptake by upland rice and associated weeds. Ind. J. Agro. 32 (2) : 213-217.

53. Rethinam, P. *et al.* 1976. Studies on crop-weed competition and chemical weed control in groundnut. Mad. Agr. J. 63 (8-10) : 456-457.

54. Rizvi, S. J. H. and Rizvi, V. (Ed.). 1992. Allelopathy; Basic and Applied Aspects. U. K. Chapman and Hall xx + 480 PP., London.

55. Sago, R. *et al.* 2001. Critical weed - seed density to prevent yield loss of rice grown on paddy fields dominated by annual weeds. J. Weed Sci. and Technology 46(4) 267-272. (Japan)
56. Saini, J. P., *et al.* 1993. Efficacy of atrazine at different moisture levels for weed management in sugarcane under mid-hill conditions of Himachal Pradesh. Ind. J. Weed Sci. 25 (3 & 4) : 49-55.
57. Satao. B. N. and Nalamwar, R. V. 1992. Integrated weed control in hybrid sorghum. Ind. J. Weed Sci. 24 (1 & 2): 22-25.
58. Shahi, H. N. 1978. Competitive effects of *Chenopodium album* for soil moisture and nutrients in wheat. Ind. Pest Control 20 (4) : 14-16.
59. Shiv Kumar and Kairon. M. S. 1988. Effect of time of weed removal on yield of green gram (*Vigna radiata*). Ind. J. Agr. Sci. 58 (11) : 859-860.
60. Singh, A. K., *et al.* 1993. Critical stage of weed-competition in pigeonpea/sesame inter-cropping under dryland conditions. Ind. J. Weed Sci. 25 (3 & 4) : 71-76.
61. Singh, D. K. *et al* 1994. Performance of mustard (*Brassica juncea* L.) in relation to weed growth pattern. Ind. J. Weed Sci. 26 (1 & 2) : 73-74.
62. Singh, G. and Singh, D. 1992. Weed crop competition studies in chickpea (*Cicer arietinum* L.). Ind. J. Weed Sci. 24 (1 & 2) : 1-5.
63. Singh, G. *et al.* 1971. Effect of weed competition on rainfed cotton in black cotton soils. Ind. J. Agron. 16 : 137-138.
64. Singh, H. and Kolar, J. S. 1994. Crop-weed competition studies in soybean (*Glycine max* L. Merrill). Ind. J. Weed Sci. 26 (1 & 2) : 83 - 86.
65. Singh, M. *et al.* 1978. Crop competition studies in mungbeans. Ind. J. Agron. 23 (4) : 377-378.
66. Singh, M. K. *et al.*, 2002. Methods to study crop-weed competition in experiments – A review. Ind. J. Weed Sci. 34: 264-268.
67. Singh, M.K. *et al.* 2002. Methods to study crop-weed competition experiments - A review. Ind. J. Weed Sci. 34: 264-268.
68. Singh, R. *et al.* 1993. Crop-weed competition in Japanese mint (*Mentha arvensis*) under foot hill, condition of U. P. Ind. J. Agro. 38 (3) : 443-448.
69. Singh, R., *et al.* 1993. Effect of weed removal on nutrient uptake by Japanese mint (*Mentha arvensis* L.) and associated weeds. Ind. J. Weed Sci. 25 (1 & 2) : 36-41.
70. Singh, T. and Kolar, J. S. 1993. Competitive ability of wrinklegrass (*Ischaemum rugosum* Salish.) for utilization of major nutrients (NPK) in transplanted paddy. Ind. J. Weed Sci. 25 (1 & 2) : 30-35.
71. Smith, R. J. Jr. 1974. Competition of barnyardgrass with rice cultivars. Weed Sci. 22 : 423-426.
72. Srinivasan, G. and Palaniappan S.P. 1994. Effect of major weed species on growth and yield of rice (*Oryza sativa*). Ind. J. Agro. 39 (1). 13-15.
73. Srivastava, T.K. *et al.* 2002. Critical period of crop-weed competition in sugarcane ratoon. Ind. J. Weed Sci. 34:320-321.
74. Sundari, A. *et al.* 2002. Crop-weed competition in sorghum. Ind. J. Weed Sci. 34:311-312.

75. Tewari, A. N. and Singh, R. D. 1991. Crop-weed competition in upland, direct-seeded, rainfed rice. Ind. J. Weed Sci. 23 (1 & 2): 51-52.

76. Tewari, A.N. *et al.* 2001. Crop-weed studies in chickpea under rainfed conditions. Ind. J. Weed Sci. 33: 198-199.

77. Tripathi, S.S. and G. Singh 2001. Critical period of weed competition in summer cowpea. Ind. J. Weed Sci. 33:67-68.

78. Tripathi, S.S. and Vivek. 2001. Critical period of weed competition in spring sunflower. Ind. J. Weed. Sci. 33:212-214.

79. Tripathi, S.S. *et al.* 2001. Study on crop-weed competition in pea, Ind. J. Weed Sci. 33:46-48.

80. Varshney, J. G. and Saxena, A. 1994. Allelopathic activity of *Cyperus rotundus* on germination and growth of grain legume. Ind. J. Weed Sci. 26(3-4): 52-56.

81. Vengris, J. M. *et al.*, 1958. Chemical composition of weeds and accompanying crop plants. Agro. J. 45(5): 213-218.

82. Vermani, A. *et al.* 2001. Nutrient uptake and economic weed management in garlic. Ind. J. Weed Sci. 33:225-226.

83. Walia, U.S. and L.S. Brar. 2001. Ability of wildoat and broadleaf weeds in wheat in relation to crop density and N levels. Ind. J. Weed Sci. 33:120-123.

84. Walia, U.SD. *et al.* 2001. Ability of wheat with variable populations of wild oat. Ind. J. Weed Sci. 33:171-173.

85. Wiese, A. F. and Vandiver, C. W. 1970. Soil moisture efects on competitive ability of weeds. Weed Sci. 118 (4): 518-519

86. Yadav, S. K. *et al.* 1986. Studies on removal of nutrients by weeds and their control in groundnut. Ind. J. Agron. 31(2): 177-180.

87. Yenish, J. P. *et al.* 1992. Effects of tillage on vertical distribution and viability of weed seeds in soil. Weed Sci., 40(3): 429-433.

88. Zimidahl, R. L. 1980. Weed-crop Competition - A Review. Int. Plant Prot. Centre (IPPC), Oregon State University, USA, 196 pp.

Chapter 3

THE PROPAGATION, DISPERSAL, AND PERSISTENCE OF WEEDS

A sound knowledge of the biology of weeds, with particular reference to their propagation and dispersal behaviour, is essential for planning their effective management. In the absence of this information, man can at best destroy their existing growths temporarily, without having any check on their future recurrence and persistence. This will mean an unending and haphazard warfare against the weeds, which we can ill afford.

3.1 PROPAGATION OF WEEDS

3.1.1 Propagation Through Seeds

The majority of weeds reproduce by distinct seed formation* which is prolific, particularly in the annual and biennial species. Such weeds are capable of producing easily few thousands of seeds per plant every season at the termination of their vegetative phase (Table 3.1). In the perennial species, on the other hand, the viable seed production facility is much limited, like in *Cyperus rotundus* and *Cynodon dactylon* which produce only 40-170 seeds per plant. But there are exceptions to this generalisation since the perennial weeds like *Sorghum halepense* and *Saccharum spontaneum* produce thousands of seeds per plant every year, in the same fashion as the annual weeds. In an undisturbed field, like in the no-tillage farming system, most weed seeds that fall on the ground tend to remain in the top about 1 cm soil layer. But in the conventional farming system, tillage of the field tends to distribute these evenly in the plough layer of the soil (Standifer, 1980 and Yenish, *et al.*, 1992). Some weed seeds may reach even deeper, up to 30 cm or more, by entering through the soil crevices. A weed like *Commelina benghalensis* places its seeds directly inside the soil since it produces both aerial and underground flowers and seeds. Within the soil the weed seeds are capable of retaining viability for 80-100 years, depending upon the weed species (Corn

---

* *Weedy ferns, algae, and equisetums reproduce by spore formation.*

and Farris, 1987, and Kiviban and Bandurski, 1973). For instance, *Rumex* spp. seeds showed 63-90% germination up to 50 years after these were burried 30 cm deep (Hongo, 1994), while *Echinochloa, Poa* and *Chenopodium* spp. germinated even after 25 years of their similar burrial in the soil (Suzuki, 1994).

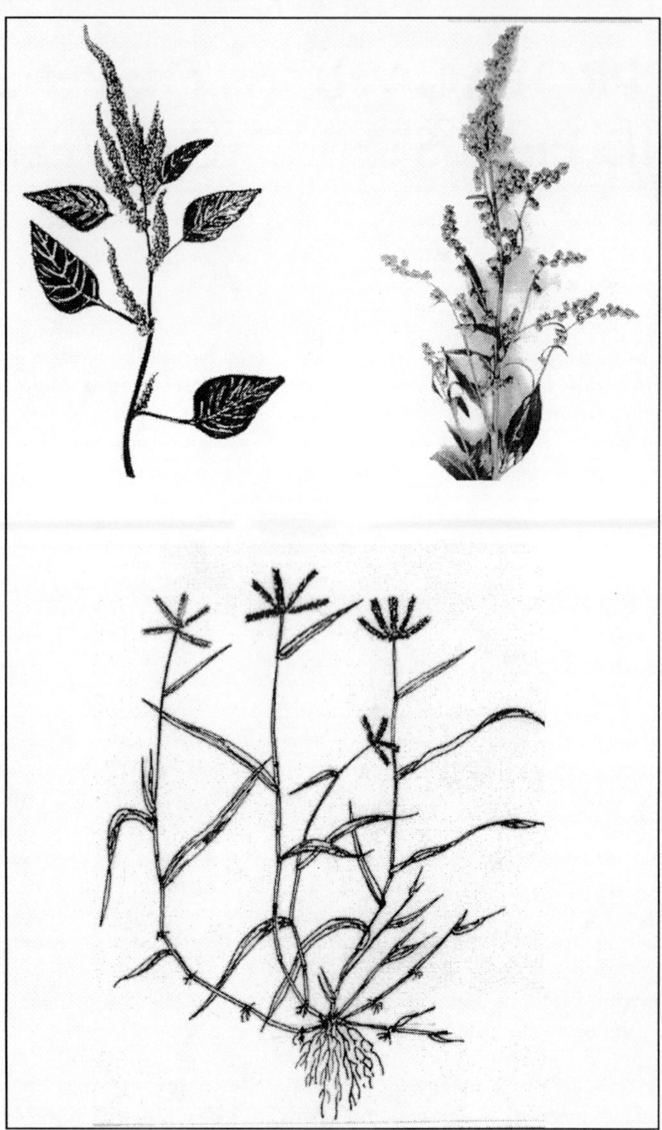

Fig. 3.1: Most weeds produce thousands of seeds per plant which helps them to multiply each year at exponential rates. Some such annual, herbaceous weeds include: *Top left = Amaranthus viridis, Top right = Chenopodium album, and Bottom = Dactyloctenium aegyptium.*

Fig. 3.1.[A]: Seed production in two common grass weeds: *Left* = *Ploypogon* sp. and *Right* = *Avena* sp. (wildoat).

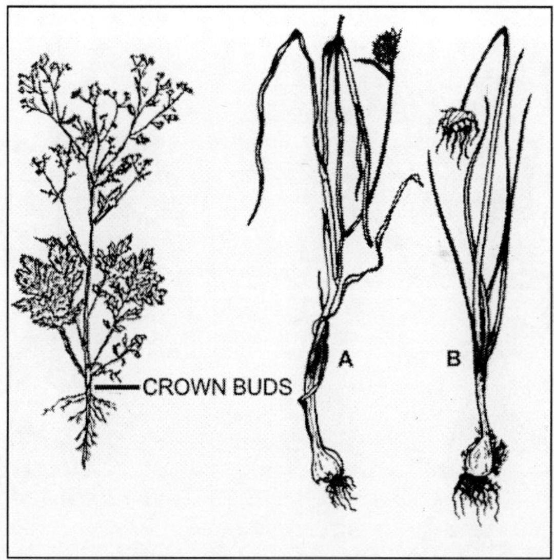

Fig. 3.1[B]: Left = *Parthenium hysterophorus*, although an annual weed reproducing by its profuse seed production, upon cutting at the ground level it can also grow from its crown buds, giving a false impression of it being a perennial weed.

Right (A) = Wild garlic (*Allium vineale*) and (B) = wild onion (*A. canadense*). The two weeds reproduce by aerial bulblets resembling wheat grains, true seeds, as well as by basal hard-shell bulbs, depending upon the weather. This makes their eradiction a long term affair.

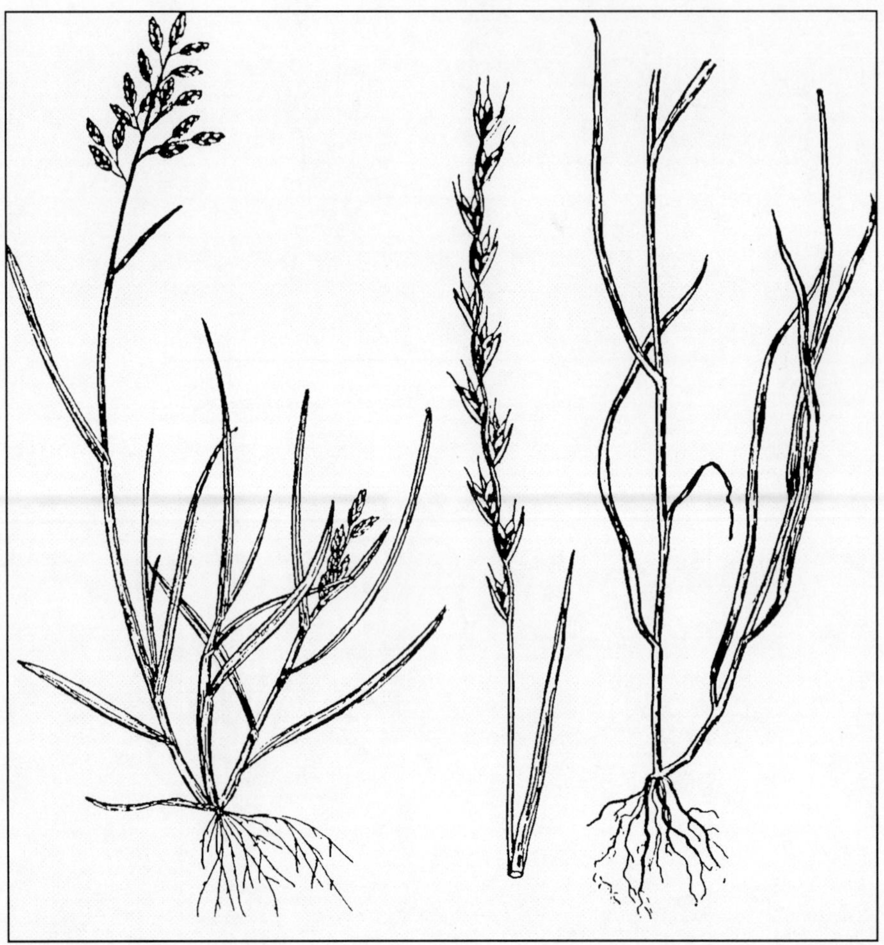

Fig. 3.1.[C]: *Left* = Flowering shoot of *Poa annua* (annual bluegrass) and *Right* = Ear of *Lolium temulentum* (ROH, USA).

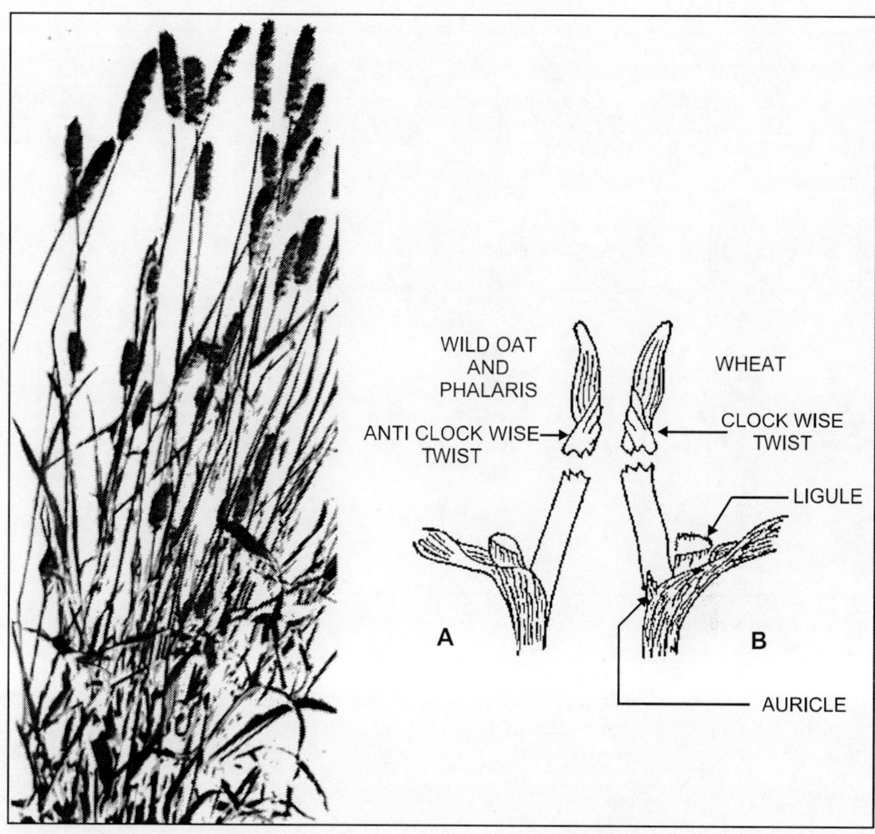

Fig. 3.1.[D]: *Left* = Ears of *Phalaris minor* (wild canarygrass). *Right* = Botanical indentification marks between wheat and wild canarygrass at their pre-flowering stages in ligule, auricle, and leaf twist. At this stage the weed apparently mimics wheat plants well enough to escape the farmer hoe.

Weed seeds (and fruits) differ widely in their shapes and sizes (Fig. 3.2) as well as in their viability. While many of these can germinate immediately after harvest, there are others which remain dormant for short or long periods before reviving their viability, like *Datura*, *Physalis,* and *Setaria* spp. Also, even in case of non-dormant weed seeds, their immediate germination behaviour differs widely with the weed species. For instance, weeds like *Eleusine* and *Bidens* spp. exhibited over 60% germination against *Cyperus rotundus* and *Cyndon dactylon* which showed only 0 and 6% germination, respectively.

In nature, the weed seeds wait for favourable environment of soil temperature and moisture before germinating and putting forth thickets of weed seedlings. But even then only those weed seeds which reside in the top 1-2.5 cm of soil, are induced to germinate at any one time, while the deeper ones remain largely dormant. However, some large-sized weed seeds, like those of *Xanthium strumarium* and *Solanum nigrum*, are able to germinate and reach the ground even from 10 cm soil depth.

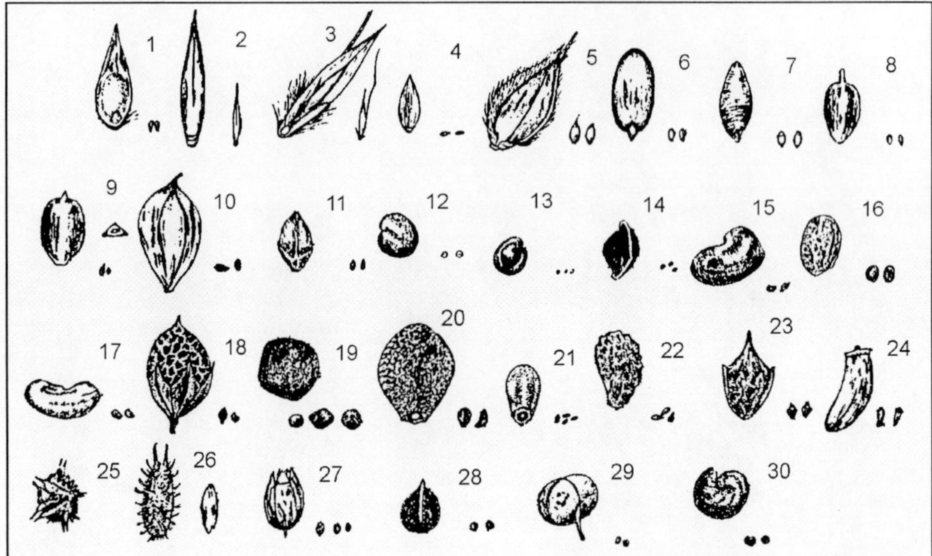

Fig. 3.2: Weeds differ widely in their shapes and sizes. Sketches of seeds/fruits of:- 1. *Agrostis alba* 2. *Agropyron repens*, 3. *Avena fatua*, 4. *Digitaria filiformis*, 5. *Echinohloa crusgalli*, 6. *Eragrostis currula*, 7. *Setaria fabri*, 8. *Cyperus esculentus*, 9. *C. rotundns*, 10. *Allium vineale*, 11. *Polygonum argyrocoleon*, 12. *Chenopodium album*, 13. *Amaranthus retroflexus* 14. *Spergula sativa*, 15. *Alhagi pseudalhagi*, 16. *Lathyrus aphaca*, 17. *Medicago sativa*, 18. *M. alba*, 19. *Vicia sativa*, 20. *Convolvulus arvensis*, 21. *Cuscuta planiflora*, 22. *Heliotropium europeaum*, 23. *Ambrosia artemissifolia*, 24. *Cirsium arvense*, 25. *Tribulus terrestris*, 26. *Xanthium strumarium*, 27. *Digera arvensis*, 28. *Argemone mexicana*, 29. *Phyllanthus fraternus*, 30. *Trianthema monogyna*, and 31. *Phalaris minor*.

Table 3.1: Seed Production Capacity of Certain Common Weeds (After Bansal and Singh, 1984, Datta *et al*., 1980; Muniyappa *et al*. 1973; Paria and Sahoo, 1981, and Yaduraju, 2005).

Weed species	Average No. of seeds per plant
Ageratum spp.	100,000
Agremone mexicana	4,000
Amaranthus spp.	196,000
Bidens pilosa	12,000
Brassica nigra	58,000
C. rotundus	40
Chenopodium album	72,000
Chromolaena odorata	13,00,000
Cirsium arvense	680
Commelina benghalensis	2,450
Conyza ambigna	33,992

Weed species	Average No. of seeds per plant
Cuscuta sp.	16,000
Cuscuta spp.	100,000
Cynodon dactylon	170
Cyperus esculentus	820
Datura stramonium	13,900
Eleusine indica	41,200
I. hispida	338
Ipomoea cynachifolia	3,340
Leucas martinicensis	12,000
Mikania micrantha	40,000
Mimosa spp.	14,000
Orobanche sp.	500,000
Parthenium hysterophorus	10,000
Phalaris minor	1,100
Physalis angulata	22,000
Portulaca sp.	193,000
Rottboellia exaltata	3,160
Rumex crispus	30,000
Setaria pallidifusca	5,120
Solanum elaegnifolium	4,500
Striga spp.	100,00,00
Trianthema sp.	52,000

3.1.2 Propagation Through Vegetative Propagules

In vegetative propagation, the weeds grow either from their stem and root fragments or through their some specific modified vegetative organs like rhizomes, root stocks, runners, stolons, suckers., offsets, tubers, bulbs, and bulbils*. Collectively these are termed as *Vegetative Propagules* (Fig. 3.3 to 3.6).

The vegetative propagation is primarily a feature of perennial weeds which employ one or more of the above cited propagules to achieve the objective, depending upon the weed species. A weed like bermudagrass (*Cynodon dactylon*) uses rhizomes under the ground, and runners and stolons over the ground surface to propagate itself into new colonies. Its rhizomes form a dense network, largely in the plough layer of the soil. But in some other weeds like tigergrass (*Saccharum spontaneum*) and Johnsongrass (*Sorghum halepense*), the rhizomes travel much deeper into the soil. Purple nutsedge (*Cyperus rotundus*) propagates by its underground, prominent tubers which are, in fact, swollen ends of its wiry rhizomes. In weeds like opuntia (*Opuntia* spp.) and dodder (*Cuscuta* spp.), the detached stems give rise to new plants. Field/bindweed (*Convolvulus arvensis*) and Canadathistle (*Cirsium arvense*) propagate typically by their extensive horizontal and vertical root system. Offsets are found in an aquatic weed like waterhyacinth

* *Any book on plant taxonomy can be consulted to define these vegetative modifications.*

(*Eichhornia crassipes*). *Hydrilla* spp. produce aerial buds called turions as additional means of its vegetative propagation.

Fig. 3.3: A plant of *Cynodon dactylon* showing its rhizomes which form the main organs in its vegetative reproduction (diagrammatic) (ROH, USA).

Besides the perennial weeds, some annual weeds can also adopt specific vegetative propagation mechanism. Such weeds vigourate their crown buds to produce new plants when the parent plants are cut at the ground level. Carrotgrass (*Partheninum hysterophorus*), lantana (*Lantana camara*), and arrowwood (*Pluchea lanceolata*) are some weeds of this type.

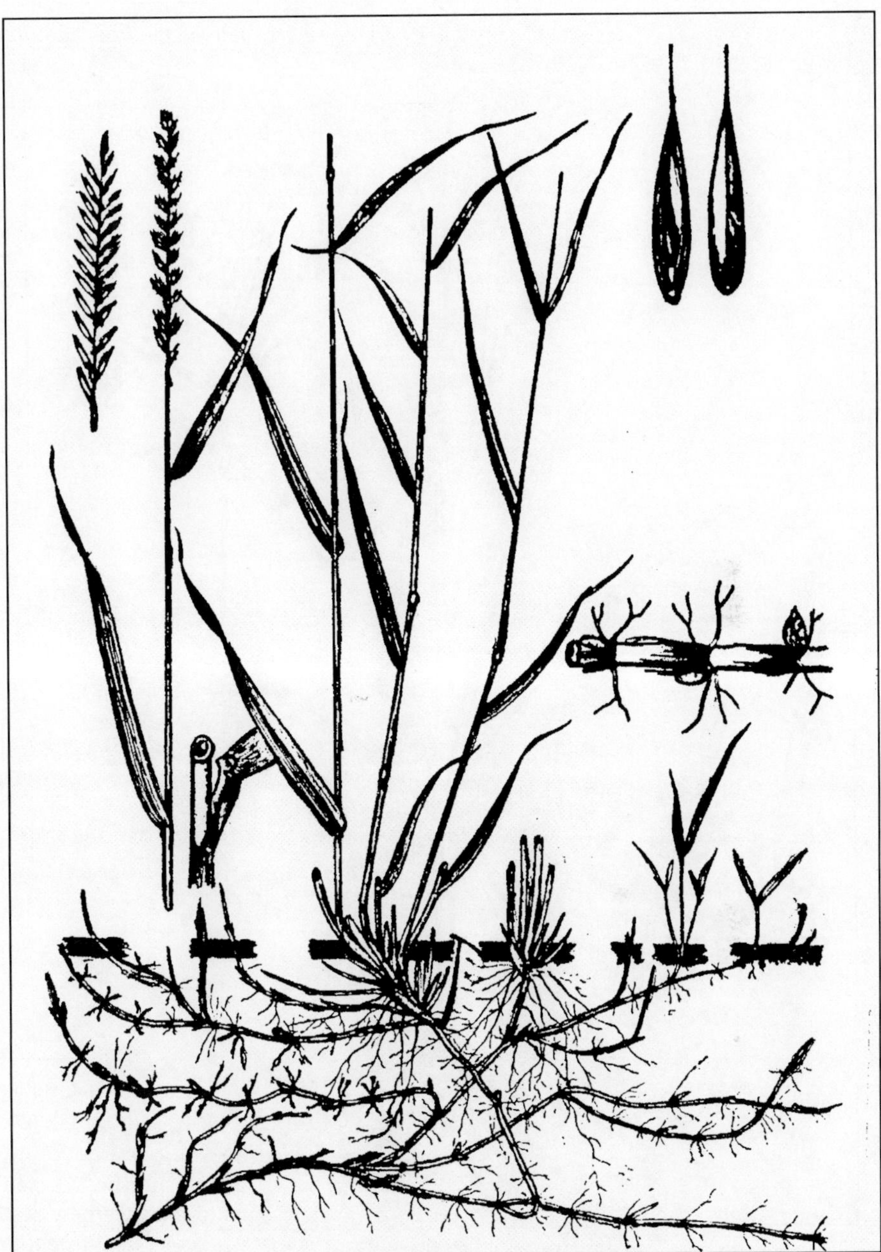

Fig. 3.4: A plant of *Agropyron repens* depicting its rootstocks as its vegetative propagules (diagrammatic) (ROH, USA).

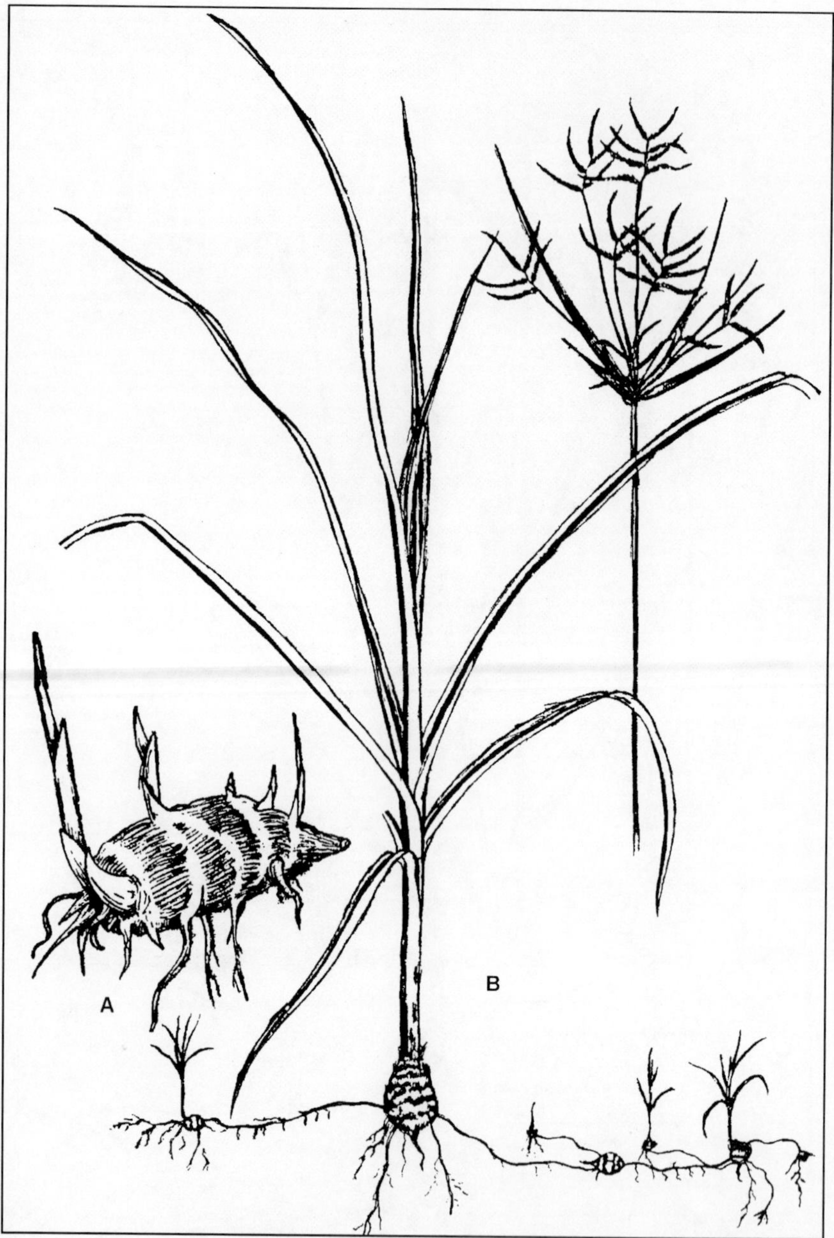

Fig. 3.5: Shoot of *Cyperus rotundus.* The plant reproduces vegetatively by its well spread tubers and stolons. A tuber has been shown on the left in enlargement (diagrammatic).

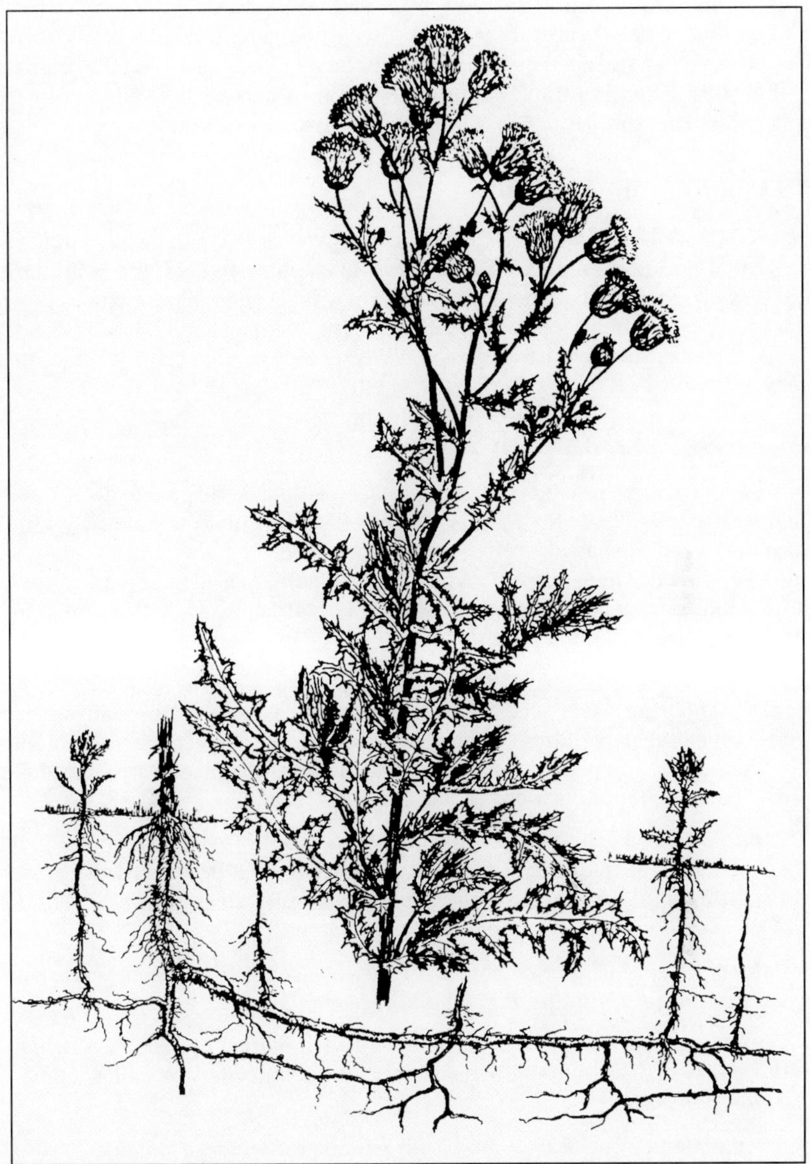

Fig. 3.6: *Cirsium arvense* reproduces vegetatively by its well wooven, underground root system. A shoot of the weed and its underground root system (diagrammtic) (ROH, USA).

Weeds equipped with vegetative propagation mechanisms are extremely difficult to manage since their propagules are located in up to 100 cm soil depth where these are not easily approachable even with deep tillage or any available herbicide. Moreover, weeds which are able to regenerate from roots will almost always be able to recover from cultivation, howsoever deep. The roots of a weed like *P. lanceolata* may hit several meters deep, and remain undisturbed by any deep tillage tool. Even if shallow roots and rhizomes of weeds are reached by tillage, it only tends to fragment and disseminate them to help their further propagation. In the destruction of perennial weeds with herbicides too, the depth of their propagules is vitally obstructive.

3.2 DISPERSAL OF WEEDS

The dispersal of seeds and vegetative propagules of weeds away from the parent plants is nature's way of providing non-competitive sites to the new individuals. If all the mature weed seeds were to fall near their mother plants, the young plants would face severe competition amongst themselves, to their great disadvantage. But, fortunately, it is not so. Weeds disperse to new sites freely, with complete disregard to the field and geographical boundaries.

3.2.1 Weed Dispersal Through Seeds

Weed seeds (and fruits) produced by the mother plants are disposed off in three ways: (A) a part of it may fall near the mother plant itself, which does not actually form a part of immediate weed dispersal. (2) A portion of it may move out of the fields as contaminants with the crop harvest, whence these get sown next season in new areas. (3) The remaining portion of the weed seeds may get dispersed with agents like wind, water, transport system, animal, man, and manure to short or long distances; sometimes thousands of kilometers away from the mother plant as follows:

1. **Wind:** Usually, the weed seeds (and fruits) that disseminate through wind possess special appendage, resulting from modifications of usually the persistent calyx, which help them to go with the wind, short or long distance away from the mother plants. Some such modifications in weeds are as follows:

    a) **Pappus:** It is a ring of fine hairs in the formation of a parachute of different shapes. It is of frequent occurrence in weeds belonging the families Asteraceae (ex. *Cirsium arvense*, *Sonchus oleracea*, and *Taraxacum officinale*) and Asclepiadaceae (ex. *Calotropis* and *Asclepias* spp.). (Fig. 3.7).

    b) **Baloon:** It is a papery, baloon like calyx enclosing loosely the weed fruit, with air around. (ex. *Physalis minima* and *P. heterophylla*).

    c) **Wings:** Certain weed fruits carry wing-like modified appendages, which allow their easier distribution on air currents. Such fruits are called Samara. (ex. *Thalaspi arvensis*)

    Besides the above special features of the windborne weed seeds/ fruits, some weed seeds are covered entirely with fine hair to enable these to fly fast with the blowing wind. This feature in weeds is called **comose** (ex. *Typha* spp. and *Saccharum spontaneum*). Then there are cases when the weed seeds are so light in weight that these can get airborne easily without possessing any special appendage for the purpose. The per thousand seed weight of such weeds may be as low as 10-20 mg or even less (ex. *Cuscuta* and *Orobanche* spp.). The *Striga* spp. seeds are almost dust particles like. About 4-5 decades back the scentists tried to quanitify the airborne capacity of such weed seeds by calculating the inverse of their densities (weight per unit surface area) and termed the values obtained as Voilure Coefficient (K). The high K value seeds (large seed surface area per unit weight) were supposed to blow easily with the wind.

High velocity wind can sometimes disperse even heavy weight weed seeds in yet another interesting manner. It may detach the whole plant of the weed from the ground and roll it over long distances, dispersing its seeds all along the way. This mode of dispersal of weed seeds is common with *Carthamus oxyacantha* 'wild safflower' and *Salsola kali* 'Russian thistle'. In *Argemone mexicana* 'Mexican poppy', the wind swings the intact plants and forces their mature pods to disperse their seeds some distance away from the mother plants. The mechanism is called **censer-mechanism**.

2. ***Water***: Aquatic weeds disperse primarily through water. They may drift either as whole plants, plant fragments, or as seeds with the water currents. Terrestrial farm weeds also frequently disperse with water in irrigation and drainage channels down the stream to new fields.

3. ***Animals***: Many weedy fruits and seeds are eaten by birds and animals. Depending upon the digestion mechanism of the animal and the nature of the weed species, 0.2 to 9.6% of the ingested weed seeds are passed in viable form with the animal excreta, which is dropped wherever the animal moves. This mechanism of weed dispersal is called **endozoochory**. Chicks digest the weed seeds most efficiently*. Several birds pick up the weed fruits and seeds on their wings, feet, and beaks and drop these during their flight. Dissemination of lantana seeds, for example, is chiefly through two birds–the Indian Myna and the Chinese turtledove. Parasitic *Loranthus* seeds stick to the beaks of the birds which are transferred to new branches of the trees when they rub their beaks against them.

   Farm animals carry weed seeds and fruits on their skin, hair, and hooves. This is aided by special appendages, such as hooks (Ex. *Xanthium strumarium*), stiff hair (Ex. *Cenchrus* spp.), sharp spines (Ex. *Tribulus terrestris*), scarious bracts (Ex. *Achyranthus aspera*), and sticky glands (Ex. *Boerhavia repens*). Ants carry a large number of certain weed seeds possessing attractive secretions, from one place to another.

4. ***Man***: Careless acts of man are greatly responsible for the dispersal of weeds. For example, when farm machinery is carried from one field to another without proper cleaning, it carries numerous weed seeds with it. Weed seeds and fruits are carried on wheels of carts, automobiles, and even aeroplanes. Too, man has carried weeds with him throughout the globe during his travels. Numerous weed seeds and fruits are dispersed by man with raw agricultural produce. This usually occurs in the case of weeds that mature at the same time and height as the host crop, and have similar size and shape of their seeds (or fruits) as the crop seeds. Such weeds are called

---

* *Chicks showed weed seed viability of 0.2% in their excreta, against 9.6% by calves, 8.7% by horses, and 6.4% by sheep.*

satellite weeds, for instance, *Avena fatua*, *Phalaris minor*, *Oryza* sp., *Cichorium intybus*, and *Cuscuta* spp. They form an integral part of specific crops.

5. **Manures and Silage:** Farm-yard manure (FYM) can be an important source of dissemination of weeds since after numerous viable weed seeds are present in the dung of farm animals. Also, there is often direct additions of mature weeds to the compost pits as farm wastes. Even under optimum temperature and acidity conditions of the compost pits, the seeds of a weed like *Convolvulus arvensis* 'field bindweed' have been reported to retain viability to the extent of 4% in the first month of composting, and up to 1%, two months later. Four months of proper composting, however, devitalized all weed seeds. But in practice, on farmer fields the optimum temperature and acidity conditions are seldom obtained in the compost pits. Therefore, a large number of weed seeds often retain viability in the FYM. In fact, it is an important source of weeds in many crop fields in India.

   Silage and hay are also found to carry considerable viable weed seeds.

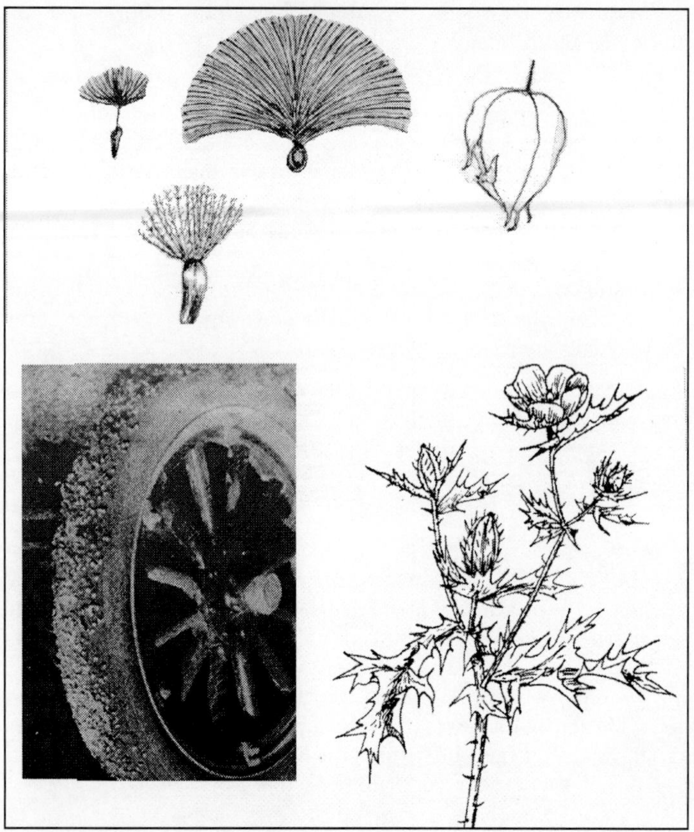

Fig. 3.7: Dispersal aids of different kinds form very important tools to aid weeds in their spread to new areas. *Top* = Parachutes and baloon, *Bottom right* = *Argemone mexicana* with censer machanism. *Bottom left* = Numerous weed seeds being carried on wheels of a vehicle.

3.2.2 Weed Dispersal Through Vegetative Propagules and Whole Plants

Careless cultivation of land is perhaps the foremost factor in the dispersal of vegetative propagules of weeds. Cultivation detaches underground organs of weeds such as rhizomes, rootstocks, and tubers and drags them to uninfested spots where they grow into new colonies. The aerial bulbs of *Allium* spp. 'wild onion' disseminate with seeds of small grains. Transplants of crops often carry weed seeds, rhizomes, and tubers hidden in their root soil. A weed like *Echinochloa* spp. 'barnyardgrass' mimics rice plants so well that it may leave rice nurseries along with the crop seedlings and get transplanted in the main field in large numbers. Aquatic weeds (whole plant, plant fragments, or vegetative propagules) disseminate largely with water currents, boats, and ships.

Besides the vegetative propagation and dispersal of perennial weeds, we have deliberately introduced in India the **whole plants** of certain weeds as ornamental plants, largely from Tropical and Subtropical America during 1980s or so in mainly Eastern India, from where, these spread to other areas. Some such alien invasive weeds with us today are: *Ageratum* spp. (agetarum), *Chormolaena odorata* (siam weed), *Eichhornia crassipes* (waterhyacinth), and *Lantana camara* (lantana). Aother perennial weed, *Salvinia molesta* (waterfern) was introduced as a botanical specimen at the Royal Botanical gardens, Calcutta during 1930s from where it got dispersed to the neighbouring areas, chiefly Kerala. One must guard against any future weed diaspora like situation.

3.3 PERSISTENCE OF WEEDS

Weeds are highly persistent* category of plants. They existed even before the first seed of any crop was planted on earth and they are with us even today, probably in larger number and with greater vigour. This speaks ample of their highly persistent nature. If a mixed growth of a crop and weeds is left to nature, soon there will be weeds all over, with no trace of the crop plants. High persistence of weeds results from their multifacet mechanisms. Important among these are:-

1. ***Prolific Seed Production***: Most weeds are prolific seed producers. For instance, the per plant seed production capacity of *Cuscuta* spp. was found approximately 16,000; *Conyza* 33,992; *Chenopodium album*, 72,000; and *Amaranthus*, 196,000. Only in few instances of some perennial weeds, the seed production was weak (Table 3.1). Further, the immediate viability of weed seeds has been found to vary from 6 to 78%. Thus, one can anticipate that in majority of cases even if a few weedy plants escaped control measures in the field, they were sufficient to produce enough seeds to continue their progeny for years to come. It is further interesting to note that weeds can set viable seeds even when they are harvested before full maturity. Perennial sowthistle (*Sonchus arvensis*) can set viable seeds even when it is cut during its flowering stage and kept in shade. Chickweed (*Stellaria media*) and

* *The persistence of an organism refers to its ability to repeatedly invade an environment even when it was apparently removed from the scene by man (or any other agent). This should be differentiated from its hardiness which refers to its ability to withstand all kinds of natural stresses at a given place. Weeds are both, persistent and hardy.*

purslane (*Portulaca oleracea*) have also been found well adapted to maturing their seeds on uprooted plants. Not only this, weeds are well adapted to premature flowering and seed setting under adverse environment conditions. A weedy plant must produce some seeds before it perishes under any stress of nature, may it be drought, biotic pressure, disease or insect pest, etc. It is commonly observed that under favourable conditions *Chenopodium album* may grow as much as 30-50 cm tall before it flowers and sets seeds. But in the event of severe drought it may grow hardly 3 cm high, and still produce some seeds before it withers.

Table 3.2: Period for Full and Partial Maturity of Certain Weeds When They Can Be Harvested Without Loss of Their Seed Vitality (After Chakrawarti, 1966)

Weed species	Period of full maturity after flowering (days)	Minimum maturity period after flowering (days)
Anagallis arvensis	25	15
Argemone mexicana	50	35
Asphodelus tenuifolius	40	15
Lathyrus aphaca	35	15
Melilotus indica	35	20
Solanum nigrum	45	15
Vicia hirsuta	30	15

2. ***Dormancy* of Weed Seeds and Other Propagules in Soil:*** As stated earlier, the majority of weed seeds lying below about 5 cm soil depth remain dormant, and act as source for future flushes of weeds. Permanent experiments laid out for up to 10 decades have shown that depending upon the weed species, the weed seeds retained viability for 2 to 100 years, to different levels. Perhaps, the oldest seed burial experiments were laid out in 1879 by late Dr. W. J. Beal in USA. The latest viability tests from thecse experiments were reported by Kiviban and Bavdurski (1973). Thus, the soils, both agricultural and otherwise, acted as "reserve banks" for the weed seeds and their other propagules. The phenomenon of dormancy and consequent longevity of weed seeds in soils is a very important tool with weeds to ensure their everlasting existence against all odds of nature (and man). If all weed seeds present in the soil were to germinate at one time, a single tillage operation could wipe these out of the scene. But contrary to it, only a fraction of weed seeds present in any soil germinate at any one time, leaving others to germinate later. Also, a few weedy plants which escaped attention in a field are often sufficient to recoup the seed banks in the soil. In this context, the old gardener's saying. "one year seeding is seven years' weeding", still holds good.

   Within the soil, weed seeds can remain dormant for three reasons, as follows:-

   a) ***Enforced dormancy:*** Enforced dormancy in weed seeds is due to their placement deeper than 5 cm, resulting usually from tillage of the field. Weed seeds under this kind of dormancy germinate readily whenever these are restored to the top 3

* *Dormancy is a state of seeds (or other propagules) in which these are alive but not ready to germinate/sprout. In other words, "dormancy is development suspended".*

to 5 cm layer of soil by tillage, provided adequate soil moisture and congenial temperatures were available in this zone of the soil. Enforced dormancy is a non-specific character of the seeds and it is caused by the absence of red light (r) under the ground, which otherwise induces germination in seeds by activating their phytochrome system (P), comprising a responsive chromophore blue pigment attached to the protein molecule in seeds. Far-red light (fr) deactivates the system and thus induces dormancy in seeds.

$$Pr \underset{red}{\overset{far\ red}{\rightleftarrows}} Pfr$$

Cultivation counters enforced dormancy by bringing the weeds to surface where they are exposed to full sun-light spectrum, besides better aeration. Higher soil temperature and NO_3 content of surface soil may further help in breaking the enforced seed dormancy.

b) ***Innate dormancy***: Innate dormancy is a genetically controlled character and it is a feature of specific weed seeds. Innate dormant seeds will fail to germinate even if they were present in the top 3 to 5 cm soil and adequate soil moisture and temperature conditions were provided to them. Innate dormancy usually results for reasons of either hard seed coats, like in *Setaria*, *Ipomoea*, and *Xanthium* spp., or immature embryos, as observed in *Polygonum*, *Juncus*, and *Eleocharis* spp. In certain weed seeds, particularly those of xerophytic origin, the presence of specific germination inhibitors is responsible for their innate dormancy. In nature the innate dormancy of weed seeds is overcome with either passage of time, or under the influence of some climatic pressure.

c) ***Induced Dormancy***: Induced dormancy results from some sudden physiological change in otherwise non-dormant weed seeds under the impact of factors like a marked rise in soil temperature, increased CO_2 content of the soil, low O_2 pressures, waterlogging, etc. Certain weed seeds, like those of wildoat (*Avena fatua*), exhibit all the three kinds of dormancies.

3. ***Vegetative Propagation:*** Many weeds are extremely persistent because of their ability to propagate by vegetative means. When the above ground parts of such weeds are destroyed, their deeply placed vegetative propagules put forth new shoots as soon as the external stresses are removed and favourable conditions revive. Even if some kind of deep tillage is employed in an attempt to destroy these, it will be a futile exercise since fragments of the weed propagules get easily dispersed to new areas where they initiate fresh colonies.

4. ***Rapid Dispersal***: Dispersal is a very important means of persistence of weeds. It exposes them to different ecosystems so that each weed species can choose its most favourable environment and put up a hard struggle for existence in nature. Dispersal is the key factor in developing a persistent weed population for every possible niche in the environment. Dispersal aids persistence of weeds in proportion to the dispersal agents and adaptations available to them.

5. ***Inherent Hardiness:*** To be widely successful a weed species must adapt itself to diverse environmental conditions. Weeds seem to possess some kind of built-in mechanism to survive against the vagaries of nature, like extreme cold, heat, drought, biotic stress, and soil abnormalities. This is inherent hardiness of weeds. It is hard to find weeds damaged under a night's severe frost, or destroyed because of attack by some insect pest, disease organism, or nematode. Weeds are rarely seen to either develop chlorosis or any other mineral deficiency or toxicity symptoms, even though the soil may be actually abnormal in its mineral composition. Also, poor quality water declared unfit for irrigating crops, fails to injure weeds. In fact, in crop fields all abnormal features of soil and water help weeds to grow vigorously in spaces vacated by the stunted growth (or death) of the crop plants. The mechanisms involved in this inherent hardiness of weeds are not much known. Further, several weeds of tropical origin, *eg Cyperus* and *Amaranthus* spp.,* have the advantage of adopting C_4 pathway of CO_2 fixation (Paul and Elmore, 1984), which is devoid of photorespiration. Several weeds have exceptionally high transpiration efficiency, low nutrient requirements, and slow rates of translocation of food and minerals. Such adaptations in weeds help them to persist in adverse weather conditions. High rates of elongation in certain weeds, particularly in the initial stages of growth, improve their competing ability and persistence. But a common aspect of inherent hardiness of all weeds seems to be their numerous generations of natural selection through climatic stresses in the struggle for survival of the fittest, advocated by Charles Darwin in the year 1859.

6. ***Evasiveness:*** Many a weed is capable of evading destruction by animals and man because of their *bitter taste, disagreeable odour, spiny nature, and mimicry* (Barrett, 1984).

7. ***Self Regeneration:*** Weeds are self-sown plants. They don't require any artificial, friable seedbeds for their germination. Detached from the mother plants, weed seeds and other propagules germinate profusely on undisturbed soils whenever the environment is favourable for the purpose.

8. ***Selective Invasion:*** Weed species differ widely in their soil and climatic requirements. But in the first instance, the weed flora composition depends upon the chance a particular weed had to reach a particular site. The nature then makes a critical selection out of the lot and allows only those weed seeds to germinate at a time which were most adapted to the environment prevailing then. (Tiwari and Besen, 1984; Singh, 1981, and Holzer and Numata, 1982). The seeds of rest of the weed species wait in soil till the environment outside changes. At this stage, suddenly another set of weed species takes over the ground. The major environment factors which determine the weed species composition on the ground comprise the available soil moisture, soil pH, temperature, photoperiod, and solar energy. To cite some examples, in a typical dry farming situation the weed flora often comprises moisture hardy species like *Tribulus terrestris, Argemone mexicana, Eragrostis cilianesis, Euphorbia hirta, Celosia argentea,* and *Heliotropium eichwaldii.* When

---

**Most of the grass weeds possess C_4 mechanism of CO_2 fixation. A complete listing of such weeds is aviable in Weeds Today (USA) 15(4):34.*

such fields are brought under irrigation, soon these weed species are replaced by the better moisture responsive weeds like *Trianthema monogyna*, *Phalaris minor*, *Asphodellus tenuifolius*, *Malva parviflora*, *Commelina benghalensis*, and *Brachiaria ramosa*, depending upon the season. Further, if such fields are irrigated still more intensively and turned into paddy fields by ponding the water, there shall be another shift in weed species. In this situation weeds like *Echinochloa*, *Caesulina*, *Butomus*, and *Eclipta* spp. will dominate the scene. Likewise, weeds in sugarbeet grow on salty soils are specific to such soils, for instance, *Chenopodium murale*, *Salsola kali*, *Taraxacum officinale*, *Polygonum* spp. and *Distichalis stricta*. Weed species also get specific to soil texture. For instance, *Celosia argentea* and *Tribulus terrestris* are dominant on sandy and light texture soils, but weeds like Trianthema monogyna and Amaranthus viridis infest heavy and fine texture soils. Weed species also differ with the microclimate offered by a particular crop. For instance, *Coronopus didymus* and *Cichorium intybus* prefer closely sown and frequently irrigated crops like lucerne and berseem, and they avoid open row crops like chickpea and mustard. Likewise, an early sown crop is likely to be infested with weed flora that is quite different from a timely or late sown crop in the same place. Climatic and seasonal changes in an environment also force rapid diversion in the weed flora towards the most adapted species. To sum up, weeds are able to dominate in every situation by choosing and putting forth the most befitting species. The mechanism of such an armour available to weeds seems to be a perfect, remote sensing system, leading to their observed persistence. They may develop in agricultural fields in response to repeated use of a herbicide in the same field in two major ways. First, within the vast population of a weed species certain amount of chance crossing is a usual natural phenomenon, resulting in few individual sthat may be resistant to a herbicide to which its primary weed population was quite susceptible. When this herbicide is applied repeatedly on such a weed growth, slowly the resistant biotypes, called chemotypes, multiply in the spaces vacated by the herbicidal control of their, primary, susceptible weed population. When the field is eventually infested largely with the chemotypes of the weed species in question, weed succession or weed shift is said to have occurred. Currently in India, wide spread of isoproturon – resistant chemotypes of *Phalaris minor* in wheat fields is a major weed succession problem of this nature chiefly in her N-W states (see also Chapter 21). At the global level, chemotypes of as many as 155 weed species belonging to different families have been placed on record.

Second, in any crop when a selective herbicide is applied to a mixed growth of different weed species, it frees the crop of most of the weeds to give acceptable, high crop yields. However, during the process one or two weed species, which initially existed in extremely low and ignorable relative density, may prove tolerant to the applied herbicide. Every thing looks fine at this stage in the field but, during course of repeated use of the same herbicide for 2-3 years, the few individuals of one or two resistant weed species may multiply fast enough to occupy niches in the field created by the control of the susceptible weed species. At this stage, a weed species shift of immediate concern to farmers is said to have occurred. Many examples of such alarming wed species successions have recently been recorded in the country, particularly in wheat, rice and soybean.

9. ***Weed Succession:*** In nature, the individuals of a weed species often have chance to cross breed to variable levels. This leads to the development of a few plants of

different genetic make-up, forming new races within a species. Such races of weeds are called **agricultural ecotypes.** When herbicides (or bioagents) are used continuously to destroy the "normal" races of a weed species, their newly developed ecotypes may sometimes prove tolerant to the herbicides used, whence they get chance to gradually expand in numbers, each season. Such agricultural ecotypes are then called **chemotypes**. The chemotypes greatly aid a weed species to persist.

Weed succession can also occur amongst different weed species themselves in response to long term adoption of an agricultural practice, including the use of herbicides. This leads to the destruction of the susceptible group of weed species, leaving behind few plants of the resistant species to gradually build up their population and finally emerge as the dominant weed flora of the area. In India, several examples of this kind have been recorded in recent years. Singh *et al* (1993) reported that in the Punjab, in wheat fields, population of *Avena fatua* 'wild oat' was on increase because of several years' herbicidal control of *Phalaris minor*. Likewise, in paddy fields, the continuous use of butachlor has led to increase in the tolerant weed, *Ischaemum rugosum*, 'wrinklegrass' (Singh and Kolar, 1992). In Tamil Nadu, the reapeated use of butachlor in paddy fields has led to increase in *Cyperus rotundus*, 'nutsedge' and some other perennial weeds (Kathiresan, 1993). Likewise, in West Bengal, *Echinochloa* spp. 'barnyardgrass' is no more a major weed since it is being replaced fast by weeds like *Cyperus*, *Scirpus*, *Fimbristylis*, *Eleocharis*, and *Sphenocloa* spp. In Jabalpur (Madhya Pradesh), in a similar situation herbicidal control in rice was reported to have enhanced population of *Sehima nervosum*, *Cyperus iria*, and *C. communis*. Similarly, at Palampur (Himachal Pradesh) long term adoption of paddy- wheat sequence has led to the march of weeds like *Polypogon*, *Alopecurus*, and *Poa* spp. In wheat fields in North India, in general, the long term use of 2,4-D in wheat fields has led to switch over to comparatively tolerant weeds like *Lathyrus*, *Anagallis*, *Melilotus*, *Convolvulus*, *Medicago*, *Cirsium*, and *Rumex* spp. Also, the continued use of isoproturon to control certain grasses in wheat fields has given boost to tolerant weeds like *Anagallis*, *Digitaria*, and *Medicago* spp. *Thus, weed succession is a very important tool in the persistence of weeds against all hurdles placed by the farmer*. Even a long term change of a crop or cropping practice will lead to shift in the weed flora composition.

Finally, the overall persistence of a weed depends upon its capability to adopt one or more of the above cited features. A weed species that embodies majority of these factors is surely a horrible weed, for instance, *Sorghum halepense* and *Saccharum spontaneum*.

SUMMARY

The perpetuation of a plant species depends upon its ability to reproduce despite the many factors which direct towards its suppression. Weeds have tremendous perpetuation capacity with various methods of reproduction and dispersal of their propagules. They propagate themselves sexually, asexually, as well as vegetatively. The vegetative propagules comprise roots and aerial or underground modified stems *eg* rhizomes, stolons, tubers, and bulbs. Many weeds reproduce both by seeds and vegetative propagules.

Weeds, as different from crops, are equipped with several mechanisms of dispersal to long and short distances, away from their mother plants. Wind, water, birds, animals, and men are common dispersing agents of weeds and their propagules. Dispersal gives weeds two important advantages. *First,* it reduces the intra-weed competition. *Secondly,* it provides them opportunity to exploit new situations.

A plant usually becomes a weed because of its persitence against odds present amongst the crop plants or in open situations. The hardy nature of weeds is largely due to their prolific seed production capacity, seed dormancy, vegetative reproduction, dispersal, inherent hardiness, evasiveness, self-regeneration, numeral impact, and high genetic variability.

With discussions offered in Chapters 1 to 3, it is now possible to view in nutshell the persistent nature of WEEDS in comparison to CROPS, as follows:

1. *Weeds* are the result of very long time natural selection under highly competitive conditions, whereas the present day *crop* varieties are invariably bred in almost competition-free environment.
2. *Weeds,* with their tremendous seed producing ability and vegetative means of propagation, have very high regeneration capacity. Most *crop* plants, on the other hand, produce comparatively much lesser number of seeds, and there are only a few species that can be propagated vegetatively. Also, *weed seeds* retain viability for years, while the *crop seeds* lose viability soon unless these were stored properly.
3. *Weeds* have several means of dissemination, but *crops* have none except their purposeful introduction by man.
4. *Weeds* are self-sown plants whereas *crops* are required to be planted by man, with intense care.
5. *Weeds* grow best in an undisturbed environment, but normally *crops* cannot be grown without alteration of the environment by man to suit individual crop species and variety.
6. By their very nature, the weedy plants are naturally adapted to local conditions to thrive at the expense of our more refined edible and ornamental crops.

SELECTED BIBLIOGRAPHY

1. Albrecht, H. 2005. Development of arable weed seedbanks during the 6 years after the change from conventional to organic farming. Weed Research 45: 339-350 (U.K.).
2. Bansal, G. L and Singh, C. M. 1984. Germination, growth, and development of three grassy weeds of wheat. Ind. J. Weed Sci., 16 (2) 121-123.
3. Barrett, S. C. H. 1984. Rice mimicry in barnyardgrass. Weeds Today 15 (1) 6.
4. Barrett, S. C. H. 1992. Genetics of weed invasions. (IN) Applied Population Biology (Ed) Jain, S. K., Kluwer Academic Publishers 91-119.
5. Bhatia, R.K. *et al.* 2002. Soil seed bank dyanamics of *Phalaris minor* as influenced by different herbicides in wheat. Proc. Int. Workshop on Herbicide Resistance and Zero Tillage held March 4-6, 2002, at HAU, Hisar (India), 63 -66 (India).

6. Chakrawarti, S. C. 1996. Certain observations on the germination of immature weed seeds. Proc. 2nd All India Weed Control Seminar held, Feb. 14-17, at HAU, Hisar (India) 38.
7. Corn, J. S. and Farris, M. L. 1987. Seed viability and dormancy of 17 weed species after 21 months in Alaska. Weed Sci. 35 (4) 524-529.
8. Datta, S. C. *et al.* 1980. Reproductive potential of some Indian weeds. Seed Res. 8 11-18.
9. Davis, A. S. *et al.* 2005. Weed seedbank and community shifts in a long-term cropping systems experiment. Weed Sci. 53: 296-306 (USA).
10. Delonit, Richarel 1970. Illustrated Taxonomy Manual of Weed Seeds, Wisconsin Pub.,
11. Geetha, T. *et al.* 2003. Enrichment of soil weed seed-bank by goat manure. Abst. Bienn. Conf. ISWS, held 12-14 March 2003 at G.B.P. Univ. Agri. Technol, Pantnagar (India): 60.
12. Gupta, O.P. 2006. Fundamentals of Weed Science. Agrobios. (India), Jodhpur. 364 p.
13. Holzer, N. and M. Numata, 1982. Biology and Ecology of Weeds. The Hague, Netherlands. 461 p.
14. Hongo, A. 1994. Longevity of buried seeds of three *Rumex* species over a fourteen year period. Weed Research (Tokyo) 39 (1) 52-53.
15. Jain, K. K. and Timari, J. P. 1993. Floristic composition of soybean- weed ecosystem and influence of tillage on weed dyanamics. Ind. J. Weed Sci. 25 (3 & 4) 44-48.
16. Kathiresan, Rm. 1993. Weed shifts in rice - blackgram system. Ind. Agro. News VI (4) 4.
17. King, L. J. (ed). 1966. Weeds of the World. Interscience Publishers Inc. N. Y. 10003, 529 p.
18. Kiviban. A. and Bavdurski, R. S. 1973. The ninety year period for Dr. Beals' seed viability experiment. Am. J. Bot. 60 140-145.
19. Kolar, J. S. and Mehra, S. P. 1992. Changing scenario of weed flora in agroecosystem of Punjab. (IN) Changing Scenario of Our Environment (EdS) Dhaliwal, G. S. *et al.*, PAU, Ludhiana (India) 252- 262.
20. Malik, N. *et al.* 1987. Growth and development of false cleavers (*Galium spurium* L.). Weed Sci. 36 (4) 490-495.
21. Muniyappa, T. V. *et al.* 1973. Seed production potential of some common weeds and screening of herbicides for their control. Paper presented at the All India Weed Control Seminar, 11th – 14th June, 1973, at HAU, Hisar (India).
22. Naidu, V.S.G..R. and J. G. Varshney, 2007. Weed Seed Atlas. I.C.A.R. National Research Centre for Weed Sci., Jabalpur (India).
23. Nandlal, D. P. and Singh, C. B. 1993. Changes in the weed flora of rice-wheat cropping system. Ind. J. Weed Sci. 25 (1 & 2) 22-28.
24. Paria, N. and Sahoo, S. K. 1981. Reproductive capacity of certain weeds. Geobios 8 135-137.
25. Parsons, W. T. and Cuthbertson, E. G. 2001. Noxious Weeds of Australia. CSIRO Pub., Australia. 712 p.

26. Paul, R. and Elmore, C. D. 1984. Weeds and the C_4 syndrome. Weeds Today 15 (1) 3-4.

27. Porwal, M. K. and Gupta, O. P. 1989. Phenology of weeds in wheat as influenced by weed control. Mad. Agr. J. 76 (11) 630-635.

28. Singh, D. N. 1981. Ecological Approaches to Indian Weeds. Geobios Int., Jodhpur (India), 300 pp.

29. Singh, T. and Kolar, J. S. 1992. Growth behaviour of *Ischaemum rugosum* Salisb. (wrinklegrass) in competition with transplanted paddy. Ind. Weed Sci. 24 (1 & 2) 59-61.

30. Singh, T. *et al.* 1993. Weed flora of wheat fields in the Punjab. Ind. J. Weed Sci. 25 (1 & 2) 17-21.

31. Standifer, L. C. 1980. A technique for estimating weed seed population in cultivated soils. Weed Sci. 29 (2) 134-158.

32. Suzuki, M. 1994. Observations on germination ability of upland weeds burried into soil at a 30 cm depth during 25 years. Weed Research (Tokyo) 39 (91) 34-39.

33. Tewari, J. P. and Besen, C. R. 1984. Ecology of *Parthenium hysterophorus*. Ind. J. Weed Sci. 16 (3) 203 - 206.

34. Umarani, R. *et al.* 1994. Studies on dormancy and germination of *Trianthema portulacstrum*. Ind. J. Weed Sci. 26 (3 & 4) 82-88.

35. Wanger, L. K. 1988. Germination and seedling emergence in *Spergula arvensis*. Amer. J. Bot. 75 (4) 465-475.

36. Wilson, R. G. *et al.* 1985. Potential for using weed seed content in the soil to predict future weed problems. Weed Sci. 33 171-175.

37. Yenish, J. P. *et al.* 1992. Effects of tillage on vertical distribution and viability of weed seeds in soil. Weed Sci. 40 (3) 429 – 433

Chapter 4

THE CLASSIFICATION AND DISTRIBUTION OF WEEDS

There are over 30,000 species of plants designated as weeds in specific situations around the world, of which about 18,000 are reported to cause serious losses in agriculture. Had each of these weed species needed a specific control measure it would have been impossible for man to control them, economically. Fortunately, several weed species often respond alike to a common weed control measure because of similarity in some aspect of their ontogeny, physiology, or morphology. This enables us to generalize the effectiveness or failure of a weed control practice against weeds as a class, instead of individual weed species. Of course, while considering weeds in groups some exceptions and overlappings must always be expected.

4.1 CLASSIFICATION OF WEEDS

There are many ways weeds can be grouped for the convenience of planning, interpreting, and recording control measures against them. Some important classifications of weeds used by the weed scientists the world-over for different purposes are as follows:

4.1.1 Classification According to Ontogeny of Weeds

Depending upon their life cycle, weeds can be classified as (i) *annuals*, (ii) *biennials* and (iii) *perennials*. Weeds belonging to any one of these classes have specific mode of propagation, dispersal, and persistence which (a) determine the gravity of the weed problem and (b) dictate their most vulnerable stage to specific control measures.

1. ***Annual weeds:*** Annual weeds grow and mature within a year of their germination; more commonly in one season itself. New plants of such weeds regenerate the next season from additional seeds present in the soil. An annual weed can either be a *summer annual* or a *winter annual*, depending upon part of the year when it puts forth its major growth. A few examples of summer annual weeds are *Trianthema* spp. 'carpetweeds', *Setaria glauca 'foxtail'* and *Digera arvensis* 'digera'. Weeds like

Chenopodium sp. 'lambsquarters', *Vicia* spp. 'vetches' are typical winter annuals. A weed like *Amaranthus viridis* 'amaranthus' may grow round the year near irrigation channels and other moist places, but primarily it is a summer annual plant. Majority of annual weeds take one full season to mature, though a weed like *Phyllanthus fraternus* 'niruri' completes its seed to seed cycle within two or four weeks. Such short-lived annuals are called **ephemerals**. The ephemerals can escape even closely spaced weedings and drought periods.

In general, the annual weeds reproduce by abundant seed production; however, some like *Allium* spp. 'wild onion 'and' wildgarlic', may grow also form bulbs and bulbils. Another important characteristic of many annual weeds is that they fail to regrow when they are cut close to the ground level. Such annual weeds are called *simple annuals*. In variance with these, several annual weeds possess crown buds which sprout into new shoots soon after the mother plant is topped. The annual weeds are comparatively easy to control, provided one is determined to do so. Such weeds must be destroyed before they set seeds each year to gradually reduce their seed population build-up in the soil. Annual weeds usually produce thousands of seeds on each plant. Buried in soil by deep tillage, these weed seeds can remain dormant for several years. This makes weed eradication almost infeasible. Therefore, a farmer must be particular about minimising weed seed setting on his farm.

2. ***Biennial weeds:*** Biennial weeds complete their life cycle in two years; in the first year they remain vegetative and in the second year they produce flowers and set seeds. The influence of environment, however, may alter this usual behaviour of biennial weeds when they may either bolt in the first year itself, or may delay flowering up to the third year of their growth. The usual feature of biennial weeds to flower in the second year of growth limits their dispersal with crop seeds, very much. It is so because they get harvested along with the crop plants before they get a chance to set seeds. But when a biennial weed like *Cichorium intybus* bolts every year, its dissemination through crop seeds is as important as in any annual weed. Some other common examples of biennial weeds are; *Daucus carota, Cirsium vulgare, Cichorium intybus, Cirsium vulgare, Carduus nutans, Gnaphalium obtusifolium, Senecio jacobaea, Centaurea diffusa* and *Verbascum* spp.

   A weed like *Malva neglecta* exhibits features of both annual and biennial weed. Also, at times a biennial weed like *Cichorium intybus* may behave as an annual, or even perennial, depending upon the prevailing environment. Still, in general, the identification of biennial weeds as a separate class of plants, holds good. The biennial weeds must be controlled in the first year of growth before these have a chance to store food in their roots.

3. ***Perennial weeds:*** Besides through seeds, the perennial weeds reproduce vegetatively from underground, specialised organs. They grow for three or more years before they wither. In tropical areas the perennial weeds remain green throughout the year although in the subtropical regions they may undergo dormancy during the low temperature periods. Usually, perennial weeds flower for the first time in the second year of their growth and thereafter each year regularly. Depending upon the depth of their underground growth, the perennial weeds may further be classified as (a) *shallow rooted* and (b) *deep rooted species. Cynodon dactylon* 'bermudagrass', *Agropyron repens* 'quackgrass', *Paspalum distichum, Sporobolus spp., Agropyron*

repens, Andropogon virginicus, Scirpus sp., Cyperus esculentus, Carex lasiocarpa, Lepidium darba, Allium vineale, Hypericum perforatum, and *Rumex crispus* are common examples of the shallow rooted perennial weeds. Their roots and rhizomes are limited mainly to the furrow slice of soil. *Cyperus rotundus* 'purple nutsedge', *Sorghum halepense 'johnsongrass', Pluchea lanceolata, Sonchus arvensis, Taraxacum officinale, Cirsium arvense, Convolulus arvensis, Solanum elaegnifolium, Euphorbea esula,* and *Mikania micrantha* on the other hand, are deep rooted perennial weeds. The depth of rooting of perennial weeds is very important in deciding about their control measures. Difficult perennial weeds are also called **pernicious weeds.**

The control of perennial weeds is much more difficult than the annual weeds since neither tillage nor the present day selective herbicides can reach their deep roots and underground, modified shoot system. Therefore, attempts to suppress such weeds are usually made during the fallow season by deep summer tillage along with the application of suitable herbicides. Scientific studies on the food storage behaviour of many perennial weeds have been made to determine the optimum time of tillage and herbicide treatments to rapidly exhaust the underground, food storage organs of such weeds (Chapter 8). Also, all attempts to check the seed formation in perennial weeds, particularly of the wind-borne types, are as important as in annual weeds. Many perennial weeds spread long distances through seeds and then persist there by their underground propagules.

4.1.2 Classification According to Cotyledon Character

The discovery of 2,4-D (and MCPA) as a highly selective translocated herbicide in the 1940s gave strong recognition to two great classes of weeds, namely (i) *the monocots* and (ii) *the dicots.* In general, the monocots were found to be tolerant to the foliage applicalion of 2, 4-D, whereas the dicots proved susceptible to it. This classification of weeds is used widely even today to generalise the effect of weed killing chemicals. The dicot weeds are often referred to also as *broadleaf weeds*, and the monocot weeds as *narrow leaf* or *grass weeds*. Exceptions to this are sedges and cattails which although narrowleaved, are not grasses. They belong to the familly Cyperaceae and Typhaceae, respectively. Likewise, waterhyacinth (*Eichhornia crassipes*) is a monocot weed though it possesses prominant broad leaves. Still this classification of weeds holds good, rather most popularly, worldwide.

4.1.3 Classification According to the Nature of the Stem

Depending upon the development of bark tissues on their stems and branches, weeds are classified as (i) *woody*, (ii) *semi-woody*, and (iii) *herbaceous* species. The woody weeds include shrubs and under-shrubs, and are collectively called **brush weeds**. *Lantana camara* 'lantana' *Acacia arabica* ' 'acacia', *Prosopis juliflora* 'mesquite', *Zizyphus rotundifolia* 'wildplum', *Rhus* spp. 'poisonoak', *Rosa multiflora* 'multiflora rose', *Rubus allegheniensis* 'blackberry', *'Chrysothamus* spp. 'rabbitbrush', *Lonicera japonica* 'honey sickle', and *Haplopappus tenuisectus* 'burroweed' are common examples of brush weeds in India. In variance with woody and semi-woody weeds, the herbaeeous weeds have green, succulent stems, and are of most common occurrence around us. Recognition of brush weeds as a distinct class is useful since their control measures are entirely different form those of herbaceous weeds.

4.1.4 Classification According to Associations

According to this classification there are three types of weeds *viz.*, (1) Season-Bound Weeds, (2) Crop-Bound Weeds, and (3) Crop-Associated Weeds.

The *season-bound weeds* grow in specific season of the year with disregard to the crop species cultivated. These weeds may be either summer annuals or winter annuals. In the case of perennial weeds, the period of their major vegetative growth is taken as their growing season. For example, *Sorghum halepense* is a summer perennial weed whereas *Cirsium arvense* is a winter perennial weed.

The *crop-bound weeds* are those species of weeds which usually parasitise the host crops. They depend for their survival upon their host plants for nutrition, partially or fully. *Cuscuta* sp. 'dodder', *Orobanche* spp. 'broomrape', and *Striga* spp. 'witchweed' are the most common crop-bound weeds of the tropics.

The *crop-associated weeds,* like crop-bound weeds, are also crop specific, but for different reasons. They may be associated with certain crops for one or more of the following reasons:

1. ***Need for specific microclimate:*** Weeds like *Cichorium intybus* 'chicory' and *Coronopus didymus* 'swinecress', require for their best growth shady, cool, and moist habitat which is amply available in crops like lucerne and berseem. Such weeds, therefore, are associatad with these crops.
2. ***Mimicry:*** *Oryza sativa var. fatua* 'wildrice' in paddy fields and *Avena fatua* 'wildoat' and *Phalaris minor* 'canarygrass' in small grain crops survive because of their similarity in morphology with the host crops. So is true of *Loranthus* in the tea gardens. This mechanism is called **mimicry**. A weed like wildoat tends to grow to the height of winter grains and adjusts its ripening time to the crop over a wide varietal range. This kind of mimicry is called phenotypic mimicry.
3. ***Ready contamination of crop seeds***: *Allium* spp. 'wild onion' and 'wild garlic' and *P. minor* mature their seeds at the same height and time as the winter grains and, thus, they easily contaminate crop seeds at harvest time.

   The crop-bound and crop-associated weeds are recognized separately because they fall easy prey to a weed control measure like crop rotation.

4.1.5 Classification According to Habitat

Depending upon the place of their occurrence there can be nine important groups of weeds. A weed scientist usually specializes in the study and control of one of these groups of weeds. These groups are (i) *Crop land weeds*; (ii) *Fallowland weeds* (iii) *Grassland, Pasture or Rangeland weeds*; (iv) *Noncropland weeds* (also called *Industrial weeds*), (v) *Aquatic weeds*; (vi) *Forest and Woodland weeds*; (vii) *Lawn and garden weeds*; (viii) *Orchard and Vineyard weeds*; and (ix) *Plantation weeds*. Several weed species overlap the above classes. Despite it, this classification is important because for each situation different weed control measures are usually employed even though the target weed species may be the same.

4.1.6 Classification According to the Origin of Weeds

Many of our weeds in India originated in some other part of the world. They were introduced from their native land or from some other countries where they had earlier migrated. *Eichhornia crassipes* 'waterhyacinth', *Parthenium hysterophorus* 'carrotgrass', *Argemone mexicana* 'Mexican poppy', *Croton bonplandianus* 'crotons' and *Lantana camara* are some of highly troublesome, *introduced* or ***alien** weeds* in India.

As against the introduced weeds, *native weeds* occur within the geographical limits of their origin. Origin of many a weed is not known. The distinction between native and introduced species of weeds is of main interest to the biological weed control workers. They find biological control of introduced weeds comparatively easier. Also, the quarantine people need to identify alien weeds to check their movement from one country to another.

Table 4.1: The Origin of Important Weeds (After De Bach, 1964)

Weed species	Probable origin
Alternanthera philoxeroides	Sourth America
Convolvulus arvensis	Eurasia
Cirsium arvense	Europe, North Africa & Eastern Asia
Cyperus rotundus	Eurasia
Centaurea repens	Near East
Eupatorium odoratum	West Indies and Tropical America
Euphorbia esula	Europe
Eichhornia crassipes	Tropical America, Brazil
Halogeton glomeratus	Western Asia
Lantana camara	Central America/Tropical America
Opuntia spp.	Western Hemisphere/ south America
Orobanche sp.	Europe
Pluchea sp.	South-western U. S. A.
Senecio jacobaea	Europe.
Sorghum halepense	Southern Europe and Asia
Tribulus terrestris	Southern Europe /Africa/Medeterrian region
Ulex europaeus	Europe

Many alien weeds become so aggressive as to fast displace the indigenous flora of the new ecosystem. These are called **Invasive Alien Weeds (IAW)**. In other words, an IAW threatens the native biodiversity of the area it infests. It is amazing to note that although hardly 0.01% of the alien weeds really turn invasive yet, this apparently minute looking figure is sufficient to disturb any nation.

In India, the top 13 alien weeds recently notified as invasive (IAW) are listed here in their alphabetic order. It may be noted that four of these weeds belong to a single family 'asteraceae' (=crucifereae). All these are native to some region or the other of Tropical America.

1. *Ageratum houstonianum* Mill. (Fam. Asteraceae)

2. *Alternanthera philoxeroides* (Mart.) Griseb. (Fam. Amaranthaceae).
3. *Chromolaena odorata* (L) K.R. (Ex. *Eupatorium* sp.) (Fam. Asteraceae).
4. *Eichhornia crassipes* (Mart) Solms (Fam. Pontederiaceae).
5. *Lantana camara* L. (Fam. Verbenaceae).
6. *Mikania micrantha* H.B.K. (Fam. Asteraceae).
7. *Mimosa* spp. (Fam. Leguminosae)
8. *Parthenium hysterophorus* L. (Fam. Asteraceae).
9. *Salvinia molesta* Mitchell. (Fam. Salviniaceae).
10. *Solanum elaegnifolium* Cav. W (Fam. Solanaceae).
11. *Cuscuta* spp. (Fam. Convolvulaceae)
12. *Ipomoea carnea* (Jacq.) (Fam. Convolvulaceae)
13. *Phalaris minor* (Retz.) (Fam. Poaceae)

4.1.7 Classification According to Soils

Of the several variables of soils, pH is implicated most frequently with the distribution of weed species over areas of similar agroclimate. On highly acid soils, **acidophile** weeds such as *Rumex acetosella* and *Pteridium* spp. tend to dominate the weed flora, while on the saline and alkali soils **basophile** weeds like *Taraxacum stricta* are known to flourish well. However, most of our common weeds are **neutrophiles**. They grow over a wide range of soil pH suited to crop production. However, the dominance of certain weed spccies on a soil of particular pH does not necessarily prove their preference for it. In many instances the weed dominance may result from the absence of other weed species that were susceptible to the soil pH in question. For example, *Spergula arvensis* will grow luxuriantly on low pH soils just because other weed species cannot survive well there although it also grows very well on high pH soils. As such, it will be more appropriate to classify weeds as *salinity and acidity tolerant weeds*, rather than the acidity and salinity loving weeds.

The texture of the soil, and consequently its water holding capacity, also determines to a great extent the weed flora of a place. For example *Tribulus terrestris* and *Euphorbia* spp. are dominant on coarse texture soils whereas *Sorghum halepense* grows abundantly on heavy, moisture retentive soils. *Echinochloa colonum* and *Fimbristylis* require wet soils for their best growth. Prominence of certain weeds on particular texture soils is largely due to their ability to withstand moisture and air conditions prevailing in the soil in question.

Some weeds tend to respond also to the nutrient status of the soil. *Desmodium* and *Stellaria* spp. are highly sensitive to low P and K levels in soil, but *Crotolaria, Ipomoea, Carolina,* and *Cassia* spp. are very tolerant to low soil P levels. Likewise, *Plantago* and *Rumex* spp. survive well on low K soils.

In summary, the preponderance of certain weeds in a field is an interplay of several factors, and one should not rush to assign it to a particular soil parameter.

4.1.8 Classification According to Plant Community

Facultative weeds are those weed species that grow primarily in wild communities but often escape to cultivated fields, associating themselves closely with man's affairs, for instance, *Opuntia* spp. *Obligate weeds*, on the contrary, occur only in the cultivated or otherwise disturbed land. They cannot stand competition from volunteer vegetation in a closed community. *Convolvulus arvensis* 'field bindweed' is an obligate weed. If a heavy infestation of such a weed is abandoned for sufficiently long, it can eventually be outgrown to the point of elimination by some facultative weeds. The facultative weeds are also called **apophytes**.

4.1.9 Noxious and Objectionable Weeds

A *noxious weed is a plant arbitrarily defined as being especially undesirable, troublesome, and difficult to control* (WSSA, 1966). The status of a plant as noxious weed will vary according to legal interpretations of a country or state, as well as with the development of new weed control technology. The noxious weeds have immense capacity of reproduction and dispersal, and they adopt tricky ways to defy man's efforts to get rid of them. These are sometimes also referred to as Special Problem Weeds. (see Chapter 23). Some common noxious weeds in the tropics today are: *Cyperus rotundus*; *Pennisetum clandestinum*, *Orobanche* spp., *Eichhornia crassipes, Eupatorium odoratum, Saccharum spontaneum, Imperata cylindrica, Lantana camara, Pluchea lanceolata, Striga spp., Solanum elaegnifolium, Parthenium hysterophorus*, and *Cynodon dactylon.*[*]

An *objectionable weed* is a noxious weed whose seeds are difficult to separate, once mixed with crop seeds. However, often the terms 'noxious', 'abnoxious', and 'objectionable' weeds have been used as synonyms in the weed science literature.

4.2 DISTRIBUTION OF WEED FLORA

India, with her great variety of agroclimatic situations spread over her length and breadth, is blessed with favourable conditions for the cultivation of a variety of crops. But, by the same token, we also have in the country numerous, widely differing weed species (Gupta, 2007). An examination of the weed flora composition reported in literature from different countries fully supports this (Appendix 1). So much so that even in the same crop the weed composition is found to differ widely in different places. Several known and unknown factors govern the weed composition obtained at a given place and time. Many of these facts were discussed in Chapter 3 and, therefore, these are given here only in brief, as follows:

1. **Extent of Dispersal:** The weed composition available at a given site is governed by the kind of weed seeds and other propagules present there in the soil. This depends upon the extent to which dispersal of different weeds to new areas had taken place. The absence of a weed from particular place does not necessarily mean that it was not adapted to that farming situation. A weed could be missing from a place just because its seeds (or other propagules) had not yet reached that site. For example, a

---

***Footnote:**[*] The Seed Certification Agency of GOI has specified certain crop-wise, objectionable weeds, which are quoted in Table 5.2.*

few years back *Parthenium hysterophorus* was limited to wastelands in some southern state of India. But now it occurs throughout the country, and in a state like Maharashtra it is now also a serious weed of crop fields. In this respect sowing of weed contaminated crop seeds and the use of uncleaned farm machinery and equipment are important in weed distribution on the farms, besides the weed dispersal mechanisms discussed in Chapter 3.

2. **Climatic elements:** Climatic elements control the distribution of plants in general on the earth. Weeds are no exception to it except that their adaptability is much wider. As a result, the pressure of climatic elements on weeds is less intense than on the crops.

3. **Soil moisture:** This is the most dominant factor influencing the weed flora composition in a field. The drylands, irrigated lands, and the paddy lands afford completely different kinds of weed flora because of differences in the soil moisture strata. Even the amount and time of rainfall affect the weed community composition. Water table also controls the kind of weed species present in the field.

4. **Soil type:** Moisture retention capacity of soil, pH, salinity, drainage, and nutrient status have their own role to play in the dominance of weeds at a place. A very common observation in this regard is the prominance of *Chenopodium album* on normal soils and of *C. murale* on the somewhat salt affected soils.

5. **Agronomic practices:** This a very strong factor controlling the kind and intensity of weed flora present in different fields. In the same crop grown by different agronomic practices, the weed flora is found to vary sharply. Rice cultivation, which is conducted in several fashions in the country, is a very common example of variation in weed flora in this crop. Similarly, potato grown on flat beds usually have different weed problems than the ridge planted crop. So is true of small grains sown after a pre-sowing irrigation as against when these are sown in dry soil and irrigated thereafter. Crop rotations and monocultures also exhibit distinct differences in weed flora and weed intensity. Likewise, the date of sowing and duration of the crop grown govern the type and intensity of weeds. The extent of soil tillage is also important in this respect.

6. **Weed succession:** Weed flora is not static. It changes with an alteration in one or more of the above cited factors whence the new weed flora frequently replaces the older one. When the modern herbicide use is introduced in the system, the change in weed flora is further hastened (Chapter-3).

SUMMARY

An attempt has been made in this chapter to characterize important classes of weeds according to their growth behaviour, situation, soil, climate, etc. The importance and examples of each classification have been given. Important classes discussed are: annual and perennial weeds; monocot and dicot weeds; herbaceous and woody weeds; season-bound, crop-bound, and crop-associated weeds; crop land and non-crop land weeds; native and introduced weeds; salt-tolerant and salt-susceptible weeds; facultative and obligate weeds; and noxious and objectionable weeds.

In the second part of the chapter, factors governing the distribution of weeds in an area are discussed; *viz.*, the extent of weed dispersal, climatic factors, soil factors, agronomic practices, and weed succession.

SELECTED BIBLIOGRAPHY

1. Abbasi, S. A. 1993. World's Worst Weeds. IBD, Dehradoon (India)
2. Anon. 1968. Weeds of the North Central States. Agr. Expt. Sta. Illmois, USA, Circ. 718; 262p.
3. Anon. 1970. Selected Weeds of United States. Agr. Handbook No. 366, USDA, Washington, USA; 463 p.
4. Baruva, I.C. *et al.* 2002. A study on the weed flora of pointedgourd fields under shifting cultivation in Assam. Ind. J. Weed Sci. 34: 104-109.
5. Britto, S.J. 2002. *Senna uniflora* (Mill.) H.S. Irwin & R.C. Barneby - a new plant record for Tamil Nadu. J. Economic and Taxonomic Botany 26(1): 133-135. (India)
6. Chakre, O. J. 1983. Exotic weeds: The green cancers in natural ecosystems. Sci. Reporter. CSIR., Dec. 682-689 and 693.
7. Dangol D.R. *et al.* 2002. Phytosociology of mulberry field weeds in central Nepal. Ind. J. Weed Sci. 34:100-103.
8. Dangol, D.R. 2001. Phytosociology of weeds of cotton in Kumber farm, Bardiya, Western Nepal. Ind. J. Weed Sci. 33:160-163.
9. Datta, S. C. and Chakrabarti, 1983. Survey of weed flora and associated weeds in jute crop of Lembucherra Farm in Tripura. Ind. J. Weed Sci. 15 (1) 94-100.
10. De Bach, P. 1964. Biological Control of Insect Pests and Weeds. Chapman and Hall Ltd., 11, New Fetter Lane, London, 666 p.
11. De, G. C. and Mukhopadhyay, S. K. 1984. Weed flora in sub-humid lateritic belt of West Bengal, India.
12. Devendra, R. *et al.* 1986. Comparative growth pattern of *Echinochloa* spp. in rice monocultures. Ind. J. Weed Sci. 18 71-78.
13. Devendra, R. *et al.* 1987. Growth pattern of *Solanum elaegnifolium* and *Oxalis latifolia*. Ind. J. Weed Sci. 19 (3 & 4) 233-237.
14. Diwakar, P.G. *et al.* 2002. *Argemone ochroleuca* Sweet: a new record for Maharashtra. J. Economic and Taxonomic Botany 26(1) : 117-118. (India)
15. Downey, D. *et al.* 2004. Weeds accurately mapped using DGPS and ground-based vision identification. California Agri. 58(4): 218-221 (USA).
16. Felfoldi, E. M. 1993. Identifying the Weeds Around You. Inkata Press, Australia.
17. Gibson, K. D. *et al.* 2004. Detection of weed species in soybean using multispectral digital images. Weed Technol. 18(3): 742-749 (USA).
18. Gogoi, A.K. *et al.* 2003. Database on weeds - significance and importance. Abst. Bienn. Conf. ISWS held 12-14 March 2003 at Pantnagar (India) : 59.
19. Gupta, O. P. 2007. Fundamentals of Weed Science. Agrobios (India), Jodhpur, 379 p.

20. Jan, P. K. and Sen, D. N. 1981. Ecology of Indian arid zone weeds IX. *Echinopes echinatus* Roxb. Geobios. 8 69-71.
21. Kumar, S. and Singh, V. 1983. Phytosociological studies on the weeds of maize fields. Ind. J. Weed Sci. 15(1) 101-108.
22. Latchama, A. 1983. The major weed flora in certain winter crops of Prabhani area Ind. J. Weed Sci. 15(1) 87-93.
23. Legere, A. *et al.* 2005. Diversity and assembly of weed communities-contrasting responses across cropping systems. Weed Res. 45(4): 303-315.
24. Maheshwari, J.K. 1966. Illustrations to the flora of Delhi, CSIR, New Delhi 282 p.
25. Moody, K. 1981. Major Weeds of Rice in South and South-East Asia. Puh. IRRI, Phillipines. 79 pp.
26. Pangtey, Y. P. S. *et al.*1987. On the occurrence of *Rumex crispus* L. (Polygonaceae) in North India. Ind. J. Forestry. 10(1) 58-59.
27. Paradkar, N. R. *et al.* 1989. Survey of *kharif* weeds in Rewa division of M. P. (India). Ind. J. Weed Sci. 21 (1 & 2) 31-36.
28. Paradkar, V. K. *et al.* 1994. Weed flora associated with mandarin orchards in Setpura Plateau of M. P. Ind. J. Weed Sci. 26 (1 & 2) 60-63.
29. Rana, M.C. and N.N. Angiras 1994. Dyanamics of weed flora in soybean and wheat + pea due to imazethapyr application. Ind. J. Weed Sci. 26 (3-4); 64-70.
30. Reddy, C.S. and V.S. Raju 2002. Additions to the weed flora of Andhra Pradesh. Indian. J. of Economical and Taxonomic Botany 26(1) : 195-198. (India)
31. Rodgers, E. G. 1974. Weed prevention is the best control. Weeds Today 5(1) 8 and 22.
32. Saraswat. V. M. 1980. Ecology of India. PANS 26 (1) 45-50.
33. Sharma, M. 1981. Weed flora of Punjab. II. Weeds of *kharif* crops. Ind. J. Weed Sci. 13(1) 26-31.
34. Siddiqi, M. *et al.* 1986. Weeds of *kharif* crops in Kashmir valley. Ind. J. weed Sci. 17 (3) 22-34.
35. Stone, C. *Fimbristylis accuminata* vahl - an addition to sedge flora of Tamil Nadu, India. J. of Economic and Taxonomic Botany 26(1) : 236-238. (India).
36. Subudhi, H.N. and J. Mitra. 2002. *Mitracarpus villosus* (Sw.) DC - a new record for Rajasthan. J. Economic and Taxonomic Botany 26(1) : 193-194 (India).
37. Tewari, J. P. 1984. weed flora in winter crops at Narsinghpur (M. P.), India. Ind. J. Weed Sci. 16 (3) 139-147.
38. Thakur, C. 1984. Weed Science, 2nd Edition. Metropolitan (India), 495 p.
39. Thomas, C. G. and Abrahm, C. T. 1990. Common Weeds of Rice Ecosystem in Kerala. Pub. Kerala Agri. University, 55 p.

Chapter 5

WEED PREVENTION

Weed prevention adds enormously to the effectiveness of weed management. It should form a critical component of all cropping systems. It is based on taking specific actions to forestall the inevitable occurrence of weeds in our agricultural fields and other situations.

Weed prevention comprises all measures which deny the entry and establishment of weeds in an area. While this is an accepted definition of weed prevention, in practice, it also includes farm hygiene that prevents the every year production of seeds, tubers, and rhizomes of the weed species already present on the farm. In other words, all practices that help discourage the weeds from becoming a problem over time, form the subject of weed prevention. Thus, any physical or chemical method adopted with the main objective of not allowing the weeds to set viable seeds, is to be considered a part of weed prevention. Weed prevention reduces the farmers' efforts in controlling weeds later by physical, chemical, or other methods. It obviously makes no sense in being careless initially, allow the weeds to establish on the farm, and later destroy them laboriously during the crop season. Prevention of weeds becomes all the same more important when one realises that it is often difficult to control weeds at some prescribed optimum time in order to harvest good crops. The weed prevention measures are all the same more essential against noxious weeds which once allowed to establish, become extremely difficult to control and eradicate afterwards.

Farmers have usually adopted some kind of weed prevention for long, but these methods have been largely ineffective. It is during the last two decades that the scientific principles of prevention of weeds have been better understood than before and translated into package of practices for farmers' benefit. The success of these practices depends upon how rigidly the principles of weed prevention are practised and upon the mode of dispersal of weed species in question. For example, the weeds that disseminate with farm machinery or crop seeds can be brought under the banner of weed prevention but those disseminating with wind, usually escape it. Further, the prevention of weeds proves most effective when it is adopted on some large area simultaneously, involving cooperation of several small land owners. In *operation, weed prevention is necessarily putting a break to weed dissemination.* As such, a thorough knowledge of dissemination behaviour of weeds (Chapter 4) of the area in question is a pre-requisite to practising weed prevention.

5.1 ELEMENTS OF WEED PREVENTION

5.1.1 Use Weedfree Crop Seeds

One important way the weeds spread on the farmlands is through crop seeds, contaminated with the weed seeds. Some weed seeds always go with certain crop seeds, for example, *Avena fatua* and *Brassica* and *Sinapis* spp. with small grains. Lucerne (alfalfa), Egyptian clover (berseem), and other small seed forage legumes and grasses are particularly prone to easy contamination with specific weed seeds of similar sizes and shapes. Bigger crop seeds like maize, cotton, and soybean are less likely to carry weed seeds with them. Therefore, the crop seed judging score cards show highest weightage for weed contamination in the case of forage legumes, forage grasses, and small grains (Table 5.1 and Appendix-18).

Table 5.1: Weightage to Weed Seed Contamination Allotted in Score Card for Judging Quality of Common Crop Seeds (After Dungan and Bolin, 1950)*

Crop	% marks	Crop	% marks
Barley	35	Maize	0
Cotton	0	Oat	35
Cowpea	30	Potato	0
Forage grasses	45	Soybean	10
Forage legumes	55	Sorghum	25
Linseed	12	Wheat	35

It is very important to have a hard look into the seed-drill boxes and seedbags before planting. An apparently small **weed content** of, say 1% in wheat, will plant 1 kg weed seeds per ha. With usually very low test weights of weed seeds, this quantity of weed seeds is sufficient to infest the land with additional few thousand of weed plants. In the case of microscopic sized weed seeds of dodder and striga, even one gram of weed seed is enough to infest a hectare of cropland. And when the contaminant in crop seed is a noxious weed, the presence of even a single weed seed in the drill seed is enough to start an unmanageable weed infestation on the farm. It is, therefore, highly undesirable to plant new areas with crop seeds carrying any noxious weed seeds (Table 5.2 & Appendix-20).

Footnote:* *Measurement of weed seed admixture in crop seeds*: The extent of weed seed admixture in agricultural seeds is usually given as percentage by weight of the initial test sample. This is called *total weed content*. The chief drawback of this measurement is that it does not give the weed seed population of individual weed species in the given test sample. For similar total weed contents of the given test samples, there can be widely differing populations of weed seeds because the weed seeds vary greatly in their 1000 grain weight (Muniyappa *et al.*, 1973). As an alternative to total weed content, Wellington (1959) suggested a more refined index of stating weed seed admixtures, callcd ***seed analysis***. It is based on counting the number of weed seeds in each kg test sample. Knowing the seed rate of a crop, one could know by seed analysis the total number of weed seeds one is likely to sow per ha. This method, is obviously laborious, though desirable. As such, now it is used for the estimation of total and specific noxious weed seeds in the sample by the Seed Certification Agencies.

Table 5.2: Weed Species Designated as Objectionable According to Seed Act 1966 (of India) and their Maximum Permissible Limits in *Certified Seeds* Against The Total Weed Seed Permissible Limits in Certain Crops. (See also **Appendices-18 & 19**)

Crop	Objectionable Weed*	Permissible seed admixture limits	
		Objectionable Weeds	Total Weeds
Paddy (*Oryza sativa*)	Wildrice or redrice (*O. sativa var. fatua*)	0.02% (5)	(20)
Wheat (*Triticum aestivum*)	(*Convolvulus arvensis & Phalaris minor*)	0.01% (5)	(20)
Rape and Mustard (*Brassica campestris* and *B. Juncea*)	Mexicanpoppy (*Argemone mexicana*)	0.1% (10)	(20)
Egyptianclover (*Trifolium alaexandrinum*)	Chicory (*Cichorium intybus*)	0.05% (10)	(20)
Lucerne (*Medicago sativa*)	Dodder (*Cuscuta* spp.)	0.05% (10)	(20)
Methi (Fenugreek) (*Trigonella foenum-graceum*)	Senji (*Melilotus alba*)	0.2% (5)	(20)
Lettuce (*Lactuca sativa*)	Wildlettuce (*Lactuca serriola*)	0.2% (5)	(10)
Cucurbit (*Cucurbita* spp.)	Wildcucurbit (*Cucurbita* spp.)	0.0 (0)	(0)
Okra (*Abelmoschus esculentus*)	Wildokra (*Abelmoschus* spp.)	0.0 (0)	(0)

*A noxious weed whose seeds are difficult to separate when mixed with the crop seeds.
**Figures in % show proportion of weed plants to crop plants by number
**Figures in brackets show number of weeds seeds per kg crop seeds.

The prevention of weeds that disperse with the crop seeds can be achieved in two ways, *viz.* (i) by the production of weedfree crop seeds at the Government farms or at the farmer's field itself, and (ii) by cleaning the crop seeds of weeds before storage as well as at the time of sowing. Both these measures require motivation of the farmer to earmark separate area for multiplying his crop seeds suiting to his future needs. This crop seed nursery should be maintained completely weedfree, employing all weeding methods available on hand, with extra attention, by the farmer. The present practice of simply storing a part of general produce as future farm seeds pravailing in many developing countries, should be abandoned.

(i) Seed Cleaning Devices

Crop seeds infested with even an extremely low content of noxious or new weed seeds should be cleaned, both before its storage and before its planting. If possible, one should avoid the purchase of such crop seeds in the first instance to avoid the trouble of cleaning it later. But when cleaning must be done, the weed screenings should be collected carefully and destroyed by burning them in a container, using kerosene. In no event, the weed screenings should be permitted to reach the soil, manure pits, or animal feed; the weed seeds are not fully devitalised in the manure pits and digestive tracts of animals.

Many methods of separating weed seeds from crop seeds are available. These methods utilize some basic differences in the physical forms of crop and weed seeds, for instance, shape, size, density, nature of surface, colour, and electrical properties. Important seed cleaning methods are:-

1. *Sieving*: The most common device of separating weed seeds in seed-houses is screening. Vibrating sieves of various mesh sizes and shapes are used for this purpose. In places where combines are used to harvest grains, the produce is automatically cleaned by screening and the cleaned seeds are directly filled in separate bags. On small farms, a set of hand sieves may be used during winnowing of seed crops. Screening separates the weed seeds that are distinctly different in size from the crop seeds, and it is a general purpose method of seed cleaning. For weed seeds that are of similar size as the crop seeds, other devices that are specific in functioning may be resorted to.

2. *Salt solution separation:* Seeds of widely differing densities can be separated by simply dipping them in a 5-10% common salt solution. The heavy crop seeds settle to the bottom of the bucket while the light weed seeds float to the surface. The crop seeds thus separated must be washed with plenty of fresh water, immediately.

3. *The specific gravity pneumatic and aspirator separators:* These separators remove weed seeds that are of different specific gravity than the crop seeds, irrespective of their shapes and sizes. A stream of air is used to discriminate between seeds of different weights. The stratified seeds of different species are collected in different trays.

4. *Dented plates*: When weed seeds are much different in shape from the crop seeds, they can be separated by passing the seed mixture over dents made on discs, cylinders, or metallic sheets. The dent shape and size can be varied to catch specific weed seeds.

5. *Velvet rollers:* Seed surfaces differ in their texture. Some seeds may be rough while others smooth. When the weed seeds to be removed are rough-surfaced, like those of dodder, these can be separated from the smooth seeds of a crop like lucerne, by passing the mixture between two rollers covered with velvet cloth and rotating in opposite directions. The weed seeds are caught on the velvet while the crop seeds fall below.

6. *Conveyer belts:* Conveyer belts made of velvet cloth are used to clean crop seeds off weed seeds on the same principle as the velvet rollers.

7. *Electrical separators:* Seeds often differ in their ability to conduct electricity or hold a surface charge. When a thin layer of seeds is passed through a high voltage electric field, the low surface charge seeds fall off and the high surface-charge seeds continue on the conveyer belts revolved around a pulley.

8. *Magnetic separators:* The magnetic separators can remove rough, cracked, and sticky weed seeds from the smooth crop seeds. The device consists of slightly moistening the seed mixture and mixing some iron powder with it. The iron powder will adhere to the rough surfaces of weed seeds. When a strong magnet is passed through the iron treated seed mixture, it sweeps out the weed seeds covered with the iron dust.

9. *Horizontal disk separators:* Disk separators sort out seeds on the basis of their ability to slide or roll when they are subjected to centrifugal force in the separating drums.

5.1.2 Avoid Contamination of Manure pits

Dispense with the common practice of adding mature, or even blooming, weeds and their vegetative propagules to the manure pits in the hope of recovering their manurial value. In most cases the weed seeds do not lose their viability in the manure pits and the resulting farmyard manure (F.Y.M.) serves as a notorious source of adding weed seeds to crop land. A composting temperature of 65-90°C, maintained for 4-5 months, is needed to devitalise most weed seeds. An alternative method of destroying weed propagules in F.Y.M. is to treat it with chemicals like acrocyanamide (= 70% hydrated lime, 20.6% N_2), SMDC (=metham), DMTT (=mylone), ammonium thiocyanate or uramon (synthetic urea). These chemicals shall kill weed propagules and dissipate from the treated compost in about 6-8 weeks' time.

5.1.3 Prevent Movement of Weeds with Other Farm resources

Do not permit livestock to move form the weed-infested areas directly into clean areas because they can always drop weed seeds and fruits attached to them or those ingested by them earlier. The farm machinery, for similar reason, should be cleaned properly before moving it from one field to another. Same is true of the movement of nursery stock, gravel, sand, and soil from weed-infested areas to the new ones. The nursery stock should be properly inspected for the presence of weed propagules of, particularly, perennial weeds. The weedy rhizomes and tubers are often transplanted with nursery transplants into the main fields. Even seedlings of weeds like *Echinochloa colonum* and *Oryza sativa var. fatua*, are transplanted with rice seedlings, unless the nursery beds were kept weedfree and the crop seedlings were inspected time to time.

5.1.4 Keep Non-Crop Areas Clean

The irrigation and drainage ditches, fence lines, farm boundries, bunds, and other like uncropped areas are often neglected by farmers. These places offer a perpetual weed nursery for the cropped plots. This should be prevented by extending the weed control efforts to non-crop areas on the farm. Sometimes, it is necessary to destroy seeds of even mature weeds to prevent their dissemination to the main fields. For example, acid arsenicals can devitalise *Convolvulus arvensis* 'bindweed' seeds and the herbicidal oils, the *Tribulus terrestris* 'puncturevine' seeds. 2,4-D has been reported to inflict similar damage to maturing seeds of many grass and other weeds.

5.1.5 Keep Vigilance

A farmer should inspect his farm area periodically and should be wary of any strange looking weed seedlings. The search for them should be extended into standing crops even if herbicides or cultivators were used to control weeds there. No sooner than any strange looking weed seedlings are noticed, they should be uprooted by digging as deep as their roots may have penetrated the soil, and the soil in these spots should be treated with a suitable sterilant.

New weeds may enter an area in numerous ways, some of which may be beyond our control (Chapter 3). For instance, a noxious weed may be introduced by a farmer with fodder purchased from outside, or through a packet of ornamental seeds received by post. Visitors to farms often bring new weed seeds in the folds of their clothes and shoes. Many weeds are introduced on farm area for their ornamental or experimental values, such as for breeding crop plants. All such weedy plants should be kept under close watch to prevent their escape as regular weeds.

The weed prevention, conscious countries of the west have divided the noxious weed seeds into two classes; the 'Prohibited Noxious Weed Seeds' and the 'Restricted Noxious Weed Seeds. The *'prohibited noxious weed seeds'* are seeds of perennial weeds that reproduce by seeds as well as by vegetative propagules, and once established, are difficult to control by good cultural practices (*ex. Cirsium arvense* and *Agropyron repens*). The *'restricted noxious weed seeds'*, on the other hand, are the seeds of weeds that though objectionable in agriculture, lawns, and gardens, yet can be controlled by good agricultural practices (*ex. Cuscuta arvensis* and *Phalaris minor*).

5.1.6 Invoke Legal Measures

Legal measures are necessary to check inter-state and inter-country movement of noxious weeds if the cost of having to control additional alien weeds is to be waved. Unfortunately, thus far, in most parts of the tropical and subtropical world, noxious weeds have not been subjected to strict quarantine laws. This has resulted in the introduction and spread of some of the costliest weeds of the world. Special mention may be made of introduction of fast spreading weeds like *Parthenium hysterophorus* in non-crop areas, and *Phalaris minor*, *Poa annua*, and *Polypogon* sp. in wheat fields of India and some other countries during the past decade. The introduction of waterhyacinth as an ornamental plant by Warren Hasting's wife to India is well known. Very recently the Indian Plant Quarantine Authorities have made it compulsory to declare plants at the time of disembarking in India. Similar views already exist in advanced countries, since long. Other countries must follow it soon for International prevention of long distance movement of weeds.

SUMMARY

The forestalling the spread of weeds is essential for obtaining long term, economic control of weeds on farmland and in other situations, It is especially true of obnoxious weeds which are extremely difficult to control. Prevention of weeds requires cooperative efforts of several land owners, but there are many things that farmers may practise individually to prevent the introduction of new weeds, and dispersal of the existing ones on their farm. Of the more than 13 recognized practices of weed prevention, particular emphasis has been laid on (i) the use of weedfree crop seeds, (ii) care in the use of farmyard manure, (iii) vigilance, and (iv) legal measures. Several small and large scale devices are available for separating weed seeds from crop seeds which utilize some major differences in the physical feature of crop and weed seeds *e.g* texture, size, shape, colour, and electrical properties. Methods of preventing dissemination of weed seeds with farm-yard manure are given in the text.

Besides, a farmer must be weed conscious. He should be alarmed at the site of some strange looking weed seedlings around his land and destroy them by digging and sterilizing the spots suitably. Weeds already present on the farm must be prevented from maturing their seeds.

Legal measures to check the inter-country and interstate movement of weeds and weed seeds have been wanting in India. These must be enforced as soon as possible.

The Sanitary and Phytosanitary (SPS) Agreement of the World Trade Organisation (WTO) confers the member countries the right to take sanitary and phytosanitary measures to the extent necessary to protect human, animal or plant life or health, provided these measures are based on scientific evidence. Several countries are busy preparing the list of quarantine weeds as much for preventing introduction of noxious weeds in to the country as for facilitating trade. Australia, New Zealand, and the USA have developed a reasonably good weed risk analysis system but unfortunately, many other countries, including India, do not have one yet. Several exotic weeds, many of them potentially harmful, have gained entry into India in the recent past in varied ways. In the modern era of globalization, trade, transport, travel, and tourism have sharply accelerated the rate of weed species movement to farm distant to new habitats and become 'alien' or 'invasive alien' species. This must be checked. (Yaduraju, *et al.*, 2005).

SELECTED BIBLIOGRAPHY

1. Chand, M. *et al.* 2000. Interception of weed seeds in wheat imported from Australia. Ind. J. Weed Sci. 32: 210-212.
2. Department Agri. (Rajasthan). 2006-07. Seed and Organic Production Certification Technology. DOA, Pant Krishi Bhawan, Jaipur Pub. 45 p.
3. Dungan, G. E. and Bolin, C. E. 1950. Judging Crop Quality. Inter-state Printers & Publishers, USA, 288 pp.
4. Hitchings, S. 1959. The control and eradication of weeds in seed crops. (IN) Harper, J. L. (ed.), The Biology of Weeds. Blackwell Scientific Publications, Oxford 108-115.
5. Moss, S. R. and Clarke, J. H. 1994. Guidelines for prevention and control of herbicide resistant blackgrass. Crop Protection, 13(3) 230-234.
6. Muniyappa, T. V. *et al.* 1973. Seed production potential of some common weeds and screening herbicides for their control. (Paper read at) the All India Weed control Seminar, 11-14 June, Hissar, India.
7. National Academy of Sciences, 1968. Weed Control: Principles of Plant and Animal Pest Control. Vol. 2: 49-68.
8. Parker C. 1976. Weed research requirements of developing countries. British Crop Protection Conf. Proc. 801-807.
9. Rodgers, E.C. 1974. Weed prevention is the best control. Weeds Today, 5(1) 8 and 22.
10. Singh, V. P. *et al.* 2004. Effect of period of *soil solarization* and weed control measures on weed growth and productivity of soybean. Ind. J. Agric. Sci. 74(6): 324-328.
11. Singh, V. P. and N. T. Yaduraju, 2004. *Soil Solarization.* NRC (Weed Science), Jabalpur (India) Tech. Bull. No. 2, 23 p.
12. Tunwar, N. S. and Singh, S. V. 1988. Indian Minimum Seed Certification Standards. The Central Seed Certification Board, Minist. Agri., GOI, New Delhi. 388 p.
13. Wellington, P.S. 1959. Assessment and control of the dissemination of weeds by crop seed. (IN) Harper, L. J (Ed.). The Biology of Weeds. Blackwell Scientific Publ. Oxford 94-107.

Chapter 6

THE ELEMENTS OF WEED CONTROL

Man discriminated between useful and unwanted plants even when he was primitive, about a million years ago. He then strove to remove shrubs and tall grasses with his simple stone tools to reach the edible nuts and fruits. This, incidentally, allowed more light to reach the useful plants for photosynthesis and reduced plant competition. Cultivation of food, in preference to collecting it, led to the dawn of civilization about 10,000 years ago. The crop cultivation at that time comprised mainly two operations, viz., planting of certain food plants and pulling out the associated volunteer vegetation—the weeds. In other words, farming started with a fight with weeds, and this fight continues even today. However, during all these years, man has slowly, but surely, improved upon his capacity to deal with the weeds. About a thousand-fold increase in human population from the time agriculture started on earth and advancements in man's standard of living are closely associated with his ability to produce additional food and fibre by proper management of the vegetation in which weeds form the major component. It is truly said: ***agriculture is a controversy with weeds.***

6.1 WEED CONTROL, WEED ERADICATION, AND WEED MANAGEMENT

Weed control is the process of limiting weed infestations so that crops could be grown profitably and other activities of man conducted efficiently. The word 'crop' is not restricted here in its meaning to maize, sugarcane, or wheat, but it means any plant community that is serving some useful purpose to man and his affairs at the place of its occurrence. It could be either those low growing grasses and brush on roadsides and uncultivated areas that bind the soil and obviate erosion hazards, or, in certain situations, the tall grasses, reeds, and sedges, that shelter the charming birds and other wild life and provide pleasing variation to landscape and waterbodies. In weed control thus we seek to limit the growth of unwanted plants, both in space and time, without any attempt to eliminate them from the scene. The extent to which any weed growth is desired to be limited will depend upon the cost of weed control and the benefits anticipated from the operation. In other words the aim of weed control is to manage the vegetation on land and in waterbodies in such a way as will encourage the growth of plants beneficial to our interests at a particular place and time, and will suppress the remaining, relatively unwanted, plant species. Indiscriminate application of control measures against plants is not the objective of weed control; a land without natural vegetation will not be much worth living on. Thus, before bringing any plant under a control measure we must be able to non-erroneously identify gains to our lives that may result from limiting the growth of an apparently unwanted plant. This gain may be either the removal of immediate obstruction in man's affairs, obviating a future threat to nearby areas that may otherwise result from rapid propagation and dissemination of the weed, or improving agricultural production.

In variance with weed control, ***weed eradication*** is complete removal of all live plant parts and seeds of a weed from an area, which may be a field/farm/village/geographical region, depending upon the need. Although very attractive, it is a very expensive adventure sine it will often cost more than the land was worth. Moreover, total destruction of weeds is considered undesirable even from crop fields since many weeds harbour predators of crop pests, or secrete in soil nematodicides, while all of them hold soil nutrients against their leaching losses during fallow periods. As such, nowhere in the world, eradication of common weeds is practised. However, the heavy expense of weed eradication is justified against noxious weeds such as *Striga*, *Cuscuta*, and *Lantana* spp., to prevent their dispersal to additional millions of hectares of useful land and waterbodies. Against the common weeds, we employ only control measures. But when required, a weed eradication programme should begin when the weed growth is still limited. Once the weed has invaded large, continuous areas, its eradication becomes uneconomical. The weed eradication is accomplished in more than one year; it requires intensive initial efforts to destroy all plant parts of the weed, followed by many years' of vigilance to prevent the new weed seedlings from establishing into adult plants. In variance with it, weed control is an every year, constant rate programme. Of course, with proper preventive measures, efforts required for eradication of weeds can be reduced to a very low level, in due course of time.

During the recent past it has been progressively realised that for sustainable agriculture we must develop and practise the concept of ***weed management*** in variance with the conventional 'weed control' approach. While weed control aims at only putting down the weeds already present by some kind of physical or chemical energy, weed management is a system approach whereby whole land use planning is done in advance to minimise the very invasion of weeds in aggressive forms and give crop plants a strongly, competitive advantage over the weeds. Further, against weed populations that stll occur, the various weed control options are pre-included in the system in optimum proportions. For this, sometimes specific cropping plans may have to be chosen. The objective here is to keep the overall weed population dyanamics in view and plan long term strategies so as to gradually lower the occurrence of weeds on the farm (and in other situations). This *systems approach* is also called *integrated weed management*[*]. There are four major principles of Integrated Weed Management on farmlands:

Footnote: [*] *The FAO, Rome has defined the integrated pest management as a method whereby all*

1. Manipulation of crop habitat by utilising some biological difference between the crops and weeds, with the objective to place the former in a competitive advantage over the latter.
2. Measures should be directed to break the survival mechanism of the weed in the soil.
3. Crop husbandry practices should be incorporated which will discourage the establishment of colonies of perennial and parasitic weeds, *eg* crop rotations, etc. (see later).
4. Any individual element of weed management should be as far as possible eco-friendly, *ie* it should be innocuous to our environment.
5. Any formulated plan of weed management should be quite flexible to accommodate the possible innovations and practical experiences of the progressive farmers.

In essence, the integrated weed management, or the systems approach, should form a part of advance land and crop planning and improvement programme. Although in IWM, usually herbicides dominate the scene, yet these should not be considered as substitutes for the physical and other methods of weed control. Rather the herbicides should act as complements to the other weed control options available on hand, particularly the physical ones, in any good IWM system.

6.2 METHODS OF WEED CONTROL

6.2.1 Good Crop Husbandry Control of Weeds

In any weed control system on crop land there is no substitute to good crop husbandry methods. These methods are also some times referred to as *Ecological Control Methods*. They weaken the growth of weeds by crop competition and, thus, indirectly help in improving the efficacy of other methods of weed control. Good crop husbandry methods involve (i) selective stimulation of crops, (ii) stale seedbeds, (iii) crop rotations, (iv) summer fallowing, (v) competitive cropping, and (vi) suitable time and method of planting crops. These methods will be discussed in detail in the next chapter. Selective stimulation of crops is achieved by planting proper crops and crop varieties, maintaining high crop plant populations, and applying adequate fertilizers and amendment to the soil to the benefit of the crop. A seedbed management method that induces crops to germinate ahead of the weeds and smother them, is an important part of crop husbandry methods of weed control. Crop rotations also aid weed control; they change the crop environment and avoid building-up of unmanageable weed populations.(see Chaptar-7).

6.2.2 Physical Control of Weeds

Physical methods of weed control utilise manual energy, animal power, or fuel to run implements that dig out weeds. They are sometimes distinguished as (i) manual and (ii)

---

economically, ecologically, and toxicologically justifiable methods are employed to keep harmful organisms below the threshhold level of economic damage, keeping in the foreground the continuous employment of natural limiting factors.

mechanical methods of weed control. Since these methods as well as those mentioned in previous section, do not involve chemicals, these practices can also be grouped as *non-chemical methods* of weed control.

The physical methods of controlling weeds are by far the oldest, and the most practical, methods available even today. These are followed widely the world-over. The implements used for the physical control of weeds vary from simple hand tools to complex, multitined weeding machines run with tractors. The physical control of weeds is safe to crop, environment, and to the user. It does not involve any great skill on the part of the farmer to use weeding tools and implements. However, the manual weed control is a labour-intensive method. Also, an important requirement of its success is its timely operation when the weeds are still young. But in practice, this is usually limited by the presence of too wet or too dry soil condition at the time when crops needed weeding (see also Chapter-8).

Another major limitation of physical control of weeds is that tillage of the land fragments the rhizomes and roots of the perennial weeds, which give rise to new plants. Also, the operation turns under the soil weed seeds which otherwise lay on the soil surface, and stores them as future source of infestations.

6.2.3 Herbicidal Control of Weeds

Herbicides are chemicals capable of killing or inhibiting the growth of plants. In the last 50 years or so, man has greatly improved upon his weeding efficiency by supplementing the conventional weeding methods with herbicides. It has saved farmers of undue, repeated inter-cultivations and hoeing, and has helped him in obtaining satisfactory weed control where physical methods often fail. Today, we have over 150 herbicides in common use for selective and non-selective weed control in different areas. These chemicals vary greatly in their (a) molecular structures, (b) mobility within plants, (c) selectivity, (d) fate in soils, and (e) response to environment. Important properties and uses of some common herbicides in use today are discussed later in Chapter 13.

Many chemicals have shown high codes of selectivity to certain crops, killing the weeds effectively. But proper selection of the herbicide, its rate, time, and method of application are very important to obtain the desired degree of weed control and crop selectivity.

Herbicides are tools, and any tool must be used with care. Many developing nations have made a good beginning in the use of herbicides in agriculture, but more comprehensive research needs to be done before extending it to new situations.

1. ***Benefits of herbicides:*** Herbicides were developed in the western world primarily to overcome the shortage of farm labour for weeding crops. However, during the past four decades, slowly the utility of herbicides has also been realised in the labour-rich tropical world, for varied reasons. Given adequate labour and money to remove weeds manually, still many advantages accrue from the judicious use of herbicides. Important among these are the following:-

   a) In monsoon season incessant rainfall may make physical weeding infeasible. Herbicides can be used to ensure freedom of crops from weeds under such a condition. Also, during the early crop growth period when many fields need weeding simultaneously, even in labour-rich countries like India, Pakistan,

Bangladesh, Nepal, Nigeria, and Sudan, there is certainly a weeding bottleneck in crop production. The soil applied herbicides can be of great help in these regions in boosting crop production.

b) Herbicides can be employed to control weeds as they emerge from the soil to eliminate weed-crop interference even at a very early stage of crop growth. But by physical methods weeds are removed after they have offered considerable competition to the crops, and rarely at the critical time. Thus, herbicides provide benefits of timely weed control.

c) Herbicides can kill many weeds that survive by mimicry, for example, wildoat (*Avena* spp.) in wheat and barnyardgrass (*Echinochloa* spp.) in rice. Weeds that resemble crop plants usually escape physical weeding.

d) Herbicidal control does not dictate strict row spacings. In physical weed control, on the other hand, the crop rows have to be sufficiently wide to accommodate weeding implements, else handweeding and hand-pulling of weeds has to be resorted to.

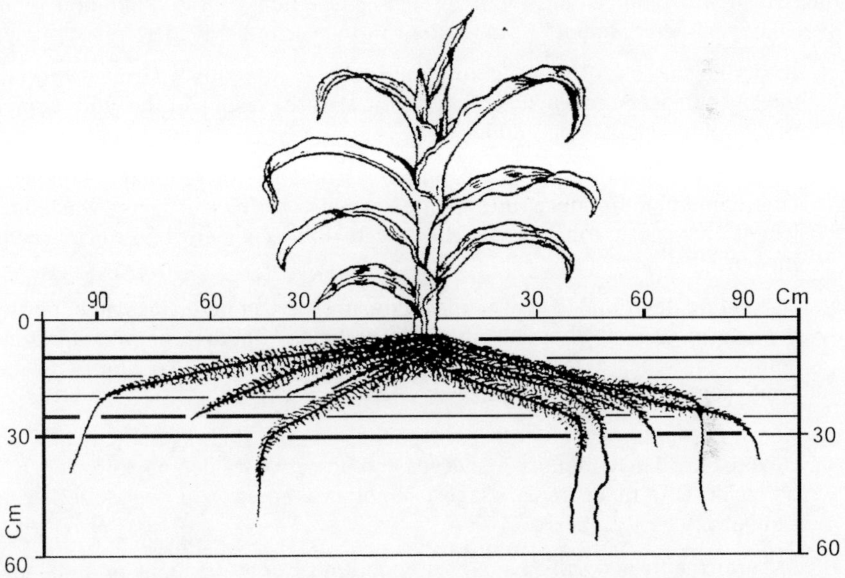

Fig. 6.1: When cultivators or hoes are worked hard in an attempt to uproot the established weeds, they may cut many feeding roots of a crop like maize, which are appreciable in the first 10 cm depth of the soil. Their lateral growth fully occupies the inter-row spaces.

e) Herbicides bring about longer lasting control of perennial weeds and brushes than is possible with any physical control method. Many modern herbicides can translocate considerably deep in the underground system of weeds and damage them.

f) Herbicides are convenient to use on spiny weeds which cannot be reached manually.

g) Herbicides are safe on erodable lands where tillage may accelerate soil and water erosion. Excessive tillage, in any case, spoils soil structure, reduces organic matter content, and depletes moisture status of the soil.

h) Herbicides kill weeds in *situ* without permitting their dissemination. Tillage on the other hand, may fragment the vegetative propagules of the weeds and drag them to new sites.

i) Herbicide sprays easily reach the weeds growing in obstructed situations, such as utility-rights-of-way, under fruit trees, and on undulating lands.

Some other benefits of using herbicides include (a) fewer labour problems, (b) greater possibility of farm mechanization, (c) easier crop harvesting and (d) lower cost of farm produce. In dryland agriculture, effective herbicidal control ensures higher water use by crops and less crop failures due to drought.

2. ***Limitations of herbicides:*** Like any other method of weed control, herbicides have their own limitations. But with proper precautions these limitations can be overcome, markedly. Important limitations in the use of herbicides are as follows.

a) In herbicidal control there is no automatic signal to stop a farmer who may be applying the chemical inaccurately till he sees the results in the crops sprayed or in the rotation crops that follow.

b) Even when herbicides are applied accurately, these may interact with environment to produce un-intended results. Herbicide drifts, wash-off, and runoff can cause considerable damage to the neighbouring crops, leading to unwarranted quarrels.

c) Depending upon the diversity in farming, a variety of herbicides must be stocked on a farm to control weeds in different fields. On the contrary, for physical control of weeds a farmer has to possess only one or two kinds of weeding implements for his entire farm.

d) Above all, herbicidal control requires considerable skill on the part of the user. He must be able to identify his weeds and possess considerable knowledge about herbicides and their proper usages. Sometimes, an error in the use of herbicides can be very costly.

e) In herbicide treated soils, usually, crop failures cannot be made up by planting a different crop of choice. The selection of the replacement crop has to be based on its tolerance to the herbicide already applied.

f) Military use of herbicides is the greatest misfortune of their discovery. In Vietnam, 2,4-D and 2,4,5-T, for example, were used for defoliating forests and crops, leading to miseries to the innocent civilians. In future, the chemical warfare with residual herbicides may be even more devastating, which must be avoided at all costs.

6.2.4 Biological Control of Weeds

About the begining of this century, some biologists used insects to control certain *alien* weeds which were causing serious damage in their new environment. The scientists called it biological method of weed control. The control of *Opuntia* spp. 'pricklypear' in Australia and that of *Lantana camara 'lantana'* in Hawaii with certain insect bioagents are two spectacular examples of early period biological control of weeds. Later, *Hypericum perforatum* 'St. Johnswort' and *Alternanthera philoxeroides* 'alligatorweed' were brought under the banner of biological control with specific insects. Lately, besides insects, certain carp fish, snails, mites, and fungi have also been employed successfully for the control of some other aquatic and terrestrial weeds (Chapter-9).

The operation of biological control of weeds is chiefly a responsibility of technicians; the farmer has little to contribute to it. The discovery of suitable bioagents is very expensive, involving visits to native land of the weed in search of its natural enemies followed by their subsequent screening at home. But its operational cost is rather limited.

6.2.5 Allelo-Chemical Control of Weeds

Allelopathy – a controversial word that has existed within the community for over last four decades – has still not been acknowledged by most scientists. Nevertheless, many weed scientists and agricultural chemists continue, rather enthusiastically, to exploit the naturally occurring allelochemicals in certain plants to suppress specific, target weeds. This has been termed *'allelo chemical control of weeds'*. Four approaches to this have so far been reported.

- *First*: Initially it was considered useful to breed varieties of crops possessing strong allelochemicals capable of stunting weeds growing in their vicinity. But soon it was realised that these allelochemicals may eventually become autotoxic. As such, this approach of allelo-chemical control of weeds was dropped.
- *Second*: Finding by research some weedy plants possessing allelochemicals strong enough to inhibit or destroy the target weed, and using such donor weeds directly in the form of their dry powder. The scheme was tried and found successful under laboratory conditions to deal with specific aquatic weed species. For instance, dry powder of shoots of *Parthenium hysterophorus* and *Coleus amboinicus* to waterbodies have been found to casue rapid withering of waterhyacinth (*Eichhornia crassipes*). This is attributed to allelochemicals present in the two plants with strong negative effects on waterhyacinth. Hopefully, in future, more of such plants with effective allelochemicals shall be discovered and feasible methods of their field – use shall be developed.
- *Third*: In this approach specific allelochemicals were identified and extracted from relevant plants and sprayed on the target weeds. Although the technique gave very eoncouraging results in the laboratory yet, under field conditions, the very large doses of such allelochamicals needed to obtain desired weed kill proved uneconomical and infeasible. Therefore, this approach of allelochemical control of weeds remained only of academic interest.

- *Fourth*: In this approach, fresh formulations of specific bacteria and fungi, capable of releasing desired allelochemicals were sprayed on target weeds. The technique proved so successful under field conditions that in the western world it has been adopted commercially to contain certain noxious weeds invading some high value crops. The technique is more commonly considered under bioherbicides Macias (2007) optimistically opined that field-success with allelo-chemical control of weeds may be in reach within this decade. (see Chapter-9).

6.2.6 Crop Breeding for Weed Control

Plant breeders, thus far, have engaged themselves in evolving crop varieties tolerant to specific pathogens, insects, nematodes, and even birds. But hardly any attempt has been made to breed crop plants tolerant to competition from weeds. In recent years attention of a group of Asian and African plant breeders has been drawn towards breeding millet varieties tolerant to *Striga* sp. Also, since the competing ability of plants is now considered a genetic character, controlled by polygenes, screening of crop germplasms against competition form weeds should be possible. Plant canopy features leading to weed suppression should be identified for each crop, besides searching for allelopathic and other bio-tolerances amongst the crop plants. It should be further useful to breed crop varieties tolerant to highly potent herbicides to achieve selective control of specific, problem weeds.

6.2.7 Non-living Mulches

Mulching stunts or kills the weeds by cutting light to them. Straw, hay, dry sugarcane leaves, farm-yard manure, rice hull, saw dust, and bark dust are natural, partial mulch materials, which can at best stunt the weed growth. Even when these are spread in thickness of 6 to 12 cm, the perenninal weeds grow through them easily. Also, the natural mulches tend to harbour insect pests and disease organisms and obstruct farm operations. Synthetic mulches, namely black paper or polythene film mulches provide stronger mechanical barriers to all kinds of germinating weeds. Black, plastic-coated, craft paper mulches are now preferred on newly prepared fields to suppress weeds. These are made in rolls of different widths which can be spread on the seedbeds and then crop seedlings can be transplanted through holes made into them. Presently mulching with synthetic materials is costly, so its economic use is limited to certain high value vegetables and ornamentals.

6.2.8 Burning and Flaming

Burning is the cheapest method of eliminating mature, unwanted vegetation from rangelands and non-crop situations like roadsides and ditchbanks in dry seasons. Weed seeds that have already shattered on the ground before flaming will not be killed by it. Burning is limited in its value because it is a potential source of fire hazard. In variance with it, *flaming* is a momentary exposure of green weeds to as high as 1000°C temperature from flame throwers. Flaming kills plants by coagulating their cell protoplasm. In some western countries, flaming is used for selective control of inter-row weeds in onion, soybean, grain sorghum, castorbean, cotton, sesame, and certain fruit orchards. For selective weed control, flaming must be done when weeds are in their seedling stage and the crop plants are well established. The flame should be directed towards the weeds under hood covers. Based on propane gas flamers, 99% reduction in weed population required 60-73 kg gas/ha against young weeds and 93-106 kg/ha in the case of older weeds (Ascard, 1992).

Flaming has proved useful in destroying dodder-infested crops of lucerne. In grasslands, woody shrubs and patches of perennial weeds can be destroyed by spot flaming. Flaming is also helpful in weeding farm ditches and many other difficult non-crop situations. It is believed that repeated light applications of flame to plant shoots can destroy even roots of the perennial weeds. The process is called **searing**.

Burning of certain weeds, however, may give out smoke containing poisonous elements. *Cannabis sativa,* a difficult to flame weed, for instance, produces dense smoke containing a poisonous chemical, tetahydrocannabional, which reacts with the brain during its inhalation by people present around the burning operation.

6.2.9 Soil Solarisation

Soil solarisation, also called *solar soil heating,* is another method of utilising solar energy for the desiccation of weeds in fallow fields during the hot summer months. It differs from hot weather tillage control of weeds described earlier in two major aspects: (i) It is effective mainly against weeds from seeds. (ii) It usually does not involve any tillage of the field.

The technique of soil solarisation involves covering the soil with transparent, polyethylene (PE) film during the hottest part of summer months, for 2-4 weeks*. This has potential of raising the surface soil temperature by up to 10-12°C over the unfilmed, control fields, which is adequate for desiccating numerous weed seeds present in the top, about 5 cm soil layer. The sudden rise in soil temperature is due to hinderance created by the film in permitting back-radiation of solar, long waves from the soil and prevention of heat loss otherwise incurred in the evaporation of soil moisture. Thin polyethylene sheets of 20-25 mm thickness are ideal for achieving the desired rise in soil temperature, although the thicker ones, of up to 100 mm thickness, have been also successfully used. One pre-filming irrigation has been found to augment its soil solarisation effect, both by trapping more heat and by making the weed seeds more susceptible to the thermal effects.

Not all weeds are equally susceptible to soil solarisation. The scientists have provided lists of soil solarisation susceptible (SSS) and soil solarisation tolerant (SST) weed species (Yaduraju, 1993). Fortunately, our several annual grass weeds, including *Phalaris* and *Avena* spp., as well as broadleaf weeds, are found to succumb to soil solarisation. Weeds with hard seedcoats, like *Melilotus* spp., are difficult to damage by this technique. Also, the rhizomes and tubers of perennial weeds are not much hurt by soil solarisation (Kumar *et al.,* 1993).

Soil solarisation may improve crop yields both by aiding the control of weeds from seeds, as well as by damaging insect pests and disease organisms, besides improving the nutrient and biological activity in the soil. These aspects are difficult to separate, though.

---

* *Compare 'mulching' in Section 6.2.7.*

6.3 GENERAL CONSIDERATIONS IN WEED MANAGEMENT

Each of the above units of weed management involves certain principles which must be well understood by the weed managers in order to make best of the system. Since the principles have been dealt with at length in chapters ahead, here it should be sufficient to enlist the general pre-requisites of a successful weed management programme, as follows:

1. One must gain knowledge of the ontogeny of weeds under attack before choosing a system for their control. This is with a view to find highly vulnerable points in their life cycles. The weed species, as was explained in Chapter 3, differ widely in their modes of propagation and dispersal; hence they require different control approaches.
2. The nature of weed problem must be surveyed in the target area. It should reveal an inventory of weeds, their time of germination in relation to planting time of crops, rainfall and irrigation pattern of the area, and period of growth of the weeds.
3. Weed control measures must be planned for the whole farm and not just against weeds in a field. Also, the weed control should extend to irrigation channels, roadsides, and other non-crop surroundings on the farm. General weed sanitation is essential to check perpetuation of weeds and to avoid having to spend more money to control them each year.
4. Weed control system must include follow up programme of weed prevention measures (Chapter 5).

SUMMARY

The chief objective of weed control is to allow or induce the growth of right plants at the right place and time to suit our interests, limiting the growth of other plants in the process. The intensity of weed control should commensurate with its present and future benefits, else we are not really interested.

Weed eradication, as different from weed control, is the complete elimination of all live plants, plant parts, and seeds of the weed in question from an area. It is often costlier than the land is worth, and is, therefore, limited to dealing with some highly noxious (orobnoxious) weed species.

There are four common methods of weed control, namely (1) Good crop husbandry methods, (2) Physical methods, (3) Biological methods, and (4) Chemical methods. Besides these other methods like Solarisation of the soil, Allelopathic control, Burning and flaming, Crop breeding, and Mulching have been defined and their important features revealed.

Emphasis has been laid on the systems concept of weed control where a combined attack with two or more suitable methods of weed control is planned in a proper sequence against the target weed problem, as a part of advance land use planning. On crop lands it has more commonly come to be known as Integrated Weed Management (IWM). No doubt, in the IWM still the herbicides dominate the scene as *complements* to the other methods of weed control but never as substitutes to these.

Lastly, it is very important to survey and analyse the weed problem before choosing a particular method for controlling it.

SELECTED BIBLIOGRAPHY

1. Anbumani, S. *et al.* 2000. Solarisation - A tool for non-chemical weed management. Abst. National Seminar on the sustainability of Weed Control Options Millenium, Annamalai Univ. Annamalainagar (India), 87-88 pp.
2. Anon. 1989. Biological Suppression of Weeds. Bull. Biol. Control. Cent. (ICAR), Bangalore (India), 27 p.
3. Ascard, J. 1992. Flaming for weed control. Weed Abs. 1993, 42(2); 104 (item 873).
4. Bond, W. and A. C. Grundy, 2001. Non-chemical weed management in organic farming system. Weed Research 41: 383-405 (U.K.)
5. Brar, L. S. and Walia, U. S. 1989. Economic evaluation of weed control systems in different field crops. Pesticides 23(5) 27-30.
6. Carter, J. and Johnson, C. 1988. Influence of different types of mulches on egg plant production. Hort. Sci. 23(1) 143-145.
7. Chandrakumar, S.S. *et al.* 2002. Weed management through soil solarisation in sunflower. Ind. J. Weed Sci. 34: 231-235.
8. Channabasave. Gowda. R. *et al.* 2003. Utilisation of alien weeds for compost -- Assessment for quality and evaluation on crop growth. Abst. Nat. Sem. Alien Invasive Weeds held AAU Jorhat, April 27-29, 2003, 50 p.
9. Dubolia, S.P. *et al.* 2003. Problems in adoption of timely weeding in paddy. Abst. Bienn. Conf. ISWS held 12-14 March 2003, at G.B.P. Univ. Agr. & Technol. Pantnagar (India): 64.
10. Green, M. B. 1973. Are herbicides too expensive? Weeds Today 4(3) 14-16.
11. Hakansson, S. 2003. Weeds and Weed Management on Arable Land: An Ecological Approach. CAB International. 288 p.
12. Kassasian, L. 1971. The place of herbicides and weed research in tropical agriculture. PANS 17 26-29.
13. Katan, J. and De Vay, J. E. (Ed.) 1991. Soil Solarization. CRS Press Inc., 267 pp.
14. Kathiresan, Rm. 2000. Abst. National Seminar on the **sustainability** of weed control options for the New Millenium held 20-21, Dec. 2000. Annamalai University, Annamalainagar, Tamil Nadu (India), 93 p.
15. Kathiresan, Rm. 2002. Allelopathy - Optimism to Realism. Bull. Annamalai Univ., Annamalianagar, T.N. (India).
16. Kathiresan, Rm. 2002. Allelopathy-Optimism to Realism. Annamalai University, Annamalai Nagar, Tamil Nadu (India).
17. Macias, F.A. *et al.* 2007. Allelopathy – a natural alternative for weed control. Pest Mgmt. Sci. 63: 327-348.
18. Mauromicale, G. *et al.* 2005. Soil solarisation to control branched broomrape (*Orobanche ramosa*) and improve the yield of tomato. Weed Sci. 53(6): 877-883.
19. Melander, B. *et al.* 2005. Integrating physical and cultural methods of weed control. Weed Sci. 53(3): 369-381.

20. Moss, S. R. and Clarke, J. H. 1994. Guidelines for the prevention and control of herbicide-resistant blackgrass. Crop Prot. 13(J). 230-234.

21. Moss, S. R. and Rubin, B. 1993. Herbicide-resistant weeds: a world-wide perspective. J. Agr. Sci. 120(2) 141-148.

22. Mukhopadhyay, S. K. 1991-92. Emerging problems and advances in weed management Proc. 79th Ind. Sci. Cong. Part-II; 1-16 pp.

23. Nimje, P.N. and V. Agrawal 2002. Effect of soil solarization on weed density and growth of chilli brinjal and marigold. Ind. J. Weed Sci. 34: 324-326.

24. Parker, C. 1976. Weed research requirements of developing countries. Brit. Crop Proc. Conf. Proc., 801-807.

25. Porwal, M.K. 2002. Relative economics of weed management system in winter sweet potato *(Ipomoea batatas)* in Rajasthan. Ind. J. Weed Sci. 34: 88-91.

26. Prasad Babu, M.B.B. and N.T. Yaduraju 2000. Decision support system - a tool for sustainable weed management. Ind. J. Weed Sci. 32: 119-120.

27. Prather, T. S. and Callihan, R. H. 1993. Weed eradication using geographic information systems. Weed Technol. 7(1) 265-269.

28. Regnault-Roger, C. *et al.* (eds.) 2005. Biopesticides of Plant Origin. Lavolsier Publishing, France (W.A.) 54(10), 3978.

29. Rodgers, E. G. 1974. Weed prevention is the best control. Weeds Today 5(1) 7 & 22.

30. Singh, U. and Misra, S. G. 1987. Herbicides - Scope and Hazards. Ecology of Rural India. Vol. 1 (Ed.) Pramol, S. Arid Pub. House, N. Delhi 189-197.

31. Singh, V. P. and N. T. Yaduraju, 2004. Soil Solarisation NRC (WS), Jabalpur (India) Tech. Bull. No. 2, 23p.

32. Singh, V. P. *et al.* 2004. Effect of period of soil solarisation and weed control measures on weed growth and productivity of soybean. Ind. J. Agri. Sci. 74(6): 324-328.

33. Singh, V.P. *et al.* 2003. Influence of duration of soil solarisation and weed control measures on weed and productivity of wheat under soybean - wheat system. Abst. Bienn. Conf. ISWS, held 12-14 March 2003 at G.B.P. Univ. of Agr. & Technol., Pantnagar (India): 65.

34. Singh, Y. *et al.* 2002. Evaluation of herbicides in zero-till wheat. Ind. J. Weed Sci. 34: 121-122.

35. Timmons, F. L. 2005. A history of weed control in the United States and Canada. Weed Sci. 53: 748-761. (U.S.A.)

36. Westing, A. H. 1984. Herbicides in War-The Long Term Ecological And Human Consequences. SIPRI Publishers, 210 pp.

37. Yaduraju, N. T. 1993. The role of soil solarisation in weed management. Proc. Int. Symp. of Ind. Weed Sci., held at Hissar (India), Nov., 18-20, Vol. 1: 343-349.

38. Yenish, J. P. *et al.* 1992. Effects of tillage on vertical distribution and viability of weed seeds in soil. Weed Sci. 40(3) 429-433.

39. Young, D. *et al* 1978. Selecting approparíate weed control systems for developing countries. Weed Sci. 26(3) 209-212.

Chapter 7

WEED SUPPRESSION THROUGH GOOD CROP HUSBANDRY

Good crop husbandry is more than half the weed control envisaged on any farmland. While directly it induces a healthy growth of crops, indirectly it maintains a crop environment that is as detrimental to weeds as possible. The weeds that develop under a dense and vigorous growth of crops are usually weak and can be easily controlled with limited physical and chemical energy. On the contrary, when fundamental principles of good crop husbandry are ignored from the point of view of weed suppression, and an attempt is made to depend solely upon controlling weeds directly with physical or chemical methods, often the weed control obtained is very disappointing and the practice proves highly expensive. In gappy crop fields the weeds grow through the crop plants in large numbers, and when the crop growth is week for some reason, their (weed) growth becomes vigorous. Some important crop husbandry practices that can lead to the suppression of weeds, and which can be easily incorporated in practical weed control programmes in farming systems, are discussed in this chapter.[*]

7.1 PROPER CROP STAND AND EARLY SEEDLING VIGOUR

Ready and uniform germination of crop seeds and their development into vigorous crop seedlings leave less spaces for the weeds to grow amongst the crop plants. Uneven and low crop populations and weak crop seedlings, on the contrary, permit thick growth of weeds. A vigorously growing crop aids weed control by weakening the weeds by offering competition (Fig. 7.1). In areas of thin crop stands or seeding skips, weeds may not be controlled even by the use of herbicides.

Important steps in obtaining good germination, optimum stand, and spatial uniformity of crops are (i) selection of most adapted crops and crop varieties, (ii) the use of high

---

Footnote:[*] *Before going through this chapter the reader is advised to study Chapter - 2 on the Nature of Weed-Crop Competition.*

viability seeds, (iii) preplant seed and soil treatment with pesticides, dormancy breaking chemicals, and germination boosters, (iv) adequate seed rates and (v) proper planting time and method. Despite these practices if some gaps are still seen in the crop rows, these must be filled as soon as possible. Row spacings of crops should be as narrow as agronomic recommendations will allow so that the crops closein early (Angiras and Sharma, 1993 and Jadhao and Nalamwar, 1993). Unnecessarily deep plantings of crop seeds should be avoided as it results in slow germination, and often, in weak seedlings.

Fig. 7.1: *Top* = An early, dense growth of a crop is congenial to suppressing the later germinating weed seedlings. *Bottom* = Non-gappy crop rows leave no intra-row spaces for weeds to germinate. Gappy crops, on the contrary, offer ready spaces for the dense growth of weeds, which become almost impossible to control later even with herbicides.

7.2 SELECTIVE CROP STIMULATION

In any system of uncontrolled weed-crop competition it is well known that weeds inflict much more damage to crops than the crops to weeds (Chapter-2). This imbalance of nature can be manipulated by man in favour of crops by suitably modifying their soil and cropping conditions, leading to selective stimulation of crop growth. Vigorous crop plants compete better with the weeds and they closein the ground quickly. Selective crop stimulation can be achieved in many ways. To start with, correction of soil condition to favour crop growth by the application of soil ammendments like gypsum or lime, as the case may be, is an important step towards favouring crop growth. Addition of farm-yard manure or synthetic soil conditioners to very light or very heavy soils may be useful in improving crop growth by ameliorating the soil structure and, thus, maintaining better air-water relationships.

Table 7.1: Effect of split application of nitrogen in pearlmillet on the Growth of Weeds at Hisar (Pooled data of 1985 & 1986) (After Rathee *et al.*, 1992)

	Time of application of N (at total of 120 kg/ha)	**Dry weed biomass (45 d. a. s. q/ha)**
1.	Full dose at 3 w. a. s.	9.25
2.	1/2 at sowing + 1/2 at 3 w. a. s	11.50
3.	1/4 at sowing + 3/4 at 3 w. a. s.	10.71

Comment: *Treatment No. 2 is the agronomic recommendation of N application in pearlmillet. But, unfortunately, it also helps the weeds to grow more vigorously.*

Application of suitable fertilizers and manures in adequate quantities improves plant growth very much. But when these are applied uniformly to soil, they may benefit the crops and weeds alike (Rathee, *et al*, 1992). Therefore to make fertilizers available mainly to the crop, these should be banded or side dressed. Weeds growing 20 cm or more away from the fertilized bands usually fail to make use of even a mobile nutrient like N. Such weeds remain stunted in comparison to the close growing weeds. Foliar application of fertilizers to wide row crops like maize, sugarcane, and cotton, also amounts to their selective stimulation. Sometimes, the absence of a nutrient from fertilizer mixture applied to a crop may cause its selective stimulation. For example, application of a fertilizer mixture devoid of nitrogen to pulse and other legume crops offen puts them in a strong competitive position with the non-legume weeds. Inoculation of crop seeds with suitable nitrogen fixing and P solublising cultures may further aid selective stimulation of such crops. There are other avenues whereby selective crop stimulation can be achieved.

7.3 PROPER PLANTING METHOD

Any planting method that leaves the soil surface rough and dry will discourage early weed growth. For example, in India when winter grains are planted in seedbeds prepared after a pre-sowing irrigation, it leaves the top 3 to 5 cm of soil above the crop seeds in rough and dry tilth. Such a physical condition of soil defers the germination of the weeds

(Fig. 7.2). By this time the crop plants are sufficiently grown-up to fight weeds. In variance with this sound practice of planting crops, when a farmer plants his crops in dry soil and irrigates the field soon thereafter, he lands himself into serious weed problems. The weeds then germinate along with the crop seedlings and compete severely with them. Very frequently they overrun and shade the crop seedlings, fully. The same thing happens in the rainy season crops when both the crop and the weeds germinate, simultaneously. In fact, in rainy season, the weed seeds may begin sprouting even before the land is opened for seedbed preparation. The sprouting weed seeds are not destroyed by tillage and many a time the weed seedlings can be seen in fields before the crop seeds have germinated. Therefore, to give rainy season crops an equal chance of germination along with the weeds, farmers should complete their seedbed preparations and planting of crops with minimum time lapse (Cook, 1962).

Fig. 7.2: A dry and loose soil in the inter-rows, as seen in the hands of the authour, is helpful in postponing weed emergence and, thus, in permitting a sturdy crop seedling growth. This is achieved in crops like winter grains by irrigating the field and quickly preparing it for sowing the crop. The postplant irrigation is then delayed till about a month later.

Table 7.2: Effect of Narrow-Row spacing in Wheat on the Yield of Weeds at Palampur (Pooled data of 1989 and 1990)

Treatments (Row spacing)	Dry weeds biomass (q/ha)		
	Lolium sp.	**Phalaris sp.**	**All weeds**
A. Angiras and Sharma (1993)			
15 cm	7.79	5.67	NA
20 cm	8.84	6.94	NA
C. D. (P = 0.05)	0.29	0.55	-
B. Jadhao and Nalamwar (1993)			
15 cm	-	-	6.05
22.5 cm	-	-	6.68
Cross sowing at 22.5cm	-	-	5.47
C. D. (P=0.05)	-	-	0.44

Comments: *In wheat, 20-22.5 cm row spacing is widely practised. Reducing the row spacing to 15 cm, or cross-sowing wheat, reduced the weed growth. (But this may not necessarily be associated with increased crop yields).*

Plough-planting and other minimum tillage planting methods have often proved very useful in minimising early weed problems. The plough-planting of crops leaves the inter-row soil loose which delays weed germination but favours the growth of crop roots. Even when a rain falls immediately after the crop is planted by this method, the weeds can at best germinate along with the crop seeds and not before it (Gupta and Saroha, 1971).

In the summer season, furrow planting of crops is a very useful method of reducing the weed problems. It is so because in this method the irrigation water is restricted initially to the furrows. This leaves the inter-row crop spaces dry where weeds fail to germinate. After the crop seedlings are well established, the fields can be irrigated, uniformly.

In transplanted crops the farmer gets opportunity to prepare a weedfree field for the placement of healthy crop seedlings. This gives a definite advantage to the crop over the later germinating weeds.

7.4 PROPER PLANTING TIME

In every agroclimate there is a peak period of germination of seasonal weeds. This period usually is also the optimum time of planting of several crops of the season. In fields with a bad history of weeds, crops can be made to escape early weed-crop competition by planting them either a little earlier or later than their normal planting time. With the availability of photo-insensitive varieties of many crops, manipulation of planting time of crops so as to avoid the first heavy flush of weeds should be easy. For instance, when rainy season crops like maize and cotton are planted about 15 days before the break of monsoon with the help of a pre-sowing irrigation, the crops germinate in weedfree environment. And by the time the weeds germinate with the onset of rains, the crop seedlings are well up. Late planting of dwarf varieties of wheat in winter season likewise reduces competition from the common farm weeds. Effects of late planting of wheat on the occurrence of wildoat (*Avena fatua*) are discussed by Yaduraju and Mani (1987).

7.5 CROP ROTATION

Crop rotation is defined as a system of growing different kind of crops in recurrent succession on the same land. The help that crop rotations offer in weed control isn't always recognized, even though the practice has been recommended for long.

Hauser (1974) stated that with each crop appear certain typical weeds which are much less serious in some crops These weeds increase in proportion rapidly if their favourable crop is grown continuously, but can be subdued by a change of the crop.

Crop rotations are effective in controlling crop-associated and crop-bound weeds such as *Avena fatua* 'wildoat' and *Cuscuta* spp. 'dodder', respectively. Wildoat can be driven away from small grain fields by using pea and gram as break crops for 2 to 3 years. Dodder, on the other hand, can be eliminated from lucerne by turning the land to grain crops for some time. *Cirsium arvense* 'Canadathistle' can be controlled by incorporating crops like berseem and lucerne in crop rotations. Sometimes, a break crop in rotation may be the one in which herbicides are available for specific weed control. For example, pea and wheat give the farmer an opportunity to treat Canadathistle with MCPA. This herbicide cannot be applied to gram or potato.

Leys are sometimes recommended as break crops for eradicating perennial weeds. But they are usually ineffective in controlling these weeds from seeds. Leys preserve the dormant weed seeds till the field is returned to arable crops.

7.6 STALE SEEDBED

A stale seedbed is one where 1 to 2 flushes of weeds are destroyed before planting of any crop. As earlier stated, most weed seeds germinate from top 4 to 5 cm of surface soil. If a finally prepared seedbed is withheld from planting and it contains adequate moisture in its top 4 to 5 cm of soil, a flush of young weed seedlings will appear on it, in about a week's time. These weed seedlings can be destroyed either with a contact herbicide like paraquat (Chapter 13) or by a shallow non-inverting type of tillage implement like, spiketooth harrow, treader-packer, springtooth harrow, corrugated iron land-roller, weeder-mulcher, and sweeps. Depending upon the time available, one or two flushes of weeds can be destroyed in this manner before planting of crops in the stale seedbeds (Gupta and Bacchawat, 1976). The main advantage of stale seedbeds is that crops germinate in weedfree environment, and if they are selectively stimulated, they may close in before subsequent flushes of weeds appear on the land. Stale seedbeds can be highly effective in controlling weeds in crops planted in a rainless period with the help of irrigation, *eg* berseem, lucerne, potato, and opium poppy. In rainy season, an odd shower may make stale seedbeds too compact to plant crops without further tillage of the land. Besides, rainy weather will transplant many weed seedlings dislodged during the preparation of the stale seedbeds. Still, Saiki and Pathak (1993) found that stale seedbed prepared 30 days before sowing rice with the help of paraquat was very useful in suppressing the weeds in a specific situation. It may, however, be noted that even a freshly finalised stale seedbed is susceptible to airborne weed seeds from elsewhere. Application of FYM or compost after final preparation of stale seedbed may have similar effects since these carry numerous viable weed seeds.

7.7 SMOTHER CROPPING

The smother crops germinate quickly and develop large canopy, capable of efficient photosynthesis, in relatively short period. They possess both surface and deep roots. Also called competitive crops, they suppress the weed seedlings by excluding light beneath and utilizing large quantities of nutrients from the soil, rapidly. However, to utilize such competitive crops for weed suppression, one must ensure that weed seedlings appear after the crop has closed in, else the weeds can easily overrun even a competitive crop. The chief point of difference between a competitive and a non-competitive crop is that the former closes in much faster than the latter, hence, lesser efforts are needed to control weeds in the competitive crops in comparison to the wide row crops. Cowpea, lucerne, berseem, other clovers, millets, sudangrass, and barley are common smother crops. Besides, fodder crops of pearlmillet, maize, and sorghum have substantial weed smothering effects. Attempts have been made repeatedly to use a smothering crop as an inter-crop to suppress the weeds in the main crop. But, almost in all cases, it has failed to do so, unless additional weeding efforts were made alongside (Thakur, 1994), In coconut-banana plantations, however, raising cowpea as a smother crop could check the weed growth up to three months (Savithri, *et al.*, 1994). Good reviews on the subject are presented by Chatterjee and Maiti (1984) and Hosmani (1991).

An important role of smother crops in agriculture is to suppress perennial weeds in crop field after they were weakened by intensive tillage during the preceeding fallow period. Preconditioning of weeds by tillage (or chemicals) gives smother crops a chance to establish themselves ahead of the weeds and then exert their smothering influence on the later appearing weed shoots. In the United States, bindweed (*Convolvulus arvensis*) has been very successfully controlled by combination of tillage and smother crops. Crossplanting of two smother crops in the same field, such as cowpea and millets, gives more rapid cover to the ground than their unidirectional planting. Bendixen (1988) found soybean helped herbicides to control johnsongrass (*Sorghum halepense*) by its smothering effect.

The success of any smother crop in suppressing weeds is judged best at its harvest time. An effective smother crop leaves the ground weedfree, as against a wide row grain crop which leaves many weeds maturing.

7.8 SUMMER FALLOWING

Farmers in India, as in many other tropical countries, have used for decades hot months of April, May and June to expose their lands to sun in order to control many soil-borne pests, including weeds. Roots, rhizomes, and tubers of shallow rooted perennial weeds like bermudagrass and nutsedge are desiccated when these are brought to surface by tillage and exposed to air temperatures of 40 to 45°C. However, to be really effective, summer fallows must be managed properly. The land should be opened by deep ploughing immediately after harvesting winter crops and it should be left in a cloddy condition. A sod mouldboard plough is very suitable for this purpose. As the soil clods bake in hot sun, the weed roots and rhizomes embodied in them are desiccated. To expose the vegetative propagules of the weeds hidden beneath the clods, as well as to break the dry clods and further expose the contained weed propagules to the hot sun, land should be ploughed subsequently once or twice at an interval of fortnight, with a heavy wooden plough or blade harrow. During all this process of exposure of weeds to solar energy, one must ensure that the field under treatment does not get any water, say from leaking irrigation channels. In the hot sun the weed roots and rhizomes are killed by desiccation and *not* by any direct effect of high temperatures on the cell protoplasm.

Summer fallowing for the control of perennial weeds is unadvisable on light soils for fear of erosion. Also, such soils cannot be turned into dry clods required for effective desiccation of the weedy rhizomes.

Weed control through summer baking should be followed by cropping of the land with narrow row crops. If a wide row crop must be planted, it should be intercultivated, hard.

Intensive cropping with 3 to 4 crops a year, which is opposed to summer fallowing, is prone to heavy infestation with perennial weeds.

7.9 MINIMUM TILLAGE

Deep and frequent tillage may be useful for some reasons, but it serves to (i) bring more of dormant weed seeds and rhizomes to the soil surface, and (ii) preserve, the new ones deep inside the soil for the future. Both these things are undesirable. One should aim at keeping the weed seeds as close to the soil surface as possible so that they germinate in large numbers at any one time and, thus can be killed with a suitable herbicide in one operation. In this context, tillage should be no deeper and more frequent than is absolutely necessary for growing crops. **zero tillage** planting of crops, as practised in some countries like U.S.A. and U.K., completely avoids burying of weed seeds and reduces persistence of annual weeds. But it often induces vigorous growth of perennial weeds.

Of late, zero-tillage has gained popularity in Northern and Western India in her wheat-rice cropping systems. From the weed dynamics point of view, the zero-tillage cultivation in rice-wheat cropping system has been of advantage to our farmers in reducing incidence of our one of the most problematic weeds, *Phalaris minor*, in wheat. Several research results have been reported positive in this respect, particularly in U.P. and Haryana.

Tillage on the farm should be minimised, keeping the above aspects in view.

7.10 LOWERING AREA UNDER BUNDS

Soil bunds made in fields for the purpose of irrigation are ideal places for the rapid growth of weeds. Soil dug or scraped for making these carries numerous weed seeds that germinate readily on them soon after the fields are irrigated, and establish into thick weed populations. These weeds form potential source of every year weed seeds on the farm since the application of herbicides and cultivations are usually restricted to the net cropped ground.

One way to tackle the problem of weeds on bunds is to level the land well so that less number of bunds are needed to irrigate the fields, uniformly. Another way that has been used in rice fields in Japan is by replacement of soil bunds by the portable, plastic ones. Incidentally, plastic partitions also increase the net area available for cultivation.

7.11 FLOODING AND DRAINAGE

Flood kills weeds by excluding air from their environment. Some weed species are more susceptible to it than the others. *Flooding* is a world-wide crop husbandry method of controlling weeds in rice fields. In some parts of Madhya Pradesh (India), deep flooding of fallow fields with rain water is practised continuously for 2-3 months. After that the water is let out and the winter grains are planted. The practice, locally called *Haveli,* is considered very effective in controlling weeds, besides conserving moisture. The technique, however, can, be used as a weed suppression measure only in limited situations.

In variance with flooding, *drainage* is used for controlling aquatic and semi-aquatic weeds in rice fields, channels, canals, and ponds. In rice fields, where both terrestrial and aquatic weeds may be common, a judicious combination of the two can be practised.

SUMMARY

Good crop husbandry is an inevitable component of practical weed management plan in any agricultural system. Ready and uniform germination of crop seeds with spatial uniformity and rapid development of crop seedlings into large foliage give crops competitive advantage and reduce survival and growth of weeds. Competitive crops may be produced by (i) manipulation of soil conditions to meet the optimum requirements of crop growth, (ii) selective placement of manures and fertilizers, (iii) maintaining high crop populations, (iv) sowing on stale seedbeds, (v) practising proper crop rotations, (vi) plough-plant planting of crops, (vii) field levelling, etc. Besides, practices like minimal tillage and summer fallowing are helpful in suppressing the weed growths. All these aspects of good crop husbandry have been discussed in this chapter in relation to practical weed control on the farms.

SELECTED BIBLIOGRAPHY

1. Angiras, N. N. and Sharma, V. 1993. Effect of cultural manipulations and weed control methods on crop-weed competition in wheat (*Triticum aestivum* L.). Ind. J. Weed Sci. 23 (3 & 4) 6-10.
2. Bendixen, L. E. 1988. Soybean (*Glycine max*) competition helps herbicides control johnsongrass (*Sorghum halepense*). Weed Technol. 2(1) 46-48.
3. Bhan, V.M. *et al.* 2003. Influence of seeding depth on emergence pattern of dodder (*Cuscuta* spp.) in linseed. Abstr. Bienn. Conf. ISWS held 12-14 March, 2003 at GBP Univ. of Agri. & Technol, Pantnagar (India), 60 p.
4. Chatterjee, B. N. and Maiti, S. 1984. Intercropping And Weed Management. (IN) Cropping Practice. Oxford IBH Pub. Co., Calcutta.
5. Chaudhary, B. M. *et al.* 2005. Effect of weed management practices and seed rates on weeds and yield of chickpea. Ind. J. Weed Sci. 37 (3&4): 271-272.
6. Colbach, N. *et al.* 2005. How to model the effect of farming practices in weed emergence. Weed Res. 45(1) : 2-17 (U.K.).

7. Gupta, O. P. and Bachhawat, N. M. 1976. Weed control in berseem using stale seedbed, EPTC, and MCPB. PANS 22(3) 386-390

8. Gupta, O. P. and Saroha, M. S. 1971. Changing concepts of tillage and role of herbicides there in. Agri. and Agro. Industries J., April 1971; 1-7.

9. Hauser, E. W. 1974. Postemergence activity of three thiocarbonate herbicides in relation to depth of placement in soil. Weeds Today 5(1) 14-15.

10. Hosmani, M. M. 1991. Cultural Methods of Weed Management. Manohar Printing Press, Dharwad, 79 pp.

11. Jadhao, S. L. and Nalamwar, R. V. 1993. Studies on weed management in irrigated wheat as affected by plant geometry, genotype, and manual weeding. Ind. J. Weed. Sci. 25(3 & 4) 18-21.

12. Kumawat, S.K. *et al.* 2002. Weed dyanamics and NPK uptake by blonde psyllium (*Plantago ovata*) as influenced by sowing methods, N, and Weed Management. Ind. J. Weed Sci. 34: 254-256.

13. Liebman, M. *et al.* (eds.). 2001. Ecological Management of Agricultural Weeds. Cambridge University Press, Cambridge (U.K.)

14. Malik, R. S. *et al.* 2005. Efficacy of fenoxaprop and competing ability of wheat cultivars against wildoat. Ind. J. Weed Sci. 37 (3&4): 256-257.

15. Misra, J.S. *et al.* 2001. Effect of water submergence and its levels on weed dyanamics and yield of transplanted rice. Ind. J. Weed Sci. 33: 189-190.

16. Olsen, J. *et al.* 2005. Increased density and spatial uniformity increased weed suppression by spring wheat. Weed Research 45 : 316-321 (U.K.).

17. Rathee, S. S., *et al.* 1992. Effect of time of N application and weed management on pearlmillet. Ind. J. Weed Sci. 24 (1 &2) 17-21.

18. Renu, S. *et al.* 2000. Stale seedbed technique for the management of *Sacciolepis interrupta* in semi-dry rice. Ind. J. Weed Sci. 32: 140-145.

19. Saiki, T. P. and Pathak, A. K. 1993. Integrated weed management in rainfed, direct seeded, upland rice (*Oryza sative*). Ind. J. Agro. 38(2) 300-301.

20. Savithri, K. E. *et al.* 1994. Weed management in coconut-banana intercropping system. Ind. J. Weed Sci. 26 (3-4) 57-63.

21. Thakur, D. R. 1994. Weed management in intercropping systems based on maize (*Zea mays*) under rainfed, mid-hill conditions. Ind. J. Agro. 39(2) 203-206.

22. Verma, O. P. S. *et al.* 1988. Effect of planting density, fertilizers, and weed control in transplanted rice. Ind. J. Agro. 33(4) 372-375.

23. Walia, U.S. *et al.* 2005. Weed control efficiency in herbicides in zero-tillage wheat. Ind. J. Weed Sci. 37 (3&4): 167-170.

24. Yaduraju, N. T. and Mani. V. S. 1987. The influence of delayed planting and seedbed preparation on the competition of wildoat in wheat. Ind. J. Agro. 32(3) 299-301.

Chapter 8

THE PHYSICAL CONTROL OF WEEDS

A farmer with a hoe shall be respected for all times to come.

8.1 HISTORICAL

The physical control of weeds is as old as agriculture itself. It began in the form of *handpulling* in about 10,000 B.C. when man started to cultivate crops. Interestingly enough, this primitive practice of weeding exists with us even today, particularly in nurseries, lawns, and flowerbeds. When handpulling of weeds is aided by a fork, sharp blade or tip of a sickle, it is called *spudding*.

In about 6,000 B. C., primitive hand tools were used to till the land and destroy the weeds. Somewhat later, hand blades with 7-10 cm wide cutting edge, sickles, pickaxes, and spades were fashioned for hand weeding. In the western agriculture, hand-hoes with long, wooden handles and scythes were used instead of hand-blades for handweeding (Fig. 8.1). *Hand-weeding* is a very effective method of weed control; it removes every blade of unwanted grass growing among the crop plants. Besides, handblades and pickaxes stir the soil up of 2.5 to 6 cm depth. In fact, the efficacy of any new method of weed control on crop land is still compared with hand-weeding. Nevertheless, hand-weeding is a very slow and tiresome process which must be replaced by some more efficient weeding methods. Early in the eighteenth century, Jethro Tull (1731)[*] invented the first animal-drawn weeding implement, the horse-hoe. It was during this period that crops were planted in rows so that animal would not walk on the crop plants. Soon the horse-hoes replaced the laborious job of hand-weeding, at least in the wide row crops. Since its invention, the original horse hoe has been greatly improved in its working efficiency, leading to the present day harrows and cultivators. The introduction of tractors in 1920's gave further fillip to mechanical weeding and new weeding implements like several kinds of cultivators, harrows, weeding blades, finger weeders, rotary hoes, rod-weeders and the like, were developed. In narrow row crops like winter

[*] *Horse Hoeing Husbandry, Berkshire, MDCC, 33 p.*

grains, jute, rice, and certain vegetables, however, hand-weeding is commonly practised in the tropical world, till date.

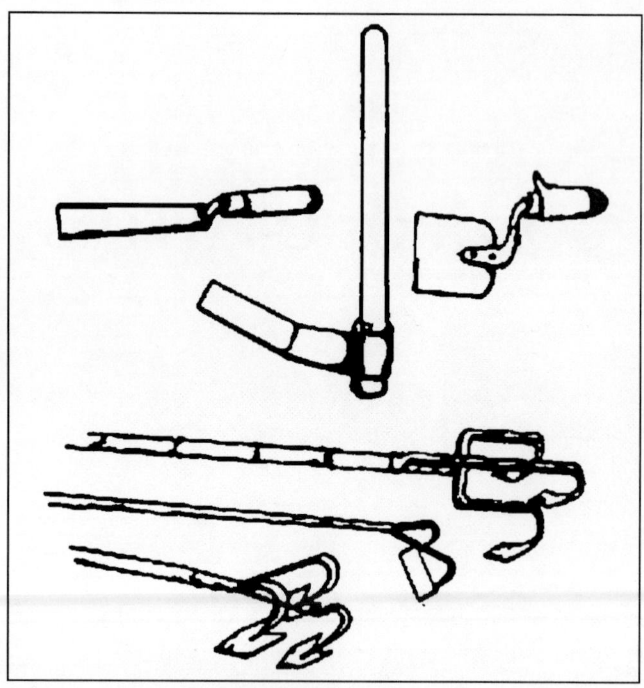

"Now in this age of knowledge where did I wrongly go? All advice was taken, but ....I should have used a hoe? **(Mrs. Beste)**.

Fig. 8.1: Some common hand-blades and hand-hoes used in India for weeding different crops. The choice of the tool depends upon the crop and soil type.

8.2 PRE-PLANT TILLAGE CONTROL OF WEEDS

The primary function of any tillage operation is to control weeds although, besides it, it may also achieve some other objectives like the incorporation of manures and fertilizers into the soil; breaking of soil pans, forming ridges, etc.

Pre-plant tillage is usually conducted in two phases, *viz.*, the *primary tillage* and the *secondary tillage*. The primary tillage is conducted effectively with either a soil inverting plough or a disc. The secondary tillage, on the contrary, is performed with lighter implements like harrows, cultivators, weeder-mulchers, and corrugated rollers. The primary tillage can help in the control of weeds by:

1. Burying the existing weeds, which in turn, eases the post-plant tillage and the application of preplant herbicides.
2. Bringing the weed seeds to soil surface for germination and their subsequent destruction by suitable, secondary tillage operations.

3. Incorporating preplant herbicides.
4. In the case of perennial weeds, delaying or obviating the need of post-plant tillage.

The role of secondary tillage in weed control is mainly to dislodge the germinating weed seedlings.

8.3 POST-PLANT TILLAGE CONTROL OF WEEDS

For a long time, besides the control of weeds, at least three more functions were assigned to the post-plant tillage, more popularly called *row cultivations*. These functions are: (i) conservation of soil moisture, (ii) enhanced soil aeration, and (iii) mixing of fertilizers and manures with the soil (Blake, 1963). The development of chemicals to control weeds made it possible to separate the weed control effects of row-tillage from its other effects in field experiments. These experiments revealed that contrary to the earlier belief, in most soils, tillage did not help to hold any more moisture by forming dust mulch than fields not hoed but kept weedfree. Even in the absence of row-tillage, the soil capillary continuum was disturbed after its 2 to 5 cm surface layer became dry, thus preventing the loss of soil moisture by evaporation. However, in heavy soils that crack badly, inter-row tillage offers benefits beyond weed control by erasing the soil cracks and preventing the uninterrupted evaporation loss of deep seated soil moisture through them. Likewise, on the lower ends of fields where the soil remains wet for considerable period after a rain or irrigation, intercultivation may be helpful in early disruption of the capillary loss of moisture.

The majority of agricultural soils of the world are adequately aerated. But compaction of the fine textured soils under either heavy traffic or beating by the rain can lead to poor soil aeration. Therefore, on very heavy soils the crops have been found to benefit from row-tillage directly even if the weeds were controlled by other methods. For example, on heavy soils early row-cultivation will often improve the number of tillers per plant in a crop like sugarcane. Further, row cultivation is considered beneficial for mixing the top dressed fertilizers and manures with the soil in the inter-rows. But it can also be accomplished equally well with the help of irrigation (or rainfall) since largely water soluble nitrogenous fertilizers are used for top dressing the crops. Top dressing with castor cake and other high analysis manures may, however, benefit crops only after their physical incorporation with hoes and cultivators.

From the foregoing discussion it can be concluded that the chief benefit of row cultivations is the control of weeds; other benefits that may accrue from it are limited to specific situations. Direct benefits of row-cultivations, other than weed control, have been difficult to demonstrate.

8.3.1 Row-Cultivation Implements

1. ***Spiketooth Harrow***: Spiketooth harrow, also called drag harrow and pegtooth harrow, uproots the germinating weed seedlings, breaks the soil crust, and stirs the soil to 1-5 cm depth. It is made of about 32 cm long steel pegs (or spikes) fixed on a frame. The angle of the pegs can be altered at will, according to the soil condition, with the help of a hand-lever. A pair of bullocks can easily draw 1 to 1.2 m wide

spike harrow, whereas a tractor-drawn spike harrow can be as much as 7.2 m wide, made in 2 to 4-folding sections (Fig. 8.2).

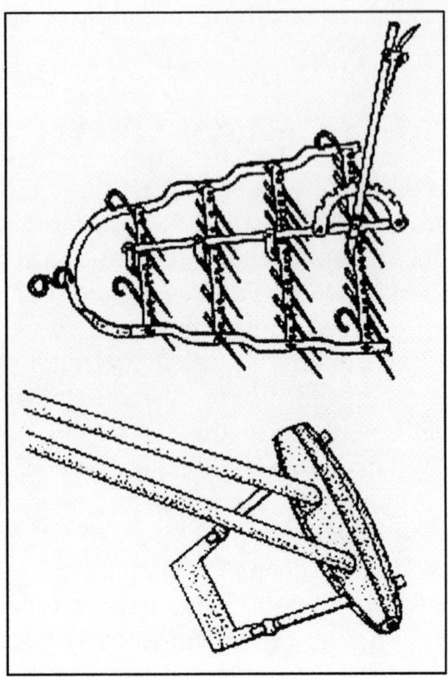

Fig. 8.2: *Top* = A bullock-drawn spiketooth harrow. The angle of the iron pegs is adjustable to suit the soil condition and weed size. The equipment is good for graminaceous crops at their flexible, seedling stages. *Bottom* = A bullock-drawn blade-harrow for preplant and inter-row weeding. Tractor-drawn models of blade-harrow are also available.

Spiketooth harrow is employed once as a rapid, economical method of controlling weed seedlings before row cultivations begin in crops like maize, cotton, soybean, groundnut, and grain sorghum. It can be used any time up to 7 to 10 cm crop height. Spiketooth harrow is run both parallel and across the crop rows to remove weed seedlings growing closest to the crop plants. The implement shall not injure the crop seedlings to any appreciable extent. When worked properly, a spiketooth harrow can create complete weedfree environment for the crop seedlings.

Other tractor-run implements, very similar to spiketooth harrow in their functioning, are (a) finger-weeder, (b) rotary thinner, and (c) rotary weeder.

2. ***Spring-Tine Harrow***: Spring-tine harrow, also called spring-tooth harrow, consists of elliptical spring tines with triangular and sharp, free ends. It is used for the same purpose as spiketooth harrow but it may stir the soil up to 7.5 cm depth (Fig. 8.3).

3. ***Rotary-Hoe Cultivator***: A rotary-hoe cultivator is made up of two gangs of hoe wheels or spiders, one placed behind the other. Within each gang there are row units with spaces between them to protect the crop seedlings. Rotary-hoe cultivator is a tractor-drawn implement designed to run fast, accomplishing adequate soil movement to dislodge the weeds. It is used to break hard crust that usually forms over the crop seeds after a rain but during this process it also destroys the sprouting

weeds. Also, a rotary-hoe cultivator is employed to destroy germinating weeds and grasses in the rows, as well as those growing close to the young crop plants (Fig. 8.4).

4. ***Wheel-Hoe***: A wheel-hoe comprises a wheel, two handles, and a tine with either a reversible shovel, a 3-prong fork, or a rake as its cutting tool. It is a manually operated weeding tool. Man behind the handles pushes the hoe between the crop rows a short length at a time, uprooting the very young weeds and grasses in the process. The wheel hoe is suitable for weeding only small vegetable gardens and some flower beds.

5. ***Blade-Harrow***: Bladeharrow is an animal-drawn, row cultivation implement. Its cutting tool is in the form of 30 to 95 cm long and 5 to 6 cm wide sharp blade which works almost like sweep of a cultivator. It cuts the weeds 7.5 to 10 cm below the ground and leaves them on the soil surface as mulch, without causing any inversion of the soil (Fig. 8.2).

   In India, bladeharrow is a common row weeding implement on heavy, black soils of Madhya Pradesh, Southern Rajasthan, Tamil Nadu, and Maharashtra. With little design variations, it is locally called as *'bakkhar'*, *'guntaka'*, *'daura'*, and *'dantula'*, in different states. A 45 cm wide blade harrow can intercultivate about 1 ha crop field in 8 to 10 hours.

6. ***Cultivator*** (***horse-hoe***): Cultivator is primarily a secondary tillage implement for seedbed preparation. But many cultivator designs are also used widely for inter-row weeding in wide row crops. Wooden ploughs used in India and many developing nations of the world are, in fact, cultivators, and are frequently used both for seedbed preparation and inter-row weeding. But now specially designed, multi-tined iron cultivators have replaced the wooden ploughs for inter-row weeding in many areas. These are also called horse hoes (Fig. 8.3). Horse hoes are very efficient inter-row weeding implements. These vary in sizes from single row, five-tined cultivators to those capable of weeding several crop rows at a time. The tractor-drawn cultivators (Fig. 8.4) can cover several hectares of crop area in a day, as against about 0.5 to 1 ha per day covered with an animal-drawn, five tined cultivator. In India, single row, 3 to 5-tined cultivators are used widely by the farmers. A cultivator is made up of all steel parts. Its tines are fitted with either shovels or sweeps as the cutting tools. While sweeps sever weed roots, up to 10 cm below ground, the shovels uproot them from about 7 cm depth. The, sweeps cause minimum soil upheaval in the crop rows. Sweeps are often more effective in controlling weeds, particularly the established ones, than shovels. The distance between the tines of a cultivator can be varied with a hand lever to suit particular crop row spacings. The depth of working of cultivators is adjusted according to the soil type with the help of front sliding wheel, as well as by varying the length of hook chain. Hoeing with a cultivator is most effective at a time when weeds are in seedling stage. The weed seedling growing adjacent to the crop plants are disturbed by cultivators by moving some loose soil into the crop rows. In crusting type of soils, weed seedlings present near the crop plants are uprooted along with the lifting of crust pieces by the farthest shovel of the cultivator.

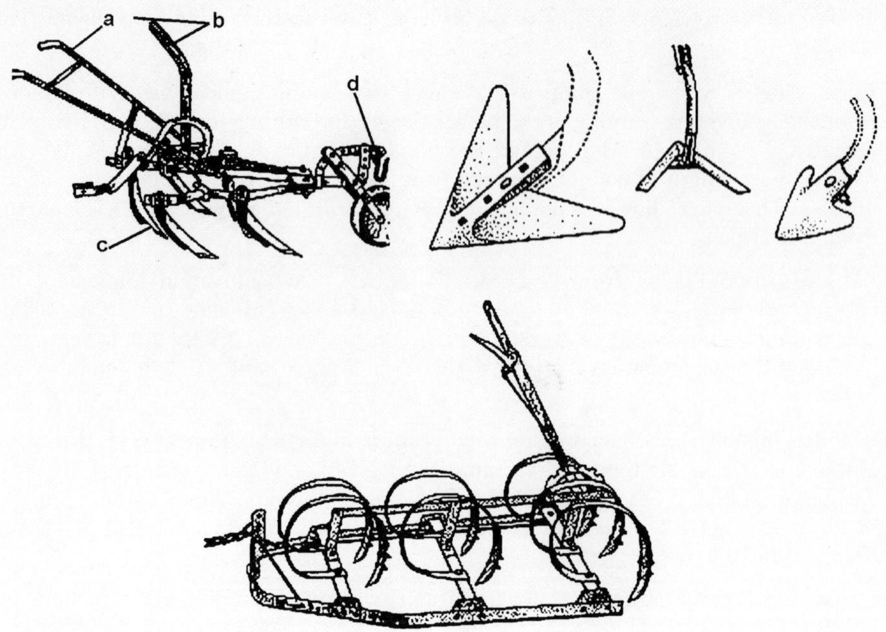

Fig. 8.3: *Top left* = A bullock-drawn, five tine horse-hoe, commonly called 'cultivator'. *Top right* = Three kinds of sweeps which, when needed, may replace the tines in the cultivator. *Bottom* = Bullock-drawn, spring-tine harrow. The depth of working of the tines is adjustable by forward and backward motion of the hand lever. More established weeds require deeper operation than the younger ones.

Horse-hoes or cultivators are not suited to removing established, grown-up weeds standing close to the crop plants. If an attempt is made to uproot the close growing weeds by widening the gap between the cultivator tines and working the shovels and sweeps close to the crop rows, the crop plants may be injured and even uprooted. First inter-cultivation with horse-hoe can be done after the crop plants are 15 to 20 cm tall. It can then be repeated two or three times during the season till the crop height will permit, without damage to the crop plants. Intercultivations prove most effective in controlling weeds when they are preceded by either a spiketooth harrow or application of a soil-active herbicide to stunt the early growth of weeds.

7. ***Rice rotary weeder***: Rice rotary weeder, as the name indicates, is a specific tool for weeding rice crops. It is made available in two sizes, *ie* single row and double row weeders (Fig. 8.5). It is worked manually with back and forth movement in between rice rows in wet fields. When rice is planted at a spacing of about 25 x 25 cm, the rice rotary weeder can be worked both parallel and across the crop rows. With a single row rice rotary weeder, one man can remove weeds from about 1 ha of rice field. Rice rotary weeder is less strenuous than hand-weeding.

Fig. 8.4: *Top*: = A Tractor-drawn rotatory hoe in operation for destroying early weeds. *Bottom* = Close-up of a tractor-drawn rotary hoe.

Besides the above equipment, some additional tools for physical weed control are now available under new names like, dryland weeders, peg weeders, twin wheel hoe, and the grubber or three tined hand cultivator.

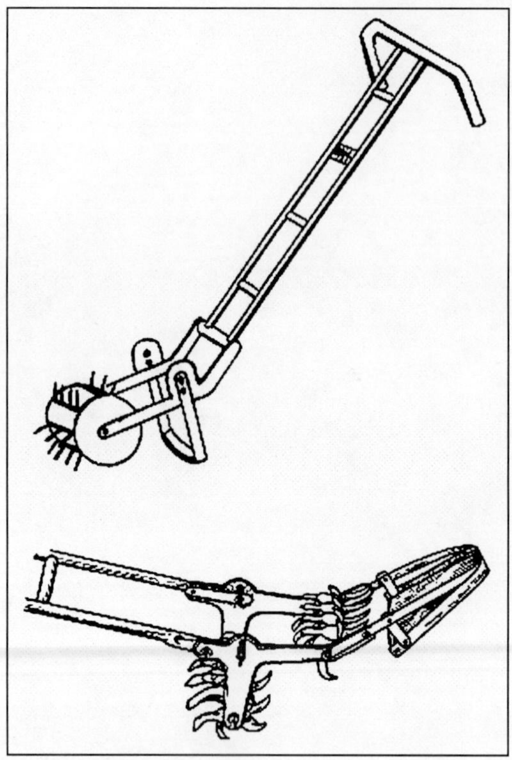

Fig. 8.5: *Top* = A hand-pushed roller-weeder for weeding row crops grown on light soils. *Bottom* = A paddy, hand pushed-pulled rotary weeder.

8.4 PHYSICAL CONTROL OF PERENNIAL WEEDS

8.4.1 Control of Deep Rooted Perennial Weeds

The control of deep rooted, perennial weeds by tillage methods involves rapid depletion of their underground food reserves. Scientists agree that young shoots of perennial weeds draw heavily upon their root reserves for some days after their emergence, till active photosynthesis begins in them. At this stage they stop importing food and begin exporting it to their underground storage organs. Hence, if a deep rooted perennial weed is topped repeatedly, each time just before its shoots begin to feedback their photosynthates to the roots, its underground food reserves shall be eventually exhausted. The practice of destroying the weed shoots as soon as they were seen over the ground is faulty since then it will take much longer to starve the weed. In Kansas (USA), cultivation performed each time *Convolvulus arvensis* 'field bindweed' shoots were 12 days old, eliminated the weed in about 16 operations as compared to 33 cultivations needed when the weed was topped every time immediately after its emergence. These scientists further found that the actual number of tillage operations needed to eradicate a perennial weed varied with (1) the volume and depth of rooting of the weed when tillage was begun and (2) the soil and environmental conditions that determined rapidity of the weed regrowth. The weed eradication was easier in the high water table, sandy, and low fertility soils than in the otherwise ones. In India, the periodical changes in the food reserves of *Cyperus rotundus* 'purple nutsedge' tubers grown in pots, beginning their planting and until 61 days after emergence have been examined. It was found that the starch content in nutsedge tubers at planting was 29.8% (dry weight basis), which dropped to a minimum of 17.4% after 18 days of their germination. The starch content of tubers then rose to 28.9%, 26 days after emergence and to 30.7%, 40 days after emergence. Thus, the destruction of nutsedge shoots everytime these were 18 to 20 days old was recommended.

The choice of the implement for topping of perennial weeds is very important. The objective should be to cut the weeds evenly a little below the ground-level. A set of sharp and flat sweeps is ideal for this purpose. Deep tillage of perennial weeds is highly undesirable, for it delays its emergence, thus prolonging its eradication time. Also, in the case of *Cirsium arvense* 'Canadathistle', deep tillage has been found to induce the weed to grow its roots deeper than usual.

8.4.2 Control of Shallow-Rooted Perennial Weeds

The control of the comparatively shallow rooted perennial weeds like bermudagrass (*Cynodon dactylon*) and quackgrass (*Agropyron repens*) (Chapter 3) by tillage requires much different kinds of operations than those described for the control of the deep rooted ones. In this case the infested land is tilled with a suitable soil inverting plough, bringing in the process as much of the weedy propagules on the soil surface as possible for their desiccation under the hot sun. In North India, mid-April to mid-June is a suitable period for this operation. The first tillage should be done at a time when the soil is dry enough to form clods, which embody in them some rhizomes and roots of the weeds. These clods dry fast with the solar energy, and the trapped weed propagules are thus subjected to desticcation. After some interval of about 15 days, second tillage with a harrow can be performed to break open the large clods into smaller ones and expose the damaged weed propagules further to the hot sun for their final desiccation. A third tillage may sometime be useful after another forthinght or so. Care should be taken not to allow any source of water to pass near the field under treatment, else the whole exercise may go waste (Chapter-7).

Sometimes it may be necessary to rake-out the exposed rhizomes and root fragments from the soil surface and collect these in one corner of the field for their immediate burning.

Finally, it may be noted that tillage control of bermudagrass and like weeds is not without risks. The vegetative fragments of such weeds, which escaped their complete desiccation for one reason or the other, may be spread here and there to initiate new colonies of weeds and aggravate the problem. Therefore, hot-weather cultivation to control specific perennial weeds need be practised with due care, and strictly as per recommendations.

8.5 MOWING, CUTTING, CHAINING, AND DREDGING

1. ***Mowing***: Mowing is cutting of a uniform growth of weeds from entire area at the ground-level. Its chief purpose is to improve look and accessibility to the area, and in certain cases to prevent multiplication of weed seeds. Also, repeated mowings can weaken the underground parts of perennial weeds.

   Mowing is usually practised in non-crop areas, lawns, and gardens, but it can also prove useful in removing weeds from rows of certain established crops. Common mowing tools and implements are sickle, sword, scythe, machete, lawn mower, and reciprocating type rotary-bar mower. Mowing is effective against only erect, herbaceous type of weeds. It is preferred over tillage control of weeds on land susceptible to erosion since it does not produce any bare land.

2. ***Cutting***: In variance with mowing, cutting is topping of the weeds above the ground level. It is most commonly practised against brushes and trees with the help of axes and saws. In aquatics, under-water weed cutters are used to cut weeds up to 1 m below the water surface. Both cutting and mowing are short-lived in their effects; the topped weeds regrow soon from their crown region and underground buds. Therefore, these operations must be repeated often to keep the weeds and grasses low.

3. ***Dredging and Chaining***: These two physical control methods are used against aquatic weeds growing in shallow ditches. Dredging constitutes mechanical pulling of weeds with their shallow roots and rhizomes covered in mud. In chaining, on the other hand, a very heavy chain is pulled over the bottom of the ditch with the help of two tractors, one moving on either bank of the ditch. The chain fragments the rooted weeds by its rubbing action, and the weed fragments float to the water surface. From here these can be collected down the stream by nets and hooks.

SUMMARY

The physical control of weeds involves the use of manual or mechanical energy for destroying weeds. It is the oldest, but most common method, of weed control. Although the physical methods of controlling weeds have undergone spectacular advancements, yet hand-pulling and hand-weeding with simple hand tools are common, particularly in the broadcast sown and narrow-row crops, nurseries, lawns, and home gardens. For weeding the wide row crops, a variety of implements run with animal or tractor power have been developed during the last 200 years or so. These include several designs of horse-hoes, cultivators, and blade harrows which are effective in removing weeds from between the crop rows when the crop plants are at least 15 to 20 cm tall. But the row cultivation implements tend to leave established weeds standing within the crop rows in the intra-row spaces. In addition to the general as well as specific row weeding implements, the use of several implements for preplant and early season control of weeds are presented in this chapter.

The physical control of deep rooted perennial weeds should aim at exhausting their food reserves present in their underground organs. This is best achieved by repeated *shallow tillage* of the weed infested area with sweeps, each time the weed shoots grow to the point of maximum import of food from their underground roots and rhizomes. *Deep tillage* is undesirable for controlling such weeds, (save the shallow rooted ones where the objective is to bring their underground parts over the ground for either their collection or desiccation under the hot sun).

Tillage control of weeds is the most common practice in agriculture, and it will remain so for long time to come.

In aquatic environment, physical methods of weed control commonly used are dredging, chaining, cutting, and collecting.

SELECTED BIBLIOGRAPHY

1. Blake, G. R. 1963. Objectives of soil tillage related to field operations and soil management. Netherland. J., Agric. Sci. II (2) 130 - 139.
2. Blake, G. R. 1964. Soil compaction-is it critical? Crops and Soils. April-May, 1964.
3. Buchanan, G. A. and A. E. Hiltbold. 1977. Response of cotton to cultivations. Weed Sci. 25 : 132 - 135.
4. Das, N. R. 2007. Tillage and Crop Production. Scientific Pub. (India), Jodhpur, 300 p.
5. Egley, G. H. 1983. Weed seed and seedling reductions by soil solarisation with transparent polyethylene sheets. Weed Sci. 31, 304-409.
6. Hosmani, M. M. and Habeeburrahman, P. V. 1992. Soil solarization: a new tool for weed control. UAS, Dharwad, India Bull. 18 pp.
7. Kumar, B. *et al.* 1993. Effect of soil solarisation on the weeds and nematodes under tropical conditions. Weed Res. 33 423-429.
8. Majid, A. *et al.* 1987. Effect of different tillage techniques on wheat production after rice. Pak. J. Agri. Res. 8 (2) 199-203.
9. Manian, R. *et al.* 2004. Development and evaluation of weeding cum earthing up equipment for cotton. Agric. Mechanisation in Asia, Africa and Latin America (AMA), 35(2): 21-25 (Japan) (W.A. 54(4), 1557).
10. Michael, A. M. and Ojha, T. P. 1966. Principles of Agricultural Engineering. Vol. 1, Jain Bros., Jodhpur, 209-228 p.
11. Mishra, J.S. 2004. Tillage and Weed Management. NRC (Weed Science), Jabalpur (India), Tech. Bull. No. 1. 33 p.
12. Powles, S. B. *et al.* 1988. Solar heating (solarisation) of the soil surface. Effect on weed control and yield of Phaseolus vulgaris. Plant Prot. Qtly. 3(1) 31-35.
13. Rubin, B. and Benjamin, A. 1984. Solar heating of the soil. involvement of environmental factors in the weed control process. Weed Sci. 32 138-145.
14. Smith, H. P. 1964. Farm machinery and Equipment. Mc Graw-Hill Book Co. N. Y. 154-164 and 209-235 pp.
15. Sthool, V. A. and P. H. Shinde. 2004. Performance evaluation of pegtooth weeder in dryland agriculture. J. Maharashtra Agric. Univs. 29(1): 113 (India).
16. Swanson, C. L. W. and Jacobson, H. G. M. 1952. Herbicides - a new tool for use in studying soil physical properties affecting crop growth. Weeds 1(2) 174-184.
17. Thakur, C. *et al.* 1955. Tillage control of nutgrass in relation to its organic reserves. Bihar Acad. Agri. Sci. Proc. Vol. 4.

Chapter 9

THE BIOLOGICAL CONTROL OF WEEDS

An important reason for the abundance and the aggressive nature of at least certain weeds is paucity of their natural enemies.

The biological control of weeds involves the use of living organisms, such as insects, herbivorous fish, other animals, disease organisms, and competitive plants to limit their infestations. Currently, there are two approaches to this method of weed control, viz., (i) the classical biological control philosophy approach, and (ii) the bioherbicide philosophy approach. Any biological control approach shall yield best results when it is integrated with a comprehensive weed management programme.

9.1 CLASSICAL BIOLOGICAL CONTROL PHILOSOPHY

In nature, often the growth of many a weed remains limited due to constant biotic stresses on them from chiefly insect pests and disease organisms. When a weed disperses to an alien geographical area, leaving its enemies back in its native habitat, the chances are it will spread rapidly in the new situation and invade large areas in relatively short time, provided the climate was suitable for its propagation. Eventually, many alien weed species turn noxious. *The classical biological weed control aims at restoring the balance between the target alien weed and its natural enemies in the ecosystem by purposeful introduction of suitable, exotic bioagents.* The immediate response to successful introduction of a native bioagent is a decrease in the weed population, followed after some period by a decline in the bioagent population due to its food shortage. Then often the weed population tends to recover. The process continues in a cyclic fashion till the bioagent-weed populations get stabilized at a low level. At that time, man enters the cycle and he puts the cleared area to some economic use. The biological weed control should not be expected to eliminate the target weed from an area; in fact, success of biological control of weeds depends upon continued presence of the weed existing in small numbers and shifting with time. The method being a slow opreating one, is persently used mainly in non-crop situations. On crop lands, even if successful, the bioagent will not get opportunity to work on the host weed because of frequent use of insecticides and fungicides in modern agriculture. Otherwise, *Cyperus rotundus* can possibly be controlled in crop fields with a moth borer, *Bactra verutana*. Another promising example of selective biocontrol in crop fields is complete denudation of *Ludwigia parviflora* 'waterpurslane' by *Haltica cyanea* Web. 'steelblue beetle', in rice fields.

An important aspect of biological weed control is that at a time, it is applicable to the control of only one major weed species that has spread widely. Also, one should be prepared to accept cyclic resurgence of the weed under attack by the classical biocontrol approach. Further, while with perennial weeds the main objective of biocontrol is the destruction of the existing vegetation, in the case of annual weeds prevention of their seed production is generally more important.

9.1.1 Criteria of a Successful Bioagent

A successful bioagent is (i) host specific, (ii) adjustable to the new environment, (iii) rapid destroyer of the target weed, (iv) easy to multiply, and (v) effective on several taxa of the weed in question.

1. ***Host Specificity***: Biocontrol agents recommended for weed control should be host-specific, *i. e.* they should not attack other plant species, particularly the economic ones. The bioagents released so far (chiefly insects) had successfully passed the 'starvation tests' before they left the laboratories for field use. They were found to prefer to starve to death rather than feed upon plant species other than the target weed. Starvation test is a good safeguard against an introduced bioagent becoming a pest on some economic crop plant. For example, *Teleonemia scrupulosa*, though found a very good insect bioagent for the control of lantana, yet in India it is found likely to damage teak (*Tectona grandis*) and sesame (*Sesamum indicum*). Therefore, it was not released in the country. Similarly, *zygogramma bicolorata* Pallister, although an effective, leaf eating bioagent of *Parthenium hysterophorus*, 'carrotgrass', it is found to attack sunflower (*Helianthus annus*) in India, because of which it was not released. However, there is also a view that unless the teak trees and sesame crop were located next to some large tract of lantana under a biocontrol programme, and *T. scrupulosa* bred there prolifically, the damage to the two economic plants would only be transient. Similarly, feeding a few plants of sunflower by *Z. bicolorata* beetle did not justify dropping of the project of biocontrol of carrotgrass with this insect (see also Chapter 23). In fact, in recent years the importance of subjecting a promising bioagent to very rigorous starvation tests has been questioned by certain biological weed control workers. According to these scientists, in the first instance even when a bioagent engaged itself in feeding upon a plant of economic value, it does not mean it will also breed upon it. Secondly, one must weigh the damage and losses caused by the target weed and difficulty in controlling it by other means, against some possible damage that may be inflicted by the bioagent to some plant of economic value. In substance, a latitude is recommended in the conventional starvation tests of the otherwise promising bioagents, although not too liberally.
2. ***Bioagent Hardiness***: It is important that a classical bioagent withstands elements of its new environment in which it is transplanted. This includes freedom from its own

parasites and predators. Further, the bioagent should be hardy enough to survive short and long periods of food shortage when the target weed population is brought to a low level. This has a significant implication in the case of carp which cannot survive even a short starvation period. To continue their survival, the grasscarp must be shifted to a new weedy waterbody soon after the weed biomass in the previous one is lowered sufficiently.

3. ***Feeding Habit***: Great stress has been placed on the selection of insects as bioagents that attack either the flowers and seeds of the weed or bore into their stems. Insect bioagents with such feeding habits have been found more host specific and efficient in controlling weeds than the leaf or root feeders. But lately certain leaf eating insects have been found equally valuable in the control of weeds, particularly of the perennials. Likewise, insects that attack roots are likely to be very effective on perennial weeds but insufficient attention has been paid to them. In any case, the destructive capacity of a bioagent on the weed should be very high so that its small population could destroy large weed infestations.

4. ***Ease of Multiplication***: High rate and ease of natural reproduction of bioagent is important in insects, pathogens, snails, and competitive plants. But it is very much unwanted in the case of carp employed for aquatic weed control because their excessive population may compete with cultivated fish. Fortunately, all present researches indicate that a bioagent carp like the Chinesegrasscarp, is a extremely slow, natural breeder in the tropics and sub-tropics, although under artificially controlled conditions it can be multiplied rapidly (Gupta, 2001).

9.1.2 Kinds of Classical Bioagents

Four kinds of bioagents have thus far been successfully used for controlling weeds, both terrestrial and aquatic. These are (i) insects, (ii) carpfish, (iii) fungi, and (iv) competitive plants.

1. ***Insects***: Insects have been more frequently used than other animals for the biological control of weeds. The first successful example of weed control with deliberately introduced insects was reported from Hawaii in 1902 when a project for the control of *Lantana camara* L. was initiated with a moth, *Crocidosema lantana* Busck. Since then insects belonging to widely different families and genera have been employed to control some other noxious weed species. Alien weeds have been the main subject of biocontrol with insects imported from the evolutionary centres of the weed concerned. But there is at least one example when a native weed has been brought under control with an alien insect species. The weed is manuka, *Leptospermum scoparium* Forester, and it was controlled on its native land, Newzealand, with mealybug *Eriococcus orariensis* Hoy, introduced from Australia.

   Insects selected as biocontrol agents of weeds are largely host specific *ie* one insect species is employed to destroy only one weed species.

2. ***Carp fish***: Certain fresh water carp fish consume large quantities of aquatic weeds and they are very suitable for relieving waterbodies of their massive growth of noxious, aquatic vegetation. Whiteamur (Chinesegrasscarp) *Ctenopharyngodon idella* Val is the most promising species of carp for aquatic weed control. Whiteamur eats

more than its own body weight in weeds daily and it grows at a rate of 5 kg/year, attaining 50 kg or more body weight at its full size. The high potentiality of white amur for aquatic weed control has been tested in many countries, including India, and it has successfully cleared many weed-infested waterbodies. Unlike insect bioagents, the herbivorous fish are not much food-specific. They feed upon a wide range of plants and, therefore, they control a variety of aquatic weeds, simultaneously. This food habit of grass carp may be undesirable in waterbodies having some plants of economic value, like waterchestnut (*Trapa natans*) and lotus (*Nelumbo* sp.) which, of course, are also classed as weeds in most situations. A good review on this bioagent is given by Gupta (2001).

3. ***Plant Pathogens***: Many fungi are observed to attack specific weed species, but examples of successful, practical weed control with fungi are few. Of late, it has been discovered that *Acacia glauca* could be controlled successfully by injecting a suspension of spores of *Cephalosporium zonatum* Sawada. The ranchers of Hawaii are already using this practice on commercial scale. Control of skeletonweed (*Chondrilla juncea* L.) by introducing a rust causing fungus, *Puccinia chondrillina* Bubak & Syd in Australia is another examle of successful biological control of weeds employing fungi.

4. ***Competitive Plants***: Certain plants may be highly competitive in nature; capable of suppressing some specific weed/s wthout causing any meaningful hinderance to our interests. (Dear, 1984). Yeo (1972) found that *Eleocharis acicularis* 'slender spikerush' possessed these two characters. It is a short, very fast growing, aquatic plant that could cover the canal bottom rather rapidly, disallowing the obstructive tall weeds from establishing there. Likewise *Panicum purpurascens* Raddi is found competitive to *Typha* spp. in marshlands. More recently marigold (*Tagetes* spp.) plants have shown potential of displacing parthenium (see also Chapter 23).

9.1.3 Outstanding Examples of Classical Biocontrol of Weeds

1. ***Lantana* (*Lantana camara* L.)**: Lantana was the first weed controlled successfully with certain insect bioagents in Hawaii. This bushy weed is a native of Central & North America. In Hawaii it had invaded such large areas of rangelands that it was causing great concern. In 1902, Albert Koebele visited Mexico and Central America to find insects destructive to *Lantana*. R. C. L. Perkins conducted tests with insects sent by A. Koebele and finally selected eight species for release on lantana infestations. Of these, *Crocidosema lantana* Busck, a moth, was found prominent in destroying flowers and seeds of lantana, which formed the chief organ for dispersal this weed. The insect greatly curtailed the spread of lantana and thinned its existing infestations. Fifty years later, the entomologists in Hawaii made further attempts to find and introduce new insect species to destroy lantana; this time from areas other than the native land of the weed. They found seven more insects feeding on lantana. Of these, *Hypena jussalis* Guenoe was an excellent feeder of lantana leaves. It defoliated all sizes of lantana plants rapidly. Since then many other insects have been screened for the destruction of lantana in Hawaii, and the weed has been brought under control on her different islands. Biological control of lantana has also been adopted successfully in Australia and other places. In Australia, three highly successful insect biocontrol agents are: hispine beetles (*Octotoma scabripennis*

Guerin and *Uroplata girardi* Pic.) and tingid or lantana bug (*Teleonemia scrupulosa* Stal). These insects are causing severe damage to the susceptible taxa of *Lantana,* which are receding fast there (Fig. 9.1). In Andhra Pradesh (India), lantana has been successfully controlled with some of these insects, besides the lantana seedfly (*Ophiomya lantanaea*) (Thakur, 1992).

Fig. 9.1: Lanatna bush has been destroyed successfully with several biogent insects, particularly in Hawaii and Australia. *Top* = Defoliation of the weed with *Teleonemia scrupulosa. Bottom* = Lantana stem gridled by larvae of *Plgiohammus spinipennis* (Photo: courtesy KLSH, Australia).

2. ***Pricklypear* (*Opuntia* spp.):** In Australia, biocontrol of *O. inermis* with a moth, *Cactoblastis cactorum* (Berg) transformed 24 million ha land from wilderness to a scene of prosperous endeavour. At the present, in Australia only occasional plants and few larger patches of pricklypear can be found. The recovered land has returned to a useful agriculture there. In Tamil Nadu and Maharashtra (India), 40,000 ha of land infested with *Opuntia dillenii* was recovered from the weed by releasing *Dactyloplius tomentosus* Auct. (*D. ceylonicus* Green) 'cochineal scale insect' as its bioagent. Other species of *Opuntia* were not attacked by this insect (Fig. 9.2).

The primary damage to *Opuntia* with insects can be combined with secondary attacks by bacterial and fungal parasites for further eroding the weed. These secondary bioagents are *Cleosporium anatum* E & E, *Phyllosticta concava* Seav. and *Montegnella oppuntiorum* Speg.

Fig. 9.2: *Top* = Opuntia All Over. *Bottom* = Opuntia's All Over, by *Cactoblastis cactorum* within 3 years (courtesy WHH, Australia)

3. ***Carrotgrass (Parthenium hysterophorus*** **L.)**: It is an exotic alien weed which is considered one of the seven most dreaded weeds of the world. Originally a native of tropical America and West Indies, it has spread in many countries, including India. Ever since its first appearance in India in 1956 at Pune, it has spread alarmingly in almost every part of the country. It is primarily a weed of all possible neglected non-crop areas, including grazing grounds, where it has covered vast areas with devastating effects on health and environment. Carrotgrass has now also spread to some agricultural lands, fallow fields, and orchards. Parthenium is poisonous and allergic in its effects on humans.

The biological control of Parthenium using a Mexican beetle, *Zygogramma biclorata*, is found very promising (Fig. 9.3). Large patches of land heavily infested with this menace have been cleared off by the beetle in several parts of the country. Its optimum level of population release is 50-100 beetles/plant of carrotgrass. Management of Parthenium through biocontrol may be considered as the most preferred, cost-effective, and self-sustaining method.

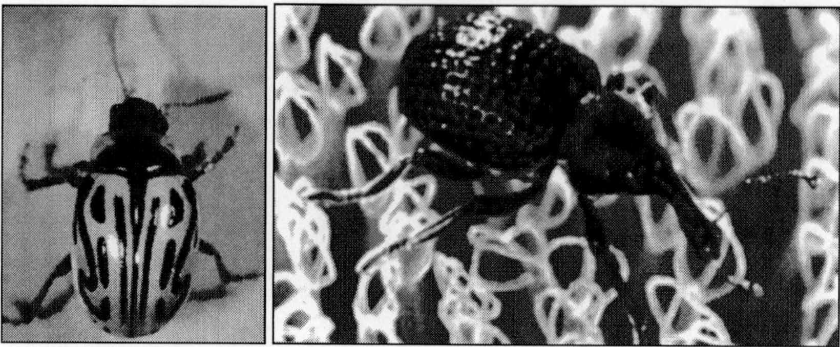

Fig. 9.3: Two successful insect bioagents used in India. *Left*: *Zygograma bicolorata* against *Parthenium hysterophorus* and *Right: Cyrtobagous salviniae* against *Salvinia molesta*. (In the background of the right side picture are seen typical, much enlarged leaf hair of salvinia weed which obstruct penetration of herbicides in the plant.

4. ***Alligatorweed (Alternathera philoxeroides)***: Alligatorweed is a very prolific, aquatic plant of the tropics and sub-tropics. In Florida, (U.S.A.) it has been very effectively controlled with fleabeetle (*Agasicles hygrophyla* Selman & Vogt)) and several bayous have been cleared of this weed there. The fleabeetle larvae feed on the leaves of alligatorweed and finally bore into its bare stems to pupate. The feeding performance of the beetle is improved greatly when the alligatorweed is pre-treated with 2,4-D or diquat which soften the weed foliage. Besides fleabeetle, the alligatorweed thrips, *Anynothrips andersoni* O' Neill and a phycitid stem borer, *Vogtia molloi* Pastrana, have proved very effective in controlling the alligatorweed.

5. ***Waterhyacinth (Eichhornia crassipes)***: Waterhyacinth, a worldwide aquatic weed, infests transplanted paddy fields in many countries, including India. Several attempts have been made on the biological control of this weed; both by pathogens and insects. Most success in this respect has been met in Florida (USA) with a hyacinthmoth, *Sameodes albiguttalis* B. Benner, which is a native of South America. The bioagent exhibits its rapid reproduction ability in field conditions. Its larvae feed upon young leaves and apical buds of waterhyacinth, rather severly.

   Besides the hyacinthmoth, two beetles, *viz., Neochetina eichhorniae* Warner. and *N. bruchii* Atustache, are also damaging to waterhyacinth, but these are not as fast in building their populations as the hyacinthmoth.

6. ***Salvinia (Salvinia molesta)***: In Kerala (*India*), fresh water courses and paddy fields have been cleared of this noxious fern, using curculionid beetle (*Cytrobagous salviniae* Sands) as a very effective bioagent (Fig. 9.3). The beetle is native of South

America. It is released in waterways by collecting some beetle-infested *Salvinia* plants from either the beetle rearing ponds or some old infestations, and scattering these on the target, salvinia infestations. It takes 4-6 months for the salvinia mats to turn yellow, and another six months to sink, completely. The young larvae of the beetle damage the terminal buds, rhizomes, and petioles of salvinia. The biological control of salvinia has made lives of over 5 million people in Kerala more comfortable than before.

In addition to the above mentioned examples of outstanding achievements and wide interest in the biological control of weeds, there are many more successes on hand at various stages of research and field use. These are given in Table 9.1.

Table 9.1: Some Additional Examples of Promising Bioagents of Weeds (From different sources cited in bibliography)

Weed	Bioagent	Reporting Country	Kind of bioagent
Chondrilla juncea	*Puccinia chondrillina*	Australia	Plant pathogen
Cirsium arvense	*Septoria cirsii*		Plant pathogen
Cyperus rotundus	*Bactra verutana*	India, Pakistan, USA	Shoot boring moth
Echinochloa spp. (In rice fields)	i) *Emmalocera* sp. ii) *Tripos* spp.		i) Stem boring moth ii) Shrimp
Eupatorium riparium	*Entyloma compositarum*	USA	Plant pathogen
Hydrilla verticillata	*Hydrellia pakistanae*	USA	Shoot fly
Orobanche cernua	*Sclerotinia* sp.	USA	Plant pathogen
Rumex spp.	i) *Uromyces rumicis* ii) *Gastrophysa viridula*	USA USA	Plant pathogen Beetle
Tribulus terrestris	*Microlarinus lareynii* and *M. lypriformis*	USA	Pod weevil

9.2 BIOHERBICIDE PHILOSOPHY OF WEED CONTROL

Bioherbicides, in variance with the *Bioagents*, are herbicidal chemicals released by some living organisms. At the present, these organisms comprise largely certain microbes (fungi/ bacteria) because of which the bioherbicides are also termed as *Mycoherbicides*. (It may be recalled here that earlier in Chapter-6, the possibility of contolling weeds with exudates of certain higher plants, called allelochemicals, was discussed. According to the current, comprehensive definition of allelopathy, the bioherbicides, in a way, are also allelochemicals).

The mycoherbicides were first promoted by certain corporates in the USA as 'made to order' products to control specific noxious weeds. Upon receiving the order from the client, the companies multiply the spores of the required microbes under controlled conditions and then supply these as formulated spore suspensions. Sometimes, the mycoherbicides are also offered as fermentation products of the relevant microbes. In either case, the farmer is advised to spray the formulation, after making recommended dilutions, on the target weed just like a herbicide, soon after procuring it, to obtain best results. It may be brought home here that mycoherbicides act like synthetic, contact herbicides, requiring repeat applications to tackle the new flush of the weed, if any.

Some proprietary bioherbicide products used in the western world, along with their active microbes and the target weeds, are listed in Table 9.2. All the released bioherbicides are supposed to be highly host-specific.

The *bioherbicide philosophy* differs from the classical biocontrol philosophy referred to earlier, in certain ways as follows:-

1. Bioherbicide remains active only on the current weed populations, without any chance of cyclic perpetuation of the weed (or of the bioagent); each new flush of the weed thus requiring retreatment with it.
2. Bioherbicide can be developed for selective control of weeds in a crop just like any other selective herbicide, which is not the case with the classical philosophy bioagents.
3. The development of bioherbicides is of great interest to industrialists since it involves every season requirement of the product for field use. In variance with it, the classical biological control approach has no incentive to the private, profit-oriented organisations; it must depend solely upon public sector support.

Table 9.2: Some Commercial Mycoherbicides in Use Abroad (From literature cited in bibliography)

Product	Content	Weed controlled
De-Vine	A liquid suspension of fungal spores of *Phytophthora palmivora* Butler. It causes root rot in the weed.	Stranglevine (*Morrenia odorata*) in citrus orchards
Collego	Wettable powder containing fungal spores of *Colletotrichum gloesporiodes* Penzig & Sacc. sub sp. aeschynomone	Jointvetch (*Aeschynomone* sp). in rice fields. The bioherbicide causes stem and leaf blight in the weed
Bipolaris	A suspension of fungal spores of *Bipolaris sorghicola*	Johnsongrass (*Sorghum halepense*)
Biolophos	A microbial toxin produced as fermentation product of *Streptomyces hygroscopicus*	Non-specific, general vegetation
Biomal	*Colletotrichum gloesporiodes* sp. *maluae*	*Malva passilia* (roundleaved mallow) in winter crops
Luboa-2	*C.g.* sp. *cuscutae*	*Cuscuta* spp. (dodder vine) in soybean
Methoxyphenone	*Streptomyces* sp.	*Echinochloa crusgalli* (barnyardgrass) in rice

Parasitic weeds, allergenic weeds, crop mimics, and narcotic plants are excellent targets for activating the bioherbicidal approach. Besides, it has always been the goal of scientists to develop products also for broad-spectrum weed control in agriculture, competitive to chemical herbicides. But thus far it has been elusive, save a few individual weeds that have been successfully curbed with bioherbicides in agriculture and horticulture (Table 9.2).

One way to increase the virulence of bioherbicides is to increase the spore load in the spray. Another, and probably better, way is to genetically modify the microorganism by genetic engineering to a very high potency level (Hallett, 2005). No doubt the transgenic bioherbicides will have to face serious scrutiny, and may be required to be equipped with some fail-safe mechanism in tandem with the enhancement genes (Gressel, 2001).

9.3 BIOLOGICAL VERSUS OTHER METHODS OF WEED CONTROL

The initial cost of biological weed control appears to be high, but in comparison to the cost of developing a new herbicide, it is quite reasonable. Unfortunately, at the present the biological control of weeds is given a last resort consideration for dealing with some difficult weed problems on grasslands and in non-crop situations where other weed control methods have either failed or were found infeasible. The last resort approach to biological control methods has been largely due to fear of man about the introduced bioagent becoming a pest on some economic plant which was not included in the starvation tests. Also, an equally important reason for it is the conflicting interests of man in the target plant. A plant may be a serious weed in one area, but it may be of high value as an animal feed, soil binder, or as a fence plant in the neighbourhood. Pricklypear (*Opuntia* spp.), for example, is a serious weed of rangelands in many areas and it can be controlled, as though by magic, by *Cactoblastis cactorum*. But in the neighbouring areas, where this plant is used either as fence or as a forage plant, the people may object to the release of the insect for its control. Whereas physical and chemical methods of weed control can be limited to the terrain to be cleared of a given weed, the insect and other bioagents can move the to non target lands and destroy the host plant there. For this reason, in Hawaii, *Cactoblastis* is not allowed to be released for the control of *Opuntia*. Likewise in Australia, lantana is not allowed to be controlled by biological methods in her rangelands where it is a noxious weed, just because in banana plantations it forms a useful cover plant. Despite such limitations of biological control of weeds, with improvements in technology and the relative costs of weed damage and value of the benefits from the control of weeds, it is now considered a folly to treat biological control of weeds as the last resort method. In fact, because of its eco-friendly nature, the biological control of weeds is bound to get new impetus, particularly when there is growing concern about the pollution hazards associated with, at least, certain pesticides.

SUMMARY

The biological control of weeds involves the deliberate use of some suitable living organisms to curb their population to acceptable limits. This approach was first examined in 1902 in Hawaii (USA), and since then very efficient bioagents have been discovered and used. Insects have been the most favourite bioagents discovered thus far against a variety of noxious weeds, in addition to certain carp employed for the control mixed aquatic vegetation. This approach to biocontrol of weeds is known as *Classical biocontrol* philosophy. The classical philosophy bioagents have to be fast multipliers in nature, save the carp. Some highly noxious weeds of the world controlled through such bioagents include, lantana, pricklypear, carrotgrass (earlier congressgrass), St. Johnswort, alligatorweed, salvinia, and waterhyacinth. The carp have been employed for non-specific aquatic weed control.

Of recent, a new approach to biocontrol of weeds, called *bioherbicide philosophy*, is gaining momentum. In this approach certain plant pathogen preparations, called mycoherbicides, are used. These are applied on the target weeds just like any organic herbicide. Unlike the classical philosophy bioagents, which once released continue their population cycles on their own in tune with the weed populations, the mycoherbicides control only the weeds present at the time of their spray and then wither away, just like a contact herbicide. A bioherbicide is from *native range* to control a native or naturalized problem weed. The transgenic races of the active pathogen and application of increased spore loads are basics to obtain virulent effect of the bioherbicide on the target weed. In either approach, a bioagent is required to be host-specific, weather hardy, and fast acting.

The major mycoherbicides made available commercially in some western countries are Devine, Collego, Bipolaris, Biolophos Biomal, Luboa-2 and Methoxyphenone for the control of, respectively, stranglevine in orchards, northern jointvetch in rice fields, Johnsongrass, mixed weed growth on non-croplands, roundleaf mallow in winter crops, cuscuta in soybean, and barnyardgrass.

It is unfortunate that presently biocontrol of weeds, which is an environmentally compatible approach, is given a last resort effort treatment in weed control programmes after the other approaches, some with considerable potential of polluting our environment, have failed. It has been primarily so because of the slow and highly climate dependent action of most of the classical bioagents. However, with more rapid development of bioherbicides and other fast acting bioagents, this thinking is bound to change.

SELECTED BIBLIOGRAPHY

1. Abhasher, A and Sauerborn, J. 1992. *Fusarium nygamai*, a potent bioherbicide for *Striga hermonthica* control in sorghum. Biological Control 2 (4) 291-296.
2. Amsellem, Z. *et al.* 2002. Engineering hypervirulence in a mycoherbicidal fungus for efficient weed control. Nat. Biotechnology 20 : 1035-1039.
3. Andres, L. A. 1982. Integrating weed biological control agents with a pest management programme. Weed Sci. 30 (Suppl.) 25-29.
4. Anon, 1993. Biological control of paddy weeds. Newsletter-Food Fertilizer Technology Center No. 99, 5-7. (novel)
5. Anon. 1993. New Control Agents Against *Parthenium*. Weed. AQIS Bulletin 6(4) 11-12.
6. Bosch, R. Van Den *et al.* 1982. An Introduction to Biological Control. Plenum Press, N. Y. 247 pp.
7. Boyette, C. D. 1988. Biocontrol of three leguminous weed species with *Alternaria cassiae*. Weed Technol. 2 414-417.
8. Buttae, G.S. and N. Aggrawal. 2005. Bioherbicides - A review. Pestology 29(6) : 27-35.
9. Center, T. D. 1982. The waterhyacinth weevils. Aquatics 4(2) 8.
10. Charudattan, R. 1982. Biological Control of Weeds With Plant Pathogens. John Wiley & Sons, N. Y. 293 pp.

11. Dear, 1984. Using plant competition to control aquatic weeds. IPM Practioner 6(1) 2-3.
12. Duke, S. O. and Lydon, J. 1987. Herbicides from natural compounds. Weed Technology 1: 122-128.
13. Duke, S.O. *et al.* 2002. Chemicals from nature for weed management. Weed Sci. 50 : 138-151.
14. Froude, V.A. 2002. Biological control options for invasive weeds of New Zealand protected areas. Science for Conservation No. 199, 68 pp. (New Zealand)
15. Frush, T. *et al.* 1996. Natural products as pesticides: two examples of stereo-selective synthesis. Pesticide Sci. 46(1): 37-47.
16. Gautam, R.D. 2002. Investigations on the release of exotic beetle for control of *Parthenium hysterophorus* in Delhi. Ind. J. Weed. Sci. 34 : 259-263.
17. Greaves, M.P. *et al.* 1989. Mycoherbicides : Opportunities for genetic manipulation. Pest. Sci. 26 : 93-101.
18. Gressel, J. 2001. Potential fail-safe mechanisms against the spread and introgression of transgenic hypervirulent biocontrol fungi. Trends Biotechnol. 19 : 149-154.
19. Gupta, O. P. 2001. Weedy Aquatic Plants : Their Menase and Management. Agrobios (India), Jodhpur, 237p.
20. Hallett, S.G. 2005. Where are the bioherbicides? Weed Sci. 53 : 404-415 (U.S.A.).
21. Hershenhorn, J. *et al.* 1993. *Septoria cirsii*, a potential biocontrol agent of Canadathistle and its phytotoxin, p-nitropropionic acid. Pl. Sci. (Limerick) 94 (1-2) 227-234.
22. Hoagland, R.E. (ed.). 1990. Microbes and Microbial Products as Herbicides. ACS Symposium Series 439, Washington D.C., American Chemical Society Publishing.
23. Kennedy, A.C. *et al.* 2001. Host range of a deleterious rhizobacterium for biological control of dwony brome. Weed Sci. 49(6): 792-797. (USA)
24. Khodayari, K. and Smith, R. J. Jr. 1988. A mycoherbicide integrated with fungicides in rice (*Oryza sativa*). Weed Technol. 2: 282-285.
25. Kumar, R. 1992. Microbes and microbials: the resurgence of a new era in biological control. Discovery and Innovation 4(2) 4-12.
26. Maniappan, R. and Viraktamath, C. A. 1986. Status of biological control of the weed *Lantana camara* in India. Trop. Pest Management 32(1) 40 42.
27. Mc Fadyen, R. C. 1992. Biological control against parthenium weed in Australia. Crop Prot. 11(5) 400-407.
28. Paul, N. D. 1992. Making biological herbicides more effective. 1992. J. Biol. Education 26(2) 94-99.
29. Rodgers, P. B. 1992. Potential of biopesticides in agriculture. Pesticide Science. 39(2) 117-129.
30. Room, P. M. 1986. Biological control in solving the world *Salvinia molesta* problems. Weed Abs. 36 (2) 1987, item 511.
31. Samways, M. J. 1981. Biological control of Pests and Weeds. Studies in Biology No. 132 (Ed). Arnold, London, 55 pp.

32. Sharma, P.K.S. and Mishra, S. C. 1986. Biological control of forest weeds in India-retrospect and prospects. Ind. Forester. 11(2) 1088-1093.

33. Singh, R. V. and H. R. Sardara, 2003. Safer packing, labeling and use of pesticides for minimizing toxicity risks. Pesticides Informatinon 29(1): 16-18.

34. Singh, S.P. 2002. Role of biocontrol agents in pest management in the millennium. (IN) Crop Pest and Disease Management: Challanges for the Millennium (eds. D. Prasad and S.N. Puri). (India)

35. Te Beest, D. O. (ed.), 1991. Microbial Control of Weeds. Chapman and Hall Ltd., London.

36. Te Beest, D. O. 1993. Biological Control of Weeds With Fungal Plant Pathogens. (In) Exploitation of Microorganisms (Ed.), Jones D. G., London.

37. Templeton, G. E. 1982. Biological herbicides. Weed Sci. 30: 430-433.

38. Tewksbury, L. *et al.* 2002. Potential for biological control of *Phragmites australis* in North America. Biological Control 23(2) : 191-212. (USA)

39. Thakur, M. L. *et al.* 1992. Lantana weed (*L. camara*) and its possible management through natural insect pests in India. Ind. Forester 118(7) 466-488.

40. Visalakshy, P.N.G. and K.P. Jayanth. 2002. Suppressing *Cyperus rotundus* Linn. by augmentative releases of *Bactra venosana* Zeller. J. Biological Control 16(1) : 85-86.(India)

41. Yaduraju *et al.* 2005. Major Invasive Alien Weeds of India. NRC Weed Science (ICAR), Jabalpur, 52p.

42. Yeo, R. R. 1972. Plants might help eliminate aquatic weeds. Crops and Soils 24(8) 24.

43. Zimmermann, H.G. *et al.* 2001. The renowned cactus moth *Cactoblastis cactorum*, its natural history and threat to native Opuntia flora in Mexico and USA. Florida Entomologist 84(4): 543-551. (South Africa).

Chapter 10

DIVERSITY OF HERBICIDES, THEIR APPLICATION METHODS, AND USE PRECAUTIONS

10.1 HISTORICAL

Common salt, ash, smelter waste, and like cheap materials have been used for centuries to control weeds on roadsides, fence rows, and pathways. But selective control of weeds in agriculture was first conceived in 1896 with the chance observation of some farmer in France that Bordeaux mixture sprayed on grapevines for protecting it from downy mildew, damaged certain broadleaf weeds. Soon it was found that copper sulphate present in the Bordeaux mixture was responsible for its weed killing effect. Further tests in France, Germany, and U.S.A. established that copper sulphate could indeed be used for selective control of broadleaf weeds in small grains; wheat, barley, and oat.

Between 1896 and 1908, several other inorganic salts, as also sulphuric acid, were found selective to small grain cereals. Of these, in Europe, a 6 to 10 per cent solution of sulphuric acid continued for considerable time as a satisfactory herbicide for broadleaf control in cereals, but it corroded the containers and sprayers. In the U.S.A.., salts like sodium chlorate, carbon bisulphide, sodium arsenite, kainite, and calcium cyanamide were developed for non-selective eradication of perennial weeds, particularly, *Convolvulus arvensis* 'fieldbindweed' and *Cirsium arvense* 'Canadathistle'. In Hawaii, sodium arsenite solution was found highly effective for weed control in sugarcane plantations. Between 1930 and 1940, some boron compounds, thiocyanates, dinitrophenols (DNC and DNBP), ammonium sulphate, and certain mineral salts were developed in the west for selective and non-selective weed control. DNC and DNBP were used extensively in Europe in small grains for broadleaf weed control, even though these chemicals dyed the hands and clothes of the users to yellow colour, almost permanently.

A real breakthrough in selective chemical weed control was achieved in 1945 with the announcement of simultaneous discovery of 2,4-D and MCPA in the U.S.A. and England, respectlvely, after the World War II. The discovery of these two sister compounds is said to have been affected much earlier than 1945 although it was then kept a war time secret till it was divulged later for agricultural use. While studying NAA for its growth regulatory effects on wheat in pot house, W. G. Templement of England observed in 1941 that it killed a few *Brassica kaber* 'wild mustard' plants growing as weeds in wheat pots. This induced him and W.A. Sexton at the Jealotts Hill Research Station, England to search for some more potent growth regulators than NAA for broadleaf weed control in small grains. IAA and NAA could not be used as field herbicides because these were found oxidised within the plants by oxidases enzymes. Their elaborate trials finally yielded 2,4-D and MCPA as potent growth regulator type of herbicides, the scientists were looking for. In the U.S.A., 2,4-D was discovered independently by P.W. Zimmerman and A.E. Hitchkock at the Boyce Thompson Institute. Both 2,4-D and MCPA were found highly selective to cereals and phytotoxic to the broadleafs. They killed broadleaf weeds at very low rates. Besides, these compounds were (a) non-corrosive, (b) non-flammable, (c) non-explosive, and (d) non-toxic to man. Therefore, the two sister compounds rapidly replaced all the earlier used selective herbicides in small grain crops. 2,4-D stayed in the U.S.A., while MCPA in the European countries. In fact, the chemical control of weeds got a spurt with the introduction of 2,4-D (& MCPA). Within ten years of discovery of 2,4-D, the U.S.A. alone produced about 30,000 tonnes of this herbicide, annually. Since then 2,4-D has been introduced in several other countries of the world, and today hundreds of thousand tonnes of 2,4-D and MCPA are used round the globe to control herbaceous, broadleaf weeds in different situations. In the agriculturally developed countries, herbicides form over 45% of the total pesticides used. Against this, in India, herbicides share only about 8% of the total pesticides consumed; the insecticides contributing to almost 77% of the total pesticide consumption. In absolute terms, in India we use an average of only about 40 g herbicide per ha per year, against 675-1350 g/ha/year used in many advanced countries. In Japan, as much as 5000g herbicide is used per ha, annually.

The spectacular acceptance of 2,4-D and MCPA for weed control in graminaceous crops in the world gave impetus to researchers to discover additional herbicides, resulting in a spate of new herbicides in certain agriculturally advanced countries. Today there are over 400 different herbicide molecules at global level, belonging to varied chemical families and groups; the latest being the sulfonylureas and their derivatives (Chapters 12 & 13). Over 100 private companies are involved in research and development of these herbicide compounds, largely in the western world. The research is ongoing to invent new herbicide structures to deal with the everemerging new weed problems. In India, at the present, 42 approved herbicides are in either active use or at various levels of testing (Appendices 2, 3, 5 & 11).

10.2 PROCEDURE OUTLINE AND COSTS OF INVENTING NEW HERBICIDES

The invention of new herbicides with novel modes of actions is a priority assignment in plant protection research. Almost all herbicides in the world are invented by private companies in the first instance, but often the Universities and public and Government research groups are latter involved in their further testing and development. The invention of each successful herbicide requires, on an average, testing of over 7000 compounds, though in most cases a company starts with 10,000 molecules. A common means to getting to such a huge number of new chemical structures is to synthesize homologues and analogues of a proven phyto-active material. But, once in a while completely new chemical structures are also tried. Often plant's native chemicals, particularly, the hormone and enzyme structures, form the basis of developing new herbicides. From the planned synthesis of new structures, and their numerous variants, come candidate herbicides. The large companies, as a routine, screen these chemicals in greenhouses for their biological and pesticidal activity which suddenly reduces their number to about 40 or so. The remainder chemical structures are filed for future reference.

For active compounds identified in greenhouse screenings, the crucial point is to tread the most efficient path in determining herbicides' target sites, chances of success, and time and research costs.

The selected compounds are then subjected to more extensive laboratory and small field plot tests, using a large number of plant species. Of these compounds, one or two are finally selected for their introduction in field studies on manufacturers' own farms located at different places in the country. The chemical process research and pilot plant production are then taken up. Concurrently, analytical techniques are developed to detect any possible residues of candidate compound in the treated crops. Also, feeding tests on animals are conducted. The bio-chemical studies on the fate of compounds in plants and soils are also made. At this stage the herbicide under investigation is offered to the Government laboratories and experiment stations as test compound for their independent evaluation.

If the data from the above evaluation schemes are still favourable, an application is made to the appropriate Government agencies for temporary permit to allow field tests in a variety of geographic conditions. Finally, when a compound has passed through all these tests successfully, a registration from the Government is sought. For instance, in the U.S.A., Pesticide Regulation Division (PRD) and the Environmental Pollution Agency (EPA) of USDA are involved in pesticide clearances.

The above complex procedure of discovering herbicides calls for the combined efforts of the chemists, physiologists, agronomists, toxicologists, and environmental biologists for an average period of six and a half years. And during this time the company has spent a few million dollars. These figures, incidentally, are tending to increase from year to year.

10.3 OBJECTIVES AND SCOPE OF HERBICIDE USAGE

The primary objective of introducing herbicides in any country has been to replace the torturous and back-breaking, manual weeding and to give the farmer the much needed leisure, of which he has been deprived since ages. The spared labour could be utilized more effectively for bringing additional land under cultivation and improving the irrigation, fertilization, and other pesticide application practices, enhancing thus the overall agricultural production in the country. The swelling costs of hired labour and limited supply of fuel for mechanical weed control, are two other reasons for introducing herbicides in agriculture.

The herbicides are not aimed at substituting the physical, biological, or good crop husbandry methods of weed control. They are meant to bridge the gaps in these methods and act as added production tools in agriculture. Practical weed control is a combined effect of good crop husbandry, herbicides, and other techiques.

Herbicides have ample scope in vegetation management, both on crop lands and non-crop lands. On crop lands, herbicides are used as aids in seedbed preparation for destroying the established weeds before they have a chance to infest the crops. Later, these can be used to raise weedfree crops with several advantages, already enumerated in Chapter-6. Outside the crop field, herbicides can be employed to maintain weed sanitation as part of weed prevention work for the main fields. Also, herbicides form useful tools in limiting the unwanted vegetation in industrial areas, roadsides, along the rails, and in several other like situations. In waterbodies too, herbicides can be efficiently employed to free them of their weedy vegetation that hinder proper water use. In summary, where there is need to manage vegetation efficiently, there is scope of using herbicides, along with the other inputs.

10.4 ECONOMICS OF HERBICIDE USE IN AGRICULTURE

Any new technology proposed to be introduced in agriculture, or other places, should be cost-effective, and yield a Benefit-Cost ratio (B:C) that is sufficiently high to attract the client towards its adoption. Introduction of herbicides in cropping plans is no exception to it.

Research work conducted so far with different crops has clearly shown that employment of herbicides for controlling weeds is a very rewarding proposition from its economics point of view. Some data on B:C ratios of this technique are summarised in Table 10.1. It may be noted from these data that, despite the fact that hand-weeding resulted in greater crop yields than herbicides, yet because of high, and ever increasing wages and comparatively lower herbicide costs, the use of herbicides resulted in higher B-C ratios. In different crops it varied from 9.0 to as high as 87.9; being especially high in the case of high value, vegetable crops. The B-C ratios of hand-weeding varied in different crops from 3.5-12.5.

Table 10.1: Economics of Herbicide Use in Different Crops

Treatments	Wheat		Paddy		Soybean		Pea		Mungbean	
	Yield (q/ha)	**B:C**	**Yield (q/ha)**	**B:C**	**Yield (q/ha)**	**B:C**	**Yield (q/ha)**	**B:C**	**Yield (q/ha)**	**B:C***
Unweeded (Check)	27.6	-	29.72	-	6.38	-	11.91	-	3.1	-
Hand-weeded (twice)	41.7	10.1	46.12	4.5	15.13	4.5	19.0	3.5	8.6	3.96
Herbicide	41.0 (2,4-D)	33.5	45.70 (Butachlor)	9.0	11.95 (Fluchloralin)	5.7	20.01 (Pendimethalin)	9.9	6.9 (Pendimethalin)	17.0
Reference	Gupta, *et al.* (1969)		Sharma, *et al.* (1994)		Chandrakar and Urkurkar (1993)		Kundra, *et al.* (1993)		Patro and Prustry (1994)	

* *See Chapter 27 for calculation of B:C.*

Table 10.1 Contd.....

Treatments	Potato		Onion		Garlic		Cauliflower	
	Yield (q/ha)	**B:C**	**Yield (q/ha)**	**B:C**	**Yield (q/ha)**	**B:C**	**Yield (q/ha)**	**B:C**
Unweeded check	135	-	90	-	6.1	- 41.60	-	
Hand-weeded (twice)	188	2.1	165	8.1	24.7	6.91	67.40	12.55
Herbicide	199 (Metribuzin)	28.4	148 (Oxyfluorfen)	87.9	21.2 (Oxyfluorfen)	19.8	69.9 (Oxyfluorfen)	13.44
Reference	Singh and Lal (1994)		Singh, *et al.* (1992)		Porwal (1995)		Porwal and Singh (1993)	

It may be pointed out here that B:C ratios of the most popular input in agriculture *viz.*, the fertilizers, is only between 2.0 and 3.0 Obviously, in comparison to it the B-C ratios of herbicide use are 5 to 15-folds.

10.5 CLASSES OF HERBICIDES

10.5.1 Selective and Non-Selective Herbicides

A selective herbicide is one that will kill some plant species when applied to a mixed plant population, without causing serious injury to the other species. 2,4-D, atrazine, EPTC, trifluralin, and alachlor are few of the battery of selective herbicides used on crop land. A non-selective herbicide, on the other hand, is one that kills plants without regard to species, for example, paraquat, sodium chlorate, weed oils, and acrolein. Selective herbicides are used in crop areas, lawns, gardens, and grasslands; whereas the non-selective herbicides are employed for general vegetation control on industrial sites, fallow land, and in aquatics. Certain selective herbicides when applied at high rates, can act as non-selective plant killers, for instance, simazine and diuron. Today, the field of selective herbicidal control has reached such an advanced stage that a weed of grass family can be controlled in the crop of the same family, for instance, *Avena fatua* 'wildoat' in wheat. Besides such occasional, inherent selectivity amongst herbicides, man has been able to purposefully induce selectivity in some herbicides to specific crops by modifying their mode of application. (see chapter 16).

10.5.2 Narrow Spectrum and Broad Spectrum Herbicides

A narrow spectrum herbicide, upon application to a mixed population of weeds, proves active on one, or a very limited number of species. Most of the other weed species remain tolerant to such herbicides. The narrow spectrum herbicides are very useful against specific noxious weeds. But their development and manufacture proves remunerative only when the susceptible noxious weed is of global importance. Metoxuron, difenzoquat, and diclofop are very successful examples of narrow spectrum herbicides. These are widely used against specific weeds like *Phalaris minor* and *Avena fatua*. A limitation of the narrow spectrum herbicides is the need to employ additional herbicides to control mixed weed species, which may contribute to greater environment pollution. A broad-spectrum herbicide, on the other hand, controls a wide-spectrum of weedy flora at a time. Most of our herbicides today belong to this group of herbicides since these find wide-spread use in agriculture.

10.5.3 Soil-Active and Foliage-Active Herbicides

A soil-active herbicide is one that is applied primarily to the soil rather than to the vegetation. Inside the soil it kills weeds as they germinate or inhibits sprouting of their rhizomes, stolons, and tubers. Therefore, in crop fields a soil-active herbicide eliminates early weed-crop competition for the period it remains active in the soil. This period is usually 4 to 8 weeks, depending upon the herbicide and its rate used. The soil-active herbicides are largely applied at the time of planting of crops, but in some cases these may also be applied to the weedfree inter-rows of established crops to obtain extended period of weed control. A few, common soil-active herbicides used in crop fields are simazine, alachlor, trifluralin, and EPTC. On non-crop lands, the soil-active herbicides used are largely the *soil sterilants and fumigants*.

A Foliage-active herbicide is applied to weeds after their emergence from the soil. They are absorbed by the plant foliage and, in many cases, these are translocated to the other plant parts. At normal rates the foliage-active herbicides are most effective against young weeds in their seedling stages but at high rates these may kill even the established weeds. Paraquat, diquat, MCPB, amitrole, and herbicidal oils are common examples of foliage-active herbicides. There may be some herbicides that are both soil-active and foliage-active, for example, 2,4-D, picloram, and atrazine.

The soil-active herbicides are becoming increasingly popular with the farmers in preference to the foliar herbicides because of three reasons: (i) The soil-active herbicides control weeds even before they emerge from the soil, thus, eliminating early period weed competition. (ii) They maintain weed control for considerable period after application, usually for 3-4 weeks. (iii) The soil-active herbicides often provide better selectivity to the treated crop.

10.5.4 Contact and Translocated Herbicides

A contact herbicide kills plants primarily by contact with the plant tissue rather than as a result of its translocation. Thus, a contact herbicide applied to the foliage of a plant will not kill its roots, though in simple annuals the roots of the treated plants may die because they were deprived of their shoots. The established weeds will regrow from their crown buds, roots, or rhizomes, shortly after treatment with a contact herbicide. Some common contact herbicides are paraquat, diquat, propanil, and petroleum oils.

In contrast to a contact herbicide, *a translocated (or systemic) herbicide moves within the plant from the point of treatment to its other parts, to variable extent.* It often kills the entire plant even if only a portion of the plant was treated with the herbicide. Therefore, the translocated type of herbicides are of particular importance in controlling the perennial weeds. Also, the translocated herbicides can be applied as low volume sprays to control annual weeds because they need not wet the entire plant foliage, as against the contact herbicides which must drench the weeds fully for bringing about their effective kill.

Some herbicides may exhibit both, contact and translocation activities. For example, atrazine is a translocated herbicide when absorbed by the weed roots from the soil, but a contact herbicide when it is sprayed on the plant shoots.

10.5.5 Residual and Non-residual Herbicides

A residual herbicide maintains its phytotoxic effects in soil for considerable time after its application. This residue period may be three to four weeks in some herbicides, such as 2,4-D and EPTC, and much longer, up to several months, in others. In intensive crop rotations, usually herbicides with three to six week's residual activity in soils are used. In variance with the residual herbicides, *a non-residual herbicide is inactivated in soil immediately, or within a few days, after it reaches the soil.* Paraquat, diquat, amitrole, DSMA, and weed oils are non-residual or very short persistence herbicides. The non-residual herbicides are good for a quick knock-down of the existing weeds; they do not provide any extended period of weed control. In agriculture their chief importance lies in destroying weed infestations occurring either before planting or before germination of the crops. The persistence of herbicides in soils is a function of herbicide structure, rate, soil type, and climatic conditions.

10.5.6 Soil Sterilants and Fumigants

A *soil sterilant prevents the growth of plants when present in the soil.* Their soil sterilizing effects may be either temporary or relatively permanent. The *temporary soil sterilants* sterilise the soil for up to 16 weeks, whereas the *permanent soil sterilants* remain active much longer, sometimes for two or more years. The temporary soil sterilants are usually volatile compounds which leave the soil in vapour form after a few days to a few weeks of application. During this period these are supposed to have killed all live plant parts in the soil. Such soil sterilants are also called *soil fumigants*. MB, metham, and dazomet are good examples of soil fumigants used in agriculture and horticulture for the treatment of seedbeds and pot soil. Permanent soil sterilants, on the other hand, find their chief use in causing bare ground in industrial and other non-crop areas for one or more seasons. Sodium chlorate, substituted ureas, several symmetrical triazines, arsenics, and borates are the major permanent soil sterilants in use currently.

10.6 METHODS OF APPLICATION OF HERBICIDES

Methods of application of herbicides are decided largely by their modes of action and selectivity. Environmental factors, convenience, and cost are other important factors in deciding the method of application of a herbicide. An improper method of application of a herbicide can result in poor weed control and/ or severe crop injury. Important methods of application of herbicides to crop and non-crop lands are given, as follows:-

10.6.1 Soil Application of Herbicides

1. ***Surface Application:*** Soil-active herbicides are commonly applied to the surface of the soil where they may be either left undisturbed or incorporated into the soil, physically. Even when left on the soil surface, the applied herbicide should be able to move into upper 3.5 to 4 cm of soil under the influence of rain (or irrigation) to

kill the germinating weeds (Fig. 10.2). Many substituted triazine, urea, and anilide herbicides form our common surface applied herbicides in crop production. Sometimes, a surface applied herbicide may have to be physically incorporated into the soil for varied reasons. For example, in dry weather the triazine herbicides perform better when these are mixed lightly with the treated soil. There are other soil-applied herbicides which must be incorporated into the soil to prevent their rapid volatilization and/or photodecomposition losses. Carbamate and toluidine herbicides are typical preplant, soil-incorporated compounds for this reason. The physical incorporation of herbicides can be achieved with pickaxes in small areas, and with animal or power-driven implements in larger fields. The optimum depth of incorporation of different herbicides for achieving selective control of weeds varies considerably. For example, EPTC is incorporated 5 to 7.5 cm deep in soil, whereas trifluralin and nitralin are incorporated not beyond 5 cm depth. Diallate and triallate herbicides, on the other hand, are mixed with soil only up to 2.5 cm depth. While most herbicides are incorporated into the soil physically, EPTC and fluchloralin can be incorporated also with irrigation water.

2. ***Sub-Surface Layering:*** It is the application of a herbicide in a concentrrated band, about 7-10 cm below the soil surface. The technique has proved effective in controlling certain perennial weeds with conventionally, soil-incorporated herbicides which are usually employed to control only annual weeds. The concentrated layer of the herbicide inhibits the growth of new shoots of specific perennial weeds. *Cyperus rotundus* and *Convolvulus arvensis* have been effectively controlled by this technique using carbamate and nitralin herbicides, respectively. The immediate use of the technique is probably in orchards and vineyards, besides certain wide-row crops like sugarbeet and tobacco. The subsurface layering of herbicides is achieved with special flood nozzles introduced below the soil, under the cover of sweep hoods (see Chapter 11).

3. ***Broadcast and Band Application:*** *Broadcast application* of herbicides is their application over the full surface area, without leaving any intentional gaps. In variance with it, the *band application of* a herbicide constitutes its application to a restricted band along the crop rows, leaving an untreated band in the inter-rows (Fig. 10.1). The band application of herbicides is primarily a cost saving device since it reduces the quantity of herbicide in the ratio of the treated band width to the crop row width. For example, a 30 cm wide band of a herbicide applied over crop rows that were spaced 90 cm apart, will require one third of the quantity of herbicide needed for its application by the broadcast method. The herbicide band width is usually 30-35 cm.

   In the band method of application of herbicides the inter-rows must be cultivated later to remove weeds from the unsprayed areas. This will also help in the control of perennial, and some other weeds, which may be resistant to the herbicide.

4. ***Soil Fumigation:*** Dependnig upon the nature of the soil fumigant, it can be applied either (1) by soil injection (Ex. chloropicrin); (2) by releasing it under sealed, plastic covers (Ex. methyl bromide); or (3) by direct soil surface application (Ex. metham). Details of these methods of fumigating soils are given in Chapter-23.

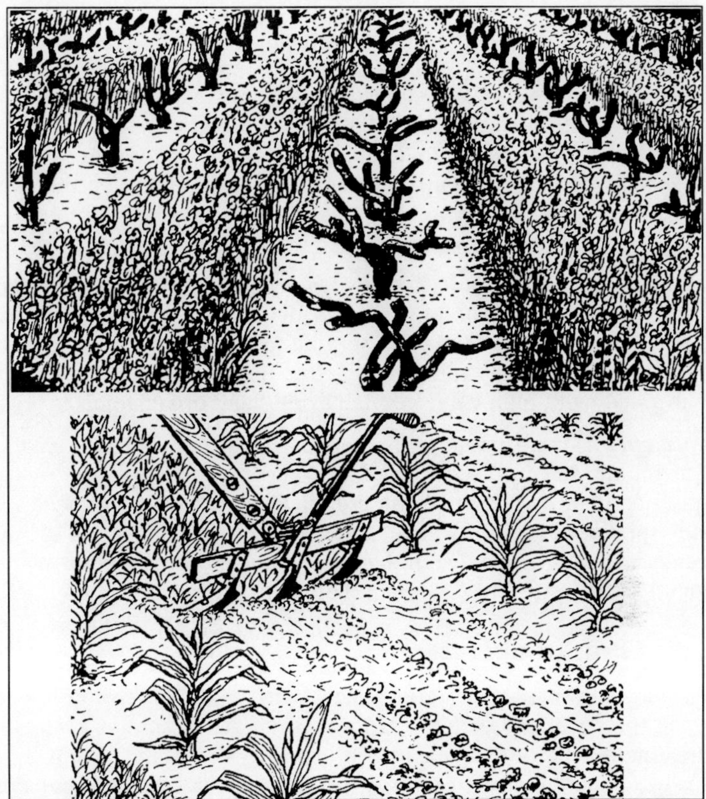

Fig. 10.1: In both the figures above, the herbicide was applied in **bands** over the crop rows only (diagrammatic). While it kept the area along the crop plants weedfree, in the inter-rows weeds must be removed later by some physical means. *Top* = A grape vineyard. *Bottom* = A maize field. The band application of herbicides is considered both a cost saving and a pollution controlling device.

10.6.2 Foliage of Application of Herbicides

1. ***Blanket Application:*** Blanket (or over-the-top) application of herbicides is their uniform application to standing crops with disregard to the location of the crop plants. Only highly selective herbicides are applied by this method, *eg* 2,4-D in wheat, MCPB in pea, 2,4-DB in lucerne, and picloram in sugarcane *cf* surface application of herbicides.

2. ***Directed Spraying:*** It is the application of herbicides to chiefly weeds growing in the inter-rows of crops, avoiding the crop foliage as much as possible. Directed spraying is accomplished by setting nozzles low with spray patterns fashioned to intersect at the base of crop plants, just above the soil line. This saves the crop plants from herbicide injury and improves weed kill. In potato and soybean, vine-lifters are used to improve the accuracy of directed spraying. One important pre-requisite of directed

spraying is that farmer must get his row crops well up over the weeds at the time of treatment. This calls for a good seedbed preparation and planting so that crops will emerge rapidly and gain a height advantage over the weeds. Orchards and plantations are good venues of directed herbicide sprays. Usually, the directed spraying is adopted with herbicides that are only partially selective to the treated crops. But, when feasible, one should apply even selective herbicides by this method to place most of the herbicide on the weeds. Herbicide falling on the crop plants is, obviously, a waste.

3. ***Protected Spraying:*** Non-selective herbicides can be employed to obtain selective weed control in distantly planted vegetables and ornamentals by covering the non-target plants before application of the herbicide with plastic or metallic covers. This can be done in 3-4 rows at a time and shifting the covers to the untreated rows each time. This method is called *protected spraying.* It is somewhat laborious but it pays itself when weeding of high value vegetable crops and ornamentals is involved.

4. ***Spot treatment:*** Spot treatment is the application of herbicides to small patches of weeds, leaving the weed-free gaps untreated. The method is used for treating patches of noxious, perennial weeds in certain crop fields with potent herbicides. To identify the already sprayed spots in the field and avoid possible duplication of the spray, one may pre-add methylene blue dye in the spray tank. Spot treatment is of value also in the non-crop areas to prevent wastage of herbicide in the weed-free spaces.

10.6.3 Treating Brush and Trees

Brush weeds and unwanted trees are treated with herbicides by different methods, depending upon the situation. *Foliage treatment* is the most common method of treating brush. The treatment is best done when the brush leaves are fully expanded, though still growing actively. Ground sprayers can cover up to 2.5 m high brush. On taller trees and brush, aerial spraying is needed. A better method of dealing with tall brushes is to treat their basal 30 cm of stem, preferably after peeling off their bark, to the point of liberal run-off. This is called *basal bark treatment.* Sometimes the more hard to kill brush are first subjected to foliar treatment and then these are retreated by the basal bark method.

The third method of application of herbicides to brush is the *cut-stump treatment.* It comprises sawing of the tree above the ground followed by liberal application of the herbicide on the cut surface. Other ways by which the concentrated herbicides are applied to unwanted trees are, *frill, notch,* and *injection* methods. The frills and notches are made with sharp tools into the sapwood at convenient stem height and filled with herbicides. The herbicide injections are made into holes made in the tree trunk. Usually, one herbicide injection per 2.5 cm stem thickness is adequate. The frill, notch, and injection methods are adopted on thick stem trees which are 8 cm or more in diameter. The treatment of stems by any one of the above methods is practised when either selective brush control is important or when foliage application of herbicides is not feasible.

10.6.4 Other Methods of Herbicide Application

1. **D.C.A. (Direct Contact Application):** D.C.A. includes all techniques involving *wiping, rubbing,* and smearing of herbicide onto the target plant surfaces. It may be

achieved by using *herbicide wax bars, herbicide cloth mulch, herbicide rouging gloves,* etc. The herbicide-laden wax bars are dragged against weeds growing much taller to the crop plants. Herbicide cloth mulches are spread in the crop inter-rows. The rouging gloves carry arrangement to smear herbicide onto the weed gripped by the worker. Many other ways of DCA of herbicides can be designed to suit specific situations.

2. ***Soil injection:*** Herbicides like ethylene, carbon bisulphide, and vernolate are applied by soil injections, at prescribed spacings, before planting of the crops.

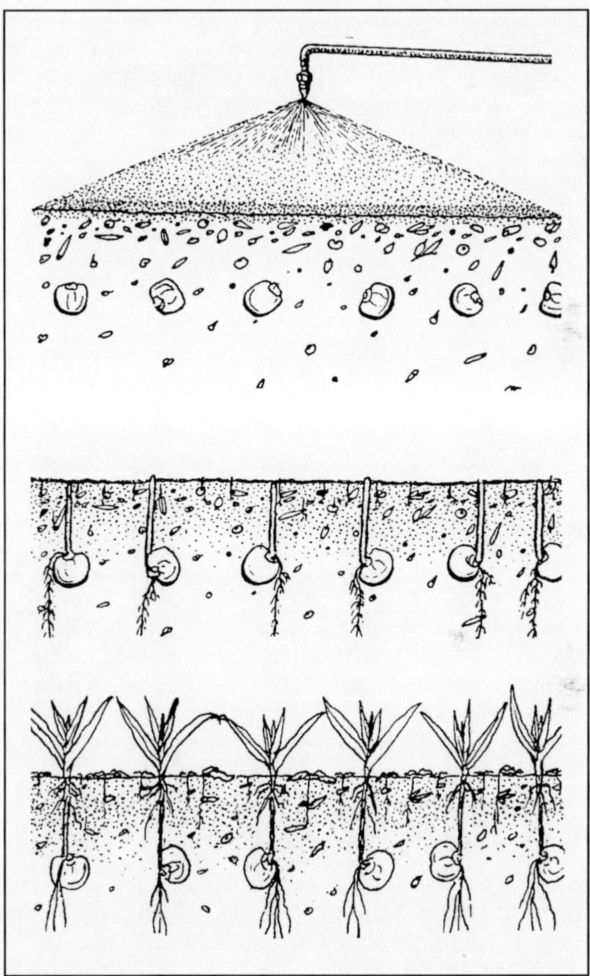

Fig. 10.2: [A] = Preemergence application of a herbicide (diagrammatic). Note, neither the weed seeds nor the crop seeds have yet germinated from their respective zones in the soil. [B] = Both weeds and crop seedling are ready to penetrate the even film of the herbicide applied on the soil surface. [C] = While the susceptible weed seedlings wither away, the tolerant crop seedlings emerge through the soil and grow in a weedfree environment.

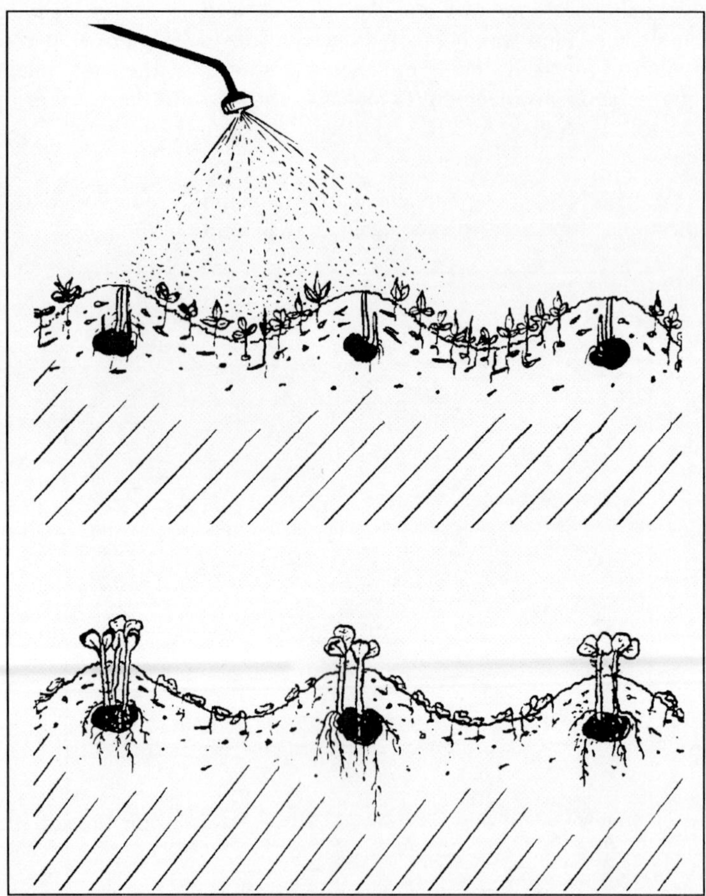

Fig. 10.3: Early postemergence application of herbicides. *Top* = A non-residual herbicide being applied after the weeds have emerged but before the crop (potato) has done so (diagrammatic). *Bottom* = The emerged weeds killed with the herbicide while the potato shoots emerge through the soil after 1-3 days, safely.

10.7 TYPES OF HERBICIDE TREATMENTS

1. ***Preplant treatment:*** *A herbicide treatment made any time before the crop is planted is called a preplant treatment.* There are two types of preplant treatments, namely (a) preplant desiccation and (b) preplant incorporation treatment. In the former method herbicides are applied to destroy the standing vegetation as an aid to seedbed preparation. *In the preplant incorporation method (PPI), on the other hand, herbicides are mixed with the soil in weedfree seedbeds to obtain residual control of weeds during the crop season.* Sometimes preplant soil incorporation of the herbicide may not be considered necessary or desirable. In soil incorporation of the herbicide, the crop to be planted should possess a very high level of physiological selectivity to

it. Else the herbicide should be left on the bare soil unincorporated and crop be sown as such.

2. ***Preemergence treatment***: *Application of a herbicide soon after planting of the crop, when neither the weeds nor the crop have germinated, is called preemergence treatment* (Fig. 10.2). But sometimes, a preemergence treatment is further specified as 'preemergence to weeds', when the herbicide may be applied to standing young crop prior to the germination of weeds. A fine, trash-free soil tilth is the first requirement of a successful preemergence treatment. Besides, the soil must be adequately moist to induce weed seed germination and move the herbicide 1-1.5 cm deep in to the soil, in a uniform film. The land under treatment, in general, should be levelled without leaving any undulations. Otherwise the herbicide shall collect in the depressions where it may damage the crop.

   In a way, while both 'preplant' and 'preemergence' treatments are soil treatments, the former is executed before sowing of the crop, and the latter, after its sowing. In either case, the weeds are killed as they germinate and come in contact with the thin herbicide film. Both kinds of treatments, to be effective, require adequate soil moisture; a fine, levelled seeded; and other conditions conducive to the rapid germination of the weed seeds. It may be noted that an uneven application of the herbicide on the soil surface shall result in uneven weed control and, sometimes, also in crop injury in spots having received the overlap sprays.

3. ***Postemergence treatment:*** *Postemergence treatment is the application of herbicide after the emergence of both the crops and the weeds*. But when the weeds grow before the crop plants have emerged through the soil, and these are knocked with a herbicide, the treatment is called **early postemergence treatment** (Fig. 10.3). Herbicides used for the early postemergence treatment are usually non-residual types, *eg* paraquat and diquat.

   When herbicides are applied on the weeds growing outside the crop fields, it is usually termed *foliage treatment* (of weeds), instead of postemergence treatment, although in either case the herbicide acts on the weed shoots.

4. ***Lay-by application:*** *It is the application of herbicides after the last cultivation in crops,* such as, after ridging in sugarcane and cotton.

10.8 HERBICIDE FORMULATIONS (=CONCENTRATES)

Most of the herbicides cannot be applied in the field in their technical grade form; these have to be made in forms suitable and safe for their field use. Such forms are called *herbicide formulations*. The herbicide formulations are diluted by the user, more generally in water but sometimes also in oil, before their application in the target area. Dry granules of herbicide formulations, however, are applied either as such or after their dilution with dry sand, and like material.

A herbicide formulation is prepared by the manufacturer by blending the toxicant (=active ingredient) with substances like solvents, invert carriers, surfactants, antifoaming agents, stickers, stabilizers, etc. The two major objectives of formulating herbicides are to ensure their (a) ease of handling and (b) high controlled activity on the target plants.

A herbicide formulation may be in one of the following forms:-

1. Emulsifiable concentrate (EC)
2. Water soluble concentrate (WSC)
3. Wettable powders (WP)
4. Dry flowables (DF)
5. Flowable liquid (FL)
6. Granules (G)
7. Emulsion in Water (EW)
8. Wettable Dispersable Granules (WDG)
9. Supension Concentrate (SC)
10. Others - Capsules, wax bars, soluble mulches, foam pieces, aerosols, etc.

Herbicides are not used in dust forms for fear of their drift hazards, which may be intense.

10.8.1 Sprayable Concentrates

A sprayable concentrate may be in the form of a (i) soluble concentrate, (ii) emulsifiable concentrate, (iii) wettable powder, or (iv) dry flowable. In water as carrier these herbicide concentrates form solutions, emulsions, or suspensions, as the case may be. They are collectively designated as *spray materials*. A *herbicide solution* is a physically homogenous mixture of herbicide concentrate and the carrier (usually water). A *herbicide emulsion*, on the other hand, is a herbicide concentrate dispersed in carrier (and *vice-versa*), where each component maintains its original identity as minute globules. In variance with solution, an emulsion is a heterogenous system and to stablize it, an emulsifying agent must be added to it (see Chapter 17). In a *herbicide suspension* the fine particles of the wettable powder* are dispersed in a suitable carrier. To prepare a suspension, first the wettable powder is turned into a slurry with limited amount of the carrier and then it is extended to required volume by adding remainder of the carrier to it. Both suspensions and emulsions of herbicides require mild agitation in the spray tanks. *Dry flowable* (DF) formulations disperse easily in water in the spray tanks.

10.8.2 Flowable Liquids

Herbicides like acrolein and aromatic solvents are applied in waterbodies as *flowable liquids*, direct from the container under pressure, without any dilution. These are known

---

* *A wettable powder (WP) is one in which the active ingredient is carried on small, solid particles which can be suspended in a liquid carrier.*

as flowable liquid formulations. In the waterbody under treatment, these form either emulsions, solutions, or both (triple phase system), as the case may be.

10.8.3 Granular Herbicides

The granular formulations of herbicides have sprung into limelight during the last over two decades. These are made by loading the toxicant on some dry, inert material, usually attaclay. The herbicide granules vary in size from 0.04 mm to 1.0 mm in diameter. Herbicide granules smaller than 0.04 mm are not used because they drift easily with wind. The maximum granule size that may be acceptable from weed control point of view depends upon the extent to which its herbicide can move laterally in soil around each granule. The farther it can move from the parent granule, the bigger can be its granule size. Granular herbicide formulations are usually as effective as the corresponding spray liquids in controlling weeds but, in many situations they have shown some added advantages. Among these *advantages of granular herbicides* are the following:

1. The foremost advantage of granular herbicides is their application convenience. This is particularly true for odd situations, like rice paddies, hilly terrain, and waterbodies. Herbicide granules obviate problems of hauling water, mixing chemicals, and opening clogged nozzles. In fact, in wetland rice fields, herbicide granules are fast replacing the herbicide sprays because of the ease of their application.

2. Most herbicide granules neither irritate skin nor corrode or eat through the containers as do, at least, some liquid herbicides. Also, these are easy to transport and possess good storage properties.

3. Herbicide granules are safe to the non-target plants because of their freedom from drift hazards. Also, the granular herbicides provide better selectivity to the standing crop plants than sprays since the granules bounce-off the crop foliage.

4. Granular forms of volatile herbicide molecules like EPTC and trifluralin are saved much longer in soil.

5. Herbicide granules are easy to mix with fertilizers, when required.

Despite many advantages, the granular herbicides have not been able to fully replace the herbicide spray systems because of their certain inherent *weaknesses,* as follows:-

1. Granular herbicides are low analysis compounds; usually they contain 2 to 10% active ingredient as against 20 to 90% in the sprayable herbicide concentrates.

2. Combinations of two or more herbicides are difficult to make with granular formulations.

3. Granular herbicides require more soil moisture to activate them than the spray liquids.

4. Calibration of mechanical granule distributors is much more difficult than the sprayers. The distributors must be recalibrated each time the granules of a different grain size and analysis are used.

5. Only soil active herbicides can be used at the present in the granular forms.
6. Certain herbicides, such as triazines, persist in soils in granular form much longer than their spray liquids. This increases chances of causing serious injury to the susceptible, rotation crops.

10.8.4 Slow Release Formulations

Of recent, herbicides have been formulated so as to regulate their release into the target environment at slow rates. This enables extended period of weed control and reduction of volatile and leaching losses of certain herbicides. Some herbicides have been even encapsulated for this purpose with prescribed diffusion patterns.

10.8.5 Choosing a Herbicide Formulation

Different commercial formulations of the same herbicide structure can vary in their performance because of variations in *adjuvants* and *solvents* used in the product (Chapter-18). Also, they may differ in their toxicant content. Some important points that must be born in mind while making a choice from the available herbicide formulations in the market are:-

(i) Cost per unit weight of the active ingredient, (ii) differential crop and weed tolerances, (iii) volatility and leaching behaviour, (iv) resistance to washing down from foliage by rain, (v) shelf life, and (vi) safety to man and the non-target organisms.

Active ingredient (A.I.): *A chemical in commercial product that is directly responsible for its herbicidal effect is called active ingredient.* Active ingredient of each herbicide concentrate or formulation is displayed by the manufacturer on the container. The container labels also read the quantity of active ingredients present per unit weight of the product. The active ingredient may also be given as per cent by weight or volume. A herbicide concentrate marked 40% W/V contains 400 g of active ingredient per litre of the liquid product. In other words, to apply 1 kg *a.i*/ha of the herbicide through this product, one must use 2.5 1 of the commercial formulation.

Acid equivalent (A.E.): Some herbicide structures are active organic acids, for example, phenoxyalkanoic acids, picloram, chloramben, cacodylic acid, and MAA. But often many of these are employed in the form of their salts and esters for the ease of their field application or for obtaining better selectivity to crops. For instance, instead of 2,4-D in its acid form, which is water insoluble, we use its sodium and amine salts and esters. *The theoretical yield of parent acid from such a herbicide formulation is called its acid equivalent.* Thus the acid equivalents (*a.e.*) of sodium salt and BEE of 2,4-D are 92.5% and 68.5%, respectively. However, it has become customary with the herbicide manufacturers to display acid equivalents of the acid type herbicides in relation to their final product in the container *ie.* the herbicide concentrate. Thus, a herbicide concentrate like 'Weeder 96', constituting dimethylamine 2,4-D and labelled as 72% W/V *a.e.*, means that each litre of 'Weedar 96' contains 720 g 2,4-D in the form of its specific amine salt.

10.9 RATE OF APPLICATION

Rate is the amount of active ingredient (or acid equivalent) of a herbicide applied to a unit area of land or waterbody. It is usually given in terms of Kg *a.i.* or *a.e.*/ha, since for most herbicides, particularly on crop lands, it is the total quantity of chemical reaching the target area that is important and not its spray concentration. However, on non-crop lands where the weed growth is scattered, it is convenient to state the herbicide rates in terms of their spray concentrations. The margin of selectivity of herbicides to crops is usually within a very narrow range of rate. Over-rates of herbicides may be undesirable not only for the crops sprayed, but it may also leave dangerous amounts of residues in the soil for the rotation crops. Sometimes, the adverse effects of over-rates of herbicides are seen several weeks after the treatment, such as of 2,4-D in wheat. Therefore, it is important to stick to the locally recommended rates of herbicides in question.

Over-rates of herbicides may further prove undesirable on perennial weeds where these may injure their leaf vascular tissues so severely as to reduce the translocation of the applied herbicide to the weed roots. Under-rates of herbicides, on the contrary, will reduce control of all types of weeds, though these may improve crop selectivity. The over-and under-rates of herbicides result primarily from inattention to details, faulty calibration of the equipment, and carelessness on the part of the spray men. Uneven application of a herbicide, even at correct rates, will result in '*hot spots*' of localized over-rates causing injury to the crop plants, and '*cold spots*' of localized under-rates where poor or no weed control is obtained (see also Chapter 18).

The herbicides developed and used by us initially, about five decades back, were effective at about 1-2 kg/ha rates. But the modern herbicides developed are so potent that their effective rates of application are only a few gram per ha. Sometimes, such herbicides are termed as *micro-herbicides*. In any case, both the conventional and modern herbicides are used today in agriculture equally well, depending uon the situation. The micro-herbicides have the advantage of being of very low environment pollution possibilities, although their field measurements and application require very sensitive judgements.

10.10 CARRIER (=DILUENT)

Carrier is the liquid (or solid) material used to increase the volume of a chemical compound so that it can be applied uniformly over the target area. The universal carrier of herbicides is water, although in special cases certain petroleum oils may fully or partially replace it. Water is universally popular as a herbicide carrier because of its negligible cost and freedom from undue interactions with the toxicant. Carrier oils are used in herbicide work only for specific purposes, such as for a quick knock-down of weeds in non-crop situations. The carrier oils, because of their low surface tensions (40), creep on the sprayed vegetation and easily enter the crowns and rosettes of the grasses and sedges growing in open stands. The carrier water with its high surface tension (75.6) and consequent, strong driving action, proves superior on the dense growth of weeds.

Hard water should not be used for spraying herbicides since it may precepitate the herbicide.

In recent years, air has been used as carrier for herbicide concentrates. Motorized ground sprayers and aerial sprayers equipped with specially designed exhaust nozzles (Chapter-11) are used for this purpose. The air atomizes the liquid concentrate into 30-150 micron diameter droplets and ejects them out of the nozzle. The air-carried droplets, unlike the water and oil carried droplets, do not have sufficient momentum to immediately hit the target; they settle by gravity and are prone to drift. The chief advantage of employing air as carrier of herbicides is low spray costs on account of saving of time and labour otherwise spent in handling of large amounts of water.

10.11 SPRAY VOLUME

Spray volume refers to total quantity of liquid applied per unit area. Generally speaking, it is the total quantity of the toxicant reaching the target weed or soil that is more important than the spray volume, inasmuch as the toxicant is uniformly distributed over the target area. A large choice of sprayers is available to achieve even spread of a herbicide with spray volume deliveries varying from less than 5 l/ha to over 1000 l/ha. The spray volumes for herbicides have been classified into five classes from high volume to ultra low volume sprays (Table 10.2). The high volume sprays provide thorough coverage of the target plants to the point of runoff or drip. This is essential when weeds are treated with a contact type of herbicide. The translocated herbicides, however, should be applied in low or medium volume sprays, because with such herbicides it is not necessary to wet complete foliage of the weed. Spray volumes in excess of the spray retention capacity of a weed canopy usually amount to herbicide wastage and, sometimes, to injury to the treated crops. But it may be useful while treating some undesirable brush species. Also, in dry weather, high spray volumes may prove superior to the low volumes for preemergence treatments. High volume sprays are also sometimes necessary to improve solubility or suspendibility of a herbicide.

The operational cost of applying herbicides is less for the low volume sprays. This has given impetus to directing research efforts towards developing the low volume and ULV spray. The LV and ULV sprays use air as carrier which turns them into extremely fine droplets. This may be good for uniform distribution of the toxicant on the weed foliage but at the same time, very fine droplets of herbicide sprays entail serious drift hazards (Chapter-11).

Lately, a controlled droplet application system (C.D.A.) has been developed to apply herbicides in as low as 10 l/ha volumes, but with droplets of 250 microns mean diameter. This droplet size is not so susceptible to drift hazards.

Table 10.2: Classification of Spray Volume As Per Indian Standard Institute Norms

Class	Volume
High-Volume (HV) or full coverage spray	560 l/ha and above
Medium Volume (MV) or semi-low volume, or semi-concentrated spray	56 to under 560 l/ha
Low Volume (LV) or concentrated spray	5.6 to under 56 l/ha
Ultra Low Volume (ULV) spray	Over 0.56 and under 5.6 l/ha
Ultra-Ultra Low Volume (U-ULV) spray	Under 0.56 l/ha

10.12 HERBICIDE ROTATIONS AND COMBINATIONS

In Chapter-3 it was revealed that weed flora at any place was never static. It changes with a change in the ecosystem around it. One important factor pointed out in this respect was the repeated use of a specific herbicide for weed control in a particular crop. Several examples of ecoshifts, in fact chemoshifts, were cited in the country. To obviate such possible **chemoshifts** in weed flora from bad to worse, *herbicide rotations* and *herbicide combinations* are recommended (Maurice and Billett, 1991). Sometimes, the fields may carry mixed categories of weeds (grasses, broadleafs, sedges) even before introducing the herbicide use when herbicide combinations (also called mixtures or associations) involving two or more molecules may have to be deployed.

10.12.1 Herbicide Rotations

Herbicide rotation is the practice of following a systematic, rotational sequence of herbicides in the same field (Hauser, 1974). It may involve either- (i) change of a herbicide in the same crop, or (ii) change of the crop in the same field so that a different herbicide could be used. The chief objective of herbicide rotation is to curb a wide spectrum of weeds. With repeated use of one or two kinds of herbicides in the same field, often, some tolerant weed species that were insignificant earlier, become prominent. Weed species shifts are also caused by no-tillage planting systems, as well as by periodic changes in rainfall and temperature. Herbicide rotations put a break to undesirable ecological shifts in weed flora in an area. Sometimes, even within a weed species there are ecotypes that respond differently to a commonly used herbicide. They are called **chemotypes**. Herbicide rotation is essential to control chemotypes too. To make herbicide rotations really effective, it is necessary to prepare a farm map showing both, major and minor weeds. Herbicide rotations should then be put in black and white for each field based on the crops involved, weeds likely to be present in each season, alternative economic herbicides, cultivation programme for each crop, and possible residual phytotoxicity of each herbicide. Of these, a few profitable schemes may be finally selected.

10.12.2 Herbicide Combinations

Often two or more herbicides are applied mixed for agronomical, environmental, and financial reasons with the following possible objectives:

1. To broaden the spectrum of weed control. *Examples:* atrazine and alachlor for preemergence weed control in maize; clodinafop with metsulfuron in wheat; butachor with bensulfuron in transplanted rice, and glyphosate with carfentrazone on non-crop lands.

2. To get synergistic action. *Examples:* amitrole with ammonium thiocyanate (=amitrole-T); CDAA with TCBC (=randox-T); atrazine with paraquat; fortified oil emulsions; and 2,4-D with 2,4,5-T.

3. To prevent rapid detoxification of active herbicide component. *Examples:* Boron to reduce rapid microbial detoxification of 2,4-D in soils; and amitrole to retard metabolism of dalapon in plants.

4. To improve herbicide safety. *Examples:* Arsenic trioxide in acid arsenical reduces corrosive action of sulphuric acid; and AMS reduces fire hazards of sodium chlorate.
5. To economise on spray costs of individual pesticide.

10.13 HERBICIDE COMPATIBILITY

When tank mix of two or more herbicides widens their weed control spectrum involving larger number of weed species, without affecting adversely the crop selectivity, the component herbicides are considered compatible. On the contrary, when such a combination lowers or narrows down the crop selectivity, the herbicide components are considered incompatible. Some prominent examples of compatible and incompatible herbicide mixtures as well as herbicide and other pesticide associations, are cited in Table 10.3.

Table 10.3: Some examples of Compatible and Incompatible Herbicides

	Kind	Herbicide components		Kind	Herbicide components
A.	Compatible	1. Clodinafop - propargyl with metsulfuron - methyl, carfentrazone - ethyl, Sulfosulfuron.	B.	Incompatible	1. Fenoxaprop-p-ethyl with metsulfuron methyl
		2. Fenoxaprop-p-ethyl with carfentrazone – ethyl, sulfosulfuron.			2. Clodinafop with 2,4-D, metribuzin.
		3. Trifluralin with dithiopyr isoproturon, chlorsulfuron.			3. Fenoxaprop with 2,4-D, metribuzin
		4. Pendimethalin with chlorsulfuron			4. Propanil with many insecticides
		5. Glyphosate with carfentrazone			5. Diuron with phorate (insecticide)
		6. Bensulfuron-methyl, with butachlor, almix.			6. Nicosulfuron with terbufos (insecticide)
		7. Clomazone with 2,4-DEE			7. Chlorsufluron with malathion (insecticide)
		8. Bentazon with Blazer			

10.14 AN IDEAL HERBICIDE

Herbicides differ widely in their phytotoxicities. The foremost criterion of a *good herbicide* is its capability to kill the target plants for a desired period with acceptable selectivity to the non-target plants (and other organisms.). Some other important criteria of a good herbicide are: It should be (1) economical to use and adequately cheap to be within the purchasing power of the farmer, (2) safe to man and his animals, (3) safe to rotation crops, (4) free of any interaction with herbicides applied to soil the previous season, and (5) resistant to changes in weather conditions. It is almost impossible to pack all these good features of a herbicide in one container. Therefore, one must assess a herbicide according to one's needs, keeping the above points in view.

10.15 HERBICIDE HAZARDS

In a way every chemical, including table salt, is toxic to human beings when ingested in improper quantities. Weight for weight, aspirine is more toxic to man than most herbicides. The LD_{50} values (for rats) of majority of herbicides have been found to vary from 200 to 75,000 mg/kg body weight (Table 10.3). This means that a man weighing about 80 kg will have to ingest about 53 g of 2,4-D or 6 kg of simazine to reduce his body weight by 50%. Some of the more toxic herbicides with low LD_{50} values are: piperphos, diquat, paraquat, 2,4,5-T, PMA, allyl alcohol, DNBP, DNOC, MB, and acrylaldehyde. These herbicide molecules possess high potential toxicity for the users in terms of poisoning. LD_{50} should be considered only indicative of toxicity potential of any chemical. A high LD_{50} value only shows comparatively less toxicity since it *still* is capable of killing or stunting the growth of 50% of the test animals. Also, when wrongly handled, even a high LD_{50} value herbicide can prove heavily hazardous. Besides, the conventional LD_{50} values relate to only oral intake hazards. A herbicide may also be hazardous on skin and respiratory system of human beings and animals. For this reason now dermal LD_{50} values are also determined and quoted, along with the oral LD_{50} values.

Table 10.4: The Oral LD_{50} values of Some Common Herbicides (compiled from literature of herbicide manufacturers)

Herbicide	LD_{50} (mg herbicide per kg body weight of test animal)	Toxicity class
Alachlor	1200	M
Atrazine	3080	M
2,4-D	666	M
Dalapon	8450	S
Diquat	420	H
Diuron	3400	M
Fluchloralin	6400	M
Fomesafen	7000	S
Glyphosate	4320	M
Isoproturon	4640	M
Oxadiazon	8000	S
Oxyfluorfen	5000	S
Pendimethalin	1250	M
Piperphos	240	H
Simazine	7500	S
Sulfonyl	5000	S
2,4,5-T	300	H
Trifluralin	10000	S

Comment: *Pesticides have been classified on the basis of their oral LD_{50} values as: (a) 1 to 50 = extremely toxic (E); (b) 51 to 500 = highy toxic (H); (c) 501 to 5000 = moderately toxic (M); (d) Over 5000 = slightly toxic to non-toxic (S).*

*Lastly, it may be noted that all LD_{50} values of herbicides are based on rats and rabbits as the test animals, considering that man and his domestic animals will react likewise.

Some herbicides, chiefly 2,4-D and 2,4,5-T, are reported hazardous to grazing animals, indirectly. These herbicides may make the otherwise discarded, poisonous weeds more palatable; for instance, *Senecio* sp. 'ragwort' is known to become sweeter upon treatment with 2,4-D. In sorghum 2,4-D may increase its dhurrin glucoside content to fatal levels. In *Eupatorium maculatum*, its nitrite content may increase to toxic levels by 2,4-D. Application of sodium arsenite as a herbicide to grasslands is beset with its obvious, direct hazards.

10.16 PRECAUTIONS IN STORAGE AND HANDLING OF HERBICIDES

1. Store herbicides away from fertilizers, seeds, food, feed, and children, in cool and well ventilated places. The left-over herbicides must be retained in original, well labelled containers. The container must be closed airtight to avoid herbicide caking, oxidation, and fuming. The herbicide stores must be checked periodically for possible leaks.
2. While preparing to use a herbicide, read the label carefully. Do not transport herbicides from store to the field on body; better use a hand trolley.
3. Prepare herbicide dilutions in open spaces, away from source of irrigation water. Wear rubber gloves, a pair of eye glasses, and cover your nose with a cloth. Always use a stick to stir herbicide solutions, and never your hand. Bury the empty containers deep in any wasteland (Appendices 12 & 14).
4. Keep lots of fresh water and soap handy to meet any emergency.
5. In the western world wearing of full protective clothing is a must for every man applying herbicide. Such a heavy protection, however, is infeasible in the hot and humid areas. In the tropics, a pair of shoes, gloves, sunglasses, a light head dress, and a cloth put around the mouth and nose, can be considered adequate precautions, besides of course, each worker must wear a long sleeve shirt and full trousers.
6. Do not smoke or eat during and in-between the spray intervals. Also, never use mouth to blow the clogged nozzles. Bathe and wash the clothes thoroughly as soon the spray work is over for the day.
7. If there is an accident, provide first-aid to the patient and contact the nearest doctor at the same time. Lie down the patient in shade and remove his all tight clothings and masks. Wash the affected body parts immediately with plenty of fresh water and soap (do not use soap in the affected eyes). In the case of oral intake of a herbicide, induce quick vomiting by any locally available method. When a toxic herbicide has been inhaled, wash the nose and ask the patient to gargle with fresh water. Do not surround the patient; give him artificial breathing, if needed. When the doctor

---

Footnote: * While *toxicity of a herbicide is its inherent potential, the hazard is the effect of that potential. The latter can be manipulated to a zero level by practising their recommended precautions.*

arrives, he must be shown all available literature of the herbicide in question to enable him to choose a proper antidote. Usually antidotes are available for most herbicides.

8. Avoid herbicide drifts from reaching the non-target crops, wild life, and man.

Fig. 10.4: Some minimum safety measures are essential to protect the herbicide spray-men from possible drift hazards. In tropical and subtropical areas, a simple dress like the one shown here will cover the body adequately, without causing any discomfort to the worker during the operation.

SUMMARY

Farmers in many countries have been thinking of getting rid of the tiring operation of uprooting weeds from their fields, for decades. During all this period they intended, and wished, to come across some chemical to help them out of this situation. Starting with their attempts with ash and common salt, they struck at copper sulphate and sulphuric acid about 100 years ago, for selective control of some herbaceous weeds in small grains. Not sufficiently satisfied with such inorganics, some scientists in the U.S.A and England made the first, major dent in the form of two evergreen organic compounds 2,4-D and MCPA in 1945 or so, as highly effective and selective herbicides for broadleaf weed control in cereals. Since then over 300 herbicide molecules have been developed and registered, the world-over, for weed management in different situations, including for the control of weeds belonging to the same family as the crop. The search for even better herbicides is continuing at the global level with about 100 private companies, despite heavy expenditure of a few million dollars involved in developing each, new compound.

The herbicidal control of weeds in agricultural fields has been found highly remunerative, with B:C ratios of 9 to 88 in different field crops and vegetables.

Herbicides have been classified, depending upon their properties, as (i) narrow-spectrum and broad-spectrum herbicides; (ii) soil-active and foliage-active herbicides; (iii) contact and translocated herbicides; (iv) residual and non-residual herbicides; and (v) soil sterilants and fumigants.

Herbicides can be applied either to the soil or to the weed foliage, depending upon their modes of action. The soil active herbicides are applied as (i) surface treatment; (ii) sub-surface layering treatment; and (iii) soil injection and fumigation treatment. The surface treatment can further be either (a) broadcast (=overall) treatment or (b) band treatment, depending upon the need. The foliage active herbicides are applied as (i) blanket (=overall) treatment; (ii) directed spray treatment; (iii) protected spray treatment; and (iv) spot treatment. The brush or woody weeds are treated with herbicides by special methods like, (i) the cut-stump treatment; and (ii) the basal-bark treatment. Besides these regular methods of application of herbicides, sometimes these are applied also by wiping, smearing, or rubbing these directly on to the target weeds.

The time of application of a herbicide in relation to the weed and crop stages is termed its mode of application. This could be a (i) preplant treatment (to soil), with or without its incorporation; (ii) preemergence treatment; (iii) early postemergence treatment; and (iv) lay-by treatment. All these modes of application have been described, with appropriate examples.

Herbicides are formulated for easing their application and providing safety to the user. The common formulations include: (i) sprayable liquid concentrates; (ii) wettable powders; and (iii) dry flowables, Water is the most common carrier used for applying these formulations. Limited herbicides are also formulated as flowable liquids, dry granules, capsules, waxbars, soluble mulches, aerosols, etc.

Repeated use of a herbicide in the same field is beset with the problem of development of resistant weed species and races. The use of two or more herbicides in the form of either a rotation or a combination, can obviate such chemoshifts in weed flora to a great extent.

Herbicides, like any other pesticide, when handled carelessly, can be hazardous, even though there are very few herbicides with potential toxicity. Several necessary precautions in handling and storage of herbicides have been enumerated to completely avoid their possible hazards.

Communicating weed science takes into account at least six major aspects. These are: (i) relative advantages of the technology over the existing one; (ii) its reproductibility; (iii) its observability; (iv) its feasibility and compatibility with the existing farming situations (*eg* farm size, farm income, and its tenurial status), (v) easy availability of technology inputs, and (vi) communication sources within the reach of the farmer.

The success of technology communication is measured in terms of extent of adoption by the farmers who are a mixed lot of: innovators, early and late adopters, and laggards. All these categories of adopters demand tailor-made communication strategies to commensurate with their socio-economic and psychological profiles, besides their access to different communication channels.

UNSOLVED EXERCISES

Ex. 1. A herbicide formulation contains active ingredient of 0.4 kg/l and the desired rate of application is 1.5 kg/ha. Calculate the volume of herbicide formulation required for l ha area.

Ex. 2. You want to apply a herbicide in a 30 cm band with 90 cm crop rows. The recommended application rate is 1.0 kg/ha. How much material would you need to cover a hectare area at this rate?

Ex. 3. You are applying a preemergence herbicide and find that 4 l have been applied on sixteen, 100 cm rows, each 440 m long. What is the application rate?

Ex. 4. You have to conduct one experiment for weed control with nitrofen at rates of 1,2, and 3 kg *a. i.*/ha. You have with you liquid Tok-E 25 that contains 250 g/l nitrofen in it. If the plot size in the experiment is 1/250 ha, calculate the total quantity of Tok E-25 you need for four replications. Also, indicate the manner in which you will distribute this quantity in each plot.

Ex. 5. Calculate the amount of Eptam-6EC containing 0.6 kg of active ingredient (S-ethyl dipropylthiocarbamate) per l, for an area of 5 ha. The application rate is 1.5 kg *a.i.*/ha.

Ex. 6. Calculate the amount of lorax—a wettable powder of linuron containing 50% *a i.*– required for 30 plots, each 20 sq m in size. The desired rate in the experiment is 2 kg *a.i.* per ha.

Ex. 7. Calculate the amount of Weedone Concentrate-48 containing 34.2% 2,4-Dichlorophenoxyacetic acid by weight, or 0.3 kg of the acid per l required for 6 plots of maize, 30 sq m each. The desired rate of 2,4-D is 2.0 kg/ha.

Ex. 8. How much area can be covered with 3 kg of amiben granules containing 21.6% 3-amino-2,5 dichiorobenzoic acid equivalent by weight applied at 2 kg *a.e.*/ha? The treatment is to be made on 15 cm wide band in crop rows spaced 30 cm apart.

Ex. 9. Arrange the following herbicide formulations in decreasing order of preference, from their cost point of view:

Formulation	Price per kg (Rs.)	*a.i.*
A	50	60%
B	70	90%
C	40	50%
D	75	80%

Ex. 10. You want to apply a 2 per cent solution of 2,4-D to ditch-bank weeds. It is estimated that 1000 l per ha of the spray volume will be needed to wet the weeds completely. Calculate the active herbicide needed to treat a 4 m wide and 2.5 km long ditch-bank.

Note: To talley your answers see Appendix-3.

SELECTED BIBLIOGRAPHY

1. Ahrens, J. F. 1972. Granular herbicides. Weeds Today 3(2): 12-13.
2. Anon, 1985. The Pesticide Chemical News Guide. Food Chemical News, INC-1982 (202) 554-1980
3. Anon, 1987. Safe Use of Pesticides. Publishers ICAR, New Delhi (India), 29 pp.
4. Bennemann, N. B. 1992. Controlling residues: Communicating the importance to farmers. Tobacco Int. 194(17) 32-38.
5. Cessna, A. J. 1991. Residues of triallate in garlic cloves following preplant incorporation. Cand. J. Pl. Sci. 71 (4) 1257-1261.
6. Cessna, A. J. 1992. Residues of mecoprop in postemergence treated wheat and oat. Pesticide Science 36 (1) 31-33.
7. Chandrakar, B. L. and J. S. Urkurkar. 1993. Efficacy and economics of weed control in soybean (*Glycine max* L.) under vertisols of Chhatisgarh region. Indian J. Weed Sci. 25 (3 & 4) 32-35.
8. Clipsham, I. E. 1985. Effects of surfactants on uptake and movement of 14_c difenzoquat in *Avena fatua*, wheat, and barley. Aspects of Applied Biol. 9:141-148.
9. Cofman, C. B. and Genter, W. A. 1980. Persistence of several controlled release formulations of trifluralin in greenhouse and field. Weed Sci. 28(1) 21-23.
10. Devine, M. D. and Rashid, A. 1993. Antagonism of tralkoxydim activity in *Avena fatua* by metsulfuron methyl. Weed Res. (Oxford) 33(2) 97-104.
11. Dhaliwal, G. S. and Balwinder, S. 1993. Pesticides: Their Ecological Impact in Developing Countries. Commonwealth Pub., N. Delhi (India).
12. Doane, W. M. 1992. Encapsulation of pesticides in starch by extrustion. Industrial Crops and Products 1(2-4) 83-87.
13. Duke, S.O. and Lydon, J. 1987. Herbicides from natural compounds. Weed Technol 1(2) 112-128.
14. Fernandez, P. and F. Walker. 2004. Mixing and associating plant protection products. Phytoma No. 574: 41-45 (France). (W. A. 54(2), 634).
15. Green, M. B. 1973. Are herbicides too expensive? Weeds Today 4(3) 14-16.
16. Grosswann, K. 2005. What it takes to get a herbicide's mode of action. Physionomics, a classical approach in a new complexion. Pest Mgmt. Sci. 61(5): 423-431.
17. Grover, R. and Cessna, A. J. (Eds). 1991. Environmental Chemistry of Herbicides Vol. II, CRC Press, Boca Raton, 302 pp.
18. Gupta, O.P. *et al.* 1969. Evaluation of herbicide efficiency of a new preemergence compound BV-201 in comparison to 2, 4-D in wheat. Ind. J. Agro. 14(2) 193-195.
19. Hauser, E. W. 1974. Crop-herbicide rotations curb weeds. Weeds Today 5(1) 14-15.
20. Jordan, *et al.* 1978. Factors affecting performance of preemergence herbicides. Weed Sci. 16(4) 457-462.
21. Kennedy, M. V. 1978. Disposal and Decontamination of pesticides. ACS Symposium Series No. 73, Washington DC, USA, 158 pp.

22. Kuldeep, S. and Khosla, S. N. 1987. Comparative evaluation of 2,4-D slow release herbicide. Ind. J. Forestry 10(4) 256-261.
23. Kundra, H. C. *et al.* 1993. Efficacy of weed management practices in pea. Ind. J. Weed Sci. 25(1 & 2) 1-6.
24. Kutze, F. W. *et al.* 1992. Selected pesticide residues and metabolites in urine from a survey of the U. S. general population. J. Toxicology and Environmental Health 37(2) 277-291.
25. Lassiter, R. D. and Coble, H. D. 1987. Carrier volume effects on the antagonism of sethoxydim by bentazon. Weed Sci. 35(4) 541-546.
26. Liang, T. and Lou, X. 1990. Studies on the residues and degradation behaviour of the herbicide bentazon in rice. Chinese J. Rice Sci. 4(2) 84-88.
27. Maurice, D. and Billett, D. 1991. Herbicide Resistance. Agri-fax N. 640-7, 4 pp.
28. Mishael, Y. G. *et al.* 2002. Slow-release formulations of sulfometuron incorporated in micelles adsorbed on monmorillonite. J. Agric. & Food Chem. 50(10): 2864-2869.
29. Palmer, M. 1987. Spray overall and save time; band spray and save money. Prt. Sugarbeet Review 55(1) 4-6.
30. Patro, H. and Prustry, J. D. 1994. Integrated weed management in mungbean. Ind. J. Weed Sci. 26(1 & 2) 81-82.
31. Porwal, M. K. and Singh, M. M. 1993. Efficacy of herbicides for weed control in cauliflower (*Brassica oleracea* L.). Indian J. Weed Sci. 25(1 & 2) 55-60.
32. Porwal, M.K. 1995. Cost-effective integrated weed management in garlic (*Allium sativum*) under vertisols of Southern Rajasthan. Proc. in VI Biennial Conference of ISWS 1994, held at Annamalai University, Annamalainagar, (Tamil Nadu) in Feb. 9-10, 1995.
33. Sankaran, S. *et al.* 1993. Herbicide Residues. Gandhi Book House, Coimbatore.
34. Schreiber, M. M. *et al.* 1978. Efficacy and rate of release of EPTC and butylate from starch encapsulated formulations under green house conditions. Weed Sci. 26 (6) 679-686.
35. Schrieber, M. M. *et al.* 1994. Efficacy of starch encapsulated formulations of atrazine containing two or three herbicides in same granule. Weed Technol. 8(1) 105-113.
36. Sharma, U. C. *et al.* 1994. Effect of integrated weed management on yield and nutrient uptake by rainfed rice in acid soil in Nagaland. Ind. J. Agro. 39(4) 553-556.
37. Singh, C. P. *et al.* 1987. Studies on the mode of application of some herbicides on wheat: I-effect on weeds. Ind. J. Agro. 32(1) 71-73.
38. Singh, K. and Lal, S. S. 1994. Herbicidal weed control efficiency and nutrient removal by weeds in potato under N. E. Hills conditions. Ind. J. Agro. 39(2) 336-339.
39. Singh, S. and Lall, A. C. 2001. Studies on technological gaps and constraints in adoption of weed management practices for rice-wheat system. Ind. J. Weed Sci. 33: 116-119.
40. Singh, S. K. 1993. Economics of weed control in transplanted, rainfed, lowland rice in West Bengal, India. Proc. Int. Symp. Integrated weed Management for Sustainable Agriculture, ISWS, held at Hissar (India), Nov. 1993, Vol. III 51-53.

41. Singh. S. J. *et al.* 1992. Studies on weed management in onion. Ind. J. Weed Sci. 24 (1 & 2) 6-10.

42. Valkenburg, W. V. 1973. Pesticide Formulations. Marcel Dekker Inc. N. Y.

43. Wilso, H. P. *et al.* 1988. Efficacy comparisons of alachlor and metachlor formulations in the field. Weed Technol. 2(1) 24-27.

Chapter 11

HERBICIDE APPLICATION EQUIPMENT AND THEIR CALIBRATION

Herbicides are primarily applied as sprays, save some dry granules and herbicide concentrates. Several kinds and makes of sprayers are available from small hand-operated to large, ground and aerial sprayers but only a few of these have come in popular use. Common herbicide sprayers, their components, and calibration form the chief subject of this chapter.

11.1 MAJOR COMPONENTS OF SPRAYERS

The major components of a sprayer are: (i) pump, (ii) power source, (iii) tank, (iv) pressure gauge and (v) pressure regulator.

11.1.1 Pump

Any spray liquid must be atomized before it leaves the spray nozzle. A pump provides the necessary pressure for this purpose. Two kinds of pumps are generally used in herbicide sprayers, as under.

1. *Air Compression or Pneumatic Pumps*: These pumps force air into an airtight tank containing the spray liquid. The air pressure moves the spray liquid into the nozzle where it gets atomized before leaving the sprayers as fine spray.
2. *Hydraulic or Positive Displacement Pumps*: These pumps take in a definite volume of spray liquid and force it through the delivery system under pressure. The pumps differ in the pressure they produce.

11.1.2 Source of Power

A source of power is needed to run the sprayer pumps. This source of power may be either (a) *manual*, (b) *traction*, (c) *motor*, (d) *tractor engine*, or (e) *aircraft engine*.

11.1.3 Spray Tank

A sprayer may have either a built in tank or separate tank to carry the spray liquid. The tank should be large enough to avoid frequent refilling but, at the same time, not unwieldy to carry. Depending upon the kind of sprayer, the tank size varies from 25 to 2250 litres and sometimes even more. A tank is provided with a large opening, fitted with strainer and a cap to fill the spray liquid. Small tank openings can make filling and cleaning of the tank difficult.

11.1.4 Agitator

Most spray tanks carry an agitator. It may be either a mechanical or hydraulic type. The agitator keeps the spray liquid components in homogenous mixture. The mechanical agitators are usually made in the shape of a metal rod with a fan or rings at its distant end. In hydraulic agitation, on the other hand, there is a pipe with several side holes but closed at its free end. It is placed in the spray tank and is fed under pressure with the spray liquid from the pump. The jet of liquid thus formed provides the necessary agitation to the spray material. Hydraulic sprayers are provided only in large, tractor-mounted spray tanks. Agitators are most essential for the application of herbicide emulsions and suspensions.

11.1.5 Distribution System

A distribution system of a sprayer includes nozzles, spray lance (or spray boom), and hose.

(1) Nozzle: The function of spray nozzle is to break the pressurized spray liquid into droplets for application to the target. Nozzles are identified by their (1) droplet size, (2) delivery, and (3) spray pattern that they produce. Of the three characteristics, the spray pattern is fixed for a given nozzle (except in the case of tripple action nozzle). The droplet size and delivery of the nozzle will vary with the pump pressure. Usually, data for delivery and droplet size of nozzles at variable pressures are provided by the manufacturer. These droplets are classified according to their Volume Mean Diameter (VMD)* as follows:

Aerosol	=	below 50 micron
Mist	=	below 100 micron
Fine spray	=	101-200 micron
Medium spray	=	201-400 micron
Coarse spray	=	Over 400 micron

In general, smaller the spray droplet size, more the herbicidal phytotoxicity. Konche (1994) found this to be particularly true for the translocated type of herbicides, monocot weeds, and waxy foliage weeds in comparison to the otherwise ones, *ie* contact herbicides, dicot weeds, and non-waxy foliage weeds, respectively. While in this respect the finer sprays may be desirable, these have the drawback of being prone to spray drift

---

* *VMD is that droplet size that divides the spray volume into two equal parts; one half containing droplets smaller than this diameter, and the other half containing larger droplets.*

hazards. Besides, if the herbicide under spray is an ester formulation, there shall be added risk of volatile drift (see Chapter 19).

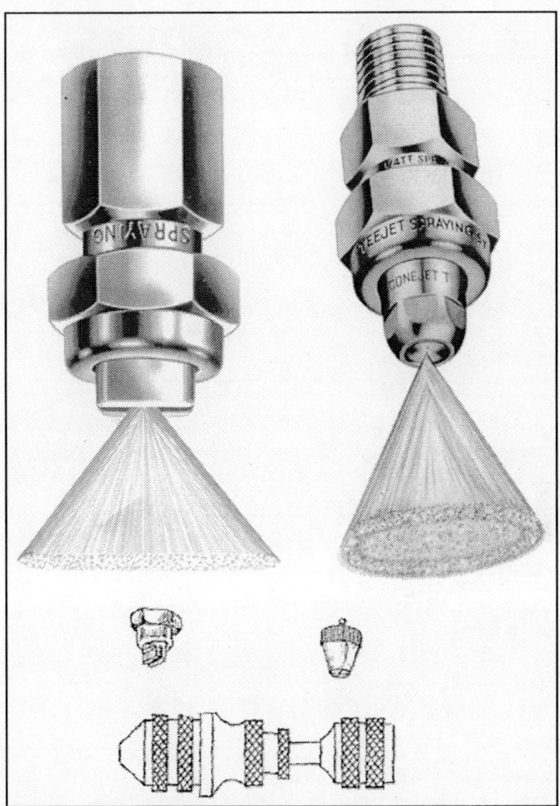

Fig. 11.1: There are several kinds of spray nozzles available in the market for specific herbicide spray application. Of these, the two most commonly used are: *Top left* = the solid cone spray nozzle and *Top right* = the flat fan, tapered edge spray nozzle. *Bottom* = A tripple action spray nozzle, used commonly with the pedal sprayers (see Fig. 11.6).

There are at least six major types of nozzles in use for the application of herbicides. These are (a) flat-fan nozzles, (b) solid cone nozzles, (c) flood-jet nozzles, (d) low volume nozzles, (e) centrifugal nozzles, and (f) blast nozzles.

The *flat-fan nozzles* are again of two types, namely, the '*tapered edge*' and the '*rectangular pattern*' nozzles. While the tapered edge ones provide an even application of herbicides on the soil surface, the rectangular pattern nozzles are good for their band applications (Chapter-10). The flat-fan nozzles of both kinds lack the vegetation penetrating capacity. These are, therefore, preferred for the preemergence application of herbicides. However, these can also be used for postemergence application of the translocated type of herbicides which do not require penetration of the weedy vegetation.

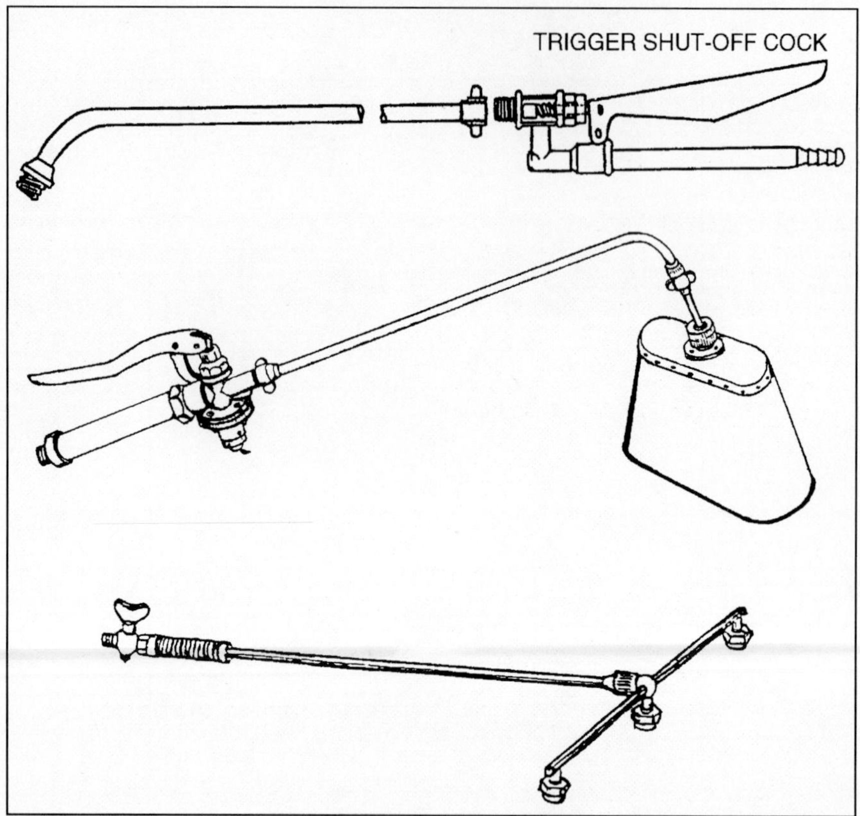

Fig. 11.2: *Top* = A spray lance with trigger cut off device. *Middle* = A lance fitted with plastic spray shield. *Bottom* = A hand-carried spray boom with three nozzles.

In variance with the flat-fan nozzles, the *solid cone nozzles* provide good vegetation penetrating ability to the sprays, thereby, making these useful for application of the contact type of herbicides on dense, weedy patches.

The *flood-jet nozzles* produce medium droplet sprays, reducing thus, their drift hazard potentials. These nozzles are commonly used for sub-surface application of herbicides.

The *low volume nozzles*, as the name indicates, are designed to apply herbicide concentrates without much dilution. *Centrifugal nozzles* are meant for spraying viscous spray liquids like invert emulsions (see Chapter 17). Motorized mist blowers employ *blast nozzles* which feed the spray liquid into the air stream to split it into droplets and carry them as mist, off the delivery pipe.

(2) Lance: It is a brass rod, about 90 cm long, attached to delivery hose of the sprayer and fitted at its free-end with a replaceable nozzle. In many cases the spray lance is bent at the nozzle-end to form a goose neck. At the hose-end it is provided with various types of trigger mechanisms to shut-off the flow of the liquid. For specific purposes, the spray lance may be fitted with plastic shields at its nozzle end to prevent spray drifts.

(3) Boom (or spray bar): A boom is essentially a horizontal pipe with two to several nozzles on it. Usually, these nozzles are spaced 50 cm apart. The boom length (distance between nozzles at the two ends of the boom) may vary from 1 m to 15 m. Short booms with 2 or 3 nozzles are used with manual sprayers, while the longer ones are attached to the tractor-mounted sprayers. A spray boom obviously covers in each trip a wider spray swath than a lance. (Spray swath is the total width of land wetted by a boom. It is slightly more than the boom length). The vertical height of the boom and nozzle spacings on the boom can be adjusted to obtain either an overall spray, or a directed spray, or a band spray of the herbicide, as per requirement.

(4) Pressure Regulator: Power-driven sprayers are usually fitted with a pressure regulator so as to push the liquid at a constant, desired pressure. Without a pressure regulator, a nozzle will deliver more liquid at one time and less at the other, in the same trip. Moreover, some herbicides are prescribed to be applied at specific pressures to obtain best results.

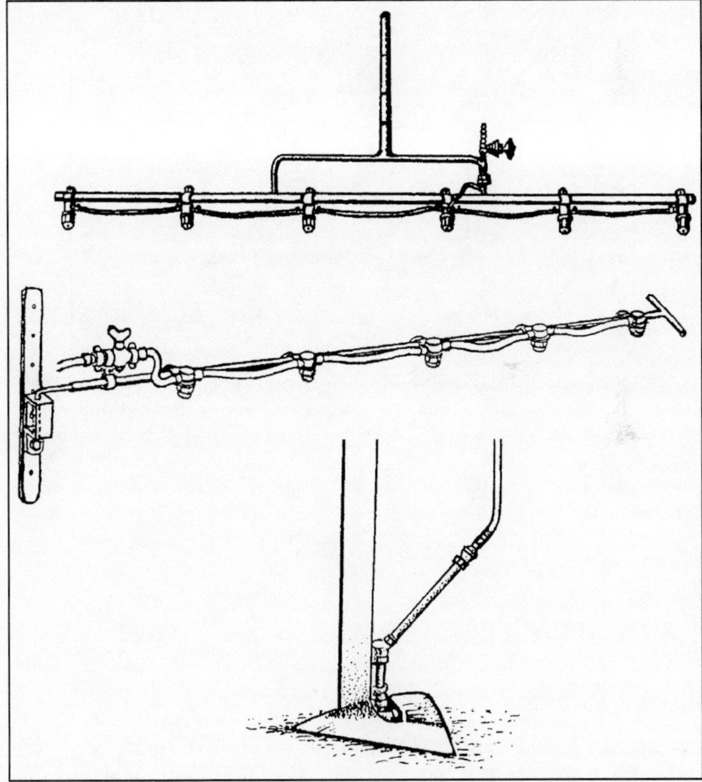

Fig. 11.3: *Top and Middle* = Two kinds of tractor-mounted multi-nozzle spray booms. *Bottom* = A spray nozzle fitted to a sweep for sub-surface application of a herbicide.

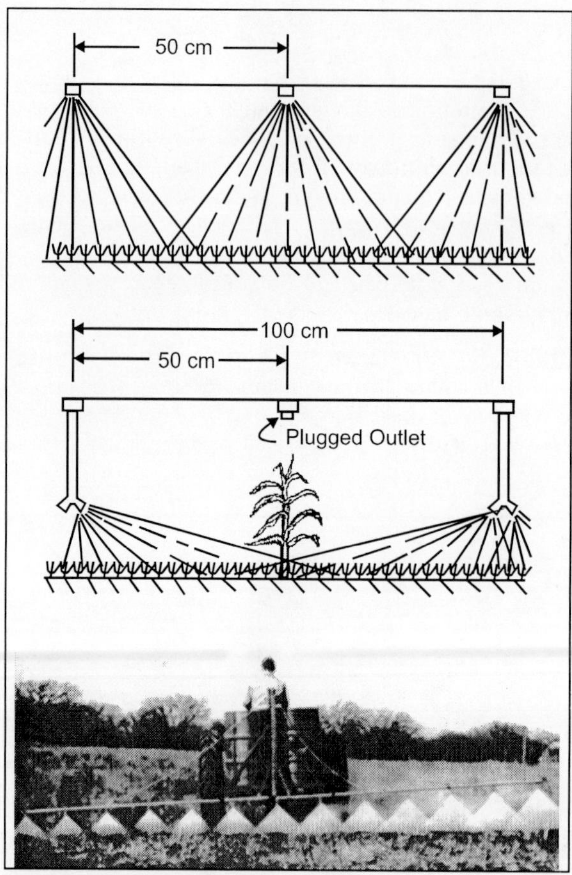

Fig. 11.4: A tractor-mounted spray boom fitted in two fashions. *Top* = Spray boom fitted too low, causing overlap sprays. This should be avoided. *Middle* = Spray boom well adjusted to avoid spray falling on the crop foliage but wet the weeds completely without any gaps or overlaps (diagrammatic). *Bottom* = A tractor-mounted sprayer in action with its boom tilted, by fault. The result is a gappy spray pattern towards the left and undue overlap sprays towards the right. The spray pattern from the middle three nozzles alone is appropriate (Butter and Bowers, 1961).

11.2 KINDS OF SPRAYERS

11.2.1 Knapsack Sprayers

Knapsack sprayers are loaded on the back of the worker during the operation. Usually they carry metallic tanks, but these are also available with plastic tanks to reduce weight. The plastic tanks are prone ot damage by rats though. Three types of knapsack sprayers in vogue today are: (i) hydraulic sprayers, (ii) manual pneumatic sprayers, and (iii) motorized pneumatic sprayers.

1. ***Hydraulic Knapsack Sprayers***: A hydraulic knapsack sprayers is a manually operated sprayer which works under hydraulic pressure. Its tank capacity is up to 122.5 litres, with provision for mechanical agitation of the spray liquid. One tank full of spray liquid can cover an area of about 600 sq m. The worker uses his left hand to operate the lever handle of the sprayer as he walks, while holding the spray lance in his right hand. With practice it is usually possible to deliver the spray at almost constant pressure. The output is usually 0.4 ha per man day. But it is possible to obtain higher output by replacing the lance with a 2-3 nozzle boom. The hydraulic knapsack sprayer is primarily a high volume sprayer, unlesss special low volume nozzles are fitted to it. It can develop a pressure of up to 12 kg cm^{-2}, but with practice one could spray at 3 to 4 kg cm^{-2} pressure to prevent a possible spray drift. Hydraulic knapsack sprayer is a low cost, easy to maintain, and a small holding farmer sprayer. It is particularly satisfactory for spot treatment and band application of herbicides. Its spray volume is about 250 l/ha.

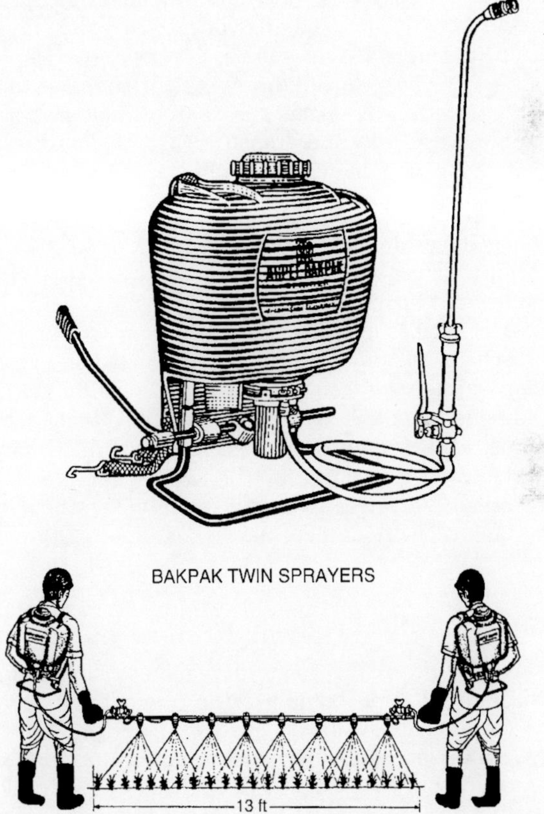

Fig. 11.5: *Top* = A hydraulic, knapsack sprayer with a plastic tank and spray lance. *Bottom* = A manual device of obtaining multi-nozzle, spray boom action (diagrammatic). The arrangement requires harmonious movement of the two workers.

The main drawback of a hydraulic knapsack sprayer is its three way tiring action on man, *viz* a load on the back, one hand engaged in operating the pump, and the other one in directing the lance.

2. ***Pneumatic (or Compressed System) Knapsack Sprayers***: Pneumatic knapsack sprayers are comparatively easy to work with since they are pressurised before loading on the back of the worker. This allows a free hand to the operator. The tank is first filled to about 2/3 capacity with the spray liquid. Then it is pumped with either a built in pump or from an external source like a charge pump or CO_2 cylinders. A big drawback of pneumatic sprayers is the decreasing spray pressure that develops in their spray tanks as the spray work is advanced. This may cause uneven spray. Also, the mouth of these sprayers is small which makes cleaning of the tank cumbersome.

   The pneumatic knapsack sprayers are useful tools to spray herbicides in odd situations like paddy fields, jute fields, hilly terrain, and water banks.

3. ***Motorized Pneumatic Sprayers* (=Blowers)**: A motorized pneumatic sprayer is a low volume sprayer suitable for spraying concentrated spray liquids. The blast of air acts as carrier of the herbicide concentrates in these sprayers, which are, therefore, also called blowers. The air is forced throught the spraying jet of the delivery hose of the blower and a nozzle tube ejects the spray liquid in this blast. The air blast atomizes the spray liquid into fine droplets. Thus, in these sprayers air acts as the carrier. Faster the air is pumped into the spraying jet, more vigorous is the atomization. The equipment is fitted with petrol engine of about 1.2 H.P.

   When a blower produces droplets in the size range of 50-100 microns, it is called a *mist blower*. A mist blower causes considerable loss of the herbicide as spray drift. The main advantages of knapsack blowers are: (i) low volume spray and consequent reduction in loss of time in refilling tanks, (ii) comfortable working, and (iii) fast spraying. The discharge of a blower is about 0.3 to 2.5 liter per minute (lpm), which can be regulated with the dosage sleeve. It has a swath of 7-8 m. One needs hardly 60 1 of spray liquid to cover one hectare of land with a knapsack blower. This means that the user must walk fast enough to keep pace with its discharge. Low volume spraying with blowers is not as uniform as with high volume sprayers. Therefore, knapsack blowers are suited for spraying mainly the shoot translocated type of herbicides. The tank capacity of these blowers is up to 22 l, with a spray volume of 10-150 l/ha.

11.2.2 Foot Sprayers (=Pedal Pump Sprayers)

The foot sprayers are very popular in many developing countries for the application of herbicides on comparatively large holdings. The pump lever of a foot sprayer has a pedal. The lever is conveniently worked with foot. The sprayer has provision for 1-2, long delivery hoses, each fitted with either a lance or a 3-6 nozzles boom. A pedal pump sprayer uses an external spray tank through an intake pipe fitted with a sieve at its sucking end. It develops a spray pressure of 17-21 Kg cm^{-2} and its output with one lance is about l ha per day of 8 hours.

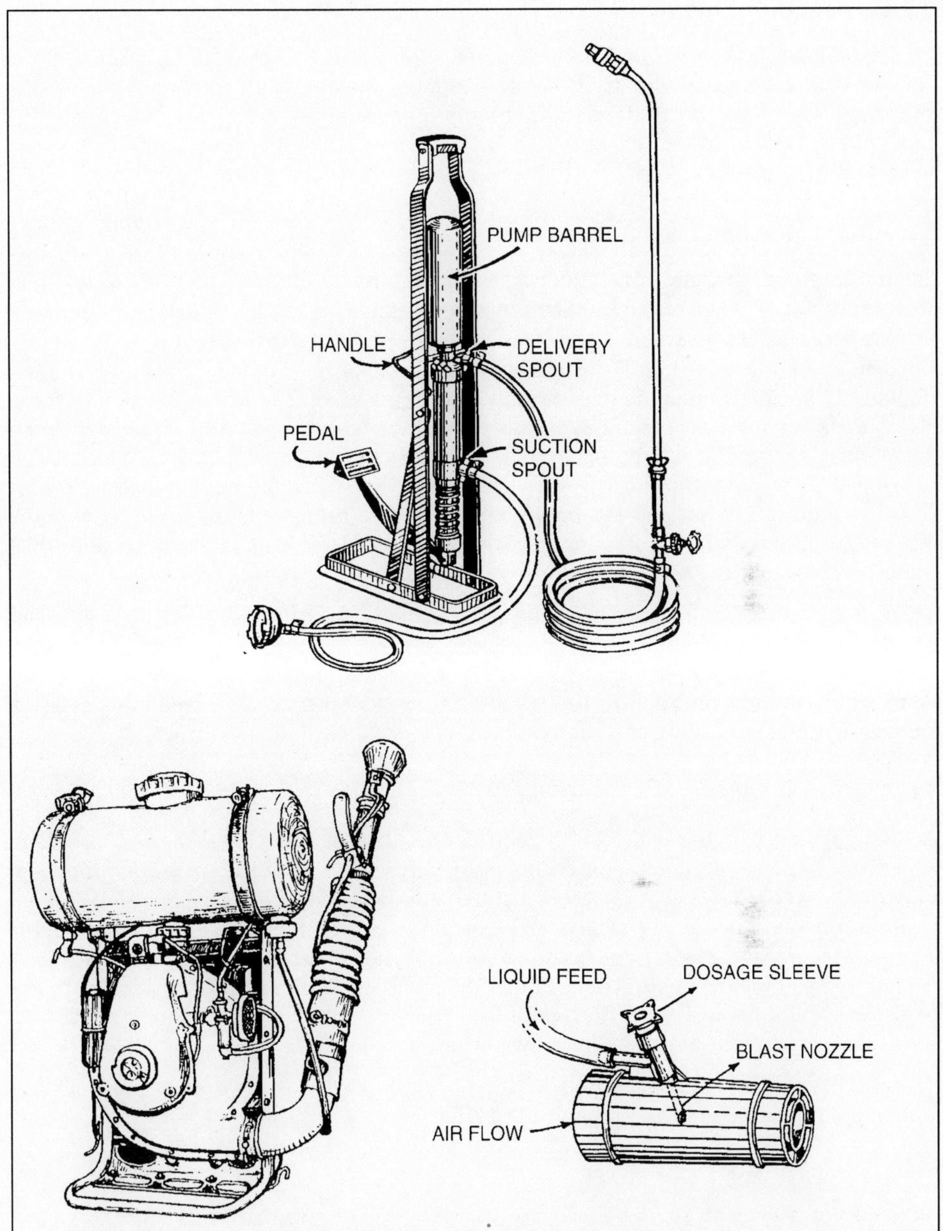

Fig. 11.6: *Top* = A foot sprayer, or pedal pump sprayer, with one delivery hose. When required, it has also provision to use two delivery hoses to hasten the work. Usually, such sprayers employ tripple action nozzles (Fig. 11.1). *Bottom left* = A motorised knapsack sprayer. *Bottom right* = Spraying jet system of a motorised knapsack sprayer.

11.2.3 Traction Pneumatic Sprayer

The Indian Institute of Sugarcane Research, Lucknow developed an animal-drawn sprayer with a six nozzle boom. It has two pumps, operated with the moving wheels as the animals advance. It can develop a maximum pressure of 2.8 Kg cm^{-2}, which is suited to minimise spray drift*. The output of this sprayer is 2-3 ha per day and the spray volume is over 150 l/ha.

11.2.4 Tractor Powered Sprayers

Tractor mounted sprayers work under a spray pressure of 1.4-2.8kg cm^{-2}. These are fitted with multinozzle booms which make them very useful herbicide application equipment for the large holding farmers. Other advantages of tractor-run sprayers include high uniformity of the spray and utilization of the tractor during idle time. Their main drawbacks are high equipment costs and high level of skill required to operate these. The success of the tractor-mounted sprayers lies in their proper calibration and boom adjustment to avoid overlapping and gappy sprays. The spray pattern should be so developed as to obtain uniform spray. For directed spraying the nozzles falling on the crop rows are turned off and the boom height is so adjusted as to avoid the crop plants but spray the weeds to the maximum. These sprayers have tank capacity of 365-400 l. Their pump output is 32 l/min, with a spray volume of over 150 l/ha.

The tractor-mounted sprayers fitted with *tilted booms* are used to spray total weed killers on the roadside vegetation. In recirculating type of sprayers- the excess herbicide delivered form the nozzles during spraying is collected in the recovery boxes. This excess spray liquid is then returned to the spray tank for its reuse. The recirculating types of sprayer is useful in treating specific weeds that grow taller to the crop rows.

11.2.5 Aerial Sprayers

Aerial application of herbicides is limited to either treating stretches of aquatic weeds or some very large, continuous land occupied by single crop variety. Large, non-crop areas under undesirable brushes can also be treated with herbicides this way. Spray drift is the main limitation of aerial application of herbicides. On crop lands it should be limited to extensive sugarcane plantations, paddies, and the like. Special aerial spray discs have been developed for the application of liquid formulation of molinate (a herbicide) in rice fields in standing water, with negligible drift. In this technique the herbicide falls in a *solid stream* and sinks to the sediment-water interface.

The output of aerial sprayers is 300-1200 ha per day. Their spray volume is as low as 1 l/ha although it can be increased up to 150 l/ha.

Footnote: * *With mechanical sprayers it is desirable to maintain a spray pressure of 1.4-2.8 kg cm^{-2}, with an average of 2.1 kg cm^{-2}. Higher than 2.8 kg cm^{-2} will induce spray drift, while very low pressure will create difficully in proper wetting of the target plants.*

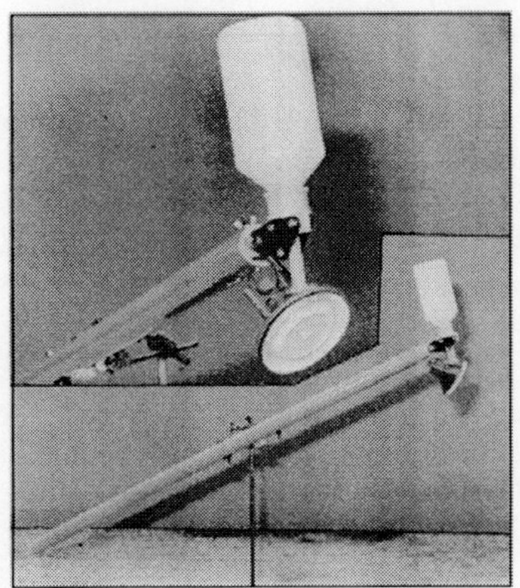

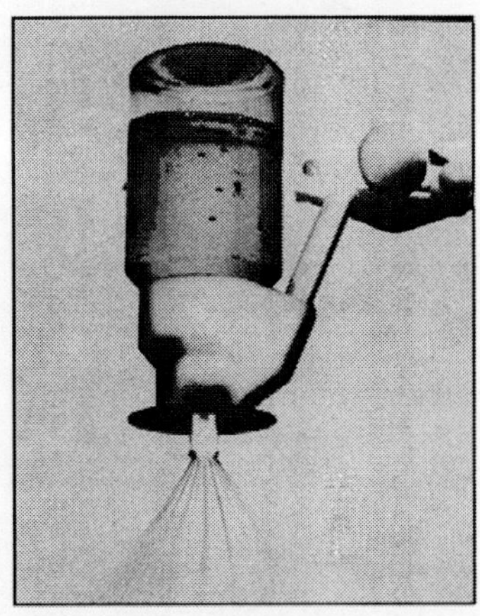

Fig. 11.7: *Top left*: A granule applicator. *Top right* = A spinning disc, hand-held sprayer operated with a battery. *Bottom left*: A manual ethylene injector developed for controlling parasitic striga in Africa. *Bottom right* = An Electrodyn, battery-operated sprayer for treating small plots. The liquid is fed by gravity to a nozzle to which a high positive charge, which is capable of spreading out the herbicide droplets on the target vegetation, is applied.

11.2.6 Hand-Held Sprayers

Most of the tropical and subtropical countries are characterised by small farm holdings and low manual output. In such areas a large number of farmers may prefer low volume, light weight, hand-carried, battery-operated sprayers. Two choices of such sprayers available to the farmers are:-

1. ***Vibrajet:*** Vibrajet, with a discharge of 100-200 l/ha, is designed to produce a coarse spray, comprising droplets of volume mean diameter of 400 microns and above, which are drift-resistant. It is very suitable to apply herbicide solutions and emulsions but not suspensions. In vibrajet the spray liquid is fed to a special type of spray nozzle with a multihole sleeve, by gravity flow. The liquid reaching there is put to fast oscillatory action produced with a 12 Volt, battery operated motor. It breaks the solid stream of the liquid into large droplets before it leaves the nozzle orifice. Vibrajet type sprayers hold promise in areas heavily prone to the spray drift hazards.
2. ***C.D.A.:*** A Controlled Droplet Applicator (CDA) differs from vibrajet in producing a fine spray, with droplets of volume mean diameter of 250 microns. These droplets of herbicide sprays are more effective on plants than the larger droplets, but at the same time these are adequately drift tolerant. C.D.A. is a low volume sprayer (20-40 l/ha). In this sprayer the spray solution is fed to a spinning disc which has a toothed edge that flings off the discrete droplets of a precisely defined size. The spinning action is achieved with a battery-run motor.

The CDA sprayers are very handy for treating small holdings, particularly in hilly topography and wet land paddy areas. The equipment is also good for use as a research plot sprayer. Further, these are easier to maintain and they cover more area per unit time than many other kinds of sprayers.

Besides the above sprayers, some more sprayers have been recorded for use in specific weed situations. These are:- Air Assisted Sprayers, (Quanquin, 1992), Directed Sprayers (Morrison and Chandler, 1993), Tunnel Sprayers (Mathews *et al.*, 1994), and High Speed Band Sprayers (Limb, 1993).

11.3 CALIBRATION OF BOOM SPRAYERS

11.3.1 Theoretical

Three factors govern the amount of spray liquid applied through a boom sprayer. These factors are: Swath width (W); Nozzle discharge rate (NDR); and the Ground speed (S). The nozzle capacity is governed by the size of the nozzle and the pressure developed at the nozzle by the pump. The nozzle manufacturers provide data sheets showing the nozzle capacities at variable pressures. Alternatively, a blank run can be made for a minute and the discharge collected at a constant pressure, and measured. For a given spray pressure, the above variables of Application Rate (R) of the spray liquids are related as follows:

$$R(\text{l/ha}) = \frac{600 \text{ x NDR (l/min per nozzle) x N (No. of nozzles)}}{\text{W(m) x S(Km/hr)}} \quad \text{....(1)}$$

Conversely,

$$\text{NDR(l/min/nozzle)} = \frac{\text{R(l/ha) x S (km/hr) x W(m)}}{600 \text{ x N (No. of nozzles)}} \quad \text{....(2)}$$

Thus, from equations (1) and (2) it is apparent that to increase the application rate (R) of any herbicide one should either use larger capacity nozzles or reduce the ground speed.

Spray pressures of over 2.8 kg/sq cm may cause serious spray drifts.

Having decided the nozzle discharge rate and the boom length (actually swath width), one can compute the ground speed needed for the sprayer as:

$$S\,(\text{Km/hr}) = \frac{600 \text{ x NDR (l/min nozzle) x N (No. of nozzles)}}{\text{W(m) x R (l/ha)}} \quad \text{....(3)}$$

Also, the swath width can be calculated as:

$$W(m) = \frac{\text{NDR (l/min/nozzle) x 600 x N (No. of nozzles)}}{\text{R (l/ha) x S (km/hr)}} \quad \text{....(4)}$$

The above formulae can be extended to calculate the area covered during a given time or the time required (T) in spraying a given area (A) as:

$$A(ha) = W(m) \text{ x } T(hr) \text{ x } S(km/hr) \text{ x } 0.1 \quad \text{....(5)}$$

and

$$T(hr) = \frac{\text{A (ha) x 10}}{\text{W (m) x S (km/hr)}} \quad \text{....(6)}$$

In the band application of herbicides, the broadcast application rates should be reduced in proportion to the ratio of the band width to the row spacing.

$$\text{Band application rate (l/ha)} = \frac{\text{Band width (cm) X Broadcast rate (l/ha)}}{\text{Row spacing (cm)}} \quad \text{....(7)}$$

It may be noted, however, that the band application of a herbicide will not make any difference in the time taken by it in comparison to its broadcast application.

11.3.2 Field Calibration

The success of the spray operation of herbicides depends upon accurate control of the spraying rates. Heavier than necessary application of herbicides may either injure the immediate crops, or it may leave harmful residues in soil for their future damage. On the other hand, if application rates are too light, ineffective weed control will result. While it is possible from the earilier mentioned calculations to regulate the application rates by choosing the proper nozzle size, boom length, and tractor speed, yet final calibration by in-motion and stationary test runs of the sprayer is necessary to make sure of proper adjustments. The procedure for such calibrations for mechanical boom sprayers and manual sprayers are described here as under.

1. ***Mechanical boom sprayers***: Fill the supply tank with water and operate the pump. Regulate the spray pressure to desired level.

   a) Place a suitable container under each nozzle and run the sprayer in stationary position. See if all the jars fill in about the same time. If not, check for clogged or worn-out nozzles and replace them. Sometimes, very narrow boom diameter may also be a cause of uneven delivery of nozzles.

   b) Make an in-motion test run of the sprayer unit for a minimum length of 100 m at the speed to be used in the field. The course may be laid out on the area to be sprayed or on a similar area. Also, keep the height of the boom from ground as you would keep in the field since swath will be slightly more if the boom is raised and less when it is lowered. Measure the time required to make one round trip. Do not include the time required for turning the sprayer.

   The area sprayed (sq m) = Distance travelled (m) x Swath width (m) ....(8)

   i) Fill the tank with water completely.

   ii) Run the sprayer in stationary position for exactly the time taken in the test run in step-3. Make sure that the sprayer is operated at the same pressure as fixed earlier in step.1. Find out the volume of water consumed in gallons. It can be done by measuring the amount of water required to refill the tank to the original mark.

   iii) From equation-8 and step-5, determine the application rate (R) as follows:

$$R(l/ha) = \frac{\text{L to refill the tank x 10,000}}{\text{Area covered (sq m)}} \quad \text{....(9)}$$

   Should the observed gpa deviate from the intended, one should check proper working of all parts of the sprayer, or if necessary, change the nozzles, boom, ground speed, and to a limited extent, the spray pressure, using calculations given earlier. Calibration must be repeated till satisfaction. (See Appendices 2 & 20)

2. ***Manual sprayers***: Manual sprayers fitted with boom can be calibrated in a manner similar to mechanical sprayers, except that the working speed in this case will vary with experience of the worker and it cannot be controlled precisely. Usually it is about 1.8 km/hr. A test run with water in a 80 sq m area may be conducted and readjustments in spray volume be made by either adjusting the walking speed or by replacing the spray nozzle. An aural aid to govern the walking speed has been developed which gives audible signals every second to the operator to regulate his pace.

11.4 MAINTENANCE OF SPRAYERS

1. Use only clean water as carrier of herbicides.
2. Use screens at the inlet of spray tanks to prevent foreign material from entering.

3. Never use a metal object for cleaning nozzles. This will corrode them and alter their discharge.
4. Flush sprayers before using them.
5. For phenoxy herbicides use separate spray barrels to save possible injury from the left-over herbicide traces to sensitive crops sprayed later with other pesticides.
6. Clean sprayers thoroughly after each period of use.
7. Remove and clean all screens and boom extensions with kerosene, using a small brush.
8. Mix a large box of detergent with 130 litres of water in the tank and circulate it through the by-pass system for 30 minutes.
9. Replace the screen and boom extensions.
10. Fill the tank one-half with 2% household ammonia and circulate it through the pump and by-pass, allowing only a small amount to go out through the nozzles. Let the remainder of the solution stand overnight and then run it through the nozzles.
11. Flush the whole sprayer with two tankfuls of clean water by spraying through the boom, with its nozzles removed.

11.5 GRANULE APPLICATORS

Most herbicide granule applicators use gravity flow system with a rotating agitator. The agitator meters the granules over an adjustable orifice plate, causing it to flow from the hopper through a gear system. But now hand and machine operated granule blowers have replaced the gravity flow knapsack distributors. Tractor-mounted granule applicators are also available. In limited areas herbicide granules can also be applied with simple fertilizer shakers.

Several factors govern the application rate of herbicide granules, including (i) size of the metering orifice, (ii) speed of the agitator, (iii) ground speed of the applicator, (iv) nature and size of the granules, (v) roughness of the field, and (vi) relative humidity and temperature. All granules seem to look alike at first glance but there is a wide variation in their particle size and density. For this reason, in variance with the spray liquids, a different applicator setting may be necessary for each kind of granule applied. Except for the orifice setting, ground speed is the most significant factor affecting the granule application rate. It is not uncommon to find a 100 per cent variation in the application rate of granules with a speed change of 1.5 Km hr^{-1}. Calibration of herbicide granule applicators comprises the following steps:-

1. Read the container label carefully to determine the application rate and particle size of the granules.
2. Adjust delivery openings on the applicator at approximate setting and fill the hopper with granules to be applied.
3. Set ground speed as it will operate in the field.

4. Tie some suitable container under each delivery of the applicator. Operate the unit over a measured area, simulating actual application.
5. Accurately weigh the granules delivered by the outlets.
6. Calculate the application rate of granules as-

$$\text{Kg/ha} = \frac{\text{Granules collected after the test run (in Kg) x 10,000}}{\text{Area covered in test run (in sq m)}}$$

Should the result differ from the desired, recalibrate after adjusting the orifice plates and/or the ground speed, till satisfaction.

11.6 HERBICIDE INCORPORATION EQUIPMENT

11.6.1 Surface Incorporation Equipments

1. ***Physical incorporation:*** In small plots, pickaxes can be used to incorporate the surface applied herbicides, although it may not give a uniform and desired depth of incorporation. Animal and tractor-drawn implements provide a more uniform incorporation of the surface applied herbicides to precise depth. Some such common herbicide incorporation equipments are:- (1) rotary tiller, (2) wheel hoe, (3) rotary spike, (4) row wheel, (5) disc harrow (6) tendem disc and (7) mulch treader.

   The tendem disc, when set to work 10-15 cm deep, tends to concentrate the herbicide in top 5-7.5 cm of soil. Power-driven rotary cultivator operating 10 cm deep places it only in surface 2.5 cm of soil. A tiller or hoe, on the other hand, mixes the herbicide to the actual depth the blades are set to cut the soil. With most machines it is possible to apply and incorporate herbicides in a single trip over the field by attaching the spray boom in front of the soil cutting blades of the incorporator. A seedbed smothering implement like a plank may also be attached to the rear of the disc to even out the stirred soil.

2. ***Herbigation***: It is the process of applying herbicides through farm irrigation system where the water incorporates the herbicide into the soil. Most success in herbigation has been reported with EPTC in maize and lucerne.

11.6.2 Subsurface Application Equipment

Subsurface herbicide application equipment comprises a special subsurface sweep. It is 45 cm wide and has a narrow flat stem with a sharp leading edge. A flood-type nozzle is mounted vertically behind the stem and under a trailing edge which projects over the nozzle to allow the full 130 degree spray angle to develop before intercepting the soil. The sweep is 2.5 cm high, excluding the stem, which allows shallow placement of the herbicide.

11.7 RESEARCH PLOT SPRAYERS

Herbicide trials round the world conform to a similar pattern, namely, several rates of different herbicides, compared with an untreated control. These treatments are replicated. Initially, the screening trials may involve couple of crop rows or small plots of 20 sq m each. Usually, spray volume of 500 ml per plot is used in these trials. To apply this small quantity of spray liquid accurately, special research plot sprayers have been designed. Their common features are:- high accuracy of discharge, compact design, easy to operate and clean, small size, and light in weight. Some of these are hand-pumped, while others are charged with small, motor-driven pumps. There are still others which are computerised. Some of the common plot sprayers have been described by Bindra and Singh (1971) and Loussaert (1992).

In initial screening trials it is necessary that several graded rates of herbicides are tried, simultaneously. The **logarithmic sprayers** are handy for this purpose. The unit applies a constant volume of spray per unit land throughout the strip but during the course it keeps on diluting the solution, logarithmically. The system employs a two vessels arrangement. One vessel is filled with a diluent and the other with herbicide of a predetermined concentration. As the spray is discharged from the second vessel, it is constantly replaced by an equal quantity of the diluent. Thus, a logarithmic sprayer can be run over long experimental strips, and by using standard curves, herbicide concentration applied at any distance from the starting point can be determined.

11.8 ROUGING GLOVES

The rouging gloves are used for applying herbicides by touch of the weed by the hand. The technique consists of an absorbent pad glued to palm of a plastic glove which is fed with the herbicide *via* a flexible tube with the herbicidal solution contained in a drop-fed dispenser, attached loosely to the operator's wearing apparal (Daelemans, 1991).

UNSOLVED EXERCISES ON CALIBRATION OF HERBICIDE APPLICATORS

1. A sprayer, equipped with two nozzles on a 50 cm long boom was found to deliver the herbicide spray at 3 l/mt/nozzle. Calculate its application rate in l/ha when the sprayer was run at a ground speed of 6 km/hr.
2. It is decided to apply a herbicide to wheat with a tractor-mounted sprayer at an application rate of 200 l/ha. The sprayer has two nozzles placed on a 50 cm long boom. Calculate the nozzle capacity required in l/mt, if the sprayer was to be run at a ground speed of 8 km/hr.
3. A sprayer is equipped with a pump of 30 l/mt capacity. It has a 7 m long boom and is run at a ground speed of 8 km/hr. Assuming a 20% loss in by-pass hydraulic agitation, calculate the potential application rate of the sprayer in l/ha.
4. What capacity nozzle should be used on a two nozzle boom to achieve an application rate of 200 l/ha, with the sprayer travelling at 8 km/hr? The nozzles are spaced 50 cm apart.
5. A sprayer carried a 7 m wide swath. When driven over a distance of 290 m it was found to spray 90 l of the herbicide emulsion. Calculate the application rate achieved in l/ha.

6. It is desired to apply 270 l/ha of a herbicide spray liquid with a tractor-mounted sprayer, running at an average speed of 6 km/hr. It possesses a boom with nozzles placed 50 cm apart. Calculate the required nozzle capacity in l/mt.
7. In the above question No. 6, recalculate the ground speed of the sprayer required if the application rate was desired to be 360 l/ha, using the already calculated nozzle capacity. The farmer desires to treat the crop in bands of 30 cm width.
8. In a test run, a measured course of 110 m length is found to require 54 seconds for travelling forward, and 56 seconds for returning to the starting point. The sprayer carried a tank of 450 l capacity and a 12 nozzles' boom, with nozzles placed 50 cm apart. After completing the run, it was found that it consumed 45 l water from the tank. Calculate the (i) swath width, (ii) area covered by the sprayer during the test run, (iii) application rate of water, and (iv) area that could be covered if it was decided to consume the tank full water.
9. While applying a herbicide spray mixture on a 33.3 cm wide band in a 100 cm wide row spacing crop, how much spray liquid will be used for 1 ha crop area, if the application rate for the broadcast spray was recommended at 18 l/ha?
10. How fast should a tractor-mounted sprayer travel to obtain an application rate of 400 l/ha, with nozzle capacity 3 l/mt? The sprayer is fitted with a 1.5 m long boom, with nozzles placed 50 cm apart.
11. What length of boom is required on a sprayer operating at 8 km/hr to permit spraying in 32 ha crop area in 8 hrs? Consider 30% time lost in filling the tank and on the turns.
12. What minimum size of pump is required to apply a spray at 90 l/ha with sprayer travelling at 8 km/hr and equipped with a 8 m long boom? The spray tank has mechanical agitation.
13. It is desired to apply a herbicide in two crops. In crop 'a', it is to be applied as broadcast spray, and in crop 'b', in 30 cm wide bands over the crop rows. The crop row spacing was 60 cm. If the sprayer is run at a ground speed of 8 km/hr, calculate the following parameters in the two cases.
    a) Application rate (a and b)
    b) time required to spray 1.0 ha crop (a and b).
        i) A granular herbicide applicator was used to treat 30 cm wide bands in 5 crop rows at a time. After driving over a distance of 290 m, each of the five openings of the distributor was found to have delivered 0.2 kg of the herbicide granules. Calculate the dose of the herbicide applied, considering the granules to contain 20% active ingredient.
        ii) A tractor-mounted sprayer has a boom length of 5 m. It is desired to spray 2,4-D in 30 cm wide bands in the maize interrows which are 100 cm wide. Calculate the time required to treat 7 ha maize in this fashion, when the sprayer is run at a ground speed of 12 km/hr.

        Note: (For tallying the answers obtained, one may see Appendix-4).

SUMMARY

Uniform application of herbicides is as important as the herbicide itself. Several kinds of sprayers are available from the small, hand-operated ones to the large, ground and aerial sprayers to apply herbicides, accurately. Major amongst these are: Knapsack sprayers (hydraulic and pneumatic types); Foot sprayers; Tarctor-powered sprayers; Aerial sprayers; and Hand-held sprayers—Vibrajet and CDA. The basic components of a sprayer are: spray tank, agitator, source of power, and distribution system, comprising nozzles, lance, boom, and pressure regulator.

Every sprayer is required to be calibrated, both on theoretical grounds and by field test runs. The theoretical calibration is based on relationship of the number and size of the nozzles, pump pressure, ground (or aerial) speed, swath width, and the application rates.

Like any other equipment, every sprayer demands its appropriate maintenance, including adequate cleaning to avoid damage to some sensitive crops. Procedure for the same is provided.

Limited herbicides are used in dry, granular forms. These are applied evenly with blowers. Their proper calibration and maintenance are also important.

Many herbicides are applied to soil surface before planting of crops, some of which require incorporation into the soil with hand tools or farm equipment like tillers, hoes, spikes, row wheels, harrows, discs, and treaders. A few soil active herbicides are aplied directly under the ground with subsurface sweeps and soil injectors. Herbicides are also applied to soil with irrigation water; the technique being called 'herbigation'.

In lawns and flowerbeds, herbicides can be smeared to individual weed with 'rouging gloves'. Likewise, weeds taller than the crop plants can be brought in contact directly with the 'herbicide-laden wicks'.

SELECTED BIBLIOGRAPHY

1. Akesson, N. B. and Yates, W. E. 1981. Pesticide Application Equipment and Techniques. FAO Agri. Serv. Bull. No. 38, FAO, Rome, 257 pp.
2. Bernat, C. and Gil, E. 1994. Pesticide application machinery development. Vida Rural 2 63-66. (Weed Abst., 43 (9) : 489)
3. Bindra, O. S. and Singh, H. 1971. Pesticide Application Equipment. Oxford and IBH Pub. Co., N. Delhi, 397 pp.
4. Clayphon, J. E. and Thornhill, E. W. 1974. A hand-held, drift-free herbicide applicator. PANS 20 (1) 145-149.
5. Daelemans, A. 1991. The magic glove to control difficult weeds. Tropicultura 9(2) 90-91.
6. Dale, J. E. 1979. A non-mechanical system of herbicide application with a rope wick. PANS 25(4) 431-436.
7. Deutsch, A. E. and Poole, A. P. (Eds.). 1972. Manual of Pesticide Application Equipment. Iny. Plant Prot. Cent., Oregon State Univ., Oregon, USA.

8. Filetsam, J. F. W. *et al.* 2004. Differential response of herbicide drift reduction nozzles to drift control agents with glyphosate. Transactions of the ASAE 47(5): 1405-1411.
9. Gupta, C. P. *et al.*, 1992. Field performance of hand-held electrostatic spinning disc sprayer. Trans. ASAE 35(6) 1753-1759.
10. Jain, S. K. *et al.* 2003. Evaluation of different designs of lever operated knapsack sprayer. New Agriculturist 14 (1/2): 107-112 (India).
11. Knoche, M. 1994. Effect of droplet size and carrier volume on performance of foliage-applied herbicides. Crop Protection 13(3) 163-178.
12. Legg, B. J. and Miller, P. C. H. 1989. Crop spraying developments. Outlook on Agri. 18(1) 18-23.
13. Limb, R. 1993. High-tech band-sprayer. Brit. Sugarbeet Review 61(4) 18.
14. Loussaert, D. 1992. Computer controlled chemical field applicator for research. Agron. J. 84(4) 759-763.
15. Mabbett. T. 1987. Portable sprayers—Everyone has its place. Agri. Int. 39(5) 162-164.
16. Mathews, G. A. *et al* 1994. Tunnel spraying: an environment favourable approach for pesticide application in orchards. Pesticide Outlook 3(3) 13-16.
17. Morrison, J.E. Jr, and Chandler, J. M. 1993. Directed sprayer for targeting pesticides. Weed Technol. 6(2) 441-444.
18. Quanquin, B. 1992. Less drift on target with the twin system. Paper - Am. Soc. Agri. Engg. No. 92-1564, 9 pp., USA.
19. Rabcewicz, J. and P. Wawrzynczak. 2004. The use of ultra-low volume atomisers for weed control in fruit production. J. of Fruit & Ornamental Plant Research 12 (April): 167-172 (Poland). Weed Abst. 54(11), 4409.
20. Rahate, R. H. *et al.* 2003. Effect of blade inclined angles on performance of power weeder. Bioved 14 (1/2): 87-90 (India).
21. Robinson, L. R. and Mulliner, H. R.1972. Sprinkler applied herbicides do good job in Nebraska tests. Weeds Today 3 (1) 6-7.
22. Thornton, M.E. 1983. A simple method of applying herbicide spot treatments. Trop. Pest Management 29(3) 271-273.
23. William, V. 1987. A rotary herbicide wiper for postemergence weed control in perennial horticultural crops. Weed Technol. 1(4) 319-322.

Chapter 12

IMPORTANT HERBICIDE FAMILIES AND MOLECULES

Any approved herbicide is known by three names *viz.*, (i) the common name, (ii) the chemical name, and (iii) the trade name. The common name of a herbicide is a technically accepted abbreviation of its chemical name. The chemical name of a herbicide reads out its full molecular structure. The trade names of herbicides, on the other hand, refer to their formulation offered by the chemical companies for the consumers. Often, the same herbicide structure is cited in the literature by more than one systematic chemical name, depending upon the authority *eg* CAS (Chemical Abstract Services) and IUPAC (international Union of Pure and Applied Chemistry). Then there are organizations like the International Organization for Standardization (ISO), British Standards Institute (BSI), and American National Standard Institute (ANSI) to approve the *common names* of the herbicides. The common and chemical names used in this book are largely those preferred by the CAS or listed by the Weed Science Society of America (Anon., 2002 and www.wssa.net). The unapproved candidate herbicides are known by certain code numbers. An illustration of the nomenclature of one herbicide is cited below.*

Example:

Common Name	:	Triasulfuron
Chemical Names	:	
(i) IUPAC	=	1-[2-(2-chloroethoxy) phenylsulfonyl]-3-(4-methoxy-6-methyl-1,3,5-triazin-2yl) urea
(ii) CAS	=	2-(2-chloroethoxy)-*N*-[[(4-methoxy-6-methyl-1,3,5-triazin-2-yl) amino] carbonyl] benzenesulfonamide
Trade Name	:	Logran (and some others in different countries)

Often, several herbicides have certain similarities in their structural formulae. Many of them are homologues and analogues of some basic structure. Herbicides belonging to one chemical family tend to have similar modes of action on plants and behaviour in

* *For current listing of common and chemical names of herbicides approved by the Weed Science Soc. Of USA, one may visit www.wssa.net.*

soils, though some herbicide members may be distinctly different form the rest. This is a great help to systematic understanding of the possible behaviour of new herbicides belonging to a particular chemical group and to develop new compounds with somewhat pre-chosen properties.

The scheme of chemical classification of herbicides mentioned in the following pages embodies over 100 herbicides that are currently in common use in different countries. Besides, some herbicide structures have been grouped as miscellaneous herbicides.

12.1 THE SUBSTITUTED PHENOLS

Example:

Dinoseb	=	2-sec-butyl-4, 6-dinitrophenol
DNOC	=	4,6-dinitro-*o*-cresol

12.2 THE PHENOXYALKANOIC ACIDS (Fig. 12.1)

The phenoxyalkanoic acid herbicide structures comprise a benzene ring attached to an alkanoic acid through an ether linkage. Several homologues and analogues of this basic molecular structure are widely used as herbicides. Acetic acids, propionic acids, and butyric acids are common constituents of herbicidal phenoxyalkanoic acids. These herbicide structures are further divided into alpha (∝) and omega (ω) phenoxyalkanoic acids, depending upon the position of carbon on the alkanoic chain involved in ether linkage. The omega carbon refers to the last alkyl carbon on the acid chain, whereas the alpha carbon denotes the first alkyl carbon, adjacent to the carboxyl group. In the case of phenoxyacetic acid and propionic acid derivatives, only the alpha carbon ether linkage phenoxy compounds show herbicidal properties, whereas among the phenoxy butyric acids, the omega (or 4) carbon ether linkage phenoxy compounds are found as active herbicides.

α-phenoxyalkanoic acids*

Ex.	2,4-D	= (2, 4-dichlorophenoxy) acetic acid
	MCPA	= (4-chloro-2-methylphenoxy) acetic acid
	Dichlorprop	= (±)-(2-(2, 4-dichlorophenoxy) propanoic acid
	Diclofop	= (±)-2-[4-(2,4-dichlorophenoxy) phenoxy] propanoic acid
	2,4-DP	= 2-(3,4-dichlorophenoxy) propanoic acid
	Mecoprop (MCPP)	= (±)-2-(4-chloro-2-methylphenoxy) propanoic acid
	Silvex (2,4,5-TP)	= 2-(2,4,5-trichlorophenoxy) propanoic acid

---

*.Alkanoic acids are from saturated hydrocarbons like the CH_4, C_2H_6, and C_3H_8 yielding, respectively, acetic, propanoic, and butanoic acids.

ω-phenoxyakanoic acids**

Among the ω-phenoxyalkanoic acids, even number carbon chain compounds with no more than eight carbons in their acid chains, are useful as herbicides. The odd number carbon acid chains of ω-phenoxyalkanoic acids are degraded within plants by β-oxidation to non-phytotoxic phenol structures.

But similar β-oxidation of the even number carbon chain ω-phenoxyalkanoic acid compounds yields phytotoxic acetic acid herbicides in the susceptible plants.

Ex. 2,4-DB = 4-(3,4-dichlorophenoxy) butanoic acid
MCPB = 4-(4-chloro-2-methylphenoxy) butanoic acid

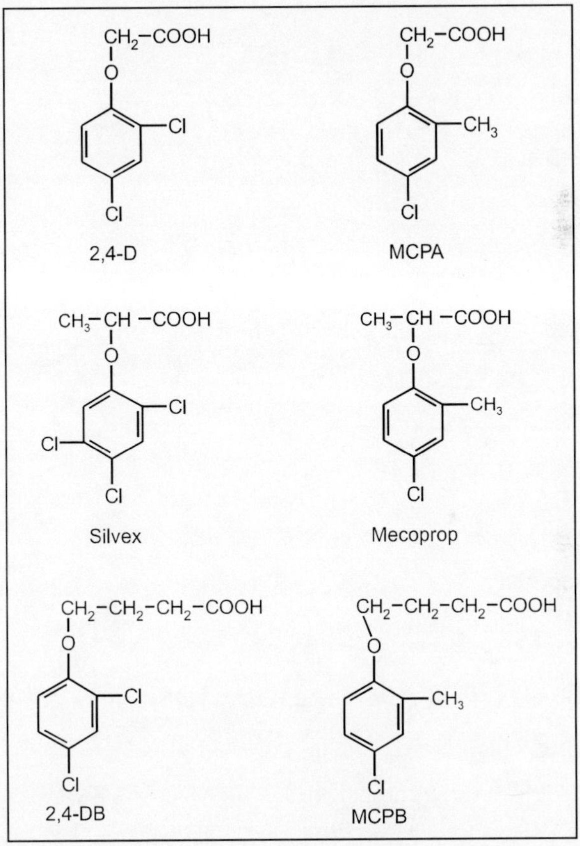

CH_2-COOH, O, Cl, Cl — 2,4-D

CH_2-COOH, O, CH_3, Cl — MCPA

$CH_3-CH-COOH$, O, Cl, Cl, Cl — Silvex

$CH_3-CH-COOH$, O, CH_3, Cl — Mecoprop

$CH_2-CH_2-CH_2-COOH$, O, Cl, Cl — 2,4-DB

$CH_2-CH_2-CH_2-COOH$, O, CH_3, Cl — MCPB

Fig. 12.1: Molecular structures of six phenoxyalkanoic acid herbicides; the top four of α types and the bottom two of ϖ types.

** In the molecular structures of 2,4-DB and MCPB sometimes instead of ω,4 is written.

12.3 THE PHENYLALKANOIC ACIDS (Fig. 12.2)

Phenylalkanoic acids, unlike the phenoxyalkanoic acids, do not possess an ether linkage; their side chains are directly attached to *para* carbon of the respective benzene rings.

Ex. Fenac = 2, 3, 6,- trichlorobenzeneacetic acid

The phenoxy and phenyl herbicides are available in different salt and ester forms. The esters vary in their volatility, depending upon the length of the chain. Some common salts and esters of phenoxy and phenyl herbicides are as follows, where 'R' represents the phenoxy or phenyl ring, as the case may be.

Salts

Sodium salt, $R—CH_2COONa$

Triethylamine salt, $R—CH_2COONH\ (C_2H_5)_3$

Triethanolamine salt, $R—CH_2COONH\ (C_2H_4OH)_3$

High volatile esters

Methyl ester, $R—CH_2COOCH_3$

H
|
$CH_2COOC(CH_3)_2$

Isopropyl ester, $R—CH_2COOC(CH_3)_2$

Butyl ester, $R—CH_2—COOC_4H_9$

Octyl ester, $R—CH_2—COOC_8H_{17}$

Low volatile esters

Butoxyethanol ester, $R—CH_2COOC_2H_4—O—C_4H_9$

Propyleneglycolbutylether ester, $R—CH_2COOCH_2CH(OH)CH_2O—C_4H_9$

12.4 THE SUBSTITUTED AROMATIC ACIDS (Fig. 12.2 contd.)

Benzoic acids and anisic acids***

Ex. Acifluorfen = 5-[2-chloro-4-(trifluoromethyl) phenoxy]-2-nitrobenzoic acid
Chloramben = 3-amino-2, 5-dichlorobenzoic acid
Dicamba = 3, 6-dichloro-2-methoxybenzoic acid

*** Anisic acid = methoxybenzoic acid.

**** 'Methylphenoxy' is also called 'tolyoxy', as per IOS.

12.5 PHTHALIC AND PHTHALAMIC ACIDS

Ex. Endothall =.7-oxabicyclo [2,2,1] heptane-2, 3-dicarboxylic acid
DCPA = dimethyl 2,3,5,6-tetrachloro-1,4-benzenedicarboxylate
Naptalam = 2-[(1-naphthalenylamino)carbonyl] benzoic acid

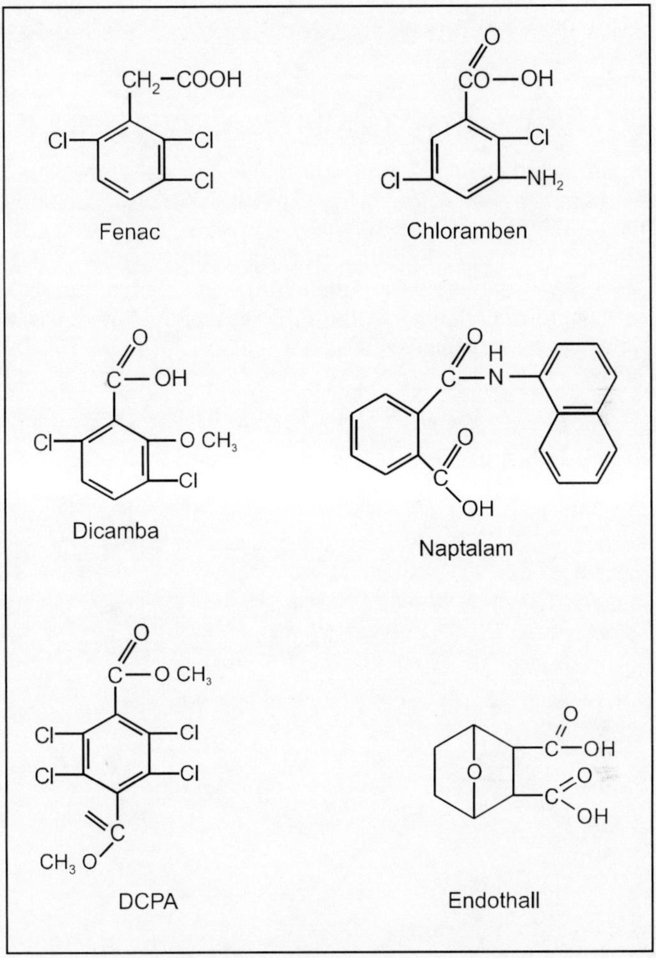

Fenac
Chloramben
Dicamba
Naptalam
DCPA
Endothall

Fig. 12.2: *Top left* = Molecular structure of fenac; a phenylalkanoic acid herbicide. *Remainders* = molecular structures of five substituted, aromatic acid herbicides.

12.6 CHLORINATED ALIPHATIC ACIDS (Fig. 12.3)

Ex. Dalapon = 2,2-dichloropropanoic acid

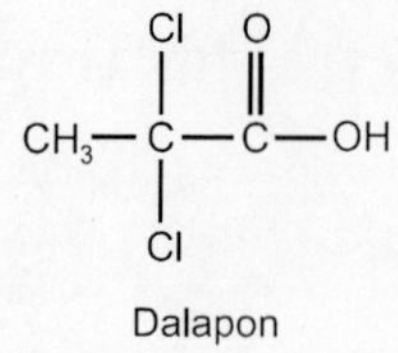

$$CH_3-\overset{Cl}{\underset{Cl}{C}}-\overset{O}{\overset{\|}{C}}-OH$$

Dalapon

Fig. 12.3: Molecular structure of dalapon.

12.7 SYMMETRICAL AND ASYMMETRICAL TRIAZINES (Fig. 12.4)

Symmetrical triazines are heterocyclic nitrogen molecules with three N atoms alternating with three C atoms in the central ring. There are two amino substitutents at two of the ring carbon atoms. At the third carbon, three alternative substituents present are: Cl^-, $O.CH_3$, $S.CH_3^-$, (or $S.C_2H_5$). Depending upon these substituents, the *S*-triazine herbicides are classified as chloro, methoxy, and methylthio (and ethylthio) compounds. The common names of herbicides falling in the three groups of *S*-triazines are suffixed by words-azine, -tone, and -tryn, respectively.

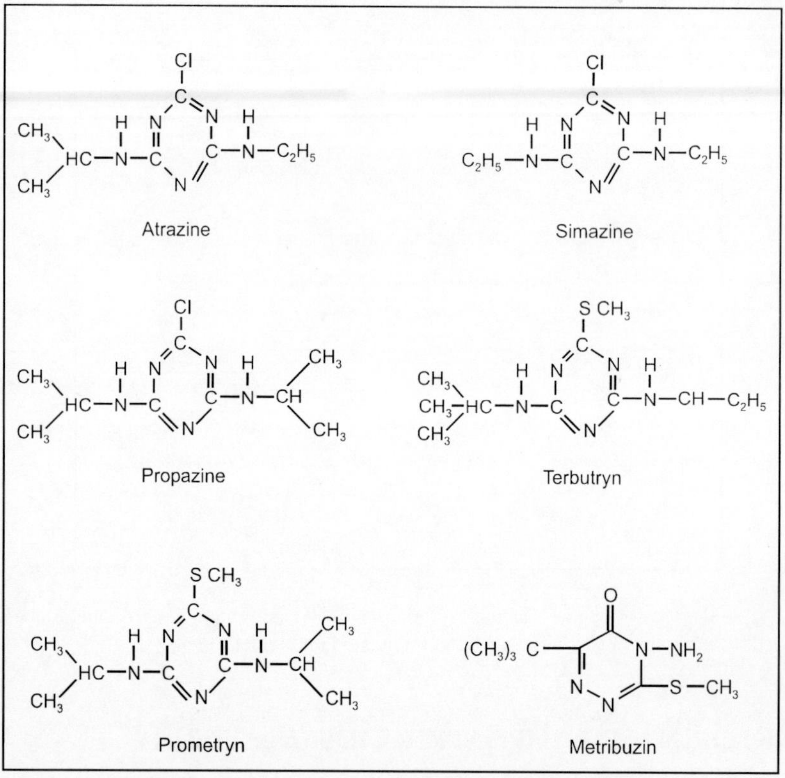

Atrazine

Simazine

Propazine

Terbutryn

Prometryn

Metribuzin

Fig. 12.4: Molecular structures of six common triazine herbicides

In asymmetrical triazines, the positions of N atoms do not alternate with those of C atoms.

Symmetrical Triazines

Ex.	Atrazine	6-chloro-*N*-ethyl-*N*′ -(1-methylethyl)- 1, 3, 5-triazine-2, 4-diamine
	Propazine	6-chloro-*N*, *N*′-bis (1-methylethyl)-1, 3, 5-triazine-2, 4-diamine
	Simazine	6-chloro-*N*, *N*′-diethyl-1, 3, 5-triazine-2,4-diamine
	Prometryn	*N*′, *N*′ -bis (1-methylethyl) -6 (methylthio)-1, 3, 5-triazine-2, 4-diamine
	Terbutryn	*N*-(1,1-dimethylethyl)-*N*′ -ethyl-6-(methylthio) -1, 3, 5-triazine-2, 4-diamine
	Prometon	6-methoxy-*N*, *N*′-bis(1-methylethyl)-1,3,5- triazine-2,4-diamine

Asymmetrical Triazine

Ex.	Metribuzin	4-amino-6-(1,1-dimethylethyl)-3-(methylthio)- 1, 2, 4-triazine-5 (4*H*)-one

12.8 THE SUBSTITUTED DIAZOLES AND TRIAZOLES (Fig. 12.5)

The diazoles and triazoles are five member, ring compounds. While diazoles contain 2 N atoms, the triazoles carry 3 N atoms.

Ex.	Difenzoquat	= 1, 2 dimethyl-3, 5-diphenyl-l *H*-pyrazolium
	Methazole	= 2-(3, 4-dichlorophenyl) -4-methyl-1, 2, 4-oxadiazolidine-3, 5-dione
	Amitrole*	= 1*H*-1,2,4-triazol-3-amine

12.9 THE SUBSTITUTED DIAZINES (Fig. 12.5)

The diazines are four carbon and two nitrogen atoms ring compounds.

Ex.	Bentazon	= (1-methylethyl)-(l *H*)-2, 1, 3-benzothiadiazin -(4) (3*H*)-one 2, 2-dioxide
	Dazomet	= tetrahydro-3, 5-dimethyl-2 *H*-1, 3, 5-thiadiazine-2-thione
	Pyrazon	= 5-amino-4-chloro-2-phenyl-3 (2*H*)-pyridazinone

Fig. 12.5: Molecular structure of one diazole (*Top right*), one triazole (*Top left*), and two diazine (*Bottom*) herbicides

12.10 PYRIDINES AND PYRIDINOLS (Fig. 12.6)

The pyridine herbicide molecules are five carbon atoms and one nitrogen atom, ring compounds. The pyridinols are hydroxylated forms of pyridines. The carboxylic acid of pyridine is called picolinic acid.

Ex. Fluridone = 1-methyl-3-phenyl-5[3-(trifluoromethyl) phenyl]-4 (*lH*)- pyridinone
Picloram = 4-amino-3, 5, 6-trichlo-2-pyridinecarboxylic acid

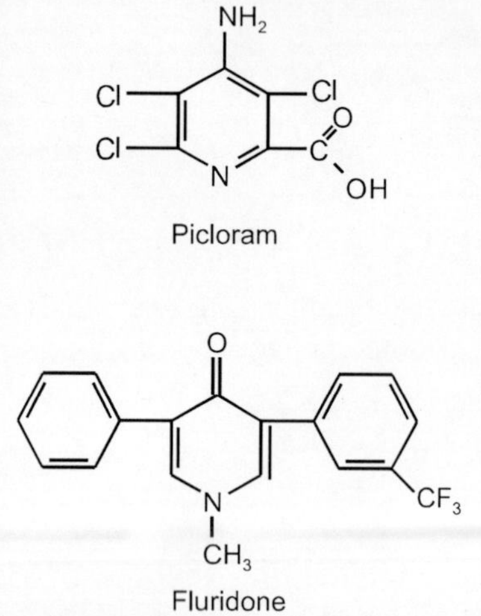

Picloram

Fluridone

Fig. 12.6: Molecular structures of three pyridine herbicides

12.11 THE QUATERNARY AMMONIUMS (=DIPYRIDYLS) (Fig. 12.7)

When all H atoms of an ammonium radical (NH_4^+) are substituted by other kinds of atoms, the resulting compound is called a quaternary ammonium compound. It carries, like NH_4^+, a positive charge, and the resulting herbicides are, therefore, cationic in nature.

The successful herbicides from such substitutions are ring structured. Three H atoms of NH_4 molecule are occupied by three bonds of the ring and the fourth one either by a bond of another ring or by any other moiety. In other words, such herbicides carry one or more rings with one N atom in each. That way, these herbicides can also be termed as dipyridyls, each molecule comprising two pyridine rings.

Ex. Diquat* = 6, 7-dihydrodipyrido [1, 2-∝:2′, 1′-c} pyrazinediium ion
Paraquat* = 1, 1′-dimethyl-4,4′- bipyridinium ion

---

* Diquat is usually formulated as a dibromide salt, whereas paraquat is made available as dichloride and dimethylsulphate salts.

12.12 THE URACILS (Fig. 12.7 Contd.)

The molecular structures of uracil herbicides are similar to those of diazines, except that they carry two additional oxygen atoms at positions 2 and 4 of the heterocyclic ring.

Ex. Bromacil = 5-bromo-6-methyl-3-(1-methylpropyl)-2,4(1*H*, 3*H*) pyrimidinedione
Terbacil = 5-chloro-3-(1,1-dimethylethyl)-6-methyl-2,4(1*H*, 3*H*) pyrimidinedione
Isocil = 5-bromo-6-methyl-3-(1-methylethyl)-2,4-(1*H*, 3*H*)-pyrimidine dione
Lenacil = 3-cyclohexyl-6,7-dihydro-1*H*-cyclopenatapyrimidine-2,4(3*H* 5*H*)-dione

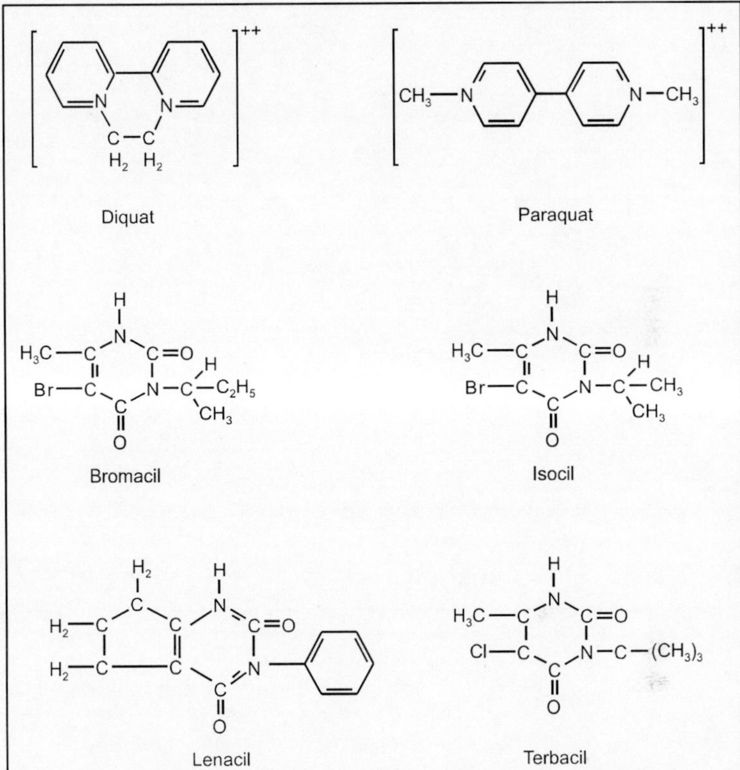

Fig. 12.7: Molecular structures of two quaternary ammonium herbicides (*top row*) and four uracil herbicides (*middle* and *bottom* rows)

12.13 THE SUBSTITUTED UREAS (Fig. 12.8)

By substituting a urea molecule with different substituted phenyl and alkyl moieties, a variety of useful herbicides have been obtained.

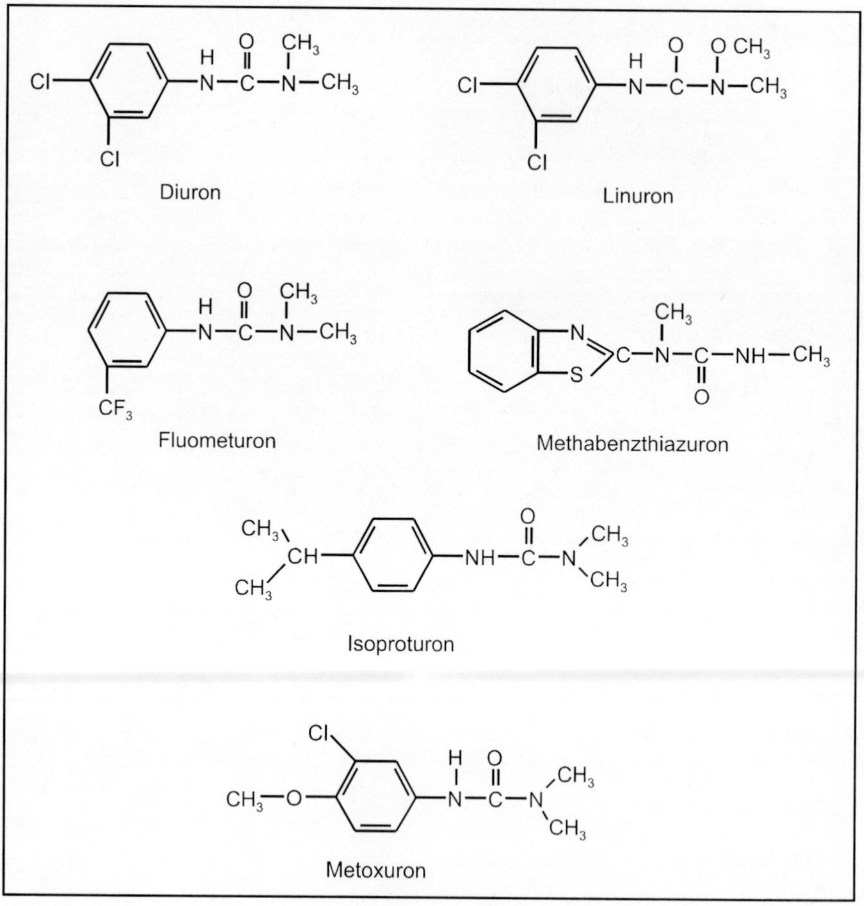

Fig. 12.8: Molecular structures of certain substituted urea herbicides

Ex.

Chlorotoluron	= *N*-(3-chloro-4-methylphenyl)-*N*,*N*-dimethylurea
Chloroxuron	= *N*′-[4-(4-chlorophenoxy) phenyl]-*N*,*N*-dimethylurea
Diuron	= *N*′-(3, 4-dichlorophenyl) -*N*,*N*-dimethylurea
Fenuron	= *N*,*N*-dimethyl-*N*-phenylurea
Fluometuron	= *N*,*N*-dimethyl-*N*′-[3-(trifluoromethyl) phenyl] urea
Isoproturon	= *N*,*N*-dimethyl-*N*-[4-(1-methylethyl) phenylurea
Linuron	= *N*-(3,4-dichlorophenyl)-*N*-methoxy-*N*-methylurea
Methibenzuron	= *N*-2-benzothiazolyl-*N*,*N*-dimethylurea
Metoxuron	= *N*-(3-chloro-4-methoxyphenyl)-*N*,*N*-dimethylurea
Monuron	= *N*-(4-chlorophenyl)-*N*,*N*-dimethylurea
Metobromuron	= *N*-(4-bromophenyl)-*N*-methoxy-*N*-methylurea

12.14 THE CARBAMATES AND CARBAMOTHIOATES (Fig. 12.9)

Several herbicides have been derived from carbamic and carbanilic acids (=phenylcarbamic acids) by substituting their amine and carboxylic moieties. It is conventional to read the chemical name of a carbamate or carbanilate herbicide beginning from the substituent at carboxylic moiety. It is separated from the substituent at amine moiety which is appended to the word 'carbamate'. Thus, isopropyl phenylcarbamate is different from isopropylphenyl carbamate and isopropylphenylcarbamate. Of these three compounds, only the first one is a herbicide, called 'propham'*.

A carbanilate differs from carbamate in having a phenyl ring substituent at amine moiety of its parent carbamic acid. It is also called a phenylcarbamate.

When a sulphur atom replaces oxygen of hydroxyl group of carbamic acid, it is called thiocarbamic acid. Likewise, in dithiocarbamic acids, another sulphur atom replaces the second oxygen of carbamic acid.

Carbamates

Ex. Asulam = methyl [(4-aminophenyl) sulfonyl] carbamate
Barban = 4-chloro.-2-butynyl 3-chlorophenylcarbamate
Chlorpropham = 1-methylethyl 3-chlorophenylcarbamate
Phenmedipham = 3-[(methoxycarbonyl) amino] phenyl (3′-methylphenyl) carbamate
Propham = 1-methylethyl phenylcarbamate

Thiocarbomates

Ex. Butylate = *S*-ethyl bis(2-methylpropyl) carbamothioate
Cycloate = *S*-ethyl cyclohexyl ethylcarbamothioate
Diallate = *S*-2,3-dichloro-2-propenyl) bis (1-methylethyl) carbamothioate
EPTC = *S*-ethyl dipropylcarbamothioate
Molinate = *S*-ethyl hexahydro-1 *H*-azepine-l-carbothioate
Pebulate = *S*-propyl butylethylthiocarbamothioate.
Triallate = *S*-(2, 3, 3,-trichloro2-propenyl) bis(1-methylethyl) carbamothioate
Thiobencarb = *S*-[(4-chlorophenyl) methyl] diethylcarbamothioate
Vernolate = *S*-propyl dipropylcarbamothioate

Dithiocarbamates

Ex. Metham (SMDC) = methylcarbamodithioic acid
CDEC = 2-chloro-2-propenyl diethylcarbamodithioate

---

* ***Footnote***: *While 'di' indicates two substituents present on the same moiety, 'bis' indicates each of the two present on separate moieties.*

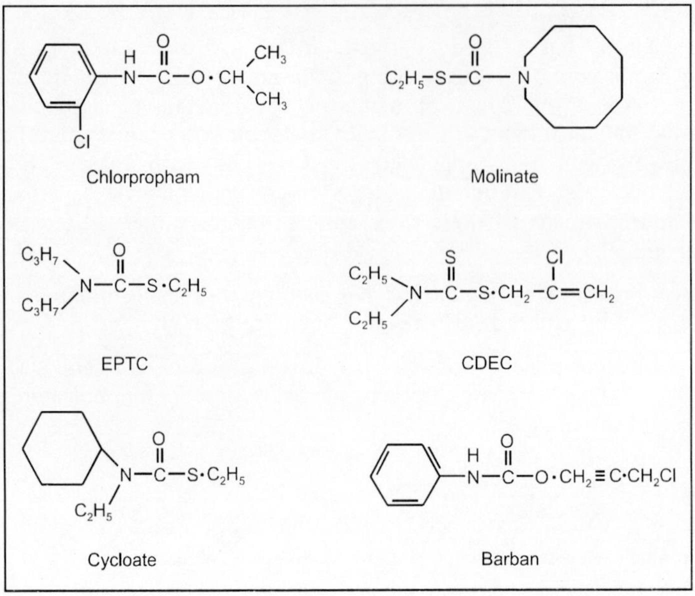

Chlorpropham

Molinate

EPTC

CDEC

Cycloate

Barban

Fig. 12.9: Molecular structures of common carbamate and carbamothiate herbicides

12.15 THE SUBSTITUTED AMIDES AND ANILIDES (Fig. 12.10)

When the hydroxyl group of an organic acid is substituted by an NH_2^+ (amino) group, an amide is formed. Thus, from acetic acid one derives acetamide, and from acrylic acid an acrylamide. Further substitution of an amide with a phenyl ring yields an anilide. Several substituted amides and anilides are selective herbicides.

Substituted Amides

Ex. CDAA = 2-chloro-*N*,*N*-2-propenylacetamide

Diphenamid = *N*,*N*-dimethyl-∝-phenyl benzeneacetamide

Mefluidide = *N*-[2, 4-dimethyl-5-[(trifluoromethyl) sulfonyl] amino] phenyl] acetamide

Napropamide = *N*, N-diethyl-2-(1-napthalenyloxy) propionamide

Oryzalin = 4-(dipropylamino)-3,5-dinitrobenzenesulfonamide

Pronamide = 3, 5-dichloro (*N*-l, l-dimethyl-2-propynyl) benzamide

Perfiuidone = 1,1,1-trifluoro-*N*-[2-methyl-4-(phenylsulfonyl) phenyl] methanesulfonamide

Alachlor = 2-chloro-*N*-(2,6-diethylphenyl)-*N*-(methoxymethyl) acetamide

Butachlor = *N*-(butoxymethyl -2-chloro-*N*-2, 6-diethylphenyl) acetamide

Metolachlor = 2-chloro-*N*-(2-ethyl-6-methylphenyl)-*N*-(2-methoxy-1-methylethyl) acetamide

Propachlor = 2-chloro-*N*-(1-methylethyl)-*N*-phenylacetamide

Propanil = *N*-(3,4-dichlorophenyl) propanamide

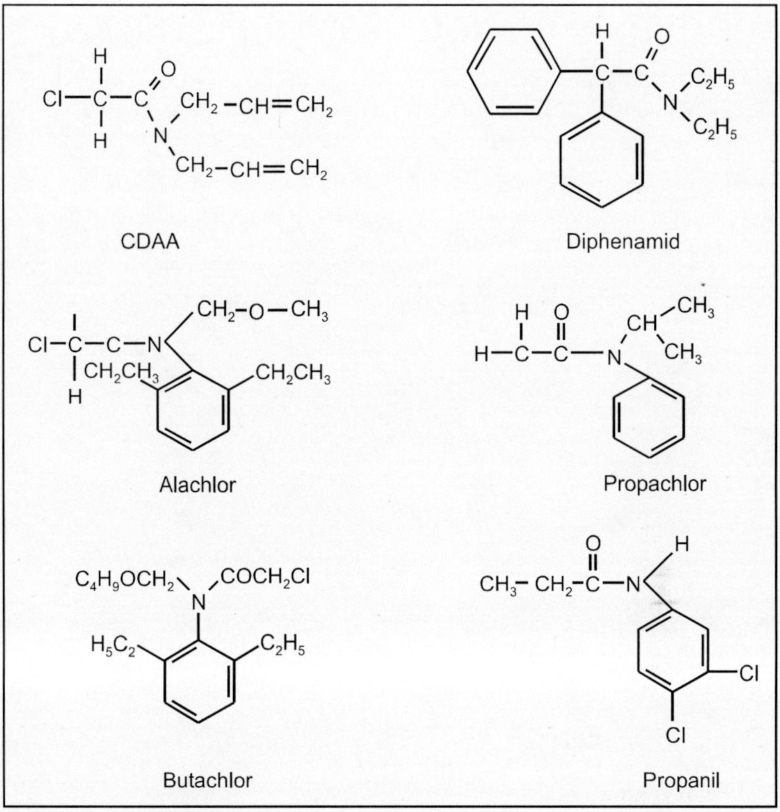

Fig. 12.10: Molecular structures of common substituted amide and anilide herbicides.

12.16 THE BENZONITRILES (Fig. 12.11)

As the name of this group of herbicides indicates, benzonitriles comprise a nitrile moiety (C = N) attached to a benzene ring through a single bond.

Ex.		
	Bromoxynil	= 3, 5-dibromo-4-hydroxybenzonitrile
	Cyanazine*	= 2-[[4-chloro-6-(ethylamino)-1,3,5-triazin-2-yl] amino] -2 methylpropanenitrile
	Dichlobenil	= 2, 6-dichlorobenzonitrile
	Ioxynil	= 4-hydroxy-3, 5-diiodobenzonitrile

Footnote: **Cyanazine is also considered as a s-triazine herbicide.*

12.17 THE ANILINES AND TOLUIDINES (Fig. 12.11 contd.)

When an amino (NH_2^+) group is connected to a benzene ring through a bond, it forms an aniline (benzenamine). Toluidines are ortho, para, or meta-methyl derivatives of aniline.

Ex.

Benefin	= *N*-butyl-*N*-ethyl.-2, 6-dinitro-4-(triflurometbyl) benzenamine
Fluchloralin	= *N*-(2-chloroethyl)-2, 6-dinitro-*N*-propyl-4-(trifluoromethyl) benzenamine
Pendimethalin	= *N*-(l-ethylpropyl)-3,4-dimethyl-2, 6-dinitrobenzenamine
Trifluralin	= 2,6-dinitro-*N,N*-dipropyl-4-(trifluoromethyl) benzenamine.

Ioxynil

Cyanazine

Fluchloralin

Trifluralin

Pendimethalin

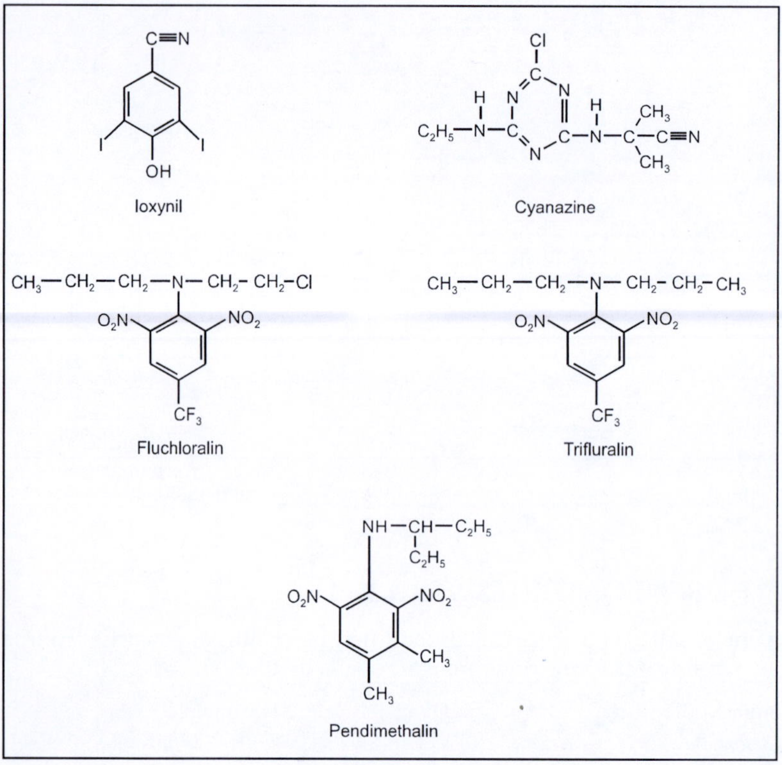

Fig. 12.11: Molecular structures of two benzonitrile (*top row*) and four aniline and toluidine (*remainders*) herbicides

12.18 THE ETHERS (Fig. 12.12)

There are some interesting herbicides developed by introducing ether linkage (oxygen linkage) between two phenyl rings and substituting them suitably with nitro group, chlorine, etc.

Ex. Oxyfluorfen = 2-chloro-1-(3-ethoxy-4-nitrophenoxy)-4-(trifluoromethyl) benzene
Fluorodifen = 2-nitro-1-(4-nitrophenoxy)-4-trifluoromethylbenzene

Flurorodifen

Oxyfluorfen

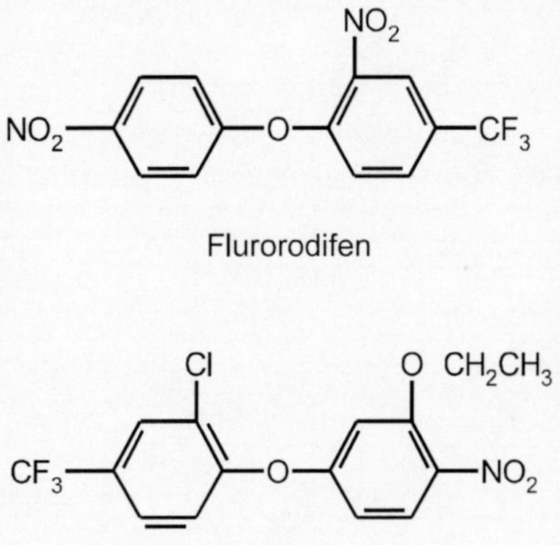

Fig. 12.12: Molecular structures of two common ether herbicides

12.19 THE IMIDAZOLINONES* (IMI)

Ex. Imazaquin = 2-{4, 5-dihydro-4-methyl-4-(1-methylethyl)-5-oxo-1*H*-imidazol-2 yl]-3-quinolinecarboxylic acid

Imazethapyr = 2[4, (-5-dihydro-4-methyl-4(1-methylethyl)-5-oxo-1 *H*-imidazol-2-yl]-5-ethyl-3-pyridinecarboxylic acid

Imazapyr = (±) -2-[4, 5-dihydro-4-methyl-4-(1-methylethyl)-5-oxo-1 *H*-imidazol-2yl] -3- pyridinecarboxylic acid

12.20 THE SULFONYLUREAS*

Ex Chlorimuron = 2-[[[[4-chloro-6-methoxy-2-pyrimidinyl) amino] carbonyl] amino] sulfonyl] benzoic acid

Chlorsulfuron = 2-chloro-*N*[[(4-methoxy-6-methyl- 1, 3, 5-triazin-2-yl) amino] carbonyl] benzenesulfonamide

Metsulfuron = 2-[[[4-methoxy-6-methyl-1, 3, 5-triazin-2-yl) amino] carbonyl] amino] sulfonyl) benzoic acid

12.21 THE ORGANIC ARSENICALS (Fig. 12.13)

Ex. Cacodylic acid = dimethyl arsenic acid
CMA = calcium salt of MAA

Foodnote: * *For chemical structures of imidazolinones and sulphonylurea herbicides, see section 12.25.*

DSMA	= disodium salt of MAA
MAA	= methylarsonic acid
MAMA	= monoammonium salt of MAA
MSMA	= monosodium salt of MAA

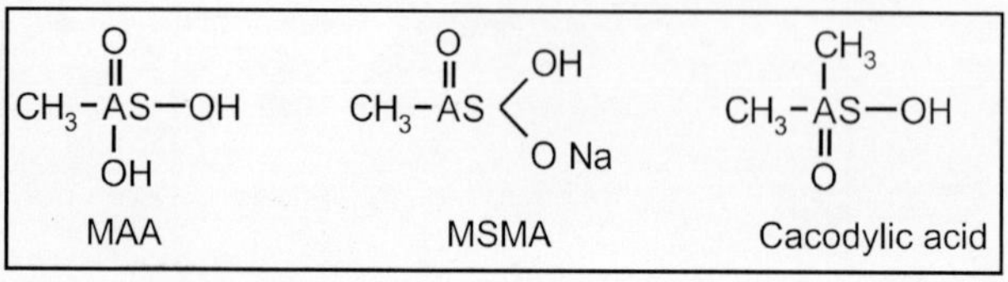

$$CH_3-\overset{\overset{O}{\|}}{\underset{\underset{OH}{|}}{AS}}-OH \qquad CH_3-\overset{\overset{O}{\|}}{AS}\langle^{OH}_{O\,Na} \qquad CH_3-\overset{\overset{CH_3}{|}}{\underset{\underset{O}{\|}}{AS}}-OH$$

MAA MSMA Cacodylic acid

Fig. 12.13: Molecular structures of three organic arsenical herbicides

12.22 THE ARYLOXYPHENOXYPROPANOIC (APOP) ACIDS*

Ex. Diclofop = (±)-2-[4-(2,4-dichlorophenoxy) phenoxy]propanoic acid
Dichloroprop = (±)-2-(2,4-dichlorophenoxy) propanoic acid
Fluazifop = (±)-2-[4-[[5-(trifluoromethyl)-2-pyridinyl] oxy] phenoxy] propanoic acid
Fluazifop-p = (*R*)-2-[4-[[5-(trifluoromethyl)-2-pyridinyl] oxy] phenoxy] propanoic acid
Haloxyfop = (±)-2-[4-[[3-chloro-5-(trifluoromethyl)-2-pyridinyl] oxy] phenoxy] propanoic acid

12.23 THE CYCLOHEXANEDIONES (CHD)*

Ex. Sethoxydim = 2-[-(ethoxyimino) butyl]-5-[2-(ethylthio) propyl]-3-hydroxy-2-cyclohexen-1-one
Tralkoxydim = 2-[1-(ethoxyimino) propyl]-3-hydroxy-5-(2,4,6-trimethylphenyl)-2-cyclohexen-1-one

12.24 SOME MISCELLANEOUS APPROVED HERBICIDES (Fig. 12.14 contd.)

Ex.

1. Acrolein = 2-propenal
   $(CH_2 = CH - \overset{\overset{O}{\|}}{C} - H)$
2. Allyl alcohol = 2-propen-1-ol
   $(CH_2 = CH—CH_2OH)$
3. AMS = Ammonium sulfamate
4. Anilofos = *S*-4-chloro-*N*-isopropylcarbaniloylmethyl *O,O*-dimethyl phosphorodithioate (IUPAC)
5. Benzoylprop = *N*-benzoyl-*N*-(3, 4-dichlorophenyl)-*DL*-alanine

---

* *Molecular structures are available in Sec. 12.25.*

6. Difenzoquat = 1,2-dimethyl-3, 5-diphenyl-1 *H*-pyrazolium
7. Flamprop = *N*-benzoyl-*N*-(3-chloro-4-fluorophenyl) *DL*-alanine
8. Fomesafen = 5-[2-chloro-4-(trifluromethyl)phenoxy]-*N*-(methylsulfonyl)-2-nitrobenzamide
9. Fosamine = ethyl hydrogen (aminocarbonyl) phosphonate
10. Glyphosate = *N*-(phosphonomethyl) glycine
11. Hexaflurate = Potassium hexafluoroarsenate
12. Hexazinone = 3-cyclohexyl-6-(dimethylamino) -1-methyl-1, 3, 5-triazine-2, 4(1*H*, 3*H*)-dione
13. Lactofen = (1)-2-ethoxy-1-methyl-2-oxoethyl-5-[2-chloro-4-(trifluromethyl) phenoxy]-2-nitrobenzoate
14. Oxadiazon = 3-[2,4-dichloro-5-(1-methylethoxy) phenyl]-5-(1,1-dimethylethyl)-1,3,4-oxadiazol-2(3*H*)-one
15. Piperphos = *S*-2-methylpiperidinocarbonylmethyl *O,O*-dipropyl phosphorodithioate

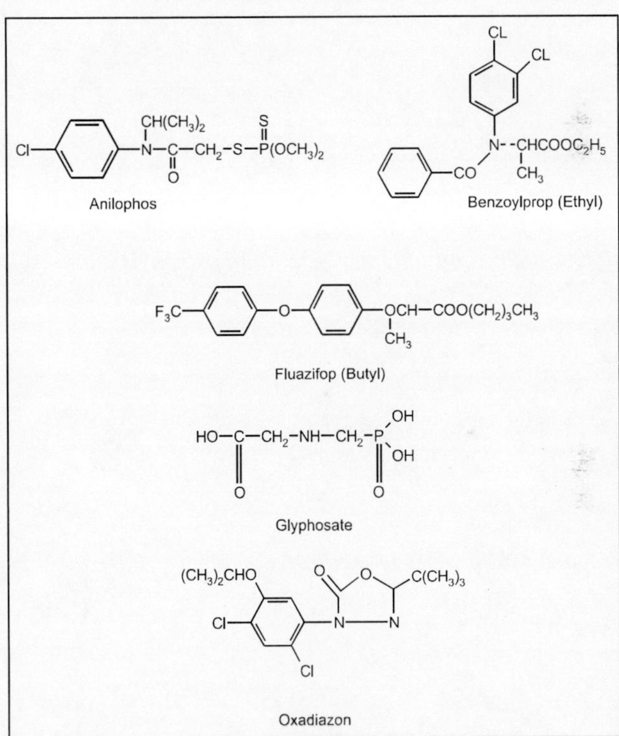

Fig. 12.14: Molecular structures of certain miscellaneous herbicides

12.25 STRUCTURES OF CERTAIN CURRENT HRBICIDE MOLECULES IN INDIA

Acetochlor

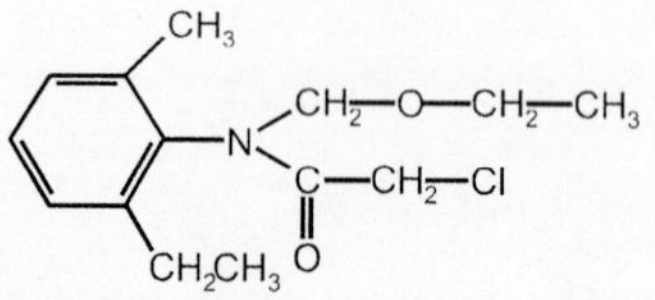

2-chloro-N-(ethoxymethyl)-N-(2-ethyl-6-methylphenyl)acetamide

Chlorimuron-ethyl

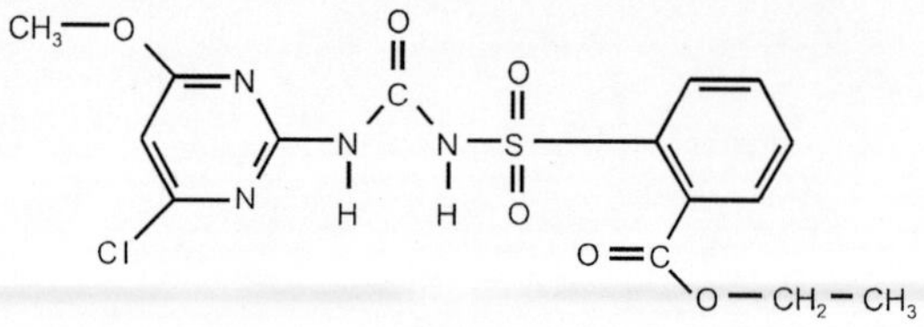

Ethyl 2-[[[[(4-chloro-6-methoxyprimidine-2-yl)amino] carbonyl] amino]sulfonyl]benzoate

Chlorsulfuron

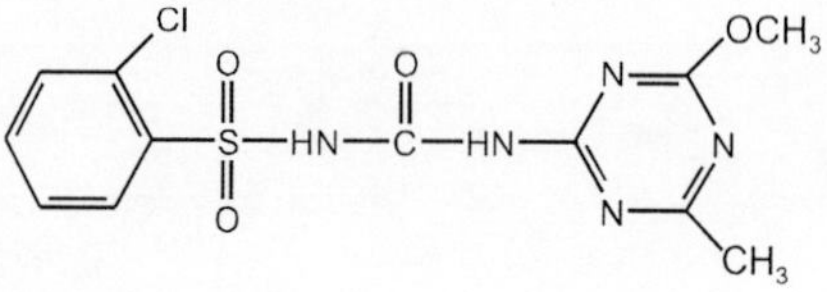

1-(2-Chlorophenylsulfonyl)-3-(4-methoxy-6-methyl-1, 3, 5-triazin-2-yl)urea

Clodinafop - propargyl

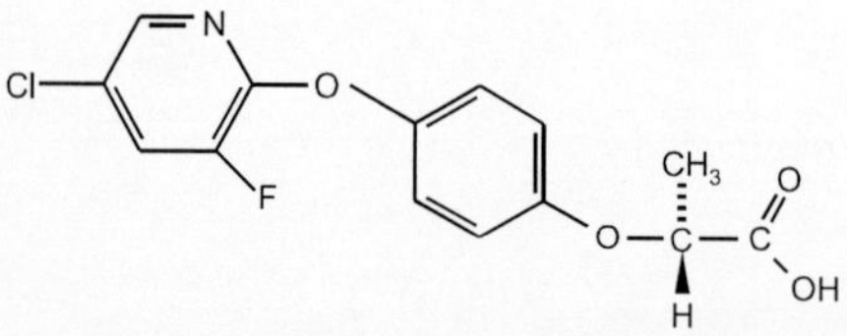

(R)-2-[4-[(5-chloro-3-fluoro-2-pyridinyl)oxy]phenoxy]propanoic acid

Cyhalofop-butyl

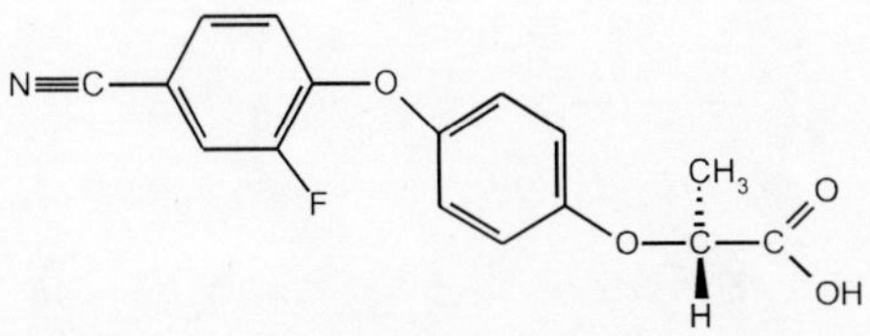

(R)-2-[4-(4-cyano-2-fluorophenoxy)phenoxy]propionic acid

Dithiopyr

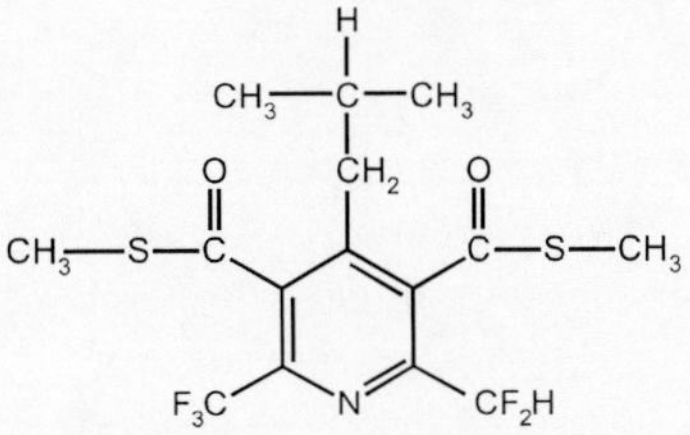

S,S,dimethyl 2-(difluoromethyl)-4-(2-methylpropyl)-6-(trifluoromethyl) 3,5-pyridinedicarbothioate

Fenoxaprop-P-ethyl

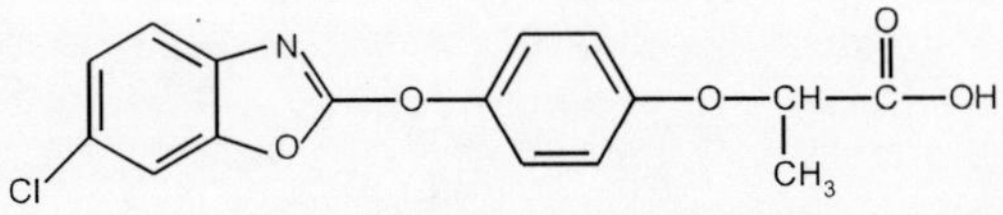

(R)-2-[4-(6-chloro-1, 3-benzoxazol-2-yloxy)phenoxy]propionic acid

Fluroxypyr

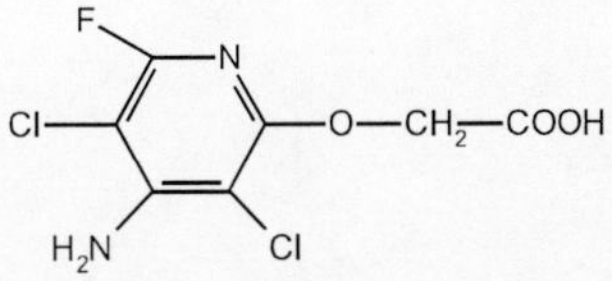

[(4-amino-3,5-dichloro-6-fluoro-2-pyridinyl)oxy] acetic acid

Glufosinate

2-amino-4-(hydroxymethylphosphinyl)butanoic acid

Imazapyr

2-[4, 5-dihydro-4-methyl-4-(1-methylethyl)-5-oxo-1H-imidazol-2-yl]-3-pyridinecarboxylic acid

Imazaquin

2-[4, 5-dihydro-4-methyl-4-(1-methylethyl)-5-oxo-1H-imidazol-2-yl]-3-quinolinecarboxylic acid

Imazethapyr

2-[4, 5-dihydro-4-methyl-4-(1-methylethyl)-5-oxo-1H-imidazol-2-yl]-5-ethyl-3-pyridinecarboxylic acid

Iodosulfuron – methyl-sodium

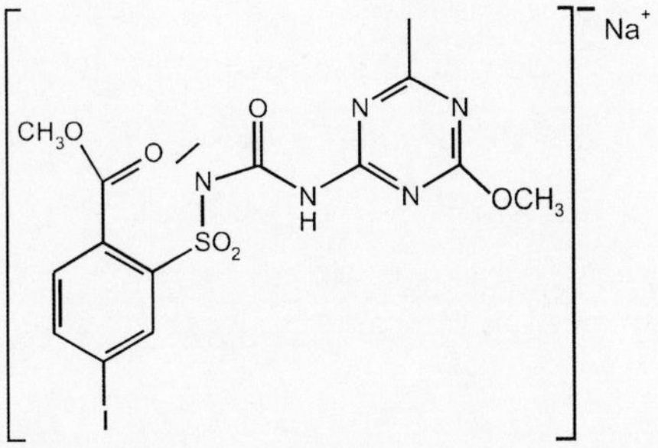

Methyl-4-iodo-2-[3-(4-methoxy-6-methyl-1, 3, 5-triazin-2-yl)-ureidosulfoyl]benzoate, sodium salt

Mesosulfuron-methyl

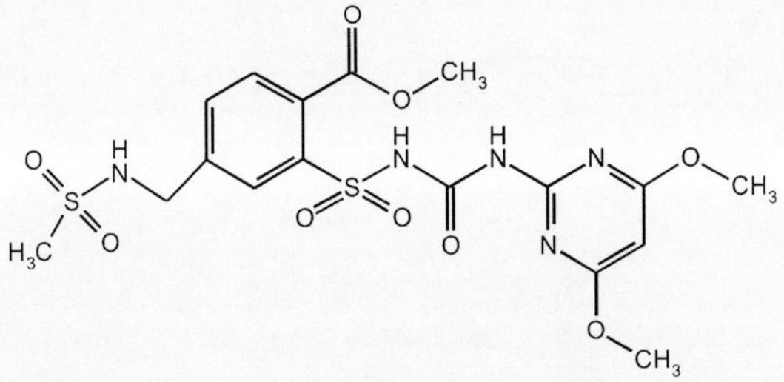

2-[[[[(4-6-dimethoxy-2-pyrimidinyl)amino]carbonyl]amino]sulfonyl]-4-[[(methylsulfonyl)amino]methyl] benzoic acid

Metamitron

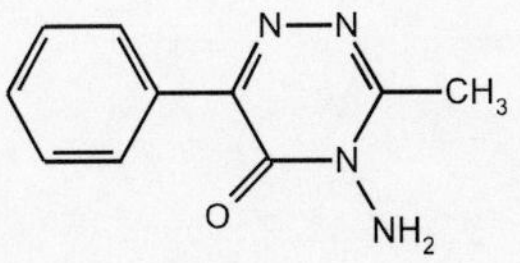

4-amino-3 methyl-6 phenyl-1, 2, 4-trazin-5 (4H)-one

Metsulfuron-methyl

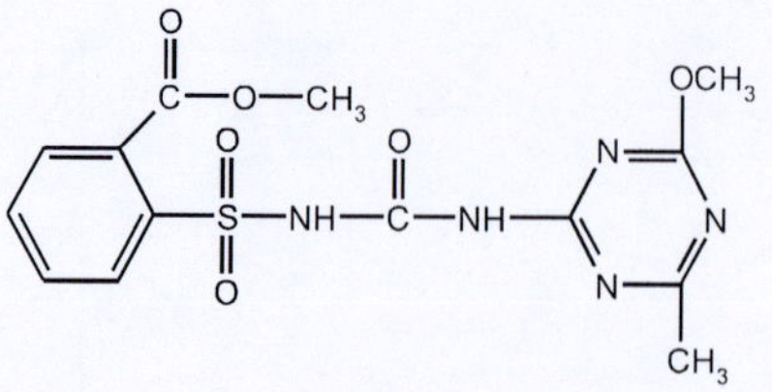

2-[[[[(4-methoxy-6-methyl-1,3,5-triazin-2-yl)amino]carbonyl]amino]sulfonyl] benzoic acid

Oxadiargyl

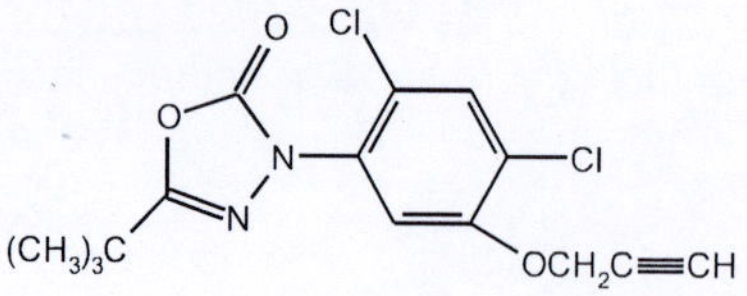

3-[2,4-dichloro-5-(2-propynyloxy)phenyl]-5-(1,1-dimethylethyl)-1,3,4-oxadiazol-2(3H)-one

Quinclorac

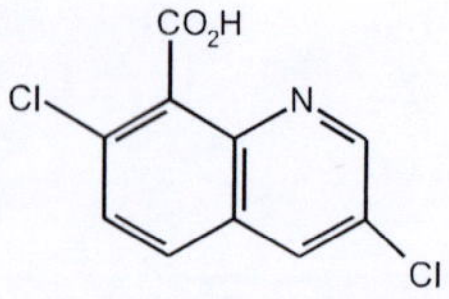

3, 7-dichloroquinoline-8-carboylic acid

Quizalofop-P-ethyl

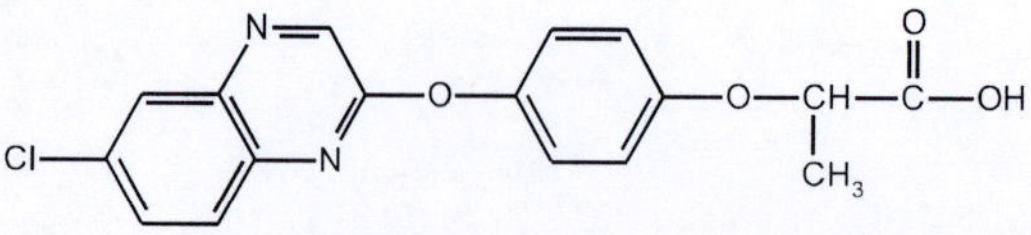

Ethyl(R)-2-[4-(6-chloroquinoxalin-2-yloxy)phenoxy] propionate

Sulfosulfuron

N-[[(4, 6-dimethoxy-2-pyrimidinyl)amino]carbonyl]-2-(ethylsulfonyl)imidazo [1, 2-a]pyridine-3-sulfonamide

Thiazopyr

methyl-2-(difluoromethyl-5-(4,5-dihydro-2-thiazolyl)-4-(2-methylpropyl)-6-(trifluoromethyl)-3-pyridinecarboxylate

Thiobencarb

S-4-chlorobenzyl diethyl(thiocarbamate)

Triasulfuron

2-(2-chloroethyxy)-N-(((4-methoxy-6-methyl-1, 3, 5-triazin-2-yl)amino) carbonyl)benzenesulfonamide

Triclopyr

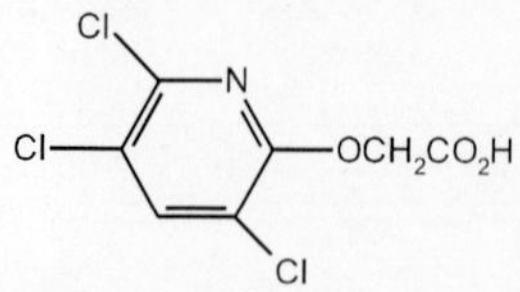

Cl, N, Cl, OCH$_2$CO$_2$H, Cl

[(3, 5, 6-trichloro-2-pyridinyl)oxy] acetic acid

Trifloxysulfuron

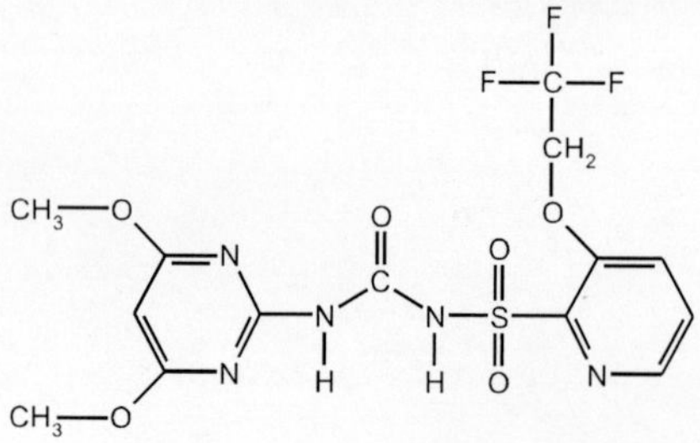

F, F—C—F, CH$_2$, O, CH$_3$—O, N, O, C, N, N, H, N, S, O, O, H, N, CH$_3$—O

1-(4, 6-dimethoxypyrimidin-2-yl)-3-[3-(2, 2, 2-trifluoroehoxy)-2-pyridylsulfonyl]urea

Imazamox

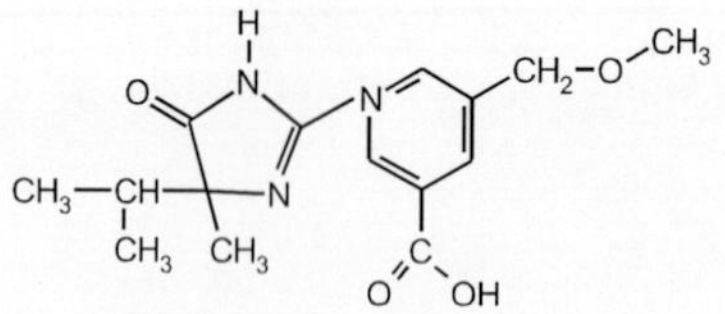

H, N, O, N, CH$_2$–O–CH$_3$, CH$_3$—CH—N, CH$_3$, CH$_3$, C, O, OH

2-[4,5-dihydro-4-methyl-4-(1-methylethyl)-5-oxo-1H-imidazol-2-yl]-5-(methoxymethyl)-3-pyridinecarboxylic acid

Flufenacet

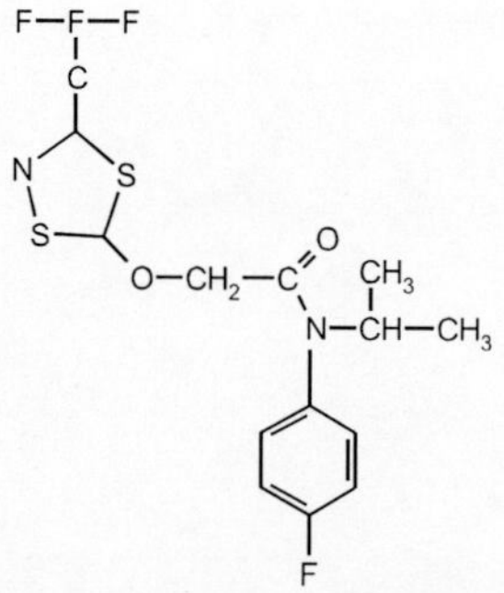

F—F—F, C, N, S, S, O–CH$_2$—C, O, CH$_3$, N–CH—CH$_3$, F

N-(4-fluorophenyl)-N-(1-methylethyl)-2-[[5-(trifluoromethyl)-1,3,4-thiadiazol-2-yl]oxy] acetamide

Clopyralid

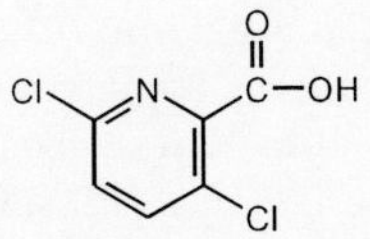

3,6-dichloro-2-pyridinecarboxylic acid

Tribenuron

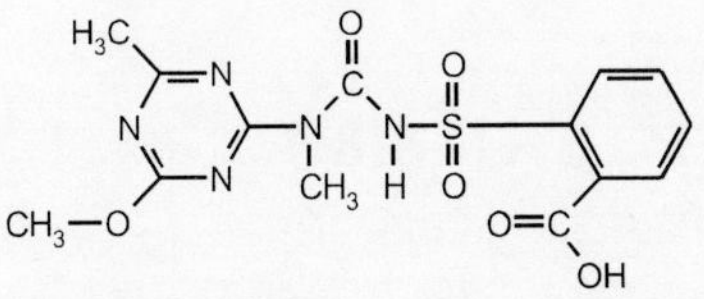

2-[[[[(4-methoxy-6-methyl-1,3,5-triazin-2-yl)methylamino]carbonyl] amino]sulfonyl] benzoic acid

Carfentrazone

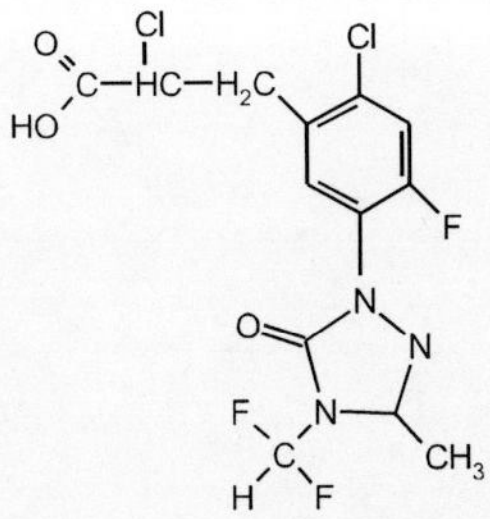

α,2-dichloro-5-[4-(difluoromethyl)-4,5-dihydro-3-methyl-5-oxo-1H-1,2,4-triazol-1-yl]-4-fluorobenzenepropanoic acid

Tralkoxydim

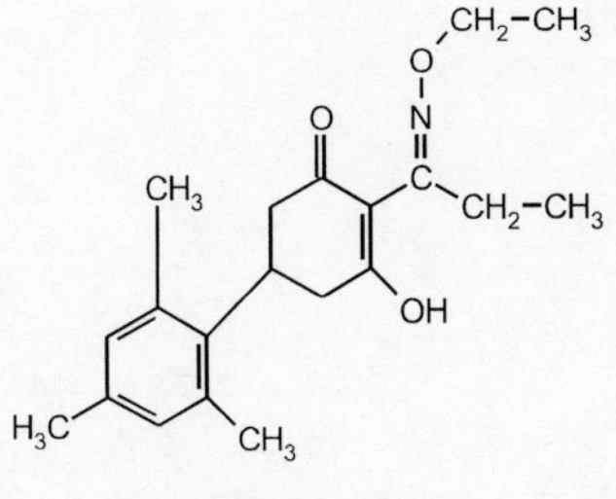

2-[1-(ehoxyimino)propyl]-3-hydroxy-5-(2,4,6-trimethylphenyl)-2-cyclohexen-1-one

SUMMARY

Any approved herbicide is known by three kinds of names, *viz.*, (1) the chemical name, (2) the common name, and (2) the trade name. Also, it is represented by its molecular structure. Many herbicide molecules have some common structural features that enable the scientists to put them together into typical classes for ease of understanding their common behaviour in plants and soils. Over 200 herbicides have been classified in this manner into 25 classes in this chapter. Molecular structure of at least one representative of each class has been provided. Some basic molecules and terms used in describing the chemical structures of herbicides are given in the Appendix-17. An exhaustive listing of herbicides appeared in Weed Science volumes 43 (1995) and 50 (2002). Also, more recent herbicides and their chemical names are available in individual issues of Weed Science, Weed Abstracts, *etc.*

SELECTED BIBLIOGRAPHY

1. Ardend, W. *et. al.*1989. Pesticides: Composition, Use and Hazards. Agromisa, 113 p.
2. Hepworth, H. H. and Fine, R. R. 1971. Herbicide Use And Nomenclature Index. Int. Plant Protection Centre, Oregon State, State University, USA, 185 p.
3. Shree Ramulu, U.S. 1982. Chemistry of Herbicides. Oxford IBH Pub. Co., New Delhi, 120 p.
4. Anon., 2002. Common and chemical names of herbicides approved by the Weed Science Society of America. Weed Sci. 50: 824-829.

Chapter 13

THE FUNCTIONAL FEATURES OF COMMON HERBICIDES

A herbicide can be used more effectively and in a safer way if its major properties were known to its users, over and above its available field recommendations.

13.1 PHENOLS

DNBP: Dinoseb is recommended for weeding pea, groundnut, soybean, besides strawberry, certain forages, and woody ornamentals. Its common rates are 6 to 20 kg/ha for the preemergence treatment and 1 to 3 kg/ha for the postemergence treatment. The herbicide proves most selective to the treated crops when the air temperature is below 25°C and the weather is dry and sunny. At higher temperature, it may seriously injure the treated crops. Applied in aromatic oils, it acts as a potent non-selective weed killer.

DNBP is highly toxic to mammals. It irritates eyes and nose, and can stain skin, hair, and clothes, almost permanently to an orange-yellow colour. It leaches rapidly in soil. Its persistence is 2 to 4 weeks.

13.2 PHENOXYALKANOIC ACIDS

Phenoxy herbicides form 48 per cent of all herbicides used in the world. 2,4-D and MCPA are the oldest and yet the most common representatives of this group of herbicides.

In general, the phenoxyalkanoic acid herbicides are translocated, foliage active compounds although some of these may be active also through the roots. Their foliar application damages chiefly the broadleaf plants and some sedges. Grasses are relatively tolerant to these herbicides. In broadleaf plants they induce rapid epinastic effects by causing differential growth rates of their internal tissues. The treated plants may remain malformed for days together without browning off but the affected plants stop new growth within hours. Nutsedge shoots are affected without showing any epinasty since their leaves possess limited internal tissues to respond differentially to the phenoxys.

2, 4-D: 2, 4-D is an excellent, selective, postemergence herbicide for the control of herbaceous, dicot weeds and nutsedge shoots in *small grains*, sugarcane, grasslands, lawns, and roadsides. When used as a preemergence herbicide, it will also control many grasses from seeds for a couple of weeks.

Certain dicot crops such as cotton, tobacco, tomato, and chickpea (gram) are extremely sensitive to 2,4-D. On non-cropland 2,4-D is an important component herbicide for general vegetation control. It is also used in waterbodies, particularly for the control of *Eichhornia crassipes* 'waterhyacinth'.

2,4-D *per se* is not easily soluble in water. However, its sodium and amine salts and esters are water soluble. These formulations differ considerably in their foliar activity. Usually, to obtain equal phytotoxicity on the susceptible plants, the rates of esters, amine salts, and sodium salt of 2,4-D are in the ratio of 1: 1.5 : 2. The ester formulations of 2,4-D stunt weeds within hours of their application. The higher potency of esters, in comparison to salts of 2,4-D, is due to their low polarity which facilitates herbicide absorption by the plant leaves. It also reduces chances of their washing down by rain falling within few hours after the treatment. But the esters are usually costlier than the salts. Besides, the short chain esters of 2,4-D are volatile, which may cause vapour drift hazards to the nearby, non-target crops. The long chain esters of 2,4-D, however, are low volatile compounds.

Applied to soil, plant roots absorb salts of 2,4-D more readily than its esters. It is so because plant roots have no cuticle on them. But the ester formulations of 2,4-D resist leaching in soil and thus prove safer to the crops as preemergence herbicides than the salts of 2,4-D which easily leach under the influence of rain or irrigation. Hence, in light and medium textured soils, preemergence application of esters of 2,4-D is often recommended. The selective rates of 2,4-D are 0.5 to 2.0 kg/ha, depending upon the formulation used and the weed flora. In non-crop areas up to 4 kg/ha of 2,4-D is used. At selective rates, its persistence in soils is 2 to 4 weeks. 2,4-D is made available also in granular form, besides its conventional wettable powder and liquid forms.

MCPA: MCPA is very similar to 2,4-D in its action but certain crops like *rice* and *oat* are relatively more tolerant to it than 2,4-D. Likewise, it is also more effective on weeds like *Cyperus rotundus* 'nutsedge' and *Ranunculus repens* 'buttercup' than 2,4-D.

Mecoprop and dichlorprop: Mecoprop and dichlorprop are similar in action to MCPA and 2,4-D but these are more potent on some difficult dicot weeds, such as *Plantago* spp. 'plantains', *Polygonum aviculare* 'knotweed' and *Glechoma hederacea* 'ground ivy'. These compounds are particularly useful in *lawns* and *turfs*. Its recommended rates are 1.5-2.0 kg/ha.

2,4-DB: 2,4-DB *per se* is only slightly phytotoxic but many non-legume, dicot plants apparently convert it into 2,4-D by its enzymic β-oxidation (see Chapter 16), which proves phytotoxic. Contrary to this, certain leguminous plants do not metabolise 2,4-DB into 2,4-D in phytotoxic quantities. Therefore, such plants escape 2,4-DB injury. *Lucerne*, certain clovers, and pea are some such plants with proven tolerance to 2,4-DB. Linseed, though not a legume, is also found tolerant to 2,4-DB at its common application rates of 0.5 to 2.0 kg/ha.

MCPB: MCPB is similar in its action and uses to 2,4-DB, but it is often more selective to clovers and pea than 2,4-DB. Also, MCPB is found more effective on *Cirsium arvense* than 2,4-DB.

Diclofop: Diclofop is marketed as its methyl salt. It forms primarily a late stage *wildoat* herbicide in wheat and barley at their fully tillered stage. Also, it is registered for annual grass control in soybean.

13.3 PHENYLALKANOIC ACIDS

Fenac: Fenac is largely used as a soil sterilant against hard-to-kill brondleaf weeds on *non-crop lands* and for draw-down treatment of lake margins at rates of 10 to 20 kg/ha. The herbicide has proved very effective against *Tribullus terrestris* 'puncturvine'. On crop land fenac at 2 kg/ha has been used in sugarcane and maize particularly against *Striga* spp. but in general, the long persistence of this herbicide greatly limits its practical use in crop fields.

Fenac resists leaching as well as its degradation in soils.

13.4 CHLOROBENZOIC AND ANISIC ACIDS

Herbicides belonging to this group of compounds produce many morphogenic responses similar to 2,4-D (or MCPA). But the benzoic and anisic acid herbicides are more potent than it.

Acifluorfen: Acifluorfen controls a number of weeds selectively in *soybean, peanut,* and rice when applied as over-the-top postemergence treatment.

Dicamba: Dicamba is a highly root and shoot mobile herbicide. It proves superior to 2,4-D in the control of young growth of certain difficult broadleaf weeds such as *Centaurea repens* 'Russian knapweed', *Cirsium arvense, Convolvulus arvensis* and certain brush species. Its postemergence application is selective at 0.06 to 0.2 kg/ha to maize, sorghum, *wheat, barley,* linseed and common turf grown on heavy soils. Sometimes it is applied mixed with 2,4-D and MCPA. Preemergence application of dicamba at 0.5 to 3.0 kg/ha will control many annual weeds. On non-cropland, dicamba is applied as foliage spray at 0.5 to 1.0 kg/ha to control many perennial broadleaf and brush species.

13.5 PHTHALIC AND PHTHALMIC ACIDS

Endothall: Endothall is largely a contact herbicide but, it is selective to sugarbeet, onion, soybean, potato, cole crops, groundnut, and carrot. Endothall is also used as a turf and aquatic herbicide, particularly in the fishery waters. In mixture with AMS, it forms a good non-crop land weed killer. Endothall persists in soils for 8 to 10 weeks.

DCPA: DCPA is useful as a preemergence, contact herbicide for the control of annual grasses and certain broadleaf weeds in cotton, fieldbean, mungbean, potato, maize, wheat, upland rice, soybean, transplanted tomato, onion, turf, and ornamentals. A special use of DCPA is for the control of *Cuscuta* sp. 'dodder' in *lucerne*. It resists leaching in soil. Its persistence in soils is 10 to 14 weeks, and its common rates are 4.5 to 12 kg/ha.

Naptalam (NPA): Naptalam (2-6 kg/ha) is a preemergence herbicide against a wide range of annual weeds. On medium to heavy texture soils, it has proved selective to *cucurbits, asparagus*, soybean, groundnut, castorbean, irrigated cotton, established woody ornamental nursery stock, and turf. Granular formulations of naptalam are also used for the control of weeds in established sweet potato and Irish potato.

Combined with dinoseb as 'dyanap', naptalam forms a very good preemergence and 'cracking stage' herbicide in groundnut and soybean. In soybean, the mixture can be used even as over-the-top spray at its second trifoliate leaf stage. Dyanap is an eye irritant, and poisonous to humans. Naptalam is also combined with other herbicides such as alachlor, oryzalin and bensulide for dealing with specific crop-weed situations. It is easily leached in soils. Its persistence in soils is 3 to 8 weeks.

13.6 ALIPHATIC ACIDS

Dalapon: Dalapon is active on plant shoots. It finds its maximum use against young grasses in *jute, coffee*, citrus, deciduous fruits, some stone fruits, and under grapevines. On non-crop land, combined with 2,4-D, dalapon (10-20kg/ha) forms a very good general weed killer. Split application of dalapon has often proved more effective on perennial grasses and cattails than its one time application. Its persistence in soils is 2 to 4 weeks. In plants, dalapon molecules are comparatively stable.

13.7 TRIAZINES

Triazine herbicides in use today are largely symmetrical species although a couple of these are also asymetrical compounds. Among the *s-triazines*, there are three types viz., the chloro, methoxy, and methylthio triazines. The chloro-*s*-triazines are primarily root active, whereas the methoxy and methylthio-*s*-triazines are active through both roots and shoots. Also, the chloro and methylthio-*s*-triazines form largely selective herbicides while the methoxy-*s*-triazines are non-selective herbicides. Long persistence and rapid leachability of the methoxy compounds make them particularly important in the control of deep rooted noxious weeds.

Simazine: Simazine is a preemergence herbicide developed basically for use in *maize, apple*, sugarcane, and sorghum. These crop plants detoxify simazine rapidly. Simazine is now also used in *pineapple*, rosery, tea, *coffee*, established lucerne, asparagus, artichoke, grasslands, turf, citrus, deciduous fruits, nuts, and olive. Common selective rates are 1 to 2 kg/ha, although maize and apple will tolerate up of 6 kg/ha of simazine. At high rates, simazine residues in soils can injure the susceptible rotation crops. Also, on sandy, high pH soil of dry areas, simazine can injure even a normally tolerant crop like maize. On non-crop lands, at 1 to 40 kg/ha simazine forms a temporary soil sterilant. Simazine is also a potent *algaecide* which is safe to fish.

Atrazine: Atrazine differs from simazine in possessing also some contact action on shoots of juvenile weeds. Its shoot activity can be further enhanced by including a phytobland oil in the spray when even established annual weeds can be severely damaged. Atrazine is more water soluble than simazine (atrazine, 33 ppm; simazine, 5 ppm), which provides it an edge over the latter in dry areas. For this reason atrazine will leach more in soils; up to 30 cm or so. Lastly, *Panicum dichotomiflorum* 'fall panicum' is found tolerant to atrazine while it succumbs to simazine. This is probably true of all grasses belonging to the sub-family Panicoideae.

Atrazine is used in almost the same crops as simazine but it is usually avoided in coffee and tea plantations where its shoot activity may injure the bush leaves. For the same reason atrazine is preferred over simazine as a component herbicide in no-till planting of *maize*.

Propazine: Propazine (0.25-20 kg ha) is evry similar to simazine in its action on weeds but it is particularly selective to *sorghum* and other millets, carrots, celery, and grapevines In vineyards, up to 10 kg/ha of propazine can be used to control perennial weeds, without damage to the vines. Propazine resists leaching in soils and persists there for 12 to 18 months. This hinders its use in the double cropping agricultural systems.

Prometon: Prometon is a *non-selective* weed killer, active through both roots and shoots. Its common rates are 1.1 to 6.6 kg/ha. This herbicide is more leachable and persistent in soils than simazine and atrazine. Traces of prometon have been found in soils several years after its application.

Desmetryn: Desmetryn is absorbed and translocated both by roots and shoots. Its major use in agriculture is in pre-and post-emergence broadleaf weed control in *Brassica* crops. Postemergent desmetryn is applied at 3 to 4 leaf stage of the crop. Its recommended rates are 0.35 to 0.5 kg/ha and the persistence in soils is 5 to 10 weeks.

Ametryn: Ametryn is absorbed through both foliage and roots but it is translocated only acropetally in xylem. It forms an effective, directed postemergence herbicide against young weeds in *pineapple*, sugarcane, banana, coffee, citrus, and ornamentals. It is also promising as preemergence herbicide in groundnut and tea. Its common rates are 0.5 to 4.0 kg/ha, and the persistence is short.

Terbutryn: Terbutryn forms both a preemergence and postemergence herbicide, mainly for the control of annual grasses and difficult broadleafs in *wheat*. Recommended rates are around 1 kg/ha. Preemergent terbutryn is also found selective to *sunflower*, pea, blackgram, and potato. Its persistence in soils is 3 to 10 weeks.

Prometryn: The primary utility of prometryn as herbicide is in postemergence control of young weeds in *carrots*, celery, leek, and wheat. Its usual rates are 0.5-0.7 kg/ha.

Prometryn is also promising as preemergence and directed postemergence herbicide in cotton and maize. At high rates, it provides a good, short term, industrial weed control. Its persistence in soils is 1-3 months, and leaching is low.

Hexazinone: A systemic herbicide, developed primarily for weed control in plantation corps, including *sugarcane*. Sugarcane is tolerant to hexazinone up to its 5 leaf stage at 0.2 to 0.9 kg/ha. In *non-crop areas*, hexazinone at 2 to 8 kg/ha will control perennial grasses and brushes. Also, it provides residual control of *Parthenium* spp. at 1 kg/ha.

Metribuzin: Metribuzin is both a root and shoot mobile herbicide, with prolonged soil residual activity of 6-12 weeks. Its main importance lies in the postemergence control of young, annual grasses in *tomato, potato*, sugarcane, carrot, asparagus, soybean, and lucerne. Its selective rates are 0.75 to 3.0 kg/ha.

13.8 TRIAZOLES

Amitrole: Amitrole is a highly shoot mobile herbicide. It is easily translocated to deep-seated rhizomes of many perennial weeds to injure their axillary buds. Amitrole is largely employed to control perennial weeds like *Cirsium arvense, Cynodon dactylon, Agropyron repens,* and *Rhus* spp. *Cyperus rotundus* has proven susceptible to a mixture of amitrole and atrazine. Combination of amitrole and dalapon are used against *cattails.* Amitrole can be fortified with ammonium thiocyanate and phytobland oils. Amitrole is a very short peresistence herbicide (about 2 weeks). It is, therefore, used in no tillage planting systems and in established orchards and ornamentals against perennial weeds. Its common spray concentration is 0.2 to 1.0 per cent.

13.9 DIAZOLES

Difenzoquat: Difenzoquat is a foliage contact herbicide. Its speciality lies in its capacity to control wildoat (*Avena fatua*) up to its initial tillering stage in wheat and barley. Its common rates are 0.8- 1.2 kg/ha. Split application of difenzoquat will accomodate control of two flushes of wildoat.

Methazole: Methazole is primarily a *cotton* herbicide where its preemergence application, followed by one directed postemergence treatment, can provide season-long weed control. Its common rates are 1.5 to 3.5 kg/ha. Postemergent methazole (up to 2 kg/ha) can be combined with MSMA to broaden the weed control spectrum. Its peresistence in soils is 60 days or less.

13.10 DIAZINES

Pyrazon: Pyrazon is a root translocated and shoot contact herbicide. Its major use is in the control of annual broadleaf weeds in *sugarbeet* and *redbeet.* To achieve simultaneous control of grasses, it can be combined with diallate. In addition to beets, pyrazon can be tried in pea, potato, sunflower, sorghum, and wheat. It is sometimes mixed with chlorbufan for weed control in onion, leek, tulip, and gladioli. Its common rates are 2.5 to 4.0 kg/ha and persistence in soils is 4 to 8 weeks.

Bentazon: Bentazon is a selective herbicide for postemergence control of difficult, broadleaf weeds in *rice, wheat,* vegetables, pea, groundnut, soybean, maize, sorghum, and flax. Rice is most tolerant to it. The recommended rates are 1 to 2 kg/ha. Bentazon leaves no residual toxicity in soils. It is miscible with common phenoxy herbicides for use in cereals and millets.

Dazomet: (See Chapter 23).

13.11 PYRIDINES

Picloram: Picloram is a highly root and shoot translocated herbicide. It is extremely active on perennial dicot weeds; about 100 times more so than 2,4-D. At rates of 0.02 to 0.03 kg/ ha, picloram is used for postemergence control of broadleaf weeds in sugarcane, cruciferous crops, small grains, grasslands, and turfs. At 1 to 3 kg/ha, picloram will control *Cirsium arvense* and *Convolvulus arvensis* on non-crop lands. At still higher rates, it forms a persistent *brush killer*. Picloram is sold as its K salt in the form of pellets for use in grasslands and non-crop areas, and as emulsifiable concentrate for use in crop fields.

13.12 QUATERNARY AMMONIUM COMPOUNDS

Diquat and Paraquat: Diquat and paraquat are cationic herbicides with zero persistence in soils. They desiccate green portions of the plants, quickly. Therefore, these form the basic herbicides in preplanting destruction of vegetation in any no-till planting system of crops. Also, these are used for (i) early postemergence application in *potato*, sugarcane, and sugarbeet; (ii) weed control in *dormant lucerne*, peppermint, and grasslands; and (iii) directed application around deciduous fruit trees, tea, coffee, forest trees. Paraquat and diquat can be combined with diuron to obtain simultaneous residual weed control in many orchards and established plantations. The two herbicides are sold as liquid concentrates containing cationic wetting agents and corrosion inhibitors since their technical grades badly corrode the metal sprayers. These herbicides are highly poisonous to humans, and irritate skin and eyes, severely.

Diquat and paraquat also form good aquatic herbicides. But where fish are important, only specific formulations devoid of any wetting agent should be employed. Gramoxone-S is one such formulation of paraquat. Diquat and paraquat are not decomposed inside plants. Therefore, the treated vegetation should not be fed to animals. However, the portion of the herbicides lying unabsorbed on leaf surfaces undergo rapid photo decomposition. The same is true for their presence in water exposed to sun.

Roberts *et al.* (2005) reported that in soils parquat was subjected to biodegradation in water present inside the soil pores and that it played an important role in its field dissipation.

13.13 URACILS

In general, uracils are soil active, translocated herbicides. They are phytotoxic at very low concentrations. Both annual and perennial weeds can be controlled with uracils by adjusting their doses. Their persistence in soils is usually long.

Bromacil: Bromacil (1.5-6.5 kg/ha) finds it maximum use in the control of annual weeds in establised citrus orchards. Its repeat applications will control perennial weeds too. Also, bromacil finds its use against young weeds in *pineapple*. On non-crop lands, bromacil (5-25 kg/ha) will provide total weed kill. It achieves control of deep rooted weeds by leaching deep into the soil. Its persistence in soils is 20 to 24 weeks at selective rates, and over one year at the non-selective rates.

Terbacil: Terbacil is similar to bromacil in its weed control effects, but it is highly selective to *peppermint* (*Mentha peperita*), spearmint (M. *spicata*), and sugarcane. Also, it is used for ring weeding 3 years' or older apple, peaches and citrus *orchards*. Its persistence in soils is over a year. The common rates are up to 3.5 kg/ha against annual weeds and up to 9 kg/ha on the perennial weeds.

13.14 SUBSTITUTED UREAS

Substituted urea and triazine herbicides combined, form 14% of total herbicides consumed in the world. Most of the substituted urea herbicides are soil active compounds with limited shoot activity. At rates of 0.5 to 5 kg/ha they constitute useful selective herbicides, and at higher rates they form potent soil sterilants. The selectivity to crops is largely dependent upon rainfall, soil type, and leaching behaviour of particular herbicide. Their persistence in soils varies from four weeks to over one crop season.

Fenuron: Fenuron is a highly water soluble compound (3850 ppm), leaching easily in soils to damage the deep roots of perennial weeds and brush species in non-crop areas of moderate rainfall. On crop land, the herbicide can be used only for spot treatment of perennial weeds. Fenuron persists for long in soils.

Monuron: Monuron is less leachable in soils than fenuron. At low rates (2 to 5 kg/ha) it has been used as a preemergence herbicide in *asparagus*, mint, sugarcane, pineapple. snapbeans, spinach, citrus, avacados, and grapevine on medium to heavy soils of limited rainfall areas. Of these crops, asparagus is especially tolerant to monuron.

At high rates monuron forms a persistent soil sterilant. It should be used at least 15 metres away from any useful trees.

Diuron: Diuron is less leachable than monuron and fenuron. Its maximum use has been made as a preemergence herbicide in *cotton*. Combined with a wetting agent, it is also used for directed, postemergence weed control in this crop. Besides, diuron can be tried in same crops as listed for monuron wherever the latter compound is considered unsafe because of its leaching behaviour. Diuron is also used on water banks and for sterilising drainage channels.

Linuron: Linuron is a selective preemergence herbicide in soybean, maize, grain sorghum, carrot, and parsnips grown on medium heavy soils, under medium rainfall conditions. Its leachability in soils is the same as of diuron, and the persistence is about 12 weeks. Like diuron, the foliage action of linuron can be enhanced on young weeds by addition of a suitable surfactant.

Fluometuron: Fluometuron is an excellent preemergence herbicide in *cotton* where diuron will injure the crop. In addition to cotton, it is recommended for use in grain sorghum, sugarcane, sunflower, established coffee, rubber, sisal nurseries, raspberries, pineapple, and cherries. This herbicide has appreciable foliar activity even without a surfactant. It is sometimes used with DSMA as a directed spray to eliminate young weeds.

Fluometuron persists in soils for 8 to 20 weeks. Its common rates are 0.5 to 2.5 kg/ha.

Chloroxuron: Unlike the above substituted ureas, chloroxuron resists leaching in soils. It can be used for selective weed control in heavy rainfall areas and medium to heavy soils. Preemergence chloroxuron has proved selective to a number of vegetable crops, *eg* carrot, pea, set onion, set garlic, potato, okra, limabean, snapbean, strawberry, grain sorghum, groundnut, certain ornamentals, citrus, apple and mango. Like fluometuron, chloroxuron has considerable foliar activity; therefore it can be used for directed postemergence control of young weeds in these crops, particularly on heavy soils. Its common rates are 3 to 4 kg/ha.

Siduron: Siduron is chiefly a preemergence herbicide for treating established turfs. It is effective against annual grasses. Foxtail (*Setaria* spp.) barnyardgrass (*Echinochloa* spp.), and crabgrass (*Digitaria* spp.) are particularly susceptible to it. Its effective rates are 2-12 kg/ha.

***Norea* (=Noruron)**: At 1 to 2 kg/ha, norea is an effective preemergence herbicide against mainly annual grassses. It is selective to cotton, grain sorghum, soybean, sugarcane, and certain ornamentals. In sorghum, broadleaf weed control with norea can be improved by combining it with atrazine in heavy soils and with propazine in light soils. In cotton, norea is sometimes combined with MSMA for directed postemergence treatment.

Norea is a short persistent herbicide (2 to 4 weeks).

Methibenzuron: A very promising postemergence herbicide for the control of annual grasses in *small grains*, certain beans (*Phaseolus*, and *Vicia* spp.), pea, garlic, and onion. High susceptibility of *Phalaris*, *Lolium*, *Poa* and *Alopecurus* spp. are the chief plus points of methibenzuron. Its common rates are 1-3.5 kg/ha and the persistence in soils is 3-6 months.

Metoxuron: Metoxuron is successful in postemergence control of *Phalaris minor* and *Avena fatua* in *winter grains*. Certain cultivars of wheat, *eg* WG-357, WG-377, and WP-833 are found susceptible to it. Its common rates are 1-1.5 kg/ha.

Isoproturon: Isoproturon is a versatile herbicide for the control of annual grass weeds, particularly, canarygrass (*Phalaris minor*) and wildoat (*Avena fatua*), in *wheat* and *barley* fields. Besides, it will also control some broadleaf weeds like *Anagallis*, *Melilotus*, *Convolvulus*. and *Chenopodium* spp. It is active on the susceptible weeds, both as preemergence and postemergence treatments, though, in India its maximum use has been made in the latter form. It is very commonly applied as spray treatment, 30-35 days after sowing winter grains; soon after the first irrigation of the crop. The annual grasses at this stage are young and susceptible to isoproturon. Its effective rates are 0.75-1.0 kg/ha on medium soils and up to 1.5 kg/ha on the heavy ones. Isoproturon can be combined with 2,4-D to imrove broadleaf weed control, if required. (In USA, isoproturon is not recommended anymore for use on feed and food crops).

13.15 CARBANILATES AND CARBAMATES

Propham (IPC) and Chlorpropham (CIPC): IPC and CIPC are soil incorporated herbicides although they also possess some foliage activity on many young weed seedlings. These herbicides are primarily used to control *Avena fatua* in pea, *Cuscuta* sp. in *lucerne*, and seedling grasses in established lawns and grasslands. CIPC has also been used for the control of annual grasses in lettuce, okra, pumpkin, limabean, snapbean, onion, carrot, garlic, spinach, safflower, maize, cotton, and soybean. Effective rates are 4.5 to 9 kg/ha for IPC and 2 to 7 kg/ha for CIPC. Its selectivity to the crops is largely positional.

CIPC is retained in top 2.5 cm of soil, but IPC leaches deeper. Also, during the summer months CIPC is more persistent (3 to 8 weeks) than IPC (2 to 4 weeks) in soils.

Barban: Barban was the first postemergence herbicide discovered for the control of *Avena fatua* seedlings in wheat, barley, sugarbeet, and certain oil and pulse crops. Besides wildoat, barban kills *Phalaris arundinacea*, and certain difficult broadleaf weeds. Common rates of the herbicide are 0.28 to 1.12 kg/ha which must be applied as low volume spray.

Karbutilate: Karbutilate is a non-crop land herbicide. Its effective rates against the herbaceous and woody species are 2-20 kg/ha; the lower ones being for the former and the higher ones for the latter weeds.

EPTC: EPTC is a preplant incorporated herbicide. It controls many annual grasses and some broadleaf weeds, *eg Chenopodium*, *Portulaca*, *Amaranthus*, and *Ipomoea* spp. It also inhibits *Cyperus roundus* tubers.

EPTC is recommended for weed control in *potato*, maize, some beans, lucerne, *Egyptian clover*, certain nursery stock ornamentals, sunflower, and safflower. EPTC + 2,4-D granules have been formulated for broad spectrum weed control in transplanted rice. EPTC is a very volatile herbicide, particularly so on moist soils. It must be incorporated into the soil immediately after its application, about 5 to 7.5 cm deep. Its common rates are 2 to 4 kg/ha and the persistence is 4 to 6 weeks in moist soils and 12 to 16 weeks in dry soils.

Vernolate: Vernolate is very similar to EPTC in its action on weeds. It has been found selective to groundnut. In some soils it can also be used in sweet potato. Its common rates are 2.3 to 4.6 kg/ha.

Pebulate (PEBC): Pebulate is recommended for preplant control of annual grasses in transplanted *tobacco* and *tomato*. It has also shown adequate selectivity to sugarbeet and redbeet. Its common rates are 3.5 to 6 kg/ha.

Cycloate and Butylate: While cycloate is most selective to *sugarbeet* and *spinach*, butylate is so to maize. The effective rates of the two herbicides are 3 to 4 kg and 2.5 to 3.5 kg/ha, respectively.

Diallate and Triallate: Diallate and triallate were developed as soil incorporated herbicides for the control of *Avena fatua* in linseed, small grain (particularly barley), lentil, pea, potato, safflower, and certain forage legumes. Common rates of these two herbicides are 1.7 to 4.5 and 1.12 to 2.24 kg/ha, respectively. The persistence in soils is 4 to 6 weeks.

Phenmedipham: Phenmedipham combines two carbanilate radicals in one molecule. As a postemergence herbicide it marks an extraordinary selectivity between broadleaf weeds and *sugarbeet*.

Thiobencarb: This herbicide possesses high degree of inter-generic selectivity between *rice* and grass weeds like barnyardgrass (*Echinochloa colonum* and *E. crusgalli*). Germinating weeds, in no more than 1-leaf stage, are most susceptible to the herbicide. Its most common time of application is within 4 days after transplanting paddy. The effective rates are around 1.5 kg/ha. Although of little mobility in soils, yet thiobencarb should be avoided on very low clay and organic content soils since rice crop may be injured on such soils.

13.16 AMIDES AND ANILIDES

Amides and anilides are largely soil active herbicides, although the latter also exhibits shoot activity against annual grasses and a few broadleaf weeds, belonging to the families Chenopodiaceae and Asteraceae. The amides are readily leached in light soils under the influence of rainfall, so they are used only on medium to heavy textured soils. Anilides, on the contrary, resist leaching and so they are preferred on light soils.

Diphenamid: Diphenamid forms primarily a preemergence herbicide in vegetable crops, particularly in tomato, pepper, okra, potato, and sweet potato. In addition, it is used in groundnut, tobacco, strawberries, soybean, cotton, woody ornamentals, *Dichondra* lawns, citrus, apple, and peach. Its common rates are 4 to 6 kg/ha and persistence in soils is 12 to 24 weeks. Diphenamid leaches rapidly in sandy soils where its split application is advisable.

Napropamide: Napropamide brings about a long lasting, selective control of annual weeds in fruits, almond, grape, and tomato. It resists leaching in soils. Effective rates for trial are 1 to 2 kg/ha.

CDAA: CDAA is suitable for preemergence control of annual grasses in maize, sorghum soybean, limabean, snapbean, *transplanted tomato*, sugarcane, cabbage, sweet potato, canning pea, onion, celery, and some ornamentals grown on heavy clay and organic matter rich soils. In maize it has given sometimes better results with trichlorobenzyl chloride (TCBC). Common rates are 4 to 5 kg/ha. CDAA leaches readily in sandy soils which may injure the treated crops. In dry soils the rotation crops may be injured because of long persistence of CDAA, although from moist soils it is lost by volatilisation. CDAA is very irritating to the skin and eyes.

Oryzalin: Oryzalin is both a soil and shoot active herbicide. Its chief use lies in its through-the-water treatment of flooded rice. It is sometimes applied with MCPA to achieve simultaneous control of certain broadleaf weeds. Oryzalin resists leaching in soils. Rates for trial are 0.3 to 1 kg/ha.

In wheat it can be tried as a preemergence herbicide to control annual grasses, including *P. minora*.

Bensulide: Bensulide is very useful for *Digitaria* spp. control in *lawns*. It is applied before weed emergence at rates of 10 to 20 kg/ha. One drawback of bensulide is its long persistence. This hinders replanting of recovered patches in lawns with some desired grass species.

In addition to lawns, bensulide is promising in a number of vegetable crops and cotton.

Propanil: Propanil is a foliage contact herbicide, discovered primarily for the control of *Echinochloa* spp. in rice. Rice plants are very tolerant to this herbicide up to dose of 6 kg/ha, although effective weed control is often achieved with half this rate. The herbicide is also promising in strawberry, small grains, linseed, onion, and cucumber.

Alachlor: Alachlor is a soil active herbicide, recommended primarily for the control of grasses and sedges from seeds, besides some broadleaf weeds. *Soybean* and maize are particularly tolerant to it. In India its maximum use has been made in the former crop. Besides, certain other oil seed crops, pulse crops, and vegetables (*eg* potato and cole crops) have also shown acceptable selectivity to alachlor. Its recommended rates are 1-2 kg/ha. The weed control may last for 4-6 weeks.

Alachlor resists leaching in soils, therefore, it may not be as effective on very heavy soils as on the medium texture soils. It is irritant to skin, eyes, and nose.

Butachlor: Butachlor is a prominent herbicide for weed control in *transplanted rice*, which possesses physiological selectivity to it. Applied within 4 days of transplanting, it will control a variety of weeds from seeds, particularly barnyardgrass (*Echinochloa colonum* and *E. crusgalil*). Butachlor resists leaching in soils and tends to reside in the top 1-2 cm of soil. The effective rates are 1-2.5 kg/ha; being higher in soils with higher clay and organic content. Weed control usually lasts for 4-6 weeks. In upland rice it can be used as a preemergence herbicide.

Butachlor is a mild skin irritant.

Metolachlor: Metolachlor is primarily a preemergence herbicide, but it is also sometimes applied for preplant soil for treatment. It has been recommended for the control of variety of annual grasses as well as *Cyperus esculentus* in crops like *maize, soybean*, groundnut, sunflower, and sugarbeet. It can be tank-mixed with atrazine to obtain simultaneous control of broadleaf weeds in maize.

Metolachlor is a short persistent herbicide.

Propachlor: Propachlor is very similar in its properties and uses to alachlor but it leaches more readily and, within limits, gives better weed control on adsorptive soils where alachlor will often fail. Its persistence in soils is 4 to 6 weeks. Propachlor has been largely used in *maize*, grain sorghum, and seed crops of soybean.

13.17 ANILINES AND TOLUIDINES

Anilines and toluidines are largely preplant herbicides with high efficacy for controlling annual grasses. These compounds have been most frequently used in cotton in several advanced countries with the hope to obtain full season freedom from weeds. Trifluralin and nitralin were the initial herbicides to gain prominence in this respect. Later, several new herbicides with variable selectivities and weed control spectrum were developed, *eg* benefin, fluchloralin, pendimethalin, and ethafluralin.

The anilines and toluidines are by and large susceptible to photodecomposition, therefore, these are preferred to be incorporated into the soil instead of leaving them on the soil surfaces.

Fluchloralin: Fluchloralin is primarily a preplant, soil incorporated herbicide but it is also sometimes used for its preemergence application. It has been found selective to a large number of crops, particularly groundnut, cumin, cotton, soybean, sunflower, certain pulses, and beans, vegetables, jute, and transplanted rice. A variety of mixed growth of annual weeds succumb to it for about four weeks. The effective rates are 1-2 kg/ha.

Fluchloralin formulations are of low mammalian toxicity. In soils, these are subjected to microbial decomposition within 4-6 weeks.

Ethafluralin: Ethafluralin is specifically recommended for weeding cotton and soybean grown on low organic matter soils.

Trifluralin and benefin: The two herbicides are found useful in cotton, soybean, some other beans, safflower, groundnut, pea, cucurbits, tomato, bellpepper, transplanted coles, citrus orchards, and certain ornamentals. Their common rates are 0. 5-1.5 kg/ha.

Pendimethalin: It is a contact herbicide, found effective against a variety of grasses and broadleaf weeds from seeds. *Cotton*, soybean, *groundnut*, pea, certain transplanted vegetables, and *sunflower* have shown physiological selectivity to it. In these crops, therefore, pendimethalin can be applied as PPI[1] treatment. But in other crops like rice, maize, wheat, rapeseed, seeded onion, carrots, cumin, and fenugreek where pendimethalin has exhibited only positional selectivity, it should be applied as a preemergence treatment. Further, in cumin and seeded onion pendimethalin has been successfully applied as *herbigation* treatment. Likewise, in cotton its directed *lay-by application* on initially cleaned soil, 30-45 days after sowing has proved very effective in withholding *Trianthema* spp. and some other weeds. The effective rates of pendimethalin are 1-2 kg/ha, depending upon the soil. It may persist in soils for up to 12 weeks. It is a skin and eye irritant and is toxic to fish. Pendimethalin is inflamable.

Dinitramine: Dinitramine is a selective, preplant herbicide recommended for the control of annual weeds in cotton and soybean. It has also been used successfully in groundnut, sunflower, transplanted rice, tobacco, and tomato. The normal rates of dinitramine are 0.4-0.8 kg/ha.

13.18 BENZONITRILES

Bromoxynil: Bromoxynil is a shoot active, contact herbicide. Its chief utility is in the postemerence control of certain difficult broadleaf weeds in small grains, linseed, grasslands and turfs. It also holds promise in sugarcane, sorghum, pea, lucerne, onion and leek. Common rates of the herbicide are 0.2 to 0.4 kg/ha.

With the development of transgenic Herbicide Resistant (HR) crops in the USA and Canada, bromoxynil also finds its use as a selective herbicide in particularly HR cotton (Chapter – 16).

Ioxynil: Ioxynil is similar to bromoxynil in its properties and uses though there may be some weed species susceptibility differences between the two compounds. Often bromoxynil is combined with ioxynil and 2,4-D for broadleaf weed control in small grains.

Dichlobenil: Dichlobenil is a powerful germination inhibitor of seeds, rhizomes, and tubers. On crop lands its preemergence application has been found selective to established *lucerne*, many orchards, nurseries, ornamentals, shelterbelts, trees, and transplanted rice. Its selective rates are 0.75 to 3.0 kg/ha in field crops, 4.5 to 6 kg/ha in orchard and other trees, and 5.5 to 17 kg/ ha in aquatics. At 10 to 30 kg/ha, dichlobenil is a good non-selective weed killer. Dichlobenil is very volatile; it should not be used in

---

[1] PPI = preplant soil incorporation

warm areas. Its leaching in soil is extremely slow, and persistence is 8 to 24 weeks. (Dichlobenil can also be employed to prevent potato sprouts in storage).

Cyanazine: Cyanazine is a short persistence herbicide for preemergence weed control in maize and potato, and as postemergence herbicide in wheat and peas. It persists in soils for 5 to 7 weeks only.

13.19 ETHER COMPOUNDS

Oxyfluorfen: Oxyfluorfen, a diphenyl ether compound, is a strong, contact herbicide, effective both as pre-and postemergence treatment. At low doses of 0.1-0.25 kg/ha, its preemergence application is found selective to *potato*, paddy, maize, sugarcane, cotton, jute, certain pulse crops, and several vegetables and seed spices. In the transplanted crops, it should be applied within 2-3 days of transplanting.

In established *orchards* and plantations, oxyfluorfen can be applied as directed, postemergence treatment on young weeds or as preemergence (to weeds) treatment. At higher doses of 0.5 kg/ ha, oxyfluorfen alone, or in combination with paraquat or MSMA, forms a total weed killer and may find place in no-till planting of crops.

13.20 SULFONYLUREAS

The discovery of sulfonylurea and associated herbicides was a significant accomplishment in the history of weed science since these provided effective weed control at very low doses of a few g/ha, with complete selectivity to the specified crops. A variety of broadleaf weeds and sedges, both annuals and perennials, succumbed to the herbicides of this group. In general, the sulfonylurea herbicides are weak on grass weeds, with some strong exceptions. These herbicides are basically foliage active compounds and possess very low manmalian toxicity and environment risks. However, their propensity to select resistant weed population threatens their long term, field utility.

Sulfonylurea herbicides exhibit considerable residual activity in soils.

The specific crop selectivities of sulfonylurea herbicides are as follows:

1. **Trifloxysulfuron (CGA – 362622)**: It is effective on several key broadleaf weeds as postemergence spray in cotton and sugarcane. Its effective rates vary from 0.005 to 0.0075 kg/ha. The herbicide is flexible in its time of postemergence application, from early to advanced growth stages of the weeds. In some sensitive cotton cultivars, this herbicide can be applied as directed/protected spray. In sugarcane, trifloxysulfuron can be premixed with ametryn to obtain simultaneous control of many grass weed species and purple nutsedge (*C. rotundus*). The premix is reported to gradually reduce tuber production and viability in the sedge.

2. **Halosulfuron**: Halosulfuron is effective particularly in the control of perennial sedges, besides some broadleafs. It is reported selective to a variety of agronomic and horticultural crops, as well as turfs. Its effective rate is 70 g/ha.

3. **Formaslfuron (AEF-130360)**: It is foliar herbicide, effective against a variety of annual and perennial grasses, and some broadleafs, in maize. Selectivity to the crop

is improved when it is used with a suitable safener like isoxadifen-ethyl. It is compatible with iodosulfuron, a broadleaf weed herbicide. The effective rates of foramsulfuron are 0.03-0.04 kg/ha.

4. **Cinosulfuron (CGA – 142464; Setoff):** Cinosulfuron is recommended primarily for weed management in rice. It is most effective when applied during 1-2 leaf and tillering stages of the crop. Its field recommended rate is 10-80 g/ha. It has low toxicity to fish, often found in paddy cultures. Its dissipation in soil is rapid.

5. **Rimsulfuron:** This sulfonylurea herbicide has exhibited excellent selectivity to most cultivars of tomato. Risks to rotation crops is minimal.

6. **Tribenuron:** A recently developed sulfonylurea herbicide with wide spectrum of selectivity to cereals like wheat, barley, and rice. It is applied as early postemergence treatment and is effective at very low doses of 10-20 g/ha. It has low persistence in soils, rendering the rotation crops sown about eight 8 months after its application, safe.

7. **Chlorimuron:** It is a sulfonylurea herbicide used for selective, postemergence control of primarily difficult broadleaf weeds and nutsedge in soybean, groundnut (pea-nut) and rice. Some grasses may also succumb to it, at least partially. The weeds should be less than 10 cm tall at time of application of chlorimuron. In groundnut apply it 60 days after crop emergence and in soybean at its first trifoliate leaf stage. The effective rates are 0.004-0.005 kg/ha. Chlorimiron may also be used effectively in non-crop areas.

8. **Pyrazosulfuron (ethyl):** This herbicide molecule is used both for *preemergence* and postemergence weed control in wet sown and transplanted rice at low doses of 15-30 g/ha. In direct sown rice it forms an effective preemergence herbicide to control a variety of weeds.

13.21 ORGANIC ARSENICALS

Herbicides belonging to this group are derivatives of cacodylic and methylarsonic acids. The cacodylic acid compounds form chiefly non-selective, shoot active herbicides whereas the arsonic acid compounds exhibit translocation effects and are selective to certain crops To get the best effects, these herbicides must be applied on warm (over 20°C) and sunny days. The organic arsenicals are inactivated in soils, rapidly.

Cacodylic Acid and its Salts: These chemicals form useful herbicides for destroying unwanted vegetation in industrial areas, old lawns and turfs, and for preplant desiccation of weeds in crop fields. The cacodylic acids are good *silvicides* too, being active on even the brown bark of trees. Their common spray concentrations are 0.25 to 0.5 per cent.

Salts of Arsonic Acids (MSMA, MAA, and DSMA): The arsonate herbicides are very effective in the control of *Cyperus rotundus*, *Xanthium strumarium*, *Tribulus terrestris*, *Cenchrus* and *Digitaria* spp., and some other common grasses and weeds. The most common use of arsonic acid compounds is postemergence control of *Digitaria* and other weedy grasses in *turf*. Currently, these are also being used extensively for directed application to young weeds in *cotton*, rubber, oil palm, citrus, coffee, and certain ornamentals. Their selective rates are 2 to 2.5 kg/ha in crops and up to 4 kg/ha in lawns. At high rates (0.2 to 0.5 per cent spray liquid), these compounds form good, general weed killers for use in non-crop areas.

13.22 MISCELLANEOUS HERBICIDES

Acrolein: Acrolein is a very potent, submersed *aquatic weed killer* in high discharge channels. It is injected in water from its container under the pressure of nitrogen. The acrolein treated water is safe for agricultural uses, but it is extremely toxic to fish. Acrolein is highly irritating to eyes and is toxic to inhale.

AMS: AMS is a non-selective, foliage active herbicide. Peculiar enough, it has contact action on herbaceous weeds and translocated action in the woody species. AMS, therefore, forms primarily a *brush killer,* particularly on farms where vapour drift of 2,4,5-T or silvex will injure crop plants. AMS is free from problem of vapour drifts. It has the added advantage of being a fire retardant.

AMS is somewhat corrosive to metallic farm sprayers which should be painted with oil before use. Its persistence in soils is 6 to 8 weeks in humid regions and longer in the dry areas.

Benzoylprop (ethyl): Benzoylprop is primarily a *wildoat* control agent in wheat and barley, although some other grasses may also be controlled with it. Fully tillered stage of small grains is most tolerant to benzoylprop. Common rates are 0.84 to 1.1 kg/ha.

Fluridone: Fluridone is both a root and shoot active herbicide. It is presently recommended as a preemergence herbicide in *cotton* to control annual grasses and sedges. Its effective rates are 0.3 to 1.2 kg/ha.

Fosamine: At 0.75 kg/ha fosamine forms an effective brush control agent. The treatment is made at the beginning of the active growth of the brush.

Oxadiazon: Oxadiazon is a shoot mobile, root contact herbicide. *Convolvulus arvensis* and *Oxalis* spp. are highly susceptible to it. Preemergent oxadiazon is active against most annual weeds, but postemergence treatment will kill mainly broadleaf weeds, save a few grasses like *Echinochloa* spp. This herbicide is recommended for preemergence treatment of *rice* at 0.6 to 1.5 kg/ha, stone-fruit orchards and vineyards at 2 to 4 kg/ha, and carnation beds at 4 kg/ha. It also holds promise in sugarcane, cotton, soybean, tobacco, bulb crops, and certain other crops. It is also recommended for ring treatment of apple and pear orchards against difficult broadleaf weeds.

Petroleum oils: Several distillates from petroleum industry contain 14% or more aromatic compounds. Such fractions are highly effective as contact, non-residual herbicides, and are known as "weed oils". Their phytotoxicity increases with rising aromatic content, total unsaturation, and molecular weight. Weed oils with more than 25% aromatic content, are non-selective, and are used for total vegetation destruction. These may be applied straight or as fortified oil emulsions. On crop lands, the non-selective weed oils can be used for early postemergence treatment of young weeds; for perplant desiccation of vegetation, and for ring weeding in orchards.

The selective herbicidal oils comprise lower contents of aromatic fractions (14 to 25%). These are called Crop Oil Concentrates (COC). The crop oils have proved particularly selective to carrot, but can also be used in onion, linseed, forest nurseries, and lawns. The crop oils are low specific gravity (over 38°C API), volatile, petroleum oils. Their common rates are 450 to 650 l/ha. High atmospheric temperatures of over 30°C may offset the selectivity of the crop oils.

Refined fractions of petroleum oils contaning less than 10% aromatic content are non-phytotoxic. The non-phytotoxic oils (NPO) are used as adjuvants, carriers (paraffinic oils), and fortifying agents. Oils with high flash point of 30°C or more are not suitable as herbicides because they invite fire hazards.

Anilofos: Anilofos is primarily a soil active herbicide for the control of annual grasses and sedges, besides some broadleaf weeds, in *transplanted rice.* To improve control of broadleaf weeds, it can be combined with 2,4-D (ester) at low dose of 0.3 kg/ha. Anilofos should be used about a week after transplanting rice but before the weeds are in their 2-leaf stage. Its effective rates are 0.3-0.45 kg/ha, depending upon the soil type.

Flamprop: Flamprop has been developed for selective control of late stage *wildoat* (*Avena fatua*) in wheat and barley. Wildoat is susceptible to it up to its 3 to 5-leaf stage. The common rates are 1-2 kg/ha.

Chlorimuron: It is a postemergence herbicide that disinguishes between *soybean* and broadleaf weeds. The selective rates are 0.33-0.66 kg/ha. A major limitation of chlorimuron is its long persistence in soils, particularly in those with high pH. This may pose limitation in the choice of rotation crops after harvesting the treated soybean.

Fluroxypyr: Fluroxypyr has been developed as an alternative herbicide in wheat to control some difficult broadleaf weeds, including fieldbindweed (*Convolvulus arvensis*), which are not so effectively controlled with 2,4-D. The effective rates are 0.2-0.3 kg/ha.

Piperphos: Piperphos is an effective herbicide for the control of sedges and grasses in *transplanted rice.* Its recommended rates are 0.6-1.0 kg/ha and the optimum time of application is 6-8 days after transplanting. Its combination with 2,4-D can provide simultaneous control of broadleaf weeds.

Glyphosate: Glyphosate is a non-selective, foliage active, highly translocated herbicide, with little persistence in soil. It is found excellent for the control of stubborn perennial weeds, both grasses and broadleaf species. Glyphosate should be applied when the weeds are young, and possess adequate foliage for herbicide absorption. Usually, at this stage the weeds have 4-6 leaves. The effective rates are 1-6 kg/ha. The affected weeds develop phytotoxicity symptoms rather slowly, often taking 10-15 days after the treatment.

Glyphosate finds its considerable use in the control of perennial weeds like *Cynodon dactylon*, *Sorghum halepense*, and *Pluchea lanceolata* during fallow periods. It is also widely used in the western world for weed control in no-till planting systems, as well as in the established orchards as a directed spray. In India, glyphosate has also been found promising in tea gardens at low doses of 0.8-1.5 kg/ha, besides in the control of aquatic weeds like waterhyacinth (*Eichhornia crassipes*) and cattails (*Typha* spp.). Glyphosate is a mild skin irritant and strong eye irritant. In soils it is subjected to rapid biodegradation.

Glyphosate was first registered as a broad-spectrum herbicide in cotton in the USA in 1997. It was recommended for postemergence application through four-leaf stage of the crop beyond which only its directed applications could be made. Maximum of two applications of glyphosate with a gap of at least 10 days were perimitted in this crop. But now it is used freely in crop fields for selective control of weeds in the transgenic soybean, maize, cotton, and canola varieties which are resistant to this herbicide (Chapter 16).

The herbicide is available as its ammine salt (Roundup) and diammonium salt (Touchdown).

Imazapyr: This herbicide is particularly good for the non-selective, postemergence control of perennial weeds at 0.50 to 1.5 kg/ha. Its residues may reside in soils for 3-5 months.

Tralkoxydim: It is a shoot active herbicide, developed for the selective control of late stage wildoat (*Avena fatua*) in *wheat*. It is applied about 30 days after sowing of the crop. The effective rates are 0.25-0.3 kg/ha.

Fomesafen: It is a selective, postemergence herbicide recommended primarily for the control of broadleaf weeds in *soybean*. It can be tank-mixed with a suitable grass killer to obtain broad-spectrum weed control. Fomesafen proves most selective to soybean at its 2 to 3-leaf stage. Its effective rates are 0.25-0.375 kg/ha.

Fluazifop-p: It is a postemergence herbicide with sufficiently high degree of safety to soybean, cotton, and groundnut. The herbicide damages chiefly grasses, both annuals and perennials. It can be combined with bentazon or other selective herbicides for obtaining simultaneous control of broadleafs. The effective rates are 0.125-0.250 kg/ha.

Lactofen: Lactofen is a postemergence herbicide found selective to soybean and groundnut. It provides effective control of broadleaf weeds, and it can be combined with a suitable grass herbicide for causing overall control of common weeds. The recommended rates are 0.8-1.0 kg/ha.

Fluminoxazin: Fluminoxazin is registered for preemergence control of broadleaf weeds in soybean and groundnut, and for preplant application in cotton. It is also being developed as a postemergence directed spray in cotton. Its effective rates are 40-60 g/ha.

Pyrithiobac: It is the first truly selective herbicide registered for postemergence control of difficult broadleaf weeds in cotton. Its effective rates are 35-140 g/ha and it generally persists in soils for less than one growing season. However, a portion of the herbicide that moves deeper in soils may come back on soil surface during tillage operations and damage the rotation crops.

Pyrithobac belongs to the pyrimidinyl (thio) benzoate family of herbicides which is similar in its mode of action to the sulfonylureas.

Clopyralid: It is a pyridine auxin herbicide, registered for selective control of composite and polygonaceae weeds in cereal crops.

Flufenacet: It is a selective, preemergence herbicide used for the control of annual grasses and small seeded dicot weeds in tomato, maize, sunflower, soybean, *etc*. It is synergistic with metribuzin (also called soybean herbicide) to achieve broad-spectrum weed control in soybean. It has low toxicity to mammals and birds. It holds potential to control *P. minor* in wheat.

Flufenacet persists in soils for 60-90 days and sometimes longer, depending upon the several soil and climatic features.

Isopropagyl: Isopropagyl is a preemergence or early postemergence herbicide found effective in the control of difficult annual grasses like *Phalaris, Alopecurus, Lolium,* and *Poa* spp. in winter grains. It is absorbed from soil by plumules of the emerging weeds.

Isopropagyl belongs to the chemical family of pyrazolemenzoates.

Imazamox: It is a broad-spectrum herbicide that is selective to maize, rape and mustard, and wheat.

Imazamox belongs to the chemical group imidolinone of herbicides.

Clomazone: Clomazone is a selective, preemergence herbicide currently labeled for use in pepper, pumpkin, soybean, cotton, tobacco, and pea. It controls many grasses and broadleaf weeds. Its effective dose is 1 kg/ha.

In cotton, clomazone has been used as a component herbicide with PPI insecticides disulfoton and phorate which are known to act as herbicide safeners in this situation.

Clomazone may persist in soils for one year or longer, making it necessary to test its selectivity to the rotation crops of the region.

13.23 FUNCTIONAL FEATURES OF SOME CURRENTLY USED HERBICIDES

Acetochlor: It is a soil applied herbicide found selective to soybean and maize. Several annual grasses, yellow nutsedge and some broadleaf weeds are reported susceptible to it. Use of a safener like 'dichlormid' shall further improve selectively of acetachlor to maize. Its effective rates are 1.5-3.0 kg/ha.

Azafenidin: At 0.240 kg/ha azafenidin forms a good preemergence (to weeds) herbicide for widespread weed control in plantations, forests and industrial areas. It can be tank mixed with a contact postemergence herbicide. Azafenidin is a triazole compound.

Carfentrazone (ethyl): At 0.02-0.025 kg/ha carfentrazone forms a good postemergence herbicide against difficult broadleafs in wheat, maize, and soybean. It is applied up to 60 days after sowing of the crop. It can be combined with 2,4-D and bentazon to further broaden its broadleaf weed control spectrum. It is an aryltriazolinone, reduced-risk (RR) herbicide.

Chlorsulfuron: It is a postemergence herbicide recommended for the control of difficult broadleaf weeds in wheat. The effective rates are 0.015-0.045 kg/ha. Its residues in soil may sometimes prove phytotoxic to a rotation crop like maize.

Cinmethylin: It is a cineole compound used as selective, preplant or preemergence (to weeds) herbicide in rice to control several annual weedy grasses for 4-8 weeks. Its effective rates are 0.075-0.10 kg/ha. It is applied 6-8 days after sowing of crop seeds or 3-

14 days after transplanting its seedlings. Cinmethylin can be mixed with 2,4-D (EE) to achieve simultaneous control of broadleaf weeds.

Clodinafop (propargyl): It is a pyridine compound used as a selective, postemergence herbicide in wheat (not in barley). It is effective against annual grasses including *Phalaris minor* and *Avena fatua* (not *Poa annua*). The two grasses are susceptible to clodinafop during their 3 leaf to early shooting stages but their best control is obtained when the grasses are actively growing and have plenty of moisture in their tissues. Wheat is tolerant to clodinafop at almost its all growth stages. The effective rates of clodinafop are 0.04-0.09 kg/ha. It is usually applied 30-40 days after sowing wheat. Addition of a suitable safener shall improve selectivity of clodinafop to the crop. The herbicide is compatible with 2,4-D and metsulfuron. Of recent, clodinafop has also been found selective to blackgram, chickpea, pea, lentil, linseed, and mustard.

Cyhalofop: Cyhalofop is primarily a preemergence herbicide developed for the control of annual grasses in rice. Barnyardgrass (*Echinochloa* sp.) is susceptible to it up to its 3-4 leaf stage. For sequential control of broadleafs, 2, 4-D can be applied at least 3 days after application of cyhalofop. Effective rates are 0.06-0.10 kg/ha.

Cyhalofop is a aryloxyphenoxy propionate herbicide. It is completely degraded in rice fields to inoccuous degrades within two weeks in soil and within three months in water. Little risk is reported to aquatic environment by the use of this herbicide in paddies.

Ethoxysulfuron: It forms an effective preemergence herbicide for the control of difficult broadleaf weeds and sedges in rice. It can be applied up to 10 days after transplanting the crop. For obtaining simultaneous control of grass weeds, it can be tank-mixed with anilophos. The effective rates are 0.01-0.15 kg/ha.

Fenoxaprop: It is a systemic herbicide with rapid shoot activity. At 0.06-0.12 kg/ha fenoxaprop shall control several annual grasses, including *Avena fatua* and *Phalaris minor* (but not *Poa, Lolium,* and *Agropyron* spp.). Fenoxaprop is presently recommended for use in wheat, rice, and soybean.

Flupropanate (Tetrapion): It is a selective, translocated, preplant herbicide found useful in the control of several annual grasses and some broadleafs in jute. Its effective rates are 2-3 kg/ha.

Glufosinate ammonium: It is a shoot active, non-selective herbicide used for the control of wide-spectrum of annual and perennial weeds as protected spray in wide-sown crops and plantations, besides in variable non-crop situations and in no-tillage farming systems. Effective rates are 0.3-0.4 kg/ha.

Glufosinate is also used in Canada and the USA as a selective herbicide in herbicide resistant canola (*Brassica* spp.) and some other crops (Chapter -16).

Haloxyfop: Haloxyfop is used for destruction of standing grasses in orchards, plantatons, forests, and on roadsides. Among field cops, it is found selective to soybean, cotton and groundnut. Effective rates are 0.0-0.25 kg/ha in field crops and up to 1.5 kg/ha in other situations.

Imazaquin: It is a imidazolinone compound used as selective, post-emergence herbicide in chiefly soybean and warm season turf to control several broadleaf weeds. Its selective rates are 0.125-0.375 kg/ha.

Imazethapyr: It is an imidazole compound used as a selective post-emergence herbicide in soybean, groundnut and certain legumenous vegetables. It is effective against mainly annual grasses. Its effective rates are 0.75-1.5 kg/ha.

Iodosulfuron (methyl-sodium): Iodosulfuron is an effective postemergence hericide for the control of some difficult, broadleaf weeds in wheat and maize. Its effective rates are 0.024-0.03 kg/ha. In maize it can be combined with foramsulfuron to obtain simultaneous control of grasses, both annuals and perennials. Mefenpyr-diethyl forms a good safener for use with iodosulfuron.

Mesosulfuron: Mesosulfuron is a potent, foliage active grass herbicide. It possesses limited activity against broadleaf weeds. *P. minor* and *A. fatua* are particularly susceptile to it. The herbicide is selective to wheat, .triticale and rye. It is compatible with iodosulfuron to achieve simultaneous control of broadleaf weeds. Its effective rates are 0.012-0.019 kg/ha.

Metamitron: It is a translocated selective herbicide; effective in the control of broadspectrum of weeds in sugarbeets. It can be applied both pre-and postemergence treatment. It is compatible with other sugarbeet herbicides.

Metazachlor: It is a selective, pre and early postemergence, chloroacetamide herbicide. It is good for controlling wide-spectrum of weeds in cruciferous crops. It is compatible with quinmerac, clomazone, etc.

Metsulfuron: It is a sulfonylurea herbicide used for obtaining selective, pre - and postemergence control of many difficult broadleaf weeds in wheat, barley and grasslands. The effective rates of metsulfuron are 0.003-0.008 kg/ha in cereals and up to 0.140 kg/ha in non-crop areas. Cereals prove tolerant to the herbicide during their 2 leaf stage to boot stage. Metsulfuron is a long residue herbicide in soil. As such, its residual effects on local rotation crops should be critically examined.

Metsulfuron can also be used in non-crop areas infested with broadleaf weeds.

Oxadiargyl: It forms a very effective preemergence herbicide for the control of a wide range of annual weeds, including sedges, in rice. Its recommended rates are 0.05-0.150 kg/ha. It is usually applied 5-7 days after seeding or transplanting of rice. Oxadiargyl is now also found selective to sugarcane and onion.

Pethoxamid: Pethoxamid forms an effective preemergence and early postemergence herbicide to control wide-spectrum of annual weeds in maize and soybean. Its effective rates are 1.0-24. kg/ha.

Propaquizafop: It is a selective postemergence herbicide recommended for use in soybean to control annual grass weeds. Its selective rates are 0.05-0.06 kg/ha. It is applied in soybean about 25 days after sowing. Besides soybean, it can be tested in groundnut, sunflower, cotton and several vegetable crops.

Quizalofop: It is a wide-spectrum, postemergence herbicide, effective against a variety of weeds from seeds. It is highly selective to soybean at its 15-25 days' seedling stages. Its effective rates are 0.025-0.0 kg/ha. Of late, quizalofop is also reported selective to chickpea, pea, lentil, linseed, and mustard.

Sulfentrazone: It is a wide-spectrum, soil-active herbicide found selective to soybean, tobacco, sugarcane, groundnut, rice, lucerne, mint, and turf. It is effective at 0.375 kg/ha.

Sulfometuron: It is largely a non-crop area herbicide to control undesirable vegetation by its postemergence and preemergence (to weeds) application. The effective rates are 0.05-0.2 kg/ha. Both annual and perennial weeds are reported susceptible to it. Sulfometuron can also be used in forests as directed spray.

Sulfosulfuron: Sulfosulfuron forms a good shoot-active herbicide against *Phalaris minor*, besides many other grass as well as broadleaf weeds in wheat. It can be applied with considerable time flexibility from 20 to 50 days after sowing of the crop. Effective rates vary from 0.025 to 0.050 kg/ha.

Tepraloxydim: It forms primarily a preemergence herbicide for the control of annual grasses in soybean. To obtain concurrent control of broadleaf weeds it can be either tank-mixed with bentazon or followed by acifluorfen. It is effective at 0.075 kg/ha.

Thiazopyr: Thiazopyr forms a selective, preemergence herbicide for the control of a variety of annual weeds in sugarcane. Its effective rates are 0.2-0.4 kg/ha.

Triasulfuron: It is a sulfonylurea herbicide found effective against a variety of difficult dicot weeds, besides some grass weeds. It is found selective to wheat and onion. Triasulfuron is used as post-emergence herbicide at 0.015-0.02 kg/ha.

Triclopyr: It is a highly translocated herbicide, useful in the control of broadleaf weeds, both weedy and herbaceous, in grasslands, plantation, rice fields and industrial areas. It is compatible with most other herbicides.

SUMMARY

In this chapter are listed some important properties and uses of over 120 common herbicides recommended for use on crop land and in various non-crop situations. Emphasis has been laid on herbicide properties, particularly sites of their active absorption and their leaching and persistence behaviour in soils. Important, approved and promising uses of each herbicide have also been indicated. To avoid duplication, soil fumigants and specific soil sterilants have been excluded from this chapter; these are discussed in Chapter 25 ahead.

SELECTED BIBLIOGRAPHY

1. Anon. 2004. Glyphosate. Pesticide News 64 : 20-21 (U.K.).
2. Bohmont, B. L. 1990. The Standard Pesticide User's Guide. Prentice Hall, xii + 498 pp.
3. British Crop Protection Council. 2001. The U.K. Pesticide Guide 2001, CAB Pub., U.K., 598p.
4. Calderband, A. 1973. The bipyridylium herbicides. Adv. Pest. Control Res. 8:127-255.
5. Fletcher, W. B. and Kirkwood, R. C. 1982. Herbicides and Plant Growth Regulators. Canada Pub. Ltd., London, 408 pp.

6. Gentner, W. A. and Damdson, L. L. 1970. Phytotoxic properties of substituted benzonitriles and their derivatives. Weed Sci. 18 (5):629-630.
7. Godley, J. L. and Kitchen, L. M. 1986. Interaction of acifluorfen with fluazifop for annual grass control. Weed Sci. 36:227-233.
8. Kobayashi, S. and Matsuura, S. 1992. Grass killer: Targa. Japan Pesticide Information, 60:7-9.
9. Munroe, C. E. and Nishimoto, R. K. 1988. Oxyfluorfen (Goal) for weed control in cabbage. Weed Abstr. 38(10):item 3142.
10. Page, B. G. and Thomson, W. T. 1994. The Insecticide, Herbicide, and Fungicide Quick Guide. Thomson Publications, 194 pp.
11. Panwar, R. S. *et al.*, 1994. Effect of tralkoxydim applied alone or as tank mixture on weed control in wheat. Ind. J. Weed Sci. 26 (1 & 2) 104-105.
12. Parmar, B. S. *et al.* 1988. Handbook of Technical Pesticides Produced in India. Soc. Pesticide Sci., India, IARI, New Delhi, 99 pp.
13. Richburg. J. S. *et al.* 1993. Toxicity of imazethapyr to purple and yellow nutsedges. Weed Technol. 7(4) 900-905.
14. Roberts, T. R. *et al.* 2005. Deactivation of the biological activity of paraquat in the soil environment. J. Agric. & Food Chem. 50(13) : 3623-3631 (U.K.)
15. Sabharwal, C. K. and Rathi, M. P. S. 1993. Manufacture of herbicides in India. Proc. Int. Symp. ISWS, Hisar (India), held Nov., 93:19-28.
16. Thomson, W. T. 1993. Agri. Chem. Book II. Herbicides 1993. (*Revision*). Thomson Publications. XXi + 309 pp.
17. Torrey, S. (ed.). 1982. Preemergence Herbicides-Recent Advances. Noyes Data Corporation, 334 pp.
18. Verma, S. B. S. and Luile, M. 1974. Bentazon - A new herbicide for chemical weed control in soybeans. PANS 20 (1) 129-132.
19. Vih, R. Y. 1975. New potent diphenyl ether herbicides. J. Agri. Food Chem. 23:5.
20. Weerd, ICVD, 1974. Basagran: a new selective herbicide for cereals and legumes. Pesticides, June 21-24.

Chapter 14

HERBICIDE AVAILABILITY AT THE ACTION SITES IN PLANTS

In the present and the subsequent two chapters it is intended to describe the herbicide behaviour in the target and non-target plants. First the mode of absorption, movement, and translocation of herbicides is considered and then their modus operandi and selectivity are discussed. It will be more helpful if the reader possesses an adequate background of plant anatomy and physiology before taking up the study of the herbicide behaviour in plants. It is out of scope of this text to present details of common physiological mechanisms in plants. These will be cited here only in brief in relation to herbicides.

To be effective a given herbicide must be absorbed[1] by the target plant and then translocated[2] to the site of its action. However, for some herbicides the site of action could be the absorption site by itself whence translocation may not be a prerequisite to witnessing their action on the plant. In this process of herbicide availability at the site of action both, the plant species and the molecular structure of the herbicide, are of paramount importance. Besides, the process is often further influenced by the variations in the environment.

Earlier the research scientists depended largely upon the morphological symptoms and anatomical changes induced by the herbicide, for recording its absorption and movement in the plant. But now labelled (usually with ^{14}C) herbicides are used to track the pathway of even a minute quantity of the herbicide absorbed by the treated plant.

Basic studies on the absorption and translocation of herbicides by different plant species provide valuable information which assists the weed scientists in predicting the most efficient method and time of application of a given herbicide to achieve the target of controlling weeds in different situations. Such researches might as well point out the

---

[1]***Absorption:*** *It is the movement of a herbicide (or other material) from the surface into the plant body in a limited zone.*

[2]**Translocation** *(or transport): It is the transfer of a herbicide, food, or other material from one part of the plant to another.*

way to chemical modifications of herbicide molecules to improve their absorption and translocation behaviour. An example would be to alter the substituted urea and triazine molecules to improve their symplastic movement (see later).

14.1 ABSORPTION

14.1.1 Pathways in Foliar Absorption

The absorption of herbicides involves their entry from plant surfaces into the cytoplasm of epidermal cells of shoots or roots. In this process a herbicide may come across five possible barriers. These are (i) surface waxes and hair, (ii) cuticle, (iii) periderm, (iv) cell wall, and (v) plasmalemma.

1. **Waxes and hair:** The outermost coverings of many plant foliage that are exposed to the atmosphere are covered with waxes and hair. The surface waxes often permeate through the cuticle below where these are called *cuticular waxes* (Fig. 14.1). Plant surfaces exposed to full sunlight develop thicker wax coatings than those exposed to low lux light. Waxes and hair are lipophilic[3] in nature and they interfere in wetting of leaf surfaces with lipophobic[3a] sprays.
2. **The cuticle:** Cuticle is an uneven, lipoidal covering on the plant leaves and branches to guard against excessive transpirational loss of water from plants. It results from deposits of metabolic excretions of plant cells outside epidermal walls, and constitutes chiefly *cutin* lamellae, impregnated with waxes. The cutin is semi-lipoidal, oxidative polymer of 18 or more carbon hydroxyfatty acids and alcohols. Thus, cuticle carries both hydrophilic (-OH, -COOH, etc.) and lipophilic (-CH_2, -CH_3, etc) groups which impart to it a hemihydrophilic character. The uppermost layer of cuticle that is exposed to the atmosphere is more oxidised than its inner layers. This creates a polarity gradient across the thickness of the cuticle. The upper, more lipohilic cuticle is called *cuticle proper* and the inner one, which is much less lipophilic, is named *cuticular layer.* The culticular layer constitutes, in addition to cutin and some waxes, hemicelluloses and pectins (polyuronides and glucans). The overall charge of the entire depth of cuticle is negative.

The leaf surface cuticle extends to the inside of the stomatal cavities as *internal cuticle.* The guard cells of stomata have no cuticle. The internal cuticle is much thinner than the leaf surface cuticle.

On the basis of the above structure of the cuticle, it is safe to assume that it is permeable to both hydrophilic (polar[4]) and lipophilic (apolar[5]) substances. A herbicide may enter

---

[3]**Lipophilic** *(=hydrophobic) : Molecules or surfaces that are attracted by oil-like surfaces and molecules, but are repelled by water.*

[3a]**Lipophobic** *(=hydrophilic): Molecules or surfaces that are attracted towards water, such as sodium chloride. They are repelled by oil-like surfaces or substances.*

[4]**Polar compound:** *Polar compounds have molecules with electropositive and electronegative regions and they tend to ionize, for example,* Na^+Cl^-, H^+Br^-, $H_2{}^+O^-$ *etc. In organic substances, groups like OH, COOH,* NH_2, *CHO and unsaturated bondages impart them polar characters. Their polarity varies with intensity of such characteristic groups and with unsaturation.*

the cuticle either through minute spaces existing between fatty acid chains of its procutin and polymerized macromolecules, or through large openings caused intermittently by thermodynamic motion of lipid molecules of the cutin. Imperfections, cracks, insect punctures, and the like may provide some direct entry of the herbicides into the cuticle but as these openings rarely traverse its whole thickness, they are not considered important for penetration of herbicides. The relative thickness and composition of cuticle on plant foliage determine the *nature of leaf surfaces*, and consequently their wettability with the herbicide spray liquids.

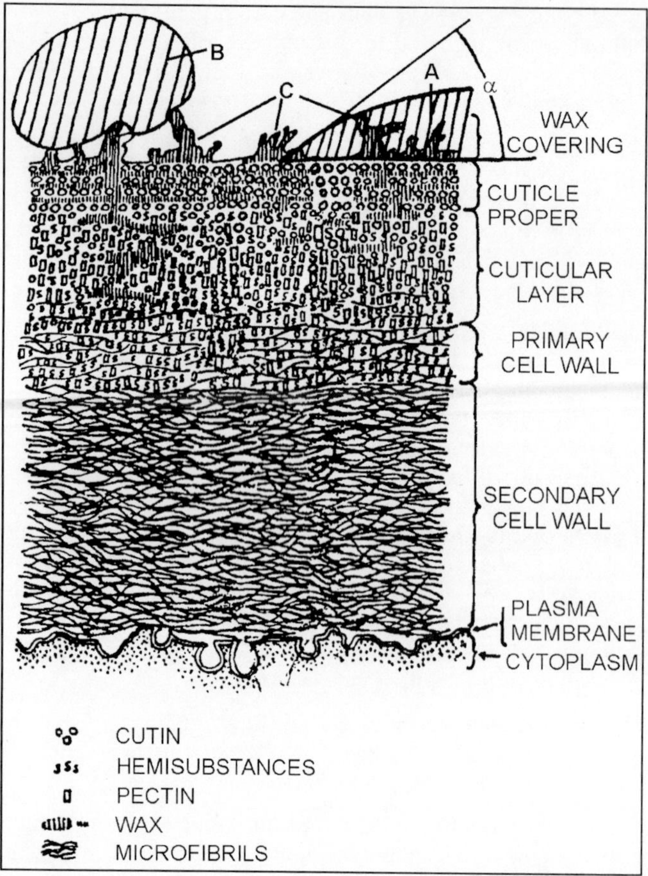

Fig. 14.1: A simplified scheme of barriers of outer wall of an epidermal cell. A = water droplet flattended with the use of a wetting agent on the waxy covering of epidermal cells because the wetting agent reduced the contact angle. B = water drop without a wetting agent held on wax rods (C) (After Van Overbeek, 1956).

---

[5]**Apolar compound:** *Molecules with no surface distribution of charge are said to be apolar (or nonpolar). Examples of completely apolar substances are aliphatic and saturated ring structure compounds e.g. hexane* (C_6H_{14}) *and cyclohexane* (C_6H_{12}).

Many organic substances are relatively polar (or apolar), for instance, benzene (C_6H_6). The majority of herbicides belong to this group of compounds.

The extent and kind of cutinization differs with plant species, age, and environment. In general, young leaves and those growing in shade are much less cutinized than mature leaves and those growing continuously in bright sun, respectively.

The roots of plants have no cuticle; therefore, they absorb hydrophilic substances more readily than the lipophilic compounds.

1. **Stomata:** Stomatal cavities increase the absorptive area of leaves. Herbicide spray drops that may enter them, pass through their thin, internal cuticle more rapidly than through the thick, surface cuticle. Besides their thickness, better absorption of the herbicides through internal cuticle may also result from the fact that stomatal cavities protect the spray drops from quick drying. However, under field conditions the herbicide droplets often find it difficult to enter the stomatal cavities because most of the time they remain filled with gases.
2. **Cell walls:** After crossing the cuticle, herbicides come in contact with cell walls of epidermal cells. The primary cell walls are rich in pectins and celluloses, hence. they are more hydrophilic than the cuticle. The secondary cell walls located outside the primary cell walls constitute largely fibrous tissues. Hydrophilic substances find easier entry through the cell walls than the hydrophobic substances.
3. **Plasmalemma:** Plasmalemma is a lipoidal, differentially permeable membrane[6] lining the plant cells just below the cell walls. It is the last barrier to the entry of herbicides into the cytoplasm of epidermal cells.

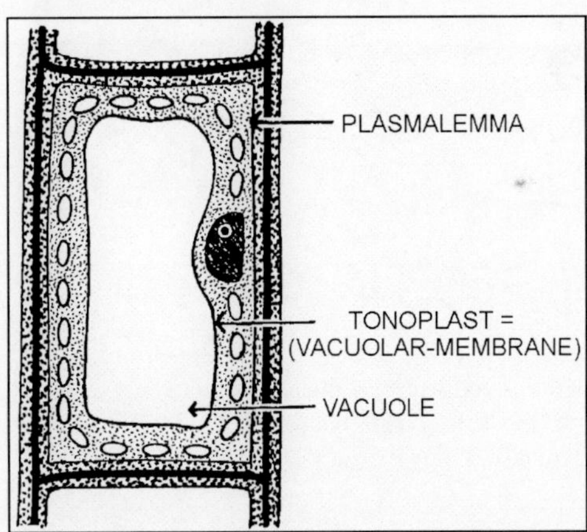

Fig. 14.2: Diagrammatic presentation of a plant cell showing position of plasmalemma and tonoplast membranes involved in the absorption of herbicides (and other solutes).

---

[6]***Differentially permeable membrane:*** *It is a membrane that allows some solutes, as well as the solvent, to pass through discriminately.*

The molecular structures and formulations of herbicides are very important in determining the foliar absorption of herbicides. In summary, the nonpolar compounds are absorbed more readily by the foliage than the polar compounds.

14.1.2 Absorption of Herbicides from Soil

The absorption of herbicides applied to soil is usually associated with roots of the plants. While this is correct, herbicides may also be absorbed by the swelling seeds and coleoptile, epicotyl, and hypocotyl of the emerging seedlings. In fact, the shoot zone of germinating plants in soil (coleoptile, etc.) has been revealed as a major site of absorption of many soil-applied herbicides (Barrentine and Warren, 1971). Prendeville *et al.* (1967) found that EPTC, chlorpropham, and trifluralin were most effectively absorbed when applied to the subsurface, shoot zone of the test plants, namely, maize and peas. But 2,4-D, simazine, and naptalam etc., were absorbed mainly from the root zone. Entry of chlorthal methyl in sorghum was primarily through its shoot zone in soil. Alachlor was absorbed by nutsedge from its part just above the tuber.

Herbicides are also absorbed by rhizomes, stolons, and tubers of perennial plants.

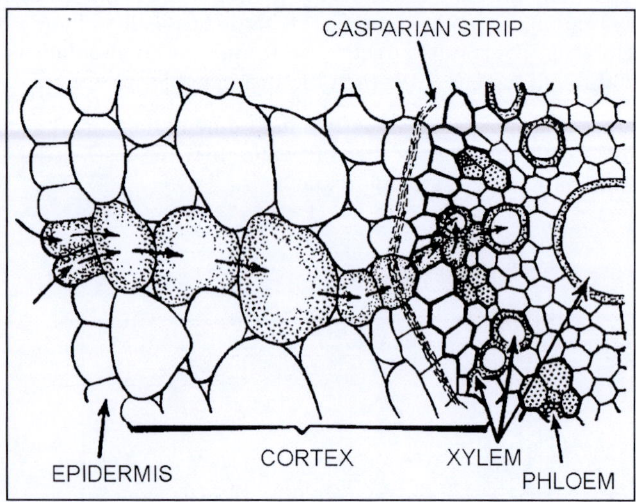

Fig. 14.3: Part of transaction of wheat root, illustrating the kinds of cell that may be traversed by herbicides absorbed from the soil before they reach the tracheary elements of the xylem. The arrows indicate the direction of the movement of herbicide solute through symplast.

In roots, the elongation zone is the chief site of absorption of the herbicides. Crown roots of grasses located above the seeds are more important in the absorption of certain herbicides than the seminal roots, but in others seminal root absorption may be sufficient to damage the plant. Data on the exact sites of absorption of soil applied herbicides can be of practical assistance in selecting the correct depth of placement of different herbicides. Unlike shoots, roots being devoid of cuticle, permit easier entry of polar compounds than the nonpolar compounds. But the polar compounds leach through the soil more easily which may sometimes cause crop injury.

14.1.3 Mechanism of Herbicide Absorption

The specific mechanisms of absorption of herbicides by plants have not yet been identified but these are believed to be largely similar to those already known for the absorption of plant nutrients (Salisbury and Ross, 1969).

1. *Absorption through cuticle and cell walls*: Hydrophilic ions and molecules enter plants by the process of diffusion[7], whereas the lipophilic substances enter by their lipid *solubizing action*. The lipophilic spray liquids solubilize the native lipid molecules of cuticle and epidermal walls and increase their permeability to the herbicide. Solubilization is a more active process of absorption than diffusion. Many adjuvants impart certain lipophilic properties to the aqueous spray liquids and aid entry of hydrophilic substances through the cuticle and cell walls. Lowering of pH of spray liquids of acid type herbicides, such as 2,4-D and silvex, also exerts an absorption enchancing effect by limiting ionization of their molecules. Herbicides are absorbed through cuticle more rapidly in molecular forms than in their ionic forms.

   It may be pointed out that herbicide absorption through cuticle and epidermal walls is reversible. A hard rain can wash out at least a portion of the absorbed herbicide, if it was still outside the plasmalemma at the time of rain.

2. *Absorption through plasmamembranes*: The plasmamembranes comprising plasmalemma and tonoplast, are made up chiefly of lipids and proteins, and are lipophilic in nature. The lipophilic herbicides such as herbicidal oils and oil emulsions pass through them easily at rates roughly proportional to their fat solubility and they reach the epidermal cytoplasm rapidly. The absorption of hydrophilic substances through the plasmamembranes, however, is much more complex. There are two probable processes by which hydrophilic herbicides may find their entry into epidermal protoplasm through plasmalemma. These are:

   a) *The passive absorption*: This involves the physical process of diffusion of substances through the plasmamembranes, and is controlled by the electrochemical potential gradient across the plasmalemma and tonoplast of the cytoplasm.

   b) *The active absorption*: This is an energy requiring mechanism, and is based on the hypothesis that certain heavy chemical carrier molecules, constituting primarily proteins and phospholipids, and possessing both positive and negative ends, occur within the plasmalemma. These chemical carrier molecules are instrumental in transporting anions, cations, and undissociated molecules of specific solutes across the plasmalemma into the cytoplasm. The tonoplast or vacuolar membrane too has a mechanism similar to the plasmalemma for transporting the absorbed solute from cytoplasm into the vacuole. But the tonoplast carrier system is comparatively very weak, hence, the solutes often bypass the vacuoles enroute the adjoining cells. In a way, it is helpful in rapid cell

---

[7]**Diffusion:** *It is the net movement of a substance from one point to another due to the random, kinetic motion of its molecules, atoms, ions, etc. It tends to occur along any free energy or chemical potential gradient regardless of how the gradient was established.*

wall movement of a solute. Compounds with high energy phosphate bonds like ADP and ATP produced by oxidative phosphorylation in the mitochondria, are essential in the synthesis, as well as functioning, of the carrier molecules. However, direct evidence of the carrier theory of the absorption of herbicides by plants is not yet available.

Absorption of herbicides through the plasmalemma into the cell cytoplasm is irreversible by rain.

There may be many shortfalls in the foregoing, briefly cited, hypotheses of the absorption of herbicides. These will undoubtedly be resolved by the future researchers.

Herbicide structures differ in the rapidity with which they are absorbed by even the same plant species. Formulations of herbicides further modify their rates of absorption. For example, Norris and Freed (1966) found that time bound absorption of four formulations of 2,4-D by bigleaf maple (*Acer macrophyllum*) took place in the decreasing order: ester, acid, amine salt, and sodium salt. The propionic acid phenoxy herbicides were absorbed more rapidly than their acetic acid derivatives by the maple leaves. Also, the trichlorophenoxyalkyl acids were absorbed less intensely than the dichlorophenoxyalkyl acid herbicides.

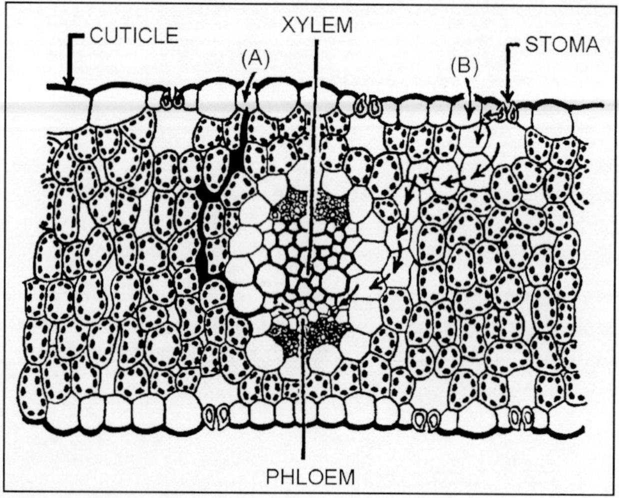

Fig. 14.4: Section of a mature isobilateral leaf showing pathways of movement of a herbicide through: (A) apoplast (B) symplast- (diagrammatic).

14.2 MOVEMENT

After a herbicide has been absorbed by the epidermal cells of plants, it moves across the thickness of the root or shoot, as the case may be, primarily in ionic form till it reaches close to vascular vessels–the phloem and xylem. This advancement of solutes is called movement. The movement of herbicides may occur either through apoplast[8] or through symplast[9]. In both cases, the movement is a process of diffusion although in the symplast, cytoplasmic streaming and active accumulation along the electrochemical potential gradient may also help the movement of herbicides. Scientists further believe that plant cells are inter-connected with plasmodesmata through which the solutes could pass freely. In the symplast the herbicide ions and molecules often by-pass the vacuoles unless the cytoplasm is overloaded with the solute in question.

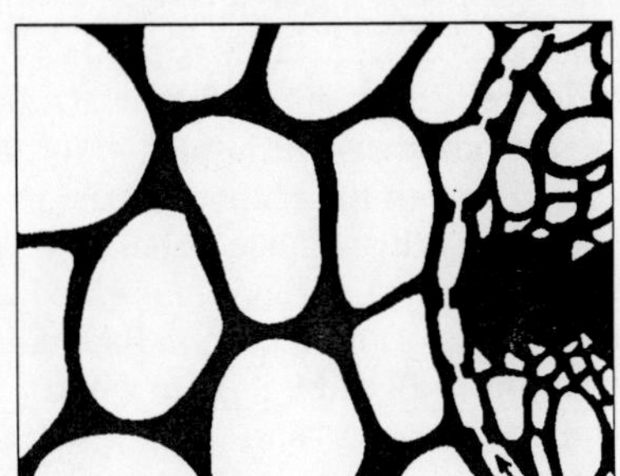

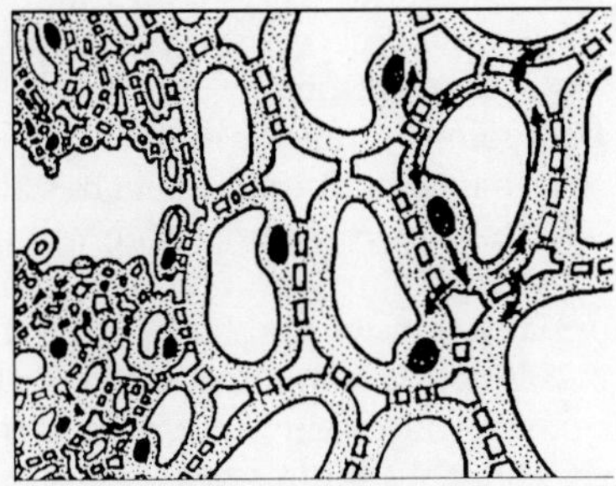

Fig. 14.5: Anatomical drawings illustrating: *Left* = Apoplast and *Right* = Symplast. Apoplast is a non-living cell wall continuum whereas symplast is the interconnected protoplasm.

14.3 TRANSLOCATION

After the herbicide ions (or molecules) have moved to the cells adjacent to the vascular vessels *ie*. the xylem and phloem tubes, they must move into appropriate conducting tissues for their translocation to distant plant parts. Herbicide structures that fail to enter into the beginnings of conducting tubes of a healthy plant do not translocate to the untreated plant parts. An important reason for this is their strong retention in certain plant cells adjoining the vascular bundles. For instance, in roots the casparian strip of the radial walls of the endodermis is responsible for serving as a physical barrier and preventing herbicides like 2,4-D and MH from moving into the xylem vessels. Herbicide molecules of substituted ureas and simazine, on the contrary, are not obstructed by casparian strip because they may be soluble in its suberin and so they are easily translocated. Also, the final secretion of herbicides from cortex cells into the vascular bundle is an energy requiring process of active accumulation. Some herbicide molecules, *eg* 2,4-D, IPC, and amitrole may be retained by cortex parenchyma cells in their vacuoles and, hence, prevent them from moving on into the xylem. Metabolic inhibitors like dinoseb, demeton, and DNP in low concentrations could lower the ability of cortex parenchyma cells to retain herbicidal molecules and consequently induce the translocation of root immobile compounds like MH and amitrole in suitable test plants. Obviously, the metabolic inhibitors check the energy requiring process of retention of the herbicide by root cells (Taylor and Warran, 1970; Sutton and Bingham, 1970). Also, at

[8]**Apoplast :** *Interconnecting cell walls and intercellular spaces, including the water (or air) filled xylem elements–a non-living system.*

[9]**Symplast :** *The system of interconnected protoplasm excluding vacuoles–a living system.*

high concentrations, capable of contact action on plant roots, 2,4-D and 2,4, 5-T translocate readily *via* xylem vessels to the plant tops (Crafts, 1961).

14.3.1 Translocation Through Phloem

The phloem mobile herbicides move along with photosynthates present in the phloem tubes; in a way "riding along" the plant food materials–the sugars and amino acids. Several mechanisms of translocation of food, and along with it the herbicides, through phloem tubes have been proposed by scientists. Of these mechanisms, the *mass flow* hypothesis is widely accepted since it is applicable to acropetal, basipetal, as well as bidirectional[10] translocation of food material and herbicides in plants. It also explains well the high rates of translocation of certain herbicides observed in plants; for instance, under favourable conditions 2,4-D may translocate through the phloem as fast as 160 cm per hour. Herbicides can translocate through only healthy phloem tubes that are in a state of active food translocation. When for some reason the phloem tubes are damaged, even a normally translocated herbicide will fail to translocate in plants. Take dalapon as an example. When it is applied at low concentration of 0.2 to 0.5 % to a healthy grass clump, it translocates easily to its roots. But when the spray concentration is high, say 1%or 2%, dalapon will quickly brown the treated foliage without translocating appreciably to the grass roots. Likewise, sulphuric acid, paraquat, and diquat herbicides are immobile in plants mainly because of their rapid phytotoxicity to leaf tissues even at low concentrations. The low phloem mobility of 2,4-D in plants is also ascribed to disruption of phloem tubes by proliferation of the adjoining cells by the herbicide (see Chapter 15).

Two important characteristics of translocation of herbicides through *phloem* are:

1. A herbicide translocates in plants along with food material, from the site of food manufacture (*ie* mature leaves) to the site of food consumption or storage, (*viz.*, growing points, young leaves, fruits, roots, and rhizomes). The site of food synthesis or food export in plants is called '*source*' and the site of its ultimate lodgement, the '*sink*'. In herbicide research, the word 'source' is also used to denote any site of application of a test herbicide on the plant, may it be stem, leaf, or root.
2. During translocation through phloem, the herbicides by-pass mature leaves because such leaves synthesize and export food but do not import it. The phloem mobile herbicides enter only the actively food importing organs of plants.

Crafts (1966) applied labelled amitrole to a leaf of an intact plant of *Zebrina pendula* and prepared its autoradiographs. The autoradiographs showed that amitrole travelled to the young leaves and roots of *Zebrina*, by-passing the mature leaves. Similar by-passing of the mature leaves was noted in many other phloem mobile herbicides. But certain herbicides like MH did not by-pass mature leaves on the treated plants. When applied to a leaf of a young plant, MH translocated even to its mature leaves. This was because MH leaked from the phloem tubes into the xylem vessels within plant shoots. From here it

---

[10]***Bidirectional translocation*** *of herbicides refers to their simultaneous, two way mobility in opposite directions through the phloem. It is opposed to their polar transport which occurs only in one direction through a living cell at a time.*

translocated to all the leaves on the plant along the transpiration stream. This phenomenon of phloem-xylem interchange of herbicides is called *circulation.*

Root and shoot tips of plants often act as final sinks for the translocated type of herbicides. But many mobile herbicides are retained in the translocation channels and are prevented from accumulating in the established sinks. Crafts (1967) observed when ^{14}C amitrole was applied to the leaves of soybean seedling, it labelled its root tips intensely, whereas MH and 2,4-D labelled the whole length of roots without any particular prominance at the root tips.

14.3.2 Translocation Through Xylem

Root mobile herbicides translocate acropetally along the transpiration stream, reaching all live leaves, both mature and immature, above the point of application of the herbicide. A labelled xylem mobile herbicide will produce a characteristic 'wedge' pattern in the autoradiograph of a leaf from the treated plant as shown in Fig. 14.2 and 14.3. Thus, a major difference in the translocation behaviour of a phloem mobile and a xylem mobile herbicide is that the latter does not by-pass mature leaves on its way to the plant tops, whereas the former does so. Also, a xylem mobile herbicide translocates only in a direction acropetal to the point of its application while a phloem mobile herbicide translocates both in acropetal and basipetal directions. But a herbicide like picloram when applied to an intact root, translocates acropetally up to its crown level and then it moves into the phloem. Once picloram has reached the phloem tubes, it can translocate both acropetally and basipetally to its sinks bypassing the mature leaves.

When a xylem mobile herbicide is placed on a plant shoot, it moves through the apoplast and is translocated upward in the xylem. It will not show any basipetal translocation unless it was capable of leaking into the adjoining phloem tubes (Crafts, 1966). To cite an example, foliar applied herbicides, atrazine and diuron, both xylem mobile, will kill only shoots of established annual grasses, leaving their crown buds, roots, and hidden meristems unhurt. This is because these herbicides do not translocate from the treated leaves, but cause contact injury to the foliage. On the other hand, when the two compounds are applied to soil, these are absorbed by the grass roots, and are translocated through xylem to the meristematic tissues, crown buds, and blades which may be damaged, seriously.

Reverse Xylem Mobility: In plants growing under intense moisture stress, such as prevailing in the arid regions, certain herbicides show 'reverse xylem mobility' *ie* they translocate rapidly from plant shoots to its roots through xylem instead of through phloem. One to two per cent solution of arsenic trioxide, borax, sodium chloride, and ammonium thiocyanate form common reverse xylem mobile herbicides. They are applied as liquids by jar method. In this method the shoots of a weed growing under an intense moisture-stress condition are bent into a jar containing the herbicide which injures the leaf surfaces and renders them so permeable that it is heavily taken in by the moisture-stressed plant into its xylem vessels and is translocated to its deep roots. In California, scientists found that the treatment of one *Alhagi pseudalhagi* plant with arsenical solution by the jar method could kill several, interconnecting *A. pseudalhagi* plants. Other weeds controlled by this curious, 'reverse xylem mobility' of certain herbicides are wild morningglory (*Convolvulus arvensis*) and poisonoak (*Rhus* *toxicodendron*). The translocation of herbicides absorbed by the cut stumps of unwanted trees is also an instance of 'reverse xylem mobility'.

The reverse mobility of herbicides in plant roots can sometime cause excretion of earlier absorbed herbicides as has been noted in the case of MCPA, 2,4-D, dalapon, picloram, and dicamba (Helling *et al.*, 1971; Hurtt, 1970). Sometimes it may have an important agronomic implication of herbicide residue toxicity to rotation crops which, of course, is very rare.

Fig. 14.6: *Left*: Three mounted soybean seedlings with arrows showing the points of application of ^{14}C tracer 2,4-D, namely, the cotelydon, epicotyl, and primary leaf. *Right*: Autoradiographs of the three seedlings depicting three modes of translocation of 2,4-D as follows:
(i) Upon application to cotyledon, the tracer 2,4-D apparently moved slowly in somewhat low intensity to the expanding trifoliate leaf and the bud. Both the primary leaves were completely by-passed. (ii) Application to the side of epicotyl resulted in selective uptake of 2,4-D into the phloem of the vascular stands and its movement was acropetal into the growing trifoliate leaf and the bud, but basipetal through the hypocotyl into the root system. (iii) Treatment of the primary leaf produced almost the above distribution except that some of the tracer 2,4-D traversed the veins of the treated leaf.
These autoradiographs provide a graphic example of bidirectional translocation of 2,4-D (Crafts, 1967).

14.3.3 Common Types of Translocated Herbicides

The translocation behaviour of herbicides differs with the herbicide structure, and sometimes it may alter with the plant species, environment, etc. Depending upon these factors, five important types of translocated herbicides are recognised:

1. ***Shoot immobile herbicides:*** These are foliar applied herbicides that translocate only in the acropetal direction through xylem. They do not translocate from leaves to the roots of the treated plants. *Examples,* atrazine and diuron.

2. ***Shoot mobile herbicides:*** These are foliar applied herbicides that show both acropetal and basipetal translocation through phloem, sometimes simultaneously. They translocate both to shoots and roots of the treated plants. *Examples,* amitrole, glyphosate, picloram, dalapon, silvex, arsonates, dicamba, TBA, and prynachlor.
3. ***Circulatory herbicides:*** These are foliar applied herbicides capable of frequent phloem-xylem interchange. *Examples* MH, 2,3,6-TBA, picloram, dalapon, and amitrole (probably as a glucose-amitrole conjugate).

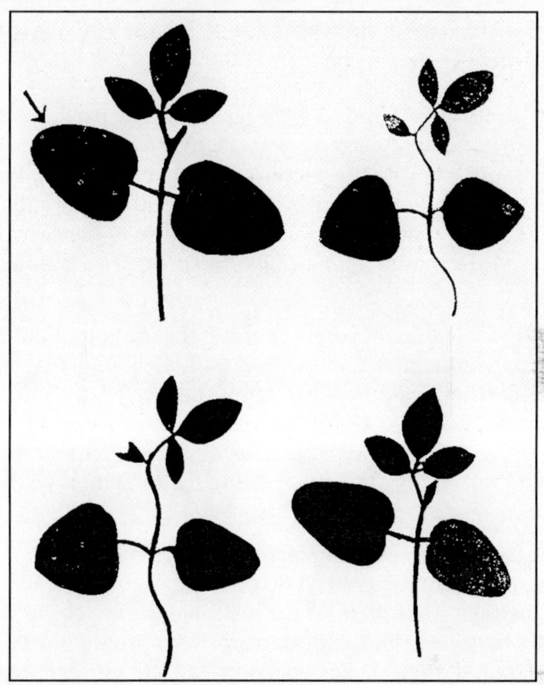

Fig. 14.7: *Top left* = A mounted soybean plant treated at its primary leaf or root with 0.1 μ mole of ^{14}C monuron or MH, in separate individuals. *Top right* = Autoradiographs of the soybean plant treated at its primary leaf with ^{14}C monuron. A characteristic wedge appeared in the treated leaf, without labelling any other leaf. The tracer herbicide obviously followed an apoplast route in the leaf and the plant failed to export it *via* the phloem to its other, untreated parts (diagrammatic). *Bottom left* = Autoradiograph of soybean plant treated with tracer monuron at it roots. The tracer was found distributed uniformly throughout the plant showing a rapid, xylem movement of the herbicide. *Bottom right* = Autoradiograph of soybean plant after its primary leaf treatment with ^{14}C MH. The tracer produced a prominent apoplast wedge in the treated leaf; a dense image in the epicotyl, stem, and terminal bud, besides a medium intensity in the trifoliate leaf. The opposite primary leaf showed light images. This depicted a xylem-phloem interchange of MH in the plant (Crafts, 1967).

4. ***Reverse xylem mobile herbicides:*** These are foliar applied herbicides that translocate to roots through xylem in acute water deficiency conditions. *Examples,* arsenic trioxide ions and sodium chlorate. Paraquat also exhibits reverse flow in xylem when

it is applied to leaf in subduded light. Desiccation of tissues in this case is much slower in comparison to its application in bright sunlight.

5. ***Root mobile herbicides:*** These are root applied herbicides that translocate freely in xylem tissues to reach the plant tops. *Examples,* dicamba, tricamba, uracils, s-triazines, and substituted ureas.

14.4 SOME REPRESENTATIVE RESEARCH FINDINGS ON ABSORPTION AND TRANSLOCATION OF PARTICULAR HERBICIDES IN PLANTS

1. Agbakoba and Goodin (1970 and 1970a) reported that partially defoliated plants of fieldbindweed, soybean, and sugarcane translocated more 2,4-D and picloram in them than their intact plants. The authors postulated that defoliation stimulated α-amylase activity in test plants, releasing more sugars which enhanced translocation of the two herbicides in phloem. Picloram *per se* also enhanced translocation of 2,4-D in fieldbindweed. Devendra *et al.* (1986) also reported similar studies with this herbicide.
2. Bhan *et al.*(1970) studied the absorption and translocation of amine 2,4-D by yellow nutsedge (*Cyperus esculentus*) leaves. The authors found that although the sedge leaves absorbed the herbicide slowly, they translocated it rapidly to the rhizomes developing around the crown region of the weed. Autoradiographs showed heavy 2,4-D labelling in rhizomes which usually develop into tubers and aerial shoots. This explained the role of 2,4-D in suppressing the growth of yellow nutsedge.
3. Crafts (1967) applied ^{14}C 2,4-D, monuron, amitrole, and MH to epicotyl, cotyledon, and primary leaf of young soybean plants and prepared their autoradiographs by standard procedures. From the pattern of labelling of the autoradiograph as shown in Fig. 14.7, he concluded that monuron translocated in xylem; 2,4-D and amitrole in phloem, and MH both in xylem and phloem. But in humid areas, the foliar applied 2,4-D has been found to translocate in xylem too. Under high humidity 2,4-D condenses on the veins of the leaves and forces its way into the xylem vessels from where it translocates to the young and mature leaves equally well, causing an accelerated weed kill.
4. Forde (1966) investigated the mode of synergism of ammonium thiocyanate with amitrole. He found that in the first 24 hours of the treatment it reduced amitrole mobility in plants. But then suddenly it invigorated the translocation of amitrole from the treated shoot to the plant roots. It seems that ammonium thiocyanate held amitrole for the first 24 hours of the treatment, and during this time it altered its molecule to a highly mobile form. It is also possible that ammonium thiocyanate induced some amitrole sparing action on the constituents of plant cells.
5. Foy (1961) studied the translocation of dalapon in cotton and sorghum and found that both roots and shoots of the test plants could absorb and translocate dalapon well. Also, dalapon exhibited circulation. Strong sinks for dalapon were loci of high metabolic activity in plants. Further, dalapon could move back from a low activity sink to a sink of high activity.

6. Hull (1969) found that in johnsongrass (*Sorghun halepense*) the foliar applied dalapon translocated most rapidly to its rhizomes between its flowering and seed maturity stages when feed-back of the food material from leaves to the rhizomes was at its peak. But herbicide absorption by johnsongrass leaves was poor at this time which was a big bottleneck in using dalapon for effective control of the weed at its flowering stage.

7. Magalhaes *et al.* (1968) applied dicamba to roots and shoots of purple nutsedge (*Cyperus rotundus*) to study its translocation in the weed. They found that dicamba translocated from roots of nutsedge to its leaves but not from leaves to the roots. Irrespective of the source, dicamba failed to reach nutsedge tubers.

8. Norris and Freed (1966) compared translocation of three formulations of 2,4-D and 2,4,5-T in bigleafmaple. They found that the maple leaves absorbed ester formulations of both the compounds faster than the amine and sodium salts. The translocation of esters was slower than of salts at the beginning but then it caught up; so much so, that the final quantities of ester formulation of either herbicide reaching the roots of the treated plants were more than those of the respective salts. Initial slow translocation of esters could be due to their rapid absorption which could temporarily inhibit the energy requiring transport system of the plant. In another experiment these authors observed decreasing order of mobility of four test herbicides in maplewood species as dichlorprop > 2,4,5-T > 2,4,D = silvex. But in the herbaceous test plants, 2,4-D was found most mobile of the four herbicides.

9. Putnam and Ries (1968) studied translocation of paraquat–a contact herbicide–in quackgrass (*Agropyron repens*). They found that in dark, foliar applied paraquat translocated in quackgrass to its shallow placed rhizomes and injured them. But in light it did not translocate to any extent and injured only the treated leaf blades. It was postulated that in light, paraquat desiccated the leaf phloem so rapidly that translocation from leaves was not possible.

10. Reid and Hurtt (1969) applied tagged 2,3,6-TBA to the leaves of drybeans (*Phaseolus vulgaris*) and detected frequent phloem-xylem interchange. The bean shoot and root tips formed strong sinks of 2,3,6-TBA. These sinks were maintained even in the case of some deep rooted species of plants.

11. Sheets (1961) studied the source to sink relationship of simazine (^{14}C) in cotton. He found that lysigenous glands present throughout the inside of cotton stems were strong sinks of foliar applied simazine which failed to reach the cotton roots. Simazine, thus, could be *selectively* absorbed by the test plants. Besides the above examples, modes of translocation of later developed herbicides have been reported by Berard *et al.* (1978) for fluridone; Bloomberg and Wax (1978) for mefluidide; Bromilow *et al.* (1993) for glyphosate; Chandrasena and Sagar (1986) for fluazifop - P; Mallipudi *et al.* (1987) for imazapyr and Reddy and Bendixen (1989) for chlorimuron.

Before closing the discussion on the absorption and translocation of herbicides in plants it may be pointed out here that all the herbicide that falls on plant foliage is not available for absorption. Norris and Freed (1966) found that in bigleafmaple hardly 10 to 30% of the applied herbicide was absorbed by the plant leaves, and of this quantity, not more than 5% was translocated to the other plant parts. The remainder of the herbicide intercepted by plant foliage was washed down by rain, volatilized, photodecomposed, or lost by chemical decomposition.

SUMMARY

Herbicides are absorbed primarily through leaves and roots of plants but many herbicides are also absorbed by the germinating seeds, coleoptiles, rhizomes, and tubers. The foliar applied herbicides have to traverse five important barriers before they can be absorbed from plant surface into the epidermal cytoplasm. These barriers are (1) surface waxes and hair, (2) cuticle, (3) brown bark, in case of mature trees, (4) epidermal cell walls, and (5) plasmalemma. Of these, cuticle is most important in determining herbicide absorption by plants. The known mechanisms of herbicide absorption by plant cuticle are (1) diffusion in the case of hydrophilic spray liquids and (2) solubilisation in the case of lipophilic sprays. The herbicide absorption mechanisms through plasmalemma are (i) active absorption involving chemical carriers and (ii) passive absorption involving electrochemical potential gradient. Movement of absorbed herbicides in plants refers to their cell to cell advancement through the thickness of leaves, stems, and roots to arrive near vascular bundles. It may take place through apoplast or symplast routes of plants, depending upon the herbicide structure and plant species.

Many herbicides enter vascular bundles and translocate to distant plant parts. While some may do so through xylem, others translocate through phloem. There are still others which display phloem-xylem interchange and circulate within the plants. Seven important types of mobility patterns of herbicides in plants have been identified in this chapter. While the xylem mobile herbicides move along the transpiration stream, in phloem they 'ride' alongside the food materials which translocate by mass flow in the assimilate stream. At the end some research findings are cited, authorwise, to exemplify absorption and translocation behaviour of specific herbicides in test plants.

SELECTED BIBLIOGRAPHY

1. Agbakoba, C. S. O. and Goodin, J. R. 1970 (a). Picloram enhances 2,4-D movement in fieldbindweed. Weed Sci. 18(1) 19-21.
2. Agbakoba, C. S. O. and Goodin, J. R., 1970. Absorption and translocation of ^{14}C labelled 2,4-D and picloram in fieldbindweed. Weed Sci. 18(1) 168-170.
3. Askew, S. D. and J. W. Walcut. 2002. Absorption, translocation, and metabolism of foliar – applied CGA 362622 in cotton, peanut, and selected weeds. Weed Sci. 50: 293-298.
4. Barrentine, W. L. and Warren, G. F., 1971. Shoot zone activity of trifluralin and nitralin. Weed Sci. 19(1) 37-41.
5. Berard, D. F. *et al.* 1978. Absorption, translocation, and metabolism of fluridone in selected crop species. Weed Sci. 26(3) 252-254.
6. Bhan, V. M. *et al.* 1970. Toxicity, absorption, translocation, and metabolism of 2,4-D in yellow nutsedge. Weed Sci. 18 (6) 733-737.

7. Bloomberg, J. R. and Wax, L. M. 1978. Absorption and translocation of mefluidide by soybean, common cocklebur, and giant foxtail. Weed Sci. 26(5) 434-440.

8. Bromilow, R. H. *et al.* 1993. phloem translocation of strong acids - glyphosate in Ricinuus communis. Pesticide Sci. 37 (1) 39-47.

9. Bunting, J. A. *et al.* 2004. Absorption and activity of foramsulfuron in giantfoxtial (*Setaria faberi*) and woolly cupgrass (*Eriochloa villosa*) with various adjuvants. Weed Sci. 52: 513-517.

10. Chandrasena, N. R. and Sagar, G. R. 1986. Uptake and translocation of ^{14}C-Fluazifop by quackgrass (Agropyron repens). Weed Sci. 34(5) 676-684.

11. Coetzer, E. *et al.* 2001. Glufosinate efficacy, absorption and translocation in amaranth as affected by relative humidity and temperature. Weed Sci. 49: 8-13.

12. Crafts, A. S. 1966. Relation between food and herbicide transport. "Isotopes in Weed Research" - Int. Atomic Energy Agency Symp., Vienna, Proc., 3-7 p.

13. Crafts, A. S. 1967. Bidirectional movement of labelled tracers in soybean seedlings. Hilgardia 37 (16) 625-638.

14. Crafts, A. S. and Foy, C. L. 1962. The chemical and physical nature of plant surfaces in relation to the use of pesticides and to their residues. Residues Review. 1:112-130.

15. Crafts, A. S. 1961. The chemistry and mode of action of herbicides. Int. Sci. Pub., N. Y. 269 pp.

16. Culpepper, A. S. *et al.* 2001. Effect of insecticides on clomazone absorption, translocation, and metabolism in cotton. Weed Sci. 49: 613-616.

17. Devendra, R. *et al.* 1986. Translocation of foliar applied 2,4-D as affected by additives and pH in Solanum elaegnifolium. Ind. J. Weed Sci. 18(3) 153-158.

18. Doll, J. D. *et al.* 1970. Herbicide and phosphorus influences on root absorption of amiben and atrazine. Weed Sci. 18(3) 357-359.

19. Foy, C. L. 1961. Absorption, distribution, and metabolism of dalapon in relation to phytotoxicity 1. Penetration and translocation of ^{36}Cl and ^{14}C- labelled dalapon. Plant Physiology 26(5) 633-697.

20. Foy, C. L. 1962. Absorption and translocation of dalapon-2:^{14}C and ^{36}Cl in Tradescantia funmoensis. Weeds 10(2) 97-99.

21. Foy, C. L. 1964. Review of herbicide penetration through plant surfaces. J. Agri. Food Chem. 12(5) 473-476.

22. Hart, J. J. *et al.* 1993. Characterisation of paraquat transport in protoplasts from maize suspension cells. Plant Physiology 103(3) 963-969.

23. Helling, C. S. *et al.* 1971. Behaviour of pesticides in soils. Adv. Agron. 23:147-229.

24. Hull, R. 1969. Translocation of assimilates and dalapon in established johnsongrass. Weed Sci., 17(3) 312-320.

25. Hurtt, C. P. P. 1970. Root exudation of herbicides by weedy plants: allelopathic implications. Nature 225(5229) 291.

26. Jacinta, C. and Prendeville, G. N. 1979. Effects of dichlofop methyl on leaf cell membrane permeability in wildoat, barley, and wheat. Cand. J. Plant Sci. 59:275-275.

27. Kohler, E. A. and B. E. Branham, 2002. Site of uptake, absorption, translocation, and metabolism of ethofumesate in three turfgrass species. Weed Sci. 50: 576-580.

28. Laties, G. G. 1969. Dual mechanisms of salt uptake in relation to compartmentation and long distance transport. Ann. Rev. Plant Physiol. 20:89-116.

29. Leonard, O. A. et. al. 1970. Translocation of herbicides and assimilates in red maple and white oak. Bot. Gaz. 127(4) 193-201.

30. Li, H. *et al.* 2005. Influence of formulation and glyphosate salt on absorption and translocation in three annual weeds. Weed Sci. 53: 153-159.

31. Mallipudi, N. A. *et al.* 1987. Absorption, translocation, and soil dissipation of imazapyr under field conditions. Weed Abstr. 36 (12) item 3738.

32. Mc Allister, R. S. and Haderlic, L. C. 1985. Translocation of ^{14}C-glyphosate and 14CO2-labelled photoassimilates in Canadathistle (*Cirsium arvense*). Weed Sci. 33:153-159.

33. Mc Elroy *et al.* 2004. Absorption, translocation, and metabolism of halosulfuron and trifloxysulfuron in green kyllinga (*Kyllinga brevifolia*) and false-green kyllinga (*K. gracillima*). Weed Sci. 52: 704-710.

34. Nissen, S. J. 1994. Imazethapyr absorption and fate in leafy spurge (E. esula). Weed Sci. 42(2) 158-162.

35. Norris, L. A. and Freed, V. H. 1966. The absorption and translocation characteristics of several phenoxyalkyl acid herbicides in bigleafmaple. Weed Res. 6:203-211.

36. Pester, T. A. *et al.* 2001. Absorption, translocation, and metabolism of imazamox in jointed goatgrass and feral rye. Weed Sci. 49: 607-612.

37. Prendeville, G. N. *et al.* 1967. Site of uptake of soil applied herbicides. Weed Research 7 (4) 316-322.

38. Preston, C. *et al.* 2005. Differential translocation of paraquat in paraquat – resistant populations of *Hordeum leporinum*. Weed Research (European Weed Research Society) 45: 289-295.

39. Price, A. J. Physiological basis for cotton tolerance to flumioxazin applied postemergence directed. Weed Science 52: 1-7.

40. Putnam, A. R. and Ries, S. K. 1968. Factors influencing the phytotoxicity and movement of paraquat in quackgrass. Weed Sci. 10(1) 80-83.

41. Reddy, K. N. and Bendixen, Leo E. 1989. Toxicity, absorption, and translocation of soil-applied chlorimuron in yellow and purple nutsedges (Cyperus esculentus and C. rotundus). Weed Sci. 37(2) 147-151.

42. Reid, C. P. P. and Hurtt, W. 1969. Translocation and distribution of picloram in bean plants associated with nastic movements. Plant Physiol. 44(1) 1393-1396.

43. Salisbury, R. B. and Ross, C. 1969. Plant Physiology. Wadsworth Pub. Co. Inc., California, USA, 747 pp.

44. Stadelmann, J. (Ed.). 1969. Permeability of the plant cell. Ann. Rev. Plant Physiol. 20:585-603.

45. Sterling, T. M. and Lownds, N. K. 1992. Picloram absorption by broom snakeweed leaf tissue. Weed Sci. 40(3) 390-394.

46. Sutton, D. L. and Bingham, S. W. 1970. Uptake and translocation of 2,4-D ^{14}C in parrotfeather. Weed Sci. 18(2) 193-196.

47. Taylor, T. D. and Warron, G. F. 1970. The effect of metabolic inhibitors on herbicide movements in plants. Weed Sci. 18(1) 68-74.

48. Van Overbeak, J. 1956. Absorption and translocation of plant regulators. Ann. Rev. Plant Physiol., 7 355-372.

49. Veerabhadraiah, G. P. *et al.* 1980. Increase of penetration and translocation of foliar applied 2,4-D into the underground parts of nutsedge. Ind. J. Agri. Sci., 50:352-356.

Chapter 15

MODES OF ACTION OF HERBICIDES IN PLANTS

Often herbicides are put to certain commercial uses before their modes of action in plants are known, just because they control certain weeds effectively. But if we learnt more about how the herbicides act within the plant system, one could find their many new agricultural and other applications. Moreover, without understanding the mode of action of herbicides, intelligent designs of combinations of two or more herbicides, or mixitures of herbicides with other pesticides and fertilizers, cannot be developed.

The biochemical modes of action of many a herbicide in popular use today in different parts of the world, have been studied by plant physiologists. Although the subject in many cases is still controversial in respect of their finer details, yet the scientists seem to have agreed upon at least on the primary modes of action of majority of herbicides. In this chapter the primary modes of action of major groups of herbicides, which can sufficiently explain their phytotoxicity, are reviewed. For a more detailed account of the subject, comprehensive reviews, such as by Eedtke (1982), Ashton and Crafts (1981), and Devine (1992) are available.

In general, the major groups of modern herbicides, *eg* triazines, ureas, bipyridyliums, benzonitriles, and uracils, besides some other herbicides, act largely by disorganising the *photosynthetic apparatus* of susceptible plants in one way or the other. (Wakabayashi and Sato, 1993). Such pesticides are likely to be less hazardous than insecticides to man and his animals. Another important biochemical mechanism of plants prone to certain herbicides is *respiration*, particularly in its stage III of electron transfer. Dinitrophenols, trisubstituted tin compounds, and copper and arsenical based herbicides are very potent in disturbing the normal course of respiration in plants. The third common mode of action of certain herbicides is interference with *mitosis*. Most carbamate and dinitroaniline herbicides, as well as MH, act in this fashion. The phenoxyalkanoic acids, benzoic acids, and related compounds interfere with plant growth controlled by *phytohormones*. Biosynthetic reactions. *eg protein synthesis, lipid synthesis,* and *carotenoid synthesis,* are inhibited by α-chloroacetamides, endothall, amitrole, and thiolcarbamate herbicides. More recently, sulfonylurea and like herbicides are known to act by mainly modifying the action sites of specific enzymes.

15.1 SYMMETRICAL TRIAZINES

The mode of action of this group of herbicides has been almost solely studied through simazine and atrazine. These herbicides accumulate in chloroplasts and interfere at or close to light reaction II of the process of photosynthesis, blocking there the electron transport (Fig. 15.1). The sequence in steps in this action is not fully known. A block in the electron transport system by simazine and atrazine leads to potentially harmful, oxidised chlorophyll molecules, both because of (i) their continuous, light activated loss of electrons and (ii) deficiency of $NADPH_2$ required to keep carotenoids, and in turn the chlorophyll, in a reduced state. It is also postulated that such effects can be accompanied by formation of secondary phytotoxic agents, *eg* certain free radicals, The immediate phytotoxicity symptom of *s*-triazines in plants, *ie,* chlorosis of actively photosynthesising leaves, margin inwards, supports the above damage hypothesis. However, plant starvation due to hampered food synthesis may further aid in bringing about ultimate death to the affected plant. A continuous source of sucrose to the simazine-treated plants may tend to prevent the herbicide phytotoxicity for sometime, but the plant is bound to die eventually.

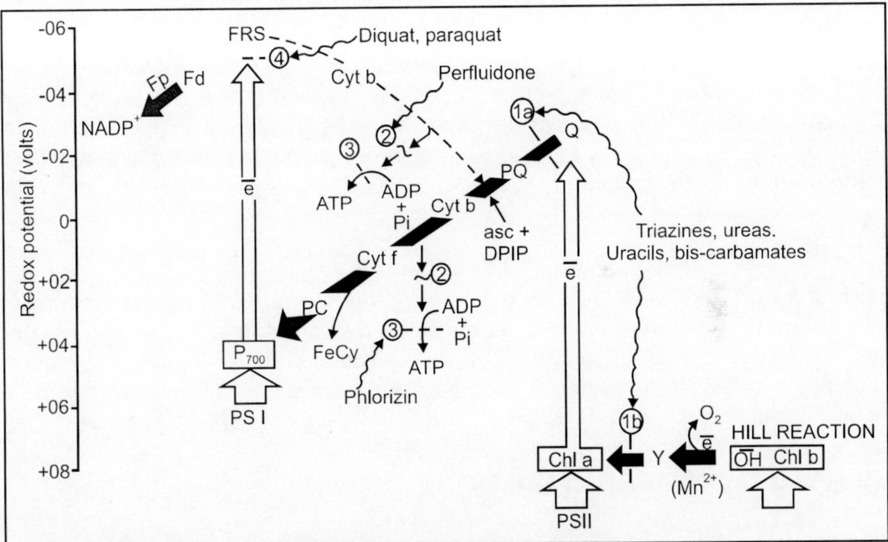

Fig. 15.1: Schematic presentation of photosynthetic electron transport chain and phosphorylation reactions considered to occur in plant chloroplast lamella. The numbers 1a, lb, 2, 3, and 4 indicate the postulated sites of action of specific herbicides. Both PS-1 and PS-2 have been of interest as target sites for some potential herbicides. Most of such herbicides, like say triazines, are inhibitors of the photosynthetic electron transport system, although some like bipyridyls act by accepting electrons from PS-1.

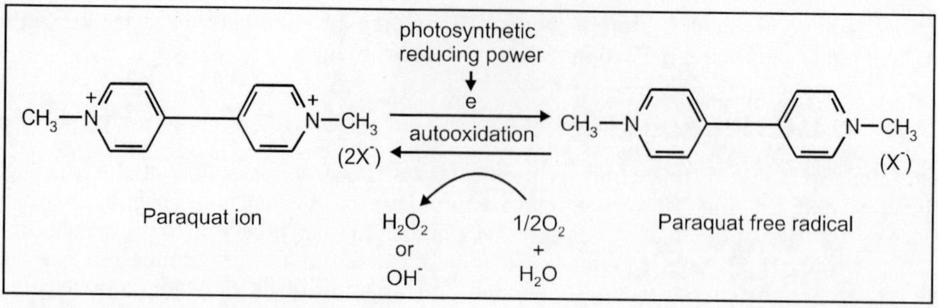

Fig. 15.2: Reversible, free radical formation from paraquat ion and its autooxidation yielding H_2O_2 or $OH^{\cdot}$. H_2O_2 in the process, causes rapid desiccation of the treated foliage. This is followed by necrosis and ultimately the death of the whole plant within 24 hours on sunny days. (Application of Fe-chelates to the paraquat-treated plant can reverse the process and protect it form herbicide injury).

There are some inconclusive evidences that *s*-triazines may also be involved in the impediment of certain other metabolic processes but, at the moment, their adverse effect on photosynthesis is considered of primary importance (Ashton and Crafts.1981).

15.2 URACILS

Uracil herbicides are found to exert their phytotoxic action by blocking electron transport in light reaction II, in a fashion similar to *s*-triazines. Also, the chloroplast envelope of the uracil treated leaves is reported destroyed, causing leakage of its contents into the cytoplasm (Ashton and Crafts, 1981). Bromacil is also implicated in causing necrosis of root meristem in the treated plants.

15.3 UREAS

Moreland *et al.* (1969) and Ponte-Freitas *et al.* (1993) reported that the major mode of action of diuron, monuron, and isoproturon in plants was similar to that of *s*-triazines, described above. Earlier, Bishop (1958) had postulated that diuron and monuron inhibited non-cyclic phosphorylation in plants. Linuron has been further found to inhibit uptake and translocation of radioactive Ca in tomato and parsnip (Hogue, 1968).

15.4 HYDROXYBENZONITRILES

Ioxynil and Bromoxynil

The two nitriles, like triazines and substituted ureas, are found to owe their phytotoxicity to inhibition of electron transport in light reaction-II of the photosynthetic apparatus of plants. Other biochemical actions of ioxynil and bromoxynil on record include (i) interference with RNA and protein synthesis and (ii) uncoupling the oxidative phosphorylation (Moreland 1967). These effects result in leaf collapse and blistered, necrotic patches on the leaves within 24 hours of the treatment with ioxynil or bromoxynil.

Dichlobenil

Dichlobenil induces dormancy in weed seeds and vegetative propagules. It is found to act as an inhibitor of synthesis and/or export of auxin by the embryonic axis as well as of proteolytic and amylase activity in seed cotyledon (Penner and Ashton, 1968). Ferrari and Moreland (1969) showed that dichlobenil was also an uncoupler of oxidative phosphorylation.

15.5 QUATERNARY AMMONIUMS (=DIPYRIDYLS)

Diquat and paraquat (methyl viologens) cause rapid desiccation of the treated vegetation. It is now certain that these herbicide molecules ionise completely in plant cells and the cations act as electron acceptors in chloroplasts, short circuiting thus the electron transfer in light reaction-I (*cf*. atrazine and diuron). The free radicals, which are extremely reactive, are then auto-oxidised by molecular oxygen back to cationic species and during the process H_2O_2 is produced. In high concentration, H_2O_2 destroys the plant tissues, usually within 24 hours of the treatment (Zweig *et al.*,1969). The chloroplast membranes of the treated leaves are further found to lose integrity, leading to wilting and bleaching of the affected tissues. As paraquat (and diquat) is not consumed during this reaction, only its catalytic amounts are required in the chloroplast for its herbicidal action. The treated plants develop symptoms within few hours of application of paraquat or diquat (when applied during period of active photosynthesis).

There is some evidence that diquat and paraquat cations can likewise be reduced to free radicals in *respiration cycle*, which may injure even the non-photosynthesising plant parts, like seeds, provided these were made to absorb into them. Reports that paraquat falling on exposed grass seeds proved phytotoxic, lends support to such hypothesis (Salazar and Appleby, 1982). Legume seeds did not respond to paraquat and diquat. Dalton (1992) reported substantial increases in the nodular glutathione content of the paraquat treated, 25-28 days old soybean plants.

Paraquat is more phytotoxic to plants with low glutathione reductase (GR) activity than those with high GR.

15.6 NITROPHENOLS

Dinoseb is a strong multi-uncoupler of phosphorylation, both in respiration and photosynthetic systems. Aslo it inhibits electron transport in photosystem II. At high concentration, dinoseb destroys cell membranes causing severe leaf wilting within minutes of the treatment.

15.7 INORGANIC COPPER BASED AND ARSENIAL HERBICIDES

Many herbicides belonging to these two groups inhibit pyruvate dehydrogenase activity during glycolysis at stage-I of the normal respiration in plants.

15.8 DIAZINES

Pyrazon

Pyrazon produces phytotoxicity symptoms similar to atrazine. The available evidence suggests that pyrazon blocks Hill reaction in the susceptible plants (Hilton *et al.*, 1969).

Table 15.1: The in *vitro* 50% Hill Reaction Inhibition Concentration of Certain Herbicides Interfering with Photosynthesis (After Corbett, 1975)

Herbicide	Concentration for 50% inhibition of Hill reaction (μM)
I. Ureas	
Chloroxuron	0.16
Diuron	0.03-0.18
Linuron	0.20
Monuron	0.50
Neburon	0.14
Noruron	1.60
II. Triazines	
Atrazine	0.25
Desmetryne	0.17
Metribuzin	0.23
Prometon	1.3-2.0
Prometryne	0.09
Propazine	0.35-4.3
Simazine	0.4-8.4
III. Acylanilides	
Propanil	0.16-0.78
IV. Hydroxybenzonitrile	
Ioxynil	0.07-10.0
V. Uracils	
Bromacil	0.49-2.0
Terbacil	0.37
VI. Pyridazinones	
Pyrazon	6-7

15.9 CARBAMATES

In general, carbamate herbicides are mitotic poisons. The soil active compounds check elongation and/or expansion of plumules of the germinating seedlings. Meristematic tissues basal to the first rudimentary leaf in the plumule is most vulnerable to this effect, (Banting, 1970). A shoot active carbamate like barban stops meristematic activity of axillary buds in wildoat (*Avena fatua*). The affected seedlings have been found low in serine, threonine, RNA, DNA, and protein levels. The treated plants die because of prolonged static condition of growth.

The thiolcarbamate herbicides like EPTC and diallate inhibit production of wax by plants although it is not certain if this could contribute to their phytotoxic action. Poorly developed lipids in cell membrane could result in leakage of cytoplasmic material. Poor development of cuticle on the leaves of EPTC treated plant is also found associated with enhanced transpiration losses of water. Foliage of cabbage sown in EPTC treated soil is reported to become susceptible to subsequent application of dinoseb because of low cuticle formation. Furest (1987) presented a detailed account on this aspect.

15.10 DINITROANILINES

Nitralin and trifluratin cause mitotic abrasions. Disruption of nuclear and cell division is a major component of their action. At molecular level, the affected tissues show reduced levels of RNA, proteins, and several enzymes. Besides, these herbicides are reported to uncouple oxidative phosphorylation.

It is typical of dinitroamine herbicides to inhibit the lateral growth of roots in the treated soil zone.

15.11 PHENOXYALKANOIC ACIDS AND BENZOIC ACIDS

This group of herbicides includes 2,4-D and related compounds. 2,4-D is a synthetic growth substance, exhibiting auxin like properties. It cannot be classed as true auxin because it is not positive on oat coleoptile curvature test (although it is so in oat coleoptile straight growth and split pea stem tests). External application of high concentration of indoleacetic acid (IAA), the only known natural auxin, to plants will produce symptoms similar to 2,4-D. Still it cannot be used as a herbicide because plants possess IAA oxidases for destroying any excessive IAA present. 2,4-D, on the contrary, is a persistent auxin-like compound which is not destroyed by most dicot plants (see Chapter 16).

Ever since the discovery of 2,4-D and MCPA in 1940's, several biochemical modes of action have been assigned to these herbicides and, probably, none is free of criticism. However, the herbicide experts do agree that plants treated with 2,4-D die slowly due to the abraded growth produced by this persistent auxin. There is a rapid proliferation of mature cambium around full length of cambium tubes in response to 2,4-D, disrupting thus the normal food translocation through them. There is a hypothesis that 2,4-D activates a cell wall enzyme in the cambium tissues, named extensin, which loosens the cell walls to allow uncontrolled, non-osmotic uptake of water. The cells thus swell, abnormally. It is further noted that mature cambium cells revive their division activity upon application of 2,4-D due to accelerated ascorbic acid oxidases activity in plants which, in turn, vigorates the protein sulphydryl synthesis. The latter is responsible for the rapid cell division of cambium tissues around phloem tubes.

Besides the phloem dislocation, 2,4-D may dislocate plant food supply in certain other ways too. Like the phloem cambium, the leaf cells may swell in response to 2,4-D and fill the intercellular spaces, checking thus the CO_2 intake by leaves. This is further aggravated by closure of stomata resulting from an attempt by plants to avoid the dehydration effects of 2,4-D. All the foregoing cytological effects of 2,4-D lead us to a 'starvation theory' of its phytotoxicity. 2,4-D often induces in susceptible plants, epinasty, rolling, and puckering within minutes of the treatment, although it takes few days before the plant actually dies (Fig. 15.3). This symptology is in agreement with the above starvation theory. A definite biochemical base to the histological responses of plants to 2,4-D is yet to be assigned.

Fig. 15.3: Cotton is highly susceptible to 2,4-D. This figure shows typical 2,4-D phytotoxicity symptoms caused by the herbicide spray drift. (Photo- Late R. D. Verma).

Fig. 15.4: Morphogenic effects of 2,4-D on *Heliotropium ellipticum*. Note the curled and drooping leaves and epinastic effects on stems and petioles (Photo- Late R. D. Verma).

2,4-D was once implicated to stimulate ethylene production in plants, but ethylene itself is not phytotoxic.

There had been much interest shown by the scientists in the past years at Illinois and Colorado (U.S.A.) in the effect of 2,4-D at the gene level, possibly by stimulating the production of messenger RNA which carries code for the synthesis of specific proteins (Hanson and Slife, 1969). However, this biochemical action could not make the plant respond to 2,4-D within minutes of its application. Moreover, simultaneous application of inhibitors of protein synthesis had not been found to dilute the 2,4-D action in plants.

Benzoic acid herbicides are known to act in a fashion similar to the phenoxyalkanoic acids.

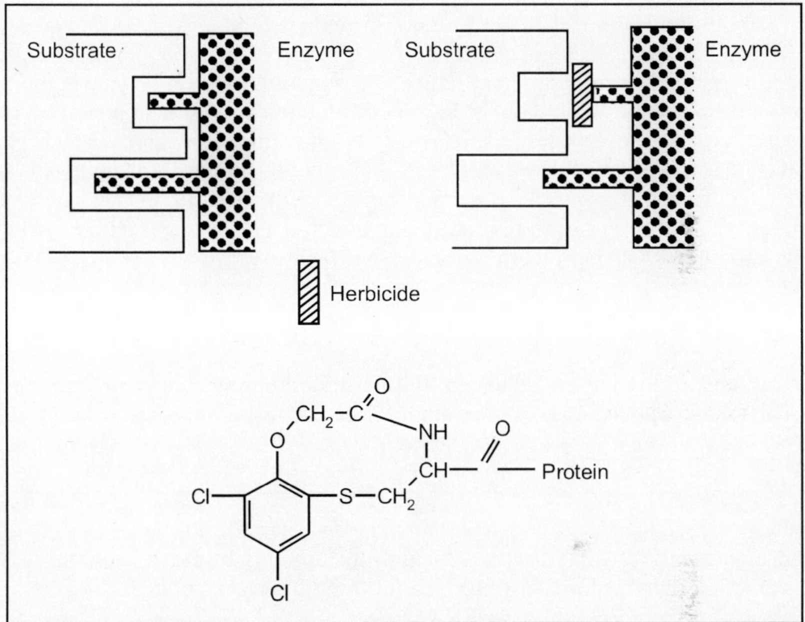

Fig. 15.5: One of the theories of action of certain herbicides like 2,4-D is disturbance in either protein synthesis (top) or structure itself (bottom).

15.12 PYRIDINES

Picloram

Picloram is a persistent, auxin-like substance. It stimulates cell elongation in the susceptible plants. The affected plants exhibit epinasty and, often split-shoots, due to tissue proliferation. The leaves are puckered and cupped in some species. The roots deteriorate and die because of abradant development of vascular bundles. At the biochemical level, picloram is reported to lower nuclease enzyme activity, resulting in abnormally high nucleic acid contents.

Fluridone

Fluridone, a pyridine compound, behaves like amitrole in its biochemical mode of action (see latter).

15.13 ALIPHATIC ACIDS

Dalapon

At low rates of application, dalapon induces growth regulator type, slow and systemic effects in plants. The leaves go chlorotic. The treated plants show inhibited levels of pantothenic acid (vitamin-B complex) which is a constituent of Coenzyme-A required in most of the metabolic reactions. But at high rates of application, the aliphatic acid causes rapid scorching and browning of leaves which inhibit it translocation through plants at high rates. Dalapon is reported to bring about conformational changes in specific enzyme proteins, leading to loss of normal permeability controls in plasmalemma and consequent leakage of cell contents into the intercellular spaces. Structural disturbance in enzymes responsible for incorporation of NH_4^+ into carboxylic acid has also been postulated, resulting in accumulation of ammonia to phytotoxic levels.

15.14 α-CHLOROACETAMIDES AND ANILIDES

The soil-applied acetamide herbicides inhibit germination and root growth of suceptible plants. The foliage-applied ones, on the other hand, cause leaf necrosis.

In general, with chloroacetamide herbicides, inhibition of protein synthesis might be a particularly important explanation of their biochemical mode of action (Furest, 1987).

Some physiologists have found that certain chloroacetamide herbicides *eg* allidochlor, inhibited incorporation of radioactive leucine into proteins in plant segments. Jaworski (1969) suggested that *s*-chloroacetamides could inhibit protein synthesis by alkylating an amino group of an aminoacyltransfer RNA.

In variance with the above general characteristic inhibition in biosynthetic reactions of chloroacetamides, certain acetamides are reported to have variable action sites. Diphenamid, CDAA, CDEA, and pronamide, for example, are found to inhibit mitosis in root tips. Contrary to this, bensulide has been found to inhibit cell elongation in root tips, but not cell division. The affected root cells showed precocious vacuolation and lignification. Propanil, besides inhibiting protein synthesis, has been found to inhibit electron transport in light reaction-II (Moreland *et al.*, 1969). Perfluidone is found an uncoupler of photophosphorylation.

15.15 PHTHALIC ACIDS

DCPA

DCPA inhibits cell division in germinating seed roots and coleoptile. The susceptible seedlings thus wither away in the treated soil.

Endothall

Endothall might act by inhibiting leucine incorporation into protein in certain plant segments. In high concentrations even lipid synthesis may be inhibited by it. The affected plants are browned to death. In seeds, endothall has been found to inhibit amylase action and in seedlings it may interfere with messenger RNA synthesis. The seedlings eventually perish in the treated soil.

Naptalam

Naptalam has characteristic effect of abolishing normal geotropism in plants; inducing the roots to grow out of the soil, besides stunting their growth. It is possible that naptalam acts by interfering with IAA transport in plants.

15.16 TRIAZOLES

Aminotriazole causes intensive inhibition of carotenogenesis in leaves. This allows free photooxidation of chlorophyll molecules during the light hours of the day. The chloroplast membranes and ribosomes are destroyed (Burns *et al.*, 1971).

The foregoing biochemical mode of action of amitrole is likely to be sufficient to explain its phytotoxicity.

15.17 ANILINES AND TOLUIDINES

Pendimethalin

Pendimethalin inhibits both cell division and cell elongation in the roots and shoot meristems of the susceptible plants. The growth is inhibited directly following absorption through hypocotyl and shoot region. The plants die shortly after germination, or emergence from the soil. The germination of susceptible weed species *per se* is not affected.

15.18 SULFONYLUREAS (SU), IMIDAZOLINONES (IMI), PYRIMIDINYL-OXYBENZOATES (POB), TRIAZOLOPYRIMIDINES (TP), AND SULFONYLAMINOCARBONYL-TRIAZOLINONES

Herbicides belonging to these five chemical families target the plastid enzyme Acetolactate Synthase (ALS) in plants which catalyses the first step in the biosynthesis of essential branched chain aminoacids (valine, leucine, and isoleucine). The ALS inhibitors thus stop cell division and reduce carbohydrate translocation in the susceptible plants. The affected plants succumb to these herbicides completely in 7-20 days.

15.19 DIPHENYL ETHERS, OXADIAZOLES, PHENYLPHTHALIMIDES, AND TRIAZOLINONES

Herbicides belonging to these groups target protoporphyrinogen oxidase (Protox) enzyme in the susceptible plant species. In plants this enzyme is responsible for catalyzing the conversion of protogen (protoporphyrinogen IX) to proto (protoporphyrin IX) inside the chloroplast membranes. Due to inhibition of the protox enzyme by the herbicide, there is thus accumulation of protogen which generates toxic oxygen radicals in the presence of light, causing irreversible, severe damage to the affected cell membranes. Some protox inhibiting herbicides are flumioxazin, acifluorfen, lactofen, and sulfentranone.

15.20 ARYLOXYPHENOXYPROPIONATES (AOPP) AND CYCLOHEXANEDIONES (CHD)

Herbicides belonging to these chemical families (*eg* diclofopbutyl and cyhalofop-butyl and lenacil, respectively) act typically through inhibition of Acetyl-CoA carboxylase (Accase) enzyme in the susceptible grasses. This enzyme is responsible in plants to catalyse the first step in the fally acid biosynthesis.

15.21 ETHERS

Oxyfuorfen

Oxyfuorfen scorches plant foliage by its contact action. Applied to soil, it kills the emerging weed seedlings.

At the cellular level the foliage applied oxyfluorfen is reported to cause (i) loss of cell membrane integrity, (ii) enhancement of leaf respiration, (iii) accelerated ethylene production, and (iv) uncoupling of non-cyclic photophosphorylation and electron transport in light reaction-II (Groske and Hopen, 1978 and Moreland *et al*., 1970). In the germinating seedling, this herbicide is found to accelerate the respiration levels.

Morphological phytotoxicity symptoms of the ether herbicides include pigment bleaching, followed by necrosis and browning of leaves. The ether herbicides are sometimes called "bleaching herbicides" or peroxidisers.

15.22 MISCELLANEOUS HERBICIDES

Clomazone

The susceptible plants upon treatment with clomazone reveal reduction in their chlorophyll (a + b) and carotenoid synthesis. This, in turn, cuts the content of light harvesting complexes; lower chlorophyll fluorescence reabsorption; and the absence of long, wavelength emission forms of PS-I; all finally leading to the death of the affected plants.

It has been recently demonstrated that clomazone metabolic products are more toxic to plants than clomazone pre se. This is why its metabolism hindering insecticides like disulfoton and phorate reduce greatly the clomazone phytotoxicity in cotton and, thus render it more selective to the crop.

Glufosinate Ammonium

Gulfosinate causes in susceptible plants inhibition of glutamine synthetase (GS) enzyme which is the key factor in ammonia assimilation in higher plants. As a consequence, there is rapid intracellular accumulation of NH 3 in plants in toxic concentrations and concomitant depletion of glutamine and several other essential amminoacids. This is followed by rapid decline of CO_2 fixation after the herbicide treatment. The affected foliage goes chloratic and necrotic.

Glyphosate

The primary mechanism of action of this foliage active, broad-spectrum herbicide in inhibition of the enzyme 5-endolpyruvyls hikimate-3 phosphate synthase (EPSP) which precludes biosynthesis of aromatic aminoacids (phenylalanine, tryasine, and tryptophan). It is estimated that approximately 20% of the CO_2 fixed by plants flows through this pathway and inhibition of this enzyme causes a shortage of compounds critical to plant growth. Also, the inhibition of lamda aminovulinic acid synthesis in barley and maize treated with glyphosate has been observed to lead to a block in synthesis of chlorophyll and other porphyrins.

Acrolein

Acrolein readily destroys the integrity of plant cell membranes, causing the affected cells to go flaccid within hours of the treatment.

Dichlofop-methyl

Dichlofop has been reported to irreversibly depolarise the membrane potential and increase the proton permeability in susceptible plant cells.

Sodium chlorate

Sodium chlorate, like many other salts, ionises the heavy metals from their salts in plants cells which can denature the plant proteins.

Petroleum oils

Petroleum oils fill stomatal openings and occupy intercellular spaces in leaves to hamper free gaseous exchange. Also, probably, the herbicidal oils exert a lipid solublising action on the cell and chloroplast membranes, forcing the cell sap and chlorophyll to leak. The affected leaves impart a water-soaked appearance.

15.23 LASER HERBICIDES

These are porphyrin containing compounds like ALA which in high doses, along with some synthetic dipyridyl chemicals, cause massive synthesis of chlorophyll in the treated plants. (In normal concentrations, as occuring in nature, ALA aids proper synthesis of chlorophyll in plants). The excessively formed chlorophylls absorb extra light during the day and produce large quantities of singlet oxygen which proves highly phytotoxic. Thus, all such compounds which bring about excessive chlorophyll formation in plants have potential of being good herbicides, and these have come to be known as *laser herbicides*.

Table 15.2: Some Important, Primary Biochemical Modes of Action of Herbicides

Biochemical action	Examples of herbicides implicated in the action
1. Interference with photosynthetic process	
(i) Electron transport blockage	(i) Triazines, ureas, pyrazon, hydroxybenzo-nitriles, dinoseb, and propanil
(ii) Electron transport deflection	(ii) Quaternary ammoniums (diquat, paraquat)
(iii) Photo-phosphorylation	(iii) Perfluidone and ethers
2. Interference with normal respiration	
(i) Uncouplers of phosphorylation	(i) Dinoseb, ethers
(ii) Inhibition of glycolysis	(ii) Copper and arsenical compounds
3. Interference with plant growth	
(i) Mitotic poisons or disrupters	(i) Carbamates, oryzalin, pronamide, CDAA, and DCPA (=chlorthal dimethyl)
(ii) Cell proliferation	(ii) Phenoxy alkanoic acids, picloram and bensulide
(iii) Anti-geotropism	(iii) Naptalam
4. Interference with biosynthetic reactions	
(i) Protein synthesis inhibition	(i) Aliphatic acids, chloroacetamides, propanil, and endothall
(ii) Lipid synthesis inhibition	(ii) EPTC
(iii) Loss of cell membrane permeability features	(iii) Dinoseb, aliphatic acids, ethers, acrolein, and petroleum oils
(iv) Carotenoid synthesis inhibition	(iv) Triazoles
5. Enzyme inhibitors	
(i) ALS inhibitors	(i) Sulfonylureas, Imidazolinones; Triazolopyrimidines
(ii) Protox inhibitors	(ii) Diphenyl ethers, Oxadiazoles, Phenyplthal imides, and triazolinones.
(iii) ACCase inhibitors	(iii) Cyclohexanediones; Aryloxyphenoxypropionic acids
(iv) EPSP synthase inhibitors	(iv) Glyphosate
6. Peroxidisers	Ethers
7. Other actions	
(i) Inhibition of enzyme activity in seeds	(i) Endothall
(ii) Denaturation of plant proteins	(ii) Sodium chlorate

SUMMARY

Herbicide structures differ widely in their modes of action in plants. Quite a few herbicides, for example, *s*-triazines, substituted ureas, pyrazon, bromacil, ioxynil, and bromoxynil disturb or block the Hill reaction in photosynthesizing plants. Certain other herbicides affect adversely important steps in respiration mechanism of plants, particularly in phosphorylation, allowing the respiration to go free-wheel. Sodium arsenite, picloram, dichlobenil, and dinoseb are herbicides of this type. Dicamba and herbicidal oils damage the differentially permeable plasma membranes of plant cells. 2,4-D is known to dislocate normal translocation of food material in plants. 2,4-D also causes alteration of nucleic acid-protein metabolism by indiscriminately activating certain otherwise repressed genes responsible for excessively accelerated metabolic activity in plants. Both picloram and 2,4-D have been found to activate ethylene production in plants. Leaf chloroplasts are destroyed directly by *s*-triazines and bromacil, and indirectly by amitrole.

CDAA, CDEA, and diphenamid act in plants primarily by dislocating normal mitotic cell division in their seedling roots and plumules. Carbamates like EPTC and bensulide inhibit cell elongation and expansion in germinating seedlings. Some other modes of action of herbicides in plants mentioned in this chapter are: inhibition of specific enzymes (*Ex.* sulphonylureas), precipitation of plant proteins (*Ex.*: dalapon); abnormal interactions with plant auxin IAA (*Ex.*: dichlobenil); inhibition of protein synthesis (*Ex.*: ioxynil and bromoxynil); H_2O_2 toxicity (*Ex.*: diquat and paraquat); and others. Further research is underway with the plant physiologists to reveal more sites of action of newer herbicides which will open new fields for their exploitation in agriculture and other areas of human activity. The new herbicide molecules are largely some specific enzyme inhibitors.

SELECTED BIBLIOGRAPHY

1. Ashton, F. M. and Crafts, A. S. 1981. Mode of Action of Herbicides. 2nd edition. Wiley-Interscience, 524 pp.
2. Askew, S. D. and J. W. Walcut, 2002. Absorption, translocation and metabolism of foliar-appied CGA 362622 in cotton, peanut, and selected weeds. Weed Sci. 50: 293-298.
3. Audus, L. J. (ed.) 1976. Herbicide Physiology, Biochemistry, and Ecology. Acad. Press, London, 564 pp.
4. Autor, A. P. 1977. Biochemical Mechanisms of Paraquat Toxicity. Acad. Press. 240 p.
5. Banting, J. D. 1970. Effect of diallate and triallate on wildoat and wheat cells. Weed Sci. 18(1) 80-84.
6. Burns, E. R. *et al.* 1971. Inhibition of carotenoid synthesis as a mechanism of action of amitrole, dichlormate, and pyriclor. Plant Physiol. 47 144-148.
7. Chang, I. K. and Foy, C. L. 1971. Effects of picloram on mitochondrial swelling and ATP-ase. Weed Sci. 19(1) 53-57.
8. Chow, P. N. P. 1976. Effects of postemergence herbicides on growth, photosynthesis, and photosynthate translocation in wildoat. Cand. J. Plant Sci. 56 429-430.

9. Corbett, J. R. 1975. The Biochemical Mode of Action of Pesticides. Acad. Press, London, 330 p.
10. Dalton D. A. 1992. Effects of paraquat on the oxygen free radical biology of soybean root nodules. Bull. Environ. Contamination and Toxicology, 45(5) 721-726.
11. Deli, J. and Warren, G. E. 1970. Uptake, translocation, and herbicidal effect of diphenamid. Weed Sci. 18 (6) 692-696.
12. Devine, M. *et al.* 1992. Physiology of Herbicide Action. Prentice Hall, XII + 441 p.
13. Eedtke, C. 1982. Biochemistry and Physiology of Herbicide action. Berlin Springer-Verlag. 202 p.
14. Ferrari, T. E. and Moreland, D. E. 1969. Effects of 3, 5-dihalogenated-4-hydroxybenzonitrile on the activity of mitochondria from white potato tubers. Plant Physiol. 44(3) 429-434.
15. Fuerst, E. P. 1987. Understanding the mode of action of chloroacetamide and thiocarbamate herbicides. Weed Technol. 1(4) 270-277.
16. Gorske, S. F. and Hopen, H. J. 1978. Effects of two diphenyl ether herbicides on common purslane (*Portulaca oleracea*). Weed Sci. 26(6) 585-588.
17. Hilton, J. L. *et al.* 1969. Modes of action of pyradazinone herbicides. Weed Sci. 17:541-547.
18. Hogue, E. J. 1968. The effect of linuron on ^{32}P and ^{45}Ca uptake in tomato and parsnip. Weed Sci. 16(2) 185-187.
19. Jaworski, E. G. 1969. Chloroacetamides. (IN) Degradation of Herbicides by Kearney, P. C. and Kaufman, D. D. Marcel Dekker, Inc. New York, 165-168.
20. Kearney, P. C. and D. D. Kaufman (eds). 1988. Herbicides: Chemistry, Degradation, and Mode of Action. Marcel and Dekker, USA. 403 p.
21. Koo, S. J. *et al.*1994. Quinclorac-induced electrolyte leakage in seedling grasses. Weed Sci. 42(1) 1-7.
22. Li, N. *et al.*, 2005. Influence of formulation and glyphosate salt on absorption and translocation in three annual weeds. Weed Sci. 53: 153-159.
23. Maffei, M. *et al.* 1993. Paraquat on carvone biosynthesis in mentha. J. Essential Oil Research 5(6) 651-657.
24. Manderscheid, R. *et al.* 2005. Glufosinate treatment of weeds results in ammonia emission by plant. Agric. Ecosyst. & Environ. 109(1) : 129-140 (Germany). (W.A. 54(10), 3984).
25. Moreland, D. E. 1967. Mechanisms of action of herbicides. Ann. Rev. Plant Physiol., 18:365-386.
26. Moreland, D. E. *et al.* 1969. Effects of herbicides on RNA and protein synthesis. Weed Sci. 17(4) 556-563.
27. Moreland, D. E. *et. al.* 1970. Effect of diphenylether herbicides on reactions of mitochondria and chloroplasts. Weed Sci. 18(5) 636-641.
28. Penner, D. and Ashton, F. M. 1968. Influence of dichlobenil, endothall, and bromoxynil on kinin control of proteolytic activity. Weeds 16(3) 323-332.
29. Perez-Jones, A. 2005. Identification of glyphosate-resistant Italian ryegrass (*Lolium multiflorum*) in Oregon. Weed Sci. 53 : 775-779 (USA).

30. Pester, T. A. and S. J. Nissen, 2001. Absorption translocation and metabolism of imazamox in jointed goatgrass and feral rye. Weed Sci. 49: 607-612.

31. Pline, W. A. *et al.* 2001. Absorption and translocation of glyphosate in glyphosate resistant cotton as influenced by application methods and growth stage. Weed Sci. 49: 460-467.

32. Ponte-Freitas, A. *et al.* 1993. Penetration of isoproturon and inhibition of photosynthesis after droplet deposition on leaf fragments. Pesticide Biochem. & Physiology 45 (1) 54-61.

33. Salazar L. C. and Appleby A. P.1982. Germination and growth of grasses and legumes from seeds treated with glyphosate and paraquat. Weed Sci. 30:235-237.

34. Sharma, M. P. *et al.* 1982. The basis for synergism between barban and flamprop on wildoat. Weed Sci. 30 147-152.

35. Smith, S. C. *et al.* 2005. Herbicidal indolizine - 5, 8 - diones : photosystem-1 redox mediators. Pest Mgmt. Sci. 61 : 16-24 (U.K.).

36. Vettakkorumakankav, N. N. *et al.* 2002. Physiological effect of clopyralid on corn as determined by bioassay and light-scattering spectroscopy. Weed Sci. 50: 713-720.

37. Vicentini, C. B. *et al.* 2005. Pyrazole derivatives as photosynthetic electron transport inhibitors : new leads and structure activity relationship. J. Agric. & Food Chem. 53(10) : 3848-3855 (USA).

38. Wakabayashi, K. and Sato, Y. 1993. Herbicides affecting the structure and function of chloroplasts (2). Japan Pesticide Information No. 61 14-19.

39. Zheng, D. *et al.* 2005. Association of the W574L ALS substitution with resistance to cloransulam and imazamox in common ragweed (*Ambrosia artemisiifolia*). Weed Sci. 53 : 424-430 (USA).

40. ZhiJIN, F. *et al.* 2005. Herbicide activity of monosulfuron and its mode of action. J. Environ. Sci. 17(3) : 399-403 (China). (WA. 54(11), 4399).

41. Zweig, G. *et al.* 1969. Mode of action of dipyridyl and certain quinone herbicides. J. Agri. & Food Chem. 17(2) 176-181.

Chapter 16

HERBICIDE SELECTIVITY AMONGST PLANTS

Different plant species often respond differently to a given herbicide and one plant species responds differently to different herbicides. Sometimes, even the plants of the same species growing in different environments may also respond differently to a given herbicide. Such phenomena are collectively called herbicidal selectivity. Herbicidal selectivity is the foundation of the phenomenal achievements made in modern, chemical vegetation management where the object is to kill some plants (the weeds) and retain the others (the crops), at the same time and place. But much as we would like to achieve it, selectivity is unwanted when it occurs within the weed species growing in a mixed population, which ultimately causes gradual build up of the tolerant ones.

The aim of this chapter is (1) to elucidate various mechanisms involved in the fascinating phenomenon of herbicidal selectivity and (2) to develop in the student an understanding of the means which can (a) improve selectivity between crops and weeds and (b) lower it within the weed species, in a given situation.

The fundamental principle of herbicide selectivity is that more toxicant reaches the site of action in an active form inside the target plants than in the non-target species. This may occur due to (1) differential absorption, (2) differential translocation, and (3) differential deactivation of the applied herbicide. Besides, some plants may exhibit innate, protoplasmic resistance to specific herbicides. These processes are, however, not mutually exclusive. A good review on the subject is provided by Baron and Gressel (1982).

16.1 DIFFERENTIAL ABSORPTION OF HERBICIDES

In laboratory, molecular peculiarities of herbicides have been found responsible for differences in their time-bound absorption by different plant species. Slife *et al.* (1962) studied the tolerance of wildcucumber (*Sicyos angulatus*) to 2,4-D in comparison to susceptible cultivated cucumber (*Cucumis sativus*). They found that 2,4-D absorption in wildcucumber was so slow that it kept pace with its metabolism easily, thus the plant proved tolerant. Similar reasons have been offered for the tolerance of honeysuckle (*Lonicera* sp.) and bigleafmaple (*Acer macrophyllum*) to amitrole as against its phytotoxicity to bean and lucerne plants. However, there are only a few examples of real, inherent differences among plant species for the absorption of a given herbicide. In field conditions differential absorption of herbicides by plants may occur for many other, more important reasons *eg*, (1) the plant species may differ in their morphology and growth habits, (2) the herbicides may be applied at different times and by different methods, (3) adsorbents and antidotes may be used to prevent herbicide absorption by the non-target plants, and (4) herbicides and their formulations may differ in their ability to contact the non-target plants. These points will be discussed here in this order.

16.1.1 Differences in Morphology of Plants

Certain morphological features of crop plants will allow limited retention of aqueous sprays of herbicides on their foliage. This offers an opportunity to obtain selective control of weed species of variable morphology that may allow easy wetting of leaves with the aqueous sprays. Important limited spray retention characteristics found in certain plants are: (i) narrow upright leaves, (ii) corrugated or finely ridged leaf surfaces, (iii) waxy leaf surfaces, and (iv) pubescent leaves. Pea, onion, wheat, cabbage, sugarcane, colocasia, and some other crop plants possess these characteristics. Aqueous sprays either bounce off as droplets from their foliage or wet them only in small spots. Crops like wheat and sugarcane are further protected against herbicide sprays by their covered growing points. The growing point in wheat plant is located at the base, initially below the soil surface, while in sugarcane it is hidden by the upper leaf sheaths.

The limited spray retention provides plants protection only against contact, selective herbicides that are sprayed in carrier water without any wetting agent. For example, limited spray retention was considered the first line of defence of wheat against postemergent ioxynil and bromoxynil which brought about selective control of many broadleaf weeds. Likewise, the selectivity of nitrofen (now banned) to many *Brassica* crops and rice was found due to differential wetting.

With translocated herbicides limited spray retention is of not much help in protecting the non-target plants from herbicide injury. It is because the translocated type of herbicides, even when they wet plant surfaces in small areas, can be absorbed and translocated to other plant parts and, thus, injure the whole plant.

In past some years the importance of limited wetting of crop plants as a factor in selective control of weeds with herbicides has diminished. In an attempt to control a wide spectrum of weeds simultaneously, several kinds of wetting agents and other adjuvants (Chapter 18) are added to herbicides to wet most leaf types equally well. Spraying through very fine nozzles, and with high pressure sprayers, has similar effect of narrowing down differences in the wetting of plants with herbicides, although it is beset with danger of spray drifts.

16.1.2 Differences in Growth Habits of Plants

Differences in Shoot Growth: When crop rows have a clear advantage in height over the inter-row weeds, directed spraying of herbicides is a common method of achieving selective control of weeds. Herbicide mulches are used in standing crop rows for affecting selective control of germinating weeds.

In slow germinating crops like potato and sugarcane, weeds often establish themselves even before crop emergence. These weeds can be controlled selectively by spraying a contact type of herbicide before more than 10 per cent of the crop plants are seen over the ground.

In more advanced stages of crop growth, sometimes specific weed species may grow much above the crop height. In crops like Egyptianclover and spinach, these tall weeds may often completely hide the crop plants. In the U. S. A. and some other countries, herbicide-laden wax bars have been employed successfully for the control of tall weeds in wide row crops. In the closely sown crops a low volume application of a contact herbicide can be made wisely to rid them of the crowding, tall weeds.

In lawns and gardens shoots of nutsedge and other erect weeds can be selectively wiped with herbicides from either a herbicide wax-bar or a clothed stick dipped in concentrated herbicide solution.

Differences in Root Growth: When herbicides are applied to soil, differences in the growth habits of underground parts of weeds and crop plants become important in determining their selective absorption. In general, weed seeds germinate from top 1.25 to 1.5 cm of soil, whereas many crop seeds are planted 5.0 to 7.5 cm deep. When a recommended preemergence herbicide is applied on the soil surface, and the soil moisture conditions are suitable to leach it to about 2.5 to 3.0 cm soil depth, it is readily available for absorption to the germinating weeds. Crop plants that grow their roots beyond 5 cm depth obviously avoid herbicide absorption and escape phytotoxicity. This is the basic principle of selectivity of most of the preemergence herbicides, and it is a function of herbicide structure, formulation, and rate besides the soil texture, organic and inorganic colloids, and the rainfall. When any one of these factors is unfavourable, the herbicide may either injure the crop plants or result in poor weed control. Sometimes, both these adverse effects may occur together when the phenomenon is called *reverse selectivity*.

The selectivity of molinate between *Oryza sativa* and *Echinochloa colonum* was chiefly due to differences in the crown root initiation levels of the two grasses. *Echinochloa* put forth its crown roots very close to the surface of the soil where most of the applied molinate resided. On the contrary, in rice seedlings the crown roots were initiated sufficiently below the soil surface in the herbicide-free zone. Likewise the selectivity between wheat (*Triticum aestivum*) and greenfoxtail (*Setaria viridis),* both grasses, with soil-incorporated trifluralin was ascribed to the fact that *S. viridis* placed its coleoptilar node within one cm of the soil surface, irrespective of the depth from which it germinated while, wheat developed the coleoptilar node much deeper. Since trifluralin is incorporated shallow in soil and the coleoptilar nodes of the above two plants are of major importance in the absorption of this herbicide, wheat got off safely without absorbing the toxicant. *Setaria*, on the other hand, absorbed trifluralin in phytotoxic amount and was killed.

16.2 DIFFERENTLAL TRANSLOCATION OF HERBICIDES

It is true that a plant can translocate through it only as much herbicide as it absorbs, and no more. But there are instances when equal amounts of herbicides are absorbed by plants but still they are translocated at different rates. It was found that 2,4,5-T was considerably more toxic to *Cucumis trigonus* than 2,4-D because it was translocated much more readily than the latter compound inside plants. The differences in the selectivity between sugarcane (tolerant) and beans (susceptible) to 2,4-D has also been explained on the basis of its slow translocation in sugarcane and rapid translocation in beans. The reverse was found true for amitrole which translocated more rapidly in *Acer rubrum* than in *Fraxinus americana*.

Better mobility of herbicides in plants, however, does not always mean a quicker plant kill. Actually, in certain instances, it may aid the plant in escaping specific herbicide action. For instance, diphenamid was found selective to *Convolvulus arvensis* because it translocated the herbicide rapidly from the roots to the shoots where it was metabolised. *Avena sativa*, on the contrary, was found susceptible to diphenamid because it failed to translocate the herbicide rapidly away from its roots which are always the site of is phytotoxic action. Similar was true for selectivity of mefluidide to *Glycine max* and its toxicity to *Xanthium* and *Setaria* spp. Diflufenican is found selective to wheat and barley because of its slow uptake and translocation in these plants (Haynes and Kirkweed, 1992). Many other similar examples are available (Delvin *et al.*, 1987; Durgesha, 1994, and Gillespie, 1994). Soybean has been found tolerant to oxyfluorfen due its slow absorption of the herbicide.

16.3 DIFFERENTIAL RATES OF DEACTIVATION OF HERBICIDES BY PLANTS

Experimental evidence is growing that herbicide selectivity is primarily a function of differential rates of deactivation of the toxicant by the target and the non-target plants before they reach their respective sites of action. This deactivation may be a process of (i) *metabolism*, (ii) *reverse metabolism*, or (iii) *conjugation* A tolerant plant species deactivates the herbicide molecule (or ion) rapidly, whereas a susceptible species does so, slowly. In some instances, reverse metabolism may be an important venue of herbicide dissipation.

16.3.1 Metabolism

Metabolism involves a change in the molecular structures of the applied herbicides inside plants to yield some non-phytotoxic products. For instance *Ribes nigrum*, which is susceptible to 2,4-D, metabolized the herbicide at rate of 2% of the applied amount in 96 hours whereas the tolerant *R. sativum* metabolised 50% of it during the same period. Likewise a striking correlation between the quantity of atrazine present in the shoots of different plant species 10 days after its application and the herbicide selectivity has been reported. Selectivity of terbacil between tolerant *Mentha piperita* and susceptible

Ipomoea hederacea was also found to be due to differential rates of metabolism in the two plants. *M. piperita* metabolized terbacil rapidly enough to show only temporary fall in its photosynthetic rates, whereas in *I. hederacea* the herbicide persisted long enough to inhibit photosynthesis to the point of plant mortality. Apple plants metabolised amitrole and simazine rapidly (Schneider *et al.*, 1993). Similar was found true for bentazon and desmedipham selectivities, as well as for many other herbicides. In summary, the faster metabolism of a herbicide in tolerant crop species (or cultivars) than in the susceptible ones is an important mechanism of herbicide selectivity (Mc Mullan and Nalewaja, 1991). Rice was tolerant to bensulfuron and *Lolium* sp. to chlorsulfuron because of their rapid metabolism inside plants.

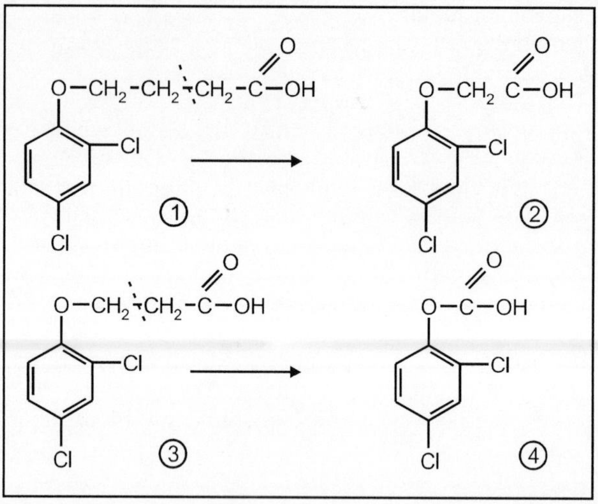

Fig. 16.1: β-oxidation of (i) 2,4-DB and (3) 2,4-DP yield, respectively, phytotoxic 2,4-D and a non-phytotoxic phenol compound. 2,4-DB thus kills only those plants which possess the β-oxidation enzymes, like several non-legume dicot weeds. The legume crop plants like lucerne, berseem, and pea escape its action. 2,4-DP is obviously non-phytotoxic to either kind of plant.

16.3.2 Reverse Metabolism

When in metabolic reactions of herbicides the intermediate chemical structures prove more phytotoxic than the parent compound, the process is called *reverse metabolism*. For instance, the even number carbon ω-phenoxyalkanoic acid herbicides like 2,4-DB and MCPB, *per se* are non-phytotoxic. But N.H. Grace in 1939 and R. L Wain in 1955 found that metabolism of these compounds in plants yielded phytotoxic acetic acid intermediates namely 2,4-D and MCPA, respectively. This reverse metabolism of 2,4-DB and MCPB was an enzymic β-oxidation process[*]. It occurred in many non-leguminous

[*] *β-oxidation:* In β-oxidation, first the carboxylic acid group (-COOH) and carbon atom adjacent to it are oxidized and resynthesized into a new carboxylic group (-COOH). This requires the presence of cofactor HS-CoA (hydroxythio coenzyme A), ATP, FAD, and NAD. This newly formed carboxyl group

plants. Certain legumes like pea, lucerne, berseem, and some other clovers, on the other hand, either lacked the necessary β-oxidation system or operated it sluggishly. Consequently, these legumes proved comparatively tolerant to 2,4-DB and MCPB. It may be pointed out that β-oxidation of odd number carbon ω-phenoxyalkanoic acid compounds, such as dichlorprop and mecoprop, yield non-phytotoxic phenol compounds. These herbicides, thus, do not exhibit any reverse metabolism.

16.3.3 Conjugation

Conjugation is coupling of intact herbicide molecules with some plant cell constituent in living plants. It takes the toxic herbicide concentration out of the main stream of the plant; and those capable of rapidly doing so obviously prove tolerant to it. It was found that ^{14}C chloramben conjugated rapidly inside the roots of soybean (*Glycine max*) with glucose molecules, forming N-glucosyl chloramben and an unknown compound chloroamiben-X. In plants susceptible to chloramben the conjugation was found to be so slow that the herbicide translocated from roots to the shoots where it proved phytotoxic. The tolerance of grasses and certain ecotypes of *Convolvulus arvensis* to foliar application of 2,4-D has also been explained, at least in part, on the basis of its conjugation with glucose and certain amino acids in these plants. With glucose, 2,4-D formed glucoside, β-D-glucose ester of 2,4-D. Binding of 2,4-D on certain protein films in a tolerant graminaceous plant like sugarcane has also been found an important mode of its selectivity. The adsorbed 2,4-D is more rapidly metabolized in plants to the non-phytotoxic compounds than the free 2,4-D molecules. Scientists working on the fate of ^{3}H, ^{14}C pyrazon in plants found that in tolerant sugarbeet and redbeet, the herbicide conjugated rapidly in their leaves with glucose forming N-glycosyl pyrazon. This conjugate, being a volatile substance, escaped from the plant cells into the atmosphere. The pyrazon susceptible test plants like tomato and millets failed to withhold pyrazon by conjugation and, therefore, succumbed to its phytotoxic action. It is further known that simazine and atrazine are also deactivated in maize, apple, sugarcane and certain millets by the process of conjugation rather than by the earlier believed mechanism of metabolism. An enzyme named Glutathione-S-transferase (GST) was extracted and purified from the leaves of maize, sorghum, sugarcane, Johnsongrass (*S. halepense*), and sudangrass (*S. sudanensis*); all of which are tolerant to simazine. This enzyme was found to catalyze the conjugation of simazine, and probably of other *s*-triazines, with reduced glutathione in foliage, forming S-(4-ethyl amino-6-isopropylamino-2-*s*-triazine) glutathione. Similar was the case with fenoxapropethylin tolerant grass species but it was found subjected to non-enzymic conjugation with glutathione (GSH) and cysteine (Tal *et al.*, 1993). Chloride ions were released during the process. Smith (1983) found rapid ^{14}C-atrazine peptide conjugate formation in certain cultivar of *Paspalum notatum*.

---

then displaces the β-carbon of the unoxidised chain (*ie*. second methyl group from right). The process repeats itself removing two carbon atoms from the chain each time, as long as two methyl moeities are available in the aliphatic acid chain. When only one methyl group is left in the chain, the process stops. Thus, β-oxidation will lead an even number carbon phenoxyalkanoic acid to phenoxyacetic acid, but an odd carbon one, to a phenol.

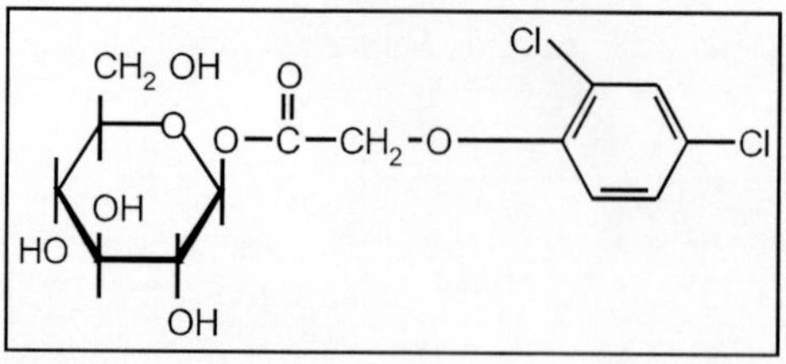

Fig. 16.2: Conjugated form of 2,4-D detected in plants, namely, β-D-glucose ester of 2,4-D. This is a selectivity mechanism against 2,4-D in at least certain tolerant plants.

16.3.4 Some Definitive Pathways of Differential Herbicide Deactivation in Plants

Substituted Ureas: Dealkylation of substituted ureas is common in the tolerant species of plants. Some scientists isolated from the leaves of cotton, plantain, broadbean, and, buckwheat–all tolerant–a microsomal, mixed function oxidase enzyme which was found to catalyze *N*-demethylation of 3-(phenyl)-l-methylurea herbicides *eg* monuron, diuron, and fluometuron. Each mole of substrate that was demethylated produced l mole each of the formaldehyde (H. CHO) and-chlorphenylurea. The latter was further metabolized to anilines which, being highly unstable, were spontaneously oxidized to nitrobenzene and other substances. Similar was found true for selectivity of fluometuron between cotton and snapbean (*Phaseolus vulgaris*). The excised roots of susceptible snapbean could not metabolize fluometuron at all. Simultaneous dealkoxylation and dealkylation of metobromuron was also reported in potato and maize. The metabolism of metobromuron yielded 4-bromophenylurea which was a nonphytotoxic compound. Sweetcorn detoxyfied sulfonylurea fast to become tolerant (Burton *et al.* 1994). Sengnil *et al.* (1993) opined that high levels of branched chain amino-acids may provide protection against bensulfuron. Sugarbeet was found tolerant to triflusulfuron due to its rapid metabolism (Withenbach, *et al.* 1994).

δ-Triazines: Simazine has been known for over a decade to get metabolized in resistant maize to hydroxy simazine with the help of a compound identified as 2,4-dihydroxy-7-methoxy-l, 4-benzoxazin-3-one (MBOA) present in the roots of such plants. The hydrolysis was found to be rapid enough to prevent the entry of intact molecules of absorbed simazine into the leaf chloroplasts of maize. However, MBOA is *not* found in other simazine tolerant plants say, *Sorghum* spp., which has diluted its importance as a general selectivity factor for simazine. Later the possibility of metabolism of simazine in such plants through monomolecular N-dealkylation of alkyl-amino side chains at the 4-C position, leading to non-phytotoxic ammelide was demonstrated. In maize, glutathione conjugation is believed to be a primary mechanism responsible for its tolerance to simazine and atrazine. Terbutryn decreased DNA content in watergrass (*Echinochloa colonum*), but increased it in maize (Bansal and Sharma, 1992).

Fig. 16.3 Glutathion-S-transferase catalysed formation of S-(4-ethylamino-6-isopropylamino-2-*s*-triazino) glutathione. In maize and like crops it is considered an important scheme of tolerance to simazine or atrazine.

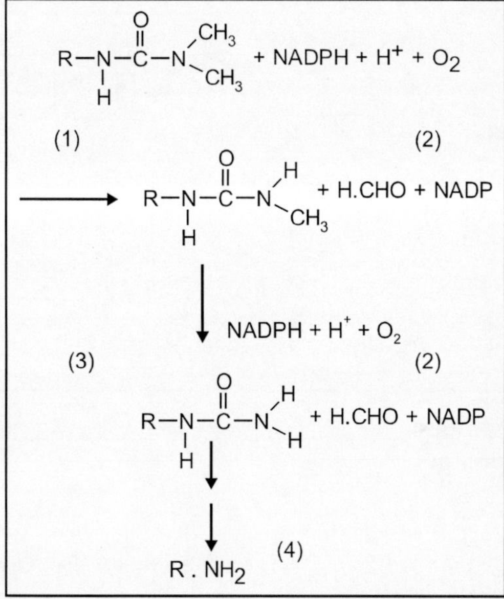

Fig. 16.4 Scheme for enzymic metabolism of substituted urea herbicides in microsomal fraction of cotton (Frear *et al.*, 1969), making the crop tolerant to a herbicide like diuron or fluometuron, within limits

Amitrole: Although amitrole is primarily a non-selective herbicide, the tolerance of some ecotypes of *Cirsium arvense* and *Convolvulus arvensis* to it aroused interest in studying its selectivity behaviour (Smith *et al.*, 1968). The studies revealed that in the amitrole resistant ecotypes (in fact, chemotypes), the herbicide molecules were subjected to photocatalysed ring cleavage in the presence of riboflavin. The exposure of the plant to high intensity light and 15-28°C temperature further stimulated amitrole metabolism in the resistant chemotypes. Ammonium thiocyanate, on the contrary, was found to inhibit amitrole metabolism in plants and, thus, it formed a very good activator of amitrole against the tolerant chemotypes.

2,4-D: The tolerant plants have been found to metabolize 2,4-D molecules by side chain degradation, followed by ring hydroxylation. The side chain degradation involves decarboxylation, demethylation, and cleavage of the ether linkage. The resulting metabolite is a non-phytotoxic dichlorophenol, with dichloroanisole as an intermediary compound. The dichlorophenol then may be either conjugated to a glucose or it may be further metabolised. The hydroxylation of 2,4-D ring at the *para* carbon is further followed by its hydoxylation at the ortho position to yield chlorocatechol. The ring is then subjected to cleavage, forming chloromuconic acid. More recently, 2,4-D (BEGE) has been reported in barley metabolised largely by its hydrolysis, followed by conjugation with sugars and higher carbohydrates. MCPA (BEGE) was, however, hydroxylated at its methyl carbon, followed by likewise conjugation.

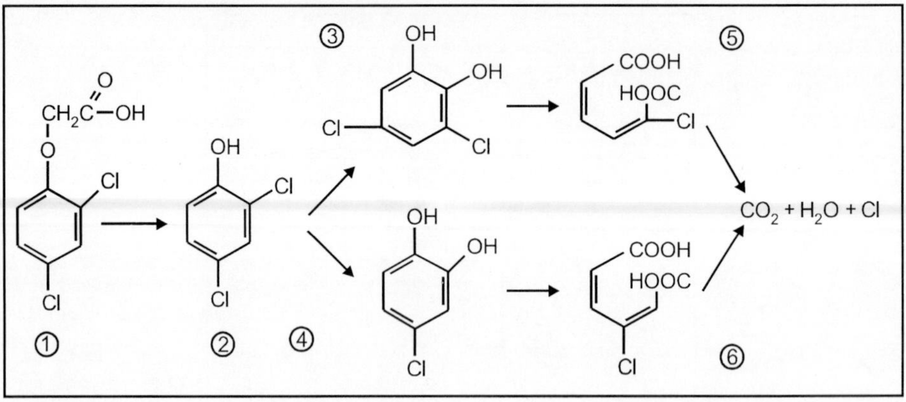

Fig. 16.5: Scheme for degradation of 2,4-D *via* catechols (2 and 3) and chloromuconic acids (5 and 6) in certain tolerant plants.

Silvex (2, 4, 5-TP): In the susceptible species silvex has been found to resist its side chain degradation more than 2,4,5-T. This is responsible for its greater phytotoxicity than of 2,4,5-T to certain woody weedy plants.

EPTC: EPTC is metabolized fast in tolerant plants, probably in the fashion it is known to biodegrade in soil (Chapter 19). Thiolalcohol, CO_2, and dialkylamine are initial non-phytotoxic metabolites. SO_2, CO_2, and H_2O are the final end products.

Propanil: Selectivity of propanil between resistant rice (*Oryza sativa*) and susceptible *Echinochloa colonum* biotypes was found to be due to differences in the arylacylamine amidohydrolase (AAAs) enzyme contents of their leaves. This enzyme is capable of hydrolysing propanil in plants to non-phytotoxic compounds, 3,4-dichloroaniline and propionic acid. The susceptible *E. colonum* leaves contained only $1/60^{th}$ the quantity of the enzyme present in the rice leaves. In rice too this enzyme level could fall greatly in response to either an abnormally high atmospheric temperature or application of certain insecticides with propanil (see Chapter 19). The resistant biotypes of *E. colonum* are found to possess mechanism similar to rice for deactivating propanil.

IPC and CIPC: Earlier IPC and CIPC were considered to affect only positional selectivity. But now the tolerant test plants have been found to metabolise these herbicide molecules to innocuous acid and aniline molecules.

Chloramben: Tolerant plants detoxify chloramben rapidly by conjugation to form *N*-glucosyl chloramben. Besides, in the roots of tolerant plants an unidentified degradation product of chloramben has also been detected.

Pyrazon: In tolerant sugarbeet, pyrazon molecule is rapidly metabolised in its leaves by dropping its phenyl ring. Also, pyrazon may be inactivated by conjugation to a glucosamine. High atmospheric temperatures accelerate absorption of pyrazon by sugarbeet which may then fail to keep pace with its deactivation mechanism, resulting in severe crop injury.

Diclofop: In tolerant wheat diclofop is aryl-hydroxylated and conjugated to an aryl glucoside. In susceptible wildoat the conjugate is neutral glucosyl ester which is easily reversible to toxic diclofop. In addition, rates of herbicide absorption and metabolism may play important role with some plant species (Boldt and Putnam, 1981).

Metolachlor: Selectivity of metolachlor between maize and yellow nutsedge was found due to chiefly differential metabolism of the herbicide. In addition, yellow nutsedge shoots readily absorbed the herbicide, while in maize it was slow (Dixon and Stoller, 1982).

Ethametsulfuron-methyl: In tolerant plants, like the rape (*Brassica napus*), this herbicide was found rapidly metabolised. The major metabolites were *O*-desmethyl and *N*-desmethyl-*O*-desmethyl of the herbicide molecule; both being non-phytotoxic compounds (Lichtner, 1995).

Glufosinate-ammonium: Despite its nonselective nature, not all weeds are controlled equally well with glufosinate. The selectivity between tolerant rigidgrass (*Lolium rigidum*) and susceptible wild sterile oat (*Avena sterilis*) has been explained on the basis of wide difference in the translocation of the herbicide in the two weed species. While rigidgrass (T) permits very weak translocation of glufosinate to its action sites, in wild oat(s) it is very fast.

The transgenic herbicide tolerant soybeans contain a gene for an enzyme phosphiothrion-acetyl-transferase, that enables the plant to metabolise rapidly glufosinate-ammonium moiety into non-phytotoxic form.

Imazamox: The differential response of tolerant joint goatgrass (*Aegilops cylindrica*) and susceptible feral rye (*Secale cereale*) to foliar applied imazamox appears to be related to differences in translocation and metabolism of the herbicide in the two weed species.

Trifloxyfulfuron sodium: The postemergence application of CGA-362622 is found selective to cotton. The mechanism of tolerance of this crop to the herbicide is assigned to its fact metabolism and slow absorption in cotton plants.

Flumioxazin: Directed postemergence application of fluminoxazin is reported selective to cotton. differential absorption, translocation, and metabolism of the herbicide at various growth stages, as well as development of a bark layer, are considered basis of tolerance of the crop to flumioxazin.

Foramusulfuron: Various hybrids of maize have exhibited differential tolerances to this herbicide applied postemergence. The phenomenon is assigned primarily to differential herbicide metabolism. The more tolerant maize hybrids metabolized the foramusulfuron to a greater degree than the sensitive hybrids. This mode of selectivity is in common to the sulfonylurea herbicides, in general.

Pyrithiobac: The selectivity of foliage applied pyrithiobac to cotton is found due to ability of the plant to metabolise it to non-herbicidal compounds rapidly enough to escape its phytotoxicity, as is generally true for other ALS-inhibiting herbicides.

Cyhalofop-butyl: It is selective to rice and is phytotoxic to weeds of the same family (poaceae) like *Echinochloa* spp. In rice (as well as in several broadleaf weeds) it is quickly metabolized to inactive diacid. But in the susceptible weedy grasses it is metabolized to herbicidally active monoacid. Besides metabolism, other modes of selectivity assigned to this herbicide are: presence of insensitive ACCase enzyme, compartmentation (active exclusion), and poor herbicide absorption or translocation in the tolerant plants.

16.4 DIFFERENTIAL PROTOPLASMIC RESISTANCE

Protoplasm of different plant species and varieties differs in withstanding abnormal deficiencies and excesses of its numerous constituents that may be induced in the presence of specific herbicide molecules. For instance, plants that show tolerance to dalapon withstand pantothenic acid deficiency and resist precipitation of their cell proteins. Likewise, plasmalemma of epidermal cells of carrot leaves resist the solublizing action of 'crop oils' much longer than many of the associated weeds.

Biophysical features of plant cells such as protoplasmic viscosity, streaming, and physical continuity also respond differently to variable herbicide structures. Buffering mechanisms of protoplasm of plants are affected differentially by different herbicides; selectivity of sulphuric acid between tolerant wheat and susceptible broadleaf weeds seems to be mainly because of the maintenance of buffering in the former and its loss in the latter. The tolerance of mustard, groundnut, and cotton to trifluralin and nitralin was assigned to their inherent protoplasmic resistance. The protoplasmic tolerance was found an important factor in the tolerance of rice plants to molinate.

16.5 MULTIFACTOR HERBICIDE SELECTIVITY IN PLANTS

From the above discussion one may tend to believe that various mechanisms of herbicide selectivity found in plants were independent of each other, and that they occurred in different plants at different times. But many plant-herbicide systems exhibit multi modes of selectivity. For example, it was established that selectivity of linuron against parsnip in comparison to tomato was both due to (i) lower absorption rates and (ii) lower pace of metabolism of the herbicide in the former crop. Similarly, selectivity of fluorodifen between resistant peanut and susceptible cucumbers was found to be due to both (i) its limited translocation from roots to leaves, as well as (ii) a more rapid metabolism of the herbicide that did reach the peanut leaves before it could enter the chloroplasts. In cucumber, fluorodifen translocation was fast but its metabolism was slow and so the plant proved susceptible to it.

Wheat is tolerant to postemergent ioxynil and bromoxynil because of three concurrent selectivity mechanisms, namely (i) limited spray retention, (ii) slow translocation, and (iii) rapid herbicide metabolism. Of course, limited spray retention is the first line of defence with wheat against the two nitriles.

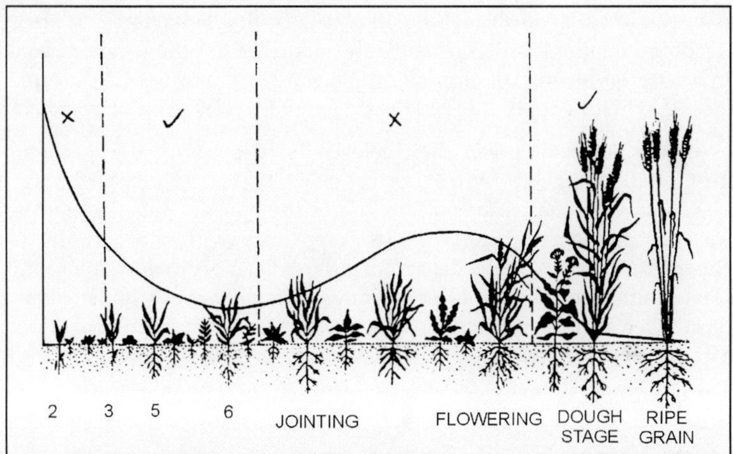

Fig. 16.6: Relatively susceptible and tolerant stages of winter grains to the foliage applied 2,4-D. The low points on the curve exhibit the tolerant stages *eg.* the tillering and dough stages, while the remainder points mark the susceptible stages. The time of application of a herbicide in relation to the crop growth stage is thus important in achieving selectivity.

Fig. 16.7: Some deformities in wheat and barley ears resulting from the wrong use of 2,4-D; like its application at the susceptible crop stages, use of higher than recommended dose, and overlap spray etc. Also, some *cultivars* of wheat may be susceptible to this herbicide.

Distribution of herbicide molecules within plants can also be an important factor in the herbicide selectivity. Perfluidone and picloram, for instance, accumulate at the site of action in the susceptible plants, but in tolerant species these are evenly distributed. In cotton leaves, lysigenous glands and trichomes hold high concentrations of certain triazine and substituted urea herbicides, thus greatly lowering their concentration at the site of their action in the treated plants.

Even if a plant possessed some mechanism to exhibit tolerance to a given herbicide, the dose of the herbicide and the growth stage of the plant at the time of treatment, are of paramount importance in dictating the final selectivity behaviour of the system. All herbicide recommendations on crop lands are identified by these two parameters. Most field research with herbicides on crop lands is devoted to finding (i) how much herbicide to apply and (ii) when to apply it to obtain a desired level of *selective* weed control.

Under-rates of herbicides improve their selectivity to crops at the cost of satisfactory weed control, while their over-rates are most likely to reduce selectivity and cause variable crop injury. It is so because at over-rates the specific defence mechanism of the plant against the applied herbicide fails to keep pace with the quantity of herbicide reaching the site of its action in active form. In the case of physiologically selective herbicides, no doubt, the range of selective rates is usually much higher than needed for obtaining best weed control, while it is very narrow for other herbicides. In fact, most of the current day selective herbicides will lose their selectivity at over-rates by even 5-10g/ha.

There are herbicide vulnerable and herbicide tolerant stages in the ontogeny of plants. It is true for both, the crops and the weeds. Only a few herbicide-crop combinations defy this generalization when the herbicide can be applied with disregard to growth stage of the crop, for example, simazine in maize and propanil in rice. In most other cases, at different stages of their growth, plants respond differently to a given herbicide. For instance, 2,4-D is selective to winter grains, first at their 3 to 6-leaf stage and again at the dough stage. At other growth stages, 2,4-D may induce in these crops malformations like onion leafing, missing spikelet ears, and rattail ears. In barley, even malting quality may be lowered by treatment with 2,4-D at a susceptible growth stage. In maize, sorghum, and other crops likewise, there are specified stages of crop growth when 2, 4-D proves most selective. (Figs. 16.6 & 16.7).

Besides the many above inherent plant factors, method of planting of crops may also determine herbicide selectivity. The ridge-planted potato is found more tolerant to preemergent 2,4-D than the flat planted crop. Likewise, soybean was found more tolerant to linuron when a slightly rounded ridge was formed over the rows than when the rows were left in the furrowed condition.

Preemergence butachlor is selective to upland, direct seeded rice but not to flood-sown rice. Similarly, the tolerance of this crop to dithiopyr is vitiated on sandy soils and when transplanted shallow. Also the application of small, concentrated droplets of thifensulfuron instead of its normal spray can damage the otherwise tolerant peas.

16.6 INDUCTION OF SELECTIVITY

16.6.1 Adsorbents and safeners

Adsorbents: Activated charcoal has been found a strong adsorbent of herbicides like 2,4-D, EPTC, 2,4,5-T, propham, pyrazon, propachlor, trifluralin, nitralin, chlorambean, diuron, neburon, simazine, and butachlor. Therefore, if the germinating crop seeds and seedlings are surrounded by a layer of activated charcoal within the soil, they can be made to escape absorption of many soil-applied herbicides (Pilshchikova *et al.*, 1991).

It offers an excellent opportunity for stretching the selectivity of herbicides to a wide variety of crops. Activated carbon was first used as an adsorbent of 2,4-D in the form of a uniform, 2.5 cm wide band over partially covered crop seed rows (Gupta, 1976). Its effective rate was 130 kg/ha on clay loam soils, and 390 kg/ha or more on sandy soils.

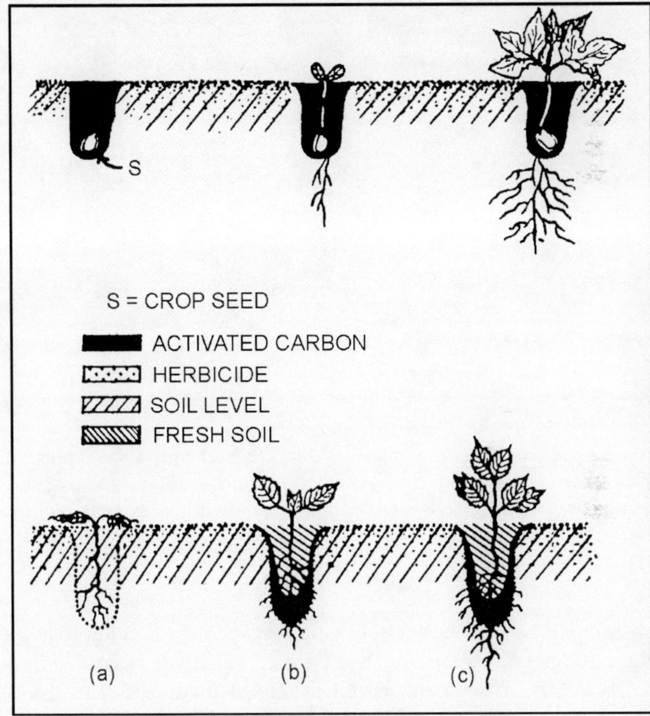

Fig. 16.8: Activated charcoal can be used to protect the crop seeds (*Top*) and crop seedlings (*Bottom*) from herbicide injury by its placement as shown in this figure (diagrammatic). The herbicide is adsorbed by charcoal in the localised region, providing a herbicide- free environment to the crop seeds/seedlings.

In dibbled vegetables activated carbon can be placed over crop seeds in the seed holes. Preemergence herbicides sprayed later are retained by carbon, thus avoiding their absorption by the germinating crops seeds. Robinson (1965) reported success with dipping roots of horticultural transplants in activated carbon before transplanting them in the herbicide treated soils. Both, 'seed hole' and 'root dip' methods of applying activated carbon for improving herbicide selectivity require much less adsorbent than the earlier mentioned 'furrow method'. Toth *et al.*(1987) reported the use of activated carbon to protect tomato seedlings against metribuzin.

Seed pelleting with activated carbon has been developed as yet another way of using this adsorbent in certain crops. In this method carbon is coated over crop seeds using gum or PVA (polyvinyl acetate). It has proven successful in improving selectivity of EPTC to maize and cowpea, and of chloramben, butachlor, and EPTC to rice (Gupta and Niranwal, 1976).

Fig. 16.9: Maize was planted in the herbicide (EPTC) treated soil in three pots. In the *left* two pots, seeds were sown after coating these with protectants R-25788 and NA, respectively. In these two pots, healthy crop seedlings were obtained, while in the extreme *right* pot, where the untreated seeds were sown, the crop seedlings exhibited stunted growth (Photo-author). This showed the crop protective action of the two compounds against EPTC.

Safeners (= Antidotes): Safeners are chemicals discovered to antagonise phytotoxicity of specific herbicides to specific plant species. Otto L. Hoffman is considered the father of 'safeners'. As early as in 1948 he observed antagonism of 2,4-D to 2,4,6-T on tomato plants. By 1969 he discovered and reported NA (1, 8-naphthalic anhydride) as highly successful safener of EPTC and butylate in maize. Later, a more maize-specific safener of EPTC and butylate, namely, R-25788 (*N, N*-dially 1-2, 2-dichloroacetamide) was discovered. It could be applied to soil as a tank-mix with EPTC without fear of protecting any EPTC susceptible weeds. NA being not so specific, must be used strictly as a seed-dress. Its effective dose is 0.5 g per kg crop seed. The dose of the soil applied R-25788 is 0.6 kg/ha (Burnside *et al.*, 1971). R-25788 has further been found an antidote of alachlor and metolachlor in protecting maize seedlings. NA seed coating has been found to provide protection to cultivated oat (*Avena sativa*) against preemergence alachlor, and to maize and sorghum against perfluidone and diclofop. CGA-43089 [α-(cyanomethoximino)-benzacetonitrile] provides safety to sorghum against metolachlor by seed treatment at 1-1.5 g/kg seed. CGA-185072 (5-chloro-8-quinolinoxy-acetic acid-1-methyl-hexyl ester) and MON-13900 (3-dichloroacetyl-5-(2-furanyl)-2, 2-dimethyloxazolidine) are some other safeners in use in specific cases. CGA-43089 provides safety to sorghum against metolachlor by seed treatment at 1-1.5 kg/ha seed. It is likely that NA, and possibly other safeners, enter the target plants and compete there with herbicide molecules for a binding site on some native enzyme. Safeners have usually proved successful only against herbicides that affect cell division in one way or the other, and not against the photosynthetic inhibiting herbicides. Now more evidence is growing that certain safeners expedite metabolism of specific herbicides in plants (Frazier and Nissen, 1994). In other cases these can reduce herbicide absorption by the tolerant species (Lee *et al.*, 1993). Good reviews on the subject have been provided by Gupta (1976), Johnson (1982), and Pallos and Casida (1978).

According to these authors, a major mechanism involved in safener action is *enhancement* of herbicide detoxification in the non-target plants (crops). Most intended herbicides are metabolised in tolerant plants by a well defined group of enzymes that catalyse various oxidative, hydrolytic, and conjugation reactions, like glutamine synthase (GS), glutathione-*S*-transferase (GST), and cytochrome P_{450} monooxygenase. The safeners support these enzyme actions to further lower or inhibit herbicide phytotoxicity in the non-target plants.

It may be noted here that safeners have been effective mainly in providing protection to the large-seeded, grass crops (*eg* maize, grain sorghum, and wet-sown rice), against particular preplant and preemergence herbicides belonging to chiefly the chemical groups, thiocarbamates and chloracetamides. However, more recently the use of safeners against sulfonylurea, imidazolinone, cylohexanedione, isoxazole and triketone herbicides in maize and wet-rice is also well established. Besides, considerable progress has been made in protecting winter grains (wheat and barley) against the postemergent sulfonylurea and aryloxyphenoxy propionate herbicides.

Table 16.1*:* Additional Herbicide Safeners Developed For the Protection of Certain Crops Against Herbicides of Specific Classes (After: Hatzois and Burgos, 2004)

	Crop	Safener	Associate herbicide
1.	Maize (= corn)	Allidochlor (CDAA)	Herbicides belonging to several different classes.
		BAS - 145138	
		Benoxacor (CGA-154281)	
		Benzenesulfonamide (2-CBSU)	
		Dichlormid	
		DKA-24	
		Furilazole (MON-13900)	
		MG-191	
		R 29148	
2.	Grain sorghum	BCS	Chloracetamide herbicides
		Dimepiperate (MY-93 or Yukamate)	
		Daimuron (SK-223, Showrone)	

	Crop	Safener	Associate herbicide
		Fenclorim (CGA-123407)	
		S-PEU	
		Flurazole	
		Fluxofenim	
		Oxabetrinil	
3.	Rice	Cyometrinil (CGA-43089, Concep-I)	Chloracetamide and Sulfonylurea herbicides
		Fluxofenim (CGA-133205, Concep. III)	
		Flurazole (MON-4606, Screen)	
		Oxabetrinil (CGA-92194, Concep-II)	
		Brassinolide	
		Mepiquatochloride	
		Fenclorium	
4.	Wheat	Cloquintocet-mexyl (CGA- 185072)	Arylphenoxypropionate and Sulfonylurea herbicides.
		Fenchlorazole (HOE-70542)	
		Mefenpyr-diethyl (HOE-107892)	

Herbicide modifiers currently approved by the WSSA of the USA include the following molecules.

1. Cyometrinil = (Z)-α-[(cyanomethoxy) imino] benzene acetonitrile
2. Dichlormid = 2,2-dichloro-*N*, *N*-di-2- propenylacetamide.
3. Dietholate = O, O,-diethyl O-phenyl phosphorothioate.
4. Flurazole = phenylmethyl 2-chloro-4- (trifluoromethyl) -5-thiazolecarboxylate.
5. NA (Naphthalic anhydride) = 1 *H*, 3 *H*- naphtho [1,8 - cd] - pyran - 1,3- dione.

(i) Structures of certain current hrbicide Safener Molecules

Benoxacor

4-(dichloroacetyl)-3, 4-dihydro-3-methyl-2H-1, 4-benzoxazine

Dichlormid

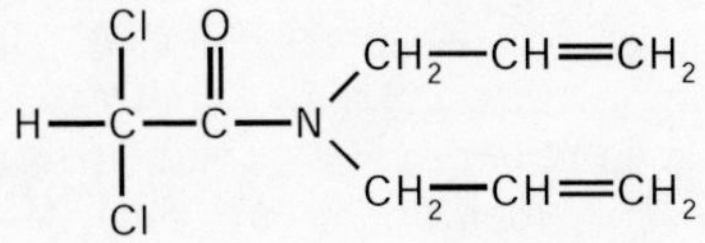

2, 2-dichloro-N-N-di-2-propenylacetamide

Fluxofenim

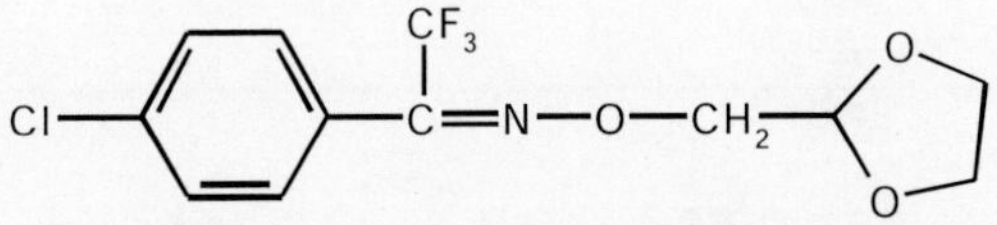

1-(4-chlorophenyl)-2, 2, 2-trifluoro-1-ethanone O-(1, 3-dioxolan-ylmethyl) oxime

Flurazole

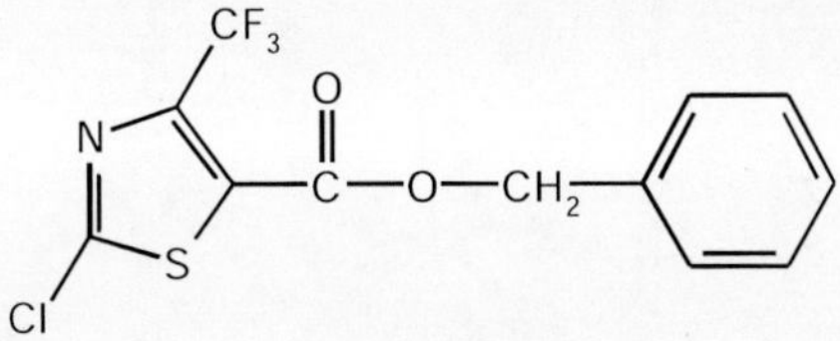

Phenylmethyl-2-chloro-4-(trifluoromethyl)-5-(thiazolecarboxylate)

Oxabetrinil

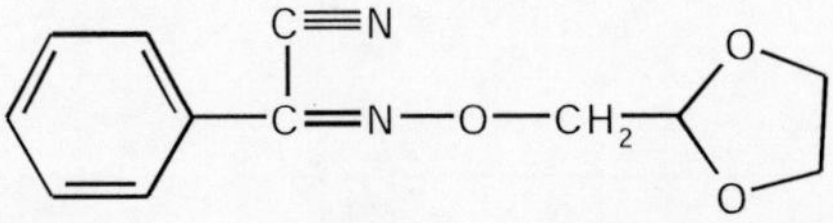

a-[(1, 3-dioxolan-2-ylmethoxy) imino]benzeneacetonitrile

R-29148

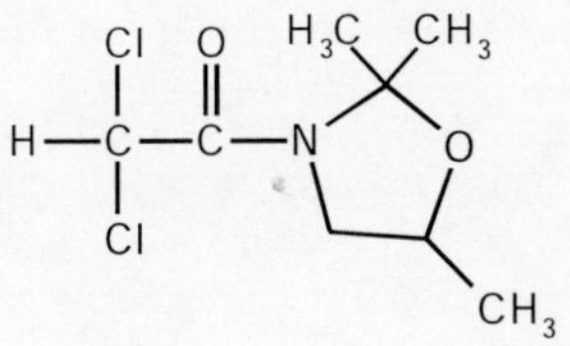

3-(dichloroacetyl)-2, 2, 5-trimethyloxazolidine

16.6.2 Use of Granular Formulations

Development of granular formulations of herbicides was a step forward towards achieving a general selectivity between established crop plants and associated germinating weeds by giving weeds the opportunity of selective absorption of the toxicant. Great success has been obtained with granular formulations of chlorpropham, dinoseb, diuron, and nitrofen in crops that would otherwise be injured by their spray liquids. The granules filter through the crop foliage, leaving little herbicide for absorption by it. They then settle on the moist ground where germinating weeds absorb the herbicide released slowly by the granules. An important desirable character of herbicides embodied in the granules is their low leachability in soils, else the toxicant may move down to the crop roots.

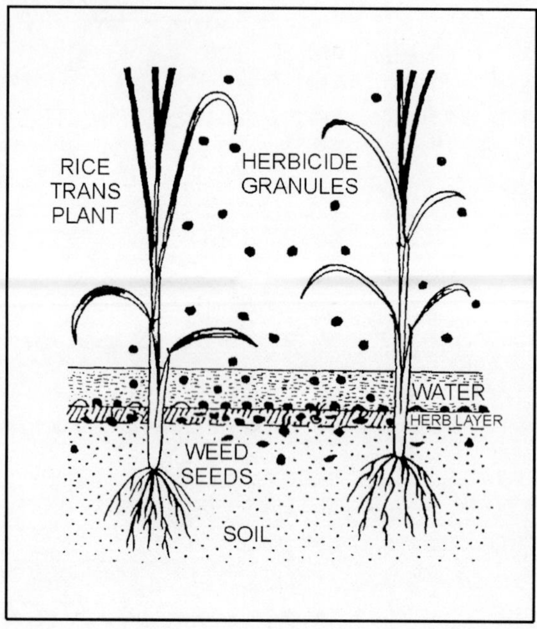

Fig. 16.10: Granular application of herbicides like butachlor and pendimethalin in transplanted paddy fields permits selective control of weeds. The herbicide granules filter through the crop canopy and fall on the ground where they act on the emerging weeds (diagrammatic).

16.6.3 Induction of Selectivity by Breeding for Herbicide Resistance

During the past one decade or so several cases of development of herbicide resistance in biotypes of certain weed species have been observed in nature. These observations on weeds gave plant breeders in some western countries idea to attempt purposeful breeding of herbicide resistant varieties of certain crops called HRCs. Both (1) *traditional breeding methods* and (2) modern *genetic engineering techniques* have been used to achieve this goal with encouraging results. In the former, usually, some resistant non-crop biotypes are used as the donors of specific herbicide resistance for the new crop varieties. But in *genetic engineering* techniques certain bacteria are used as donors of herbicide resistance genes.*

Following are the major advantages conceived in this relatively new venture of developing herbicide resistantce in crops plants.

1. A herbicide can be used in larger number of crops than is presently possible. This will save huge sums of money spent in developing new herbicides for treating additional crops.
2. Limitations in the choice of rotation crops can be greatly reduced when their herbicide resistant varieties are available. For instance, if a 2,4-D resistant cotton variety is made available in near future, there will be no problem in treating wheat in rotation with cotton.
3. A farmer will have to know about limited number of herbicides to fulfil his weed management needs.

Since the transgenic bromoxynil - resistant cotton and glufosinate - resistant canola (*Brassica* spp) were introduced in 1995 in Canada and the glyphosate resistant (GR) soybean varieties in the USA in 1996, the planting of herbicide resistant crops (HRCs) has grown substantially in the western world, particularly in these two countries, revolutionizing weed management and, often, increasing yields. In 2003, over 80% of soybean grown in the USA were GR cultivars. Also, over 10% of maize and 70% of cotton hectares were planted to glyphosate resistant cultivars.

Worldwide approximately 88 m ha are planted to transgenic crops with resistance to herbicides with different chemistries, chiefly glyphosate, glufosinate, imidazolinones, and bromoxynil.

The herbicide resistant transgenic crop varieties (HRCs) offer two major potential dangers. *First,* the crop varieties developed for resistance to single herbicide will accelerate the selection pressure on the associated weeds to evolve their resistant biotypes. Two families of herbicides for which HRCs are commercially available *viz.*, the sulfonylureas and imidazolinoes, are particularly prone to rapid evolution of resistant weeds. There is a fear that HRCs will increase the cultivated area treated with these herbicides, exacerbating the herbicide resistant weed problems. For example, with the availability of imidazolinone resistant transgenic maize, the farmers in the USA and some other countires are using this herbicide in both, maize and the naturally tolerant soybean in Maize-Soybean sequence, year after year. Earlier the farmer was using several different herbicides in maize. Thus, now the herbicide rotation system has been

---

* *The transgenic crop plants (TCP) are presently produced by Agrobacterium-mediated gene transfer technique. In this, first Agrobacterium (tumefaciens) is made to receive relevant gene for herbicide resistance from another bacterium Arthrobacter (oxidans). Such genes usually encode enzyme/s responsible for the metabolism of specific herbicide. eg glyphosate insensitive EPSPS in case of glyphosate resistant (GR) soybean and maize. Agrobacterium is then allowed to form callus on the relevant part segments of the crop plant on selection medium containing high concentration of the herbicide. The regenerated plants obtained from the callus show resistance to the herbicide since the host genome now carries the resistance factor gene.*

abandoned in maize, resulting in the development of herbicide resistance weeds, besides neglect of some environmentally safer herbicides to which maize possessed natural tolerance.

The *second* danger of HRCs is their potential to increase herbicides residues in the crop plants. This is specifically true for a crop variety engineered to provide resistance to a specific herbicide by making its active site in the plant tissue insensitive. In New Zealand, the transgenic soybean (*eg* Roundup Ready Soybean) is postulated to show increased glyphosate residues in its grain by up to 200 times. Also, another threat to Transgenic Crops is the possible insertion of modified viruses and insect virus genes into the crop.

Besides the above three major bottlenecks, there is fear that the introduced resistance genes may escape into weedy relatives of the HRCs, resulting in modulation of some *Super Weeds*. Also, the volunteer HRC plants may become problematic in subsequent seasons, and there may be potential pleiotropic effects of genetic modifications.

In recent years, several scientists have seriously questioned the real need of HRCs. A large number of herbicides are already available to treat most weed problems in almost all crops. In the USA, for instance, for use in 'maize-soybean' crop sequence, at least 30-40 herbicides are already available. In view of this, the HRCs seem largely unnecessary in our present agro-systems. *Nevertheless, a major welcome venue for the HRCs is in countries with extensive problem of parasitic and noxious weeds for which selective herbicides are not yet available.* In India and Africa, for instance, HRCs of host crops of *Cuscuta* and *Striga* spp. are very much needed to bring these parasitic weeds under effective control, the herbicide way.

Duke (2005) opined that probably the adoption of HRCs in the west during the next decade was not likely to be as dramatic as in the past 10 years.

16.7 GENERAL CONSIDERATIONS

While we want to control weeds, no one would want to injure his crops. Zero crop injury is an ideal state to aim at, but it is often very difficult to achieve despite the above discussed inherent and induced modes of herbicide selectivity. A farmer should feel satisfied if he obtained higher economical levels of crop yields from the use of herbicides than what he would have obtained without herbicides, despite some apparent or inconspicuous crop injury. This should be the approach for obtaining practical, herbicide selectivity in field conditions. Selectivity is a very relative phenomenon and it depends upon the objective of the farmer. Many farmers in the West consider it a selective weed control even if herbicide injured crops suffciently to give them only as much yield as conventional row cultivated or even unweeded crops would, just because it controlled weeds without labour and checked their further perpetuation. This, however, is an extremely liberal view of herbicide selectivity which cannot be accepted, widely.

SUMMARY

Selectivity refers to the state when upon application to a mixed population a given herbicide will kill some plant species without serious injury to the other species. The principles that contribute towards herbicidal selectivity are presented in this final chapter on herbicide behaviour in plants.

Morphological features of plants such as waxy and narrow leaves tend to repel aqueous spray liquids, and are responsible for protecting some crops against certain herbicides. Selectivity of ioxynil to wheat is a good example of this. Besides, herbicides may be applied selectively to a mixed growth of weeds and crops, wetting chiefly the former if (i) there are distinct differences in height of the weeds and crops, (ii) herbicides are sprayed on weeds before the emergence of the crop, (iii) granular formulations of herbicide are used, (iv) herbicides are applied by preemergence method and there are distinct differences in the below-ground growth of the weeds and the crops, and (v) chemical adsorbents and antidotes are used.

Although practical herbicidal selectivity is often achieved in fields by the above methods which minimise herbicide absorption by the crop plants, yet inherent tolerance of plants to herbicides, where available, is of even greater significance in obtaining selective herbicidal control. The innate or physiological tolerance of plants to herbicides may result either from (i) its failure to rapidly translocate the absorbed herbicide from the site of its absorption to the site of its action, (ii) its rapid rate of metabolism and conjugation within the plant, or (iii) insensitivity to the target enzyme.

Several examples of metabolism including 'reverse metabolism' and 'conjugation' of herbicides in plants have been cited in this chapter, along with their definitive pahways. Emphasis has been laid on the possibility of two or more of the above mentioned mechanisms of herbicide selectivity, acting simultaneously as defence mechanisms in the tolerant plants against specific herbicides. Further, selectivity is relative to proper use of herbicides and environmental factors, and it can be altered in most cases by specific agronomic treatments.

Purposeful induction of selectivity in crop plants is possible through the use of adsorbents and chemical 'safeners and modifiers, agronomic manipulations including the use of granular herbicides, and production of transgenic herbicide resistant crops (HRCs). Notable examples and advantages and limitations of each approach have been discussed.

SELECTED BIBLIOGRAPHY

1. Ashton, F. M. 1958. Absorption and translocation of radioactive 2,4-D in sugarcane and bean plants. Weeds 6(3) 257-262.
2. Bansal, G. L. and Sharma, V. K. 1992. Effect of terbutryn on maize (*Zea mays* L.) and watergrass (*Echinochloa colonum* L.). III Changes in macromolecule and phenol. Ind. J. Weed Sci. 24(1 & 2) 88-90.
3. Baron, B. M. Le and Gressel, J. 1982. Herbicide Resistance in Plants. John Wiley Inter Sci., N. Y. 100 pp.
4. Blackshow, E. *et al.* 2005. Glyphosate resistant spring wheat production systems effects on weed communities. Weed Sci. 53(4) : 451-464 (U.S.A).
5. Boldt, P. F. and Putnam, A. R. 1981. Selective mechanisms for foliar application of dichlofop–methyl-II metabolism. Weed Sci. 29(2) 237-241.

6. Briomner, T. A. *et al.* 2005. Influence of herbicide-resistant canola on the environmental impact of weed management. Pest Mgmt. Sci. 61(1) : 47-52 (Canada).

7. Buker, R. S. *et al.* 2004. Physiological basis for differential tolerance of tomato and pepper to rimsulfuron and halosulfuron: Site of action study. Weed Sci. 52 : 201-205.

8. Bunting, J. A. *et al.* 2004. Physiological basis for tolerance of corn hybrids to foramsulfuron. Weed Sci. 52 : 711-717.

9. Bunting, J. A. *et al.* 2004. Absorption and activity of foramsulfuron in giant foxtail (*Setaria faberi*) and wooly cupgrass (*Eriochola villosa*) with various adjuvants. Weed Sci. 52 : 513-517.

10. Bunting, J. A. *et al.* 2004. Physiological basis of tolerance of corn hybrids to formasulfuron. Weed Sci. 52(5) : 711-717 (U.S.A.).

11. Burnside, O. C. *et al.* 1971. Protecting corn from herbicide injury by seed treatment. Weed Sci. 19:565-568.

12. Burton, J. D. *et al.*, 1994. Sulfonylurea selectivity and safener in sweet corn. Pesticide Biochem. and Physiol. 48(3) 163-172.

13. Caretto, S. *et al.* 1993. Production and characterisation of *Nicotiana tabacum* L. cell lines and plants resistant to chlorsulfuron. J. Gent. & Breed., 47 (20 115-120.

14. Chen, T. M. *et al.*, 1968. Herbicidal action of molinate in barnyardgrass and rice. Weed Sci. 16(1) 28-31.

15. Delvin, D. L. *et al.* 1987. Differential absorption and translocation of metribuzin by downybrome (*Bromus tectorum*) and winter wheat. Weed Sci. 35:1-5.

16. Dill, G.. M. 2005. Glyphosate-resistant crops : history, status, and future. Pest Mgmt. Sci. 61(3) : 219-224 (UK).

17. Dixon, G. A. and Stoller, E. W. 1982. Differential toxicity of metolachlor in corn and yellow nutsedge. Weed Sci. 30:225-230.

18. Duke, S.O. 2005. Taking stock of herbicide - resistant crops ten years after introduction. Pest Mgmt. Sci. 61(3) 211-218 (U.K.).

19. Durgesha, M. 1994. Absorption, translocation, and metabolism of fluchloralin in groundnut and pigweed. Crop Prot. 13 (94) 286-290.

20. Edwards, R. *et al.* 2005. Differential induction of glutathione transferaces and glucosyltransferaces in wheat, maize, and *Arabidopsis thaliana* by herbicide safeners. Weed Abs. 54 (12), 4793.

21. Ellis, J. F. *et al.* 1980. Effectiveness of a new safener for protecting sorghum from metolachlor injury. Weed Sci. 28(1) 1-5.

22. Frazier, T. L. and Nissen, S. J., 1994. Influence of crop safeners on the interaction of primisulfuron and terbufos in corn (*Zea mays*). Weed Sci. 42 (2) 168-171.

23. Frear, D. S. and Still, G. G., 1968. The metabolism of 3, 4-dichloropropionanlide in plants. Partial purification and properties of an arylacylamidase from rice. Phytochem. 7:913-920.

24. Frear, D. S. and Swanson, H. R., 1970. Biosynthesis of S-(4-ethylamino-6-isopropylamino-2-*s*-triazine) and properties of a glutathione-*S*-transferase from corn. Phytochem. 9:2123-2132.

25. Frear, D. S. *et al.* 1969. N-demethylation of substituted 3-(phenyl)-1-methylureas; isolation and characterisation of a microsomal mixed function oxidase from cotton. Phytochem. 8:215-2169.

26. Gillespie, G. R. 1994. Basis for the differential response of quackgrass biotypes to primisulfuron. Weed Sci. 42(1) 8-12.

27. Gupta, O. P. 1976. Adsorbents and Antidotes. World Crops 28(3) 134-138.

28. Harker, K. Neil. 2005. Glyphosate - resistant spring wheat production system effects on weed communities. Weed Science 53 : 451-464 (USA).

29. Hassan, G. *et al.* 2002. Differential sensitivity of Italian ryegrass cultivars to fenoxaprop. Weed Sci. 50:567-575.

30. Hawf, L. R. and Behrens, R. 1974. Selectivity factors in response of plants to 2,4-DB. Weed Sci. 22(3) 245-249.

31. Haynes, C. and Kirkwood, R. C. 1992. Studies on the mode of action of diflufenican in selected crop and weed species. Pesticide Sci. 35(2) 161-165.

32. Hougue, E. J. and Warren, G. F. 1968. Selectivity of linuron on tomatoes and parsnip. Weed Sci. 16(1) 51-54.

33. Johnson, J. C. (Ed.). 1982. Plant Growth Regulators and Herbicide Antogonists. Nayes Data Corporation, Park Ridge, USA. 303 pp.

34. Kohler, E. A. and B. E. Branham, 2002. Site of uptake, absorption, translocation, and metabolism of the ethofumestate in three turfgrass species. Weed Sci. 50 : 576-580.

35. Kumaratilake, A. R. *et al.* 2002. A comparative study of glufosinate efficacy in rigid ryegrass (*Lolium rigidum*) and sterile oat (*Aveva sterilis*). Weed Sci. 50: 560-566.

36. Lee, D. J. *et al.* 1993. Mechanism of safening action of dimepiperate on clomeprop injury in rice seedlings. Weed Res. (Tokyo) 38(4) 294-299.

37. Lichtner, F. T. *et al.* 1995. Ethametsulfuron methyl metabolism and crop selectivty in spring oilseed rape. Pesticide Biochem. & Physiol. 52(1) 12-24.

38. Liphadzi, K. B. *et al.* 2005. Soil microbial and nematode communities as affected by glyphosate and tillage practices in a glyphosate - resistant cropping system. Weed Sci. 53 : 536-545 (USA).

39. Liu, L. C. *et al.* 1978. Diuron metabolism in two sugarcane cultivars. Weed Sci. 26(6) 642-646.

40. Luckwill, L. C. and Loyd-Jones 1960. Metabolism of plant growth regulators. II. Decarboxylation of 2,4-D in the leaves of apple and strawberry. Annals. Applied Biol.: 626-636.

41. Luers, H. 1991. The industry viewpoint. New Farmer & Grower 30:30-31.

42. Machado, V. S. and Bandeen, J. D. 1982. Genetic analyses of chloroplast for atrazine resistance in *Brassica campestris*-Cytoplasmic inheritance. Weed Sci. 30:281-295.

43. Marquis, L. Y. *et al.* 1979. Metabolism and selectivity of fluchloralin in soybean roots. Agri. & Food Chem. 27(6) 1148-1156.

44. Matsui, Y. *et al.* 2002. Pesticide adsorption by granular activated carbon adsorbers. Environ. Sci. & Technol. 36(15) : 3432-3438.

45. Matsunaka, S. 1969. Activation and inactivation of herbicides by higher plants. Residue Rev. 25:45-58.

46. Mc hughen, A. and Holm, F. A. 1995. Transgenic flax with environmentally and agronomically acceptible attributes. Transgenic Research 4(1):3-11.

47. McElroy, J. S. *et al.* 2004. Absorption, translocation, and metabolism of halosulfuron and trifloxysulfuron in green Kyllinga and false-green Kyllinga. Weed Sci. 52:704-710.

48. McMullan, P. M. and Nalewaja, J. D. 1991. Triallate absorption and metabolism in relation to tolerance in wheat. Cand. J. Pl. Sci. 71(4) 1081-1088.

49. Messean, A. *et al.* 2005. Impact of GMCs within cropping systems : towards a more systemic approach. Aspects of Applied Biology 74 : 191-196 (U.K.).

50. Monjardino, M. *et al.* 2005. The economic value of ghyphosate resistant canola in the management of two widespread crop weeds in a Western Australian farming system. Agric. Systems 84(3) : 297-315 (U.K.).

51. Negi, N. S. *et al.* 1964. Metabolism of atrazine by susceptible and resistant plants. Weeds 12:53-57.

52. Niemann, P. 1991. Breeding for herbicide resistance-benefits, risks, and perspectives. Plant Res. & Devp. 34 14-33.

53. Ogasawara, H. *et. al.* 1994. Introduction of a herbicide resistant gene into an apple root-stock with *Agrobacterium tumefaciens*. Bull. Faculty Agr. Hirosaki Univ. No. 57, 1-8.

54. Pallos, F. M. and Casida, J. J. (Eds.), 1978. Chemistry and Action of Herbicide Antidotes, Acad. Press. N. Y. 171 pp.

55. Pilshchikova, N. A. *et al.* 1991. The use of activated carbon for the protection of crops sensitive to herbicides. Moscow University Soil Sci. Bull. 46(1) 69-72.

56. Price, A. J. *et al.* 2004. Physiological basis for cotton tolerance to flumioxazin applied postemergence directed. Weed Sci. 52 : 1-7.

57. Rahman, A. and Ashford, R. 1970. Selective action of trifluralin for control of greenfoxtail in wheat. Weed Sci. 16 432-435.

58. Sander, K. W. and Barrett, M. 1989. Differential imazaquin tolerance and behaviour in selected corn hybrids. Weed Sci. 37(3) 290-295.

59. Sawada, H. 2002. Invasions of exotic species and releases of genetically modified crops - Introduction. Grassland Sci. 48(2): 159-160. (Japan)

60. Schafer, D. E. and Chilcote, D. O. 1970. Translocation and degradation of bromoxynil in a resistant and susceptible species. Weed Sci. 18(6) 729-732.

61. Schneider, B. *et al.* 1993. Metabolism of amitrole in apple. Pesticide Sci. 37 (1) 9-13.

62. Schulte, M. 2005. Transgenic herbicide resistant crops : a review based on 8 year's of international cropping experience. Weed Abst. 54 (8), 3267.

63. Sengnil, K. *et al.* 1992. Selection of bensulfuron methyl-tolerant rice cells and their acetopictate synthase response. Weed Res. (Tokyo) 37(3) 232-238.

64. Sengnil, K. *et al.* 1993. Bensulfuron methyl effects on amino acids and protein levels in cultured rice cells. Weed Research (Tokyo) 38(4) 259-266.

65. Smith, A. E. 1983. Differential *Paspalum notatum* cultivar response to atrazine. Weed Sci. 31:88-92.

66. Smith, L. W. *et al.* 1968. Metabolism of amitrole in excised leaves of Canadathistle ecotypes and bean. Weeds 16(4) 523-527.

67. Stephenson, G. R. and Ries, S. K. 1967. The movement and metabolism of pyrazon in tolerant and susceptible species. Weed Res. 7(1) 51-60.

68. Stoller, E. W. 1970. Mechanism for the differential transaction of amiben in plants. Plant Physiol. 46:732-737.

69. Streber, W. R. *et al.* 1994. Expression of a bacterial gene in transgenic plants confers resistance to the herbicide phemedipham. Plant Molecular Biol. 25(6): 977-987.

70. Tadic, Z. D. and Ries, S. K. 1971. Thermal and ultrasonic dealkylation of δ-triazines *via* the cyclic transition state. Agri. & Food Chem. 19(1) 44-49.

71. Tal, A. *et al.* 1993. Glutathione conjugation-a detoxification pathway for fenoxaprop-ethylin barley, crabgrass, oat, and wheat. Pesticide Biochem. & Physiol. 46(3) 190-193.

72. Toth, J. *et al.* 1987. Use of activated carbon to protect tomato against metribuzin. Weed Res. 27(5) 367-373.

73. Weimer, M. R. 1988. Metabolism as a base for differential atrazine tolerance in warm-season forage grasses. Weed Sci. 36:436-440.

74. Withenbach, V. A. *et al.* 1994. Basis of selectivity of triflusulfuron methyl in sugarbeets. Pesticide Biochemistry and Physiology 49(1) 72-81.

75. Yaduraju, N. T. *et al.* 1992. Bioefficacy and selectivity of tralkoxydim with and without 2,4-D and fluroxypyr. Pesticide Res. J. 4(2): 159-163.

Chapter 17

HERBICIDE RESISTANCE IN WEEDS

The advent of selective herbicides in agriculture proved a boon for weed management in various crops, but it soon posed the problem of spread of the naturally tolerant or resistant weed species in the spaces vacated by the susceptible ones. The phenomenon was first noticed with the auxin herbicides which although freed the cereals and sugarcane of their broadleaf weeds yet these aggravated the infestation of grasses. The development of broad-spectrum herbicides and herbicide mixtures with adequate selectivity to the specific crops eventually solved the problem. But soon a new problem cropped up when within a susceptible population of a weed species, the existence of few individuals of its resistant biotypes was noticed either in natural or evolved manner. These weed biotypes slowly kept multiplying under repeat applications of single herbicide each season, resulting in large, resistant weed populations. These evolved herbicide resistant weed populations pose today the biggest challenge to the weed scientists, the world-over.

17.1 HERBICIDE TOLERANCE VERSUS HERBICIDE RESISTANCE

The most important herbicides used in agriculture are those capable of controlling one or more classes of weeds without affecting adversely the crops in which their use was recommended. However, the selectivity of these herbicides lasts only as long as their field recommended doses are adhered to. With increasing doses the selectivity between crops and weeds may either be weakened or eliminated. This phenomenon is termed **herbicide tolerance**. It is the inheritable ability or aptitude of a plant (crop or weed) population to survive and reproduce after treatment at the *recommended or normal doses*, and can be considered as a natural population characteristic.

In variance with the above phenomenon of herbicide tolerance, some weed species, or biotypes of a normally susceptible weed population, may remain unhurt even at much *higher than the recommended doses of the herbicide.* This is termed as '**herbicide resistance**'. Thus, 'herbicide tolerance' and 'herbicide resistance' are terminologies denoting differences in the intensity of the same phenomenon. The resistance is considered as an extreme case which occurs less frequently than the herbicide tolerance

(Prado and Franco, 2004). The natural herbicide resistances in weed species or their biotypes are noticed even in fields where the herbicide was applied for the very *first* time.

Quite aside the above natural phenomena of herbicide resistance, what we are concerned in this chapter is the ***evolved capacity*** of a previously herbicide susceptible (HS) weed population to withstand an intended herbicide and complete its life cycle when the herbicide was used at its *normal* rates in an agricultural situation. Frequently, this occurs under some continuous herbicide pressure when the few individuals of a resistant weed biotype expand into resistant popuplations. How long it will take this to happen depends upon the herbicide and weed species in question. Usually, the herbicide resistance is witnessed after long, repeated use of some herbicide molecule in a given field.

17.2 CROSS-RESISTANCE VERSUS MULTIPLE RESISTANCE

Cross resistance is said to occur when a weed biotype *develops resistance to more than one herbicide possessing the same, snigle mode of action*. For instance, weeds resistant to sulfonylurea herbicides can be cross-resistant to imidazolinones, triazolopyrimidines, sulfonalides and pyrimidinylthio benzoates; all of which operate with the same mode of action, *viz.*, inhibition of the activity of the plant enzyme, ALS (see Chapter-15). The development of cross-resistance among weeds presents a serious problem. But even more disturbing is the fact that there have been a few instances of weeds developing resistance to herbicides that do not have similar modes of action. *When an individual plant biotype possesses more than one mechanism of resistance to one or more herbicides, the phenomenon is called* ***multiple resistance***. For instance Walsh *et al.* (2004) observed in Australia multiple resistance in a wild radish (*R. raphanistrum*) population to herbicides with different modes of action, involving PDs enzyme inhibiting herbicide diflufenican, the mutation causing, 2,4-D, and the photosystem II-inhibiting metribuzin and atrazine. Likewise, ryegrass (*Lolium rigidum*) biotypes exhibited resistance to ACCase and ALS enzymes inhibiting herbicides. *Kochia* and *Amaranthus* spp. biotypes are also known to display multiple herbicide resistances.

The development of multiple resistant weed populations in a field makes their management extremely difficult.

17.3 HERBICIDE RESISTANCE AND OUR CONCERNS

The development of herbicide-resistant weeds is a serious worldwide threat to agricultural production. The first case of herbicide resistant weed population to be extensively examined was that of a triazine herbicide resistant population of common groundsel (*Senecio vulgaris*) in the USA in 1969, *ie* almost two decades after atrazine and simazine were introduced in agriculture in 1950s. By 1998, the International Survey of Herbicide Resistant Weeds recorded 231 resistant weed biotypes in 45 countries. And these numbers continue to increase each year (Cranston *et al.*, 2001). The herbicide classes which have exhibited resistance in weed biotypes most frequently include triazines, imidazolinones, sulfonylureas, triazolopyrimidine sulfonailides, and bypyridiliums; implicating biotypes of over 50 weed species. The auxin herbicides like 2,4-D and MCPA which have been extensively used globally for over 50 years, are comparatively weak in exerting selection pressure and developing resistant weed populations. It may be so because of their multiple modes of action on the susceptible plants. Glyphosate, a broad-spectrum, non-selective herbicide, likewise has been on very low risk resistance list. During the past 30 years of its use only eight weed species (both grasses and broadleafs) are reported to have developed resistance to it. On the contrary, paraquat, an alternative non-selective herbicide, has already qualified for developing resistance in 20 weed species.

Perhaps the fastest development of resistance in weed biotypes has been caused by sulfonylurea and other ALS enzyme inhibiting herbicides. Within 20-25 years after their commercial introduction in 1980s, these herbicides have already been held responsible for putting forth over 64 resistant weed biotypes round the world. It seems the selection pressure of ALS inhibiting herbicides is very intense.

In India, isoproturon resistant populations of *Phalaris minor* in wheat fields and those of propanil resistant *Echinochloa* spp. in rice fields are the major herbicide resistance problems. Both, cross resistance and multiple resistance behaviour are feared to occur in these two weeds.

17.4 MECHANISMS OF HERBICIDE RESISTANCE

The most common mechanism of development of herbicide resistance in weed biotypes is an alteration or modification in the target site. This is particularly true for the enzyme inhibiting type of herbicides. The alteration in target site can be caused by point mutations that afford high level of protection while still producing the active enzyme for normal plant growth. The target site-based herbicide resistance generally endorses higher resistance levels than does the metabolism-based herbicide resistance, considered to be of secondary importance.

Understanding the mechanism of herbicide resistance in weed biotypes is important to predict the weed population dynamics and establish the resistance - management strategies.

Some representative mechanisms of herbicide resistance are given here as follows :

1. Weed biotypes exhibiting cross resistance to **ALS enzyme** inhibiting herbicides, like *sulfonylureas, imidazolinones,* and *triazolopyrimidines,* are known to cause modification or alteration of the enzyme molecules to field a less sensitive ALS such that the herbicide binds with it either poorly or not at all. Several point mutations within the gene encoding ALS can result in a herbicide resistant ALS. From investigations of numerous resistant weed biotypes, five conserved amino acids have been identified in ALS which upon substitution can confer resistance to ALS – inhibiting chemicals. (See also Table 15.2).

   (Although resistance to the ALS – inhibiting herbicides has been a bane to weed management, the knowledge of its mechanism has spurred many advances leading to the development of ALS inhibiting herbicide tolerant *crop varieties* for widening the use of herbicides.)

2. Exhaustive studies have been made on the mechanism of resistance to *acylanilide herbicides,* like say propanil, developed in biotypes of jungle rice (*Echinochola colona*) and barnyardgrass (*E. crus-galli*) in India, and several other countries, after

its very successful extensive use in rice fields since early 1960s. This developed resistance has been assigned to the elevated levels of active **enzyme AAAs (aryl acylamidase)** which is responsible for fast degradation of the acylanilide herbicides through hydrolysis. In normal populations of *Echinochloa* spp., the AAAs activity is extremely poor or absent. Hoagland *et al.* (2004) opined that some non-metabolic resistance mechanism also existed alongside, at least in ryegrass (*Lolium rigidum*) resistant biotypes in Australia.

3. It is now well established that observed resistance to *as-triazene* and *chloracetamide* herbicides in weed biotypes is the result of increased activity of **GST (glutathione-S-transferase) enzyme** which conjugates the herbicide molecule with tripeptide-glutathione to render it (herbicide) inactive and non-phytotoxic. This has been shown in resistant biotypes of velvet leaf (*Abutilon* sp.), blackgrass (*Alopecurus* sp.), giantfoxtail (*Setaria* sp.) and some other weed. Further, there is a view that two GST isoenzymes are present in the resistant biotypes which may carry out this inactivation action, instead of over expression of the GST itself.

4. To date, *diclofop* – resistant biotypes have been found in 10 weedy grass species in Europe. The resistance is mainly the result of modifications at the target site in **ACCase (Acetyl – CoA Carboxylase)** enzyme. There are now four mutants of the ACCase gene known to endow resistance to APOP and CHD herbicides (Chapter 12) which are involved in the ACCase inhibiting activity in susceptible populations (Brown *et al.*, 2002). Also, enhanced herbicide metabolism of the herbicides of these groups is postulated to cause resistant weed biotypes.

5. Resistance to *decamba* in wild mustard (*B. kaber*) biotype has been found to be due to **gene mutation** causing reduced herbicide binding with the auxin binding proteins.

6. Studies suggest that *glyphosate* resistance was likely to be due to altered cellular distribution that implicated phloem loading and plastidic import of glyphosate resulting in its overall reduced translocation. Also, inhibition of **EPSS (5-enolpyruvylshikimate-3-phosate synthase)** enzyme is noticed in the resistant biotypes (see Chapter-15).

7. Resistance to the two herbicides, *isoproturon* and *chlortoluron,* in some biotypes of blackgrass and ryegrass has been found to the caused by accelerated **Cyt P_{450}** activity which mediates herbicide detoxification. The mechanism has also been observed in other herbicides of similar chemistry, as well as in some of those with different modes of action.

8. Resistance to *paraquat* in *Hordeum leporinum* biotype is believed to be the result of its **reduced translocation** from the treated leaves to other plant parts. But paraquat resistance in annual bluegrass (*Poa annua*) biotypes is postulated to be due to **detoxification** of the highly reactive oxygen species and sequestration of the herbicide in non-chloroplast site (Prado and Franco, 2004). (*P. annua* exhibits multiple resistance to paraquat, ATA, and simazine).

17.5 REINING THE OCCURRENCE OF HERBICIDE RESISTANT WEED BIOTYPES

While the use of herbicides in agriculture cannot be denied, yet their judicious use is an essential requirement to minimize the occurrence of the problem of herbicide resistant weed biotypes. The foremost among the technologies recommended for the purpose is the use of 'herbicide combinations' and 'herbicide rotations'. The objective is to offer chemically different herbicide molecules to weeds instead of bringing them under pressure of single herbicide, repeatedly. Another very good way to prevent the development of herbicide resistant weed populations is to use herbicides as complements to the available physical weeding alternatives. Stale seedbed preparation and rotational use of non-selective herbicides like paraquat and glyphosate, when possible, can also help in effective prevention or delay in the development of resistant weed biotypes.

Of recent, there is a revolution in the development of new herbicide molecules with different modes of action to combat the herbicide resistant weed populations. Although successful, one has to guard against possibility of development of cross and multiple resistances in weeds to these new herbicides, whence more effective herbicide molecules, with completely different modes of action, shall have to be invented.

SUMMARY

The discovery of broad-spectrum, selective herbicides for use in agronomic and horticultural crops has been a big boon to farmes. But during the last three decades or so, their continuous use has revealed presence (or development) of herbicide resistant weed biotypes within a susceptible weed species population. The spread of herbicide resistant weeds has threatened the agriculturists round the world with more than 290 such weed species documented by the year 2005. India is no exception to it with her burning problem of isoproturon resistant biotypes of *Phalaris minor* in the wheat fields. So is the case with propanil resistant biotypes of *Echinchloa* spp. in rice.

Herbicide resistance has been classified as Cross Resistance and Multiple Resistance, depending upon the modes of resistance present or developed in the weed biotypes. To tackle the problem of herbicide resistant biotypes, it became necessary for the scientists to first study the resistance mechanisms relevant to different chemical groups of herbicides. These have been briefly classified and presented in the text with reference to the major chemical groups currently in use. Today there are over 290 herbicide resistant weed types on record in the world and these numbers are increasing fast with the accelerated use of herbicides. The scientists have over-powered some of these biotype populations by developing new herbicide molecules and recommending the adoption of herbicide rotations and combinations, in conjunction with physical weeding methods and no-till farming systems, wherever possible.

SELECTED BIBLIOGRAPHY

1. Avila, L. A. *et al.* 2005. Assessment of ALS tolerance to imazethapyr in red rice ecotypes and imidazolinone tolerant/ resistant rice varieties. Pest Mgmt. Sci. 61(2) : 171-178 (USA).

2. Baerson, S. R. 2002. Investigating the mechanism of glyphosate resistance in rigid ryegrass (*Lolium rigidum*). Weed Sci. 50 : 721-730.
3. Balyan, R. S. *et al.* 2000. Efficacy of sulfosulfuron as influenced by surfactants. Ind. J. Weed Sci. 32 : 190-19.
4. Bhullar, M. S. *et al.* 2000. Studies on behaviour in isoproturon resistant Phalaris minor to different herbicides. Proc. Int. Workshop on Herbicide Resistance and Zero Tillage held 4-6 March 2002, C.C.S. Haryana Agri. Univ., Hisar (India), 24-27 pp.
5. Brar, L. S. 2002. Current Status of herbicide resistance in Punjab and its management strategies. Proc. Int. Workshop on Herbicide Resistance and Zero Tillage held 4-6 March 2002, at C.C.S. Haryana Agri. Univ., Hisar (India), 6-10 pp.
6. Chaverra, E. *et al.* 2005. Dicamba-responsive genes in herbicide resistant and susceptible biotypes of kochia (*K. scoparia*). Weed Sci. 53 (2) : 139-145 (USA).
7. Cranston, H. J. *et al.*2001. Dicamba resistance in kochia. Weed Sci. 49: 164-170.
8. Dhawan, R. S. 2004. Reversal of isoproturon resistance by malathion in *Phalaris minor* Retz. Ind. J. Weed Sci. 36 (3 & 4): 260-261.
9. Dixit, A. 2004. Role of herbicide mixtures, adjuvants, and weed management. Crop Care 29(4): 6-14.
10. Duke, S. O. (ed.) 1995. Herbicide Resistant Crops. Lewis Publishers, N.Y., USA, 420 p.
11. Feng, C. C. *et al.* 2004. Investigations into glyphosate – resistant horseweed (*Conyza Canadensis*): retention, uptake, translocation, and metabolism. Weed Sci. 52 : 498-505.
12. Ferguson, G. M. *et al.* 2001. ALS inhibitor resistance in populations of Powell amaranth and redroot pigweed. Weed Sci. 49: 448-453.
13. Foy, C. L. and D. W. Pritchard, 1996. Pesticide Formulation and Adjuvant Technology. CRC Press. Boca Raton, NY (USA), 363 p.
14. Gessel, M. J. 2001. Glyphosate – resistant horseweed from Delaware. Weed Sci. 49: 703-705.
15. Hatzois, K. K. and Burgos, N. 2004. Metabolism – based herbicide resistance: regulation by safeners. Weed Sci. 52: 454-467.
16. Hoagland, R. E. *et al.* 2004. Metabolically based resistance to the herbicide propanil in *Echinochloa* species. Weed Sci. 52 : 475-486.
17. Hutto, K. C. *et al.* 2004. Annual bluegrass (*Poa annua*) resistance to simazine in Mississippi. Weed Technology 18(3), 846-849 (USA).
18. Jugulam, M. *et al.* 2005. Inheritance of picloran and 2,4-D resistance in wild mustard (*B. kaber*). Weed Sci. 53(4) : 417-423 (USA).
19. Kathiresan, Rm. and A. Guruswamy, 1996. Herbicide tolerance in rice cultivars. Proc. 2nd Int. Weed Control Cong., Copenhagen: 955-963.
20. Kern, A. J. *et al.* 2005. Dicamba – responsive genes in herbicide – resistant and susceptible biotypes of kochia (*Kochia scoparia*), Weed Sci. 53 : 139-145.
21. Koger, C. H. and K. N. Reddy, 2005. Role of absorption and translocation in the mechanism of glyphosate resistance in horseweed (*Conyza canadensis*). Weed Sci. 53 : 84-89 (USA).

22. Koger, C. H. *et al.* 2004. Glyphosate-resistant horseweed (*Conyza canadensis*) in Mississippi. Weed Technol. 18(3) 820-825 (USA).

23. Koger, C. H. *et al.* 2005. Assessment of two non-destructive assays for detecting glyphosate resistance in horseweed (*Conyza canadensis*). Weed Sci. 53 : 438-445.

24. Kuk, Y. I. and N. R. Burgos, 2007. Cross-resistance profile of mesosulfuron-methyl-resistant Italian ryegrass in the southern US. Pest Mgmt. Sci. 63 : 349-357 (USA).

25. Kumar, V. *et al.* 2005. Potency of trifluralni, chlorsulfuron, and their tank mixture against isoproturon resistant *Phalaris minor* Ind. J. Weed Sci. 37 (1 & 2): 88-90.

26. Li, J. *et al.* 2004. Physiological basis for resistance to diphenyl ether herbicides in common waterhamp (*Amaranthus rudis*). Weed Sci. 52: 333-338.

27. Malik, R. K. (ed.) 2000. Herbicide resistance management and zero tillage in rice-wheat cropping system. Proc. Int. Workshop held 4-6 March 2002 at C.C.S. Haryana Agri. Univ., Hisar (India) 210 p.

28. Malik, R. S. *et al.* 2001. Efficacy of new herbicides with and without surfactants on weeds in wheat. India J. Weed Sci. 33: 59-62.

29. Maneechote, C. *et al.* 2005. Resistance to ACCase - inhibiting herbicides on sprangletop (*Leptochloa chinensis*). Weed Sci. 53 : 290-295 (USA).

30. Marshall, M. W. *et al.* 2001. Gene flow, growth, and competitiveness of imazethapyr resistant common sunflower. Weed Sci. 49 : 14-21.

31. Mc Naughton, K. E. *et al.* 2005. Mutations in ALS confer herbicide resistance in redroot pigweed (*Amaranthus retroflexus*) and Powell amaranthus (*Amaranthus powellii*). Weed Sci. 53 : 17-22 (USA)

32. Mc Roberts, N. *et al.* 2005. An assessment of genetic diversity within and between populations of *Phalaris minor* using ISSR markers. Weed Res. 45(6) : 431-439 (UK).

33. McRoberts, N. *et al.* 2005. An assessment of genetic diversity within and between populations of *Phalaris minor* using ISSR markers. Weed Res. 45 : 431-439.

34. Mengistu, L. W. *et al.* 2005. Genetic diversity of herbicide-resistant and susceptible *Avena fatua* populations in *N. Dakota* and Minnesota. Weed Research 45(6) : 413-423 (UK).

35. Nandula, V. K. *et al.* 2005. Glyphosate resistant weeds : current status and future outlook. Outlooks on Pest Mgmt. 16 : 183-187 (USA).

36. Park, K. W. and C. A. Mallory-Smith. 2005. Multiple herbicide resistance in downy brome (*Bromus tectorum*) and its impact on fitness. Weed Sci. 53 : 780-786 (USA).

37. Parmar, B. S. and S. S. Tomar. 2004. Pesticide Formulations: Theory and Practice. CBS Pub. & Distributors, New Deli 414 p.

38. Patzoldt, W. L. and P. J. Tranel, 2002. Molecular analysis of cloransulam resistance in a population of giant ragweed. Weed Sci. 50: 299-305.

39. Perez-Jones, A. *et al.* 2005. Identification of glyphosate-resistant Italian ryegrass (*Lolium multiflorum*) in Oregon. Weed Sci. 53 : 775-779.

40. Poston, D. H. *et al.* 2001. Enhanced sensitivity to cloransulam – methyl in imidazolinone – resistant smooth pigweed. Weed Sci. 49: 711-716.

41. Poston, D. H. *et al.* 2002. Response of ALS from imidazolinone susceptible and resistant smooth pigweed to ALS inhibitors. Weed Sci. 50: 306-311.

42. Prado De, A. and R. Franco. 2004. Cross resistance and herbicide metabolism in grass weeds in Europe: biochemical and physiological aspects. Weed Sci. 52: 441-447.

43. Prado, J. *et al.* 2004. Cross resistance to ACCase herbicide in *Lolium rigidum*. Weed Abst. 54(5), 1960.

44. Prado, R. D. *et al.* 2004. Resistance to ACC case inhibitor herbicides in green foxtail (*Setaria viridis*) biotype in Europe. Weed Sci. 52: 506-512.

45. Preston, C. 2004. Herbicide resistance in weeds endowed by enhanced detoxification: complications for management. Weed Sci. 52: 448-453.

46. Preston, C. *et al.* 2005. Differential translocation of paraquat in paraquat – resistant population of *Hordeum leporinum*. Weed Research 45: 289-295.

47. Rainbolt, C. R. *et al.* 2004. Herbicide resistant grass weed development in imidazolinone-resistant wheat,. Weed Technol. 18(3) : 860-868 (USA).

48. Reade, J. P. H. and A. H. Cobb, 2004, A role for glutathione – *S* – transferases in resistance to herbicides in grasses. Weed Sci. 52: 468-474.

49. Salava, J. *et al.* 2004. The emergence of a atrazine resistant black nightshade (*Solanum nigrum* L.) biotype and molecular basis of the resistance. Plant Protection Sci. 40(3) : 94-100 (Prague). (W.A. 54(4), 1525).

50. Singh, G. and V. P. Singh 2005. Compatibility of clodinafop- propargyl and fenoxaprop-p-ethyl with carfentrazone-ethyl, metsulfuron-methyl and 2,4-D. Ind. J. Weed Sci. 37(1 &2): 1-5.

51. Tranel, P. J. and T. R. Wright, 2002. Resistance of weeds to ALS – inhibiting herbicides; What have we learnt? Weed Sci. 50: 700-712.

52. Volenberg, D. S. and D. E. Stoltenberg, 2002. Inheritance of resistance in eastern black nightshade (*Solanum nigrum*) to ALS inhibitors. Weed Sci. 50 : 731-736.

53. Walsh, M. J. *et al.*2004. Multiple – herbicide resistance across four modes of action in wild radish. Weed Sci. 52: 8-13.

54. Wang, Y. and J. C. Hall, 2001. Calcium may mediate auxin herbicide resistance in wild mustard. Weed Sci. 49: 2-7.

55. White, A. D. *et al.* 2002. Common sunflower resistance to ALS inhibiting herbicides. Weed Sci. 50: 432-437.

56. YongBing, H. *et al.* 2004. Studies on resistance of *Echinochloa cus-galli* to quinclorac in rice planting areas in China's Human Province. Plant Protection 30(3) : 48-52 (China), W.A. 54(6), 2392.

57. Zheng, D. *et al.* 2005. Association of the W574L ALS substitution with resistance to cloransulam and imazamox in common ragweed (*Ambrosia artemisiifolia*). Weed Sci. 53 : 424-430 (USA).

Chapter 18

ADJUVANTS

The Oxford dictionary defines adjuvant as a thing that helps. In herbicide formulations, adjuvants are chemicals included to improve their herbicidal effects, sometimes marking a difference between satisfactory and unsatisfactory weed control. As is known today, adjuvants do not act by increasing the innate activity of any herbicide but they merely aid its availability in the region of plants where it is needed for best results. The adjuvants may also be added to herbicides to (i) improve herbicide selectivity to the non-target plants, (ii) to render herbicides safer for the user, (iii) to prolong shelf-life of the concentrates, (iv) to activate specific herbicides, and (v) to reduce herbicide drift hazards, besides for some other similar purposes. Space in this text does not permit a detailed discussion of the chemistry of adjuvants, or even to mention all the different kinds of adjuvants available for use in herbicide formulations.

In this chapter, functions of eight important kinds of adjuvants are presented. These are (1) surfactants, (2) stabilizing agents, (3) solvents, (4) humicants, (5) stickers, (6) activators, (7) compatibility agents, (8) activators, and (9) drift control agents. Reviews on pesticidal formulations research are available that list the modern adjuvants and deal with their physical and colloidal chemistry aspects. Research organisations are continually looking for new adjuvants and new ways of using the old ones to make herbicides more effective so that their doses could be reduced and their utility extended.*

18.1 SURFACTANTS (= SURFACE ACTIVE AGENTS)

If one dips a leaf of bermudagrass (*Cynodon dactylon*) in a beaker containing pure water, one can pull it back without wetting it. Repeating the action will not wet it either. This can be demonstrated for many other plants with waxy, hairy, or thick cutin surfaces. But if you add a drop of surfactant to water in the beaker, you can readily wet the foliage of most weed species with it. The problem of wetting of leaf surfaces arises in many

---

* *Solvent, 'Co-Solvent' and 'Coupling Agent' – the three words have often been used as synonyms in literature.*

aqueous herbicide-plant combinations and it can be overcome by adding suitable surfactants to the spray concentrates. The surfactants possess surface modifying properties. They aid (a) in wetting the waxy leaf surface with the aqueous herbicide sprays (*wetting agents*), (b) in spreading the hydrophilic herbicides uniformly over the foliage (*spreaders*), and (c) in the penetration of the herbicide into the target leaves and stems (*penetrants*). Wetting and spreading are aspects of the same phenomenon and they occur simultaneously. Besides, certain surfactants have exhibited innate phytotoxicity and growth stimulating effects, depending upon the concentration used (Foy and Smith, 1965). They may strongly react with specific herbicides within or outside the treated plant surfaces. Scientists are now working on finding specific surfactant-herbicide structure phytotoxicity relationships due to which the role of surfactants in aiding weed control is measuring new dimensions (Smith *et al.*, 1967, Gould, 1967; Kudsk and Straibig, 1993).

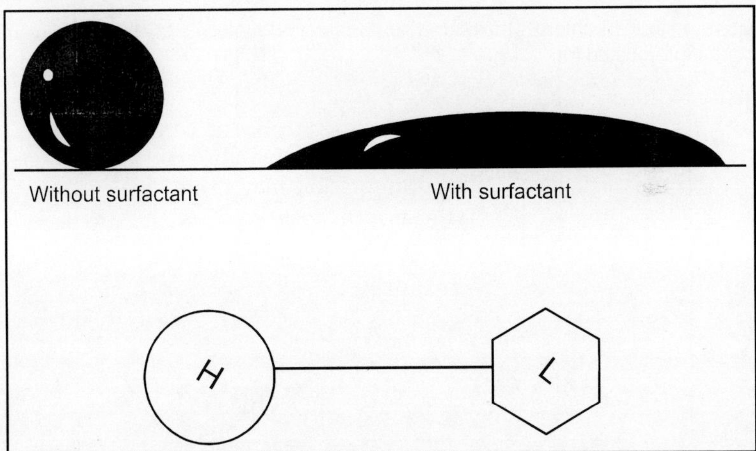

Fig. 18.1: ***Top*** = Phenomenon of surface tension of a herbicide spray drop. *Left*: A spray drop without any surfactant is held as a ball on any waxy leaf surface; touching the leaf surface to a minimum. *Right*: With the addition of a surfactant, the spray drop flattens and, thus, wets the leaf surface thoroughly; allowing its due absorption by the leaf (diagrammatic). ***Bottom*** = A diagrammatic concept of a surfactant molecule which embodies both, hydrophilic (H) and lipohilic (L) ends. The proportion of H and L group in a molecule imparts a surfactant its characteristic properties.

18.1.1 Chemical Nature of Surfactants

Surfactant molecules are amphipathic *ie* they possess both lipophilic (apolar) and hydrophilic (polar) atomic groupings within a single molecule. The hydrophilic portion gives surfactant its ionic character, *viz., anionic, cationic, and nonionic,* depending upon the ionic species they may release in solution. Some surfactants are amphoteric; their anionic and cationic properties vary with change in pH of the medium. The relative proportion of size and intensity of hydrophilic (H) and lipophilic (L) groups of a surfactant assigns it a hydrophilic-lipophilic balance value (= HLB). When the two groups just balance each other, HLB is scaled at 10. Good surfactants fall in the range of HLB of 7 to 9. The HLB of a surfactant determines the relative leaf wetting properties which it imparts to the aqueous herbicide spray liquids. This role of HLB, however, is often masked in strongly ionic type surfactants wherein the nature of the ionic species (micelles) become important in affecting their wetting properties. Hence, HLB values of monomer units of surfactants are of importance primarily in nonionic or weakly ionic surfactants.

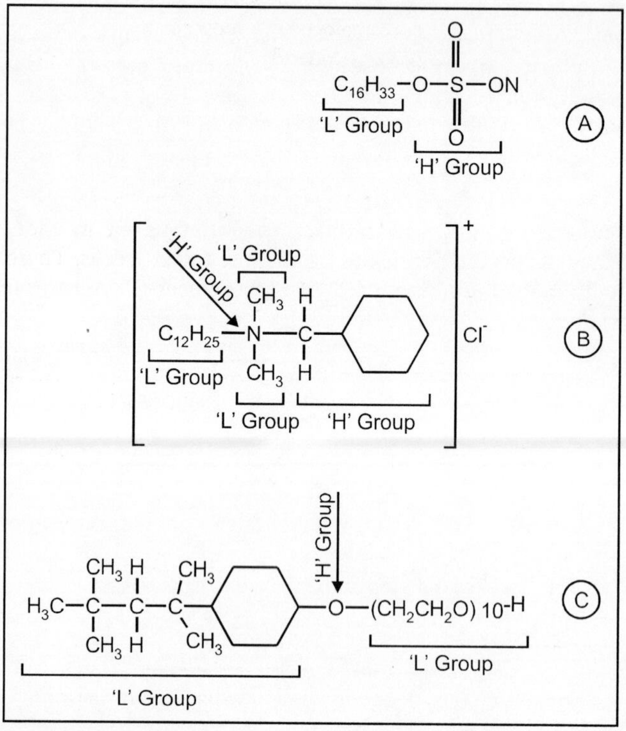

Fig. 18.2: Representative structures of three kinds of surfactant molecules *viz.*, A = anionic type, B = cationic type, and C = non-ionic type. L and H in this figure denote, respectively, lipohilic and hydrophilic portions of the molecules.

The ionic character of surfactants determines its compatibility with a particular herbicide concentrate. Cationic surfactants, such as Aliquat-4 and Quaternary-O are compatible with only cationic herbicides like diquat and paraquat. With other herbicides either anionic or nonionic surfactants (or their combinations) are used, depending upon the ionic character of the toxicant.

As will be discussed later, though numerous surfactants induce wetting of plant foliage, in recent years, specific surfactant-herbicide combinations have been found to optimize herbicidal effects. Their discovery is largely the result of trial and error called Edisonian approach.

Examples of surfactants: Of the many organic surfactants available in the market, a few are given below to give the reader an idea of their complex chemical nature.

1.	Non-ionic	
	S-145 or Tween-20	= Polyoxyethylene sorbitan monolaurate
	Surfactant WK	= Dodecyl ether of polyoxyethylene glycol
2.	**Anionic**	
	Santomerse	= Dodecylbenzene sodium sulphonate
	Vatsol-OT	= Sodiumdioctyl sulphosuccinate
	SDS	= Sodium dodecylsulphate
3.	**Cationic**	
	Quaternary-O	= Alkylimidazolinium chloride
	Aliquat-4	= Lauryltrimethylammonium chloride
	CTAB	= Hexadecyltrimethylammonium

Several new adjuvants, largely surfactants, have been tested in India and found to improve the efficacy of specific herbicides against the target weeds. These include: Triton (0.1%) for use with metsulfuron methyl; APSA-80, Agrocer-02, Agrocer-03 and Active-80 (0.1%) with atrazine; AG-F (0.5%) with glyphosate and Laffmul DA (0.2%) with varied herbicides. Then there are esterified seed oils (ESO) prepared from seed oils of maize, soybean, sunflower, maize, soybean, sunflower, castor, canola, etc. by reacting these with alcohol to form esters. (Examples – Haslen, Meth-oil, MSO, Sun-it II).

Organo-silicones (OS) form another group of surfactants. These are either pure silicones or mixtures with suitable non-ionic or other surfactants. (*Examples:* Sylgard, Silivet L-77, Kinetic, Herbex).

18.1.2 Wetting Action of Surfactants

Surfactants, by their combined polar and apolar properties in the same molecule, render compatible the aqueous liquids and lipoidal phase of leaf surfaces. Upon addition to an aqueous herbicide system, the hydrophilic ends of surfactant molecules turn inward the water surface and lower its surface tension, whereas its lipophilic ends are held towards air in the spray tanks and towards the lipophilic leaf surfaces after it has been applied to the foliage. By lowering the interfacial* tension between the carrier water drops and the leaf surfaces, the surfactant flattens the spray drops and facilitates wetting of the foliage with the herbicide solutions.

The surface tension of an aqueous solution is reduced in proportion to the concentration of the wetting agent maintained in the spray liquid. Both, too much and too little of the surfactant will reduce plant kill. An excess of the surfactant tends to deposit the spray in such a thin layer that it does not hold the required quantity of the toxicant. Too little surfactant in the spray, on the other hand, will fail to bring about proper wetting of the foliage. Usually, the optimum surfactant concentration in a spray liquid is 0.5 to 1.0 per cent.

**Interface refers to the surface common to both water and leaf (or any other lipophilic substance).*

18.1.3 Penetrating Actions of Surfactants

All surfactants induce wetting of foliage with herbicides but this is not sufficient to explain the spectacular herbicide enhancing effects of many of these. Foy and Smith (1965) showed whereas 0.1 to 0.5% of several surfactants minimized the contact angles with the aqueous sprays of dalapon, maximum herbicide activity was observed at 5.0% or more of many test surfactants. Likewise, McWhorter *et al* (1961) reported that although all surfactants caused wetting of grasses with diuron, certain surfactants also helped it (diuron) to kill the treated plants. With a suitable surfactant of the type alkyl polyoxyethylene ether or alkylaryl polyoxyethylene glycol, as little as 0.25 to 0.50 kg/ha of diuron killed the established, annual grasses and at 4 kg/ha also the perennial grasses, including *Sorghum halepense*, to the extent of 80% for 6 to 8 weeks. Without surfactant, diuron had practically no foliage action. Bayer and Drever (1965) computed a surfactant concentration of over 1% to accentuate diuron to kill grasses. Levene and Owen (1994) found UAN[**] enhanced bentazon absorption in weeds.

Radiotracer studies showed that many surfactants enhanced herbicide penetration in plants *per se*, that is, they acted as penetrants. Foy (1963) observed that maize leaves absorbed as much dalapon (^{14}C) in one hour from spray containing suitable surfactants as in two weeks from solutions without them. Expedited penetration of herbicides in the presence of specific surfactants has also been observed for certain other herbicides, for example, 2,4-D amitrole, and atrazine (Jansen, 1964). Liu, *et al.* (1995) reported sodium bisulphate ($NaHSO_4$) helped imazamethabenz to kill wildoat more actively by increasing the herbicide absorption by the weed foliage. Further, the surfactants have been found to enhance the uptake of herbicides even by plant roots which, being devoid of cuticle, do not pose any problem in wetting them with aqueous sprays. This is a direct proof of surfactant enhanced herbicide penetration in plants.

Presently there is no conclusive evidence for surfactant facilitated herbicide translocation in plants though it has been recorded that GAF-141 [(2-chloroethyl) phosphonic acid plus *N*-methyl pyrrolidone] increased basipetal translocation of glyphosate, dicamba, and aciflurofen in *Phaseolus vulagaris* seedlings. Yet to be discovered are (i) mode of penetrating action of surfactants, (ii) absorption pattern of surfactants themselves, and (iii) time when surfactants depart from the herbicides, outside or within the plant tissues. Limited experimental data available on hand show that hardly 1-3% of any applied surfactant enters plants and that it is subjected to easy metabolism (Smith and Foy, 1966).

18.1.4 Surfactants used with Soil-Applied Herbicide Sprays

Certain surfactants have been found to apparently affect percolation and leaching behaviour of some soil active herbicides. When they aid leaching of herbicides to kill deep-rooted weeds they are called *water extenders*. A common water extender available commercially is Hydro-wet. It is a compound containing alkylarylpolyoxyethylene ethers plus isopropanol. Specific surfactants can be used to reduce the capillary loss of soil

---

[**] *Urea ammonium nitrate*

moisture and hold it near the soil surface by forming an impervious layer on it. It induces germination of weeds and activates the soil-applied herbicides against them.

18.2 EMULSIFYING AGENTS

As described earlier the foliage – active herbicides, in particular, are formulated with an oil like solvent or surfactant to ensure their adequate spread and contact with the target plant. This forms the emulsion concentrate (EC). When an emulsion concentrate is added to the most common and feasible carrier *ie* water, the surfactant tends to separate out. One way to keep the toxicant evenly distributed in the carrier is to cause constant physical agitation in the spray tank. But a preferred way is to use an emulsifying agent (=emulsifier), which shall keep the toxicant well distributed through the volume of carrier water. Today, a variety of emulsifying agents is available to suit the nature of the herbicide molecule. These are usually pre-blended in the formulations. Thus, the present day emulsion concentrate comprises at least three components, *viz.*, the toxicant, the solvent, and the emulsifier.

18.2.1 Kinds and Composition of Herbicide Emulsions

There are three kinds of herbicide emulsions, namely, (1) oil-in-water (O/W) emulsion, (2) water-in-oil (W/O) emulsion, and oil in water in oil (O/W/O) emulsion. The first one is called *normal emulsion,* the second, *invert emulsion* and the third, *bivert* or *double invert emulsion*. Any emulsion has two phases *ie.* (i) a discontinuous phase comprising a liquid in the form of globules embodying the toxicant, and (ii) a continuous phase comprising another liquid surrounding these globules. In normal emulsion (O/W) the toxicant particles are embodied in oil globules and water is the surrounding continuous phase (Fig. 18.3). In invert emulsion (W/O) on the other hand, the carrier water is broken into discontinuous globules and they are surrounded by continuous phase of oil containing the toxicant. In the bivert system, each spray droplet has an oil centre, an outer layer of water, and yet another layer of oil. Herbicide may be included in either phase. This system is generally used for weed control in irrigation waterbodies. The differences in physical structures of emulsions originate from the kind of emulsifiers added to the herbicide concentrates. Emulsifiers of HLB of 4 to 6 are used for making invert emulsions and those of 8 to 18 HLB, for preparing normal emulsions. Also, the solvents used for making the two types of emulsion concentrates are different. The normal emulsion concentrates are prepared from solvents of HLB of 9 to 15 and invert emulsion concentrates from solvents of HLB of 4 to 8.

Important features of invert emulsions:

1. Invert emulsions are viscous. Their viscosity increases with increasing proportion of water and decreases upon addition of oil. Violent agitation makes an invert emulstion more viscous by subdividing its water droplets, whereas upon standing the invert emulsion thins down. High viscosity of invert emulsions reduces spray drift hazards that may occur with normal emulsions when wind is blowing fast. The invert emulsions produce sprays that contain much lower proportions of drift susceptible droplets than the normal emulsions (Table 18.1).

2. Invert emulsion sprays stick to both dry and moist foliage well and they are resistant to wash-off from the treated foliage by rain.
3. Invert emulsion sprays dry from treated surfaces rather slowly which is an important advantage in the postemergence control of weeds in summer months.
4. Invert emulsions are applied as low to very low volume sprays. This makes them very suitable for aerial application of herbicides.

Table 18.1: Per cent Proportion of Different Size Spray Droplets Contained in Sprays of Equal Volumes of Two Types of Emulsions and Total Number of Drops Intercepted Per Sq Inch at Spray Volume of 5 gpa

Type of emulsion	Droplet diameter (microns)				
	200*	200 to 600	600 to 1000	over 1000	Total No. of drops per square inch
Invert (W/O)	8.5%	67.5%	29.0%	0.0	130
Normal (O/W)	22.0%	66.0%	10.4%	1.6%	65

*This grade of droplets is considered drift susceptible.

It may be pointed out that the above first three advantages of invert emulsions in comparison to normal emulsions become perceptible only under abnormal weather conditions like high wind velocity and excessively dry or wet weather. Under normal conditions invert emulsions are about equal in their herbicidal effects to normal emulsions.

18.2.2 Nature of Action of Emulsifier

The emulsifiers influence two way action in stabilizing the emulsions. *First,* like surfactants they are *emphipathic* and reduce interfacial tension between the oil and the water. *Second,* they provide a repellent charge around the globules of discontinuous phase. This is exemplified in Fig. 18.3. If an anionic emulsifier has been added to an emulsifiable concentrate of 2,4-D and an emulsion is prepared from it, the hydrophilic portion (H) of the emulsifier will ionize to stud the globule surface with negative charges. This charge will, therefore, repel the negatively charged herbicide ions inside the oily globules, thus preventing the oil drops from 'grouping', 'creaming', or 'oiling out'. By the same token, the cationic emulsifiers will stabilize emulsion of cationic herbicide concentrates.

Choice of emulsifier is very important in forming a good emulsifiable concentrate. A good emulsifiable concentrate means (i) it should form an emulsion spontaneously, (ii) the emulsion should remain stable for at least 24 hours. (iii) it should not react with the herbicide containers**, (iv) it should not form any nozzle clogging sludges, and (v) it should not result in excessive studs in the spray tanks. Several choices of emulsifiers are available for use with different kinds of herbicides and solvents. To avoid confusion of having to choose a specific emulsifier from such a large variety, some adjuvant

** Phenolic and epoxy coatings are now used to protect herbicide containers against corrosive action of certain emulsifiers.

manufacturers have combined 2 to 3 appropriate emulsifiers in one. The combination, called *universal emulsifier*, or 2 to 3 way stabilizer, works efficiently with a large variety of herbicide emulsions. *Examples:* Altox-3406, Altox-3408, Buffer-X, Orthotronic, and Emcol emulsifier.

Emulsifiers also act as wetting agents, hence, one need not add any wetting agent to an emulsion.

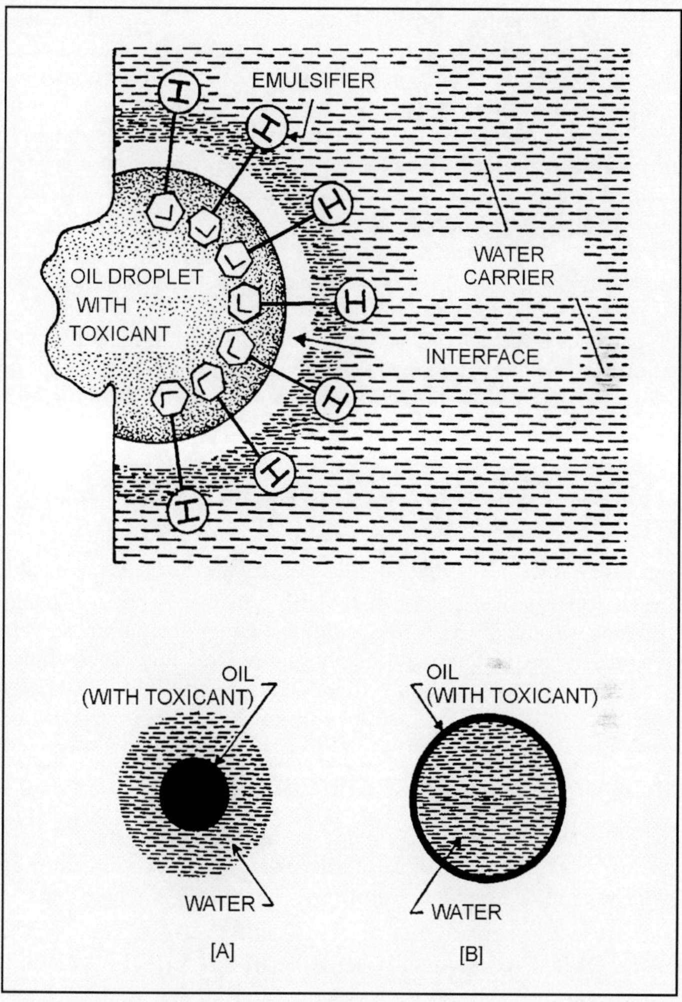

Fig. 18.3: Orientation of surfactant molecules in an Oil-Water emulsion system; H = hydrophilic and I = lipophilic groups. *Bottom left* = Common or Oil-in-Water (O/W) emulsion system. *Bottom right* = invert or W/O emulsion system (diagrammatic)

18.2.3 Preparation of Emulsion Spray Liquids

The normal or oil-in-water (O/W) emulsions are prepared by adding emulsifiable concentrates of choice to the desired volume of water in any type of spray tank. The reverse practice of first pouring a herbicide concentrate in the tank and then filling it with water will form a poor emulsion.

Invert emulsions are complex to prepare. There are two systems of preparing invert emulsions *viz.*, (i) by spinning disc spray system, and (2) by bifluid system. In the spinning disc system, the emulsifiable concentrate is poured into an empty tank and its volume is made-up by adding water, maintaining strong agitation of the emulsion from the spinning disc. In the process of agitation the oil folds itself around the water droplets. In the bifluid system, on the contrary, the two components *ie* the herbicide concentrate and water, are forced into the boom of a sprayer through separate tubes and the invert is formed at specially designed nozzle tips. The water for the bifluid system is preconditioned with sodium bisulphate.

18.3 DISPERSANTS

They keep fine particles of the *wettable powders* in suspension in water even after initial vigorous agitation has been withdrawn from the spray tank. They act by increasing the hydration of fine particles of wettable powers laden with the herbicides. *Examples*-Multifilm, Tryad, and Biofilm.

18.4 COUPLING AGENTS (=SOLVENTS AND CO-SOLVENTS)

Coupling agent is a chemical that is used to solubilize a herbicide in a concentrated form in so far as the resulting solution is soluble or miscible with water in all proportions. 2,4-D (acid form), for instance, is almost insoluble in water, but it can be dissolved in polyethylene glycol to make it water soluble. Other common solvents used for solubilizing the otherwise water insoluble herbicies are: lanolin, carbowax, benzene, HAN, xylene, petroleum ether, carbon tetrachloride, methyl chloride, various alcohols, acetone, etc.

18.5 HUMICANTS (=HYGROSCOPIC AGENTS)

Humicants prevent rapid drying of herbicide sprays on the foliage, thus providing an extended opportunity of herbicide absorption. Being hygroscopic, humicants are also called hygroscopic agents. *Example* glycerol.

18.6 DEPOSIT BUILDERS (=STICKERS OR FILMING AGENTS)

Deposit builders are chemicals added to herbicide concentrates to hold the toxicant in intimate contact with the plant surface. They also reduce washing-cff of the toxicant from the treated foliage by rain. *Examples* several petroleum oils, Du Pont Spreader Sticker, Citowett, and Chevron Spary Sticker.

18.7 COMPATIBILITY AGENTS*

With the advent and widespread use of high analysis liquid fertilizers, farmers in many countries apply plant nutrients, pesticides, and herbicides in a single spray to save cost of application. Compatibility agents like 'compex' are used to intimately mix fertilizers and pesticides in spray liquids.

18.8 SYNERGISTS (=ACTIVATORS)

In weed science the synergists are chemicals added to any herbicide formulation to enhance its phytotoxicity against the target weeds by inhibiting or slowing down its detoxification within the plant. Some recently recognised example of synergism include piperphos and anilophos applied to synergise the action of propanil against resistant populations of jungle rice (*Echinochloa colona*); isoproturon and malathion synergise action against resistant biotype of *Phalaris minor*; and Glyphosate is synergistic with 2,4-D against certain weeds.

Some other common synergists or activators are as follows:-

18.8.1 Phytobland Oils

The phytobland oils are non-phytotoxic, paraffinic oils (NPO) with less than 10% aromatic content, which act as strong penetrants. In certain plant-herbicide combinations they have proved more potent in activating herbicides than the usual surfactant activators (McGlamery, 1971). A notable example of effectiveness of phytobland oil is 25% enhancement in foliar activity of atrazine against annual grasses in its presence in comparison to its aqueous spray without the oil. The atrazine-oil emulsions are now widely used for preplant desiccation and postemergence weed control in maize and sorghum. The NPO is used at 5 to 10% by volume of the final spray liquid. It is first mixed with the herbicide concentrate, using suitable emulsifier (if the concentrate did not already contain it) to form an emulsifiable concentrate. The concentrate is then diluted with water to the desired volume.

Table: 18.2: Four Common Phytobland Oils; Their Viscosity, and Aromatic Content

Trade name	Source	Viscosity (SSU at 33°C)	Aromatic content %
Orche x 796	Humble Oil and Refining Co.	70	4
7 N	Sun Oil Co.	71	7
11 E	Sun Oil Co.	105	8
Mobilsol-ICO	Mobil Oil Co.	33	3

Besides atrazine, the phytobland oils have been found to activate amitrole, chloroxuron, fluometuron, dinoseb, and terbacil more than the usual surfactants. However, NPO has been found to reduce the phytotoxicity of MSMA + norea, and it had no effect on MSMA

* Compatible: Quality of two compounds that permits them to be mixed without any effect on the properties of either.

combinations with diuron and prometryn. This shows that NPO is superior to the usual surfactants in activating only specific herbicides. Currently research is underway to develop a 4:1::NPO:surfactant combination as a broad-spectrum activator of herbicides. Also, some researchers believe that a combination of specific vegetable and paraffinic oils will form superior phytobland oil activators, at least for some herbicides (Barrentine and Warren, 1970).

18.8.2 Isoparaffinic Oils

Burr and Warren (1971) found that an isoparaffinic oil used as diluent accelerated atrazine and dinoseb action against *Ipomoea hederacea* 16 fold, but it affected no chage in atrazine action against nutsedge (*Cyperus* spp.) and quackgrass (*Agropyron repens*). The oil carrier did not bioactivate 2,4-D although it activated dinoseb 200-fold against 40 species of plants, and linuron against nutsedge. Isoparaffinic oil carrier activated 2,4-D sufficiently to inhibit tuber production in nutsedge as well as killed some of the tubers already present. Radiotracer studies confirmed enhanced penetration of 2,4-D (^{14}C) in nutsedge tubers. Barrentine and Warren (1970) obtained almost complete kill of *Setaria faberii* with chlorpropham and terbacil in oil carrier, whereas in aqueous sprays the two herbicides were practically ineffective against the grass.

18.8.3 Ammonium Thiocyanate (NH_4SCN)

Ammonium thiocyanate is a widely used activator of amitrole and the combination is designated as 'amitrole-T. Investigating the nature of synergism, Cook *et al.* (1981) reported that ammonium thiocyanate beefed amitrole mobility in many plants from the treated leaves by preventing rapid scorching of the absorbing cells otherwise caused by amitrole. This was probably achieved by preferential oxidation of ammonium thiocyanate within the plant, thereby preventing the formation of amitrole free radicals and probably subsequent conjugation with serine and other plant constituents. Rapid mobility of amitrole from the leaves decreased its decomposition in the foliage. There is also a view that ammonium thiocyanate inhibited the formation of 3-ATAL from amitrole, which is less mobile and less phytotoxic than the parent herbicide.

Cyanide and hexacyanoferrate (ii) were also found to be very active scorch inhibitors of amitrole.

18.8.4 Trichlorobenzyl Chloride (TCBC)

Like ammonium thiocyanate, TCBC is a specific herbicide activator. Thus far it has been used successfully only with CDAA. The combination of CDAA with TCBC is named Randox-T. The mode of synergistic action of TCBC is not known.

18.8.5 Nitrogen Fertilizers

Nitrogenous fertilizers like urea, ammonium chloride, and ammonium nitrate have been employed to enhance 2,4-D and sethoxydim phytotoxicities and reduce their rates of application. It is postulated that these compounds when present in herbicide spray liquids widen the openings in the leaf cuticle by modifying ester, ether, and diether bondages between the macromolecules of its cutin. This facilitates the entry of either herbicide in the treated leaves.

18.9 ANTAGONISTS

When combination of a herbicide with another herbicide or any other pesticide reduces the herbicide action within plant, the phenomenon is called antagonism. Some recognised examples of antagonisms are: (1) Diclofop with phenoxy herbicides or metribuzin; imazmethabenz-methyl with 2,4-D or clopyralid; sethoxydin with 2,4-D or glyphosate and cyhalofop-butyl with 2,4-D.

18.10 DRIFT CONTROL AGENTS

Herbicide spray drifts may pose serious hazards to non-target plants, particularly from their aerial applications. An important way to tackle this problem is to spray herbicide liquids in large droplets. The use of invert emulsions for this purpose has already been discussed in this chapter. Besides, following chemical agents can be used to increase the droplet size of the herbicide sprays.

18.10.1 Thickening Agents

Thickening agents are large molecule, organic compounds which in aqueous system behave like gels, making the spray liquid viscous. The thickened sprays, as is true of invert emulsions, produce large drops that are less susceptible to spray drifts than the usual aqueous sprays. *Examples:* sodium alginate, hydroxyethylcellulose, and dacagin. Dacagin resists both spray and vapour drifts. It is used at 2.8 kg/100 gal spray.

18.10.2 Particulating Agent

A particulating agent comprises particles of a lightly, crosslinked, swellable (but not soluble) polymer. It imbibes liquids (both water and oil) to form 'particulate aqueous' and 'particulate oil' sprays, as the case may be. The drift potential from particulate sprays has been found less than for sprays of thickened or unthickened liquids. 'Norbak' is a particulating agent of Dow Chemical Co.

18.10.3 Foams

Foam is a liquid interface surrounding small pockets of gas, usually air. One could call it also an air emulsion system. Expansion ratio (E.R.) of a foam system per unit of original liquid volume can be raised by adding suitable adjuvants. In herbicide sprays, low expansion foams of ER of about 7 are under trial as drift control agents. (Foams of E.R. 100-400 are used as cryoptoprotectants of crops in frost-prone areas).

SUMMARY

There are 17 categories of adjuvants identified round the world comprising about 155 agricultural spray products.

Adjuvants are chemicals that improve the efficacy of herbicides. They are grouped according to the type of action as (i) surfactants (wetting agents, spreaders, penetrants), (ii) stabilizing agents (dispersants, emulsifiers), (iii) cosolvents (coupling agents), (iv) hygroscopic agents, (v) deposit builders (stickers), and (vi) activators.

Surfactants have two important functions *viz.*, (1) wetting of difficult leaf surfaces, and (2) enhancement of herbicide penetration. Some surfactants may also directly interact with herbicide action. Chemistry, nature of action, and classification of surfactants have been discussed.

Emulsifiers maintain an oil phase carrying the herbicide and an aqueous carrier phase in miscible state for sufficiently long for field application. Depending upon the kind of emulsifier added and the method used in making the emulsion, it can form either an oil-in-water emulsion (O/W), or water-in-oil (W/O) emulsion. The latter is also called invert emulsion and it is used mainly to minimize the spray drifts. Emulsifiers act by (i) reducing the interfacial tension between the oil and water, as well as by (ii) providing a repellant charge around the globules of discontinuous phase.

Spray drift can be serious when wind velocity is high. It can be minimized by enlarging the size of spray droplets. Lower than 150 micron diameter spray droplets are considered drift suseceptible. Spray droplet diameter can be increased by using (i) invert emulsions, (ii) or thickening agents, or (iii) particulating agents. A comparative statement of effectiveness of the three sources of drift control is provided in the last section of the chapter.

SELECTED BIBLIOGRAPHY

1. Balyan, R. S. *et al.* 2000. Efficacy of sulfosulfuron as influenced by surfactants. Ind. J. Weed Sci. 32 : 190-19.
2. Barrentine, J. L. and Warren, G. F. 1970. Isoparaffinic oil as carrier for chlorpropham and terbacil. Weed Sci. 18:365-372.
3. Bayer, D. E. and Drever, H. R. 1965. The effects of surfactants on efficiency of foliar applied diuron. Weeds 13(3) 222-226.
4. Burr, R. J. and Warren, G. F. 1971. Enhancement of herbicide activity with an isoparaffinic oil carrier. Weed Sci. 19(6) 701-705.
5. Cabanne, F. 2000. Increased efficacy of clodinafop by terineols and synergestic action with esterified fatty acids. Weed Res. 40: 131-152.
6. Cook, G. T. *et al.* 1981. Influence of ammonium thiocyanate on scorching and control of *Pteridium equilinum* by amitrole. Weed Sci. 29 (92) 196-199.
7. Dixit, A. 2004. Role of herbicide mixtures, adjuvants, and weed management. Crop Care 29(4): 6-14.
8. Dunne, C. L. *et al.* 1994. Primary linear alcohol ethoxylates as adjuvants for primisulfuron. Weed Sci. 42(1) 82-85.

9. Foy, C. L. 1963. The influence of formulation, exposure time, and pH on the herbicidal action of dalapon foliar sprays tested on corn. Hilgardia 35(7) 125-144.
10. Foy, C. L. and Smith, L. W. 1965. Surface tension lowering wettability of paraffin and corn leaf surfaces and herbicidal enhancement of dalapon by seven surfactants. Weeds 13(1) 15-19.
11. Foy, C. L. and D. W. Pritchard, 1996. Pesticide Formulation and Adjuvant Technology. CRC Press. Boca Raton, NY (USA), 363 p.
12. Gould, R. F. (Ed.). 1969. Pesticide Formulation Research: Physical and Colloidal Chemical Aspects. Advances in Chemistry Series-86. ACS, Washington D.C., 212 pp.
13. Harvey, L. T. 1992. A Guide to Agricultural Spray Adjuvants Used in the United States. Thomson Publications vii + 244 pp., USA.
14. Jansen, L. L. 1964. Surfactant enhancement of herbicide entry. Weeds 12 251-255.
15. Kudsk, P. and Streibig, J. C. 1993. Formulations and Adjuvants. (In) Herbicide Bioassays. (Ed.), CRC Press Inc.
16. Levene, B. C. and Owen, M. D. K. 1994. Movement of ^{14}C bentazon with adjuvants into common cocklebur and velvetleaf. Weed Technol. 8(1) 93-98.
17. Liu, S. H. *et al.* 1995. Effect of sodium bisulfate on the phytotoxicity, retention, foliar uptake, and translocation of imazamethabenz on wildoats. Weed Sci. 43(1):40-46.
18. Liu, Z. Q. 2004. Bentazone uptake into plant foliage as influenced by surfactants and carrier pH. Aust. J. Agric. Res. 55(9) : 967-971.
19. Malik, R. S. *et al.* 2001. Efficacy of new herbicides with and without surfactants on weeds in wheat. India J. Weed Sci. 33: 59-62.
20. McGlamery, M. D. 1971. The use of oils in postemergence weed sprays. Weeds Today. 2(1):13.
21. McKay, I. *et al.* 2005. Bentazone - surfactant interactions in three selected weed species of differing leaf characteristics. Weed Abs. 54(4), 1499.
22. McWhorter, C. G. *et al.* 1961. Now diuron controls emerged weeds in cotton. Agri. Res. 19(3) 10.
23. Norsworthy, J. K. and T. L. Grey. 2004. Addition of nonionic surfactant to glyphosate plus chlorimuron. Weed Technol. 18(3) : 588-593 (USA).
24. Parmar, B. S. and S. S. Tomar. 2004. Pesticide Formulations : Theory and Practice. CBS Pub. & Distributors, New Deli 414 p.
25. Scherhag, H. *et al.* 2005. Influence of rapeseed oil ethoxylate surfactants on retention and biological efficacy of glyphosate spray solutions in selected weeds. J. Applied Botany and Food Quality. 79(1) : 17-23 (Germany).
26. Schonherr, J. and Baur, P. 1994. Modelling penetration of plant by crop protection agents and effects of adjuvants on their rates of penetration. Pesticide Sci. 42(3):185-208.
27. Singh, G. and V. P. Singh 2005. Compatibility of clodinafop- propargyl and fenoxaprop-p-ethyl with carfentrazone-ethyl, metsulfuron-methyl and 2,4-D. Ind. J. Weed Sci. 37(1 &2): 1-5.

28. Smith, L. W. and Foy, C. L. 1966. Penetration and distribution studies in bean, cotton, and barley from foliar and root application of Tween-20-^{14}C, fatty acid and labelled oxyethylene. Agr. Food Chem. 14(2) 117-122.

29. Streibig, J. C. and Kudsk, P. 1992. The influence of adjuvants on herbicidal activity of alloxydim-sodium, fluazifop-butyl, and tribenuron. (In) Adjuvants for Agrichems. (Ed.) Foy, C. L. Florida, USA:513-523.

30. Taylor, L. F. 1972. Spray adjuvants make pesticides do a better job. World Fmg. 14(9) 9-10.

31. Turner, D. J. 1972. The influence of additives on the penetration of foliar applied growth regulator herbicides. Pesticide Sci. 3(3) 323-331.

32. Valkenburg, W. V. 1973. Pesticide Formulations. Marcel Dekkker Inc., N. Y.

Chapter 19

FATE OF HERBICIDES IN SOILS

In this chapter important venues of dissipation of herbicides in soils, factors affecting these, and important methods to change the course of herbicide persistence in soils are described.

Application of herbicides to soil is a common practice of weed control, particularly on crop lands. Besides, indirectly, portions of all herbicides eventually end up in the soil through (i) drip from the sprayed vegetation, (ii) spray falling in spaces between weeds and crop plants, and (iii) decay of the treated vegetation.

Of the total herbicide applied to a soil, only a small amount is actually utilized in controlling weeds. The major portion of the herbicide is diluted by soil material and is subjected to (i) *transfer* and (ii) *decomposition* processes. The two processes–transfer and decomposition–constitute the *fate of herbicides in soils.* Good reviews of herbicide interactions in soil are provided by Hanee (1980) and Scheunert (1992).

The transfer of herbicides involves division of the toxicant into parts among different phases of the soil, *viz.*, soil colloids and soil solution. It also includes movement of herbicides from the site of their initial placement to other zones in the soil. Transfer does not involve any molecular change in the herbicide structure.

Transfer of herbicide is usually followed by its decomposition in which herbicide structures are altered either biologically or chemically. Also, sunlight decomposes specific herbicides on soil surfaces by photodecomposition (= photolysis). Transfer and decomposition are essential features of pesticide usage, else these would accumulate in soils to destroy soil productivity, permanently.

The fate of herbicides in soils determines (i) their availability in soils for immediate as well as sustained weed control, (ii) selectivity to crops, and (iii) herbicide carry-over from one season to another. *An ideal fate of a herbicide in soil on crop land* is the one that brings about selective control of weeds for sufficiently long period to give competitive advantage to the crop but, at the same time, allows the herbicide to dissipate from the soil before the close of the crop season so that rotation crops could be planted safely. Very rapid loss of herbicides from soil will cause insufficient weed control, which is considered as unsatisfactory as their unduly long persistence in soils. Beside herbicide structure, soil conditions prevailing during and after the application of a herbicide, as well as herbicide application methods, influence the fate of the toxicant in soils.

The fate of herbicide in soils can be classified as follows:

I. Transfer

1. Adsorption,
2. Movement (includes leaching, seepage, capillarity, volatilization, chromatographic movement along colloidal surfaces, entry in soil cracks, and runoff and wash off),
3. Plant removal.

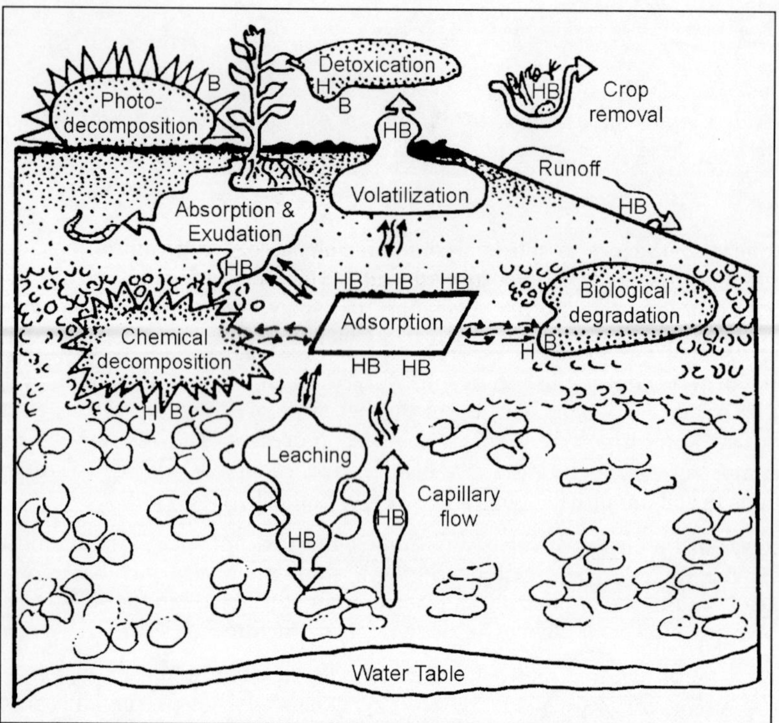

Fig. 19.1: A diagrammatic presentation of the possible fate of herbicides applied to soil (Courtesy J.B.W. of U.S.A.)

II. Decomposition

1. Microbial decomposition (intercellular and extracellular),
2. Chemical decomposition, and
3. Photodecomposition (= photolysis)

19.1 ADSORPTION

Adsorption of herbicides in soils is a physical process of accumulation or gathering of their molecules and ions at specific soil colloid-water interfaces. The portion of the herbicide thus held by the soil colloid (= particulate matter) is called 'adsorbed' herbicide, whereas that present in soil solution (or soil air) is 'free' herbicide. In many cases adsorption removes a part (sometimes all) of the herbicide added to the soil from the field of its potent action; like uptake by plants or utilization by microbes. However, with most herbicide structures adsorption is reversible and the 'adsorbed' and 'free' herbicides exchange status freely under external and internal influences, tending to maintain certain equilibrium in soil. A plot of quantity of herbicide adsorbed plotted against variable concentration of free herbicide in soil at any given time is called an *adsorption isotherm* (Fig. 19.2). The adsorption isotherms of many herbicides have been described emperically by the use of the Freundlich equation

$$x/m = Kf.\ Ce.\ 1/n,$$

where x is the quantity of adsorbate (herbicide) reversibly adsorbed by a given quantity of adsorbent, in equilibrium with the adsorbate solution of concentration Ce; Kf and n are constants and may be determined by the best line drawn through a plot of log (x/m) versus log Ce. Kf is called Adsorption (or Equilibrium) Coefficient. It depicts relative adsorption capacity of a soil for any given herbicide. An alternative adsorption isotherm equation, which has shown better fit for certain herbicides, as suggested by Lambert (1967), is

$$x/m = K_1\,Ce + K_2\,Ce^2,$$

where K_1 and K_2 are two equilibria coefficients; K_1 is the adsorption coefficient at infinite dilution (*i.e.*, Ce = O), equivalent to Kf of Freundlich equation when n=1, K_2 is adsorption coefficient when Ce has some value other than zero.

Figure 19.2 shows adsorption isotherms based on Freundlich equation of two soils differing in their Kf values. The two isotherms clearly show that at any level of application of a herbicide, more of it is adsorbed in a high Kf value soil than in a low Kf value soil, leaving less quantity of the toxicant in soil solution for weed control in the former type of soil. Therefore, higher rates of herbicides must be applied to higher Kf value soils and vice-versa to obtain similar weed control (see also Chapter 20).

The tendency of pesticides for adsorption in soils is an interplay of their electrical state and properties of soil *colloid particulates* (Barriuso and Calvet, 1992). The soil particulate of colloidal dimensions (<1 micron) alone act as adsorbent of the added pesticides. Both, soil inorganic (clays) and organic colloids (humic materials) participate in adsorption of pesticides, although the latter are generally considered functionally more important. The clay minerals constitute two major types *viz.*, the crystalline Si-Al (or Mg) clays and the amorphous Fe-Al hydrous oxide metallic clays, besides some allophanes. The crystalline Si-Al clays are further differentiated into expanding types *eg.* montmorillonite and vermiculite and nonexpanding types *eg.* kaolinite, illite, and chlorite. The expanding types offer much larger surface area for adsorption of relevant ions than the non-expanding types. The clay micelles are surrounded by isomorphic substitution and pH dependent negative charges which assign these their cation exchange capacity (CEC). The cation exchange capacity of the expandable micelles is as high as 80-150 meq/100g soil, as compared to 3-40 for the non-expanding clays. Under certain circumstances, Fe-Al hydrous oxide clays, allophanes*, and even kaolinite clays, also exhibit limited anion exchange capacity (AEC).

The negative charges on humic materials are pH dependent, arising from -COOH (carboxylic groups) and -OH (phenolic groups). In neutral to alkaline soils, hydrogen of these groups tends to be held rather loosely, and is easily exchanged for other cations. The CEC of humus ranges from 150-300 meq/100 g substrate. Pantani *et al.* (1994) reported the influence of clay minerals on adsorption of cinosulfuron.

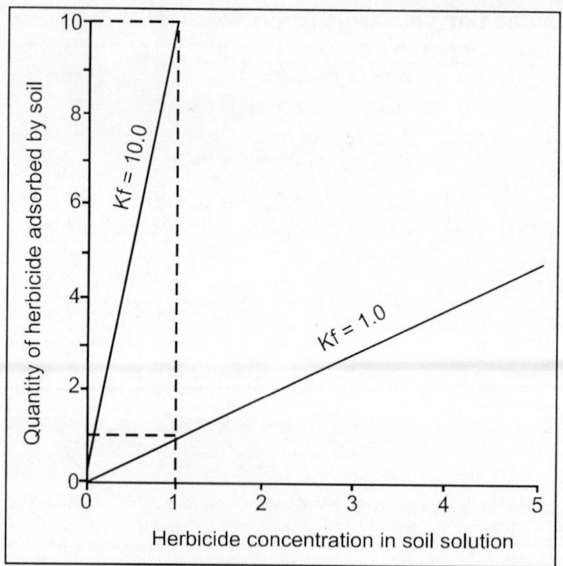

Fig. 19.2: Linear adsorption isotherms of two soils with different adsorption capacities (Kf = 1 and 10). To obtain a particular concentration of a herbicide in soil solution, a much higher dose should be applied to a high Kf value soil than to a low Kf value soil.

19.1.1 Mechanism of Adsorption of Organic Herbicides

Depending upon thir ionising characteristics, herbicides can be divided into four main groups. These are (1) Cationic (strong base) herbicides, (2) Weak base herbicides, (3) acidic herbicides, and (4) non-ionic herbicides. The mechanisms of adsorption of the four types of herbicides differ.

1. *Cationic* (*or Strong base*) *herbicides:* Cationic herbicides readily dissolve and dissociate in aqueous systems to form cationic species. Paraquat and diquat are common representatives of strong base herbicides. These are adsorbed on soil colloids by a combination of ionic and physical forces. The ion exchange is for

---

* Allophanes are amorphous Si-Al clay micelles.

cations like Na^+, K^+, and Ca^{++} in the case of inorganic colloid adsorbent (Equation-1), and for H^+ in the case of organic adsorbent in soil.

$$\text{Paraquat}^{++} + 2\text{Na-clay} \rightleftharpoons \text{paraquat-clay} + 2(\text{Na}^+) \quad \text{..........(1)}$$

The reaction goes strongly to the right but weakly to the left.

2. *Weak bases herbicides:* Herbicides such as the *s*-triazines and triazoles are weakly basic compounds which under sufficiently acid conditions can accept a proton H^+ at each of their N atoms in the ring to become cationic (Fig. 19.3 and Equation-2). The process is called protonation. Protons (H^+ ions) are donated by molecular layer of water present on the clay particles in soils. (Che *et al.*, 1992).

$$R + H \rightleftharpoons RH \quad \text{..........(2)}$$

Where, R = molecular species of a weakly basic herbicide, H = hydrogen ions; RH = protonated species.

The protonated basic herbicide molecules (= conjugate acid) dissociate in aqueous solutions to form cationic species which are adsorbed by cation exchange adsorbents according to Equation 3.

$$RH^+ + \text{X-solid} \rightleftharpoons \text{RH-solid} + X^+ \quad \text{..........(3)}$$

where, X-solid = particulate adsorbent matter with X^+ as exchangeable cation other than hydrogen, *eg.* Na^+ and K^+. The proton donating capacity of a solution increases with lowering of pH of the media; the maximum protonation occurring at pH near the pK_a[1] value of the conjugate acid, which differs markedly with the herbicide structure. The pK_a of conjugate acids of atrazine, ametryn, and amitrole, for example, are respectively 1.68, 3.93 and 4.17. Maximum adsorption of these compounds has been found to occur at pH near these pK_a values, and the amount of adsorption was also directly related to the pK_a values. A decreased adsorption at pH lower than the pH of the conjugate acid presumably represented increased competition from solution H^+ (cited by Weed and Weber, 1974). On the contrary, decreased adsorption of *s*-triazine herbicides at higher pH was attributable to decrease in the number of protonated molecules.

Like cationic herbicides, weakly basic herbicides can also be adsorbed by cation exchange in the interlayer spacings of the expanding clay mineral but they remain biologically available. Besides ionic adsorption, basic herbicides can be adsorbed in molecular form to cation exchange adsorbents through various physical mechanisms, including (a) physical adsorption (Equation-4), (b) hydrogen bonding[2] and (c) complexing with hydrogen ions on the exchange surface (Equation-5).

---

[1]1. pka = log (RH^+)/R + pH, where RH = protonated, weakly basic molecule and R = molecular species. At pH near pKa value of a conjugate acid, 50% of the species in solution are present in the cationic forms and 50% in the moleculSar forms.

[2]*Hydrogen bonding:* Carboxyl oxygens on pesticide molecules may bond to amino hydrogens or hydroxyl groups on the organic matter, assuming special arrangements permit. Other associations can be devised. Sometimes a water bridge between an exchangeable metal cation and the pesticide molecule may contribute to hydrogen bonding. Hydrogen bonding is not strong and the adsorbed mole-

$$R + X\text{-solid} \rightleftharpoons RX\text{-solid} \qquad \text{..........(4)}$$

$$\text{and } R + H\text{-solid} \rightleftharpoons RH\text{-solid} \qquad \text{..........(5)}$$

where X = exchangeable cations other than hydrogen; solid = particulate matter; and H-solid = particulate matter on which hydrogen is the exchangeable cation.

Fig. 19.3: Protonation of chloro-*s*-triazine: (1) un-protonated molecule (2) single protonated ion, and (3) double protonated ion

Other physical adsorption processes suggested to occur between basic herbicides and particulate matter surfaces include hydrophobic bonding[3] through Van der Waals forces[4] and, perhaps legand exchange[5]. Physical adsorption may make greatest contribution at higher pH when the basic herbicide molecules are not protonated.

The molecular adsorption of basic herbicides is predominant under neutral or alkaline conditions, while the ionic adsorption is predominant under acid conditions. Also, the quantity of basic herbicide adsorbed in soil is more at low pH than at neutral pH, and it further declines at higher pH. This is attributed to decrease in the number of protonated molecules in neutral and alkaline soils.

3. *Acidic herbicides* Acidic herbicides possess carboxyl or phenolic functional groups and they ionize in aqueous systems to yield anionic species. The tendency to ionize decreases at low pH. Various phenoxyalkanoic acids, benzoic acids, pthalamic acids, dalapon, phenols, and nitriles are examples of acidic herbicides. Adsorption of an acidic herbicide by basic anion exchange resins in the laboratory is rapid and is easily reversible (Equation 6).

$$R + Cl\text{-Resin} \rightleftharpoons R\text{-Resins} + Cl^{-} \qquad \text{..........(6)}$$

---

cule is easily desorbed by water.

[3]*Hydrophobic bonding:* Waxes, fats, and resins present in organic matter give it hydrophobic surfaces. Adsorption of organic molecules, particularly non-polar molecules, may occur here by physical forces. This is called hydrophobic bonding.

[4]*Van der Waals force:* It is a very weak, physical force of attraction that operates in adsorbent-adsorbate relationship. Its contribution to adsorption of herbicides increases with increase in their molecule size and molecule α capacity to adapt to the adsorbent surface.

[5]*Ligand exchange:* In this process herbicide molecule displaces water of hydration of incompletely chelated transition metals in soils.

Where R = molecular species of acidic herbicide.

In soils, ion exchange adsorption of acidic herbicides is limited mainly to non-silicate clay minerals. The herbicide anions exchange sites on these clay minerals for ions like PO_4^{-}, Cl^{-5}, and OH^{-5}. Adsorption of acidic herbicides with organic matter *via* ion exchange is not anticipated but it may occur when molecular species dominate at low soil pH by weak hydrogen or hydrophobic bonding. Thus, the adsorption of acidic herbicides would be greatest for soils with low pH and high organic matter content. However, it is still of much lower magnitude than the adsorption of cationic or basic herbicides with organic matter, and it is in competition with water. Adsorption with organic matter does not deactivate acidic herbicides although movement through soil may be impeded (Weed and Weber, 1974).

The weakly acid herbicides, *eg* dinoseb ($pk_a = 4.40$) are adsorbed more than the stronger acids like picloram ($pK_a = 1.90$), 2,4-D ($pK_a = 2.80$), and dicamba ($pK_a = 1.9$). It is because there are proportionately more molecular than anionic species in solution at a given pH for the weaker acids as compared to the stronger acids (Weber, 1972).

4. *Non-ionic herbicides:* Some herbicide structures do not ionize significantly in aqueous or soil systems, for example, substituted aniline, anilide, phenylcarbamate, phenylurea, phenylamide, thiocarbamate, benzonitrile, and ester herbicides. Considerably less work has been reported on mechanisms of adsorption of the non-ionic herbicides as compared to the ionic ones. For relatively nonpolar compounds, adsorption on organic matter is through hydrophobic bonding, while for polar, nonionic herbicides, adsorption occurs in greater competition with water.

Adsorption behaviour of specific non-ionic type herbicides is discussed elsewhere.

Quite generally, adsorption of non-ionic herbicides by soils is positively correlated with soil organic matter content but the effects of adsorption on the activity and movement of herbicides vary widely. This variability appears to be related to solubility, polarity, and to a restricted extent, molecular size (= parachor) of the herbicide. The hydrophilic-lipophilic balance (HLB) of both adsorbate and adsorbent strongly influences adsorption (Weed and Weber, 1974).

At the end it may be pointed out that the fate of adsorbed herbicides where the reaction moves strongly to the right whether or not they will be released or how fast, is only conjectural. May be these toxic substances are accumulating in small amounts.

19.1.2 Factors Affecting Herbicide Adsorption

1. ***Particulate matter:*** As earlier discussed, organic matter content is the most important single factor determining adsorption of majority of herbicides in soils leading to their lowered (a) initial phytotoxicity and (b) reduced volatilization and leaching losses (Muller *et al.*, 1992). It encourages herbicide persistence in soil. When organic matter content of the soil is very low, the inorganic colloids become important in the adsorption of herbicides in soils. However, for cationic, strong base herbicides, irrespective of the organic matter content of a soil, strong and almost irreversible adsorption is primarily dictated by clay colloids, particularly the

expandible lattice types. Jerome *et al.*, (1987) developed regression equations allowing herbicide recommendations based on soil organic matter content, or more appropriately the soil humic content.

2. ***Soil pH:*** Soil pH influences the adsorption of herbicides (a) by its effects on cation and anion exchange behaviour of soil on one hand, and (b) by determining the ionic species of herbicides on the other. Within limits, adsorption of both acidic and basic herbicides is positively related with lowering soil pH for reasons discussed earlier. Adsorption of non-ionic herbicides is not influenced by soil pH. Leux and Reed (1992) found imazaquin adsorption, and therefore its persistence, increased as the soil pH decreased from 6.5 to 4.5.

3. ***Soil moisture:*** Usually, within the available moisture range, herbicide concentration in the soil solution remains relatively stable and it decreases as the moisture level increases above field capacity because of dilution. But in high adsorption soils, irrigation may move some reversibly adsorbed herbicide into the soil solution even within available soil moisture range thus improving weed control on such soils. But in low adsorption soils, irrigation dilutes soil solution without inducing desorption of herbicides, which leads to poor weed control (Fig. 19.2). Drying the soil to below wilting point will no doubt concentrate the "free" herbicide but its total quantity will be small. The non-ionic herbicides like CDEC, CDAA and EPTC are adsorbed more on dry than on wet soils. Moisture competes for sites on colloidal surfaces with these herbicides and induces desorption. The volatile compounds thus desorbed are lost to atmosphere.

4. ***Soil temperature:*** Adsorption of herbicides by ionic exchange mechanisms is independent of changes in soil temperature. In variance with it, physical adsorption is generally weakened by rise in soil temperature. This is particularly pronounced for volatile herbicides and herbicides with negative heats of solution *ie* the ones which exhibit less solubility in the soil solution at higher than at low temperature, for example, thiocarbamate herbicides (Weber, 1972).

5. ***Aqueous solubility of herbicides:*** Weber (1972) reported an inverse relationship between water solubility of acidic herbicides and their adsorption when other soil variables were constant. He studied the adsorption of several weakly acidic herbicides by an acid muck at pH of 4 and arranged them in the order dinoseb > picloram < 2,4-D = dicamba. Water solubility of these materials is 45, 430, 650 and 4,5000 ppm, respectively.

19.1.3 Specific Adsorption Behaviour of Some Herbicides

1. ***Diquat and Paraquat:*** Diquat and paraquat, being organic divalent cations, are adsorbed ionically by soil organic matter and clay minerals through cation exchange forces. The adsorption is very strong. The chemicals cannot be removed by extraction with water, but they may be exchanged off organic matter and nonexpanding clays (such as kaolinite) with salt solutions containing exchange cations like calcium, aluminium, hydrogen, sodium, and potassium. They may not be exchanged off montmorillonite clays because they have become adsorbed between the silicate sheets and entrapped in much the same way as potassium becomes 'fixed' in certain types of micas. Paraquat and diquat adsorbed in the

interlayer spaces of montmorillonite may be partially removed by digesting the clay sample in concentrated sulfuric acid and destroying the clay mineral itself.

2. ***Atrazine and simazine:*** Atrazine and simazine are basic herbicides. In alkaline pH these compounds are present prominently in unprotonated forms, which are weakly adsorbed by soil colloids and are available for leaching and absorption by plants (Best and Weber, 1974). The adsorption is further reduced and availability to plants increased when soils are sandy and temperatures high. Very high availability of atrazine and simazine in soil solution may lead to triazine phytotoxicity to even a normally tolerant crop like maize. Also, it may result in very good control of first flush of weeds, but subsequently because of excessive leaching the weed control is poor. In acidic pH range, simazine and atrazine are profusely protonated (Fig. 19.3) and adsorbed by soil colloids by cationic exchange reactions mentioned earlier. The adsorption is maximized at pH near their pK_a values of 1.68 and 1.65, respectively. When an excess of acid is added to the system, lowering thus the pH of the media below pK_a of the conjugate acid, H^+ ions (actually hydronium ions) begin competing for adsorption sites on colloids and displace the conjugate acid ions back into solution (Equation 7).

$$H^+ + \text{RH-solid} \rightleftharpoons \text{H-solid} + RH^+ \quad \text{..........(7)}$$

The methoxy and methylthio-*s*-triazine herbicides are adsorbed on soil particulates in greater amounts than the chloro-*s*-triazines.

3. ***2,4-D:*** 2,4-D is an acidic herbicide. Like other acidic herbicides its dissociation is limited in acidic media where molecular species dominate. Undissociated 2,4-D is adsorbed primarily by organic matter and to some extent by dry silicate clay particulate under competition with water molecules. The adsorbed 2,4-D may be saved from leaching but it remains biologically available for removal by plants and microbes. Its adsorption is maximum in upper layer of soil which contains highest organic matter. At high pH, 2,4-D is completely dissociated. The anions exhibit only limited adsorption by non-silicate clays or organic matter, hence, in alkaline soils 2,4-D is subjected to easy leaching.

4. ***Phenylureas:*** The phenylurea herbicides are non-volatile, non-ionic herbicides. They show extremely weak acidic properties in aqueous systems. The adsorption of phenylurea is relatively low compared to many other non-ionic herbicides. Organic matter and charcoal are the main adsorbents, and the mode of adsorption is physical, involving Van der Waals forces. This adsorption is essentially pH independent. Water can easily induce desorption of phenylureas from organic matter. Increasing the organic matter content of the soil has been found to increase adsorption and decrease leaching, bioactivity, and volatilization of phenylureas. Adsorption of phenylureas by organic matter particulate generally is reported to be directly related to molecule, volume of the compound (= parachor) and inversely to its aqueous solubility. For example, the adsorption of three phenylureas was found to increase in the order; fenuron, fluometuron, and neburon. Their aqueous solubilities are 2900-3850 ppm, 90 ppm, and 4.8 ppm and their parachors 399, 410, and 599, respectively. Neburon is the most strongly adsorbed substituted urea herbicide used so far. It is because of its extremely low water solubility (4.8 ppm at 20-25°C).

5. ***EPTC:*** EPTC is a volatile, non-ionic herbicide. It is adsorbed by organic matter, charcoal, and dry montmorillonite fraction of the soil, and is displaced by water molecules. The adsorption of EPTC induces its loss in vapour form. Adsorption of EPTC on dry montmorillonite is through weak physical forces between carbonyl oxygen atoms of EPTC and metal ions on the clay surface. EPTC thus adsorbed was found biologically active though its adsorption on organic matter reduced EPTC bioactivity. Adsorption of EPTC in soils increased as its organic matter content increased and temperature and moisture content decreased. Also, air movement on the soil surface increased EPTC loss from the soil.
6. ***Glyphosate*** Glyphosate in soils is reversibly adsorbed on clay or organic colloids through phosphoric acid moiety.
7. ***Metolachlor:*** The adsorption isotherm of metolachlor conformed to the Freundlich equation. The Kf values increased with increase in organic matter content (Pusino *et al.*, 1992).

19.2 MOVEMENT

19.2.1 Leaching

Leaching of herbicides is their downward movement in soils as solutes with soil water. Herbicides may move in soil by the physical process of diffusion or mass flow in the liquid or vapour phase. Transport by diffusion is slow relative to mass transport by soil water movement but it may be exceedingly important over short distances. Also, under static water condition diffusion is the only means of herbicide movement within the soil profile. Soil and other factors that discourage adsorption, aid leaching of herbicides in soils. High adsorption herbicides are relatively immobile. The extent of leaching of herbicides determines (i) weed control, (ii) selectivity to crops, and (iii) their dissipation and persistence in soils. When a surface applied herbicide fails to leach even to 2 or 3 cm depth of soil, it will bring about negligible or very poor preemergence control of weeds. On the other hand, if herbicide leaching is excessive, crop seedlings may be injured. Very deep leaching may be desirable for controlling the deep rooted weeds. Usually leached herbicides reside in sub-surface soil for a long period in active form because here the conditions for degradation of herbicides are less favourable. Eventually, from sub-surface, either a herbicide may return to soil surface during deep ploughing or it may contribute to ground table. For example, Sheets (1970) observed that simazine and atrazine returned to the surface when the treated land was ploughed 12-14 weeks after herbicide application and injured the susceptible rotation crops. Laboratory apparatus used for studying pesticide leaching in soils was described by Isensee and Sadeghi (1992).

Effect of Soil Water on Leaching of Herbicides: Soil water affords the driving agency in leaching of a herbicide and then it moves it down under the impact of gravitational pull. That way, solubility of herbicides in water should be an important factor in their leaching behaviour. However, water is never a limiting factor in irrigated or adequate rainfall areas to dissolve even a very low solubility herbicide like simazine (5 ppm at 20°C) at its usual rates of application. Moreover, herbicides with similar water solubility but with different ionic and adsorption properties have been known to differ widely in their leaching behaviour. For example, benefin, trifluralin, and nitralin, though about equally soluble in water, exhibit leaching in advancing order of their listing. Conversely, phenylcarbamate herbicides are more water soluble than substituted anilines, but they are equally immobile in the soil system (Weber, 1972). The relative water solubility of herbicides with similar ionic and adsorption properties may, however, relate to a great extent with their movement (and bioactivity) in soils and aqueous systems. For example, one can relate the water solubility of fenuron (2900 ppm) and diuron (42 ppm)-both nonionic and weakly adsorbed by soil—with their relative mobility through soil. Fenuron is much more mobile than diuron. One could likewise relate leaching behaviour of acid, salt, and ester formulations of a herbicide with their water solubility. The water solubility of the three formulations of herbicides, in general, increases and mobility in soil decreases in the order, esters, acids, and salts. Also, ammonium salt of chloramben is more mobile in soils than either its amide or methyl ester form (Talbert *et al.*,1970).

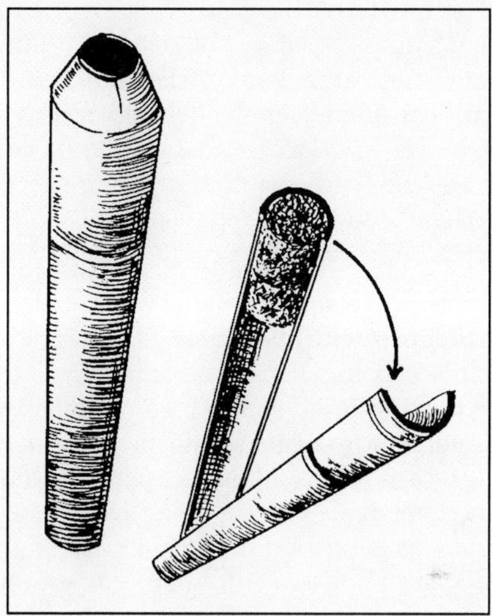

Fig. 19.4: Soil core for determining the presence of a herbicide in the soil at different depths (WRO)

The amount of water applied to a soil at a given time seems to influence the rate of leaching of herbicides more than their extent (= depth) of leaching. Variations in rapidity of application of water to a herbicide treated soil likewise, alter the total amount of herbicide that leaches under a given delta of water but not to depth of leaching. Usually, slow application of water will move larger quantity of a herbicide down the soil column than its fast application. This is so because slow moving water remains in contact with adsorbed herbicide for a longer duration to initiate desorption. For the same reason, split application of water at frequent intervals induces more leaching than its one time application. But when the interval between intermittent rainfall or irrigation is wide, upward capillary movement of herbicide, which is very considerable, may negate their leaching effects.

Although different from leaching, it may be mentioned here that herbicides may move in soils laterally, as well as upward. Ashton (1961) demonstrated very appreciable lateral movement of *s*-triazine herbicides under the influence of furrow irrigation. Lateral and upward movements of herbicides occur along with capillary water, similar to the native solutes of the soil.

The leaching of herbicides under the impact of water may be influenced indirectly by amendment of the soil with compost (Said-Pullicino *et al.* 2004).

19.2.2 Volatile Movement

A compound is said to be volatile when it changes from its solid or liquid state to the vapour state in significant amount at ordinary temperatures. The phenomenon is called volatilization. The vapour pressure of such compounds is high because of weak intermolecular attraction forces. Herbicides with vapour pressure of more than 1×10^{-5} mm of Hg at 20°C are considered volatile, for example, thiocarbamates, acetamides, toluidines, methylcarbamates and carbanilates. Trifluralin, with vapour pressure of 1.14×10^{-4}mm of Hg at 20°C, is considered moderately volatile while EPTC with a vapour pressure of 2.0×10^{-2}mm of Hg at 20°C is classed highly volatile. Volatile herbicides perform better when they are either (a) incorporated into the soil or (b) combined with an additive which imparts them slow release characteristics.

Ester formulation of herbicides are more volatile than acids and salts. Volatile herbicides upon incorporation move within the soil slowly in vapour form by diffusion through its water-air interfaces in accordance with the usual gas laws. They dissipate slowly from soil to the atmosphere after causing considerable damage to the target weeds. The dissipation of volatile herbicides from soils is commonly expedited by rise in soil temperature and air flow rate, and it declines with increase in organic matter and water content of the soil. There are a few exceptions to such relationships. Prominent among these is the volatility behaviour of EPTC. The volatile loss of EPTC enlarges on moist soils and at low temperatures, as compared to dry soils and high temperatures. This is in agreement with the active role of soil moisture and temperature in desorption of EPTC discussed earlier. The volatile loss of herbicides is lowered by soil incorporation and compaction of open structure soil, and it can be expedited by tillage. Parochetti *et al.* (1971) found less volatilization of dichlobenil from its granular formulation than from its liquid formulation.

A comprehensive review on volatilisation of pesticides from soil is provided by Spencer (1991).

19.2.3 Wash-off and Run-off

A heavy rain received immediately after the surface application of herbicides may often remove the toxicant in solution form in the runoff out of the target area. On erodable soils, runoff may be followed by wash-off. Wash off is the movement of herbicide ions (or molecules) adsorbed on soil particulate matter that is suspended in the run-off water. Water solubility and adsorption characteristics of herbicides affect runoff and wash-off losses of herbicides, respectively. Other factors being constant, wash-off of herbicides occurs in direct proportion to their rates of application and per cent area of the watershed treated. The wash-off and run-off losses of soil-applied herbicides are usually greatest in early stages of a storm as well as from bare soils. Factors that encourage herbicide leaching reduce their runoff and wash-off.

Tillage practices also influence herbicide run-off on the farms (Isensee and Sadeghi, 1993).

19.3 PLANT REMOVAL

Both crops and weeds remove portions of herbicides from soils. But adequate estimates of herbicide removal by plants in fields are lacking. Maize and sorghum grown in atrazine-treated pots showed in one experiment approximately 25% of the soil applied herbicide in the test plants. But Best and Weber (1974) recovered not more than 3.9% atrazine in maize plants from the treated soil. In field where weeds and crops grow together, the removal of herbicides by plants may be greater.

19.4 DECOMPOSITION

Transfer of herbicides does not lead to their inactivation from the soil. It may only remove herbicides from the site of their active uptake by plants, temporarily or permanently, but the herbicide structures remain biologically active at some site in the soil or atmosphere. For actual inactivation of herbicide structures it must undergo molecular change leading to its degradation. In soils, this change may be (a) microbial, (b) chemical or (c) photochemical in nature.

19.4.1 Microbial Decomposition (= Biodegradation)

Microbial action is a major mode of decomposition of herbicides in soils. Certain polar groups on the pesticide molecules, like - OH, - COO,-NH_2, and -NO_2 provide points of attack for the micro-organisms. The widely used herbicide groups, *viz.*, phenoxys, phenylureas, aliphatic acids, acetanilides, triazines, and carbamates are readily attacked by a host of soil microbes. The microbiological decomposition is characterised by an initial slow release of CO_2 from soil for some time after addition of the herbicide, called the *lag phase*, followed by increasing rates of CO_2 evolution which marks the period of rapid microbial activity. During the lag phase, the relevant microbial population proliferation and intercellular (or extracellular) enzyme built-up take place. It is possible, at least in some cases, that such enzymes may also be active on alternative substrates and, thus, continue their activity over a long period after completing the degradation of the added pesticide.

Scientists verify biodegradation of herbicides in soils indirectly by preventing microbial activity in the perfused soil by the use of a metabolic inhibitor like sodium azide. Directly they elucidate the process by isolation of specific microbes, followed by enrichment of herbicides perfused-soil with the isolates. If enrichment of the soil expedited the evolution of CO_2, biodegradation of the herbicide is usually accepted. Microorganisms often show cross adapation, *ie* one species of microorganism initiating decomposition of two or more herbicide structures.

1. ***Factors affecting biodegradation***: Microbial activity, hence biodegradation of herbicides, is activated at 20 to 30°C soil temperatures and by near field capacity

conditions. Organic matter is also essential for microbial activity in soils as a source of energy, but too much of it may reduce extracellular enzyme activity by inducing its adsorption by the organic particulates.

Herbicide structures differ widely in their biodegradation. In general, chemicals with terminal quaternary groups, non-alkyl substitutes, or extensive branching on aliphatic moiety tend to resist their biodegradation in soils. Extra large herbicide molecules are difficult to be embodied by the microbial cells. Chloride moieties are less biodegradable than methyl moieties. A study of such structural relationships is important for developing biodegradable pesticides which shall tend to persist less in our soils than the bio-resistant pesticides.

2. ***Microbial adaptation:*** The repeat applications of a soil active, biodegrable herbicide is not found to result in its build-up in crop fields, including the paddy fields. It happens so due to the phenomenon of microbial population, bringing about rapid mineralisation of the herbicide. Even strongly absorbed and bound residues of herbicides are subjected to this phenomenon of increased bio-mineralisation rates. However, the build-up of the adapted microbial population with ability to degrade the applied herbicide at increasing rates occurs chiefly in the surface soil (0-15 cm depth), for obvious reasons.

3. ***Extenders***: Extenders are microbial inhibitors employed to extend the persistence of a herbicide (or other pesticide) in soil. Such chemicals prevent the enrichment of enzyme necessary for biodegradation. Boron is a long known extender of 2,4-D. More recently, vorlex, a fungicide is found to act as an extender for linuron. Dietholate (*O,O*-diethyl-*O*-phenyl phosphorothioate) is a reported extender for EPTC in soils. Sharton *et al.* (1993) found phosphate fertilizers acted as potential inhibitors of terbutryn degradation. The objective in the use of extenders is to increase the weed control period.

Specific herbicide biodecomposition sequences

1. ***2,4-D***: Fourteen species of bacteria, two actinomycetes, and one fungus (*Aspergillus niger*) are implicated in biodegradation of 2,4-D and like compounds in normal soils. The biodegradation goes through the same sequence as traced earlier in Chapter 16 for 2,4-D metabolism in plants, releasing CO_2, Cl, and H_2O as the end products. Ester formulations of 2,4-D take a little longer for their biodegradation than their salts. This is so because their ester moieties are first metabolized by hydrolysis and oxidation to acid forms before the herbicide molecule can be biodegraded.

2. ***2,4-DB and MCPB***: 2,4-DB and MCPB are biodegraded in soils by double action of fungus *Aspergillus niger*. It simultaneously hydroxylates the ring and oxidizes its acid side chain, resulting in the formation of non-phytotoxic, 4-(and 2)-hydroxyacetic acid dervatives. These compounds are further subjected to cleavage of their ether linkage and ring structure by bacterium *Flavobacterium* spp., yielding CO_2, Cl, and H_2O. The important intermediate products of the sequence are phenol, catechol, and crotonic acid. Besides biodegradation, to some extent a bioactivation mechanism for 2,4-DB and MCPB has also been detected in soils. It constitutes exclusive β-oxidation of the butyric acids to phytotoxic acid derivatives 2,4-D and MCPA, without their simultaneous ring hydroxylation.

3. ***EPTC:*** Reaction sequence in biodegradation of EPTC shows that mercaptan (thiolalcohol), CO_2 and dialkylamine are produced as the first non-phytotoxic products in the reaction. Mercaptan and dialkylamine are further biodegraded in soils to SO_2, CO_2, and H_2O. Then SO_2 is incorporated into specific amino acids in the microbial tissues.

4. ***Substituted ureas:*** Several species of bacteria and at least two fungi (*Penicillum* and *Aspergillus* spp.) are implicated in the degradation of substituted ureas in soils. The reaction sequence involves dealkylation followed by oxidation. In the case of diuron this reaction yields metabolites *eg* 3-(3,4-dichlorophenyl)-1-methyl-urea; 3,4-dichlorophenylurea, and finally 3,4-dichloroaniline. The last metabolite is eventually decomposed to CO_2, NH_3, and Cl.

5. ***Dalapon:*** Many soil microbes can dehalogenate dalapon in soils and utilise its carbon as energy source. Its dehalogenation yields pyruvate through 2-chloro-2-hydroxypropionate. Pyruvate can either be used in microbial tissues or be liberated as CO_2. Bacterium *Arthrobacter* sp. has been isolated from soils which initiates the enzymic dehalogenation of dalapon in soils (Weightman *et al.*, 1992).

   Amitrole inhibits biodegradation of dalapon in soil.

6. ***s*-triazines:** The triazine herbicides are degraded in soils by fungi, chiefly *Aspergillus fumigatus*. It dealkylinates and deaminates branched chains of triazines to produce 2,4-dihydroxy-6-amino-*s*-triazine, which is non-phytotoxic. Behl and Khan (1994) showed degradation of atrazine by *'Phodococcus'* strain B-30. In Japan, Korpraditskul (1993) isolated two bacterial strains, including *Proteobacteria*, responsible for atrazine degradation.

7. ***Pyrazon:*** Smith and Meggitt (1970) showed that pyrazon was dephenylated by certain soil microbes to 5-amino-4-chloro-3-pyridazine, a non-phytotoxic metabolite.

8. ***Acifluorfen:*** Cultures of microbes have been identified which biodegraded this herbicide to amino-acifluorfen (Gennari, *et al.*, 1994).

9. ***Alachlor:*** Pothuluri, *et al.* (1993) found alachlor was biodegraded by fungus *Cunnighamella elegans* by N-dealkylation at the benzoic position. Metolachlor and butachlor likewise are also subjected biodegration in soils.

10. ***Trifluralin:*** Sato (1992) isolated two bacteria (*Alcali* and *Moraxella* spp.) which degraded trifluralin in culture media up to 20% and 95%, respectively, within 28 days.

11. ***Glyphosate:*** It has been reported biodegraded by *Pseudomonas* spp. and certain other bacteria.

19.4.2 Chemical Decomposition

In variance with biodegradation, chemical degradation begins as soon as a herbicide is placed in soil and it continues at a steady or declining rate, depending upon the availability of the reactant. The chemical degradation of herbicides is characterised by first order reaction. It is a less common mode of dissipation of herbicides from soils than biodegradation, save a few herbicides like simazine, trifluralin, sulfonylureas, etc.

1. ***Simazine:*** Most important step in decomposition of simazine in soils is hydroxylation of the ring at position 2-carbon, displacing chlorine atom from there. The resulting hydroxylation of simazine is favoured by its adsorption on soil colloids which is rapid at soil pH of less than 7.0. It is so because the adsorption of protonated simazine raises the electron deficiency at position-2 carbon which intensifies its hydroxylation. In high pH soils the adsorption of simazine is poor, yet preponderance of OH in soil solution initiates considerable hydroxylation of the herbicide molecules. Of course, hydroxylation of simazine is less extensive in high pH than in low pH soils. In neutral soils, hydroxylation of simazine still continues. It occurs near clay surfaces which always afford an acidic medium with disregard to neutral pH of the soil solution. Hydroxylation as a mechanism of chemical degradation of *s*-triazines is also extendable to compounds other than simazine, including methylthio and methoxy-*s*-triazines. In addition to hydroxylation, polysulphide ions can be made to displace chlorine atom from simazine to inactivate the unwanted herbicide residues in soils.

2. ***Trifluralin:*** α-α-α-triflurotoluene-3,4,5-triamine serves as the chief intermediate non-phytotoxic compound in chemical degradation of trifluralin in soils, which in aerobic conditions is produced by dealkylation of the herbicide and in anaerobic conditions by its reduction. Further chemical decomposition of triflurotoluene-triamine produces N, CO_2, H_2O, and the constituent halogens.

3. ***Sulfonylureas***: The major pathways of degradation of this group of herbicides is through chemical hydrolysis and microbial breakdown. The chemical hydrolysis occurs *via* cleavage of the sulfonylurea bridge. The process is enhanced by lower soil pH, higher soil temperature, and moist soil conditions.

4. ***Butachlor:*** Butachlor is subjected to both chemical and microbial degradation in soils, breaking even its aniline ring structure.

19.4.3 Photodecomposition (= Photolysis)

Photolysis is decomposition of a herbicide under the direct effect of solar radiation. The importance of photolysis of herbicides at the soil surface is very difficult to demonstrate because of practical difficulty in differentiating it from volatilization due to heat. Therefore, most of the studies on photolysis of herbicides have been carried out in laboratory conditions where temperatures could be kept sufficiently low to minimize volatilization of the test compound from solid bases like aluminium planchets, filter paper, glass plates, and soil surfaces. So far, photolysis as a process of significant degradation of herbicides in field conditions has been demonstrated for trifluralin, nitralin, imazaquin, and chloramben. The first two compounds are particularly susceptible to photodecomposition. Incorporation of herbicides into the soil could greatly reduce their photodecomposition losses from field applications. Of the full solar spectrum, ultraviolet component of 220 to 400 mμ wave length is most active in inducing photolysis reactions in herbicide molecules. It is so because in this endeavour light energy of 50 to 120 K Cal/mole of herbicide decomposed is needed, whereas UV rays yield an energy of 60 to 143 K Cal/mole. The UV rays are more intense on cloudy days than in open sun, and in the morning and evening hours than at noon.

From the above discussion it is evident that after a herbicide is placed in soil, it is subjected to many physical, chemical, and positional changes through varied agencies. The time-bound fate of herbicide in soil *ie,* its persistence in active form is an inter-play of herbicide structure and its ecosystem. It will be misleading to predict the longevity of a herbicide on the basis of an individual variable.

19.5 MINIMIZING HERBICIDE PERSISTENCE IN SOILS

A herbicide is said to be persistent when it may be found to exist in soil in its original, or a closely related but phytoactive form longer than one crop season after its initial application. On agricultural land, a major problem arising from herbicide persistence is injury to rotation crops. With triazine herbicides, rotation crops may be injured even 6 to 24 months after their application at normal rates. These herbicides are therefore called *notorious herbicides*. Several substituted ureas, sulphonylureas, dichlobenil, diphenamid, and 2,3,6-TBA, also often pose phytotoxic residue problems on crop land (Fent *et al.*, 1993 and Fokm *et al.*, 1992). Even a short residue herbicide like glyphosate has been reported to damage tomato transplants (Cornish, 1992). Sometimes, non-phytotoxic residues of a previously applied herbicide may damage the rotation crop by interacting with the herbicide applied to the present crop. For example, injury to lucerne from EPTC is noted in fields treated with atrazine in the previous season. Likewise, terbutryn injured wheat sown after maize that was treated with simazine or atrazine.

Table 19.1: Comparative Persistence of Commonly Used Herbicides in Terms of Their Half-Life**. (After Metcalf R. L. and Pitts J. N. 1969. Adv. in Env. Sci. Tech. 1:1-26; and Zimdahl, R. L. and Clark, S. K. 1982. Weed Sci. 30 : 345-548)

Herbicide	Approximate Half life
Alachlor and propachlor	1.9-7.3 days
Benzoic acids	2.4-12 months
2,4-D and the like	1.2-4.8,,
Metolachlor	1-1.7,,
Substituted Ureas	3.6-9.6,,
Triazines	12-24,,

Although herbicide persistence is primarily a function of herbicide structure, soil, and environmental conditions, yet there are several methods by which the weed scientists and farmers can minimise it and grow rotation crops safely.

Basically, there are two approaches to reduce herbicide residues in soils. The *first* is an indirect one. It aims at reducing the dose of the herbicide without losing its weed control effects. This can be achieved by (i) the use of chemical activators and surfactants, (ii) selection of the most appropriate time and method of application of the herbicide, (iii) selective stimulation of crops to smother the weeds, and (vi) supplementing herbicidal

** *Half life = Time needed for half the pesticide to decompose and disappear from the scene, usually soil. Each successive unit of half the remainder pesticide shall require the same time. This is in accordance with the first order reaction.*

control with tillage and other methods of weed control. The *second* approach to reduce herbicide residues in soils is by direct actions as follows:-

1. ***Molecular structure approach:*** At equal rates, volatile, photodecomposable, and biodegradable herbicide structures are less persistent than the other types of structures. In the case of volatile herbicides, their dilution in air is sought as solution to their long persistence in soil (but then they may contribute to air pollution). Thus, developing volatile, photodecomposable, and biodegradable structures of soil-active herbicides should prove helpful in lowering at least the soil pollution.

2. ***Controlled mobility approach:*** Mobility of herbicides in soils can be manipulated to dissipate the herbicide by leaching and volatilization. Heavy irrigation may leach a mobile herbicide beyond the root zone of rotation crops but then it may contribute to groundwater. In the case of EPTC and like carbamates, irrigation will induce dissipation by volatilization. Repeated deep tillage of the treated soil will hasten both volatile loss and degradation of herbicides, and it may also dilute the herbicide by mixing it with a larger volume of soil to innocuous levels. Research is needed on the role of chemical adjuvants in controlling mobility, and consequently the persistence of herbicides in soils.

3. ***Enhanced degradation approach:*** Herbicidal triazines can be degraded faster when the soil pH is lowered by the application of sulphur, but this may not be permissible under all conditions. Provision of adequate soil moisture, addition of easily decomposable organic matter, (of low C : N), and frequent tillage of the land can enhance microbial activity in soils, leading to rapid biodegradation of the herbicide residues. Weed scientists think that introduction of suitable microorganisms into the soil will be used in future to biodegrade herbicides at will. Plant enzymes that degrade certain herbicides in nature may also be synthesized and added to soils. Sodium and calcium polysulphides have been found effective in deactivating simazine and atrazine in laboratory researches by replacing chlorine radicals of the herbicide ions by S. A 50 t/ha of muck and peat added to soil may often also eliminate triazine residues from the soil. But Rouchaud (1992) found when any organic fertiliser source was added to a sandy soil, it actually increased the persistence of test herbicides by way of increasing their adsorption. More recently Martin – Laurent *et al.* (2004) reported that organic amendment did not modify atrazine mineralisation activity, which was found essentially to depend upon the soil type.

4. ***Toxicity prevention approach:*** Role of adsorbents and antidotes in preventing injury from direct application of preplant and preemergence herbicides was discussed in Chapter 17. These chemicals can be used also to protect crops from residues of many herbicides. Organic matter is a good adsorbent of many herbicides in soils. Adding organic matter to sandy soil has been reported to reduce herbicidal activity of fluometuron and fenuron in growth chamber studies, as well as in field experiments (Weber *et al.*, 1971). Possibility has also been shown of chemically enhancing the metabolism of herbicides absorbed in crop plants. For example, benzyladenine has been found to enhance the metabolism of amitrole in plants. Addition of phosphorus to soil reduced the phytotoxicity of diuron to cotton. Further research is needed for developing new metabolic agents of herbicides.

Ghauch *et al.* (1999) found the utility of fine grained zero-valent iron (Fe^o) in promoting reductive dechlorination and nitro-group reduction, of a wide range of pesticides, including herbicides, in water (and soil). It has been further reported that $Al_2(SO_4)_3$ was synergestic to the zero-valent iron in enhancing pesticide degradation. Shea *et al.* (2004) reported treatment with 5% (w/w) zero-valent iron (Fe^o) resultedin over 60% destruction of residues of herbicides like metolachlor, alachlor, atrazine, and pendimethalin within 90 days. Addition of 2% (w/w) $Al_2(SO_4)_3$ accelerated the process to over 90% decontamination of soil.

Ozone has been found promising in decontamination of groundwater of its residues of herbicides like bentazone and molinate. But the triazine residues remained unaffected by it.

5. ***Trap-crop approach:*** One obvious answer to herbicide residue problems in soils is to deliberately include crop plants in rotation that are resistant to a particular herbicide. This permits the land to stay in production and, at the same time, it hastens the dissipation of the herbicide. Such crops are called *herbicide trap crops*. For example, sugarcane, sorghum, and maize are good trap crops for eliminating residues of atrazine and simazine from soil. Crop breeding for selecting crop varieties tolerant to specific herbicides is already underway. (Chapter 16).

19.6 HERBICIDE EFFECTS ON SOIL MICROORGANISMS

Of the different kinds of herbicides, fumigants alone may inflict a drastic effect on soil microflora and microfauna. An agriculturally important group of bacteria—the nitrobacteria—are often impeded in their activity in the presence of a soil fumigant, causing accumulation of NH_3 to toxic levels. However, the nitrobacteria recover soon after the fumigant leaves the soil, sufficiently before a crop is planted.

In respect of the field-applied herbicides in crop fields it is concluded that at the recommended rates these do not have significant or consistent effects on the soil biological life (Lupwayi *et al.*, 2004). Their toxic effects are normally considerable immediately after their application when the herbicide concentration in soil is the highest. With time, the microbes take part in the herbicide degradation process, and so its concentration goes low and the soil biology returns to normal. However, there is no universal pattern of the herbicide effects on soil microbes, which somewhat vary with the herbicide chemistry (Zheng *et al.*, 2005; Milanova *et al.*, 2005). The setback to microbial population, by and large, is thus temporary except to the N-fixing bacteria which show special sensitivity to certain herbicides like prometryn (Wang *et al.*, 2004). But even these recover to normal activity eventually, without adversely affecting the crop growth.

SUMMARY

Herbicides are applied to soil primarily with the intention that they will move into the soil under the influence of either water or physical incorporation. When there is a delay in the movement of a surface-applied herbicide into the soil for some reason, certain herbicide structures may be subjected to photochemical decomposition and/or volatile loss. All herbicides from soil surface can be eroded by wind or sudden erosive storm.

Once a herbicide is in intimate contact with the soil, the particulate matter—organic and inorganic colloids—tend to adsorb a part (or sometimes whole) of it, while the remaining portion remains in soil solution in a free state in equilibrium with the adsorbed herbicide. Adsorption affects the biological activity, leaching, and volatile loss of herbicides. Cationic herbicides are ionically adsorbed to most clay minerals and soil organic matter. They are biologically available in the adsorbed state in most cases, except where they are retained on the internal surfaces of montmorillonitic clay minerals; *example-* diquat and paraquat. Weakly basic herbicides are ionically and physically adsorbed to some clays and organic colloids. Their adsorption is pH dependent and it is greater under neutral and alkaline conditions. Acidic herbicides are adsorbed sparsely by clay minerals, but in greater amounts by the soil organic matter and metallic hydrous oxides. Adsorption is greater under acid than neutral conditions. Bioactivity is not greatly affected by soil pH, except for volatile compounds such as phenols.

Adsorption of non-ionic herbicides like substituted ureas and carbamates by soil particulate matter and their movement in soil and biological activity in adsorbed forms depend greatly upon the chemical properties of the compound and the type of particulate matter involved. Compounds of extremely low water solubility are adsorbed primarily to lipohilic organic particulate materials by hydrophobic bonding and are relatively immobile. Relatively more water soluble nonionic herbicides are weakly adsorbed to clay minerals and organic matter and they are mobile in soil. In soils organic matter is most important constituent influencing adsorption of herbicides, except of cationic compounds like diquat and paraquat. Besides, soil moisture status, temperature, and pH also affect variably the herbicide adsorption on soil particulate.

Free herbicide moves within the soil in porous media by diffusion or mass flow in the liquid or vapour phases. The downward movement of herbicides is called leaching. The depth, amount, and rate of leaching of herbicides determines weed control, selectivity to crop, and herbicide persistence. Leaching of herbicides is affected by mainly herbicide structure, soil moisture status, and soil texture. Relative mobility classification of common herbicides is provided in the text.

Herbicides with vapour pressure greater than 1×10^{-5} mm Hg at room temperature are volatile. They move in soil in vapour form and dissipate slowly into atmosphere. Immediate incorporation into soil is necessary to prolong bioactivity of such herbicides.

Wash-off and plant removal are yet other venues of dissipation of portions of herbicides from soils. But neither these nor adsorption and leaching can cause permanent loss of bioactivity of major herbicides in soils. Exceptions are diquat and paraquat which are inactivated by adsorption by certain clay fractions. Volatilization amounts to only dilution of the toxicant in the environment.

Decomposition of herbicides is of chief importance in permanent bioinactivation of almost all herbicides added to soils. It may occur by either (a) chemical, (b) photochemical or (c) biological process. Because of decomposition no year to year build up of herbicides in agricultural soils of the world has been observed thus far; nor there has been any lasting change in soil microbial populations due to the application of herbicides. Sequences in decomposition of certain common herbicides in soil are outlined. Also, several ways of expediting dissipation of herbicides from soils in order to minimize possible hazardous herbicide residues have been proposed.

There is no universal pattern of herbicidal effects on soil biology. In general, the herbicides applied at the recommended rates do not have significant, persistent effects on microbial biomass and diversity.

SELECTED BIBLIOGRAPHY

1. Abdullah, A. R. *et al.* 2001. Adsorption, desorption, and mobility of metsulfuron methyl in Malaysian agricultural soils. Bull. Environ. Contam. & Toxicol. 66(6) : 762-769.
2. Accinelli, C. *et al.* 2001. Atrazine and metolachlor degradation in subsoil. Biology and fertility of soils 33(6): 495-500.
3. Aislabie, J. *et al.* 2005. Characterization of *Arthrotacter nicotinovorans*; an **atrazine** degrading bacterium from agricultural soil in New Zealand. FEMS Microbiology Eco. 52(2) : 279-286, Netherlands. (W.A. 54(7), 2743)
4. Alves, P. L. *et al.* 2004. Soil attributes and the efficiency of **sulfentrazone** on control of purple nutsedge. Scientia Agricola 61(3) : 319-325. (W.A. 53(1), 4389).
5. Anderson, B. A. *et al.* 2002. Fate of tributylin in a created tidal wetland. Environmental Toxicology and Chemistry, 21(6): 1176-1183. (USA)
6. Barriuso, E. and Calvet, R. 1992. Soil type and herbicide adsorption. Int. J. Envion. Analytical Chem. 46(1-3) 117-128.
7. Basham, G. W. and Lavy, T. L. 1987. Microbial and photolytic dissipation of imazaquin in soil. Weed Sci. 35, 865-870.
8. Behki, R. M. and Khan, S. U. 1994. Degradation of atrazine, propazine, and simazine by *Rhodococcus* strain B-30. J. Agri. and Food Chem. 42(5) 1237-1241.
9. Berger, B. Von. 1993. Bioassay for the determination of the degradation of metsulfuron methyl in soil. Weed Abs. 43(4) : 186, item 1435.
10. Best, J. A. and Weber, J. B. 1974. Disappearance of *s*-triazines, as affected by soil pH using a balance sheet approach. Weed Sci. 22:364-373.
11. Burkart, M. R. and Kolpin, D. W. 1993. Hydrologic and land use factors associated with herbicides and nitrate in near surface aquifier. J. Envion. Quality 22(4) 646-656.
12. Businelli, M. *et al.* 2000. Transport to groundwater of six commonly used herbicides. Pest Mgmt. Sci. 56(2) : 181-188.
13. Caux, P. Y. *et al.* 1995. Environmental fate and effects of MCPA : Canadian perspective. Critical Reviews in Environm. Sci. & Technol. 25(4): 313-376.
14. Che, M. *et al.* 1992. Effect of pH on sorption and desorption of imazaquin and imazethapyr on clays and humic acid. J. Envion. Quality 21(4) 698-703.
15. Comfort, S. D. *et al.* 1992. Degradation and transport of dicamba in a clay soil. J. Envion. Quality 21(4) 653-658.
16. Comfort, S. D. *et al.* 2001. Field scale remediation of a metolachlor - contaminated spill-site using zerovalent iron. J. Environ. Quality 30 (5): 1636-1643.
17. Cornish, P. S. 1992. Glyphosate residues in a sandy soil affect tomato transplants. Australian J. Exptl. Agri. 32(3) 395-399.

18. Cumming, J. P. *et al.* 2002. Clomazone dissipation in four Tasmanian top soils. Weed Sci. 50(3): 405-409.

19. Deli, J. and Warren, J. F. 1971. Adsorption, desorption, and leaching of diphenamid in soils. Weed Sci. 19(1) 67-69.

20. Donkova, R. and D. Petkova. 2003. Behaviour of herbicide **acetochlor** in three soils. Bulgarian J. Agri. Sci. 9(4) : 553-555. (W.A. 54(3), 1089.

21. Eliason, R. *et al.* 2004. Phytotoxicity and persistence of **flucarbazone**-sodium in soil. Weed Sci. 52(5) : 857-862.

22. Elmarakby, S. A. *et al.* 2001. Degradation of carfentrazone-ethyl under aerobic aquatic conditions. J. Agri. Food Chem. 49(11): 5285-5293.

23. El-Sebai, T. *et al.* 2004. Isolation and characterisation of an **isoproturon** mineralising *Methylopila* sp. TES. FEMS Microbiology Letters 239(1) : 103-110 (Netherlands). (W.A. 51(1), 239.

24. Farenhorst, A. *et al.* 2000. Earthworms and the dissipation and distribution of atrazine in the soil profile. Soil Biology and Biochemistry 32(1) : 23-33.

25. Fent, G. *et al.* 1993. Fate of the new sulfonylurea amidosulfuron in soil. Sci. of Total Environ. 132(2-3) 201-215.

26. Fokin, A. D. *et al.* 1992. Degradation and leaching of cheorsulfuron in the soil and concentration of its residual products. Soviet Soil Sci. 24 (1) 55-60.

27. Fourie, J. C. 1994. Herbigation in a vineyard–persistence of four preemergence herbicides in a sandy loam soil. S. Afr. J. Ento. & Viticulture. 13(2) 64-70.

28. Garacia, V. A. I. and J. L. Tadeo, 1999. Influence of soil moisture on sorption and degradation of hexazinone and simazine in soil. J. Agri. & Food Chem. 47(9): 3895-3900.

29. Gennari, M. *et al.* 1994. Anaerobic degradation of acifluorfen by different enrichment cultures. J. Agri. and Food Chem. 42(5) 1232-1236.

30. Ghauch, A. *et al.* 1999. Rapid treatment of water contaminated with atrazine and parathion with zero-valentiron. Chemosphere 39(8): 1309-1315.

31. Gimsing, A. L. *et al.* 2004. Chemical and microbiological soil characteristics controlling **glyphosate** mineralisation in Danish surface soil. Applied Soil Ecology 27(3) : 233-242 (WA. 54(3), 1068).

32. Guha, P. K. *et al.* 1992, Dissipation of fluchloralin in *kharif* paddy under West Bengal agroclimatic conditions. Pesticide Res. J.4(2): 165-169.

33. Gunther, P. *et al.* 1993. A bioassay technique to study the *leaching* behaviour of sulfonylurea herbicides in different soils. Weed Res. 33(2): 177-185.

34. Guo, L. *et al.* 1993. Sorption and movement of alachlor in soil modified by carbon rich wastes. J. Envion. Quality 22(1) 186-194.

35. Gupta, N. *et al.* 1998. Degradation of the OP herbicide anilophos under UV light. Pesticide Res. J. 10(1): 123-126.

36. Gupta, S. and V. T. Gajbhiye, 2002. Effect of concentration, moisture, and soil type on the dissipation of flufenacet from soil. Chemosphere 47(a): 901-906.

37. Hance, R. J. 1980. Interactions between herbicides and the soil. Academic Press, London, 249 pp.

38. Hu, J. *et al.* 2004. The isolation and identification of a Gram positive **atrazine**-degradation bacterium BTAHI. China Environmental Sci. 24(6) : 738-742. (W.A. 54(7), 1493).

39. Hultgren, R. P. *et al.* 2002. Effects of soil pH and soil water content on **prosulfuron** dissipation. J. Agric. & Food Chem. 50(11) : 3236-3243.

40. Hyun. S. H. and L. S. Lee. 2004. Factors controlling sorption of **prosulfuron** by variable-charge soils and model sorbents. J. Environ. Quality 33(4) : 1354-1361 (W.A. 53(11), 4410).

41. Isensee, A. R. and Sadeghi, A. M. 1992. Laboratory apparatus for studying pesticide leaching in intact soil cores. Chemosphere 25(4) 581-590.

42. Isensee, A. R. and Sadeghi, A. M. 1993. Impact of tillage practice on runoff and pesticide transport. J. Soil & Water Conservation 48(6) 523-527.

43. James, T. K. *et al.* 1998. Degradation and movement of terbuthylazine in soil. Weed Abst. 51(3): 127.

44. Jenkins, S. R. *et al.* 2000. Temperative effects on retention of atrazine and imazapyr on soils. Water, Air, and Soil Pollution 118 (1/2): 169-178.

45. Jerome, B. *et al.* 1987. Making herbicide rate recommendations based on soil tests. Weed Technol. 1(1) 41-45.

46. Kalpana, D. *et al.* 1999. Dissipation of pendimethalin and fluchloralin in soil and their residue in onion. Pesticide Res. J. 11(1): 76-80.

47. Knight, W. G. *et. al.* 1993. Soil-applied atrazine directly alters blue grana physiology and indirectly influences soil. N. Agro. J. 85(5) 1029-1035.

48. Korpraditskul, R. *et al.*1993. Degradation of atrazine by soil bacteria in the stationary phase. J. of Pesticide Science 18(4) 293-98.

49. Kotoula-syka, *et al.* 1993. Persistence of preemergence application of chlorsulfuron, metsulfuron, triasulfuron, and tribenuron in three soils of Greece. Weed Sci. 41(2) : 246-250.

50. Krutz, L. J. 2005. Reducing herbicide run off from agricultural fields with vegetative filter strips : a review. Weed Sci. 53 : 353-367 (USA).

51. Kulshrestha, G. *et al.* 2000. Effect of long-term field application of pendimethalin : enhanced degradation in soil. Pest Management Sci. 56(2): 202-206.

52. Li, L. F. *et al.* 2004. Clomazone dissipation, adsorption and translocation in four paddy top soils. J. Environ. Sci. 16(4): 678-682.

53. Liphadzi, K. B. *et al.* 2005. Soil microbial and nematode communities as affected by **glyphosate** and tillage practices. Weed Sci. 53(4) : 536-545.

54. Locke, M. A. 1993. Sorption-desorption kinetics of alachlor in surface soil from two soybean tillage systems. J. Envion. Quality 21(4) 558-566.

55. Loux, M. M. and Reese, K. D. 1992. Effect of soil pH on adsorption and persistence of imazaquin. Weed Sci. 40(3) 490-496.

56. Lupwayi, N. Z. *et al.* 2004. Soil microbial biomass and diversity after herbicide application. Canad. J. Pl. Sci. 84(2) : 677-685. (W.A. 53(11), 4454).

57. Martin-laurent, F. *et al.* 2004. Estimation of **atrazine**-degrading genetic potential and activity in three French agricultural soils. FEMS Microbiology Ecology 48(3) : 425-435. (W.A. 53(10), 4000).

58. Martins, J. M. F. *et al.* 2001. Degradation in soil and water and ecotoxicity of rimsulfuron and its metabolites. Chemosphere 45(4/5): 515-522.

59. Milanova, S. 2001, Persistence of diflufenican and its residual effect in soil. Weed Abst. 51(10) : 694, item 4397.

60. Milanova, S. D. *et al.* 2005. Movement, persistence, and microbial effect of **azafenidin** in soil. Herbologia 6(1) : 55-64 (Bulgaria). (W.A. 54(9), 3588.

61. Ming, Y. C. and L. Z. Fang. 2002. Adsorption - desorption behaviour of acetochlor to soils in the presence of some environmental substances. J. Environmental Sciences 14(2): 269-276. (China)

62. Muller, T. C. *et al.* 1992. Effect of concentration, sorption, and microbial biomass on degradation of the herbicide fluometuron in surface and subsurface soils. J. Agri. Food Chem. 40(12) 2517-2522.

63. Nalayini, P. and Sankaran, S. 1992. Effect of preemergence herbicides on soil micro-organisms. Ind. J. Agro. 37(3) 625-626.

64. Negre, M. *et al.* 2005. **Cinosulfuron** : chemical and biological degradability, absorption, and dissipation in flooded paddy field sediment. Pest Mgmt. Sci. 61(7) : 675-681. (W.A. 54(10), 4006).

65. Negre, M. *et al.* 2005. **Cinosulfuron** : chemical and biological degrability, adsorption, and dissipation in flooded paddy field sediment. Pest Mgmt. Sci. 61(7) : 675-681.

66. Nishimura, S. and K. Itoh. 2002. Residual levels of dioxins in soil, algae, and weeds in paddy and fallow paddyfields when chlornitrofen had been applied for years. J. Weed Science andTechnology 47(1): 47(1): 36-41. Japan)

67. Oliveira, R. S. Jr. *et al.* 2004. Fate and properties of herbicides in tropical soils. *IN* Weed Biol. and Mgmt. (ed. Inderjit), Dordrecht, Netherland. (W.A. 53(10), 4008).

68. Pang, L. *et al.* 2005. Degradation and sorption of **atrazine**, **hexazinone,** and **procymidone** in coastal sand aquifer media. Pest Mgmt. Sci. 61(2) : 133-143.

69. Pantani, O. *et al.* 1994. Influence of clay minerals on adsorption and degradation of *sulfonylurea* herbicide (cinosulfurion). Applied Clay Sci. 8(5) 373-387.

70. Papatonious, A. N. *et al.* 2005. Activity, absorption, mobility, and field persistence of **pyrithiobac** in three soils. Weed Sci. 53(2) : 212-219.

71. Parochetti, J. V. *et al.* 1971. Volatility of dichlobenil. Weed Sci. 19: 28-31.

72. Patel, R. B. *et al.* 1996. Dissipation of fluchloralin in soils and its residues in chicory. Pest. Res. J. 8(2): 182-185.

73. Patzold, S. and G. W. Brummer. 2004. Importance of earthworm macropores for translocation of the herbicide **diuron** in soils of fruit orchards. (Geman). (W.A. 54(1), 252).

74. Petkova, D. and R. Donkova, 2003. Behaviour of **metsulfuron**-methyl in soil. Bulgarian J. Agri. Sci. 9(4) : 449-454 (W.A. 54(3), 1088.

75. Poppell, C. A. *et al.* 2002. Dissipation of **microsulfuron** and **rimsulfuron** in surface soil. J. Agric. & Food Chem. 50(16) : 4581-4585.

76. Pothuluri, J. V. *et al.* 1993. Metabolism of alachlor by the fungus *Cunninghamella elegans.*
J. Agri. & Food Chem. 41(3) 483-488.

77. Prakash, N. B. and L. S. Devi. 1998. Effect of organic matter on adsorption - desorption of pendimethalin in soils. Pesticide Res. J. 10(2): 202-208.

78. Prakash, N. B. *et al.* 1999. Mobility of butachlor and pendimethalin in soil columns. Pesticide Res. J. 11(2) : 143-149.

79. Pusino, A. *et al.* 1992. Influence of organic matter and its clay complexes on metolachlor adsorption in soil. Pesticide Sci. 36(3) 283-286.

80. Rai, *et al.* 2000. Absorption - desorption of pendimethalin in six soils of India. J. Ind. Soc. Soil Sci. 48(1): 52-56.

81. Rai, J. P. N. 1992. Effects of long-term 2,4-D application on microbial population and biochemical processes in cultivated soil. Biology and Fertility of Soils 13(3) 187-191.

82. Raj *et al.* 2003. Downward movement of pendimethalin, fluchloralin, and oxadiazone in soil columns. Pesticide Res. J. 15(1) : 50-52.

83. Rajanna, K. B. *et al.* 1991. Movement of s-triazines in Karnataka soils. Current Res., UAS (Bangalore) 20(12) 254-255.

84. Reinbardt, C. F. and Nel, P. C. 1993. The influence of soil type, soil water content, and temperature on atrazine persistence. S. A. J. Plant and Soil 10(1) 45-49.

85. Roberts, T. R. *et al.* 2002. Deactivation of the biological activity of **paraquat** in the soil environment. J. Agric. & Food Chem. 50(13) : 3623-3631, USA

86. Rouchanud, J. *et al.* 1992. Influence of the organic fertilizer treatments on the soil persistence of imazamethabenz and isoxaben in wheat. W. A. 1991. 42(4) 179 (item 1463).

87. Saeki, M. and K. Toyota. 2004. Effect of **bensulfuron**-methyl on the soil bacterial community. Bio. & Fertility of soils 40(2) : 110-118 (Japan). (W.A. 54(9), 3637.

88. Sahid, I. 1992. Effects of paraquat and alachlor on soil microorganisms in peat soil. Weed Abs. 42(11)562 (item 4491).

89. Said-Pullicino, D. *et al.* 2004. Environmental fate of **triasulfuron** in soils amended with municipal waste compost. J. Environ. Quality 33(5) : 1743-1751. (USA).

90. Saikia, T. P. *et al.* 2000 Investigation on residue of atrazine and fluchloralin in maize-chickpea and maize-Indian mustard cropping sequences. Ind. J. Agro. 45(4): 653-657.

91. Sakaliene, O. 1998. Duration of persistence of herbicide clopyralid in fodder beet and soil. Weed Abst. 48(5): 200; item 1384.

92. Sanyal, D. and G. Kulshrestha. 1999. Effects of repeated acetachlor applications on its persistence in field soil and degradation kinetics in mixed microbial cultures. Biology and Fertility of soils 30(1/2): 124-131.

93. Sarmah, A. K. and J. Sabadie. 2002. Hydrolysis of **sulfonylurea** herbicides in soils and aqueous solutions : a review. J. Agric. & Food Chem. 50(22) : 6253-6265.

94. Sato, Y. 1992. Degradation of triffuralin by bacteria isolated from soil. Weed Research 37(3) 213-219.

95. Scheunert, I. 1992. Transformation and degradation of pesticides in soil. Chem. of Pl. Prot. 8, 23-75.

96. Seifert, S. *et al.* 2001. Imazaquin mobility and persistence in a Sharkey clay soil as influenced by tillage systems. Weed Sci. 49: 571-577.

97. Sette, L. D. *et al.* 2004. Biodegradation of **alachlor** by soil streptomycetes. Applied microbiology and Biotec. 64(5) : 712-717 (W.A. 53(10), 3971).

98. Sharma, A. *et al.* 2005. Effect of organic manure application on adsorption - desorption of isoproturon herbicide in different soils. Pesticide Res. J. 17(1): 77-81.

99. Sharma, R. and H. M. Mehta. 1989. Studies on pendimethalin and fluchloralin residues in soil and onion. Ind. J. Agro. 34(2): 245-247.

100. Sharon, A. *et al.* 1993. Extended terbutryon persistence and herbicidal activity effected by superphosphate fertilizer. Phytoparasitica 21(2) 111-122.

101. Shea *et al.* 2004. Accelerated remediation of pesticide-contaminated soil with zero-valent iron. Environ Pollution 132(2) : 183-188.

102. Sheets, T. J. 1970. Persistence of triazine herbicides and related problems. Res. Rev. 32: 287-310.

103. Spencer, W. F. 1991. Volatilization of pesticides from soil processes and measurement. Pesticide Research J. 3(1) 1-14.

104. Strebe, T. A. and R. E. Talbert. 2001. Sorption and modility of flumetsulam in several soils. Weed Sci. 49: 806-813.

105. Talbert, R. E. *et al.* 1970. Behaviour of amiben and dinoben derivatives in Arkansas soils. Weed Sci. 18: 10-14.

106. Torra, R. M. *et al.* 2004. Degradation of **thiobencarb, butachlor,** and **molinate** by a newly isolated *Aspergillus niger*. J. Pesticide Sci. 29(3) : 214-216 (Japan). (W.A. 51(1), 234).

107. Veletza, V. G. *et al.* 2006. Activity, adsorption, mobility, and field persistence of pyrithiocbac in three subs Weed. Sci. 53: 212-219.

108. Vicari, A. *et al.* 1994. Persistence and mobility of chlorsulfuron and metsulfuron under different soil and climatic conditions. Weed Research (Oxford) 34(3) 147-155.

109. Vouzounis, N. A. and Americanos, P. G. 1992. Effect of temperature and soil moisture on degradation of alachlor, pendimethalin, and prometryn. Tech. Bull. Cyperus Agricultural Research Institute No. 147, 5pp.

110. Wackett, L. P. 2004. Evolution of new enzymes and pathways : soil microbes adapt to **s-triazine** herbicides. *IN* Pesticide Decontamination And Detoxification (Eds. Gan, J. J. *et al.*), Washington USA, pp 37-48. (W.A. 53(10), 3970).

111. Wang, X. D. et al. 2005. Persistence and metabolism of **imazapyr** in four typical soils of Zhejiang Province (China). Int. J. Environ. Analytical Chem. 85(2) : 99-109 (W.A. 54(7), 2749).

112. Wang, X. H. *et al.* 2004. Study on the toxicity of herbicides in rice fields to nitrogen fixing blue-green algae. Agric. Sci. 22(4) : 400-405. W.A. 5497), 2791.

113. Wardle, D. A. and Rahman, A. 1992. Side-effects of herbicides on the soil microbial biomass. Weed Abs. 1993, 42(5) 235 (item 1911).

114. Weaver, M. A. *et al.* 2007. Effects of **glyphosate** on soil microbial communities and its mineralization in a Mississippi soil. Pest Mgmt. Sci. 63(4) : 388-393.

115. Weber, J. B. 1972. Interaction of organic pesticides with particulate matter. Adv. In Chem. Ser. No. 111: 55-150.

116. Weber, J. B. *et al.* 1971. What happens to herbicide in the environment? Weeds Today 4(1) 16-22.

117. Weed, S. B. and Weber, J. B. 1974. Pesticide-organic matter interactions. Paper No. 3840, Agri. Expt. Sta., NCS, Releigh, USA, 39-65.

118. Wehtje, G. R. 1993. Adsorption, desorption, and leaching of oxadiazon in container media and soil. Hort. Sci. 28(2) 126-128.

119. Weightman, A. L. *et al.* 1992. Microbial dehalogenation of TCA. Word J. Microb. and Biotech. 8(5) 512-518.

120. Yu, Y. *et al.* 2005. Fungal degradation of **metsulfuron**-methyl in pure cultures and soil. Chemosphere 60(4):460-466 (UK).

121. Zheng, R. Q. *et al.* 2005. Effects of **paraquat** herbicide on soil animal in agroecosystem. J. of Zoology 40(2) : 60-65 (China). (W.A. 5498), 3236).

Chapter 20

PLANT ENVIRONMENT AND HERBICIDE INTERACTIONS

The present chapter attempts to explain the manifold effects of environment around plants, both atmospheric and edaphic, on the chemical control of weeds and crop selectivity and communicates that one need not give up using herbicides if these failed once in a while. Rather, one should attempt to analyse the observed effects and improve upon them during subsequent years. The past observatory records, weather forecasts, and soil analyses can be very helpful in this endeavour.

Environmental factors are known to interact significantly with the performance of a herbicide, causing marked variation in its action on plants, both in space and time, even though it was applied at the same rate and by the same method. (Mc Whorter and Azlin, 1978; Putman and Rice, 1979). This herbicide-environment interaction may be caused by the elements of edaphic and atmospheric environment in two ways.

1. By affording different kind and density of weed flora and modifying morphology, physiology, and course of biochemical reactions in plants.

2. By influencing herbicide availability at the site of its uptake by plants at intended rate and in desired quantity.

In fields temperature may vary from 5 to 40°C, relative humidity from 10 to 100%, light intensity from 10,000 to 100,000 lux, wind velocity from calm to tornadic, soil organic matter from less than 1% to over 5%, and soil moisture status from wilting point to over saturation (Sylwester, 1973). When a small quantity of herbicide (usually 0.01-1.5 kg/ha) is thrown into such a plastic environment and it is distributed over more than one million plants, each sharing less than one µg of the toxicant, its effects on weeds and crops can easily deviate from anticipation.

With our present technology we cannot control the environment in our fields. But we can definitely improve upon herbicide performance in a given environment if we knew fully (not mere speculation) how different parameters of herbicides, such as their (i) molecular structures, (ii) formulations, (iii) rates, and (iv) time and methods of application, interact with the environment. It must be admitted that so far we know only incompletely about such interactions. Nevertheless, many variations in herbicidal effects caused by environment have been accounted for, which are discussed here as follows.

20.1 ELEMENTS OF PLANT ENVIRONMENT AFFECTING HERBICIDE PERFORMANCES

20.1.1 Temperature and Relative Humidity

The temperature and relative humidity influence the course of absorption, translocation, and metabolism of herbicides in plants, often simultaneously, with marked effects both on weed control and crop selectivity.

1. ***Effects on weed control***: In general, temperatures below 10°C reduce weed kill efficacy of foliar-applied herbicides, both by reducing their absorption and translocation. However, in some cases it is also found that the primary reason for a lack of response of plants to 2,4-D at low temperatures was shortage of thiamin in plants and not its slow absorption. Obviously, thiamin was related in some way to 2,4-D toxicity in plants.

   Chemical weed control usually improves with rise in atmospheric temperature; 20°C to 25°C being most suitable for the action of most herbicides. For a few herbicides like MSMA and DSMA, the optimum temperatures are 25°C to 28°C. Chloroxuron has been found to cause improved weed control up to air temperature of 30°C at relative humidity of 100% (Carlson and Wax, 1970). But in the case of amitrole, high temperatures induced its rapid metabolism in plants and, thus, reduced its phytotoxicity. Smith *et al.* (1968) likewise found that increasing the temperature from 15°C to 28°C stimulated amitrole metabolism in Canadathistle and kidneybeans (*Phaselous vulgaris*) and reduced the final plant kill. Likewise, at 30°C resistance of *Hordeum* spp. biotypes to paraquat was broken due to its enhanced movement and operation in the plant, as compared to at 15°C (Purba *et al.*, 1995).

   Like very low temperatures, very high temperatures can also reduce effectiveness of translocated herbicides. High temperatures may induce systemic herbicides to scorch plant leaves rapidly, which impedes translocation of herbicides to deep roots of the target plants resulting in their only partial control. The phenomenon becomes particularly noticeable when high air temperatures are associated with very low relative humidity. Control of broomweed (*Gutierrezia* spp.) with phenoxy herbicides is reduced at temperature above 25°C to 36.6°C. Also, for a given temperature, higher soil moisture is more conducive to weed control than lower soil moisture. But in another perennial weed, groundcherry (*Phaseolus longifolia*), more root injury was caused at higher temperature than at lower temperature when the soil fertility and moisture were high. Likewise, Prasad *et al.* (1967) reported greater uptake and translocation of ^{11}C dalapon in beans (*P. vulgaris*) at 43 ± 1°C than at 26 ± 1°C post-treatment temperatures, at constant relative humidity.

   High temperatures and low humidity produce an excessively dry climate which dries the spray droplets on plant leaves rapidly, thus reducing the absorption of applied herbicide by the target plants. In India, dry climate is a common cause of herbicidal failures during summer months. In dry climate herbicidal action can be enhanced to some extent by spraying the herbicides during evening hours, in high spray volumes. It will improve herbicide absorption during cool hours of the night and the following morning. Prasad *et al.* (1967) from their radioautographic studies observed that the test plants absorbed and translocated more dalapon at high relative humidity (88%) than at low relative humidity (28 to 60%). Rate of droplet drying and stomatal distribution behaviour in plants were apparently affected by relative humidity variations which contributed most to the observed uptake of dalapon. In the case of bean plants, cuticle dehydration was also implicated in the phenomenon of relative humidity affecting the absorption and mobility of dalapon.

Temperature also governs the success of the soil-applied herbicides. Soil temperature that is too low for profuse and synchronized germination of weed seeds in any soil, is also low for the action of perplant or preemergence herbicides. Generally speaking, suitable temperatures for weed seed germination and the activity of the soil applied herbicides are 20°C to 25°C. In cold soils, most herbicides tend to persist longer (save EPTC and like carbamate compounds) without controlling the weeds, which may prove injurious to the immediate, as well as the rotation crops.

Effects of temperature on the adsorption and desorption of herbicides in soils have already been discussed in Chapter 18 and so these will not be repeated here.

It may be worthwhile to observe here that within an area one should not expect any uniform effect of abnormal temperatures both low and high, on the herbicide-treated vegetation. It is a common observation that after the application of say paraquat to destroy a given vegetation in some large area, if suddenly cold waves set in at night, the next morning one is likely to find strips of weed kill instead of a uniform weed kill. This occurs because the cold (or hot) winds do not run uniformly over any large area uniformly.

2. ***Effects on crop selectivity***: Under excessively low and high temperatures herbicides may injure even normally tolerant crops. Low temperatures may injure crop leaf tissues and lead the herbicide directly into them, whereas at high air temperatures of over 28°C to 30°C many crops may lose their built in tolerance to specific herbicides. This is commonly seen in the case of propanil in rice, MSMA and DSMA in cotton, dinoseb in soybean, and simazine and atrazine in maize. Undue high temperatures may either (i) activate leaf scorching action of a herbicide, or (ii) over accelerate its absorption and translocation, or (iii) destroy internal mechanism of the plant to metabolize herbicides. For instance, high temperatures of 30°C destroy the enzyme, arylacylamine amidohydrolase in rice leaves which is otherwise responsible for detoxifying propanil in the crop leaves (Chapter 16). In maize, high temperatures (with adequate soil moisture) accelerate foliar and root absorption of atrazine which may exceed its normal detoxification rates. Also, high soil temperatures can activate atrazine and simazine *per se*. In the case of dinoseb and MSMA their scorching action was found activated at high temperatures. Linseed sprayed with 2,4-D or MCPA was injured more at 29.5°C than at 10°C. Alachlor can cause injury to beans at high temperature and at the same time poor weed control due to volatilization of the herbicide.

Many plants lose their protective wax deposits on leaves under the impact of high temperatures while others show marked increase in their total wax content and certain changes in the chemical composition of their cells. Crop seedlings may succumb to the soil-applied herbicides under high temperatures also because of their proliferated cell growth. There could be many other yet unidentified effects of high temperature on plants which could be held responsible for inducing herbicide susceptibility in the otherwise tolerant crops. Air temperature may also govern translocation and selectivity of herbicides. Under low temperature (and high pH) translocation of diphenamid from the roots to the shoots is hindered in tomato plants which, therefore, prove susceptible to the herbicide.

20.1.2 Rainfall (and Irrigation)

Adequate soil moisture in surface 2.5 to 3.5 cm of soil is necessary to induce uniform germination of large population of weeds before these could be effectively killed with herbicides. In the case of soil-applied herbicides, soil moisture initiates herbicide absorption by the germinating weeds, whereas in the case of postemergence herbicides it induces thick weed growth which can be killed with single application of the herbicide. Uneven weed growth in fields makes it difficult to fix the time of application of postemergence herbicides.

Soil-applied herbicides often fail completely when there is a dry spell of 10-15 days after their application. From dry soil surfaces, the preemergence herbicides may be lost by photo-decomposition, volatilization, and wind blowing. In dry weather, unless otherwise dictated by specific crops, the efficacy of preemergence herbicides can be greatly improved by *lightly* incorporating them into the soil immediately after their application. It will bring the toxicant into close contact with weed seeds, and at the same time it will minimise unnecessary loss of the chemical through photodecomposition, volatilization, and wind blowing.

While some amount of water is desirable to activate the soil-applied herbicides, excess of it may leach the herbicide to the crop seed and root zones. This may, on one side, injure crops and, on the other side, result in poor weed control. The latter is caused by washing down of the herbicide beyond the major weed seed germination zone of 2-3 cm soil depth. Also, erosive storms received soon after the application of preemergence herbicides may erode the land heavily, exposing the untreated soil below. The herbicide that moves with the eroded soil may damage crops at the low lying end of fields. Heavy showers may also wash down herbicides from the treated foliage, if the rain fell before the herbicides had a chance to be absorbed into plasmalemma (see Chapter 14). Use of filming agents or invert emulsion spray liquids can reduce removal of the herbicide from the treated foliage by rain.

Further, continuously wet weather may induce herbicide injury in certain crops by turning them over succulent. Maize plants, for example, are normally tolerant to atrazine emulsion sprays but they become susceptible to it in excessively wet weather, particularly when the air temperature is low. Extra succulence in maize plants has been found to increase atrazine absorption, and low temperatures decrease its metabolism inside plants. Both ways, atrazine could accumulate in maize in phytotoxic amounts.

Carlson and Wax (1970) likewise observed enhanced absorption of chloroxuron by leaves of certain weeds when applied after simulated rainfall.

Quality of water used for spraying herbicides may also determine herbicide action. Dusty water reduces action of paraquat and diquat while the $CaCl_2$ rich water reduces glyphosate phytotoxicity.

20.1.3 Wind

Wind initiates both spray and vapour drifts*. **Vapour drift** occurs only in case of high vapour pressure compounds like EPTC and lower alkyl ester of 2,4-D, whereas the **spray drift** is a common feature of all herbicide molecules. In either case, the wind action tends to reduce the quantity of herbicide reaching the target area and places it in the non-target area. Both these actions are undesirable. The first action results in poor weed control and the latter in crop injury. Injury to sensitive crops like cotton, tomato, and grapes from 2,4-D drift several kilometers away from the treated area is well known. In summer months in India hot winds may remove considerable portions of the sprayed herbicides from the plant and soil surfaces and, thus, reduce the weed control effects.

The distance and amount of herbicide *spray drifts* depend upon (i) the velocity of wind and (ii) the spray droplet size. Spray drift has been found to increase approximately linearly with the wind speed. Also, this rate of increase in the spray drift for a given operating pressure and sheet angle was found a function of nozzle size (Hobson *et al.*, 1993). Fine droplets (less than 0.07 mm in diameter) drift more than the medium fine droplets (0.07 mm diameter). The coarse droplets (0.28 mm to 0.56 mm in diameter) drift the least. Relationship between the spray droplet size and the wind velocity is shown in Fig. 20.1. In view of this relationship, one could think of minimising unnecessary loss of herbicide spray drift by spraying herbicides in bigger droplets. This can be achieved in several ways *eg* (1) by the use of invert emulsions, thickening agents, and particulating agents (Chapter 17), (2) spraying herbicides with low pressure sprayer pumps (< 2.1 kg cm^{-2}), and (3) maintaining a ground sprayer speed of over 6.4 hr^{-1} so that large orifice, flood type nozzles could be used in the spray booms (Chapter 11).

While increasing the spray droplet size is a good means of reducing the spray drift and placing the herbicide on the target plants, the oversize droplets are not desirable. Very large droplets do not wet the plant foliage adequately and prove less phytotoxic. Therefore, a compromise must be made between drift control and satisfactory wetting of the plants to arrive at the optimum droplet size of the spray.

Besides the above factors, spray angle is also important in determining the spray drifts. Hobson *et al.* (1993) found that there was greater spray drift from the 80° nozzles maintained 0.5 m above the crop than from the 110° nozzles operating at 0.35 m above the crop canopy, despite coarser droplets produced with the lesser spray angle nozzles.

---

* ***Spray drift:*** *Spray drift is physical movement of airborne spray particles. It occurs during the spraying operation and may continue for sometime after it.*

Vapour drift: *Vapour drift is the movement of volatile herbicide in atmosphere in vapour form from the treated surfaces.*

To sum up, the following precautions should be considered during field operations to ensure proper herbicide **spray drift management**.

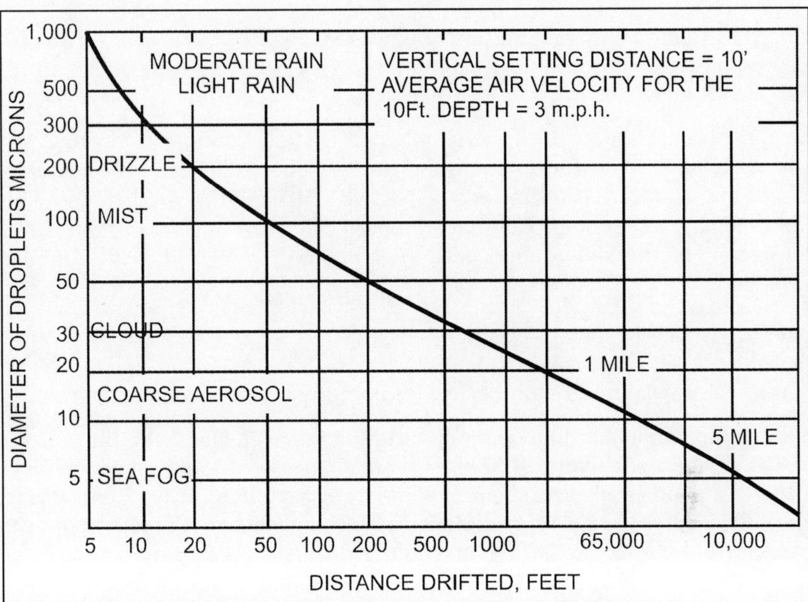

Fig. 20.1: Relationship between spray droplet size and drift distance (OSU, USA, Circular 1203)

1. Orient the nozzles at an angle between straight down and straight back.
2. Make herbicide applications at the lowest possible height that provides a uniform distribution pattern.
3. Do not use high nozzle pressures that create unnecessary small droplets that may become drift prone in the prevailing wind situation.
4. On windy days, turn the nozzles to produce coarse spray, and stop application when winds become gusty or exceed 16 km h^{-1}. At the same time, do not spray at near zero wind velocity conditions. Occasionally, in the absence of wind, the spray droplets may remain suspended above the target crop and then drift to the non-target areas when the air movement occurs after sometime.
5. Exercise caution when spraying during hot and dry weather or when RH is low. These conditions increase evaporation rates which reduce the droplet size and thus make them prone to drift.
6. Do not spray during hours of temperature inversion[1]. At this time the spray droplets remain suspended and are easily moved off the target by even minor breeze.

---

[1] *Horizontal movement of a created smoke, or the presence of fog/mist indicates temperature inversion.*

7. Leave at least a 10 m strip at the end of the target area without spray.
8. In the case of aerial applications of herbicides, operate when the wind has calmed down, and use airfoil booms (see Chapter-11).
9. Oil used as carrier of a herbicide spray produces larger proportion of drift susceptible droplets than the carrier water. Therefore, the former should be avoided on windy days (see Chapter-17).

In variance with the spray drift, ***vapour drift*** can be controlled largely by proper selection of the herbicide formulation. In general, the ester forms of herbicides are subjected to more vapour drift than the respective salts, and the short chain alkyl esters more than the long chain ones. High volatile herbicides like fluchloralin and EPTC must be incorporated in the soil immediately after application in order to minimise their vapour losses.

20.1.4 Light

Light may affect weed control with herbicides in at least three ways, as follows:-

1. It may induce photodecomposition of certain herbicides like trifluralin, fluchloralin, and chloramben (Chapter 19). This amounts to loss of the applied herbicide and consequent poor weed control. Incorporation of a photosensitive herbicide into the soil will greatly obviate its photodecomposition losses. Photodecomposition of herbicides like 2,4-D and MCPA may occur on plant foliage; in fact, it may be an important reason for failure of these compounds to kill weeds in certain situations.
2. Light often induces rapid translocation of herbicides that move with the photosynthates.
3. Light affects thickness of cuticle on the leaves. Plants growing in open sunlight usually develop thicker cuticle and respond less to contact type of herbicides than those growing in uninterrupted light. The contact type of herbicides prove more effective against plants with thin cuticle than on plants with the well developed cuticle. For instance, paraquat damaged Canadathistle (*Cirsium arvense*) more effectively in shade than in full sunlight (Lehoezki, 1991). Same was found true of this herbicide on *Mikania micrantha*. Similarly, with 70% shading, wildoat (*Avena fatua*) proved more susceptible to fenoxaprop and imazamethabenz than in the full sunlight (Xie *et al.*, 1994).
4. Light may govern the overall selectivity of herbicide to the crop. Metribuzin, for instance, is most selective to tomato when high light intensity preceeds and low light intensity follows its foliage application.

20.1.5 Soil Organic Matter

Through its effect on the adsorption of herbicides, soils with higher organic matter content require higher rates of herbicides for bringing about the intended weed control. With 1% organic matter in a soil, about 0.25 kg/ha of trifluralin was found as effective as its 1.0 kg/ha rate on a 4% organic matter soil; on high organic matter soil its 0.25 kg/ha rate gave poor or no weed control and 1.0 kg/ha injured crops that did not possess built in tolerance to trifluralin. In another experiment propachlor applied to a 7.0%

organic matter soil leached so rapidly that it failed to control crabgrass (*Digitaria* sp.), whereas alachlor leached slowly in this soil and effectively killed the grass. But on a 3% organic matter soil, both alachlor and propachlor proved equally ineffective against crabgrass. Likewise, variations in soil organic matter accounted for 94% variability in trifluralin dose effects (Moyer, 1979). As such, in general, lower rates of soil active herbicides should be used on soils low in organic matter and higher rates on soils high in organic matter.

20.1.6 Soil Texture

Next to organic matter, soil texture is important in determining the efficiency of the soil-applied herbicides. Because of their low colloidal content and open texture, lower rates of herbicides must be used on light, sandy soils in comparison to the heavy, clay soils. In light soils high rates of herbicides may injure crops by leaching to the crop seed and root zones. Conversely, in heavy soils low herbicide rates should be expected to give poor, short-lived weed control, though crop selectivity of a higher order may be obtained.

20.1.7 Soil pH

The usual recommended rates of herbicides hold good for normal agricultural soils. But when the soils are either acidic or alkaline in nature, the herbicide behaviour may change appreciably. Several herbicides have a tendency to decompose faster in acid soils, while they persist longer than usual (and some of them even get activated) in alkaline soils. For instance, atrazine and simazine absorption by maize roots is greatly activated on alkaline soils, particularly at high temperatures. This leads to herbicide phytotoxicity to maize even at their recommended rates of application (Adams and Pritchard, 1977).

In fact, in acidic and alkaline soils a marked deviation in the choice of the herbicide and its rate of application from the normal is required. For instance, at low soil pH, the phytotoxicity of metribuzin, vernolate, and dalapon is enhanced while that of dicamba, atrazine, and prometryn lowered, particularly on medium and heavy soils; requiring cautious choice of the herbicide.

20.2 OTHER ASPECTS AFFECTING HERBICIDE PERFORMANCE

20.2.1 Fertilizers

Fertilizers form important component contributing to plant environment in modern agriculture. Although these are applied for the benefit of the crop plants, the associated weeds also share their nutrients. Herbicides have been found to interact with fertilizers in fields. A typical interaction shows up when some fast growing weeds that are getting ample nitrogen develop greater susceptibility to 2,4-D, glyphosate, and dalapon than the slow growing weeds on the low fertility lands. High rates of atrazine are more toxic to soybean, maize, sorghum, and pea seedlings when applied with high levels of phosphorus than with the low P levels. Increased activity of diuron, amitrole, and simazine also results when these are applied with high rates of phosphorus (Penner, 1974). Application of phosphorus to a deficient soil often enhances the control of wildoat with barban. Such improved effect of herbicide-fertilizer interactions against weeds, however, is a real gain only when there is no corresponding increase in the susceptibility of the crop plants to the herbicide. For instance, sometimes fertilizers, particularly the nitrogenous ones, invigorate the meristematic activity in crop plants so much so that they become susceptible to certain herbicides. This is generally noted when 2,4-D is applied to a winter grain crop like wheat growing on a high fertility soil, particularly in respect of nitrogen.

20.2.2 Pesticides and Pests

Herbicides, fungicides, and insecticides may be applied together to reduce spray cost. Both synergistic and antagonistic effects of their combinations have been noted. While synergistic interaction, wherein herbicide action is enhanced, is good on weeds it may be undesirable on certain crops. For example, injury to cotton seedlings is increased by associating diuron with phorate. Another example is the loss of selectivity of propanil to rice seedlings when applied with phosphate and carbamate type of insecticides, *eg* malathion and carbaryl. This herbicide-insecticide interaction is noted in rice even when the two are applied separately at 14 days' interval. Likewise, the selectivity of nicosulfuron to maize was found reduced when it was applied following the application of insecticide, terbufos (Diehl, *et al.*, 1995). Also, malathion antagonised metabolism-based chlorsulfuron resistance in *Lolium rigidum* (Cristropher *et al.*, 1994).

Carbofuran seed treatment has been reported to enhance the phytotoxicity of alachlor and butylate in barley. Carbaryl, tank-mixed with linuron, injured carrot foliage. The cotton seedling growth was reduced with combinations of trifluralin and PNCB (a fungicide) but not with trifluralin alone (Penner, 1974).

The antagonism between certain herbicides and other pesticides may be very desirable. For example, malathion has been found to protect wheat and maize seedlings against trifluralin. Dexon (a fungicide) reduced atrazine injury to cucumber roots and soybean seedlings. Disulfoton decreased high dose phytotoxicity of fluometuron to cotton and of metribuzin to soybean.

The interactions amongst herbicides are also on record. These are sometimes antagonistic to reduce weed kill, *eg* dichlofop with 2,4-D against wildoat, or synergistic to improve crop selectivity *eg* preplant fluchloralin protecting snapbeans against preemergence metobromuron. MCPA amines (but not esters) and fenoxprop were observed to antagonise imazamethabenz against wildoat (Liu, 1995). Such synergistic and antagonistic interactions may be observed in some other herbicide combinations too, which need be recorded by the agronomists for future planning of the pesticide sprays.

In respect of the herbicide – crop pests interactions, it is usually observed that diseased and insect pest – infested crops are more susceptible to herbicides than the healthy crops, although there may be some exceptions to it.

20.2.3 Pollutants in Air

High ozone content in the atmosphere inhibits metabolism of atrazine in maize, of diphenamid in tomato, and of pebulate in tobacco, thus injuring the respective crops. Reverse interaction of ozone with benefin on tobacco has also been observed.

20.3 HERBICIDE BENEFITS OUTWEIGH HAZARDS

Despite practical precautions, the possibility of herbicide injury to crops is a part of using herbicides. A farmer who uses herbicides should not feel frustrated over a few twisted or scorched crop plants in his field. If he compared his crops with his neighbour's weed infested crops where no herbicide was applied and the weather was too wet to cultivate, he would soon realize that his benefits from herbicidal control outwighed some crop injury he incurred (Selleck, 1973). Unwanted herbicide interactions with environment is one reason of herbicide failures, but it cannot be held responsible for all the failures. Improper choice of herbicides, their rates and methods; insect and pathogen injury to crop plants; and past history of the field are often more common reasons of poor weed control and crop injury with some herbicides. Thus, one need not give up using herbicides if they failed once in a while. Rather one should attempt to analyse the observed effects and improve upon them during the following years. Past observations and records, weather forecasts, and soil analyses can be very helpful in this endeavour.

20.4 HERBICIDE IMPACT ON THE ENVIRONMENT

A very comprehensive, three volume text was made available on the pesticides in the environment by R. W. Stevens (ed.) in 1977*. This is still valid as a valuable compilation. The section on herbicides in this work concludes as follows:-

"In general, the environmental impact of herbicides is minimal. Residues are either innocuous or degraded rapidly and have only minor impact on wild life, other than destroying vegetation upon which the wild life may feed".

Also, from aquatic environment no biological magnification of herbicide residues has yet been noted. Herbicides thus far used have further been found free of causing permanent damage to the soil fauna or to its fertility. Temporary fluctuations in biopopulations in soil are soon restored to normalcy.

SUMMARY

Environmental factors are known to modify herbicidal control and crop selectivity significantly. Therefore, a sound knowledge of various herbicide-environment interactions is indispensable if herbicide failures that sometimes occur are to be scientifically accounted for and avoided in future.

Although our knowledge of herbicide-environment interactions is still incomplete, and in many cases conjectural, yet it is not altogether lacking. The scientists have gathered considerable useful information on the influence of: (i) environmental factors, particularly temperature, humidity, rainfall, soil organic matter, soil texture, pH, wind, and sunlight and (ii) inputs like fertilizers and pesticides, on the phytotoxicity and selectivity of the herbicides. These effects have been discussed briefly in this chapter.

---

* *Earlier to Stevens (1977) monumental articles on the subject had appeared in 1961 and 1966 issues of Advances in Pest Control Research. The latest review of possible herbicide residues, with particular reference to our food, is provided in* ***Chapter-25*** *of this book.*

In general, the herbicide benefits far outweigh their possible hazards and the herbicide residues are insignificant in the environment (Chapter 25) as compared to the residues of some other pesticides, chiefly the insecticides.

SELECTED BIBLIOGRAPHY

1. Adamns, R. S. Jr. and Pritchard, D. J. 1977. Influence of soil pH on the phytotoxicity of three-*s*-triazine herbicides. Agron. J. 69(5) 820-824.
2. Behrens, R. and Miller, G. R. 1971. The importance of moisture and temperature in weed control. Weeds Today, Jan/Feb., 16-18.
3. Benchley, R. C. and Appleby, A. R. 1971. Effect of magnesium and photoperiod on atrazine toxicity to tomato. Weed Sci. 19:514-515.
4. Bhan, V. M. and M. L. Kewat. 2002. Persistence of pendimethalin in medium black soil following preemergence application to soybean. Ind. J. Weed Sci. 34: 137-138.
5. Carlson, W. C. and Wax, L. M. 1970. Factors influencing the phytotoxicity of chloroxuron. Weed Sci., 18(1) 98-101.
6. Caux, P. Y. *et al.* 1995. Environmental fate and effects of MCPA : Canadian perspective. Critical Reviews in Environm. Sci. & Technol. 25(4): 313-376.
7. Coetzer, E. *et al.* 2001. Glufosinate efficacy, absorption, and translocation in amaranthus as affected by relative humidity and temperature. Weed Sci. 49: 8-13.
8. Cristropher, *et al.*, 1994. Malathion antagonises metabolism based chlorsulfuron resistance in *Lolium*. Pesticide Biochem. 49(3)172-182.
9. Diehl, K. E. *et al.*, 1995. *In vivo* and *in vitro* inhibition of nicosulfuron metabolism by terbufos metabolites in maize. Pesticide Biochem. & Physio. 51(2) 137-149.
10. El-Mahy, S. A. 2005. Degradation of clethodim, fluazifop-p-butyl and quizalofop-p-ethyl under different environmental factors. Bull. Faculty of agri. Cairo Univ. 56(1) : 157-171 (Egypt).
11. Hobson, P. A. *et al.* 1993. Spray drift from hydraulic spray nozzles. J. Agri. Engg. Res. 54(4) 293-305.
12. Ipor, I. B. and Price, C. B., 1994. Uptake, translocation, and activity of paraquat in different light conditions. Int. J. Pest Mgmt. 40(1) 40-45.
13. Ketchersid, M. L. *et al.* 1981. Influence of soil moisture on safening effect of CGA - 43089 in grain sorghum. Weed Sci. 29(3) 281-285.
14. Kieloch, R. 2004. Influence of temperature on herbicide effectiveness. Weed Abs. 54(6), 2357 (UK).\
15. Kumaratilake, A. R. and C. Preston 2005. Low temperature reduces glufosinate activity and translocation in wild radish (*Raphanus raphanistrum*). Weed Sci. 53(1) : 10-16 (USA).
16. Lehoezki, E. *et al.* 1992. Mode of action of paraquat in terms of *Conyza canadensis*. Plant, Cell, and Envion. 15(5) 531-539.
17. Liu, S. H. 1995. Effect of MCPA and fenoxprop on phytotoxicity of imazamethabenz in wildoat. Crop Prot. 14(4) 275-281.
18. Martinson, K. B. *et al.* 2005. Time and day of application effect on glyphosate and glufosinate efficacy. Crop Mgmt. July, 1-6 (USA).

19. Mattice, J. D. *et al.* 2001. Environmental implications of pesticides in rice production. Research Services. Arkansas Agri. Expt. Sta. No. 485, 88-85 pp.
20. McWhorter, C. G. and Azlin, V. R. 1978. Effect of environment on the toxicity of glyphosate to johnsongrass and soybean. Weed Sci. 36(6) 605-608.
21. Moyer, J. R. 1979. Soil organic matter, moisture, and temperature effect on wildoat control with trifluralin. Can. J. Plant Sci. 59:763-768.
22. Mulder, C. E. G. and Nalewaja, J. D. 1978. Temperature effect on phytotoxicity of soil-applied herbicides. Weed Sci. 26(6) 566-70.
23. Naik, M. C. *et al.* 2004. Seasonal effect on ^{14}C-glyphosate translocation pattern in different plant parts of *Cyperus rotundus*. Ind. J. Plant Physiology 9(4) : 367-371.
24. Penner, D. 1974. The effectiveness of pesticide interaction. Weeds Today 5(3) 13-14.
25. Prasad, R. *et al.* 1967. Effects of relative humidity on absorption and translocation of foliarly applied dalapon. Weeds 15(2) 149-156.
26. Pritchard, M. K. and Warren, G. F. 1980. Effect of light on the response of tomato and two weed species to metribuzin. Weed Sci. 28(2) 186-189.
27. Priya, G. *et al.* 2006. Effect of soil properties on the persistence of fluchloralin. Pesticide Res. J. 18(1): 95-97.
28. Purba, E. *et al.*, 1995. The mechanism of resistance to paraquat is strongly temperature-dependent in resistant *Hordeum*. Planta 196(3) 464-468.
29. Putman, A. R. and Rice, R. P. 1979. Environment and edaphic influences on the selectivity of alachlor on snap beans (*Phaseolus vulgaris*). Weed Sci. 27(5) 570-574.
30. Rahman, A. and Mathews, L. J. 1979. Effect of soil organic matter on the phytotoxicity of thirteen-*s*-triazine herbicides. Weed Sci. 27(2) 158-161.
31. Ritter, R. L. and Cable. H. D. 1981. Influence of temperature and relative humidity on the activity of acifluorfen. Weed Sci. 29: 480-485.
32. Savage, 1978. Persistence of several dinitro aniline herbicides as affected by soil moisture. Weed Sci. 26(5) 465-471.
33. Seifert, S. *et al.* 2001. Effect of tillage on microbial characteristics and herbicide degradation in a Sharkey clay soil. Weed Sci. 49: 685-693.
34. Selleck, G. W. 1973. Pesticide benefits overshadow hazards. Weeds Today 4(4) 14-15.
35. Smith, L. W. *et al.* 1968. Influence of environmental and chemical factors on ATA metabolism in excised leaves. Weed Sci. 16(4) 527-530.
36. Stevens, R. W. (Ed.) 1977. Pesticides in the environment. Marcel Dekker Inc., N. Y. Vol. 1-2.
37. Sylwester, E. P. 1973. Success or failure of herbicides. Weeds Today 4(2) 12-13.
38. Xie, H. S. *et al.* 1994. Effect of shading on activity of imazamethabenz and fenoxaprop in wildoat. Weed Sci. 42(1) 66-69.

Chapter 21

WEED MANAGEMENT PRACTICES IN FIELD CROPS AND VEGETABLES

21.1 SMALL GRAIN CEREALS

21.1.1 Rice (*Oryza sativa* L.)

The Weed Problem: The weed flora and intensity in rice differs distinctly with the methods of its cultivation which vary widely through length and breadth of the country, depending chiefly on the moisture status of the field; from dry to meter deep flood. From the weed management view point, the existing practices of rice cultivation can be grouped into three major categories *viz.*, (i) upland, rainfed, direct seeded rice, (ii) direct seeded but puddled rice with standing water, and (iii) lowland direct seeded or transplanted rice in puddled fields, with standing water. Of these situations, weeds are most aggressive in the upland rice fields, which are devoid of both puddling and standing water. In this situation, 2-3 flushes of a variety of annual and perennial grasses, sedges, and broadleaf weeds grow luxuriantly. In lowland rice, on the other hand, puddling destroys many germinating weed seeds from seedling stage of the crop. Subsequent flooding of the paddies by way of rainfall or irrigation, further creates an unfavourable environment for the establishment of weeds. However, flooding is helpful in any meaningful suppression of the weeds only when a flood height of 10-20 cm is maintained uniformly over the field for 1-3 weeks and re-flooding of the field is resorted to before any new weed is past its 1 to 3-leaf stage. Usually, such a strict flood control is difficult to practise and in that event, a variety of weeds invade the paddies 1-3 weeks after transplanting rice, some of which are of semi-aquatic nature. In rice nurseries again the weeds pose a serious problem where often heavy, labour-intensive weeding is practised.[1]

---

[1]*Note: The author takes no responsibility of crop, animal, or human damage resulting from the wrong use of herbicides listed in this, and foregoing chapters. The recommendations made here must be plot tested before their generalised application. Also, one must go through all previous chapters on herbicides before deciding upon a particular control recommendation.*

Of the several weed species recorded in rice fields, *Echinochloa colonum* and *E. crus-galli* (barnyardgrass) are of most common occurrence throughout the rice world. *Echinochloa* spp. mimic rice plants during their vegetative phase so well that these often get transplanted from rice nurseries to the main fields along with the rice seedlings. These grassy weeds are very competitive. It has been found that as low as 10 plants m^{-2} density of *Echinochloa* reduced the grain production in rice by 40% when the weed was allowed to compete for only four weeks. Number of panicles per plant, number of spikelets per panicle, and percentage of mature grains per rice panicle were adversely affected by its presence. In constantly flooded situation of rice cultivation, besides the common rice weeds, some aquatic plants like *Eichhornia crassipes, Pistia lanceolata, Salvinia auriculata*, and *Lemna minor* act as major weeds. Besides, in many transplanted rice fields, certain algae may grow so dense as to pull down the young rice transplants into muddy water, leaving a thin crop in the field.

The Weed Management: Flooding is an age old practice followed in the cultivation of low land rice. Its sole objective is to suppress weeds. Physical weeding with various tools, like the Japanese weeders, are employed to row-cultivate rice crops. In rice nurseries, handpulling is the sole weed management practice followed in almost all the developing countries. However, with the growing scarcity of labour, more rice growers are opting for the use of herbicides than before in the tropics and sub-tropics. This has been possible because of the availability of a battery of herbicides that are selective to rice plants and are effective against specific weed species.

(a) Herbicidal Control In Upland Rice: In upland *drilled rice*, a suitable preemergence herbicide should be the first choice of the farmer to get rid of annual grasses and the broadleafs. **Oxyfluorfen** (0.25 kg/ha), **dinitramine** (1-2 kg/ha), **oxadiazon** (0.6-1.5 kg/ha), **benthiocarb** (3 kg/ha), and **butachlor** (1-1.5 kg/ha) are found successful in this respect. **Anilofos** (0.4 kg/ha) can be used about 7 d.a.s rice when besides the grass weeds, sedges also pose serious problem. It can be further combined with 2,4-D to kill the dicot weeds, if any. But when the floral composition of weeds in rice comprises prominently the broadleaf weeds, pendimethalin (1.0 kg/ha) would be the right choice. It is applied about 3 d.a.s. of the crop. In some areas the broadleaf weeds and sedges invade the direct sown rice fields when a pre-packed mixture of metsulfuron and chlorimuron (0.004 kg/ha) has given excellent results. (It will not control the grass weeds). Rice is tolerant to it about 17 d.a.s. A row cultivation can be usefully combined with all the above preemergence herbicidal control treatments to obtain extended weed control in rice fields.

Propanil (3-4 kg/ha), *swep* (4-6 kg/ha), and **fluordifen** (2-4 kg/ha) form selective postemergent herbicides in rice fields for destroying young weeds. Of these herbicides, propanil will not provide any residual weed control, while others will cause three weeks' or longer residual control of weeds. Propanil is most effectively applied when a large population of weeds has germinated and they are in 2 to 3-leaf growth stage. Sometimes, repeat application of propanil is required to control a second flush of weeds. Swep is selective to rice after its 4-leaf stage. The dry-drilled rice is more tolerant to it than the wet-seeded rice. Fluorodifen is a better choice than swep when weeds must be controlled early, at 2-leaf stage of the crop. But it is a long persistence herbicide (up to 12 weeks), which may sometimes limit the choice of the rotation crops.

(b) *Herbicidal Control In Flooded Rice:* In flooded rice, as earlier mentioned, broadleafs often form the major weed flora. 2,4-D, MCPA, and silvex may be used to control solid stands of such weeds, with adequate selectivity to the crop. The phenoxys are employed in rice at fully tillered stage of the crop *ie* 4-6 weeks after transplanting rice. The selective rates are 0.75-1.5 kg/ha. While **2,4-D** and **MCPA** are active against herbaceous weeds, silvex is employed against rough weeds like *Melochia*, *Abutilon*, and *Baptisia* spp. Silvex at low rates can be used in rice fields at even earlier than fully tillered stage of the crop, if warranted. The fields should be drained before the application of any postemergence herbicide in flooded rice crops. High soil fertility and high atmospheric temperature (over 32°C) may reduce crop tolerance to the phenoxys. In Egypt, bentazon (0.96-1.92 kg/ha) has been found a successful postemergence herbicide in transplanted rice to control some difficult broadleaf weeds and sedges.

Table 21.1: Comparative Performance of Three Herbicides in Rainfed, Upland Rice (*Var.* (ARS-10372) at Hyderabad (India), During 1989 and 1990 (After Singh, 1993)

Treatments	Dry weed biomass (Mean of 2 yrs) (q/ha)	Grain yield of rice (q/ha)			% increase
		1989	1990	Mean	
Unweeded check	31.75	9.91	8.84	9.38	-
Hand-weeded (20, 40 d.a.s.)	6.05	20.00	23.67	21.84	133
Butachlor (1.5 kg/ha)	15.50	16.4	16.73	16.57	77
Butachlor + Hand-weeding (20 d.a.s.)	7.92	21.20	23.68	22.44	139
Benthiocarb (1.5 kg/ha)	17.37	15.72	16.57	16.15	72
Benthiocarb + Hand-weeding (20 d.a.s.)	8.91	19.60	22.10	20.85	122
Pendimethalin (1.0 kg/ha)	11.50	16.52	18.94	17.73	89
Pendimethalin + Hand-weeding (20 d.a.s.)	4.42	22.50	24.62	23.56	151
C. D. (at P = 0.05)	-	3.05	2.74	-	-

Note: All herbicides were applied preemergence.

Comments: *Either of the test herbicides could substitute for one hand-weeding in upland rice, which can be very helpful in view of the growing labour scarcity.*

For controlling unwanted algal growths in rice fields, copper sulphate and copper oxychloride at 8-10 kg/ha have long been used. But now more effective products like Brestan-60 (0.7-1.7 *a.i*/ha), potassium azide (3-4 ha/ka), swep, triphenyl tin acetate, and diathan D-14 are available for this purpose. Potassium azide should not be used on calcareous soils.

For the control of annual grasses and many broadleaf weeds, granular formulations of some herbicides can be applied through the flood, from before emergence of the weeds to 3-7 days after *transplanting rice*. Some such outstanding herbicides are, DCPA (2-8 kg/ha), 2,4-D ester G (0.8-1.2 kg/ha), molinate (2-4 kg/ha), **butachlor** (1.5-2 kg/ha), **pendimethalin** (1 kg/ha), oxadiazon (1-1.5 kg/ha), dichlobenil (0.75-1 kg/ha), chloramben (1.75 kg/ha), **thiobencarb** (1.5-2. kg/ha), oxadiargyl (0.1 kg/ha), and

anilofos. With a herbicide such as dichlobenil it is important not to allow the treated water to contact the rice leaves, else these may be severely scorched. In modern times many grass-effective herbicides are granulated with 2,4-D (IPE) to obtain simultaneous control of broadleaf weeds and sedges. Granules containing EPTC and 2,4-D (0.75 to 1.75:0.5 kg/ha), for example, have proved very active on annual sedges in rice fields. When it is possible to drain rice fields to expose young weeds, propanil spray can also be employed to achieve a quick knock-down of such weeds. Soon after this the rice fields should be refilled with water to weaken germination of the next flush of weeds. Thiobencarb and butachlor prove most selective to rice when healthy seedlings are transplanted 2-5 cm deep, in an even flood of 3-7 cm. The field should not be drained till 7 days later to obtain satisfactory weed control.

Some more recently reported field trials have revealed successful broad-spectrum control of weeds (involving grasses, broadleafs and sedges) with pyrazosulfuron-ethyl (0.01-0.03 kg/ha) as well as with a pre-made mixture of acetochlor and bensnlfuron-methyl (0.250 kg/ha). Acetochlor alone can be attempted at 0.1-0.15 kg/ha in transplanted rice.

Herbicidal control of perennial grasses in rice fields is yet undiscovered. These are presently controlled with 1-2 hard, row cultivations. Of recent, *Scirpus maritiums*, a perennial sedge, is reported controlled with preemergent butachlor followed by postemergent bentazon, fenoprop, or MCPP.

(c) *Herbicidal Control In Rice Nurseries:* Molinate, DCPA, and **propanil** are commonly used herbicides in rice nurseries. Molinate is incorporated into the seedbeds and then rice seeds are sown by broadcast. It can sometimes also be applied after the rice seeds have germinated. DCPA (1. 5-2 kg/ha) forms a preemergence herbicide in drilled rice beds. Propanil is employed on young weeds as over-the-top treatment in established rice nurseries. Broadcast of pyrazosulfuron (0.015 kg/ha) wettable powder mixed with sand 1 d.a.s. has been found very effective in rice nurseries.

(d) *Wild rice (O. sativa var. fatua) Control In Rice Fields:* Wild rice is a serious weed in certain rice growing areas of India, as well as in some other countries of the world. The weed survives by mimicry. Cultivation of purple-leaf rice varieties to distinguish them from the green-leaf wild rice plants has been recommended for long to get an opportunity to handpull the later. Some purple-leaf rice varieties are P-502, R-575, L-12, and CP-1. But all these varieties, unfortunately, are very poor yielders. Herbicide research to mark a selectivity between wild rice and cultivated rice is under way at IRRI, Phillipines and W.R.O., U.K. Possibility is also being sought to use antidotes to protect the rice seeds against preemergence herbicides that would destroy wild rice. Preplant incorporated molinate at 4.5-6.7 kg/ha in flooded cultures is reported to control red rice in white rice, effectively (Smith, 1981).

During the past one decade or so, butachlor and, to some extent, pretilachlor have been used in the country to achieve selective weed control in rice. The continuous use of the two herbicides, however, has now brought to light some serious weed flora shifts necessasitating testing and use of alternate herbicide molecules. Most of these weed shifts comprise displacement of certain annual weed species by the perennial ones although sometimes within annual weed species such weed shifts may also occur.

Table 21.2: Herbicidal Control in Transplanted Rice at Two Sites in Kashmir During 1986 and 1987 (After Amarjit *et al.*, 1994)

Treatments	Dry weed biomass (q/ha)					Grain yield of rice (q/ha)					
	Khudwani		Larnoo			Khudwani		Larnoo			% increase
	1986	1987	1986	1987	Mean	1986	1987	1986	1987	Mean	
Unweeded check	90	103	89	91	93	36	32	30	14	28	
Hand-weeded (20, 30 d.a.s.)	18	22	10	16	19	65	64	41	40	53	89
Benthiocarb (2.0 kg/ha)	19	21	25	23	22	61	64	38	36	50	79
Butachlor (1.5 kg/ha)	16	19	16	16	17	60	67	42	39	52	86
C.D. (at P=0.05)	18.3	15.0	13.9	15.1	-	6.9	7.3	4.8	6.7	-	-

Note: Herbicides were applied as granules within a week after transplanting.

***Comments:** Under the prevailing conditions, herbicidal control proved as effective as two manual weedings, although more usually one handweeding is still required to supplement the herbicides (Saiki and Pathak, 1993)*

The notable examples of weed successions in rice are replacement of *Sphenoclea zeylanica* and *Cyperus difformis* by *Marsilea qudrifolia* and *C. rotundus*, respectively. In some other situations, *Echinochloa* spp. have been reported replaced by *Panicum* spp. and *C. iria* by *C. difformis*. Among the dicot weeds, *Ludwigia parviflora* was displaced by *Marsilea quadrifolia*. In certain places, *Ischaenum rugosum* (a grass weed) has been reported replaced by *Fimbristylis* sp. (a sedge weed). Repeated use of pretilachlor is found to cause marked suppression of *C. iria* (a sedge) and dominance of *Caesulina axillaris* (a broadleaf weed).

The **alternate herbicides** tested successfully in India in rice nurseries and rice fields to curb new weed problems include the following. These can be used in suitable yearly rotations to prevent possible weed shifts.

1. Rice Nurseries:

   a) *Preemergence:* Pyrazosulfuron-ethyl, clefoxidim, quinclorac, and butachlor and pretilachlor with suitable safeners.

2. Transplanted Rice:

   a) *Preemergence (to weeds):* Clomazone (0.2-0.25 kg/ha), triazolopyramidine (0.015-0.025 kg/ha), oxadiargyl (0.07-0.125 kg/ha), anilophos (0.25-1.0 kg/ha), flufenacet (0.09-0.12 kg/ha), fentrazamide (0.21-0.24 kg/ha), cinosulfuron (0.02 kg/ha), ethoxysulfuron (0.01-0.15 kg/ha) and chlorimuron-ethyl (0.01 kg/ha), benbulfuron-methyl or Almix (0.004 kg/ha) with butachlor (1 kg/ha).

   b) *Postemergence* (about 10 days after transplanting): Ethoxysulfuron (0.02 kg/ha), fenoxaprop-p-ethyl (0.075-0.120 kg/ha), and cyhalofop butyl (0.06-0.75 kg/ha).

3. Direct Seeded Rice:

   a) *Preemergence:* Pretilachlor (0.750 kg/ha) with safener, butachlor (1-1.5 kg/ha) with safener, ethoxysulfuron (0.01-0.03 kg/ha), oxadiargyl (0.09 kg/ha), acetachlor G (0.2 kg/ha), thiobencarb (1.5 kg/ha), cyhalofop-butyl (0.06-0.07 kg/ha), fenoxaprop (0.06-0.07 kg/ha), almix (0.02 kg/ha), quinclorac (0.187-0.375 kg/ha), and dithiopyr (0.180 kg/ha).

b) *Postemergence (Broadleaf weed control):* Ethoxysulfuron (0.02-0.03 kg/ha), chlorimuron-ethyl (0.004 kg/ha), and metsulfuron (0.03-0.06 kg/ha).

c) *Postemergence (Grass and sedge control):* Fenoxaprop-P-ethyl (0.05-0.075 kg/ha), cyhalofop-butyl (0.12 kg/ha).

d) *Postemergence (Broadspectrum weed control):* Pretilachlor (0.75 kg/ha) and pyrazosulfuron-ethyl (0.025 kg/ha).

There may be some varietal differences in rice in respect of their tolerance to the recommended herbicides. For instance, ADT-36, ADT-38 and PY-3 varieties of rice in Tamilnadu and HPU-845 and HPU-846 in Himachal Pradesh have been found susceptible to butachlor because of their very low α–amylase contents. Similarly, cultivar IR-50 has been reported susceptible to oxyfluorfen because of its very low chlorophyll content. Such, responses of crop varieties to the herbicides should be examined before using these, commercially.

21.1.2 Winter Grains *(Wheat, Barley, and Oat)*

The Weed Problem: *Winter* grain crops are frequently infested with dense growth of a variety of weeds in the tropical and subtropical areas of the world. These weeds reduce their grain yields by 10-40%. The common weed species found in winter grain fields are the broadleafs, *eg Chenopodium album, C. murale*; *Fumaria, Vicia, Meliotus* and *Lathyrus* spp.; *Anagallis arvensis*, and the like. In many places *Carthamus oxyacantha, Cirsium arvense, Convolvulus arvensis*, and *Asphodelus tenuifolius* are particularly problematic. In Africa and other tropical areas, more difficult broadleaf weeds *eg. Fagopyron tataricum, Galium tricorne, Polygonum* spp., and *Anthemis cotula* are found. In the last two decades, besides the broadleaf weeds, at least five grass weeds have threatened wheat and barley grain production in Asian and African countries. These are: (i) *Phalaris minor*, (*ii*) *Avena fatua*, (*iii*) *Lolium temulentum* and *L. rigidum*, (*iv*) *Polypogon monspeliensis*, and (*v*) *Poa annua*. In some areas perennial grass, *Cynodon dactylon* is noxious in grain fields. In India, currently *Phalaris minor* in moisture retentive soils and *Avena fatua* in light soils are the biggest threats to her wheat production.

Of the various yield attributes in winter grains, weed-crop interference causes first a significant reduction in the ear bearing tillers (e.b.t.) of the crop. Under an increasing stress from weeds, the surviving tillers bear shorter ears, lesser number of grains per ear, and finally shrivelled grains. Weeds maturing with the crop also reduce its quality by contaminating the grain with their seeds.

The Weed Management: Because winter grains are sown either in narrow rows (22-25 cm apart) or by broadcast, manual weeding is the only physical method available to the farmer to remove weeds from these crops. Usually two weedings, one each at 4 and 6 weeks after sowing the grains are considered adequate. When only one weeding is feasible, it should be done at six weeks' crop stage. Hand-weeding is often feasible and efficient in light soils, but in heavy soils, it is a very slow and costly practice. Moreover, grass weeds like *Phalaris* and *Avena* spp. are difficult to identify from wheat and barley during their vegetative phases, many of which may thus escape attention of the farmer. Therefore, in such weed prone areas extra efforts must be made by the farmers to follow strict weed prevention and good crop husbandry practices in the cultivation of the grain crops (Chapters 5 & 7).

(a) *The use of herbicides:* Several herbicides are used in conjunction with good crop husbandry to tackle specific weed problems in small grains. **2,4-D** and **MCPA** are the most widely used alternative herbicides the world-over for the control of common broadleaf weeds in these crops. Either phenoxy herbicide is applied just after first irrigation of the dwarf varieties of wheat (or barley), which is usually adopted at their CRI stages. Normally, the safe dose limits of the two herbicides are 0.75-1.0 kg *a.e.*/ha of their sodium and amine salts, and 0.5-0.75 kg *a. e.*/ha of their low volatile esters. Often lower rates would provide adequate broadleaf control, particularly in combination with 1-3% urea. In the tall varieties of winter grains, 2,4-D should be applied 40-50 days after sowing *ie.* at fully tillered stage of the crops. Such varieties frequently tolerate up to 2 kg *a.e.*/ ha of sodium, 1.5 kg *a.e.*/ha of amine, and 0.75 kg *a.e.*/ha of ester form of 2,4-D and MCPA. If an irrigation is due to the crop, it should be given before, and *not* after the application of 2,4-D or MCPA, else leaching of the herbicide may cause crop damage. More recently, fluroxypyr (0.1-0.3 kg/ha) has been found a very good substitute to 2,4-D for broadleaf weed control in wheat. Likewise, tribenuron and thifensulfuron in minute dose of 0.09 kg/ha will provide selective control of many broadleaf weeds in these crops.

There is a second phase in the life cycle of wheat (and barley) namely, hard dough stage, when 2,4-D and MCPA can be employed to destroy late weeds like *Convolvulus arvensis* and *Carthamus oxyacantha* to prevent grain contamination with these and other common weed seeds.

Winter grains under-sown with dicot crops like Bengalgram (chickpea), linseed, pea, and broadbeans should *never* be treated with the phenoxy herbicides. Also, wheat and barley cultivars themselves may differ in their tolerance to 2,4-D and MCPA. This must be checked before a new variety is treated with either of these herbicides. For instance, in India HD 2009 cultivar of wheat has been found highly susceptible to 2,4-D and MCPA. Preemergent pendimethalin has been found successful in the control of weeds in wheat intercropped with mustard or Bengalgram.

When winter grains are infested with weeds at a very early crop stage, say at 3 to 4-leaf stage of grains, or when wheat is undersown with crops like pea and clovers, MCPB and 2,4-DB prove much safer herbicides than MCPA and 2,4-D.

Not all broadleaf weeds are completely destroyed with 2,4-D. A few like *Convolvulus arvensis* and *Asphodelus tenuifolius* are only stunted in their growth by it. However, a dense crop cover will help keep them enough suppressed to be within economic threshold levels. There are still other broadleaf weeds which are completely tolerant to 2,4-D and MCPA, for example, *Galium aparine*, *Anthemis* spp., *Stellaria media*, and *Matricaria* spp. Some herbicides found successful against such broadleaf weeds are dicamba (6-25 g/ha), bromoxynil and ioxynil (28-56 g/ha), bentazon (0.75-1.5 kg/ha), dinoseb (0.75 kg/ha), mecoprop and dichlorprop (1.5-2.0 kg/ha), **terbutryn** (0.75-1 0 kg/ha), picloram (0.3-0.42 kg/ha), and certain sulfonylureas (0.28-0.67 kg/ha) (Chapter 13).

Fig. 21.1: *Top* = Wheat infested heavily with wildoat. *Bottom* = Wheat freed of wildoat with isoproturon. (Source: NRCWS, Jabalpur)

Considerable field success has been achieved in the control of notorious weeds, wildcanarygrass (*Phalaris minor*) and wildoat (*Avena fatua*) in wheat. The most useful herbicides against these bad weeds are terbutryn (0.6-1.0 kg/ha), methabenzthiazuron (0.75-1.5 kg/ha), metoxuron (1.5 kg/ha), **isoproturon** (0.75 kg/ha), and pendimethalin (1.0 kg/ha). Of these, pendimethalin, though very effective in the control of *Phalaris*, yet being a preemergence herbicide, is difficult to use on any large scale because of rush of sowing of wheat in the season. Amongst the remaining herbicides, isoproturon is being used most commonly in India as postemergence treatment, 30-45 days after planting wheat (or barley) *ie.* at their fully tillered stage. This herbicide can also be applied in wheat as preemergence treatment, as well as just before the first irrigation scheduled for the crop. Although, isoproturon will also kill some common broadleaf weeds, yet it can be combined with 2,4-D at 0.25-0.5 kg/ha to further improve control of this category of weeds. Another good herbicide combination for this purpose comprise isoproturon at 1 kg/ha and clopyralid at 0.75-0.15/1.5 kg/ha. Some cultivars of wheat and barley may be susceptible to the above cited grass killers which may be checked before using these on a new crop variety.

Against wildoat (*Avena fatua*) some more specific herbicides are now available. Soil incorporation of diallate or triallate was the earliest recommendation in this respect. Later, these herbicides were replaced by postemergent barban, but it had the limitation of being active only on very young wildoat seedlings at their 1½ to 2½-leaf stages. The new weed seedlings appearing after the treatment, escaped and infested the crop. To obviate this, delayed postemergence herbicides were developed which killed comparatively more grown-up wildoat plants in their 3 to 5-leaf stages. By this time most of the wildoat seeds germinated and succumbed to the herbicides. These herbicides include flamprop (1-2 kg/ha), tralkoxydim (0.25-0.3 kg/ha), difenzoquat (0.8-1.12 kg/ha), benzoylprop (0.84-1.1 kg/ha), and diclofop (0.84-1.11 kg/ha).

Table 21.3: Weed Control in Wheat With 2,4-D And Isoproturon at Jorhat (India) During 1989 And 1990 (After Tiwari and Parihar, 1993)

Treatments	Dry weed biomass (q/ha)		Grain yield of wheat (q/ha)			% increase
	1989	1990	1989	1990	Mean	
Unweeded check	6.87	7.45	18.29	18.16	18.23	–
Hand-weeded 30 d.a.s.	1.26	1.45	28.93	24.66	26.80	47
2,4-D	1.63	1.79	32.13	25.33	28.73	58
Isoproturon	0.56	0.45	32.36	29.16	30.76	69
2,4-D with isoproturon	0.23	0.20	36.77	33.29	35.03	92
C.D (at P = 0.05)	0.18	0.21	3.94	1.99	–	–

Note: Herbicides were applied at 1 kg/ha each, 30. d.a.s.

Comments: *While 2,4-D was effective in the control of broadleaf weeds, isoproturon was so against Phalaris minor. The combination provided control of both the weeds and resulted in the highest wheat yields.*

Poa annua is another annual grass which is becoming increasingly problematic in wheat. It has been reported very susceptible to certain sulfonylurea herbicides at 0.28-0.7 kg/ha at its young, actively growing stage.

In general, it is agreed that to achieve a permanent control of annual grasses in winter grains, block campaigns combining (i) the use of weedfree crop seeds (ii) labour intensive uprooting of grasses at their pre-seed formation stage and feeding them to animals, and (iii) application of suitable herbicides should be organised for 2-3 years.

During the last over a decade or so, two major herbicides used by farmers in N-W wheat belt of India, almost continuously, have been isoproturon and 2, 4-D against, respectively, *Phalaris minor* (a grass weed) and certain herbaceous broadleaf weeds. But due to selection pressure of their long term use, two new weed problems have cropped-up in wheat fields of this region. These are (i) development of isoproturon resistant* populations of *P. minor* and (ii) spread of 2, 4-D semi-tolerant and tolerant broadleaf weeds like *Medicago, Circium, Trigonella, Coronopus, Silene, Fumaria, Convolvulus* and *Malvastrum* spp. Besides this, certain wheat varieties like HD-2009, WH-283, WH-1416, Sonak, HPW-56 and HS-295 have shown deformed ears after the application of 2,4-D. Both these problems forced the weed scientists to search for alternate herbicides to answer the new weed problems.

1. Alternate Herbicides for the control of **Isoproturon - Resistant Populations of *P. minor*** (besides many other annual grasses);

    a) Clodinafop - propargyl (0.45-0.09 kg/ha)

    b) Fenoxaprop-p-ethyl (0.06-0.12 kg/ha)

    c) Mesosulfuron (0.012-0.030 kg/ha)

    d) Metribuzin (0.245-0.315 kg/ha)

    e) Sulfosulfuron (0.025-0.05 kg/ha),

    f) Tralkoxydim (0.35-0.40 kg/ha).

Of these herbicides, metribuzin and sulfosulfuron are broadspectrum herbicides, being effective against both grass and considerable broadleaf weeds. The remaining four herbicides, though very potent against *P. minor* and *A. fatua*, are weak on broadleaf weeds. To obtain simultaneous control of broadleafs, mesosulfuron has been successfully combined with iodosulfuron; clodinafop with chlorsulfuron; and fenoxaprop with isoproturon. Somehow, none of the six grass herbicides is found miscible with 2, 4-D or metsulfuron. Tralkoxydim should be the choice when late stage wildoat (*Avena fatua*) is the main weed problem although it will control *P. minor* too.

---

* The resistance to isoproturon is known to have developed due to adverse gene flow in nature which transferred certain genetic code imparting capability of rapid dealkination of the herbicide molecule in some plants of *P. minor*. Such individuals probably existed among normal, large populations of *P. minor* even before the use of isoproturon. These few resistant plants then multiplied after each year use of isoproturon to appear as resistant population in spaces vacated by the susceptible population.

Table 21.4: Effect of alternate herbicides on resistant *P. minor* infestation and associated grain yield of wheat at Ludhiana during 2000-01 (Bhatia, R. K. *et al.* 2002)

Sl. No.	Treatments (applied 30 d.a.s.)	Mean Population of P. minor (m^{-2}) 70 d.a.s.	Mean Seed production in P. minor (m^{-2})	Grain yield of wheat (q/ha) (var. PBW-343)
1.	Isoproturon (0.94 kg/ha)	57.7	53.4	45.2
2.	Clodinafop (0.06 kg/la)	18.5	10.3	56.4
3.	Fenoxaprop (0.10 kg/ha)	44.1	23.60	50.5
4.	Sulfosulfuron (0.025 kg/ha)	35.1	19.70	55.5
5.	Tralkoxydim (0.35 kg/ha)	58.7	42.60	47.5
6.	Untreated control	117.1	51.2	43.2
	C.D. (at 5%)	04.7	08.0	03.7

Remarks: One should expect significant increases in crop yield from use of alternate grass herbicides only when the wheat field was infested with isoproturon-resistant population of P. minor. Else, these herbicides may obviously prove at best as effective as isoproturon. In the above experiment, resistant P. minor dominated the scene and so the results. However, probably, the weed crop- competition was not severe enough since even in untreated control high wheat yield of 43.2q ha was reported.

Further, it may be noted that there are reports of development of cross resistance in *P. minor* to clodinafop and fenoxaprop which should be used judicially and search for new herbicide molecules against it *(P. minor)* should continue.

The efficacy of alternate herbicides against *P. minor* (and *Avena* spp.) could be further enhanced by adoption of: (i) stale seedbed sowing of wheat, (ii) long duration varieties of wheat with rapid canopy formation characteristics, (iii) early planting of crop in the last week of October to the first week of November when the temperatures were still not low enough to induce germination of *P. minor*, and (iv) rotation of wheat with suitable broadleaf crops and forages to aid physical uprooting of the *P. minor* escapes.

2. Alternate Herbicides for the Control of **Difficult Broadleaf Weeds** (applied 20-35 days after sowing):
   a) Carfentrazone ethyl (0.02-0.025 kg/ha),
   b) Chlorsulfuron (0.015-0.045 kg/ha),
   c) Fluroxypur (0.2-0.3 kg/ha),
   d) Iodosulfuron (0.024-0.03 kg/ha),
   e) Metribuzin (0.175-0.225 kg/ha),
   f) Metsulfuron-methyl (0.003-0.008 kg/ha),
   g) Triasulfuron (0.015-0.02 kg/ha) and
   h) Tribenuron methyl (0.05-0.10 kg/ha),

Table 21.5: Effect of metsulfuron methyl (MSM) alone and in combination with 2, 4-D on broadleaf weeds in wheat and grain yield at Pantnagar (India) during 1997 & 1998 (After Singh *et al.*, 2002)

	Selected Treatments	Dry weight of broadleaf weeds 60 d.a.s. (kg/ha)			Mean grain yield of wheat
		(Mean of 1997 & 1998)	1997	1998	
1.	MSM (0.004 kg/ha)	68	48.7	46.8	47.7
2.	2, 4-D (EE) (0.5 kg/ha)	109	41.6	38.6	40.1
3.	MSM +2, 4-D (0.004 + 0.025 kg/ha)	54	48.8	46.0	47.4
4.	MSM with surfactant (0.004 kg/ha)	58	49.3	47.8	48.6
5.	Isoproturon (1.0 kg/ha)	297	40.1	39.7	39.9
6.	Weedfree	-	50.1	46.6	48.4
7.	Weedy control	823	23.9	20.1	22.0
	C.D. (at 5%)	-	4.0	4.0	-

Remark: In this field experiment Medicago denticulata was the dominant weed. The alternate herbicide MSM proved significantly superior to 2, 4-D in controlling it. It may however be pointed out that an alternate herbicide like MSM shall prove superior to 2, 4-D or isoproturon in crop performance only when the treatment site was infested with primarily some difficult broadleaf weed species.

Asphodelus tenuifolius, a difficult common weed in wheat in northern India can be managed by integrating (a) stale seedbed sowing of wheat, (b) good crop husbandry practices leading to early crop growth, and (c) postemergence application of 2,4-D. Outside the fields, seed production of *A. tenuifolius* can be stopped by destroying it before flowering with herbicides like oxadiazon and oxyfluorfen which are much mre potent than 2,4-D.

21.2 MAIZE AND MILLETS

Maize and millets are largely rainy season grain crops grown in various parts of Asia and Africa. Because of warm and moist weather, a variety of graminaceous and broadleaf weeds invade these crops frequently even before the crop germination is completed. The weed infestation is sometimes so bad that farmers prefer to plough down their millet fields and replant them. Parasitic weed *Striga* spp. poses a special weed problem in millets. In maize, weeds cause reduction in plant height, cob length, number of grains per cob, and in very severe cases, also in its test weight. In pearlmillet, the weedy crops produce less ear bearing tillers, shorter ears, and, sometimes, even grains with lowered test weight.

A sound weed management system in maize and millets should incorporate (a) selective crop stimulation (b) herbicides, and (c) 1-2 row cultivations with the improved implements. Sometimes it is also possible, depending upon the distribution of rainfall, to cross run a spike-tooth harrow at 3-5 cm height of the crop to dislodge the germinating weed seedlings. The crop seedlings are at this stage flexible and would survive the operation. Row cultivation, preferably with sweeps, should begin at 15 cm whorl height of maize and millets, and it can continue up to 60 cm crop height. Best results with row cultivations are obtained when a soil active herbicide is used earlier. In labour intensive areas, hand-weeding twice, 25 and 40 days after sowing the crop has been an effective weed control practice in maize, pearlmillet, and sorghum.

Herbicidal control in maize and millets can be very usefully combined with the above practices, as follows.

21.2.1 Maize (*Zea mays* L.)

Preplant soil incorporation of butylate or **EPTC** at 3-4 kg/ha, mixed with about 0.5 kg/ha of either atrazine or simazine is a very effective treatment for achieving a broad-spectrum control of weeds in maize. The treatment will also hold sedges for 3-5 weeks. However, to improve crop selectivity to the carbamate herbicides it is required to either treat the maize seeds with NA, or to add antidote R 25788 to the spray tank. EPTC formulations containing R 25788 are marketed for their direct use in maize fields. The use of antidotes is, however, unnecessary in maize grown on organic matter rich soils. Butylate should not be used in maize grown on high pH soils. Also, the crop should be planted shallow in either case.

Atrazine and **simazine** were the first highly successful preemergence herbicides in maize which replaced the earlier used herbicides 2,4-D and MCPA in 1960's. Maize possesses a high degree of tolerance to the two triazine compounds up to a dose of 5-6 kg/ha. But in practice their 1-2 kg/ha rates are commonly used to avoid phytotoxic residue hazards of these herbicides to the rotation crops. In some low organic matter soils in India the rotation crop of wheat was injured even at 1.0 kg/ha rate of simazine.

In dry areas atrazine and simazine should be slightly incorporated into the soil to improve herbicide efficacy. When fall panicum (*Panicum dichotomiflorum*) and wildcane (*Sorghum bicolor*) are important weeds, simazine should be the choice since these grasses are found tolerant to atrazine.

Alachlor and **metolachlor** (1-2 kg/ha) are more effective preemergence herbicides against annual grasses than simazine and atrazine, but these are weak against the broadleafs. Therefore, a judicious combination of the two groups of herbicides should control both types of weeds, effectively. Alachlor will suppress nutsedges too. On high adsorptive soils, a combination of propachlor and linuron is preferred over alachlor and metolachlor.

Table 21.6: Effect of Atrazine on Weed Control in Pearlmillet (var. RSB-2) And Crop Yield on an Alfisol in Andhra Pradesh (India), During 1988 and 1989 (After Kumar and Shaik, 1993)

Treatments	Dry weed biomass 60 d.a.s. (q/ha)		Grain yield of pearlmillet (q/ha)			% increase
	1988	1989	1988	1989	Mean	
Unweeded check	19.52	33.54	18.2	21.1	19.7	–
Hand-weeded 30 d.a.s.	0.81	1.20	28.8	34.1	31.5	59.6
Atrazine (PE, 0.5 kg/ha)	0.72	1.12	30.3	36.8	33.6	70.3
C.D. (at P = 0.05)	1.02	2.47	4.8	4.5	–	–

Comments: *Preemergent atrazine was found very effective for weed control in pearlmillet at low doses. At higher than 0.5 kg/ha dose, in many places crop injury may result*

Linuron is reported effective also against *Cynodon dactylon*. Pendimethalin (1.0 kg/ha) has been newly added to the list of preemergence herbicides in maize.

For early postemergence control of young weeds in maize a very good herbicide combination is 0.42 kg alachlor + 0.25 kg atrazine + 5% phytobland oil emulsion spray. Later, at 3 to 6 leaf stage of the weeds, cyanazine (0.75-2 kg/ha) can be used on even still older weeds, any time up to 25 cm whorl height of maize. Against solid stands of broadleaf weeds and nutsedge, 2,4-D or MCPA (0.25-0.5 kg/ha) should be used as directed spray between 8 cm and 25 cm whorl height stage of the crop. The treatment may make the maize plants brittle for short period. More difficult broadleaf weeds like *Trianthema*, *Portulaca*, and *Ipomoea* spp. in maize may be controlled with a mixture of dicamba and 2,4-D (or MCPA). Nutsedge in maize has proved very susceptible to herbicide combinations comprising alachlor, atrazine, and phytobland oil.

(In the USA, glyphosate is widely used in the transgenic, glyphosate resistant varieties of maize – Chapter 16).

21.2.2 Millets

Sorghum (*Sorghum bicolor* (L.) Moench) and Pearlmillet (*Pennisetum americanum* (L.) Leeke) are major millet crops in the tropics and sub-tropics. Besides, some minor millets like *Eleusine* and *Panicum* spp. are also grown. Strange enough, although the millets occupy larger area than maize in the world, yet herbicidal control research is much limited in the former..

Initial 30-45 days of seeding minor millets are considered most critical for weeding. Triazines, chiefly **atrazine**, simazine, and propazine, are most commonly recommended preemergence herbicides in millets. Their doses vary from 0.25 to 1.0 kg/ha, depending upon the soil type. Atrazine has been found effective even when applied up to 7 days after sowing pearlmillet. The use of propazine in millets is limited to one crop a year areas because of its residual phytotoxicity to the rotation crops. Some varieties of pearlmillet like GHB-27, 28, 183 and BK-560, are found sensitive to atrazine.

Table 21.7: Weed Management in Pearlmillet (*var.* MH-179) at Sumerpur (India) During 1991 and 1992 (From Research Highlights, 1992 of RAU, Bikaner, India : 30)

Treatments	**Grain yield of pearlmillet (Pooled data of two years)**	
	q/ha	**% increase**
Unweeded check	9.04	–
Hand-weeded once (20 d.a.s.)	10.04	11.1
Hand-weeded twice (20, 40 d.a.s.)	14.98	39.7
Atrazine (PE, 0.5 kg/ha)	12.81	41.70
Atrazine + Hand-weeding (20 d.a.s.)	16.74	85.2
C.D. (at P = 0.05)	2.59	–

Comments: *Two manual weedings were required to effectively curb the weeds and increase the crop yield. Combination of atrazine with one hand-weeding tended to perform even better than the twice hand-weeded crop.*

Further research has revealed new herbicides for the preemergence treatment in millets. In sorghum grown on light soils, terbutryn (1-2 kg/ha) and propachlor (1-2 kg/ha) are considered superior preemergence herbicides. Likewise, in medium to heavy soils norea (1-2 kg/ha) and fluometuron (1-1.5 kg/ha) are now recommended. In dry areas the herbicides should be lightly incorporated into the soil. It is now further made possible to use preemergent alachlor in sorghum by coating its seeds with NA (see Chapter 16).

In pearlmillet, besides atrazine and simazine, other promising preemergence herbicides are buturon, linuron, neburon, prometryn, ioxynil, lenacil, and oxyfluorfen (0.3 kg/ha).

2-4-D is a versatile herbicide for postemergence broadleaf control in millets. Against *Siriga* spp. it is employed to achieve its preventive control. The effective rate of 2,4-D is 1 kg/ha. Another difficult weed *Tribulus terrestris* in pearlmillet has proved susceptible to a mixture of 2,4-D (or MCPA) and dicamba (or atrazine.)

Aqueous spray of atrazine can also be employed for destroying mixed growth of very young, annual weeds in their 1 to 2-leaf stage, without damage to millets. More established weeds in sorghum have been found susceptible to diuron (0.5-0.75 kg/ha) when it is applied with 0.5% of a suitable wetting agent. In *ragi* (*E. indica*), in India preemergent chlorimuron ethyl (5-100 g/ha), isoproturon (0.75 kg/ha), and anilophos (0.3 kg/ha) applied 6-8 d.a.s., followed by either one hand-weeding or postemergent propanil at 2 kg/ha have proved very successful.

21.3 OILSEED CROPS

21.3.1 Groundnut (*Arachis hypogaea* L.)

Groundnut is a major oilseed crop in the tropical world. Hot and humid weather prevailing during its cultivation period affords repeated flushes of grasses and broadleaf weeds through its entire growing season. In addition to competing with the crop, weeds in groundnut hinder its pegging, compete for underground space, and make crop harvest cumbersome. The weedy crop finally produces fewer pods per plant and smaller peanuts.

Since most groundnut crops in the tropics are grown on light soils, spiketooth harrowing and hoeing are practised during early stages of crop growth. About four weeks after sowing is considered a critical stage for weeding groundnut. But once pegging in groundnut begins, no further physical method of weeding can be adopted for fear of damage to the pegs. Herbicidal control in groundnut under Indian conditions should aim at 20-25 days' freedom from weeds, followed by one row cultivation.

Certain herbicides have proved remarkably effective in providing weedfree conditions during pegging in groundnut. **Fluchloralin** (1-2 kg) vernolate (202.5 kg/ha), benefin (0.75-1.5 kg/ha), trifluralin, nitralin (0.25-0.75 kg/ha), and **pendimethalin** (2 kg/ha) are proven preplant, incorporated herbicides in groundnut. Alachlor can also be used as presowing herbicides. Choice amongst these compounds depends upon their weed control spectrum.

Table 21.8: Effect of Herbicidal Cum Physical Weed Control on The Performance of Groundnut During 1991 at Hyderabad (India) (After Kumar *et al.*, 1994) at Hyderabad (India) (After Kumar *et al.*, 1994)

Treatments	Dry weed biomass	Pod yield of groundnut	
	(q/ha)	(q/ha)	% increase
Unweeded check	64.3	8.9	–
Hand-weeded (repeatedly)	–	38.0	326.9
Fluchloralin (PPI, 1 kg/ha)	26.7	21.1	137.1
Fluchloralin + Hand-weeding 30 d.a.s.	4.5	30.4	241.6
Pendimethalin (PPI, 1 kg/ha)	25.1	22.7	155.1
Pendimethalin + Hand-weeding 30 d.a.s	5.2	29.8	234.8
C.D. (at P = 0.05)	7.93	10.4	–

***Comments:** Like in other oil seed crops, the soil-applied herbicides remain effective only for 20-25 d.a.s. Therefore, it is necessary to combine these with one physical weeding, 30-35 d.a.s. In this case, such a combination gave 7-8 q/ha additional pod yield than herbicides alone.*

Preemergence herbicides in groundnut are best applied about 6 days after planting the crop *ie.* a little before expected time of crop emergence. By this time the crop roots are as deep as 14 cm in soil. The more effective preemergence herbicides in groundnut are fluorodifen (2-4 kg/ha), alachlor (1-3 kg/ha), naptalam (2-3 kg/ha), prometryn (0.5-1.5 kg/ha), simazine (1 kg/ha), oxadiazon (1-2 kg/ha), and prynachlor, dimethazone (0.5 kg/ha), acetolachlor (0.75-1.0 kg/ha), and dimethazone (0.5 kg/ha), metolachlor (0.75-1.0 kg/ha), and butachlor (1.0 kg/ha). A mixture of **oxadiazon** and **dinoseb**, each at 1.7 kg/ha, gives excellent control of weeds besides reducing stem rot in groundnut.

Weeds that have already emerged at the soil cracking stage of the crop, can be scorched heavily with dinoseb or diphenamid (4-6 kg/ha). Care should be taken to avoid its overlap spray and avoid spraying during high atmospheric temperatures of over 30°C. Of recent, **fluazifop** (0.125-0.250 kg/ha) has been found promising for postemergence control of grasses, particularly *Cynodon dactylon*, 35-40 days after sowing groundnut. Against a mixed growth of annual weeds, imazethapyr (0.75 kg/ha) and against specifically the annual grasses, quizalofop-ethyl (0.04-0.05 kg/ha) have been lately found very effective with safety to groundnut.

21.3.2 Linseed (*Linum usitatissimum* L.)

Linseed is largely crowded by common, winter broadleaf weeds. Amine salts of **MCPA** (0.2-0.5 kg *a.e.*/ha) and **MCPB** (0.5 kg *a.e.*/ha) form primary herbicides in this crop. Linseed is most tolerant to these herbicides at just its pre-branch stage when usually the linseed plants are 8-15 cm tall. A mixture of MCPB and MCPA (1 : 1) to a total of 0.5 kg *a.e.*/ha is particularly effective against weedy thistles in linseed. Mecoprop (0.5 kg/ha), dicamba (0.125-0.25 kg/ha), and bromoxynil (0.25 kg/ha) are used against the more difficult broadleaf weeds. Postemergent, chlorpropham (4 kg/ha), and dinoseb (0.5-0.75 kg/ha) can be used to control grasses in linseed, while preplant EPTC against sedges. Diclofop (1.68 kg/ha), a wildoat (*Avena* spp) herbicide, has been found selective to linseed. More recent field research has revealed letter weed control in this crop with:

Preplant fluchloralin (1.0 kg/ha); *Preemergence* alachlor (1-2 kg/ha), methabenzthiazuron (1.0 kg/ha), pendimethalin (1.0 kg/ha), and oxadiazon (0.75 kg/ha); and *Postemergence* control of annual grasses with isoproturon (1-1.5 kg/ha). Isoproturon may also control the parasitic weed *Cuscuta* spp.

21.3.3 Rape and Mustard (*Brassica* spp.)

Rape (*B. compestris*) and mustard (*B. lcuhcea*) are fast growing crops. These are rarely infested with more than one flush of weeds. And these weeds can be hoed down easily in these row-planted crops. After initial weeding, a healthy crop of rape and mustard closes in fast to smother any further weed growth. When required, herbicides may replace hoeing in rape and mustard. **Fluorodifen** (1-2 kg/ha), isoproturon (0.75-1.0 kg/ha), oxadiazon (0.5-0.75 kg/ha), fluchloralin (0.5-0.75 kg/ha), trifluralin (0.5 kg/ha), and bifenox (1.6 kg/ha) are outstanding herbicides for the purpose. Rape and mustard are tolerant to pre-and postemergence treatments with fluorodifen at 2 to 3-leaf stage. Fluchloralin is applied as preplant treatment. Isoproturon is found effective both as preplant and preemergence treatments, while oxadiazon is so only as preemergence treatment.

When more difficult weeds like thistles invade rape and mustard, dicamba should be tried. It is applied after the crop is at least 5 cm tall but before it has initiated flowering. Grasses are usually not problematic in rape and mustard. But in specific fields with history of annual grasses, preplant trifluralin (1 kg/ha) and postemergent dalapon (4-7 kg/ha) can be employed. Against wildoat (*Avena fatua*) barban can be used. In recent years, a parasitic weed, *Orobanche*, is becoming increasingly problematic in rape and mustard. So far no effective herbicidal control of this weed is on report.

(In Canada, glyphosate is widely used in transgenic, glyphosate resistant varieties of *Brassica* spp. – Chapter 16).

Table 21.9: Comparative Efficacy of Herbicidal And Manual Weeding in Mustard During 1981 and 1992 (After Yadav *et al.*, 1995)

Treatments	Weed population (per m^2)		Grain yield of mustard (q/ha)			% increase
	1991	1992	1991	1992	Mean	
Unweeded check	2.0	3.0	12.81	11.71	12.26	–
Hand-weeded once	0.1	0.1	18.33	18.58	18.46	50.5
Isoproturon (1 kg/ha)						
a) Preemergence	2.7	3.2	17.32	18.00	17.66	44.0
b) PPI	2.0	3.0	17.46	18.08	17.77	44.9
C.D. (at P = 0.05)	1.96	2.94	1.08	0.56	–	–

Comments: *Soil application of isoproturon was as effective in boosting the mustard yield as hand-weeding it once.*

21.3.4 Soybean (*Glycine max* Merrill)

Like most summer crops, weeds pose a serious threat to soybean cultivation during early phase of the crop till almost two months after sowing. Early herbicidal control seems to be a must in this crop for harvesting acceptable bean yields. In this crop, as well as in other oil-seed crops, weeds cause reduction in the number of branches per plant, number of pods per plant, number of grains per pod and, sometimes, in the test weight.

Preplant soil incorporation of trifluralin, nitralin, **fluchloralin** (0.5-1.0 kg/ha) for controlling grasses; of vernolate (1-5 kg/ha) for suppressing sedges and grasses; and of metribuzin (0.25-0.75 kg/ha) for controlling difficult broadleaf weeds were initially recommended in soybean. Some successful **preemergence** herbicides against annual grasses in soybean are **alachlor** (1-2 kg/ha), **metolachlor** (1-2 kg/ha), clomazone (1-1.5 kg/ha), oxyfluorfen (0.1-0.2 kg/ha), dimidazon (0.5-0.75 kg/ha), oxadiazon (0.4-0.5 kg/ha), chloramben (2-3 kg/ha), chlorimuron ethyl 0.009 kg/ha, pendimethalin (0.5-0.75 kg/ha), metribuzin (0.25-1.0 kg/ha), imazaquin (0.15 kg/ha), and imazethapyr (0.15 kg/ha). Of these herbicides, chloramben is used on heavy soils, while rest of the herbicides may be used also on medium textured soils. On light soils DCPA (6-10 kg/ha) and chlorpropham (4-9 kg/ha) are safe herbicides in soybean. Dinoseb (2-3 kg/ha), with or without naptalam, and fluorodifen (4-4.5 kg/ha) are specific against difficult broadleaf weeds in soybean.

Now it is also possible to control several, broadleaf weeds effectively in soybean with **postemergent** herbicides like chlorimuron (0.033-0.066 kg/ha), lactofen (0.8-1.0 kg/ha), and fomesafen (0.25-0.375 kg/ha). **Fluazifop** (0.125-0.25 kg/ha), haloxyfop (0.125-0.250 kg/ha), quizalofop ethyl (0.05 kg/ha), and bentazon (1.5 kg/ha), form effective postemergent grass killers in this crop. Two other recently evaluated postemergent herbicides in soybean are imazethapyr (0.075 kg/ha) and imazamox (0.06 kg/ha). The postergence herbicide application is attempted about 20-25 d.a.s. Glyphosate has been successfully used for spot treatment of scattered patches of perennial grasses, if any, in soybean.

Table 21.10: Study on Weed Control in Soybean (*var.* Bragg) With Herbicides in Himachal Pradesh (India) During 1992 and 1993 (After Negi and Saini, 1994)

Treatments	Dry weed biomass (q/ha)		Grain yield of soybean (q/ha)			% increase
	1992	1993	1992	1993	Mean	
Unweeded check	12.4	32.7	5.62	10.58	8.1	–
Hand-weeded (30, 45 d.a.s.)	5.8	19.4	15.39	29.32	22.4	176.5
Alachlor (PE)	–	17.7	15.06	26.48	20.8	156.8
Metolachlor (PE)	0.95	18.7	16.30	29.47	22.9	182.8
Fluchloralin (PPI)	1.2	18.3	15.53	25.45	20.5	153.1
Clomazone (PE)	0.9	17.4	16.93	25.62	22.3	175.3
C.D. (at P = 0.05)	0.87	0.87	2.62	3.43	–	–

Note: Herbicides were applied at 1 kg/ha each.

Comments: *Of the herbicides evaluated, preemergent alachlor and metolachlor proved as effective as hand-weeding in boosting the crop yield. Fluchloralin effects were inconsistent.*

Further field research in soybean has shown superior selective weed control with: *Preplant* pursuit plus (0.8 kg/ha); *Preemergence* anilophos (2-3 kg/ha), tepraloxydim (0.75 kg/ha), clomazone (1.0 kg/ha), oryzalin (1.0 kg/ha), pendimethalin (1.0 kg/ha), alachlor (1.0 kg/ha), fenoxaprop-p-ethyl (0.07-1.0 kg/ha), and flumioxazin (0.045-0.5 kg/ha); and *postemergence* quizalofop-p-ethyl (0.05 kg/ha), sethoxydim (0.25-0.35 kg/ha) and haloxyfop EE (0.05-0.1 kg/ha) against the grass weeds, and acifluorfen (0.1 kg/ha), imazethapyr (0.75-1.5 kg/ha), lactofen (0.12 kg/ha), neburon (0.009 kg/ha) and chlorimuron ethyl (0.006-0.012 kg/ha) against the broadleafs like *Trianthema, Celosia* and *Cleome* spp.

(In the USA glyphosate is widely used as coverall spray in the transgenic, glyphosate resistant varieties of soybean – Chapter 16).

21.3.5 Sesame (*Sesamum indicum* L.)

Promising herbicides in sesame are preemergent chlorpropham (4 kg/ha), diuron (0.5-0.75 kg/ha), norea (3 kg/ha), **alachlor** (1-2 kg/ha), fluchloralin (1.0 kg/ha), oxyfuorfen (0.15 kg/ha), and pendimethalin (1.0 kg/ha). Good control of annual grasses in sesame can be achieved with postemergence isoproturon (1-1.5 kg/ha).

21.3.6 Safflower (*Carthamus tinctorius* L.)

Preplant soil incorporated EPTC (2 kg/ha), triflluralin (1-2 kg/ha), nitralin (1.5 kg/ha), and chlorpropham (3-6 kg/ha) have proved effective herbicides in safflower. Of recent, alachlor (1.0 kg/ha), fluchloralin (1.5 kg/ha), and diuron (0.85 kg/ha) have been shown as effective preemergence herbicides in this crop.

Table 21.11: Effect of Three Herbicides With One Row Cultivation in Sunflower at Navsarl (India), During 1988-89 (Patel *et al.*, 1994)

Treatments	Dry weed biomass	Seed yield of sunflower	
	(q/ha)	(q/ha)	(% increase)
Unweeded check	5.91	11.37	–
Hand-weeded	–	15.44	35.8
Row cultivation (40 d.a.s.)	2.00	13.63	19.9
Oxyfluorfen (2 kg/ha) + Tr. 3	0.58	16.80	47.8
Pendimethalin (1.5 kg/ha) + Tr.3	0.55	16.83	47.9
Fluchloralin (1.0 kg/ha) + Tr. 3	0.94	15.44	35.8
(at P = 0.05)	0.42	1.39	

Note: Fluchloralin was applied PPI, while other herbicides were applied PE.

Tr. = Treatment

Comments: *Weed control effects of one inter-cultivation was improved significantly by soil application of one of the test herbicides.*

Fig. 21.2: *Top* = Weedy sesamun. *Bottom*: Weedfree sesamum. (Source: NRCWS, Jabalpur)

21.3.7 Sunflower (*Helianthus annus* L.)

Preplant EPTC (2-3 kg/ha) fluchlordin (1.0 kg/ha), and trifluralin (0.5-1 kg/ha) are reported efficient in selective weeding of sunflower. Besides, preemergence treatment with herbicides such as chloramben (2-3 kg/ha), norea (2-4 kg/ha), prometryn (2 kg/ha), **terbutryn** (2 kg/ha), **pendimethalin** (1-2 kg/ha) alachlor (1-2 kg/ha), oxadiazone (0.5-1.0 kg/ha), metolachlor (0.75-1.0 kg/ha), butachlor (1-1.5 kg/ha), and oxyfluorfen (0.25 kg/ha) are reported selective to the crop. Against wildoat, barban is recommended in sunflower.

21.3.8 Castorbean (*Ricinus communis*)

The more promising herbicide treatments recommended in castorbean are (1) *preplant* **fluchloralin** (0.75-1.5 kg/ha), EPTC (2 kg/ha), and naptalam (4 kg/ha), and (2) **preemergent** CDAA (6 kg/ha), DCPA (6-12 kg/ha), **alachlor** (1-1.5 kg/ha), metolachlor (1.0 kg/ha), pendimethalin (1.5 kg/ha), and butachlor (1.0 kg/ha). Glyphosate can be spot sprayed to take care of patches of the perennial weeds.

21.3.9 Niger (*Guizotta abyssinica* Cass.)

Parasitic dodder (*Cuscuta* sp.) has been found controlled in niger with preemergent chlorpropham, pronamide (1.5 kg/ha), and fluchloralin (1.5-2.0 kg/ha). Preemergent thiobencarb (0.75 kg/ha) and isoproturon (1-1.5 kg/ha) are also reported selective to niger.

21.4 GRAIN LEGUME CROPS

21.4.1 Chickpea or Bengal gram (*Cicer arietinum* L.)

Both dryland and irrigated chickpea crops are badly infested with weeds because of their short growing nature. Narrow rows of these crops make mechanical weeding almost out of question, although hand-weeding, particularly in light soils, is feasible. Under irrigated conditions the crop is often infested with repeated flushes of broadleaf weeds, requiring 2-3 manual weedings to keep the crop weedfree. But in dryland gram, the weed growth is limited, and it usually requires only one manual weeding to obtain acceptable crop yields. Effective herbicidal control in irrigated chickpea has been achieved with preplant soil treatment with fluchloralin or trifluralin at 0.75 kg/ha. Among the preemergence herbicides, pendimethalin, prometryn, terbutryn, chloramben, and linuron hold promise. In specific situations where weeds in irrigated chickpea germinate late, fluchloralin can also be applied in the inter-row spaces, just before first irrigation. The irrigation water will bring about the necessary incorporation of the herbicide in the soil. Bentazon (1.0 kg/ha) has been found effective in chickpea when applied 7-8 days after sowing. Quizalofop – ethyl (0.04-0.05 kg/ha) on the other hand forms a very effective postemergence herbicide to control annual grasses in this crop.

Fig. 21.3: *Top* = Weedy niger. *Bottom:*Weedfree niger. (Source: NRCWS, Jabalpur)

21.4.2 Beans (*Vigna* and *Vicia* spp.)

In recent years, herbicidal control research has been extended to bean crops like blackgram, greengram (mungbean), dwarfbean, and fieldbean. Preplant incorporation or preemergence application of **pendimethalin**, trifluralin, and **fluchloralin** (0.75-1.0 kg/ha), has shown considerable selectivity to these crops. Amongst other promising preemergent herbicides are linuron (0.75 kg/ha), acetochlor (1.0 kg/ha), imazethapyr (0.1 kg/ha), alachlor (1-2 kg/ha), metolachlor (0.5-0.75 kg/ha), chloramben (1 kg/ha), terbutryn (0.5 kg/ha), fluorodifen, oxyfluorfen, and pendimethalin (0.5 kg/ha). The crop selectivity and weed control are greatly dependent upon soil type, atmospheric temperature, and rainfall. In summer season, usually both, crop selectivity and weed control effects of preemergence herbicides are less consistent in beans.

Table 21.12: Effect of Different Weeding Methods on The Yield of Irrigated Chickpea (*var.* C-235) at Durgapura (India) During 1989-90 to 1991-92 (From Research Highlights 1992 of RAU, Bikaner (India) 41-42)

Treatments	Grain yield of chickpea (Pooled data of 3 yrs)		B : C
	(q/ha)	(% increase)	
Unweeded check	4.05	–	–
Hand-weeded twice (25, 45 d.a.s.)	14.77	264.7	8.12
Fluchloralin (0.5 kg/ha) + Hand-weeding (45 d.a.s)	13.74	239.3	6.56
Fluchloralin (0.75 kg/ha) + Hand-weeding (45 d.a.s.)	15.46	281.7	6.23
C.D. (at P = 0.05)	1.99	–	–

Note: Fluchloralin was applied as PPI.

Comments: *Preplant incorporation of fluchloralin at 0.5-0.75 kg/ha could replace one operation of hand-weeding in chickpea to give pulse yield equal to the twice hand-weeded crop. Herbicidal use in this crop can obviate problem of labour scarcity wherever it is so.*

Table 21.13: Effects of Herbicides and Physical Methods of Weed Control On the Performance of Blackgram (*var.* Krishna) During 1982 at Udaipur (India) (After Gupta and Chaudhry, 1986).

Treatments	Dry weed biomass 40 d.a.s	Grain yield of blackgram		B : C
	(q/ha)	(q/ha))	(% increase)	
Unweeded check	12.54	3.65	–	–
Hoed twice (30, 45 d.a.s.)	6.21	6.95	100.0	9.62
Hand-weeded (4 times)	4.48	7.67	110.1	1.67
Fluchloralin (PPI, 1.5 kg/ha) + Hoed once	2.95	11.08	203.6	4.11
Terbutryn (PE, 0.5 kg/ha) + Hoed once, 30 d.a.s.	3.61	10.75	194.5	13.90
Pendimethalin (PE, 0.5 kg/ha) + Hoed once,30 d.a.s.	3.87	10.34	183.3	4.69
C.D. (at P = 0.05)	1.02	0.75	–	–

Comments: *Herbicidal cum physical control of weeds in blackgram proved significantly more productive than the physical methods alone, with resulting Benefit/Cost ratios of 4.11 to 13.90. Since most of the soil-applied herbicides hold back the weeds for about 30 days, one hoeing at this stage is essential to prevent crowding by the second flush of weeds. (This is true for most of other crops too).*

Postemergence treatment with bentazon (0.75-1.5 kg/ha) at 2-trifoliate leaf stage of mungbean is found suitable for the control of solid stands of broadleaf weeds and sedges in this crop. Other promising postemergence herbicides in beans include fluazifop-p-butyl (0.25-0.375 kg/ha), clodinafop (0.375-0.75 kg/ha), and quizalofop-ethyl (0.5-1.0 kg/ha).

Table 21.14: Role of Metolachlor for Weed Control in Greengram at Bhatinda (India) During 1989 & 1990 (After Sandhu *et al.* 1993)

Treatments	Dry weed biomass (Pooled data of two years) (q/ha)	Pulse yield of mungbean (q/ha)		
		1989	1990	Mean
Unweeded check	9.81	5.1	6.5	5.8
Hand-weeded (20, 40 d.a.s.)	6.19	12.7	9.6	11.1
Metolachlor (PE, 0.75 kg/ha)	8.26	11.01	9.27	10.1
C.D. (at P = 0.05)	4.01	2.27	0.66	1.5

Comments: *Preemergent metolachlor gave as good greengram yield as the twice hand-weeded crop. But more usually, one weeding is stll required after the use of a preemergence herbicide.*

21.4.3 Pigeonpea (*Cajanus cajan* L.)

Pigeonpea is comparatively longer duration pulse crop than other pulses. Therefore, it often requires 2-3 hand-weedings to keep the crop weedfree in initial stages of its growth, before it closes in. Herbicides are now available which can replace 1-2 manual weedings in this crop. These are all soil active herbicides applied either as preplant or preemergence treatments. Two herbicides found promising in tests conducted in India are **pendimethalin** (0.75-1.0 kg/ha) and **alachlor** (1-1.5 kg/ha). Quizalofop-ethyl (0.04-0.05 kg/ha) has proved a good postemergence herbicide against annual grasses in pigeonpea.

Table 21.15: Weed Control in Pigeonpea Through Pendimethalin in Karnataka (India) During 1989-90 (After Itnal *et al.*, 1993)

Treatments	Pulse yield (q/ha)	% increase
Unweeded check	3.60	–
Hand-weeded (20, 40, 60 d.a.s)	13.16	265.6
Pendimethalin (PE, 1 kg/ha)	9.16	154.4
Pendimethalin (PE, 1 kg/ha) + Intercultivated once (30 d.a.s.)	11.15	209.7
C.D. (at. P = 0.05)	0.94	-

Comments: *A long duration crop of pigeonpea responded positively to three manual weedings. A preemergence herbicide could substitute for two of these.*

Table 21.16: Role of Herbicidal Control in Pigeonpea at Bangalore (India), During 1988 (After Maheswarappa and Nanjappa, 1994)

Treatments	Dry weed biomass (q/ha)	Pulse yield (q/ha)	% increase
Unweeded check	34.1	4.35	–
Hand-weeded (25, 45 d.a.s.)	0.35	16.02	268.3
Alachlor (PE, 1 kg/ha) + I hand-weeding (45 d.a.s.)	0.45	15.26	250.8
C.D. (at P = 0.05)	–	1.04	–

***Comments:** Herbicidal control in pigeonpea could substitute effectively for one hand-weeding; a step towards integrated weed management.*

21.4.4 Pea (*Pisum sativum* L.)

MCPB is a widely used herbicide in pea against broadleaf weeds, including thistles. Applied at 5 to 6-leaf stage, the field pea will tolerate up to 1-1.5 kg/ha of the herbicide. A major precaution in its use is not to use more than 250 l/ha water in the spray solution. The idea is to prevent MCPB from falling on the soil where it gets biodegraded to MCPA which is phytotoxic to the pea plants. Against dense growth of perennial thistles a mixture of MCPB and MCPA (3:2) applied at early bud stage of the weed, has proved superior to MCPB although it may cause some crop injury.

Another herbicide that has found favour for broadleaf control in pea is **dinoseb** (Na or amine salt). It is applied at 2.25 kg/ha when pea plants are 5-15 cm tall. When annual grasses become problematic in pea, preemergence herbicides like chlorbromuron, prometryn, chloroxuron, linuron, propazine, dinoseb, and alloxydim may be tried. Preplant diallate is specific to wildoat control in pea. Of late, preplant **fluchloralin** (1-1.5 kg/ha) has proved excellent in the selective control of a mixed growth of weeds in this grain legume.

Table 21.17: Comparative Weed Control in Pea Through Herbicides at Ludhiana (India) During 1989-90 and 1990-91 (After Kundra *et al.*, 1993)

Treatments	Pooled data of two years		B : C
	Dry weed biomass (q/ha)	Pulse yield (q/ha)	
Unweeded check	32.2	11.91	–
Hand-weeded (20, 35 d.a.s.)	4.3	19.00	4.5
Pendimethalin (PE, 0.75 kg/ha)	3.80	20.01	9.9
Methibenzuron (PE, 1.31 kg/ha)	5.7	19.05	10.2
C. D. (at P = 0.05)	3.4	1.70	–

***Comments:** The herbicidal control in pea was almost 2.5 to 3.0 times more remunerative than manual weedings.*

21.4.5 Lentil (*Lens culinaris* Medic.)

The weed problems in lentil are very much similar to those given above for the field pea. Of the herbicidal possibilities, the prominent ones are: *Preemergent* pendimethalin (0.5 kg/ha), linuron (0.5-1.0 kg/ha), trifluralin (0.5-1.0 kg/ha), and isoproturon (0.5 kg/ha); and *Postemergence* quizalofop-ethyl (0.04-0.05 kg/ha).

Table 21.18: Efficacy of Pendimethalin for Weed Control in Lentil (*var.* 9-12) at Ludhiana (India) During 1989 (After Parmar *et al.*, 1994)

Treatments	Dry weed biomass (q/ha)	Pulse yield of lentil (q/ha)	% increase
Unweeded check	48.0	3.6	–
Hand-weeded	–	13.5	275.0
Pendimethalin (PE, 1.0 kg/ha)	15.21	13.2	266.7
C.D. (at P = 0.05)	1.5	1.4	–

Comments: *herbicidal control was as productive in lentil as manual weeding. (Number of weedings not mentioned in the paper).*

21.4.6 Rajmash (*Phaseolus vulgaris* L.)

Cultivation of rajmash beans has gained wide popularity in India, particularly in her hilly tracts and adjoining northern plains. Very effective weed control has been reported in this crop with *preemergence* alachlor (0.75-1.0 kg/ha), pendimethalin (0.45-1.0 kg/ha), and metolachlor (1.5 kg/ha).

21.4.7 Dolicus beans (*Dolichus lablab*)

Preemergence fluchloralin (0.5-1.0 kg/ha) and oxadiazon (0.5 kg/ha) have been found in field research highly selective to dolicus bean, with acceptable weed control.

21.4.8 Cowpea (*Vigna ungiculata* Walp.)

Cowpea (also called Southern pea), is considered a fast germinating, smother crop, with capability to suppress the latter germinating weeds. But in situations where the weeds germinate along with the crop, even this smother crop requires early weeding; else cowpea itself may be smothered by the weeds. To guard against the situation, early freedom of the crop from weeds can be achieved with: either *preplant* fluchloralin (1.0 kg/ha) or *Preemergence* oxadiazon (0.4 kg/ha), butachlor (1.5 kg/ha), trifluralin (1.0 kg/ha), and alachlor (0.75 kg/ha).

21.4.9 Clusterbean (*Cyamopsis tetragonoloba* (L.) Taub)

Although a grain legume, clusterbean is not exactly a pulse crop in the country. It is highly adapted to the drylands of Indian plains as a feed, fodder, and commercial gum crop. It is invaded by several summer weeds in its early growth period. Usually one hand-weeding about 30 d.a.s. is sufficient to save the crop from competition form weeds, though in irrigated situation, a second weeding about 45 d.a.s. may also be needed.

Amongst the herbicides tried thus far, preplant soil incorporation of **fluchloralin** (1-1.5 kg/ha) and preemergent **pendimethalin** (0.5-0.75 kg/ha) have held promise in clusterbean. Other preemergent herbicides worth trial are chloroxuron, DCPA, diphenamid, linuron, and trifluralin.

Table 21.19: Effect of Weeding Methods on The Performance of Clusterbean (*var.* HG-75) at Bawal (India) During 1992 (After Anon, 1994)

Treatments	Dry weed biomass (at crop harvest) (q/ha)	Grain yield of clusterbean (q/ha)	% increase
Unweeded check	14.1	9.9	–
Hand-weeded (30 d.a.s.)	3.5	14.8	49.5
Fluchloralin (PPI, 1.0 kg/ha	2.2	21.3	115.2
Pendimethalin (PE, 0.5 kg/ha)	8.8	13.2	33.3
C.D. (at P = 0.05)	1.8	3.2	–

***Comments:** In clusterbean, fluchloralin proved at par with hand-weeding and significantly superior to pendimethalin.*

21.5 SUGAR CROPS

21.5.1 Sugarcane (*Saccharum officinarum* L.)

The Weed Problem: Sugarcane takes about 30 days to germinate. During this long period a variety of summer weeds, including nutsedge, invade the sugarcane fields. These weeds reduce crop germination and early crop vigour, probably by competing for soil moisture and/or by exerting their adverse allelopathic effects on the cane sprouts. Subsequently, frequent irrigations and high temperatures induce a number of new flushes of weeds, both grasses and broadleafs. Johnsongrass (*Sorghum halepense*), bermudagrass (*Cynodon dactylon*), and several species of morningglories (*Ipomoea* spp.) pose special weed problems in sugarcane in different areas. Sugarcane tonnage is reduced heavily up to 80% or more at the hands of weeds, if these were left uncontrolled. This damage is by way of reduced length and girth of internodes and less number of millable canes per unit area. Besides, the stunted weedy canes become bunchy because of forced germination of their buds on the shoots. A weedy 'plant cane' leads to a weedy 'ratoon cane'.

The Weed Management: A healthy crop stand is primary to any weed management programme in sugarcane. In weak and gappy cane adequate weed control is hard to achieve.

Physical control of weeds in sugarcane begins with a 'blind hoeing' before the cane sprouts are seen over the ground. Later, during the tillering phase of the crop, manual and mechanical row cultivations are done 2-3 times during the season. Finally the crop is earthed up, just before it enters its grand growth period. By this time a healthy crop of cane should close in sufficiently to smother any new weed seedlings. *Ipomoea* sp. and the like trailing weed species, may, however, still survive by climbing the cane plants. Herbicides can be very usefully employed to supplement physical control of weeds in sugarcane to achieve higher yield targets and lower labour days. Preplant soil incorporation of **vernolate** (3-4 kg/ha) will provide effective control of nutsedge and many annual grasses for 4-6 weeks. Simazine (0.5-1.0 kg/ha) may be combined with it to achieve simultaneous control of broadleaf weeds. Another substitute to blind hoeing in sugarcane is the application of a mixture of **atrazine** (0.25 kg/ha) and **2,4-D** (1 kg/ha), couple of days before crop emergence. Nutsedge and broadleaf weeds prove particularly susceptible to the mixture. The same treatment can be applied to ratoon cane after shaving off. Inclusion of phytobland oil (5%) in the mixture will further improve control of young grasses. Paraquat, diquat, MSMA, DSMA (2-3 kg/ha), amitrole (0 2 to 1% solution), and herbicidal oils (450-650 1/ha) can also substitute blind hoeing in sugarcane. The choice among these alternatives depends upon the weed species present at the time of treatment.

Successful preemergence herbicides in sugarcane include **atrazine**, simazine, thiazopyr, pendimethalin, CDAA, metribuzin, and terbacil. Atrazine and simazine (1-2 kg/ha) will hold the weeds for 4-6 weeks. It is important that these herbicides are applied after, and not before, a due postplant irrigation. CDAA (3-5 kg/ha) is used in cane grown on heavy, organic matter rich soils. It is effective mainly against annual grasses. To improve its broadleaf control capability, atrazine may be combined with CDAA. **Metribuzin** (0.75-3 kg/ha) has been found a superior preemergence herbicide in sugarcane. Terbacil (3.5 kg/ha) is also found highly selective to sugarcane. Broadleaf weeds in established sugarcane can be knocked with 2,4-D, picloram, silvex, thiazopyr, or metribuzin, depending upon the weed species and the crop growth. 2,4-D (up to 1 kg/ha) can be applied as a semi-directed spray at about eight weeks' age of sugarcane, **Picloram** has proved superior to 2,4-D against the perennial dicot weeds. Sugarcane is tolerant to its over-the-top application at 2-2.5 kg/ha rates. Silvex (0.75-1 kg/ha) is employed in ratoon cane after shaving-off, to control certain rough broadleaf weeds. A mixture of isoproturon (1-2 kg/ha) and 2,4-DEE (0.25-0.3 kg/ha) applied 9 days after planting cane has also been reported highly effective.

Asulam has been announced successful against grasses as an over-the-top treatment of grass infested sugarcane. Limited patches of perennial grasses in sugarcane can be destroyed with 0.5-1.0% dalapon or glyphosate spray.

21.5.2 Sugarbeet (*Beta vulgaris* L.)

In variance with sugarcane, sugarbeet is a winter season crop in tropical countries. Broadleaf weeds, such as *Chenopodium album, C. murale,* and *Amaranthus* spp. are particularly troublesome during the early establishment of the crop.

A combination of herbicide and row-cultivation seems the most practical answer to the weed problem in sugarbeet in the developing countries. **Pyrazon** (2.5-4 kg/ha) and **endothall** (0.75-1.5 kg/ha) are versatile herbicides for broadleaf weed control in sugarbeet. Besides their preemergence use, pyrazon can also be applied after the first true leaf develops in sugarbeet, but before thinning of the crop. Endothall (3-6.5 kg/ha), likewise, can be applied at 4 to 6-leaf stage of beets. Metamitron (1-2 kg/ha) and phenmedipham (1-2 kg/ha) are applied at 3-leaf stage of the crop. Ethofumesate is another good selective, postemergence herbicide for the control of broadleaf weeds in sugarbeet. For preplant broadleaf weed control in this crop currently EPTC and trifluralin are registered.

To control annual grasses in sugarbeet, (i) *preplant* cycloate (3-4 kg/ha), (ii) *postemergent* phenmedipham (1-2 kg/ha), alloxydim (sodium) (1.25-2.5 kg/ha), and dalapon (2-4 kg/ha); and *preemergent* lenacil (0.4-1 kg/ha) are found satisfactory. Against wildoat (*Avena fatua*), postemergent barban is more effective.

Table 21.20: Effect of Selected Weed Control Treatments on The Weed Density And Yield of Sugarcane (var. Co-419) at Udaipur (India) During 1989-90 And 1990-91 (From Research Highlights, 1992, RAU, Bikaner (India) 53-54)

Treatments	Weed density per sq m 80. d.a.s. (Mean of two years)	Sugarcane yield (t/ha)			% increase
		1989	1990	Mean	
Unweeded check	94.5	57.3	56.7	57.0	–
Hand-weeded once + Hoed twice	–	105.6	110.2	107.9	89.3
Atrazine (PE, 1 kg/ha)	10.1	74.2	90.1	82.1	44.0
Atrazine + Hoeing (60 d.a.s.)	8.5	123.7	109.1	116.4	104.2
C.D. (at P = 0.05)	–	10.51	5.24	–	–

Comments: *In a long duration crop like sugarcane, three manual weedings were needed before earthing up of the crop for getting desired weed control. Preemergent atrazine with only one manual weeding could give even better sugarcane yields than three weedings, which clearly supports the need for integrated weed management.*

21.6 FIBRE CROPS

21.6.1 Cotton (*Gossypium* spp.)

Early competition from weeds can drastically curtail the fibre yield of cotton, far more than the reduction in its vegetative growth might suggest. At the end of growing season, late weeds can interfere with mechanical picking of cotton, cause staining of lint, and induce ginning problems. In India, the weed problem in cotton is more serious in the monsoon-planted crops. In summer cottons the first irrigation is applied 30 to 45 days after sowing, which delays the main flush of weeds sufficiently to allow the crop plants to establish themselves. In some fields, however, nutsedge and bermudagrass can be serious in the summer period. In the monsoon sown cotton crops, on the contrary, a variety of annual grasses and broadleaf weeds invade the fields right at the time of crop emergence.

In most cotton growing areas of Africa, Asia, and Latin America weeds are controlled by repeated intercultivations with manual, animal, or tractor power. Within the crop rows, weeds are then removed by labour intensive hand hoeing. In hill-planted cotton of equal row and plant spacings, however, cross cultivation can be adopted. A good seedbed preparation and timely planting of cotton can reduce considerable burden of intercultivations.

Herbicides can very well supplement row cultivations in cotton to further improve crop production and quality. Being a cash crop, farmers can afford even a sequential herbicide treatment in cotton.

Trifluralin (0.5-1.0 kg/ha), **fluchloralin** (0.75-1.5 kg/ha), and pendimethalin (1.2-1.5 kg/ha) are notable preplant incorporated herbicides for early suppression of annual grasses in cotton. Trifluralin is known to reduce lateral root development in cotton in the treated zone, but it does not affect its fibre yield. On the contrary the morphological change in roots makes the crop more tolerant to a preemergence herbicide by limiting its uptake by cotton.

A dinitroaniline application to cotton fields is often followed by a preemergence application of **diuron** (0.5-1.5 kg/ha) or **fluometuron** (1-1.5 kg/ha). Besides, the substituted ureas, acetanilides such as alachlor and propachlor, and triazines such as prometryn, cyanazine, and dipropetryn are also used as preemergence herbicides in cotton but to a limited extent. Dipropetryn and prometryn are particularly preferred in cotton grown on light soils. Alachlor is the choice when nutsedge is problematic, in addition to annual grasses. Pendimethalin has also been used as a preemergence herbicide.

It may be pointed out that in summer cotton crops in India, preemergence herbicides often remain ineffective because of dry soil surface at the time of treatment. In this season, therefore, postemergence herbicides should be considered. In the monsoon-planted cotton crops too, despite the use of preemergence herbicides, the pressure from weeds is often so great that further weed control measures are needed following early crop establishment. Row cultivation is one good choice for this purpose. Alternatively, diuron or fluometuron could be sprayed against annual, young weeds after the cotton plants have grown 15 cm or taller. The diuron (0.5 kg/ha) spray must carry 0.5% of a suitable wetting agent in the spray solution. Arsenicals, MSMA, and DSMA are developed to control perennial weeds like *Cyperus rotundus* and *Sorghum halepense*, as directed spray treatments. The arsenicals are miscible with fluometuron and diuron and they can be applied any time up to the flowering time of cotton.

Glyphosate (3.5 kg/ha) is a choice for dealing with more obnoxious perennial weeds like *Cynodon dactylon*, standing between the cotton rows. It is applied as directed spray through hooded sprayers.

Of late, metribuzin, bentazon, and methazole are introduced as postemergence herbicides for broadleaf control in cotton. Likewise, norflurazon, perfluidone, fluridone, ethalfluralin, **pendimethalin**, methazole, butachlor, metolachlor, oxyfluorfen, thiazopyr, acetochlor, and tetrafluron are new preemergence herbicides at various stages of testing in cotton. Pendimethalin has been specifically used for the control of *Trianthema* spp. as lay-by treatment. Glufosmate ammonium and glyphosate are recommended in cotton as directed spray for broadspectrum control of young weed growths. Postemergent pyrithiobac for broadleaf control and fluazifop butyl for grass control are also lately recommended in cotton.

Table 21.21: Effect of Pendimethalin on Weed Control and Cotton Yield During 1991 and 1992 in Haryana (After Panwar *et al.*, 1995)

Treatments	Dry weed biomass (q/ha)	Seed cotton yield (q/ha)			% increase
	(Mean of 2 yrs.)	1991	1992	Mean	
Unweeded check	22.0	10.2	14.40	12.3	–
Handweeded twice	–	21.0	26.7	23.8	93.5
Pendimethalin (PE, 1.5 kg/ha)	12.2	17.1	19.5	18.3	48.8
Pendimethalin (PE 1.5 kg/ha) + Hoed once (30 d.a.s.)	6.8	18.4	22.7	20.6	67.5
C.D. (at P = 0.05)	–	3.8	4.8	–	–

Comments: *Preemergent pendimethalin could substitute for only one manual weeding to get yields equal to the twice hand-weeded crop. Without combining the herbicide with one hand-weeding, the seed cotton yields were reduced. This is because the hot, desiccating winds prevailing at the time of sowing cotton in April/May, aggravate herbicide volatile loss. Much improvement is needed to make herbicidal control in this crop more attractive under Indian conditions.*

(In the USA, glyphosate is used widely in the glyphosate resistant transgenic, cotton varieties – Chapter 16).

21.6.2 Jute (*Chorcorus* spp.)

Weeding is the most costly input in the cultivation of jute. And invariably the period of maximum labour demand for weeding jute is during 30-55 days after sowing, which coincides with the transplanting of paddy. Since the farmers have to give preference to the latter operation, the jute crops frequently continue to suffer from weeds. The jute farmers in India and Bangladesh, therefore, look forward eagerly to an effective herbicidal control, even though it may cost little more than manual weeding. Most research on herbicides in jute has been conducted at the Indian Central Jute Research Institute (Barrackpore). The first successful herbicide accepted widely by the jute growers was **dalapon**. It is recommended to be applied as a semi-directed spray at 7.5 kg/ha when the jute plants are 3 to 4 weeks old. Dalapon destroys most species of young weeds, particularly grasses. Addition of 0.5% of a suitable weeting agent to the spray tank should improve weed control. The treatment also partly substitutes manual crop thinning. Postemergent MSMA at 4 to 4.5 kg/ha has often proved superior to dalapon in jute but it is applied strictly as directed spray through shielded nozzles. A mixture of dalapon and MSMA, each at half the dose, can also be used the same way.

Early tests with preplant incorporated herbicides *eg* EPTC, pebulate, and molinate gave encouraging results. Later, preplant **tetrapion** was found much superior to these herbicides as well as to dalapon and MSMA in jute. Its effective rates are 3 to 4 kg/ha and it is to be incorporated in fields 10 days before seeding jute (Saraswat and Ray, 1980). Another successful preplant herbicide in jute is **fluchloralin**. At 0.45-0.9 kg/ha it has provided excellent selective control of weeds in this crop (Mukhopadhyay and Ghosh, 1979). More recent researches have shown postemergent **fluazifopbutyl** effective in controlling grasses, at 0.4-0.5 kg/ha. **Pendimethalin** at 0.75 kg/ha has been found a very effective preemergence herbicide in this fibre crop.

Table 21.22: Efficacy of fluazifop butyl in Weed Control in Tossa Jute in West Bengal (India) During Two Years (After Das *et al.*, 1994)

Treatments	Dry weed biomass (q/ha)	Fibre yield of jute (q/ha)			% increase
	(Mean of two years)	1987	1989	Mean	
Unweeded check	154	9.38	7.49	8.5	–
Hand-weeded twice (21, 35 d.a.s.)	0	33.08	23.52	28.3	232.9
Fluazifopbutyl (0.4 kg/ha, 21 d.a.s.) + Hand-weeded once	0	29.29	18.51	23.9	181.2
C.D.(at P = 0.05)	–	4.92	9.29	–	–

***Comments:** Postemergent fluazifop butyl could substitute for one manual weeding in jute to get fiber yields equal to the twice hand-weeded crop.*

21.7 STIMULANT CROPS AND SEED SPICES

21.7.1 Tobacco (*Nicotiana* spp.)

There are two major weed problems in tobacco cultivation. *First*, a thick growth of mixed species of weeds in the nurseries. *Second*, invasion of tobacco by parasitic *Orobanche* in the fields. The most prevalent practice of weeding tobacco nurseries in tropical and subtropical countries is hand-pulling. In the western world, however, temporary soil sterilants like methyl bromide (5-10 kg 100 m^{-2}), metham ((2-5 kg 100 m^{-2}), calcium cyanamide (50-70 kg 100 m^{-2}) or a pretransplant, incorporated herbicide like diphenamid (3-6 kg/ha) are advocated for raising weedfree tobacco nurseries. The waiting period before tobacco seeds can be sown in the treated nurseries varies form 2 to 30 days, depending upon the compound used. In the main field, tobacco transplants have shown tolerance to benefin (1-1.5 kg/ha), metobromuron (1-2 kg/ha), and pebulate (3.5-4.5 kg/ha) for general weed control.

Table 21.23: Weed Control in Flue-cured Tobacco Through Diphenamid, During 1978-81, at Rajamundri (India) (After Raghavaiah and Sannibabu, 1991)

Treatments	Pooled data of four years		% increase
	Weed control efficacy (WCE)**	Yield of cured leaf tobacco (q/ha)	
Unweeded check	–	2.93	–
Hand-weeded	71.8	13.73	368.6
Diphenamid (6 kg/ha, 7 d.b.t.)*	53.3	13.35	355.6
C.D. (at P = 0.05)	–	2.66	–

Note: *dbt = days before transplanting.

** Orobanche spp. was not present in this experiment.

***Comments:** Diphenamid was a very suitable herbicide for the control of common weeds in transplanted tobacco.*

Against *Orobanche* (broom rape) in particular, soil fumigation with DMTT granules at 300-350 kg/ha, about 30-40 days before transplanting tobacco, is found effective. But the treatment is infeasible on any large scale.

Tests have been made from time to time with postemergence herbicides to destroy established *Orobanche*. In this respect, glyphosphate (50-500 g/ha), MH-T (1.5% spray), and **allyl alcohol** (0.1-0.2%) have been very promising (see also Chapter 23).

21.7.2 Opium Poppy (*Papaver somniferum*)

Establishing opium poppy is a gamble in weeds. Initially its seedlings grow extremely slow for a month and, thus, get easily crowded by weeds. Thereafter, its leaves grow horizontally close to the ground for considerable period and the crop continues to be prone to weeds. Further, poppy being a crop of heavy soils, it is visited by several flushes of weeds.

The first agronomic improvement needed in opium poppy production is the development of a suitable, soil active herbicide with adequate residual activity to keep the weeds in check for at least initial four weeks. Thus far, preemergent **chlortoluron** and **asulam** have shown promise in this respect in the initial tests conducted in India (Singh and Turkhede, 1981). Their selective rates are 0.5-1.0 kg/ha. These herbicides can also be tried for postemergence treatment of poppy. While chlortoluron is more effective against broadleaf weeds, asulam is more so against the monocots.

21.7.3 Cumin (*Cuminum cyminum* L.)

Cumin is largely sown by broadcast. The emerging crop seedlings are so badly infested with weeds that farmers have to often abandon the sown fields. In India, besides several common winter weeds, *Jeeri* (*Plygonum pumila* Wild) is a very notorious weed in cumin. Its seeds resemble very much the cumin seeds, which are difficult to separate from the crop seeds. Also, during the vegetative phase, *P. pumila* plants resemble the cumin plants and, thus, escape manual weeding. But, fortunately, now herbicides are available which kill *jeeri* weed without harming cumin.

Table 21.24: Herbicidal Control in Cumin at Junagadh (India) During 1981 to 1983 (After Kavani *et al.*, 1989)

Treatments	Pooled data of 3 years		B : C
	Dry weed biomass at crop harvest (q/ha)	Grain yield (q/ha)	
Unweeded check	27.55	2.51	–
Hand-weeded (per ha 278 labour days)	–	5.10	(–)
Fluchloralin (PE, 0.9 kg/ha)	7.86	4.67	4.24
Oxadiazon (PE, 1.0 kg/ha)	4.63	4.93	8.48
Benthiocarb (PE, 2.0 kg/ha)	8.18	4.63	5.17
C.D. (at P = 0.05)	–	1.05	–

Comments: *Herbicidal control in cumin was a highly remunerative proposition, with B:C of up to over 8.0, against a total loss in the manually weeded crop.*

Preplant **fluchloralin** and trifluralin have been found versatile herbicide in this respect. Their effective rates are 0.75 to 1.0 kg/ha. Fluchloralin can also be applied in cumin with first irrigation, either simultaneously or just after it. Besides fluchloralin, preemergence herbicides, mainly oxadiazon (1 kg/ha), benthiocarb (1-2 kg/ha), oxyfluorfen (0.2-0.5 kg/ha), pendimethalin (1 kg/ha) and terbutryn (0.5-1.0 kg/ha) are reported selective to the crop.

21.7.4 Fenugreek (*Trigonella foenum-graceum* L.)

In a slow growing and frequently irrigated crop like fenugreek, several common winter weeds grow profusely and pull down its yield to less than half. Although two manual weedings, 20 and 40 d.a.s. can save the crop from this menace, yet because of the growing shortage of labour, often one, or both manual weedings are neglected by the farmer, with consequent depressed growth of the crop. More recently, herbicidal control in fenugreek has met with success, particularly, in Rajasthan. Of the different herbicides, preemergence application of pendimethalin at 0.75 kg/ha has proved the best, with higher remunerative potential than manual weeding. Besides, preemergent oxadiazon (0.5 kg/ha) and metribuzin (0.15 kg/ha) have recently been found very promising in this spice crop.

Table 21.25: Herbicidal Control of Weeds in Fenugreek (*var.* Nagouri) at Jobner (India) During 1982 & 1983 (After Maliwal and Gupta, 1989)

Treatments	Pooled data of two years		B : C
	Dry weed biomass (45 d.a.s.) (q/ha)	Grain yield (q/ha)	
Unweeded check	13.03	5.73	–
Hoed twice (20, 40 d.a.s.)	0.06	13.30	2.84
Pendimethalin (PE, 0.75 kg/ha)	3.28	11.86	3.54
C.D. (at P = 0.05)	–	1.34	–

Comments: *Preemergent pendimethalin was a more remunerative proposition than manual weeding in fenugreek.*

21.7.5 Coriander (*Coriandrum sativum* L.)

Like in other seed spices, weeds pose a serious problem in the cultivation of coriander. These weeds can be controlled effectively by 2-3 manual weedings in the early phase of the crop. But labour for the purpose is often not available and the crop suffers heavy yield losses. Now economical, selective control of weeds in coriander has been rendered possible with certain herbicides. In this respect, preplant application of fluchloralin (0.6-1.5 kg/ha) and preemergent pendimethalin (1.0-1.5 kg/ha) are of particular importance. Other herbicides reported successful at different places in India include: preemergent oxyfluorfen (0.08 kg/ha), pretilachlor (1.5 kg/ha), atrazine, prometryn, and trifluralin; and postemergent linuron and propanil.

21.7.6 Cardamom (*Elettaria cardamomum*)

In Kerala, one application of glyphosate (0.8 kg/ha) or three applications of paraquat (0.4 kg/ha) have been found highly effective treatments for weed management in cardamom.

21.7.7 Isabgol (*Blonde psillium*)

Preemergence: Isoproturon (0.5-0.75 kg/ha)

Postemergence: Oxadiargyl (0.05 kg/ha)

27.7.8 Java Citronella (*Cymopogon winterianus*)

Preemergence: Atrazine (2.0 kg/ha)

21.7.9 Coleus (*Coleus amboinicus*)

Preemergence: Oxyfluorfen (0.15 kg/ha)

21.7.10 Asgand (*Withania somnifera*)

Preemergence: Isoproturon (0.25-0.5 kg/ha)

21.8 FORAGE CROPS

21.8.1 Lucerne (*Medicago sativa* L.) and Berseem (*Trifolium alexandrinum* L.)

The Weed Problem: Weeds often pose a major problem in establishing new lucerne (alfalfa) and berseem (Egyptianclover) crops. During the first two cuttings, the lucerne and berseem forages frequently constitute 60% or more weeds in their biomass. Since in the tropics and subtropics lucerne and berseem are sown in the early phase of winter season, the weed flora in the first cutting comprise largely the summer broadleafs like *Amaranthus* and *Trianthema* spp. Later, at the second and subsequent cuttings, winter weeds like *Chenopodium* spp., *Cichorium intybus,* and *Coronopus didymus* dominate. High quality milch animals refuse to feed upon the weed-infested berseem and lucerne.

The lucerne crop is additionally infested with parasitic dodder (*Cuscuta* spp.). In fact, for the farmers in India and other like countries, *Cuscuta* spp. is the primary enemy of lucerne. Another weed of great concern in both lucerne and berseem is *Cichorium intybus*. It fouls the milk and milk products of animals feeding upon it. During the dormancy period of lucerne too, the weeds may grow luxuriantly. Unless controlled, such weeds weaken the lucerne clumps, sometimes to the extent of eliminating them altogether.

Weed Management Practices: (a) *Cultural aspects:* To keep weeds in low vigour in lucerne and berseem always use weed-free crop seeds to start with. This is particularly true for reducing *Cuscuta* infestation in lucerne. Weed seeds get easily mixed-up with lucerne and berseem seeds. The surest way to obtain weedfree forage seeds is to induce the farmers to reserve their own seed plots, which, of course, must be maintained completely weedfree, employing all available weeding methods.

Crop rotation is equally important for weed management in lucerne and berseem. In fact, it is the most practical method of eliminating *Cuscuta* from lucerne farms. *Cuscuta* fails to infest other winter crops like wheat and gram, although it germinates readily with them. In rotation with these crops, the parasite is, thus, forced into a 'suicide'.

Of the several seed cleaning devices available (Chapter 5), two are specially suited to clean lucerne and berseem seeds. The first method consists in dipping the seeds in a 5-10% solution of table salt for five minutes. Light weight weed seeds, like of chicory, dodder, and swinecress (*Coronpus* spp.) float, while the heavy forage seeds settle down at the bottom. It is important to freely wash the forage seeds thus cleaned with plenty of fresh water immediately to remove traces of the salt. The second method of seed cleaning is specific to separating dodder seeds from lucerne seeds. This requires a simple equipment with two felted rollers. While the *Cuscuta* seeds stick to the felt, the lucerne seeds being smooth, fall away from the rollers.

Planting of lucerne and berseem in stale seedbeds using paraquat to destroy weeds that germinate before seeding of the crops, has been found a very effective way of establishing lucerne and berseem. But the technique requires an extra irrigation. Besides, it would delay forage sowing by 7-10 days (Gupta and Bachhawat, 1976).

(b) *Herbicidal control:* Preplant soil incorporation of EPTC (1.5 kg/ha) or benefin (0.75-1.5 kg/ha) in plant lucerne has been successful in the selective suppression of common weeds. EPTC can also be used in berseem. Benefin is considered more selective to lucerne than EPTC. EPTC should not be used in fields where a triazine herbicide was applied the previous season since the two herbicides may interact to injure lucerne (and probably also berseem). Pendimethalin (0.5 kg/ha), fluchloralin (0.75 kg/ha), butachlor (2.0 kg/ha) and oxadiazon (0.5 kg/ha) have proved effective preemergence herbicides in plant crops of lucerne.

2,4-DB in lucerne (0.5-7.5 kg/ha) and MCPB in berseem (0.5 kg/ha) form most common postemergence herbicides for the control of broadleaf weeds. The 3 to 4-trifoliate leaf stages of lucerne and berseem are most tolerant to the two phenoxys. At this stage, if the weeds were very young, these could also be controlled with propham granules (4-5 kg *a.i.*/ha). Crop leaves should be dry at time of application of propham granules. More difficult broadleafs in lucerne can be hit with bromoxynil (0.4 kg/ha) or dinoseb (0.75/1.5 kg/ha). Dinoseb may injure lucerne at over 25°C. Simazine (0.75-1.0 kg/ha) can be employed as a preemergence herbicide in dense stands of lucerne during its early dormancy period. Late in the dormancy period, before the new lucerne shoots break through the ground, soil incorporation of trifluralin or nitralin (0.75-1.0 kg/ha) can provide season long weed control. Alternatively, at this time EPTC (1.5 kg/ha) can be applied by metering it through the irrigation channels. This avoids soil incorporation problems often encountered with trifluralin and nitralin.

Dodder control in lucerne with herbicides is gaining momentum in the developing countries. Farmers want to check this menace at any cost. Before the dodder has infected the lucerne shoots, granular application of chlorpropham (2 kg/ha) or pronamide (1.7 kg/ha) will prevent dodder development in lucerne for 3-5 weeks. Pronamide effect is somewhat longer lasting. The lucerne plants at the time of treatment should be at least

10 cm tall and its foliage should be dry. In the ratoon lucerne, the dose of chlorpropham can be increased up to 6 kg/ha, if needed. The ground should be sealed by irrigation immediately after application of the chlorpropham or pronamide granules. While chlorpropham acts by killing the germinating dodder seedlings, pronamide prevents circumnutation of dodder seedlings around the lucerne plants.

Dichlobenil (2 kg/ha) and DCPA (up to 10.0 kg/ha) granules are cleared for dodder control in lucerne grown for seed production, but not for forage production. These are used in the same manner as chlorpropham and pronamide.

In established lucerne the dodder infestations cannot be destroyed by any of the above mentioned herbicides. For this, paraquat (0.10-0.2% spray) is the best choice, at the present. It will desiccate both dodder and lucerne within 24 hours. But lucerne being a perennial plant will soon regrow from its crown buds after an irrigation while the sprayed dodder will fail to recover. Often a second application of paraquat is needed to contact the hidden and left-over dodder shoots. The practice of desiccating the weed with paraquat is superior to harvesting the weedy crop for animals since it prevents dissemination of dodder.

The destruction of dodder with paraquat may be followed by the application of chlorpropham or pronamide granules in lucerne to prevent its reinfestation from millions of dodder seeds present in the field.

21.8.2 Shaftal (*T. resupinatum*)

The weed problems in Shaftal or Persian clover are almost similar to those described for lucerne and berseem. The promising herbicides reported in this forage crop include pendimethalin (1.25 kg/ha), butachlor (1.0-1.5 kg/ha), and fluchloralin (0.67 kg/ha).

Table 21.26: Effect of Preemergence Herbicides on The Weed Biomass And Foage Yield of Maize During 1987 to 1989 (After Singh and Prasad, 1994).

Treatments	Dry biomass of *Trianthema* sp. 30 d.a.s. (Mean of 3 years) (q/ha)	Green fodder yield of maize (t/ha)				% increase
		1987	1988	1989	Mean	
Unweeded check	29.1	8.5	5.9	9.0	7.8	–
Hand-weeded twice	0	18.8	28.4	11.9	19.7	152.6
Atrazine (PE, 1.0 kg/ha)	0	34.3	45.1	37.4	38.9	398.7
Pendimethalin (PE, 1.0 kg/ha)	0	29.8	44.5	33.1	35.8	358.9
C.D. (at P = 0.05)	–	2.5	5.9	9.0	–	–

Comments: *Herbicidal control in fodder maize proved significantly superior to hand-weeding. In the manually weeded crop, the weeds regrew after second weeding while it was not so in the herbicide treated plots.*

21.8.3 Sorghum and Maize (fodder crops)

In comparison to their grain crops, very limited research work has been conducted on the forage crops of sorghum and maize. At the present, atrazine (0.5-0.75 kg/ha), both for preemergence and postemergence (at initial growth of forages) application, is found a very effective herbicide for ensuring weedfree establishment of these crops.

Herbicidal control in forage crops in India, in general, is unlikely to catch since still most farmers here do not hesitate feeding weeds to their animals.

21.9 INTER-CROPPING SYSTEMS

Inter-cropping is a part and parcel of Indian farming system, particularly in the dryland agriculture regions. The majority of research work on weed management in agriculture has been conducted with monocultures of different crops. It is so both because of the fact that in dryland agriculture there is hardly any scope of any new input beyond an odd, manual weeding. As such, whatever limited research work on this aspect has been reported, relates to inter-cropping farming in either irrigated or heavy rainfall areas. Some of the herbicides found suitable in specific intercropping systems are given below:-

1. Groundnut + Pigeonpea
   a) *Preemergence*: Pendimethalin, nitrofen, alachlor, fluchloralin
   b) *Postemergence*: Fluazifop-P.
2. Groundnut + Sunflower
   a) *Preemergence*: Alachlor, fluchloralin, metolachlor, trifluralin, pendimethalin.
   b) *Postemergence*: Fluazifop-P
3. Groundnut + Sorghum
   a) *Preemergence*: Alachlor, fluchloralin, pendimethalin
4. Cotton + Greengram or Blackgram
   a) *Preemergence*: Fluchloralin
5. Maize + Turmeric
   a) *Preemergence*: Pendimethalin
6. Potato + Wheat
   a) *Preemergence*: Isoproturon, pendimethalin
7. Wheat + Mustard
   a) *Preemergenee*: Pendimethalin, Oxyfluorfen
   b) *Postemergence*: Isoproturon
8. Maize + Soybean
   a) *Preemergence*: Fluchloralin, alachlor, oxyfluorfen
9. Maize + Pigeonpea
   a) *Preemergence*: Metolachlor
10. Chickpea + Linseed

a) *Preemergence*: Pendimethalin, isoproturon

11. Potato + Linseed

a) *Preemergence*: Pendimethalin, isoproturon

12. Potato + Mustard

a) *Preemergence*: Pendimethalin + Isoproturon, oxyfluorfen

13. Groundnut + Pigeonpea

a) *Preemergence*: Pendimethalin, oxyfluorfen (particularly to check *Trianthema monogyna*)

14. Wheat + Chickpea or Linseed

a) *Preemergence*: Pendimethalin + Isoproturon

15. Pea + Mustard

a) *Preemergence*: Pendimethalin, metolachlor, oxyfluorfen

16. Pigeonpea + Sorghum

a) *Preemergence:* Metribuzin + Metolachlor, pendimethalin, oxyfluorfen

17. Pigeonpea + Soybean

a) *Preemergence*: Pendimethalin, metribuzin, alachlor, oxyfluorfen

b) *Postemergence*: Fluazifop-P for the control of *Sorghum halepense*.

18. Greengram + Pearlmillet

a) *Premergence*: Pendimethalin

21.10 VEGETABLE CROPS

Most vegetables are initially slow growing crops, incapable of offering any competition to the aggressive weeds. Dense growth of weeds in vegetables hides fruits, which (i) are variously discoloured in the absence of natural light, (ii) become over-ripe, and (iii) finally rot. For harvesting vegetables at their intended development stage, the visibility of vegetables should not be hindered by weeds. Root vegetables are malformed in the presence of weeds because of underground competition for space. Insanitation due to weeds also increases burden of insect pests and diseases in vegetables.

Hand-weeding is the most common practice of weed control in vegetables in the country. Despite its high cost, it is sometimes favoured because of high cash returns from these crops. However, in summer and rainy season vegetables, repeated flushes of weeds make the operation ineffective, whence the farmers eagerly look forward to some selective herbicides.

Chemical control of weeds in vegetable farming is relatively new. Still, quite a few herbicides are made available for weeding vegetables, but unfortunately, no single herbicide controls all the weed species that may plague a vegetable field. Therefore, a system that combines herbicides with cultivation and other good crop husbandry practices like proper field selection, crop rotation, stale seedbeds, good land preparation, sanitation, and other cultural practices should be adopted.

Table 21.27: Promising Herbicide Recommendation in Common Vegetable Crops*

Type of treatment	Herbicide	Remark
21.10.1 VEGETABLE NURSERIES		
Fumigation	Metham (1 kg 20 m^{-2})	Treat the beds and drench with water for 48 hours. Cultivate 5-7 days later, and seed 7-15 days after it. Low temperatures (10°C) will reduce weed kill.
	Methyl bromide (1 kg 20 m^{-2})	Fumigate for 24 hours and seed 3 days later.
21.10.2 FIELD VEGETABLES		
1. **Arrowroot** (*Maranta arundinacea*)		
Preemergence	2, 4-D	
2. **Cabbage And Cauliflower** (*Brassica oleracea var. capitata* and *botrytis*)		
Preplant:	Nitralin, butralin, trifluralin, fluchloralin	Incorporate. Treat only direct seeded crops.
Preemergence:	Alachlor, CDAA, propachlor, CDEC, chlorpropham, DCPA, oxyfluorfen, butralin	
Pretransplant	Oxadiazon, pendimethalin	
Posttransplant:	Alachlor, CDAA, CDEC, DCPA, nitrofen	Apply as directed spray a week after transplanting. Do not use any wetting agent.
	Simazine, desmetryn	Apply at 3 to 4-leaf stage of the transplants.
3. **Carrot** (*Daucus carota var. sativa*).		
Preplant:	EPTC, trifluralin, flluchloralin.	Incorporate rapidly.
Preemergence:	Chlorbromuron, propham, linuron, metolachlor, metobromuron, metoxuron, oxyfluorfen, prometryn, propazine, chloroxuron, and pendimethalin.	
Postemergence:	Chlorbromuron, prometryn, Stoddard solvent	Apply at l-leaf stage of the crop.
	Chlorbromuron, chloroxuron, linuron, nitrofen	Suited to 3 to 4-leaf stage crop.
	Prometryn	Suited to 4 to 6-leaf stage of the crop.
4. **Cantaloupe** (*Cucurbita melo*)		
Preplant:	Vernolate	Incorporate rapidly.
Preemergence:	Naptalam, chloramben, CDEC	

* Note: For dose ranges of herbicides in this table please refer to Chapter 13.

Type of treatment	Herbicide	Remark
Postemergence	Naptalam, trifluralin, CDEC	Use only granular forms.
5. **Cassava** (*Manihot esculenta*)		
Preplant:	2,4-D (ester), chloramben	
Preemergence:	Several substituted triazine and urea herbicides hold promise, particularly fluometuron.	
6. **Colocasia** (=Taro) (*Colocasia* and *Xanthosoma* spp.)		
Preemergence:	Propanil	
Postemergence:	Ametryn, prometryn, triazine, prometone, diuron, and trifluralin	
7. **Cowpea** or **Southern pea** (*Vigna unguiculata*)		
Preplant	Trifluralin, pebulate	Incorporate rapidly.
Preemergence	Chlorthal, linuron	
8. **Cucumber** (*Cummis sativus*)		
Preplant:	Bensulide, trifluralin, fluchloralin	Incorporate quickly
Preemergence:	CDEC, dinoseb, nitralin, naptalam	Nitralin may-be mixed with soil.
9. **Dwarf bean** (*Phaselous vulgaris*)		
Preplant	Trifluralin, EPTC	Incorporate rapidly.
Preemergence:	Several substituted ureas, CDAA, CDEC, diphenamid, and chlorthal	
Early post emergence:	Dinoseb	Apply at crook stage of the crop.
10. **Brinjal** (*Solanum melongena*)		
Directed post-emergence:	DCPA	
Post-transplant	Alachlor, fluchloralin, oxyfluorfen, pendimethalin and metolachlor	Apply after the transplants are established but before weed emergence.
11. **French beans**		
Preemergence:	Fluchloralin, butachlor	
12. **Gourds**		
Preemergence:	Fluchloralin, butachlor, alachlor, oxadiazon	
13. **Ginger** (*Zingiber officinale*)		
Preemergence:	Simazine, diuron.	
14. **Lady's finger** or **Okra** (*Hibiscus esculentus*)		
Preplant:	Trifluralin, fluchloralin, EPTC	Incorporate quickly.
Preemergence:	Diphenamid, alachlor, prometryn, trifluralin, metolachlor, fluchloralin, pendimethalin, oxadiazon	
15. **Lima bean** (*Phaseolus lunatus*)		
Preplant:	Trifluralin	
Preemergence:	CDAA, CDEC, chlorpropham, chloramben, dinoseb (amine), chlorthal.	

Type of treatment	Herbicide	Remark
16. **Muskmelon** (*Cucumis melo*)		
Preplant:	DCPA, dinoseb	Incorporate two weeks before planting melons.
17. **Onion** and **Garlic** (*Allium* spp.)		
Pretansplant:	Nitralin, trifluralin, alachlor, oxyfluorfen, fluchloralin, bensulide, oxadiazon, pendimethalin	Apply 2-3 days before transplanting. Trifluralin should be limited to garlic. Do not incorporate oxyfluorfen and alachlor.
Pre-sowing:	Oxyfluorfen	Apply 2-3 days ahead of sowing seeds at 0.2 kg/ha and repeat 30 days latter at 0.15 kg/ha.
Preemerence:	CDDA, chlorpropham, allidochlor, DCPA, chloroxuron, pendimethalin, butachlor, alachlor, oxyfluorfen, pendimethalin, oxadiagryl, metolachlor, pretilachlor (with safener).	
Post-transplant:	Oxyfluorfen,	Apply 2-3 days after transplanting.
	Chloroxuron. nitrofen, propachlor	Apply about 25 days after transplanting.
18. **PEA** (*Pisum sativum* L.)		
Preemergence:	Pendimethalin, alachlor, isoproturon	Limit the row spacing to 30 cm.
19. **Pepper, Paprica, Chilli** (*Capsicum annum*)		
Preplant:	Bensulide, dazomet	Use in direct-seeded crops. Incorporate the herbicide.
	Nitralin, trifluralin, fluchloralin	Incorporate 4-6 weeks before transplanting.
Preemergence:	Bensulide, chlorpropham, diphenamid, alachlor, oxadiazon	
Postemergence:	Diphenamid	
Post-transplant:	Chloramben, bensulide, DCPA. Diphenamid, oxyfluorfen, pendimethalin, metolachlor	Apply as directed spray.
20. **Potato** (*Solanum tuberosum* L.)		
Preplant:	EPTC, fluchloralin	Incorporate rapidly. EPTC induces greater proportion of large tubers in the harvest.
Preemergence:	Metobromuron, alachlor, linuron, diphenamid, MCPA, pendimelhalin, isoproturon, metribuzin, oxyfluorfen, clomazone, chlorimuron-ethyl, CDAA, CDEC.	More selective on ridge-planted crops and on medium to heavy texture soils. Adjust the dose suitably, depending upon the soil types.
(Preemergence in seed potatoes	Atrazine, isoproturon, pendimethalin)	
		Specific against annual grasses.
Early postemergence:	Paraquat, diquat	Apply well before 10% emergence of the haulms, but after weed

Type of treatment	Herbicide	Remark
		emergence.
21. **Pumpkin** (*Cucurbita pepo*)		
Preemergence:	Chloramben, butachlor	
Pre-transplant:	Trifluralin	incorporate rapidly.
22. **Spinach** (*Spinacia oleracea*)		
Preplant:	Cycloate, propham	Use high seed rate. Incorporate the herbicide.
Preemergence:	CDEC, chlorpropham, dinoseb, endothall, monuron, norea, naptalam, trifluralin, alachlor, lenacil, propham, diuron	
Postemergence:	Propham	Apply at 2 to 4-leaf stage of the crop.
23. **Lettuce** (*Lactuca sativa*)		
Preemergence	Lenacil, propham, diuron	
24. **Squash** (*Cucurbita maxima*)		
Preplant:	Bensulide	Incorporate
Preemergence:	Chloramben, dinoseb, naptalam, butachlor	
Postemergence:	DCPA	Apply to weedfree rows, 4-6 weeks after seeding.
25. **Sweet potato** (*Ipomoea batatas*)		
Preplant:	EPTC, vernolate, fluchloralin	Incorporate
Post-transplant:	Chloramben, Chlorbromuron, CDAA, DCPA, diphenamid, EPTC, vernolate	Apply before weed emergence. Incorporate EPTC and vernolate.
Preemergence:	EPTC, pendimethalin, alachlor	Mix with soil.
26. **Tomato** (*Lycopersicum esculentum*)		
Preplant:	Pebulate, diphenamid, trifluralin, nitralin, bensulide, CDEC, napropamide, fluchloralin, Oxyfluorfen	Napropamide has long persistence. Do not incorporate oxyfluorfen.
Preemergence:	Bensulide, diphenamid, metribuzin, fluchloralin, alachlor	
Postemergence:	Diphenamid, trifluralin, nitralin	Apply as directed spray, after thinning the crop, but before weed emergence. Diphenamid can be applied as over-the-top treatment.
Pre-transplant:	Diphenamid, nitralin, pebulate, trifluralin	Apply 4-6 weeks before transplanting and incorporate.
At transplanting:	Bensulide, CDAA, CDEC, DCPA, oxyfluorfen	
Post-transplant:	Chloramben, diphenamid, linuron, metribuzin, pendimethalin.	Apply as directed spray about 3 to 30 days after transplanting.
27. **Turnip** (*Brassica campestris* var. *rapa*)		
Preplant:	Trifluralin	Incorporate rapidly.
Postemergence	Prometryn, chloroxuron	

Type of treatment	Herbicide	Remark
Preemergence:	DCPA, alachlor, diuron, trifluralin, linuron.	
28. **Radish**		
Preplant	EPTC	
Preemergence	Alachlor (12.0-1.5 kg/ha), metolachlor (1.0-1.5 kg/ha), TCA, trifluralin, diallate, linuron	
Postemergence	Nitrofen, prometryne, (at 3 leaf crop stage) chloroxuron (at 15 day's crop growth stage).	
29. **Watermelon** (*Citrullus vulgaris*)		
Preplant:	Bensulide, trifluralin	Incorporate quickly.
Preemergence:	CDEC, naptalam	
Postemergence:	DCPA	Apply 4 weeks after seeding.
30. **Yam** (*Dioscorea alata*)		
Preemergence:	Atrazine; chloramben, diuron	
Post-transplant:	DCPA	

Table 21.28: Evaluation of Herbicidal Control in Okra at Palampur (India) During 1985 (After Singh *et al.*, 1993).

Treatments	Dry weed biomass (q/ha)	Fruit yield of okra (q/ha)	B : C
Unweeded check	13.9	10.94	–
Hand-weeded	0	106.82	7.2
Fluchloralin (PPI, 1.25 kg/ha)	3.5	72.71	20.1
C.D. (at P = 0.05)	–	16.26	–

Comments: *Herbicidal control in okra proved about 3 times more remunerative per Re. spent on weeding, despite its lower production than by hand-weedings. This was because of higher cost of labour than herbicides.*

Table 21.29: Effect of Herbicidal Control in Transplanted* Onion (var. Pusa Red) at Dholi (India) During 1987 & 1988 (After Singh *et al.*, 1992)

Treatments	Dry weed biomass (Mean of two years) (q/ha)	Yield of onion (t/ha)			B : C
		1987	1988	Mean	
Unweeded control	9.4	9.3	8.6	9.0	–
Hand-weeded (20 & 40 d.a.s.)	2.1	16.5	14.5	15.5	8.1
Oxyfluorfen at 0.12 kg/ha, 3-5 d.b.t.	3.8	16.4	13.2	14.7	84.0
C.D. (at P = 0.05)	–	3.85	3.78	-	–

Note:* December end

d.b.t. = days before transplanting; d.a.s. = days after transplanting

Comments: *Herbicidal control in onion was about 10 times more remunerative than manual weeding, despite equal yields. High wages caused this effect.*

Table 21.30: Effect of Herbicidal Control on Performance of Potato (*var. Kufri Badshah*) at Kota (India) During 1990 and 1991 (From Research Highlights 1992, RAU, Bikaner, India: 72-73.

Treatments	Pooled data of two years		B : C
	Dry weed biomass (q/ha)	Tuber yield (q/ha)	
Unweeded check	28.22	226.8	-
Hand-weeded twice	1.61	248.3	2.44
Fluchloralin (PPI, 1 kg/ha)	2.87	382.5	33.96
Pendimethalin (PE, O.75 kg/ha)	2.83	274.2	12.05
Paraquat (EPOE, 1 kg/ha)	2.59	333.3	23.14
Isoproturon (PE, 1 kg/ha)	2.70	304.3	24.32
C.D. (at P = 0.05)	-	15.14	-

Note: EPOE = early postemergence

Comments: *Herbicidal control in potato proved 5-15 times more remunerative than manual weeding.*

SELECTED BIBLIOGRAPHY

1. Agiras, N. N. and Rana, M. C. 1990. Weed and phosphorous management in **gobhi sarson** (*Brassica napus*) under mid hill conditions of Himachal Pradesh. Ind. J. Weed Sci. 22:57-64.

2. Aldhous, J. R. 2000. Pesticides, Pollutants, Fertilizers, and Trees. Their Role inForests and Amenity Worldlands. Baldock, UK Research Studies Press Ltd. 588 p.

3. Amarjit, S., *et al.* 1994. Weed control in transplanted **rice** (*Oryza sativa*). Ind. J. Agro. 39(1):16-18.

4. Anantha Kumari, P. and Rao, V. N. 1993. Effect of different herbicides on weed control in lowland **rice**. Ind. J. Weed Sci. 25(2 & 3): 105-107.

5. Angiras, N. N. and S. Kumar, 2005. Efficacy of pyrazosulfuron-ethyl against weeds in **rice nursery** under mid-hill conditions of H.P. Ind. J. Weed Sci. 37(3 & 4): 202-204.

6. Anon, 1994. Performance of fluchloralin and pendimethalin in **clusterbean**. Ind. J. Weed Sci. 26(3-4):139-142.

7. Bajpai, R. P., *et al.* 1992. Weed control in upland drilled **rice**. Ind. J. Weed Sci. 24 (1 & 2) 69-71.

8. Bali, A. S. *et al.* 2006. Efficacy of herbicides in transplanted, medium-duration **rice** under sub-tropical conditions of Jammu. Ind. J. Agro. 51(2): 128-130.

9. Balusamy, M. *et al.* 1991. Economic weed control in **sugarcane**. Bharatiya Sugar 16(9):13-15.

10. Balyan, R. S. 2001. Evaluation of new herbicides against mixed weed flora in **wheat**. Ind. J. Weed Sci. 33:104-106.

11. Balyan, R. S. and Malik, R. K. 194. Chemical weed control studies in **barley** (*Hordeum vulgare*). Ind. J. Weed Sci. 26 (182): 1-5.

12. Balyan, R. S. *et al.*, 1994. Atrazine as postemergence herbicide for weed control in **maize**. Ind. J. Weed Sci. 26(3-4):35-39.

13. Banga, R. S. and A. Yadav. 2004. Effect of fenoxaprop and sulfosulfuron alone and as tank mixture against complex flora of weeds in **wheat**. Ind. J. Weed Sci. 36 (3) : 163-165.

14. Banga, R. S. B. *et al.* 2003. Compatability of clodinafop with metsulfuron and 2, 4-D against wildoat in **wheat**. Abst. Bienn. Conf. Ind. Soc. Weed Sci. held G.B. Pant University of Agr. & Technol., Pantnagar (India) during March 12-14, 2003:17.

15. Behera, U. P. *et al.* 2005. Influence of weed control method on productivity of rainfed **soybean** in verhsal of central India. Ind. J. Agro. 50(3): 221-224.

16. Bhadoria, R. B. S. and Chauhan, D. V. S. 1994. Effect of fertilizer and weed control in **India mustard** (*Brassica juncea*). Ind. J. Agro. 39(4):690-691.

17. Bhardwaj, A. K. *et al.* 2004. Weed management in zero-till sown **wheat**. Ind. J. Weed Sci. 36 (3 & 4): 175-177.

18. Bindra, A. D. *et al.* 2002. Bioefficacy of promising herbicidal molecules in direct seeded, sprouted, puddled **rice**. Ind. J. Weed Sci. 34:39-41.

19. Brar, L. S. and Walia, U. S. 1993. Bio-efficacy of S-ureas against *Phalaris minor* Retz. in **wheat**. Ind. J. Weed Sci. 25 (3 & 4) 1-5.

20. Brar, L. S. *et al.* 1991. Integrated weed control in **toria** (*B. campestris* var. *toria*). Ind. J. Weed Sci. 23 (1 & 2):69-60.

21. Chatha, R. P. S. and Y. R. Chanana 2003. Studies on wood management in young peach orchards. Abst. Bien. Conf. ISWS held 12-14 March, 2003 at G.B.P. Univ. Agr. & Technol. Pantnagar (India): 90.

22. Chauhan, R. S. and Singh, G. B. 1993. Chemical weed control in spring planted **sugarcane**. Ind. J. Weed Sci. 25(1 &2):47-50.

23. Chauhan, Y. S. *et al.* 2002. Effect of herbicides on weeds and **soybean**. Ind. J. Weed Sci. 34:213-216.

24. Chauhan, Y. S. *et al.* 2005. Weed management in Indian **mustard** (*B. juncea*). Ind. J. Agro. 50(2): 149-151.

25. Chela, G. S. and Gill, H. S. 1990. Chemical control of *Echinochloa crusgalli* in transplanted **rice** (*Oryza sativa* L.) Ind. J. Weed Sci. 12(1):7-14.

26. Chhokar, R. S. and Malik, R. K. 2002. Isoproturon-resistant littleseed canarygrass (Phalaris minor) and its response to alternate herbicides. Weed Technol. 16 : 116-123.

27. Chin, D. V., Pandey, J. 1991. Effect of pre-and post-emergence herbicides on weeds and yield of **blackgram** (*Phaseolus mungo*). Ind. J. Agro. 37:276-277.

28. Chopra, N. and N. K. Chopra, 2005. Bioefficacy of fenoxaprop, clodinafop, metribuzin, and carfentrazone, alone and in combination, against weeds in **wheat**. Ind. J. Weed Sci. 37 (3 &4): 163-166.

29. Chopra, N. *et al.* 2001. Effect of herbicides and weeding on weeds in **chickpea**. Ind. J. Weed Sci. 33:194-197.

30. Choubey, N. K. *et al.* 2001. Relative performance of cyhalofop butyl for weed control in direct seeded **rice**. Ind. J. Weed Sci. 33:132-135.

31. Das, K. *et al.* 1994. Weed management in tossa **jute** (*Corchorus olitorius*) Indian J. Agro., 39(10):87-92.

32. Deka, N. C. 2003. Alien **invasive weeds**: man made renewable biologicaql threat. Souvenir Nat. Sem. Alien Invasive Weeds in India held April, 27-29, 2003 at AAU Jorhat (India):20-22.

33. Deshpande, R. M. *et al.* 2006. Integrated weed management in rainfed **cotton**. Ind. J. Agro. 51(1): 68-69.

34. Deshveer, C. L. and L. S. Deshveer 2005. Weed management in **pearlmillet** with special reference to Trianthama portulacastrum. Ind. J. Weed Sci. 37 (3 & 4): 212-215.

35. Dhar, S. *et al.* 2005. Productivity and plant stand of perennial **lucerne** under different weed control measures during establishment year. Ind. J. Agro. 50 (3) : 243-246.

36. Dheer, S. and Sharma, K. C. 1990. Economics of **soybean** cultivation under different methods of weed control. Ind. J. Weed Sci., 22:7-11.

37. Dhyani, V. C. *et al.* 2005. Response of rice to crop establishment and weed management. Ind. J. Weed Sci. 37 (3 &4): 260-262.

38. Dinakar, V. S. and Ahuja, K. N. 1987. Studies on the rate and time of isoproturon application in relation to first irrigation in **wheat**. Ind. J. Agro. 32(3):241-244.

39. Dubey, M. P. 2002. Bioefficacy and phytotoxicity evaluation of anilofos and metolachlor in **soybean**. Ind. J. Weed Sci. 34 : 53-57.

40. Dungarwal *et al.* 2002. Herbicidal weed management in **fenugreek**. Ind. J. Weed Sci. 34:247-250.

41. Dungarwal, H. S. *et al.* 2002. Chemical weed control in **chickpea**. Ind. J. Weed Sci. 34:208-212.

42. Dungarwal, H. S. *et al.* 2002. Herbicidal management in **fenugreek** Ind. J. Weed Sci. 34 : 247-250.

43. Dutta, R. and Gogoi, A. K. 1994. Integrated weed control in direct-seeded upland **rice** (*Oryza sativa*). Ind. J. Agro. 39(4):639-641.

44. Gaikwad, R. P., V. S. Pawar 2002. Chemical weed control in **soybean**. Ind. J. Weed Sci. 34:297-298.

45. Giri, A. N. *et al.* 2006. Effect of cultural and integrated metters of weed control on **cotton** intercrop yield, and weed control efficiency in cotton-based cropping systems. Ind. J. Agro 51(1): 34-36.

46. Gogi, A. K., *et al.* 1992. Effect of browth promoter and herbicides on yield of **carrot** (*Daucus carota* L.). Ind. J. Weed Sci. 24 (1 & 2):104-105.

47. Gogoi, A. K. and Kaltia, H. 1990. Integrated weed control in direct seeded upland **rice**. Ind. J. Agro. 35(4):433-34.

48. Gogoi, A. K. *et al.* 1991. Weed management in **blackgram** (*Phaseolus mungo*). Ind. J. Agro. 36(4):601-602.

49. Gogoi, A. K. *et al.* 1992. Chemical weed control in *capsularis* **jute**. Ind. J. Weed Sci. 24(3, 4): 68-70.

50. Gopinath, K. A. and J. Pandey. 2004. Weed management in transplanted **rice** and its residual effect on weed and yield of succeeding wheat. Ind. J. Agro. 49(4): 226-229.

51. Gupta, O. P. and Chaudhry, N. K. 1986. Herbicide evaluation in **blackgram**. Trop. Pest. Management. 32(2):167-170.

52. Ithal, C. J. *et al.* 1992. Weed management in groundnut and sunflower **intercropping**. Ind. J. weed Sci. 24(1 &2):75-77.

53. Itnal, C. J. *et al.* 1993. Integrated weed management in irrigated **pigeonpea**. Ind. J. Weed Sci. 25(1 & 22):95-97.

54. Jacob, T. *et al.* 1994. Performance of some herbicides in (pigeonpea + cowpea)-(Wheat) **cropping system**. Ind. J. Weed Sci. 26(3-4):11-17.

55. Jain, H. C. and Tiwari, J. P. 1992. Influence of herbicides on the growth and yield of **soybean** (*Glycine max*) under different spacing and seeding rates. Ind. J. Agro. 37(1):86-89.

56. Jena, S. N. *et al.* 2002. Integrated weed management in direct seeded, rainfed, lowland **rice**. Ind. J. Weed Sci. 34:32-35.

57. Kathiresan, Rm. 2002. Weed management in rice-blackgram **cropping system**. Ind. J. Weed. Sci. 34:220-226.

58. Kathiresan, Rm. and I. Gnanavel. 2004. Integrated weed management on *Coleus amboinicus aromaticus* (Benth.) Ind. J. Weed Sci. 36 (3 & 4): 253-255.

59. Kewalanand, C. S. and Pandey 2001. Chemical weed control in Chamomile (Matricaria chamomilla L.) Ind. J. Weed Sci. 33:156-159.

60. Kewat, M. L. *et al.* 2000. Economics and eco-friendly weed management in **soybean**. Ind. J. Weed Sci. 32:135-139.

61. Kothe, S. S. 2001. Integrated weed management in **onion**. Ind. J. Weed Sci. 33:26-29.

62. Krishnamoorthy, *et al.* 1995. Chemical and cultural weed control in irrigated **soybean** (*Glycine max*). Ind. J. Agro. 4(1):127-128.

63. Kulmi, G. S. and P. N. Tiwari. 2005. Integrated weed management in **Asgandha** (*Wilhane somnifera* Dunol). Ind. J. Weed Sci. 37 (1 & 2) : 77-80.

64. Kulmi, G. S. and Jain, H. C. 1993. Evaluation of bentazon and oxadiazon in transplanted **rice**. Ind. J. Weed Sci. 25(1 & 2):73-77.

65. Kumar, A. and K. S. Thakur. 2005. Influence of intercropping and weed control measures on weeds and productivity of rainfed **maize**. Ind. J. Weed Sci. 37 (1 & 2): 65-67.

66. Kumar, A. *et al.* 2005. Efficacy of herbicides on weeds and seed yield of **fenugreek**. Ind. J. Weed Sci. 37 (3 & 4): 279-280.

67. Kumar, B. V. 1992. Chemical weed control in **groundnut**. Ind. J. Weed Sci. 24(1 &2):72-74.

68. Kumar, B. V. and Shaik, M. 1993. Efficacy of herbicide sprays as an alternative to manual weeding in **pearlmillet** (*Pennisetum glaucum*). Ind. J. Agro. 38(2):218-222.

69. Kumar, B. V. *et al.* 1994. Chemical control of horsepurslane (*Trianthema portulacastrum*) and barnyard grass (*Echinochloa crusgalli*) in **groundnut** (*Arachis hypogaea*). Ind. J. Agro. 39(3):491-493.

70. Kumar, K. and H. C. Kundra 2001. Chemical weed control in summer **moong** (*Vigna radiata*) and summer **urd** or mash (*V. mungo*) in Punjab. Ind. J. Weed. Sci. 33:200-202.

71. Kumar, N. and N. Ramawat 2005. Weed management in **shaftal** (Trifolium resupinatum) under mid-hill condition of Himachal Pradesh. Ind. J. Weed Sci. 37 (3 & 4): 244-246.

72. Kumar, S. *et al.* 2001. Differential response to sulfosulfuron under different irrigation frequencies to control weeds in **wheat**. Ind. J. Agro. 46:480-484.

73. Kumar, Y. *et al.* 2003. Integrated weed management in irrigated **groundnut**. Ind. J. Agro. 48(2): 117-119.

74. Kundra, H. C. and Gill, H. S. 1990. Comparative efficacy and selectivity of herbicides for weed control in **field pea** (*P. sativum* L.). J. Res. Punjab Agri. Univ. 27:207-212.

75. Kundra, H. C., *et al.* 1993. Efficacy of weed management practices in **pea** (*Pisum sativum* L.) Ind. J. weed Sci. 25 (1 &2): 1-6.

76. Kurchania, S. P. *et al.* 2001. Bioefficacy of postemergence herbicides for weed control in **soybean**. Ind. J. Weed Sci.33:34-37.

77. Kushwah, S. S. and M. D. Vyas. 2005. Herbicidal weed control in **soybean**. Ind. J. Agro. 50(3): 225-227.

78. Maan, S. S. and Thind, I. S. 1995. Effect of atrazine on weeds, growth and forage yield of *Sorghum X Sudan grass hybrids*. VI Biennial Conference of Indian Society of Weed Science 1994, held at Annamalai University, Annamalai Nagar, Tamilnadu in Feb. 9-10, 1995., p. 87.

79. Mahadevaswamy, *et al.* 1994. Integrated weed management in **sugarcane** (Saccharum officinarum). Ind. J. Agro. 39(1):83-86.

80. Mahere, J. *et al.* 2000. Chemical weed control in linseed with special reference to **Cuscuta.** Ind. J. Weed Sci. 32:216-217.

81. Maheswarappa, H. P. and Nanjappa, H. V. Relative efficacy of herbicides in controlling the weeds infesting **pigeonpea** (*Cajanus cajan* (L.) Millsp). Ind. J. Agron 39(4): 662-664.

82. Malik, K. S. *et al.* 2005. Efficacy of clodinafop, fenoxaprop, sulfosulfuron, and triasulfuron alone and as tank mixture against weeds in **wheat.** Ind. J. Weed Sci. 37 (3 &4): 180-183.

83. Malik, M. *et al.* 2002. Evaluation of dithiopyr for control of weeds in direct seeded **rice**. Ind. J. Weed Sci. 34:287-289.

84. Malik, R. S. *et al.* 2001. Efficacy of new herbicides with or without surfactants on weeds in **wheat.** Ind. J. Weed Sci. 33:59-62.

85. Malik, R. Z. K. *et al.* 2000. Efficacy of trifluralin, linuron and acetachlor against weeds in **mungbean** (*Vigna radiata*). Ind. J. Weed Sci. 32:181-185.

86. Maliwal, P. L. and Gupta, O. P. 1989. Study on the effect of four herbicides with and without phosphorus on weed control and seed yield of **fenugreek**. Trop. Pest. Management 35(3):307-310.

87. Mane, R. B. and B. S. Raskar 2002. Effect of weed control measures on drilled **rice**. Ind. J. Weed Sci. 34:282-284.

88. Manjeet Singh and Chandel, A. S. 1995. Effect of weed control method on **soybean** (*Glvcine max*). Ind. J. Agron 40(1):55-58.

89. Manuel, R. I. and P. Panneerselvam. 2001. Bioefficacy of acetachlor in transplanted **rice**. Ind. J. Weed Sci. 33:182-184.

90. Mehta, H. M. *et al.* 1995. Effect of methods of sowing and weed management on yield of **chicory** (*Cichorium intybus*). Ind. J. Agro. 40(1):147-149.

91. Mehta, J. P. *et al.* 2003. Influence of weed management and N application on productivity of **fennel** (*Foeniculun vulgaris*), Bien. Conf. ISWS, held March 12-14, at G.B.P. Univ. Agri. & Technol. Pantnagar (India):41.

92. Mehta, R. K., *et al.* 1993. Weed management in rainfed lowlands **rice**. Ind. J. Weed Sci. 25 (3 & 4):99-101.

93. Meyyappan, M. and Rm. Kathiresan. 2005. Integrated weed management in maize + blackgram **intercropping** system. Ind. J. Weed Sci. 37 (3 &4): 209-211.

94. Mishra, J. S. and N. T. Yaduraju, 2005. Bio-efficacy of sulfosulfuron against weeds in **wheat** in vertisols. Ind. J. Weed Sci. 37(1 & 2):23-25.

95. Mishra, J. S. *et al.* 2004. Bioefficacy of herbicides against cuscuta in **blackgram** (*Vigna mungo* (L.) Hepper). Ind. J. Weed Sci. 36 (3 & 4): 278-279.

96. Mishra, J. S. *et al.* 2005. Effect of tillage practices and herbicides on weed dynamics and yield of **wheat** under transplanted rice-wheat system in vertisols. Ind. J. Agro. 50(2): 106-109.

97. Modak, Rita, *et al.* 1995. Method of weed management on weed biomass, yield of **blackgram** (*Phaseolus mungo*), and nitrogen uptake. Ind. J. Agron. 40(1):114-115.

98. Mondal, D. C. *et al.* 2005. Chemical weed control in **onion** (Allium cepa L.) inWest Bengal. Ind. J. Weed Sci. 37 (3 & 4): 281-282.

99. Moorthy, B. T. O. and S. Saha. 2002. Evaluation of pre - and postemergence herbicides for their effects on weeds and upland, direct seeded **rice**. Ind. J. Weed Sci. 34:197-200.

100. Moorthy, B. T. S. and S. Saha, 2002. Bioefficacy of certain new herbicide formulations in puddled, seeded rice. Ind. J. Weed Sci. 34:46-49.

101. Moorthy, B. T. S. *et al.* 2004. Effect of different densities of *Cusanta chenensis* on lentil and **chickpea**. Ind. J. Weed Sci. 36 (3 & 4): 221-223.

102. Mukherjee, D. and R. P. Singh, 2005. Effect of micro-herbicides on weed dyanamics, yield and economics of transplanted **rice**. Ind. J. Agro. 50(4): 292-295.

103. Mukhopadhyay, S. K. 1990. Weed management in **rice** ecosystems in India. Agroecosystems Management, 227-235 pp.

104. Mundra, S. L. *et al.* 2003. Effect of postemergence herbicides on weed management in **soybean**, Ind. J. Weed Sci. 34(1&2):62-66.

105. Muniyappa, T. V. *et al.* 2003. Management of weeds in golf course. Abst. Bienn. Conf. ISWS held 12-14 March 2003 at G.B.P. Univ. of Agr. & Technol, Pantnagar (India): 89.

106. Murray, M. W. *et al.* 1994. Early broadleaf control in **potato** with herbicides. Weed Technol. 8(1):165-167.

107. Nandal, T. R. and R. Sharma 2005. Integrated weed management studies in **tomato** crop of subtropical conditions of Himachal Pradesh. Ind. J. Weed Sci. 37 (3 & 4): 283-284.

108. Nandal, T. R. *et al.* 2005. Integrated weed management in **cabbage**. Ind. J. Weed Sci. 37 (3 &4): 240-243.

109. Nandanassbabady, T. and O. S. Kandaswamy 2002. Evaluation of herbicides and cultural methods for weed control in **cotton**. Ind. J. Weed Sci. 34:143-145.

110. Nandlal, T. R. and R. Singh 2002. Integrated weed management in **onion** under Himachal Pradesh conditions. Ind. J. Weed. Sci. 34:72-75.

111. Nanjappa, H. V. *et al.* 2003. A non-herbicidal approach for weed management in **sunflower.** Abst. Bienn. Conf. ISWS, held 12-14 March 2003 at G.B.P. Univ. Agr. & Technol., Pantnagar (India):67.

112. Negi, S. C. and Saini, J. P. 1994. Studies on integrated weed control in **soybean**. Ind. J. Weed Sci., 26(3 & 4): 100-103.

113. Nepalia, V. and G. L. Jain. 2000. Effect of weed control and S on yield of Indian **mustard** (*B. juncea*). Ind. J. Agro. 45:483-488.

114. Orasad, K. and Srivastava, V. C. 1991. Weed management in pure and mixed crops of **pigeonpea** (*Cajanus cajan*) and **soybean** (*Glycine max*). Ind. J. Agril. Sci. 61(60):374-378.

115. Pahalwan, D. K. *et al.* 2003. Assessment of weed management in **soybean** on farmers' participatory mode. Abst. Bienn. Conf. ISWS held 12-14 March 2003 at G.B.P. Univ. of Agr. & Technol. Pantnagar (India):85.

116. Paikray, R. K. *et al.* 2000. Weed management in **niger** (*Guizotia abyssinica*). Ind. J. Weed Sci. 32:208-209.

117. Pal, C. *et al.* 2000. Weed control studies in pearlmillet-pigeonpea **intercropping.** Ind. J. Agro. 45:662-668.

118. Palmer, C. 2002. Controlling weeds around the woodland environment. Forestry & British Timber 31(2) : 28-30. (UK)

119. Pandey, A. K. and V. Prakash 2002. Weed management in maize and soybean **intercropping** system. Ind. J. Weed Sci. 34:58-62.

120. Pandey, A. K. *et al.* 2006. Evaluation of snlfasulfuron and metribuzin for weed control in irrigated **wheat**. Ind. J. Agro. 51(2): 136-138.

121. Pandey, I. B. and K. Kumar. 2005. Response of **wheat** to seeding methods and weed management. Ind. J. Agro. 50(1): 48-51.

122. Pandey, I. B. *et al.* 2005. Economics of tillage and weed management system for **wheat** after lowland rice. Ind. J. Agro. 50(1): 44-47.

123. Panwar, R. S. *et al.* 1988. Chemical weed control in **cotton**. Ind. J. Agro. 33(2):205-208.

124. Panwar, R. S. *et al.* 1994 (1) Efficacy of fluroxypyr as influenced by the time of application for weed control in **wheat**. Ind. J. Weed Sci. 26(3-4): 112-114.

125. Panwar, R. S. *et al.* 1994. Effect of clopyralid with isoproturon on weed control in **wheat**. Ind. J. Weed Sci. 26(3-4 1-5).

126. Panwar, R. S. *et al.* 1995. Effect of application time and hoeing on efficiency of pendimethalin in **cotton** (*Gossypium* spp.). Ind. J. Agro. 40(1).

127. Panwar, R. S. *et al.* 2001. Chemical weed control in **cotton**. Ind. J. Weed Sci. 33:14-17 and 164-167.

128. Panwar, R. S. *et al.* 2001. Effect of new herbicides for weed control in **cotton**. Ind. J. Weed Sci. 33:89-90.

129. Paramjeet, S. S. *et al.* 2003. Integrated weed management studies in **toria**. Bienn. Conf. weed Sci. held G.B.P.A.T., Pantnagar (India) March 12-14, p. 33.

130. Parmar, J. S., *et al.* 1994. Weed control studies in **lentil** (*Lens culinaris* M.). Ind. J. Weed Sci. 26(1 &2): 49-50.

131. Patel, I. S. *et al.* 1996. Weed management in **blonde psyllium** (Plantago ovata) under N. Gujarat condition. Ind. J. Agro. 41 : 476-479.

132. Patel, R. H. *et al.* 2005. Influence of irrigation schedule and weed management practices on growth and yield of **fenugreek**. Ind. J. Weed Sci. 37 (3 & 4): 237-239.

133. Patel, S. M. and T. N. Barevadia 2003. Chemical weed control studies in **chilli** nursery and their residual effect on succeeding crop. Abst. Bienn. Conf. ISWS held 12-14 March, 2003 at G.B.P. Univ. Agr. & Technol. Pantnagar (India):83.

134. Patel, Z. G. *et al.* 1994. Effect of weed control methods on yield and yield attributes of **sunflower** (*Helianthus annus*). Ind. J. Agro. 39(2):330-331.

135. Patro, H. and Prustry, J. C. 1994. Integrated weed management in **mungbean** (*Vigna radiata* L.). Ind. J. Weed Sci. 26(1 &2):81-82.

136. Ponnuswamy, K. *et al.* 2003. Effect of herbicides on weeds and productivity of rainfed **sorghum**. Abs. Biew. Conf. ISWS held 12-14 March 2003 at G.B.P. Univ. of Agr. & Technol. Pantnagar (India):

137. Porwal, M. K. and Singh, M. M. 1993. Efficacy of herbicides for weed control in **cauliflower** (*B. oleracea* L.). Ind. J. Weed Sci. 25 (1 & 2): 55-60.

138. Prakash Ved, *et al.* 1991. Chemical weed control in **soybean**. Ind. J. Weed Sci. 23(1 & 2):29-31.

139. Prakash, V. *et al.* 2001. Integrated weed management in **okra**. Ind. J. Weed Sci. 33:49-51.

140. Prakash, V. *et al.* 2003. Integrated weed management in **capsicum** under mid-hill conditions of N-W Himalayas. Ind. J. Agro. 48(2): 139-141.

141. Prasad, R. *et al.* 2003. Effect of weed management treatments in **sorghum** for fodder and associated weeds. Abst. Bienn. Comp. I.S.W.S. held March 12-14 at G.B.P. Univ. of Agri. & Technol. at Pantnagar (India) : 43.

142. Punia, S. S. *et al.* 2001. Efficacy of dinitroaniline herbicides against weeds in **sesame**. Ind. J. Weed Sci. 33:143-146.

143. Punia, S. S. *et al.* 2002. Performance of chlorsulfuron as tank mixture in **wheat**. Ind. J. Weed Sci. 34:168-171.

144. Punia, S. S. *et al.* 2003. Chemical weed control in lentil. Abst. Bienn. Conf. Ind. Soc. Weed Sci. held 12-14 March at G.B.P. Univ. Agri. & Technol. Pantnagar (India):26.

145. Punia, S. S. *et al.* 2005. Efficacy of tank mixtures of sulfosulfuron with clodinafop and fenoxaprop on weeds in **wheat**. Ind. J. Weed Sci. 37(182): 6-8.

146. Punia, S. S. *et al.* 2005. Evaluation of prometryn at metribuzin against weeds in **wheat**. Ind. J. Weed Sci. 37(1 &2): 26-28.

147. Purshotam, S. and Hosamani, M. M. 1990. Weed management in transplanted **rice**. Ind. J. Agro. 35(3):305-306.

148. Raghavaiah, C. V. and Sannibabu, M. 1991. Efficacy of herbicide mixtures in weed control and flue-cured **tobacco** yields. Ind. J. Weed Sci. 23(1 & 2):32-37.

149. Raghavaiah, C. V. and Subbarao, 1986. Herbicidal control of weeds in monsoon-grown barely **tobacco**. Ind. J. Agro. 31(4):331-334.

150. Raj, V. C. and Patel, Z. G. 1995. Integrated weed management in forage **lucerne** (*Medicago sativa* L.) VI Biennial Conference of Indian Society of Weed Science, 1994 held at Annamalai University, Annamalai Nagar, Tamilnadu in Feb. 9-10, 1995, p. 87.

151. Rajkhowa, D. J. *et al.* 2005. Evaluation of carfentrazone-ethyl 40 DF and glyphosate as tank mixture for weed control in tea. Ind. J. Weed Sci. 37(1 &2): 157-158.

152. Rajput, A. L. 2000. Integrated weed management practices in white **jute**. Ind. J. Agro. 45:782-786.

153. Rajput, A. L. and Pandey, B. P. 1994. Chemical weed control in **pigeonpea** (*Cajanus cajan*). Ind. J. Agro. 39(1): 27-30.

154. Rajput, H. D. *et al.* 2003. Irrigated weed management in **chilli**. Ind. J. Agro. 48(2): 136-138.

155. Raju, R. A. 2003. Bioefficacy of new herbicidal molecules in wetland (transplanted) **rice**. Abst. Bienn. Conf. ISWS held 12-14 March 2003 at GBP Univ. of Agr. & Technol., Pantnagar (India):72.

156. Raju, R. A. and B. Gangwar. 2005. Long term effect of herbicidal rotation on weed strift, crop productivity and energy efficiency in **rice-rice** system. Ind. J. Agro. 49(4): 213-217.

157. Ram, H. *et al.* 2002. Investigations on the chemical control of wildoats in irrigated **barley**. Ind. J. Weed Sci. 34:24-27.

158. Ramamoorthy, K. *et al.* 1994. Performance of sethoxydim as early postemergence herbicide on weeds and yield of rainfed ***Phaseolus mungo***. Indian J. Agron. 39(2):318-320.

159. Ramamoorty, K. 1991. Effect of integrated weed management on nutrient uptake by upland **rice** and associated weed. Ind. J. Agron. 36:213-217.

160. Rameswar, *et al.* 2002. Evaluation of herbicides for weed control and economics of **onion** in Himachal Pradesh. Ind. J. Weed Sci. 34:68-71.

161. Rana, M. C. and Angiras, N. N. 1993. Effect of weed control and phosphorus management on **gobhi sarson** (*Brassica napus*) and associated weeds. Ind. J. Weed Sci. 25 (1,2): 84-89.

162. Rana, S. S. 2002. Evaluation of promising herbicide combinations for weed management in **Rajmash** under dry temperate conditions of H.P. Ind. J. Weed Sci. 34:227-230.

163. Rana, S. S. 2002. Integrated weed management in **pea** under Sangla valley conditions of H.P. Ind. J. Weed Sci. 34:204-207.

164. Randhawa, J. S. *et al.* 2002. Crop-weed studies in summer **blackgram** (*P. mungo*). Ind. J. Weed Sci. 34:299-300.

165. Raskar, B. S. and P. G. Bhoi. 2002. Bio-efficacy and phytotoxicity of Pursuit plus herbicide against weeds in **soybean**. Ind. J. Weed Sci. 34:50-52.

166. Rath, G. S. and R. P. Sharma 2003. Bioefficacy of fenoxaprop-p-ethyl and chlorimuron ethyl alone and in combination for weed control in **soybean**, Abst. Bienn. Conf. Weed Sci., held at G.B.P. University of Agr. & Technol., Pantnagar (India) March 12-14, p. 32.

167. Rathee, S.S. *et al.* 192. Effect of time of N application and weed management on **perlmillet**. Ind. J. Weed Sci. 24 (1&2): 17-21.

168. Rathi, J.P.S. *et al.* 2004. Integrated weed management in **blackgram** (*Vigna mungo* L.) Ind. J. Weed Sci. 36 (3 & 4): 218-220.

169. Rathor, P.S. *et al.* 1990. Effect of weed control measures on growth and yield of **cumin**. Ind. J. Agro. 35(4):304-305.

170. Reddy, C.N. *et al.* 2000. Efficacy of various herbicides on weed control and yield of **brinjal**. Ind. J. Weed Sci. 32:150-152.

171. Reddy, C.N. *et al.* 2003. Effect of Fenoxaprop-p-ethyl on transplanted **rice**. Ind. J. Weed Sci. 35(1&2):117-118.

172. Reddy, M.D. *et al.* 2001. Integrated weed management in **okra**. Ind. J. Weed Sci. 33:217-219.

173. Sagarka, B.K. *et al.* 2005. Integrated weed management in **coriander**. Ind.J. Weed Sci. 37 (3 & 4): 231-233.

174. Sagarka, B.K. *et al.* 2005. Weed management in **isabgul** (Plantago ovata). Ind.J. Weed Sci. 37 (3 & 4): 287-288.

175. Saimbhi, M.S. *et al.* 1991. Studies on weed control in **pea** (*Pisum sativum* L.). Haryana J. Hort. Sci. 19:198-201.

176. Saini, J.P. 2005. Efficacy of cyhalofop butyl alone and in combination with 2,4-D against mixed weed flora in direct-seeded upland **rice** (*oryza sativa*). Ind. J. Agro. 50(1):38-40.

177. Saini, J.P. and N.N. Angiras, 2002. Evaluation of ethoxysulfuron against broadleaf weeds and sedges in direct seeded, puddled **rice**. Ind. J. Weed Sci. 34:36-38.

178. Saini, J.P. and N.N. Angiras, 2002. Evaluation of fenoxaprop-p-ethyl for weed control in direct seeded, puddled **rice**. Ind. J. Weed Sci. 34:131-132.

179. Saini, J.P. and N.N. Angiras. 2005. Standardization of dose of sulfosulfuron (MON 37503) in controlling weeds of rainfed **wheat** under mid-hill conditions of Himachal Pradesh. Ind. J. Agro. 50(1) : 41-43.

180. Sandhu, K.S. *et al.* 1993. Studies on weed control in **mungbean** (*Vigna radiata* (L.) Wilzeck). Ind. J. Weed Sci. 25(1 &2):61-65.

181. Sardana, V. *et al.* 2001. Management of broadleaf weeds in **wheat**. Ind. J. Weed Sci. 33:69-71.

182. Sarma, J.S. and Dhillon, S.S. 1993. Effect of different diluent on bioefficacy of isoproturon in **wheat**. Ind. J. Weed Sci. 25(3 & 4): 102-103.

183. Savithri, K. E. *et al.* 1994. Weed management in coconut-banana **intercropping** system. Ind. J. Weed Sci. 26(3-4):57-63.

184. Shaikh, A.R. 2005. Integrated weed management in rabi **chilli** (C. annum). Ind.J. Weed Sci. 37 (3 & 4): 285-286.

185. Shanmughavelu, K.G. *et al.* 1985. Weed Management in Horticultural Crops. Agrobios (India) Jodhpur, 114 p.

186. Sharma, G.D. *et al.* 2004. Evaluation of alachlor, metolachlor, and pendimethalin for weed control in **rajmash** (*Phaseolus vulgaris* L.) in cold desert of N-W Himalayas. Ind. J. Weed Sci. 36 (3 & 4):287-289.

187. Sharma, J. and Nayital, S.C. 1993. Weed Management in maize-blackgram **intercropping** in mid hills, sub-humid zone of Himachal Pradesh Ind. J. Weed Sci. 25(1 & 2):43-46.

188. Sharma, R. and Mehta, H.M. 1994. Chemical weed control in **onion**. Ind. J. Weed Sci. 26 (1 & 2):44-45.

189. Sharma, R. and S.S. Pahuja 2001. Bioefficacy of chlorsulfuron, metsulfuron methyl and metribuzin in **wheat**. Ind. J. Weed Sci. 33:112-115.

190. Sharma, R. and S.S. Pahuya. 2001. Effect of weed control measures by crops and weeds in **wheat** Ind. J. Weed Sci. 33:174-176.

191. Sharma, R. and U.S. Upadhyay 2002. Bioefficacy of acetachlor in transplanted **rice**. Ind. J. Weed Sci. 34:184-186.

192. Sharma, R. *et al.* 2002. Effect of sulfurylurea herbicides applied alone and tank mix with metribuzin on weeds in **wheat** and their residual effect on succeeding crop of sorghum. Ind. J. Weed Sci. 34:178-183.

193. Sharma, R.P. *et al.* 2001. Effect of weed management and P levels in Indian **mustard** (*B. juncea*). Ind. J. Weed Sci. 33:147-150.

194. Sharma, S.D. *et al.* 2004. Effect of doses and stages of application of isopropagyl on *Phalaris minor* in **wheat**. Ind. J. Weed Sci. 36(3) : 171-174.

195. Sharma, S.D. *et al.* 2004. Efficacy in halofop-butyl against weeds in **rice** nursery. Ind. J. Weed Sci. 36 (3 & 4): 181-183.

196. Sharma, S.K. and R.C. Gautam 2003. Integrated weed management in pearlmillet. Ind. J. Weed Sci. 35(1&2):135-135.

197. Sharma, U.C. *et al.* 1994. Effect of integrated weed management on yield and nutrient uptake by raqinfed **rice** (*Oryza sativa*) in acid soils of Nagaland. Ind. J. Agron. 39(4):553-556.

198. Sharma, V. and D.R. Thakur 2001. Evaluating herbicides for weed control in **gobhi season** (*B. napus*) under rainfed, mid-hill conditions of H.P. Ind. J. Weed Sci. 33:5-8.

199. Shekhar, B.G. *et al.* 2002. Weed management in transplanted **onion** under protective irrigation situation. Ind. J. Weed Sci. 34:327-328.

200. Shekhar, J. and B.S. Mankotia. Efficacy of some new herbicides in wet seeded **rice**. Ind. J. Weed Sci. 37 (1 & 2): 58-60.

201. Sheoran, P. *et al.* 2003. Weed management studies in Indian **mustard.** Abst. Bienn. Conf. Weed Sci. held at G.B.P.A.T., Pantnagar (India), March 12-14, p. 33.

202. Singh, A. *et al.* 200. Integrated weed management in turmeric (*Curcuma longa*) planted under popular plantation. Ind. J. Weed Sci. 34: 329-330.

203. Singh, A. *et al.* 2001. Selectivity of pendimethalin and oxyfluorfen in **Artemisia annua**. Ind. J. Weed Sci. 33:215-216.

204. Singh, A.K. and Singh, R.A. 1994. Weed management in **rice** (*Oryza sativa*) - **lentil** (*Lens culinaris*) sequence under dryland conditions of Varanasi. Ind. J. Agro. 39(4):608-611.

205. Singh, B. and N.S. Rana, 2003. Bioefficacy of sulfentrazone against weeds in **sugarcane**. Ind. J. Weed Sci. 35(1&2):82-86.

206. Singh, B.B. 2001. Effect of metribuzin on weed control and grain yield of **wheat**. Ind. J. Weed Sci. 33:180-181.

207. Singh, C.M. *et al.* 1993. Study on the weed management in **okra** (*Abelmoschus esculentus* (L.)). Ind. J. Weed Sci. 25(1&2):92-95.

208. Singh, D. and Singh, G. 1993. Spike malformation and grain yield of **wheat** in relation to time of 2,4-D application under different dates of sowing. Ind. J. Weed Sci. 25 (1 & 2): 77-81.

209. Singh, D.P. *et al.* 1994. Weed control in white **jute** (*Corchorus capsularis*). Ind. J. Agro. 39(3):437-441.

210. Singh, *et al.* 1998. Control of isoproturon-resistant biotypes of Phalaris minor by chlortoluron and clodinafop. Resistant Pest Mgmt. 10 : 15-18.

211. Singh, G. and Prasad, R. 1994. Studies on the control of *Trianthema portulacastrum* L. in fodder **maize**. Ind. J. Weed Sci. 26(1 &2):64-67.

212. Singh, G. and Singh, D. 1992. Weed control efficacy of oxyfluorfen, acifluorfen, metribuzin, and linuron in **soybean**, Ind. J. Weed Sci. 24(1,2): 97-99.

213. Singh, G. and Singh, O.P. 1993. Effect of weed control method on rainfed, lowland, direct seeded **rice** and associated weeds. Ind. J. Weed Sci. 25 (3 & 4):123-125.

214. Singh, G. and Singh, O.P. 1994. Herbicidal control of weeds in transplanted **rice** (*Oryza sativa*) in rainfed lowland conditions. Ind. J. Agron. 39(3):463-465.

215. Singh, G. *et al.* 1993. Weed control in **cauliflower** (*Brassica oleracea* L.). Ind. J. Weed Sci. 15:1-6.

216. Singh, G. *et al.* 2000. Effect of herbicidal weed management in direct-seeded **rice**. Ind. J. Agro. 45:470-476.

217. Singh, G. *et al.* 2001. Bioefficacy of clomazone and metribuzin in **soybean**. Ind. J. Weed Sci. 33:191-193.

218. Singh, G. *et al.* 2001. Effect of doses and stages of application of fluazolate on weeds and **wheat** yield. Ind. J. Weed Sci. 33:234-235.

219. Singh, G. *et al.* 2002. Bioefficacy of flumetsulam, cloransulam and diclosulam in **soybean**. Ind. J. Weed Sci. 34:293-294.

220. Singh, G. *et al.* 2002. Bioefficacy of haloxyfop on **soybean** and associated weeds. Ind. J. Weed Sci.:34:217-219.

221. Singh, G. *et al.* 2002. Bioefficacy of herbicides in zero till **wheat** in rice-wheat cropping system. Ind. J. Weed Sci. 34:5-8.

222. Singh, G. *et al.* 2002. Effect of doses and stages of application of sulfosulfuron on weeds and **wheat** yield. Ind. J. Weed. Sci. 34:172-174.

223. Singh, G. *et al.* 2002. Effect of metsulfuron methyl alone and in combination with 2,4-D and surfactant on non-grass of weeds and **wheat** yield. Ind. J. Weed Sci. 34:175-177.

224. Singh, G. *et al.* 2004. Bio-efficacy of metribuzin and promebyn in **wheat** Ind. J. Weed Sci. 436 (3 &4): 178-180.

225. Singh, G. *et al.* 2005. Effect of denoxaprop-p-ethyl with and without surfactant on weeds and **wheat** yield. Ind. J. Weed Sci. 37(1 & 2):13-16.

226. Singh, G. *et al.* 2005. Effect of weed management practices on direct-seeded **rice** Ind. J. Agro. 50(1):35-37.

227. Singh, H. *et al.* 2001. Weed management in **Brassica** species. Ind. J. Agro 46:533-537.

228. Singh, I. *et al.* 2005. Herbicidal control in **blond psyllium** (*Plantago ovata*) grown on arid soils under irrigated condition. Ind. J. Agro. 50(3): 247-248.

229. Singh, K. and Lal, S.S. 1994. Herbicidal weed control efficiency and nutrient removal by weeds in **potato** (*Solanum tuberosum*) under N.E. hills condition. Ind. J. Agro. 39(2):336-339.

230. Singh, M.K. *et al.* 2004. Influence of crop geometry, cultivor, and weed management practices on crop weed competition in **chickpea**. Ind. J. Agro. 49(4): 258-262.

231. Singh, O.N. and Singh, R.P. 1993. Integrated weed management in direct sown upland **rice**. Ind. J. Weed Sci. 25 (1 & 2):70-73.

232. Singh, P.P. and Prasad, R. 1991. Weed control in **pearlmillet**. Ind. J. Agro. 36(2):286-88.

233. Singh, R. and T.R. Nandlal 2002. Studies on weed management in **garlic.** Ind. J. Weed Sci. 34:80-81.

234. Singh, R. *et al.* 2003. Weed management studies in **lentil.** Ind. J. Weed Sci. 35(1&2):70-73.

235. Singh, R. *et al.* 2005. Effect of weed management practices on ripening-planted **sugarcane**. Ind. J. Agro. 50(3): 236-238.

236. Singh, R.D. *et al.* 2000. Chemical weed control in *Cynodon dactylon* lawns. Ind. J. Weed Sci. 32: 146-149.

237. Singh, R.K. *et al.* 2001. Integrated weed management in **pearlmillet**. Ind. J. Weed Sci. 33:206-208.

238. Singh, R.P. *et al.* 2005. Efficacy of oxyzalin on weeds and yield of **wheat**. Ind. J. Agro. 50(4): 300-302.

239. Singh, R.V. and Arya, M.P.S. 1994. Studies on the chemical weed control in **fingermillet** under rainfed conditions. Ind. J. Weed Sci. 26(3 & 4):45-51.

240. Singh, R.V. and Arya, M.P.S. 1995. Chemical weed control in Japanese **barnyardmillet** (*Echinochloa frumentacea*). Ind. J. Agro. 40(I):51-54.

241. Singh, R.V. *et al.* 2003. Weed control in **chickpea** under late sown condition. Ind. J. Agro. 48(2): 114-116.

242. Singh, S. *et al.* 2003. Effect of cinosulfuron on weeds and transplanted **rice**. Ind. J. Weed Sci. 35(1&2):117-118.

243. Singh, S. *et al.* 2003. Effect of doses and stages of application of pyrazosulfuron ethyl on weeds in transplanted **rice**. Ind. J. Weed Sci. 35(1&2):27-29.

244. Singh, S. *et al.* 2005 (a). Performance of tank mixture of chlorsulfuron and demitroaniline herbicides for the control of weeds in **wheat**. Ind. J. Weed Sci. 37(1 & 2): 20-22.

245. Singh, S. *et al.* 2005. Evaluation of dithicopyr alone and in combination with trifluralin for the control of weeds in **wheat**. Ind. J. Weed Sci. 37(1 & 2): 17-19.

246. Singh, S. *et al.* 2005. Performance of tank mixture of metribuzen with clodinafop and fenoxaprof for the control of mixed weed flora in **wheat**. Ind. J. Weed Sci. 37(182): 9-12.

247. Singh, S.J. *et al.* 1992. Studies on weed management in **onion** (*Allium cepa* L.) Ind. J. Weed Sci. 24 (1 & 2):6-10.

248. Singh, S.P. 1993. Weed control in rainfed upland **rice**. Ind. J. Weed Sci. 25 (3 & 4):61-64.

249. Singh, S.S., *et al.* 1992. Weed management in transplanted **rice** (*Oryza sativa*) under midland, calcareous ecosystem. Ind. J. Agro. 37:173-176.

250. Singh, V.B. and G. Giri 2001. Influence of **intercropping** and weed control measures on suppression of weeds and productivity of spring season sunflower and groundnut. Ind. J. Agro. 46:440-444.

251. Singh, V.K. and Bajpai, R.P. 1994. Influence of crop geometry and weed control methods on yield and economics of rainfed **soybean** (*Glycine max*). Ind. J. Agro. 39(4):671-673.

252. Singh, V.P. *et al.* 2004. Bioefficacy of tepraloxydim and dimethanamid in **soybean**. Ind. J. Weed Sci. 36 (3 & 4) : 271-273.

253. Singh, V.P. *et al.* 2004. Effect of fenoxaprop-p-ethyl on transplant **rice** and associated weeds. Ind. J. Weed Sci. 36 (3&4): 190-192.

254. Singh, V.P. *et al.* 2005. Effect of bensulfuronmethyl (Londax 60 DF) on sedges and non-grassy weeds in transplants **rice**. Ind. J. Weed Sci. 37(1 & 2): 40-44.

255. Sinha, K.K. and S.J. Singh, 2004. Efficacy and isoproturon with and without surfactant on weed suppression in **wheat**. Ind. J. Agro. 49(4):254-257.

256. Srivastava, T.R. 2001. Efficacy of new herbicides in spring planted **sugarcane**. Ind. J. Weed Sci. 34:318-319.

257. Subbaiah, S.V. and B. Sreedevi. 2000. Efficacy of herbicide mixtures on weed control in direct seeded **rice** under puddled condition. Ind. J. Weed Sci. 32:199-200.

258. Subramanian, E. *et al.* 2006. Effect of integrated weed management practices on growth and yield of wet-seeded **rice** and their residual effect on succeeding pulse crop. Ind. J. Agro. 51(2): 93-96.

259. Sukhadia, N.M. 2000. Integrated weed management in **crop sequence**. Ind. J. Agro. 45:253-256.

260. Sundari, A. and Rm. Kathiresan 2002. Integrated weed management in irrigated **sorghum**. Ind. J. Weed Sci. 34:313-315.

261. Tamrakar, M.K. *et al.* 2002. Efficacy of herbicides against *Cichorium intybus* in **berseem.** Ind. J. Weed Sci. 34:333-334.

262. Tewari, A.N. and Singh, R.D. 1993. Weed management in potato (*Solanum tuberosum*) intercropped with **wheat** (*Triticum aestivum*). Ind. J. Agro. 38(4): 626-627.

263. Tewari, A.N. *et al.* 2001. Effect of pendimethalin, oxadiazon and metolachlor on weeds and **onion** nursery. Ind. J. Weed Sci. 33:220-221.

264. Tewari, A.N. *et al.* 2003. Evaluation of imazethapyr in **greengram** with special reference to *Parthenium* control. Abst. Bienn. Conf. Ind. Soc. Weed Sci., G.B.P. Univ. Agri. & Technol., Pantnagar (India) held March 12-14:24.

265. Tewari, A.N. *et al.* 2005. Herbicidal control of weeds in **coriander** with special reference to Coronopus didymus Ind. J. Weed Sci. 37 (3 & 4) : 234-236.

266. Thakrai, K.K. *et al.* 1990. Evaluation of herbicides in **coriander** seed crop. Proc. First National Seminar on Seed Spices, held at Jaipur (India), Oct.24-25, 1989:109-199 p.

267. Tiwana, U.S. *et al.* 2002. Effect of butachlor, trifluralin and fluchloralin on chicory and berseem **fodder**. Ind. J. Weed. Sci. 134:251-253.

268. Tiwana, U.S. *et al.* 2006. Influence of herbicides on fodder yield and quality of Persian clover. Ind. J. Weed Sci. 38(1&2): 96-99.

269. Tiwari, R.B. and Parihar, S.S. 1993. Weed management studies in **wheat**. Ind. J. Weed Sci. 25(3 & 4): 88-90.

270. Tomar, S.S. and Namdeo, K.N. 1991. Studies on chemical weed control in **mustard**. Ind. J. Agro. 36(1): 119-120.

271. Tumbare, A.D. and S.S. Iihe. 2002. Response of **tomato** to irrigation regimes and herbicides during summer season. Ind. J. Weed Sci. 34:322-323.

272. Upadhyaya, V.B. and C.S. Bhalla. 2002. Efficacy of cultural, mechanical, and chemical weed control in **chickpea**. Ind. J. Weed Sci. 34:141-142.

273. Ushakumari, K. *et al.* 2001. Effect of spacing and weed control methods on growth and yield of **onion**. Ind. J. Weed Sci. 33:222-224.

274. Vaishya, R.D. 1993. Efficacy of some herbicides for weed control in **pigeonpea**. Ind. J. Weed Sci. 25(3 &4):120-122.

275. Vaishya, R.D. and Kumar, P. 1993. Effect of methods of isoproturon application on weeds in **wheat**. Ind. J. Weed Sci. 25 (3 & 4):115-117.

276. Vaishya, R.D., *et al.* 1992. Mechanical and chemical weed control in upland, direct seeded **rice**. Ind. J. Weed Sci. 24(1 & 2):11-16.

277. Veeramani, A. *et al.* 2000. Integrated weed management in **soybean**. Ind. J. Agro. 45:740-745.

278. Victor R. *et al.* 2001. Evaluation of glufosinate ammonium in tea (*Camellia* spp. L.), Ind. J. Weed Sci. 33: 227-228.

279. Virendra, S. *et al.* 2006. Efficacy and economics of weed management practices in blackgram under rainfed conditions. Ind. J. Weed Sci. 38(1&2): 77-80.

280. Walia, U.S. *et al.* 2005. Role of variable tillage depths on seed bank dynamics of Phalaris minor Retz. in **wheat**. Ind. J. Weed Sci. 37 (1 & 2): 33-35.

281. Warade, A.D. *et al.* 2006. Integrated weed management in onion. Ind. J. Weed Sci. 38(1&2): 92-95.

282. Yadav, R.P. 2004. Effect of herbicides alone and in combination with cultural methods on weed control in Indian **mustard.** Ind. J. Agro. 49(4):268-270.

283. Yadav, R.P., *et al.* 1995. Yield and economic analysis of weed control practices in **Indian mustard** (*Brassica juncea*). Ind. J. Agro. 40(1): 122-124.

284. Yadav, R.S. and B.L. Poonia. 2005. Effect of crop and herbicide rotations on weed dyanamics with speral reference to *Asphodelus tencifolius* in **mustard** in arid regions of Rajasthan. Ind. J. Weed Sci. 37(1 & 2): 68-73.

285. Yadav, S.S. *et al.* 2005. Comparative efficacy of herbicidal and manual weed control in **cumin** at different levels of nitrogen. Ind. J. Agro. 50(1) : 77-79.

286. Yaduraju, N.T. *et al.* 1992. Isoproturon does well in **potatoes**. Ind. Agro. News V(4) 2.

287. Yaduraju, N.T. *et al.* 2000. Evaluation of herbicides for the control of *Asphodelus tenuifolius* in **mustard**. Ind. J. Weed Sci. 32:186-189.

Chapter 22

WEED CONTROL IN ORCHARDS, PLANTATIONS, GRASSLANDS, AND LAWNS

22.1 ORCHARDS

22.1.1 The Weed Problem

Weed control is most essential in orchards around the fruit tree rings and in continuous 1.5 to 3.0 m strips down the tree rows. Here the weeds, in addition to competing with the trees, interfere with fruit picking, tree pruning, and other horticultural operations. Also, they increase damage to the surface tree roots by diseases and rodents. Further, weeds in orchards may lead to a more severe frost bite in fruits because of reduced radiation from the soil. Ultimately, the fruit trees may be crowded out by the weeds. Densely planted tall trees may smother weeds but they are no more acceptable in modern horticulture. Today's orchards are very much open type in which control of weeds is essential.

22.1.2 The Weed Management Practices

Tree bases, where freedom from weeds is most essential, are not easily accessible to mechanical cultivation. It may cause injury to the lower fruiting branches and shallow feeding roots of the trees. For this reason herbicidal control is important for ring weeding under the fruit trees. In between the tree rows, both cultivators and herbicides could be used with similar results, depending upon their economic viability. Also, suitable cover crops and sods may be grown in between the tree rows for weed suppression. Such sods should be kept low by mowing. Some gardeners like to grow vegetables in orchards, which indirectly induces them to maintain weedfree conditions. But intercropping of any kind in orchards may be undesirable in part of the year when the demand of orchard trees for mineral nutrients and water is high. At this time, black polythene mulches of 400 gauge can be used more effectively in smothering the weeds in orchards (Kaundal *et al.*, 1994)

There has been considerable progress in the development and use of herbicides in orchards, particularly around the tree bases. The selectivity of herbicides to orchard trees may be achieved in either of the following four ways:-

1. The inherent tolerance of the plant to the herbicide; for instance apple to simazine.
2. Failure of herbicides such as paraquat and diquat to penetrate the bark of trees.
3. Directed and protected application of herbicides.
4. Use of limited leaching herbicides, such as dichlobenil.

Most herbicide hazards to orchard trees result from the soil persistent herbicides. Therefore, the use of such herbicides should be avoided in orchards, particularly when the trees are in bearing. Also, herbicide sprayers should not be used for spraying other pesticides on fruit trees.

Herbicides under current recommendations in orchards are given in Table 22.1. Intelligent combinations of these can be designed to achieve broad-spectrum weed control with acceptable safety to orchards.

Table 22.1: Important Herbicide Recommendations in Orchards Arranged by Herbicides. (Key; A = annual weeds, P = perennial weeds, G = grass weeds, B = broadleaf weeds NS = nutsedge. Symbols in parenthesis show secondary susceptibility of the weeds to the herbicide in question.)

Herbicide	Type of weeds controlled	Type of treatment	Remarks
1	2	3	4
I. Contact Herbicides (with no soil residues):			
Herbicidal oils	A, P	Directed spray around the tree bases	Avoid drift to the tree trunks.
Paraquat/ diquat	A	-do-	Drift will not damage woody stems. To obtain residual control, paraquat can be combined with simazine in tolerant crops like **apple** and **peach**.
Organic arsenicals	G (PA)	Apply repeatedly before the weeds set seeds.	Good against difficult grasses
II. Soil Active Herbicides:			
The soil active herbicides should be selected according to soil and rainfall conditions to avoid their leaching to the effective root zone of fruit trees.			
EPTC (5-7.5 Kg/ha)	NS, AG	Soil incorporated	Use for ring weeding.
Dichlobenil (5-10 kg/ha)	P, A, NS	Preemergence to weeds	Use for ring weeding in established **apple** and two years' or older **pear** orchards. But it can be toxic to apple in the presence of symbiotic mycorrhizae, which is frequent.
Terbacil (2-10 kg/ha)	G. NS	Directed spray	Use for ring weeding in two years' or older apple, peach, and citrus orchards.
Bromacil	G, NS	Directed spray	Use for spot treatment in two years'

Herbicide	Type of weeds controlled	Type of treatment	Remarks
1	2	3	4
			or older **apple**, **peach**, and **citrus** rings.
Trifluralin (0.5-1.0 kg/ha)	A G	Soil incorporated	It can be used in young fruit nurseries around newly planted liners as well as for ring weeding of several orchards and **vineyards**.
Simazine (1-2 Kg/ha)	A (G,B)	Preemergence to weeds	Use in **citrus**, **apple**, and other deciduous orchards, as well as in **nuts** and **vineyards**. Established apple and **pear** are tolerant up to 5 Kg/ha simazine, once in two years.
Diuron (1-3 kg/ha)	A (G,B)	-do-	Use in **apple, pear, peach, citrus, banana**, and **pineapple** plantations, as well as in **vineyards**. Vineyards can tolerate up to 3.5 kg/ha of diuron.
Monuron (1-2 Kg/ha)	A (G,B)	-do-	It is used in **citrus** grooves in low rainfall areas only.
Ametryn (0.5-4 Kg/ha)	A (G,B)	Directed spray	It is found useful in **citrus**, **pineapple**, and **banana** plantations.
Oxyfluorfen (up to 0.25 kg/ha)	A (G,B)		Apply soon after transplanting **banana** (before weed emergence) followed by directed spray of glyphosate at 1.64 kg/ha.
III. Shoot Translocated Herbicides:			
These herbicies should be sprayed in low to medium spray volumes to wet only the weeds. Soil residues of these herbicides may harm certain fruit trees.			
Dalapon (1%)	G (P,A)	Directed spray	It is used for ring weeding four years' or older **apple** and **pear** orchards. Also, **citrus** and **vineyards** can be treated while these are dormant.
Amitrole (4-6 kg/ha)	P (G,A)	-do-	Apply in four years' or older **apple**, **pear**, and **citrus** orchards. It may be combined with simazine and diuron.
2,4-D (1-2 Kg/ha)	B (A)	Directed and protected spray	Fruit trees with exposed suckers should not be treated with it. Avoid ester formulations of 2,4-D. Apply as inverts or with drift control agents to avoid spray drift hazards.
Glyphosate (kg/ha)	A,G,B	Directed spray	Apply 2-3 times in the season for ring weeding of orchards, It can also be used to clean interrows of **strawberry**, **fig**, and **banana** orchards, particularly for bermudagrass control.

Table 22.2: Herbicides Recommended in Orchards Arranged by Crops.

Apple	:	ATA, diuron, paraquat, simazine and terbacil
Banana	:	Alachlor, ametryn, diuron, oxyfluorfen and simazine
Blueberry	:	Hexazinone, simazine and terbacil
Citrus	:	Atrazine, diuron and paraquat
Grapes	:	Atrazine, diuron and simazine
Mango	:	Bromacil, dalapon, diuron, glyphosate and paraquat
Peach	:	Dalapon, fosamine, glyphosate, paraquat, simazine and terbacil
Pear	:	Fosamine
Pineapple	:	Atrazine and bromacil
Plum	:	Atrazine, bromacil, diuron, simazine and terbacil
Sapota	:	Bromacil and diuron
Strawberry	:	DCPA and simazine

Table 22.3: Weed Control in Established Peach Orchard Through Herbicides and Mulch During 1990-91 in Punjab (India)

Treatments	**Dry weed biomass (q/ha)**		**Fruit yield of peach (kg/tree)**	**TSS %**
	Kharif	**Spring**		
Unweeded check	36.5	51.7	42.0	10.6
Hand-weeded (12) (every month)	10.4	9.2	45.5	11.0
Diuron (3 kg/ha)	10.1	9.6	50.0	12.2
Glyphosate (2 kg/ha)	8.1	7.1	51.0	12.3
Black polythene mulch (400 gauge)	2.1	1.9	58.0	13.0
C.D. (at P = 0.05)	2.2	1.5	4.1	1.65

Note: *Diuron was applied twice (July, 90 and Feb. 91) in 8 years' old orchard as PE treatment after initial cleaning. Glyphosate was applied POE during the same period on standing weeds as directed spray under the tree canopy.*

22.2 PLANTATION CROPS

22.2.1 The Weed Problem

Weeds are problematic in plantation crops till the tree or bush inter-spaces underneath are covered. This period is usually very long in such crops. In coconut and rubber, for example, it may take as much as 10 years before the ground is covered. This then requires a long term weed management programme to keep the plantation trees growing vigorously. In other crops like tea and coffee, their annual pruning exposes the ground spaces to weeds repeatedly, requiring a constant weed management programme. There may still be other plantation crops (and orchards) where it may be necessary to provide open inter-row spaces, constantly. Besides all this, the plantation crops are heavily attacked by weeds at their nursery stage. *Eupatorium odoratum*, *Imperata cylindrica*, *Pennisetum clandestinum*, *Paspalum conjugatum*, and *Oxalis* spp. are particularly noxious in plantation crops of the tropical world. Although exhaustive data on the losses in yield and quality of plantation crops caused by weeds are not available because of the long waiting periods required for even the first crop harvest, yet such losses do occur, beyond doubt. In tea and coffee, losses in leaf and seed yields of up to 40% due to weeds are on record. Besides, the weeds have been found to aggravate die-back disease in coffee (Awatramani and Mathew, 1973).

22.2.2 The Weed Management Practices

Manual weeding has been the rule in plantations since ages. But in recent years its many limitations have been realised and more and more plantations are switching over to herbicidal control. In India, 95% of paraquat, diuron, and dalapon; 100% of glyphosate and MSMA; and 60% of 2,4-D and simazine marketed are sold to plantations, particularly for tea and coffee.

Manual weeding in tea and coffee has been estimated to share 17% of the total cost of cultivation. Labour management is a big problem on plantations, in general. Besides, many plantations exist on hill slopes where physical weeding may seriously erode soils. Many plantation owners often grow cover crops in the inter-rows to protect the soil from the beating action of rain. The cover crops however, are considered competitive with the plantation crops. A better alternative to this would be to use herbicides and artificial mulches to hold the soil. Intercropping with a leguminous crop like cowpea during the initial growth stages of plantation crops has been successful in suppressing weeds in many cases (Savithri, *et al.* 1994).

Table 22.4: Important Herbicide Recommendations for Weed Control in Common Plantation Crops

Herbicides	Rates	Remarks
1	2	3
	BANANA (*Musa sapientum*)	
Diuron Oxyfluorfen	0.5-1.0 kg/ha Up to 250 g/ha	Apply preemergence to weeds in young plantations till closing-in of the crop.
	COCOA (*Theobroma cocoa*)	
Paraquat	0.1% spray	It is used for ring-weeding, both new and old cocoa plantations. To obtain extended period of weed control, paraquat may be combined with linuron or simazine in light soils and with diuron in heavy soils.
2,4-D + dalapon 2,4-D + MSMA	1 + 10 kg/ha 1 + 2 or 2.5 kg/ha	In established plantations directed spray of the mixture will control young growth of mixed weed species.
DNOC	0.1%	It is used for the treatment of cocoa trees against epiphytes like lichens and mosses.
Cu_2O	0.3-0.5%	-do-
CuOCl	0.4-0.5%	-do-
	COCONUT (*Cocos nucifera*)	
Diuron, oxyfluorfen		Apply before weed emergence
Paraquat + atrazine	0.5 + 1.0 Kg	Apply as directed spray to maintain

Herbicides	Rates	Remarks
1	2	3
(or diuron)	ha^{-1}	about 2 m diameter circle around the coconut seedlings weed-free.
Dalapon	1% spray	When perennial grasses are the main weeds, dalapon should be preferred over other herbicides. Apply it as directed spray when the coconut leaves are well above the ground.
MULBERRY (*Morus australis*)		
Diuron	1-2 kg/ha	Apply a day after its bottom pruning, but before weed emergence.
OILPALM (*Elaeis guineensis*)		
Paraquat	0.05-0.1% spray	In young oil palm plantations paraquat is often useful to establish a cover crop in the interrows. In established plantations, paraquat can be used for ring weeding oil palm of up to 5 years' age. One may combine simazine with paraquat to provide extended period of weed control; oil palm is very tolerant to the mixture.
Dalapon	1% spray	Apply as directed spray to knock down perennial grasses, both in new and old plantations.
Amitrole and MSMA	0.2-1.0% spray	When *Paspalaum conjugatum* is the chief weed problem in oilpalm circles, alternate sprays of amitrole (or MSMA) and paraquat at 2 weeks' interval have proved effective.
2,4-D	0.25% spray	2,4-D will kill stem epiphytes of oilpalm. The herbicide is also used to destroy young growth of *Eupatorium odoratum* outside the tree circles.
Atrazine and diuron	1.6-2 Kg ha^{-1}	These form good preemergence herbicides for ring weeding oilpalm.
MINTS (*Mentha piperita* and *M. arvensis*)		
Terbacil and bromacil	1.6-2 Kg ha^{-1}	Apply on young weeds a month after planting the mint. In established crops, apply terbacil after a pre-dormancy breaking cultivation, preferably in isoparaffinic oil carrier.
Prometryn	1 Kg ha^{-1}	-
Propanil	1.75 Kg ha^{-1}	-
Bentazon	2.2 Kg ha^{-1}	Repeat its applications to control a perennial weed like *Cirsium arvense*.
Metoxuron	0.4-0.8 Kg ha^{-1}	-
Terbutryn	0.5-0.75 Kg ha^{-1}	-

Herbicides	Rates	Remarks
1	2	3
Pendimethalin	1-1.5 kg ha	Apply preplant.
RAMIE (*Boehmeria nivea*)		
Atrazine + paraquat	1 = 2 Kg ha^{-1}	Apply to young weeds after individual cutting of ramie.
Atrazine + dalapon	1 +2 Kg ha^{-1}	-do-
RUBBER (*Hevea brasiliensis*)		
Paraquat	0.42-0.56Kg ha^{-1}	Apply as directed spray for ring weeding rubber. Use lower rates around mature rubber and higher rates around the immature trees. Diuron can be combined with paraquat 2-3 months after planting of the rubber seedlings.
Amitrole-T	0.2 to 1.0% spray	Apply as directed spray. Paraquat and amitrole-T are the most common herbicides used in rubber plantations.
Dalapon	13-16 Kg ha^{-1}	Use for preplanting desiccation of grasses, particularly against *Imperata cylindrica*.
MSMA (and DSMA)	2-2.5 Kg ha^{-1}	Apply as directed spray, using a wetting agent.
Neburon	2-2.5 Kg ha^{-1}	Neburon is effective in new rubber plantations which are still under the legume cover. Treat when the legume cover is about 2 months old.
Simazine, Cynazine	1-2 Kg ha^{-1}	Apply preemergence to weeds.
SISAL (*Agave sisalana*)		
Bromacil/atraton/diuron/dalapon/atrazine/ simazine/fluometuron.	At usual rates	All these herbicides have proved good for preemergence treatment of agave nurseries and plantations in different situations. By trial one can pick-up the herbicide most suited to one's agroclimate.
Dalapon	-do-	Apply six months before planting agave, particularly when a perennial grass like *Digitaria scalarum* is to be controlled.
TEA (*Camellia sinensis*) and COFFEE (*Coffea arabica*)		
Dalapon (with 0.5% of wetting agent)	7-8 Kg ha^{-1} (or 1% spray)	Use for the control of actively growing perennial grasses at their 10 cm height. Row cultivate 4-6 weeks later. Treat also the regrowth with dalapon.
Diuron (with 0.5% of a suitable wetting agent)	2.62-3.40 Kg ha^{-1}	Treat no more than 5 cm tall weeds. Avoid drift to the pruned tea bushes to avoid their forced bud break and bunly shoots. Avoid the treatment on light and erodable soils. Do not over rate

Herbicides	Rates	Remarks
1	2	3
		diuron.
Fluometuron	2.62-3.40 Kg ha^{-1}	Apply preemergence to weeds. Fluometuron is safer than diuron to coffee and is slightly less persistent in soil.
Linuron	2.25-3.35 Kg ha^{-1}	-do-
Simazine	2.25-3.35 Kg ha-1	Simazine is a very safe herbicide for preemergence control of weeds in tea and coffee. Apply 6 months after sowing in seed nursery; 2-3 weeks before sowing in clonal nursery; and during summer in established tea plantations.
Paraquat	0.25-0.4 Kg ha^{-1} (or 0.2-0.4% spray)	Apply paraquat to dense stand of young weeds no taller than 15 cm. It will kill most annual weeds and debiliate the perennials. Paraquat is supposed to suppress the further growth of *Imperata* rhizomes in tea and coffee. Repeat the treatment with half the dose, 2 to 3 times annually. Spray through flood-nozzles of knapsack sprayers to avoid drift hazards. Paraquat can injure green suckers and stem of coffee which may lead to secondary infection of *Fusarium*.
Dichlobenil	3-4.5 Kg ha^{-1}	Dichlobenil is specific to control nutsedge in tea.
Glyphosate	0.6-1 Kg ha^{-1}	Very promising against *Imperata cylindrica* and other deep rooted, perennial weeds.
Napropamide	4.0 Kg ha^{-1}	Apply after cleaning the field by hand weeding.
Methazole	0.12-0.25 Kg ha^{-1}	It is found effective in tea plantations, both preemergence and postemergence.
Oxyfluorfen	0.12-0.25 Kg ha^{-1}	It is found highly selective to coffee and tea plantations, both preemergence and postemergence.
Glufosinate ammonium	0.08-0.1%	Apply as spot treatment of problem perennial weeds.
Metribuzin	1.4-2.1 Kg ha^{-1}	It is found to control emerged weeds and also provide their selective residual control throughout the monsoon period.
MB, Metham, allyl alcohol	At usual rates	Soil fumigation before planting coffee.

Herbicides	Rates	Remarks
1	2	3
Oryzalin		Apply before weed emergence in 1 year or older coffee plantations. Coffee plants are very tolerant to this herbicide.
	CASSAVA (*Manihot aipi*)	
Fluchloralin	1.0 kg/ha	Apply preemergence
Pendimethalin	1.0 kg/ha	This can be flowered
Thiobencarb	1.5 kg/ha	
	CARDAMOM (*Elettria cardamom*)	
Paraquat	0.4 kg/ha	Apply prior to initiation of cropping
Glyphosate	0.8 kg/ha	fruiting branches.
	TURMERIC (*Curcuma longa*)	
Atrazine	0.75 kg/ha	Apply preemergence
Oxyfluorfen	0.15 kg/ha	The two herbicides have prover very promising in field trials
	GINGER (*Zingiber officinale*)	
Alachlor	1.0-1.5 kg/ha	Apply preemergence
	ROSELLE (*Hibiscus* sp.)	
Fluchloralin	1.0 kg/ha	Apply preplant
	TAPIOCA (*Manihot utilissima*)	
Oxyflucoralin	1.0 kg/ha	Apply preemergence (to weeds)
Pendimethalin	1.0 kg/ha	
Oxadiazon	2-4 kg/ha	

Table 22.5: Effect of Weed Control Methods on Leaf Yield of Mulberry And Associated Weeds in 1991-92 (After Shivakumar *et al.*, 1994)

Treatments	Dry weed biomass (Mean of 2 years) (q/ha)	Mulberry leaf yield (q/ha)			% increase
		Kharif	*Rabi*	Mean	
Unweeded check	41.11	2.77	2.57	2.67	-
Hand-weeded	0.0	8.35	8.40	8.37	213.5
Diuron* (1.2 kg/ha)	8.02	7.17	7.27	7.22	170.4
C.D. (at P = 0.05)	-	0.38	0.37	-	-

Note: **Diuron was applied preemergence to weeds a day after bottom pruning of mulberry in the kharif season only.*

22.3 GRASSLANDS

22.3.1 The Weed Problem

In India and many other tropical countries grasslands are largely left uncared, and abound in shruby and herbaceous weeds that are unpalatable and, many a time, harmful to the animals. Dutta and Singh (1970) estimated that in Bundelkhand region of India alone, brush occupied 35% of the grassland area. Weeds in grasslands compete with grasses for space and nutrients, thus, reducing their carrying capacity. In a weedy grassland, considerable portions of grasses are hidden by the bushes which remain unaccessible to the animals. Experiments conducted at the Indian Grassland and Fodder Research Institute, Jhansi, showed that a well managed grassland devoid of bushes gave a hay yield of 42 q/ha against 12 q/ha when it was infested with an average of 1800 bushes per ha and 5.5 q/ha when the bush population was 3500 per ha. This amounted to a fall in hay yield of grasslands by 70 and 87 per cent, respectively (Magoon and Dabadghao, 1973). Likewise, Singh *et al.* (1971) found that yield of forage grasses in the bush-free portion of grasslands was 35 q/ha as against 8 q/ha in the heavily infested areas. However, one should expect increased forage production from weed control in grasslands only when the intended forage grass and legume species were still present in sufficient population to spread back. James *et al.*(1991) has listed some major noxious weeds of rangelands.

Table 22.6: Weed Control in Japanese Mint (*Mentha arvensis* L.) Through Pendimethalin (After Jaindev *et al.*, 1993)

Treatments	Dry weed biomass (q/ha) during		Fresh herbage yield of mint (q/ha) during	
	1st growth	2nd growth	1st growth	2nd growth
Unweeded check	10.2	65.1	41	42
Hand-weeded (4 times)	2.8	7.0	257	152
Pendimethalin (1.0 kg/ha)	14.1	30.6	240	136
C.D. (at P = 0.05)	-	-	25	17

Comments: *Preplant pendimethalin provided adequate weed control to boost the mint yield to the level of hand-weeded crops. (In this experiment authors further reported fluchloralin as toxic to the crop).*

22.3.2 The Weed Management Practices

The weed problem in any grassland is aggravated primarily as a consequence of mismanagement, which may include over or under grazing, poor soil and water conservation, lack of fertilization, etc. Therefore, to properly manage the weeds in grasslands, weed control methods should be teamed with (a) controlled and deferred grazing, (b) proper fertilization, (c) soil and water conservation practices. The application of weed control measures in the absence of these practices may yield unsatisfactory results.

Burning is helpful in destroying undesirable brushes in grasslands in humid areas, but in dry regions it may simultaneously prove injurious to the forage component of the grassland. In such areas, physical methods of weed control like mowing, hard grazing, cabling, girdling, and grubbing should be preferred over burning. However, both burning and physical destruction of weeds are of limited utility in as much as the severed weeds may regrow vigorously after some interval from their underground portions. Also, the creeping type of weeds in grasslands usually escape the common physical weed control operations in grasslands. Merchant (1993) found 20-30 goats could graze *Juncus* sp. in 1 ha pasture in 3 years.

Biological control has been highly successful in vacating grasslands of their certain aggressive weeds, notably *Opuntia* spp., *Hypericum perforatum*, and *Senecio jacobaea* in different countries (Chapter-9). Further research is underway on the biological control of other difficult weeds in grasslands.

Herbicides are employed in some agriculturally advanced countries to recover the grasslands from weeds more efficiently than the physical methods, including flaming. (Table 22.6). *Annual herbaceous weeds*, both broadleafs and grasses, are comparatively easy to control in established grasslands when herbicides are applied either at the beginning of the growing season or after grazing of the grasslands. The weeds at this time are beginning to germinate and most of them are still young. Even if a herbicide scorches some desirable grasses in the grassland, the injury will be temporary and soon the forage regrowth will crowd out the weeds. In new grasslands no herbicide should be applied until the grass roots are established and the sod has developed.

Perennial, herbaceous weeds in grasslands are more difficult to control than the annuals. In recent years some very effective herbicides such as picloram, dicamba, and 2,3,6-TBA, have been discovered that kill the *perennial broadleaf weeds* without appreciable damage to the forage grass component of the grasslands. The timing of herbicide application to perennial weeds is very important; the objective should be to treat them at a time when their underground food reserves are at low level. This usually coincides with early bud stage of the weeds.

Chemical control of *perennial grasses* in grasslands is still a problem. Much of the perennial grass control in grasslands must still be attempted through proper grassland management techniques combined, at most, with spot application of herbicides. New perennial weeds starting from seeds must be controlled like annual weeds before they develop their perennial character.

Returns from herbicide usages in grasslands in terms of increased grass production usually cannot be obtained in the year of treatment. Depending upon the situation, one must wait for two or more years for seeing the increased grass production. During this period freedom from weeds itself should be a great satisfaction to the grassland owners.

Lastly, herbicides in grasslands often impose certain after-treament waiting periods for permitting grazing. These are usually well displayed by the herbicide companies, and one should adhere to these restrictions strictly.

Phenoxys, chiefly 2,4-D and 2,4,5-T, are reported to be hazardous to the grazing animals in varied, indirect ways. These may make the otherwise unacceptable, poisonous weeds more palatable. For instance, *Senecio* 'ragwort', and *Conium* 'hemlock' spp. are known to become sweeter upon treatment with 2,4-D. In forage sorghum, the fatal glycoside content may increase, by up to 70%. In *Eupatorium macuiatum*, the nitrite content was found to increase to toxic levels. Application of sodium arsenite as a herbicide to grasslands is beset with the obvious, direct hazards.

22.3.3 Renovation of Grasslands

When weeds and brushes have infested a grassland to render it unfit for grazing, it is called a *degraded grassland*. There is no use trying to control weeds in such grasslands in the hope of making these reuseable because there is not sufficient population of the desirable grasses left in the degraded grasslands to cover the spaces recovered from the weeds. In such a situation, one must seriously consider renovation of the grassland. The old sward must be destroyed by either deep tillage or with some non-residual, foliage active herbicide. Paraquat, diquat, and MAMA have been successfully used in the renovation of weedy grasslands. New seeds of desired grasses/legumes should then be planted soon without any additional tillage of the land, lest the recovered grassland should get reinfested soon with weeds.

The main advantage of using herbicides instead of tillage for the renovation of grasslands is to avoid soil erosion and minimise soil moisture losses, wherever these are important factors in grassland management.

Table 22.7: Herbicidal Control of Herbaceous and Woody Weeds in Grasslands (Key: B= broadleaf weeds, G = grasses, NS = nutsedges, and Br = brush weeds)

Herbicide	Time of treatment	Rate (kg/ha)*	Type of weed	Remarks
1	2	3	4	5
I. Annual Weeds				
Amitrole	Postemergence	2-2.5	G	Use only in established grasslands.
Borax	Postemergence	1000	G, B	Broadcast in weedy grasslands. The grasslands will usually recover in 2-3 years.
Bensulide	Postemergence	4.8	G	Apply during dormancy period of the grassland.
Bromacil	Preemergence	2	G.B	Apply just before the spring growth of grassland.
Chloramben	Preemergence	4-4.5	G, B	Use for weed control in new seedings of grass/ legume mixtures.
Dalapon	Postemergence	1-2	G	Use only in established grasslands.
Diuron	Preemergence	1-2	G	Apply either just after transplanting new grasslands or during the dormancy period of the established grasslands.
Diuron	Postemergence	1-2	G	Use only in established grasslands.
Fluometuron	Preemergence	1.5-2.0	G	Apply during dormancy period of the grassland.
Linuron	Preemergence	1-1.2	G	Apply during dormancy period of the grassland.
Prometryn	Post harvest	3-4	G	Apply after the last forage harvest and then leave the grassland to seed.

* unless otherwise specified.

Herbicide	Time of treatment	Rate (kg/ha)*	Type of weed	Remarks
1	2	3	4	5
Simazine (and atrazine)	Preemergence	1-3	G,B	Apply either just after transplanting a new grassland, or in dormant grasslands.
2, 4-D (ester)	Postemergence	0.5-0.75	B, NS	Apply when the forage species are in 4 to 5-leaf stage.
2, 4-DB (ester)	Postemergence	0.75-1.0	B, NS	Use it in legume/grass pastures in preference to 2,4-D.
Vernolate	Preplant soil incorporation	2-4	G, B	Use in certain forage legumes like *Lespedaza*, which is tolerant to it.
II. Perennial weeds				
Amitrole	Postemergence	0.8%	Br	Effective as spot treatment against milkweeds and thistles.
Bromoxynil	Postemergence	0.5-1.5	B, G	Apply when the forage seedlings are in l-leaf stage.
Dalapon	Postemergence	2%	G	Apply by spot treatment.
Dicamba + 2,4-D (or MCPP)	Postemergence	0.25-0.75	B	Apply at the preflowering stage of bindweed, rumex, and docks.
Dicamba	Postemergence	0.5-1.0	B, G	Apply when the forage seedlings are in 1-leaf stage.
DMPA	Postemergence	20-25	G	Apply when the forage species are 1-12 cm tall.
2,4-D (ester)	Postemergence	1-2	B	Use for the control of dandelions, bindweeds, ragwort, and wildgarlic.
MCPA	Postemergence	1.0	B	Use for the control of buttercups and like weeds.
Mecoprop	Postemergence	0.8%	Br	Useful in the control of thistles.
Picloram	Postemergence	1-1.5	Br	Apply before the spring growth of forage species.
Silvex	Postemergence	2-8	Br	Apply in oil for the control of rough weeds like *Opuntia* spp.
Simazine	Preemergence	1.5-2	G	Apply before the spring growth of forage specics.
Sodium chlorate	Postemergence	20 g m^{-2}	G	Apply as spot treatment.
2, 3, 6-TBA	Postemergence	10-20	Br	Use for the control of spurges and like weeds.
III. Brush Weeds				
Dicamba	(i) Foliage spray	0.25% - 0.5%	Br	Use as aqueous spray.
	(ii) Injection method	50%		Apply 0.5-10 ml per injection
Picloram	Soil treatment	(i) 10-20 g per brush	Br	Incorporate around each brush in 30 cm diameter circles.
		(ii) 7-10		Broadcast picloram in granule form.

Herbicide	Time of treatment	Rate (kg/ha)*	Type of weed	Remarks
1	2	3	4	5
				The treatment is effective when there is low but even population of brush in the grassland, and there is rain to incorporate the herbicide.
Picloram + 2,4-D	Foliage spray	0.25% (aqueous)	Br	Picloram should be the choice when one fails to kill a brush with cheaper compoud like 2,4-D.
Silvex	(i) Foliage spray	0.2-0.4%	Br	Use aqueous solution. It is more effective than 2,4,5-T against woody species, *eg Quercus, Acer, Rhus,* and *Opuntia* spp.
	(ii) -do-	5-7.5%		Use for aerial application in a mineral oil carrier.
Tebuthiuron	Foliage spray	1-2.25	Br	
2,4,5-T plus 2,4-D (1 : 2)	Foliage spray	0.2-0.6%	Br	Use aqueous solution.
(LVE)	Basal bark and stump treatment	1.2-1.8%		Use a mineral oil carrier.
	Injection method	4%		Use aqueous solution.

22.4 LAWNS (AND TURFS)

22.4.1 The Weed Problem

For those who have a lawn, weeds are a constant headache. Successful weeds in lawns are low growing annual and perennial species, capable of withstanding repeated mowings and closed community environment. Annual grasses and sedges, such as *Digitaria, Poa,* and *Cyperus* spp,. and broadleafs like *Oxalis* and *Taraxacum* spp. are common problem weeds in lawns in the country.

22.4.2 The Weed Management Practices

Proper mowing, fertilization, and watering are three fundamentals of good lawn management. When the three operations are teamed in a manner that would result in a dense, healthy turf, the weeds are considerably smothered. Herbicides further aid in the development of a dense turf by stunting the weeds or preventing their occurrence. Weed management practices in lawns differ with the grass species in question, locality, and season of the year. Some of the relevant common lawn management practices affecting weed control are as follows:-

1. *Planting Material*: One should use only weedfree planting material for establishing a new lawn.
2. *Mowing:* Time, frequency, and lawn height at mowing have to do much with weed control and the growth of the lawn grass. Both, too close and too high mowings

allow the weeds to become vigorous; close mowings by weakening the lawn, and high mowings by inducing the lawn grass to go stemmy. Likewise, too frequent or too delayed mowings will aggravate weed problem although the type of weeds encouraged by the two wrong practices may differ. In any case, a lawn must be mowed so as to cut the weeds before they set seeds. Clippings obtained from mowings should be removed if they were heavy enough to smother the turf; weeds tend to move into the smothered areas.

3. *Irrigation*: Frequent, shallow waterings favour shallow turf and a rampant growth of weed. The turf should be soaked to a depth of 15-23 cm and allowed to dry at the surface to give a set-back to the annual, weedy grasses and broadleafs before the next irrigation.

4. *Fertilization:* Fertilizers should not be applied to weedy lawns without first killing the weeds with an appropriate herbicide, otherwise it will stimulate the weedy grasses more than the lawn grass. Appropriate fertilization of the lawn often helps in allowing higher frequency of mowing which may weaken the weeds, depending upon the kind and time of application of the fertilizer.

5. *Use of herbicides:* Very effective herbicides are now available to suppress weeds in turfs. This, combined with adeqate fertilization, watering, and proper seeding material, should allow the turf to grow into the spaces recovered from weeds. A listing of lawn herbicides follows in Table 22.8.

Table 22.8: Herbicidal Control in Lawns and Turfs (Key symbols A = annual; P = perennial; G = grasses; NS = nutsedge; Bl = broadleaf weeds)

Herbicide	Type of weeds controlled	Type of treatment	Remarks
(1)	(2)	(3)	(4)
I. For Establishing New Lawns			
EPTC (6-8 kg/ha)	NS, G (A)	Preplant incorporation	Mix deep, with friable soil. Do not irrigate for one week. Run a roller after herbicide incorporation.
Metham (1 kg m^{-2})	Most weed specics	Preplant	Treat the soil and drench with water for 48 hrs. Cultivate 5 to 7 days later and seed 7-15 days thereafter. (May also use MB or any other suitable fumigant instead of metham).
II. For Preemergence (to Weeds) Treatment in Established Lawns			
Atrazine (or simazine (0.5-10 kg/ha)	Bl,G (A)	Spray	Irrigate immediately after treatment.
Bensulide (10-20 kg/ha)	G (A)	Spray	-do-
Benefin (2-3 kg/ha)	G, Bl (A)	Spray	-do-
DCPA (4-10 kg/ha)	Crabgrass	Spray	-do-
DMPA (10-20 Kg/ha)	G (A)	Spray or broadcast as	-do-

Herbicide	Type of weeds controlled	Type of treatment	Remarks
(1)	(2)	(3)	(4)
		granules	
Trifluralin, nitralin, or profluralin (2-3 kg/ha)	G (A)	Spray	-do-
III. Postemergence Treatments in Established Lawns			
2, 4-D (1 kg/ha)	Bl (A), NS	Spray	Use only salts of 2,4-D. Provide physical protection to ornamental beds, or use drift control additives. Don't apply 2,4-D to bentgrass lawn. To control nutsedge, combine EPTC (3 kg/ha) with, 2,4-D.
Dicamba (0.4 kg/ha)	Bl (A)	Spray	Do not use ester formulations. Avoid drift hazards to ornamentals. It is particularly effective against *Euphorbia* and *Polygonum* spp.
Endothall (3-4 Kg/ha)	Bl (A)		Use any salt of endothall. It is particularly active on *Veronica* spp.
MAA (2-4 kg/ha)	G (A), NS	Spray	Apply when the weedy grasses are 5-7.5 cm tall. Repeat the spray when needed. *Digitaria* and *Paspalum* spp. are particularly susceptible to MAA and its salts. Conduct a test spray to determine the lawn grass tolerance to MAA. Seed the recovered patches immediately with the lawn grass species.
Paraquat (or diquat) (0.5-1.0 Kg/ha)	Bl, G (A)		The treatment will cause total lawn scorch. But the perennial lawn grass shall recover soon after an irrigation. Include a residual preemergence herbicide in the spray liquid to suppress the new weeds from seeds.
Silvex (1 kg/ha)	Bl (A)	Spray	Weeds like *Euphorbia* and *Oxalis* spp. are susceptible to silvex.

SUMMARY

Orchards and plantations comprise very wide inter-row space crops, providing a completely different ecosystem to the weeds than the field crops and vegetables. This results in not only a typical, persistent weed flora but also need for a long period weed management effort till the crop canopy closes in, to maintain the tree vigour. In crops like tea and coffee which are subjected to every year pruning, an open environment for the weeds exists almost permanently. In grasslands, on the other hand, weeds meet a very closed environment. Therefore, the weed species here are absolutely different, comprising largely grasses and bushes, which can withstand not only crowded spaces, but also are capable of slowly replacing the desirable grassland species. Some prominent weed species of orchards, plantations, and grasslands have been cited.

Intercropping with leguminous plants has been successful in the suppression of weeds in certain plantations. In orchards, intercropping with vegetables and forages, although practised as an indirect method of weed control, is considered competitive to the fruit trees. In grasslands, good agronomic management, including proper grazing schedule, fertilisation, and quick gap filling, are very important pre-requisites to weed management.

Herbicidal control of weedy bushes, grasses, and herbaceous weeds has made much advancements in orchards, plantations, and grasslands. While most of these herbicides are for spot treatment, some can be applied as directed spray, and still others as overall treatment. These have been briefly tabulated in this chapter.

SELECTED BIBLIOGRAPHY

1. Aldhous, J.R. 2000. Pesticides, Pollutants, Fertilizers, and Trees. Their Role in Forests and Amenity Worldlands. Baldock, UK Research Studies Press Ltd. 588 p.
2. Anwar, C. and Bacon, B. 1986. Comparison of *Imperata* control by manual and mechanical methods for small holder **rubber** farming system. Biotrop. Special Pub. 24:307-316.
3. Awatramani, N.A. and Mathew, P.K. 1973. Herbicidal control of weeds and its effects on growth and yield of **coffee**. J. Coff. Res. 3 (3) 61-70.
4. Balakrishnan, S. and Pillai, G.R. 1976. Herbicidal control of weeds in **pineapple** variety Kew. Agr. Res. J. Kerala 14(2) 132-137.
5. Balasubramanian, R. *et al.*, 1985. Effect of chemical weed killers versus cultural operations in weed growth and yield of **coconut**. Ind. Coconut J. 16:17-20
6. Bankpur, V. M.*et al.* 1973. Simazine, dalapon, and EPTC in **vineyards**. Curr. Res. 2(1) 3-4
7. Bhutani, V.P., *et al.* 1983. Effect of herbicides and nitrogen on weed control, yield, and quality of Santa Rose **Plum** J. Res. Sci. 2:84-90.
8. Brecke, B.J. 1981. Smutgrass (*Sporobolus poiretii*) control in Bahiagrass (*Paspalum notatum*) **pastures**. Weed Sci., 29:55.
9. Brewsler, B.D. and Stanger, C.E. 1980. Bentazon for Canadathistle control in **peppermint** (*Mentha piperita*). Weed Sci. 28(1) 36-39.
10. Chacko, E.K. and Reddy, A. 1981. Effect of planting distance and intercropping with cowpea on weed growth in **bananas**. Proc. 8th Asian-Pacific Weed Sci. Soc. Conference. Pages 137-141.
11. Chatha, R.P.S. and Y.R. Chanana 2003. Studies on wood management in young **peach** orchards. Abst. Bien. Conf. ISWS held 12-14 March, 2003 at G.B.P. Univ. Agr. & Technol. Pantnagar (India): 90.
12. Chitkara, S.E. and Kamali, A.G.H. 1978. Effect of herbicides on the growth, yield, and quality of berries in perellatte **grapes**. Haryana J. Hort. Sci. 7 (1, 2) 6.

13. Crawford, M.C. and Simpson, R.J. 1993. Manipulation of the feeding value of senescing annual **ryegrass** (*Lolium rigidum*) with imazethapyr and glyphosate. Aust. J. Agri. Res. 44(7) 1653-1666.

14. Dhuria, H.S. and Leela, D. 1971. Chemical control of weeds in **banana**. Ind. J. Hort. 28 (1) 22-24.

15. Dutta, T.R. and Singh, R.P. 1970. Weed control is a must in **pastures** too. Ind. Farmer's Digest 3(1) 27-30.

16. Evans, S.G. and Workman, J.P. 1994. Optimization of **range** improvements on sagebrush and pinyon-juniper sites. J. Range Mgt. 47(2) 159-164.

17. Gautam, D.R. 1980. Effect of long term use of several herbicides on yield, quality, and storage of Santa Rose **plum**. Haryana J. Hort. Sci. 9(3/4) 122-124.

18. Ghanbari, A. and Bhullar, J.S. 1986. Relative efficacy of preemergence herbicides in **Kinnow-Mandarin**. Ind. J. Weed Sci. 17(1) 45-47.

19. Gibbens, R.P. *et al.* 1987. Field scale tebuthiuron application on brush infested **rangeland**. Weed Technol. 1: 323-327.

20. Gunathilake, H.A.J. 1985. Weed control in **coconut** lands. Planter 61 (716) 531-537.

21. Hamel, C. *et al.* 1994. Mycorrhizal colonization increases herbicide toxicity in **apple**. J. Amer. Soc. Hot. Sci. 119 (6): 1255-1260

22. Himme, M. *et al.* 1986. Nursery crops: Dwarf fruits. Weed Abstr. 36(2) 1987, item 407.

23. Jaidev, S.J.N. and Singh, G. 1993. Chemical weed control in Japanese **mint** (*Mentha arvensis* L.) Ind. J. Weed Sci. 25(1 & 2) 50-54.

24. James, L.W. *et al.* 1991. Noxious Range Weeds. Westview Press 500 p.

25. Kaundal, G.S. *et al.* 1994. Studies on weed control in **peach** (*Prunus persica* L. Batch) orchard. Ind. J. Weed Sci. 26 (1 & 2) 68-72.

26. Korikanthimath, V.S. and Venugopal, M.N. 1986. Some weeds of **cardamom** estates. Ind. J. Weed Sci. 17(3) 59-60.

27. Kuhns, L.J. *et al.* 1986. Preemergence and postemergence grass herbicides on annual flowers. Weed Abst. 32(2) 1987, item 389.

28. Leela, D. 1982. A decade of weed research in horticultural crops. Pesticides 16(10) 3-8.

29. Litwinee, J. and Grzybowska, E. 1985. Control of troublesome perennial weeds in **grasslands** and watercress. Weed Abst. 36(2) 1987, item 368.

30. Magoon, M.L. and Dabadghao, P.M. 1973. How to achieve potential **grassland** production? Indian Fmg. 23(5) 15-19.

31. Masters, R.A. *et al.* 1994. Leafy spurge control with fall-applied imazapyr, imazaquin, and imazethapyr. Weed Technol. 8(1) 58-63.

32. Merchant, M. 1993. The potential for control of the soft rush (*Juncus effusus*) in grass **pasture** by grazing goats. Grass and Forage Science 48(4) 395-409.

33. Mohapatra, S. 2005. Effect of weed control in **sabaigrass** (Eulaliopsis binata. Ind. J. Weed Sci. 37 (3 & 4): 291-292.

34. Muniyappa T.V. and Shivkumar, H.R. 1994. Nutrient uptake by **mulberry** and associated weeds. Ind. J. Weed Sci. 26(3-4) 148-151.

35. Muniyappa, T.V. *et al.* 2003. Management of weeds in **golf course**. Abst. Bienn. Conf. ISWS held 12-14 March 2003 at G.B.P. Univ. of Agr. & Technol, Pantnagar (India): 89.

36. Namdoo, K. N. and Dubey, J.H. 1979. Herbicides in renovation of **grasslands** of Madhya Pradesh, PANS (c) 16:117-120.

37. Nishimoto, R.K. 1992. Evaluation of preemergence herbicides for establishing **coffee**. Trop. Pest. Mgmt. 38 (3) 298-301.

38. Palmer, C. 2002. Controlling weeds around the **woodland** environment. Forestry & British Timber 31(2) : 28-30. (UK)

39. Patil, V.C. and Patil, S.V. 1983. Studies on weed control in **bamboo**. Ind. J. Weed Sci. 15(1) 83-86.

40. Rajkhowa, D.J. *et al.* 2005. Evaluation of carfentrazone-ethyl 40 DF and glyphosate as tank mixture for weed control in **tea**. Ind. J. Weed Sci. 37(1 &2): 157-158.

41. Ramadass, R.C. and Vaithialingam, M. 1980. Control of weeds in **banana** with herbicides. Proc. Nat. Seminar on Banana Prod. Technol., TNAU., Coimbatore, pages 93-97.

42. Randhawa, G.S. *et al.* 1982. Weed control in the first and second cutting of ***Mentha arvensis***. Ind. Perfumer (2-4) 107-111.

43. Rathore, M.S. and Pareek, O.P. 1977. Chemical control in a Thompson seedless **vineyard**. Haryana J. Hort. Sci. 6(182) 15.

44. Riepma, P. 1968. Weed control in **rubber** cultivation-A new review. PANS (C) 14:43-61.

45. Satyanaryana, N. *et al.* 1981. The potential of metribuzin as a broad-spectrum herbicide in **tea** culture. Trop. Pest. Management 27 (2) 401-404.

46. Savithri, K.E. *et al* 1994. Weed management in **coconut-banana** intercropping system. Ind. J. Weed Sci. 26(3-4) 57-63.

47. Shaikh, A.R. and O.G. Lokhande. 2005. Effect of sequential herbicide application on **banana** and weeds. Ind. J. Weed Sci. 37 (3 & 4): 289-290.

48. Shanmughavelu, K.G. *et al.* 1985. Weed Management in Horticultural Crops. Agrobios (India) Jodhpur, 114 p.

49. Sharma, B.K. *et al.* 1980. Effect of some herbicides on weed control in **Remie** plantations. Ind. J. Weed Sci. 12(2) 125-129.

50. Sharma, Y.P. 1991. Interaction effect of nitrogen and weed control treatments on yield and quality of *Shan-i-Punjab* **peach**. Haryana J. Hort. Sci. 20(1-2) 50-55.

51. Shivakumar, H.R. 1994. Effect of chemical weed control on nutrient uptake by common **mulberry** (*Morus australis*) and associated weeds. Ind. J. Agro. 32(2) 277-281.

52. Singh, A. 1982. Weed control studies in **mint**. Indian perfumer 99-103.

53. Singh, A. *et al.* 200. Integrated weed management in **turmeric** (*Curcuma longa*) planted under popular plantation. Ind. J. Weed Sci. 34: 329-330.

54. Singh, M.P. 1985. A perspective of weed control in **tea**. Two and a Bud 32 (1-2) 35-39.

55. Singh, R.D. *et al.* 2000. Chemical weed control in *Cynodon dactylon* **lawns**. Ind. J. Weed Sci. 32: 146-149.

56. Singh, R.P. *et al.* 1971. Weed problem and control in **grassland** and **fodder** crops in India. Ind. J. Weed Sci. 3(1) 45-50.

57. Srinivasan, E.B. *et al.* 1994. Effect of weed density on the nutritive value of **mulberry**. Ind. J. Sericulture 26(3) 72-75.

58. Stephenson, D.W. and Mitchell, G.J. 1993. Barley grass control with herbicides in sub-terranean clover **pasture**. Aust. J. Expt. Agri. 33(6) 737-741.

59. Ulvund, M.J. 1992. Toxic **pasture**-lands for sheep. Weed Abst. 1993. 42(11) 590 (item 4708).

60. Victor R. *et al.* 2001. Evaluation of glufosinate ammonium in **tea** (*Camellia* spp. L.), Ind. J. Weed Sci. 33: 227-228.

61. Walia, U.S. *et al.* 1980. Studies on chemical weed control in Japanese **mint**. Ind. J. Weed Sci. 12(2) 181-185.

62. Zhang, Y.S. *et al.* 1993. Experiments on controlling weeds in sown *Festuca sinensis* **grasslands** by applying 2,4-D-butyl. Grassland of China 1: 6, 47-51.

Chapter 23

NON-SELECTIVE CONTROL OF WEEDY VEGETATION

By definition, the non-selective control of weedy vegetation, also called general vegetation control, includes its indiscriminate suppression and prevention of its future growth for some target period. Non-selective weed control may be desirable on non-croplands, around water-bodies, and crop lands, with specific objectives. In practice, most of the time our objective of vegetation management in non-crop areas should be to curb only its excessive growth which is considered weedy, and to encourage the low growing, soil conserving, and better eye-appealing grasses.

23.1 WEED CONTROL ON NON-CROP LANDS

Both mechanical and chemical methods are available for the weed control in non-crop areas. The choice will depend upon a number of factors. Probably, the most important of these is the situation of the operational area. Herbicides, for instance, will impart repulsive appearance to highways by browning the vegetation, whereas mowing and cutting will maintain the natural green look by letting the low grasses grow. High power rotary mowers are used for vegetation management on highways and ditchbanks. But in many other non-crop situations, such as railway rights-of-way, petroleum farms, pavements, and air strips, herbicidal control is more convenient and desirable. In these situations, physical methods cannot reach the weeds easily, and their effects are not sufficiently long lasting. Herbicides are also important where bare soil is desired, for instance, under fence-rows and pipe lines, around electric and telegraph poles, observatory structures, forest fire-breaks, and asphalt and gravel walks. Such herbicides are called soil sterilants, which are discussed in Sec. 23.1.3.

23.1.1 Herbicides For Non-Crop Lands

1. **Dalapon and Phenoxy Herbicides:** Dalapon and 2,4-D mixtures are widely used as general, broad-spectrum weed killers. The combination causes simultaneous control

of grasses, sedges, cattails and broadleafs. The proportion of the two herbicides in combination varies with the weed species. The final combination concentration is 0.5 to 1%. Wetting agents will generally improve their herbicidal effects. Application of dalapon plus 2,4-D at 7 to 10 days' interval when earheads in grasses have just started to form, frequently provides satisfactory vegetation control. When weeds like morningglories, dandelions, wildonion, and wildgarlic are present in considerable proportion in the noxious vegetation on a non-crop land, a low volatile form of 2,4-D should be preferred over its other formulations. 2,4-D alone is useful when grasses are to be spared, such as on roadsides and ditchbanks. It can be applied both as spray (0.1-0.15%) and granules (30-40 kg/ha). Dalapon and 2,4-D mixtures persist in soils for 4-6 weeks.

2. **Picloram:** Picloram (1-4 kg/ha) is perferred over most other non-selective herbicide treatments where deep rooted broadleaf weeds must be destroyed without undue injury to grasses.

3. **Paraquat and Amitrole-T:** Paraquat and amitrole-T are practically non-residual herbicides; good for treating vegetation on ditchbanks, irrigation channels, and other like situations where toxic herbicide residues cannot be tolerated beyond a very short period. Their effective spray concentrations are 0.1-0.2% and 1.0 %, respectively.

4. **Prometryn:** Prometryn usually forms a component herbicide with 2,4-D to destroy mixed growth of perennial grasses and broadleafs. Its non-selective rates are 5-8 kg/ha. But for a more permanent weed control, follow-up treatments are necessary every five weeks or so throughout the growing season.

5. **Petroleum Oils:** Petroleum oils with over 25% aromatic content are useful for non-selective, non-residual weed control. The low viscosity herbicidal oils are particularly good for treating grasses and sedges since such oils creep down the stems into their crowns and rosettes where their growing points are located. But to avoid drifts, low viscosity oils must be applied through flood nozzles under very low pressure. The viscosity of oils is given as API. The non-selective oils of 27-38° API are considered as low viscosity oils. Over 38° API oils are too thin and lack persistent action on vegetation needed in the non-selective vegetation control. Herbicidal oils of below 27° API, on the other hand, are too viscous and pose difficulty in their application, particularly during the winter season.

6. **Fortified Oils:** Low aromatic content oils can be fortified with herbicides like DNBP, and DNOC. DNBP is added at 0.6 kg and DNOC at 1.86 kg per 455 litre of the carrier oil. Fortified oils are used to destroy low growing vegetation indiscriminately. On tall vegetation the spray volume required to wet it will often be too high to be economical. Fortified oils kill a wider spectrum of weed species than the straight aromatic oils.

7. **Fortified Oil Emulsions (F.O.E):** A fortified oil emulsion comprises (i) a high aromatic content oil, (ii) a fortifying agent, (iii) water, and (iv) an emulsifier. DNOC, S, and DNBP are effective fortifying agent to form fortified oil emulsions. A common composition of a fortified-oil-emulsion is given below:

DNOC/DNBP/S	= 1-1.8 kg
Petroleum Oil with	
40-50% aromatic content	= 18 L
Water	= 720 L
Emulsifier	= 1 kg

Fortified oil emulsions are cheaper than straight oils or fortified oils. Therefore, they prove economical for use on tall growing vegetation.

8. **Phenols:** 1-2% aqueous sprays of DNOC activated with AMS, aluminium sulphate, or sodium sulphate can be used to control young vegetation growing under partial light conditions, *eg* in deep irrigation ditches or under tall trees. On open grounds the ammonium salt of DNBP (0.5%) is more suitable than other phenols.
9. **AMS:** AMS is a general weed killer that is almost free from volatile drift to the neighbouring, useful plants. This makes AMS a superior herbicide to FOE for vegetation control on farm boundaries. However, it is a long persistence herbicide in soils.
10. **Glyphosate:** Glyphosate (isopropylamine) is a foliage-applied, highly shoot translocated herbicide that destroys the roots and rhizomes of many perennial weeds. Effective at 1.12-3.36 kg/ha, it is practically non-residual in nature.
11. **Asulam:** Asulam (sodium) at 6.72 kg/ha has been reported to destroy established *Sorghum halepense* for 2-3 months and allow rapid recolonization of the area by a low growing grass like *Cynodon dactylon*. *Asulam* holds back the weeds longer than MSMA but it is slower acting. Its effects are comparable to dalapon. Besides *Sorghum halepense*, asulam will also control *Brachiaria, Bromus, Digitaria*, and *Paspalum* spp.
12. **Imazapyr:** Imazapyr is particularly designed for obtaining non-selective control of perennial weeds by its foliage spray. Its effective rates are 0.5-1.5 kg/ha. It is likely to achieve weed control for 3-5 months.
13. **Chlorsulfuron:** It is a long persistent herbicide which makes it very good for treating unwanted vegetation in non-crop areas. It will control some difficult annual and perennial weeds, both broadleafs and grasses. The recommended rates are 0.09-0.67 kg/ha (see also Chapter-13).
14. **Carfentrazone:** When some perennial broadleaf weeds are to be eliminated from a non-crop site, carfentrazone can the priority choice. Its effective rates are 0.01-0.025 kg/ha, or more.

    Besides the above herbicides, certain triazine, substituted urea, and sulfonylurea herbicides can be used for non-selective control of unwanted vegetation at relatively higher doses.

23.1.2 Brush Weed Management on Non-Crop Land

Brush weeds refer to woody plants, underwood thickets, and small trees and shrubs. Herbicides to control brush weeds in grasslands were enumerated earlier in Chapter-22.

Besides these, there are at least four more brush killers which can be used on non-croplands. These are listed in Table 23.1.

Table 23.1: Additional Important Brush Killers For Non-Crop lands

Brush killer	Rate and method of application	Remarks
(1)	(2)	(3)
Amitrole-T	0.2% aqueous, foliage spray	It proves superior to 2,4,5-T and silvex in killing a brush weed like *Rhus* spp.
AMS	(i) 6-10% aqueous foliage spray	-do-
	(ii) 50% aqueous, stump or frill treatment	An effective arboricide to kill large trees. Absorption of AMS through bark is rapid.
	(iii) 125 g per 10 cm trunk diameter as frill treatment	-do-
	(iv) 10% aqueous foliage spray	Use for the treatment of young sprouts from the cut stumps of trees.
Bromacil	(i) 5-24 kg/ha as dry granules (ii) 2-4% aqueous spray, as basal bark treatment.	Bromacil is superior to other herbicides, including picloram, on *Quereus* spp. 'oak' and *Acer rubrum* 'red maple'. But picloram has proved more effective than bromacil on *Vaccinium* spp 'huckleberry', *Callicarpa americana* 'beanlyberry' *and Sassafras albidum* 'sassafras'.
Karbutilate	(i) 3-3.5 g (10% granules) per cm stem diameter as frill treatment. (ii) 1.8 kg/ha aqueous foliage spray.	It has provided 99% kill of several woody species on industrial sites. It is useful against 2,4,5-T tolerant brush weeds.

23.1.3 Soil Sterilants for Non-crop Areas

The aim of using soil sterilants is to obtain bare soil. Depending upon the length of time a sterilant maintains a bare ground, it can be classed as permanent, semi-permanent, or temporary soil sterilant. A permanent soil sterilant sterilises the soil for 24 months; semi-permanent for 4-24 months; and temporary sterilant for less than 4 months. While on non-cropland permanent and semi-permanent soil sterilants are used, the temporary soil sterilants are useful on croplands.

Table 23.2: Permanent and Semi-Permanent Soil Sterilants Used on Non-Croplands

Sterilant	Rate and form	Remarks
(1)	(2)	(3)
Sodium chlorate	5-12 kg 100m^{-2} (dry granules or spray)	It is both a root and shoot mobile herbicide. In soils it leaches readily. The treated vegetation becomes highly inflammable. Formulations carrying fire retardants-MBC and Atlacide- are available. While spraying sodium chlorate, use low pressure sprayers with flood type nozzles. Sodium chlorate sterilises the soil for a year or more against deep rooted, perennial vegetation. Organic manures, gypsum, and sodium nitrates are effective,

Sterilant	Rate and form	Remarks
(1)	(2)	(3)
		soil-applied antidotes of sodium chlorate.
Boron (sodium tetraborate and metaborate)	20-70 kg $100m^{-2}$	Boron compounds make the soil bare for 6-24 months. Higher rates are used against the unwanted perennial vegetation and lower rates against the annual weeds. Boron compounds resist leaching, so they are not effective against the deep-rooted weeds. Grasses are somewhat tolerant to it. After boron residues have gone low in soil, grasses tend to cover the ground rapidly. This is highly desirable on highways.
Fenuron, monuron, Diuron, Fluometuron	0.16-0.5 kg $100m^{-2}$ (dry granules or foliage spray with surfactant)	The four substituted urea herbicides sterilise the soil for 1-2 years. Guided by their leaching behaviour, fenuron is preferred in low rainfall areas and monuron in heavy soil conditions. Diuron can be used against only shallow-rooted vegetation. Fenuron, monuron, and diuron are good for sterilising drainage ditches. The ditches should be wetted before the treatment and kept under flood for 48 hours.
Prometone	0.1-0.6 kg $100m^{-2}$ (spray in water diesel oil)	It may sterilise the soil for one to several years. It should be used only against deep-rooted vegetation.
Simazine	0.05-0.12 kg $100m^{-2}$	It is suitable for high rainfall regions. Its mobility in soil being low, it is safer than prometone to nearby useful trees. It must be applied preemergence to the weeds.
Bromacil, isocil, terbacil	0.07-3 kg $100m^{-2}$	The uracils are superior soil sterilants against unwanted, perennial vegetation occurring in low rainfall areas. They are applied just before weeds begin to putforth new growth. The lower recommended rates are effective against the annuals and the higher against the perennials. They sterilise the soil for 1-2 years, but their rapid leaching may make the top soil herbicide-free whence the annual weeds may rebegin invading the treated land. To control these, bromacil and isocil may be combined with a less leachable sterilant like diuron.A mixture of 0.16 kg bromacil + 0.3 kg dalapon and 0.01 kg of a wetter m^{-2} can clear over 98% of the herbaceous weeds and brushes in early spraying and keep the land weedfree for over 6 months.
Metribuzin	0.05 kg $100m^{-2}$	Metribuzin provides as complete contol of a mixed stand of perennial grasses and broadleaf weeds as diuron, bromacil, and amitrole mixtures, mentioned above.
Fenac	0.045-4.0 kg $100m^{-2}$ (aqueous spray or dry granules)	Fenac is almost immobile, laterally. This makes it safe to the nearby trees. At low rates it is effective against annual weeds and at high rates against the perennials and other hardy species. Fenac sterilizes the soil for a year of more.

Note: 1 kg 100 m^{-2} = 100 kg ha^{-1}

23.2 NON-SELECTIVE WEED CONTROL ON CROP LANDS

On crop lands non-selective weed control may be desirable on the farm bunds and channels in the preparation of seedbeds; for weed control prior to emergence of the slow germinating crops; and to keep the fallow lands clean. Tillage, in its various forms, is yet the most common and cheap method of achieving non-selective vegetation destruction on crop lands. But in many situations, herbicides have proved superior. For example, weedfree crop nurseries and flower pots can be obtained by non-selective soil sterilization with temporary soil sterilants. Likewise, preplanting desiccation of vegetation with non-selective, non-residual type of herbicides forms a very good aid in seedbed preparation. In certain situations, even no-tillage planting of crops is made possible with non-selective herbicides. In slow germinating crops like potato and sugarcane, such herbicides are empoyed for total weed kill a little before crop emergence.

In fallow lands total weed killers prevent unnecessary moisture losses, without opening the land to the vagaries of wind erosion.

23.2.1 Herbicides For Non-Selective Weed Control On Crop Lands

1. **Herbaceous Vegetation Control:** On crop lands a total weed killer should be primarily a shoot active, non-residual herbicide. Such a herbicide can be employed to obtain total weed kill either *before planting of crops, or before germination of some slow growing crops like sugarcane, potato, and several plantation crops*. Also, the total weed killers may be used in near future for *fallow land management*.

   Paraquat, diquat, glyphosate, amitrole-T, salts of MAA, and herbicidal oils are useful as total weed killers on crop lands.

2. **Temporary Soil Sterilants:** Steam is a temporary soil sterilant. It is used in green house cultivation of vegetables and ornamentals. Calcium cyanamide is sometimes used likewise to treat nursery beds. Its effective rate is 50-70 kg 100 m^{-2}.In soil it is subjected to biodegradation to urea through two phytotoxic intermediates, hydrogen cyanamide and dihydrogen cyanamide, as follows:

   $$CaCN_2 \rightarrow HCN_2 \rightarrow H_2CN_2 \rightarrow (H_2CN_2)_2 \rightarrow CO(NH_2)_2$$

   Calcium cyanamide sterilises the seedbeds for 3-12 weeks. Frequent tillage dissipates H_2CN_2 from soil while rolling the ground preserves it. The main limitation of this temporary soil sterilant is the very high quantity of nitrogen that it adds to the soil. This limitation can be partially overcome by adding kainite (a double salt of magnesium sulphate and potassium chloride) to it in the ration of 1 : 6.

3. **Soil Fumigants:** Soil fumigants are chemicals that volatilise at field temperatures and release phytotoxic vapours in soil. The phytotoxic vapours move within the soil by diffusion, killing the weed propagules that come in contact. Eventually the toxic vapours are lost into the atmosphere whereafter the crops could be planted safely. The waiting period and fumigant efficacy on weeds vary with the fumigant and many soil factors, chiefly, soil temperature, moisture, and its physical characteristics. The most suitable temperatures for fumigating soils are 10-30°C. Higher temperature may induce rapid initial phytotoxicity to the weeds but it will accelerate its

dissipation from the soil. Both, over wet and over dry conditions reduce the fumigant action. At field capacity of soils is considered ideal for destroying weed seeds and rhizomes by fumigation. Heavy soils retain the fumigant action longer than the light soils. Likewise, tillage of the treated land tends to hasten the loss of the fumigant, while rolling and mulching have reverse effects.

Soil fumigants can be used on crop lands to treat some high value crop seedbeds. These are applied after seedbed preparation and allowing these to become firm. The soil at the time of treatment must be just enough moist to induce weeds to germinate for falling easy prey to the fumigant. Too cold and too hot soils are not good for treatment with soil fumigants. Fumigants should not be used in beds surrounded by desirable trees, within 2-3 m distance. An excellent example of the use of soil fumagant in agriculture is the control (or eradicaron) of the parasitc weed *Striga* spp., on crop lands by injecting ethylene into the seedbeds (Chapter 24).

Table 23.3: Important Soil Fumigants And Their Uses

Fumigant	Rate	Remarks
MB	5-10 kg 100m^{-2}	MB is applied as a pressurised liquid under gas proof plastic cover through a special canister opener and hose. The cover is removed after about 3 days, and the soil is worked lightly for planting crops after another 2-3 days. MB is explosive and poisonous. It is often combined with chloropicrin.
CS_2	60-65 g per hole; 3-5 holes m^{-2} area	CS_2 is applied by injection, 5-20 cm deep in soil. Irrigation is used to seal the soil. CS_2 is unsuitable in high pH soils.
Metham (SMDC)	2-5 kg 100^{-2}	Metham is applied as either dry granules or as spray and incorporated into the soil by 7-15 cm deep disking. The land should be rolled immediately and irrigated to wet the top 2.5 cm of soil. (Treat and disk only 10 sq m area at a time). Wait for 3-4 weeks. Hand hoe the beds once or twice during this period. Try test planting with the desired crop before regular planting is taken up. Metham is known to act by decomposing into phytotoxic vapours of methyl isothiocyanate (MIT) in soils. It does not kill weed seeds embodied in the farm-yard manure bits. Besides seedbeds and lawns, metham is also recommended for relieving the sewers of tree roots. The dose of metham for this purpose should be low enough to kill only the intruding roots and not the tree itself.
Dazomet (DMTT)	3-3.5 kg 100 m^{-2}	Dazomet is used for treating seedbeds and potting soils against weed seeds only. *Orobanche* is susceptible to it. It is applied as dry granules and incorporated into the seedbed with a rotary hoe. The treated beds are sealed with irrigation. Dazomet releases phytotoxic vapours of methyl isothiocyanate, formaldehyde, and H_2S. For treating a heap of potting soil, apply dazomet (as spray or granules) to every 15 cm layer of the soil. The pile is then covered with a polythene trap and left for 3 weeks. Waiting period is about three weeks.

Activities like untreated soil imported into the fumigated beds along with the crop transplants and new weed seeds planted as contaminants with the crop seeds, will undo the soil fumigation effects. Also, one should not expect the soil fumigation to kill deep-rooted perennials that may grow from soil layer below the treated zone; however, it usually takes a long time for these deep weeds to reach the ground. Soil fumigation is primarily meant to treat nurseries, greenhouse beds, lawns, and pot soils. In the main fields their use is usually uneconomical.

SUMMARY

Biodiversity in vegetation on earth (as also in aquatic environment) is fundamental to human survival. But according to our requirements we have to be choosy about it. Like in agriculture, where we aim at selective control of weeds with complete safety to the crop plants, on non-crop lands too we plan to curb the excessive growth of vegetation which may be of hinderance to man in one way or the other, as well as to suppress the less eye appealing plant species and encourage the low growing, superior ones. In other words, actually, even on non-crop lands we aim at selective control of vegetation, although we are more used to calling it as non-selective vegetation management. A bare ground is rarely needed, except in places like around electric poles and fuel pipes.

Several machines and tools are used to harvest and limit the vegetation in non-crop situations. But now a series of wide-spectrum, non-selective herbicides are available to do the job more effectively. These are described in this chapter. Where bare ground is needed, semi-permanent and permanent soil sterilants can be used.

Non-selective vegetation control may also be needed in special situations on crop fields, like on bunds and channels, fallow fields, and in minimum tillage programmes. Special herbicides for use in this situation are discussed, particularly glyphosate and paraquat. The uses of temporary soil sterilants and fumigants in high value crops and for eradicating parasitic weeds, are provided in this section.

SELECTED BIBLIOGRAPHY

1. Bogdan, A. 1954. Brush-clearing and grazing trials at Kisokan (Kenya) E. Agri. and Forestry J. 19(C) 253-259.
2. Day, B.E. *et al.* 1964. Uracil herbicides for weed control. Citrograph 49(10) 372, 380, and 382.
3. Gupta, O.P. 2001. Weedy Aquatic Plants: Their Menace and Management. Agrobios (India), Jodhpur (India), 273 p.
4. Harrington, G.N. 1972. The effect of foliar spraying of *Acacia hockil* with picloram and 2,4-D/picloram mixtures and additional treatment with picloram granules E. Afr. Agri. and Forestry J. 37(3) 197-200.
5. Harrison, S.J.T. 1963. Progress in poisonivy thinning. N.Z. Timber J. 10(2) 257.
6. Harvey, R.G. and Muzik T.J. 1973. Effects of 2,4-D and amino acids on fieldbindweed in vitro. Weed Sci. 21(2) 135-138.
7. Hodgson, J.M. 1973. Differential response of ditchbank grass to herbicides. Weed Sci. 21(4) 421-422.
8. Kelly, W.B. 1960. Australian scrub clearing methods. Unasylva, 14:179-184.
9. Leonard, O.A. *et al.* 1974. Control of tree roots. Weeds 22(5) 516-520.

10. McNeilly, D.P. 1971. Clearing the tracks for progress. Du Pont Mag. Int. Edition. 65(6) 6-9.
11. Meyer, R.E. and Bovey R.W. 1973. Control of woody plants with herbicide mixture. Weed Sci. 21(5) 423-425.
12. Meyer, R.E. and Riley T.E. 1969. Influence of picloram granules and sprays on whitebrush. Weed Sci. 17(3) 293-295.
13. Peevy, F.A. 1972. How to kill hardwoods by injection? Weeds Today 3(1) 8-9.
14. Peevy, F.A. 1972. Injection treatment for killing bottom-land hardwoods. Weed Sci. 20(C) 566-568.
15. Rice, R 1992. Nursery and Landscape. Weed Control Manual. Mittal Pub., Delhi (India)
16. Robertson, J.A. and C.H. Pedersen. 1972. Chemical control of regrowth. Trop. Grasslands. 7(2) 223-227.
17. Robertson, J.A. and Moore R.M. 1972. Thinning *Eucalyptus populnea* woodlands by injecting trees with chemicals. Trop. Grasslands 6(2) 141-149.
18. Thompson, L.Jr. *et al.* 1973. Action and fate of 2,4-D and dicamba in trumpet creeper. Weed Sci. 21(5) 429-432.
19. Wilson, J.H. 1967. The effects of basal injections of tordon on some central African indigenous trees. Rhod. Zambia Malawi J. Agri. Res. 5:301-313.

Chapter 24

SPECIFIC PROBLEM WEEDS AND THEIR CONTROL

24.1 GRASSES

Family: Poaceae

24.1.1 *Cynodon dactylon* (L.) Pers. (bermudagrass, d*oob*) (Fig. 3.3)

Biology and Habitat: *Cynodon dactylon* is a perennial weed growing largely from rootstocks and stolons. Although it produces seeds, yet these are not important in its dispersal. Bermudagrass rootstocks form dense sod inside the soil and its stolons creep over the land, extensively. The grass grows round the year, but it is particularly vigorous under warm and moist conditions.

Bermudagrass has become a serious menace in irrigated crop fields and plantations of tropical and subtropical areas as an escape from pasturelands where it is a valuable forage plant.

Control: In the semiarid tropics, exposure of *Cynodon dactylon* rhizomes to hot sun during summer months by deep tillage of the infested land, is an effective method of controlling the weed (see Chapter 8). It takes about 7-14 days to desiccate the exposed rhizomes whereafter a second tillage operation to further expose the bermudagrass rhizomes is required. Bermudagrass control by summer tillage can be improved by pre-conditioning it by the application of herbicides *eg* **dalapon**, diuron, **glyphosate**, amitrole-T, and uracils. These herbicides will aid in achieving a longer lasting and more complete kill of the weed by translocating to the underground rhizomes of the weed. But the treatment limits the choice of crops that could follow on the treated land. Glyphosate and amitrole-T, however, are comparatively short-lived in soil and offer wider crop choices. In intensive cropping systems, more appropriate herbicides for pre-conditioning bermudagrass are paraquat and diquat. These herbicides are completely non-residual types, and desiccate bermudagrass expeditiously for 15-20 days. Usually, two applications of low doses of paraquat or diquat, at one week's interval, before initiating summer tillage, are required for obtaining best results. Two to three years' efforts in summer tillage can eventually weaken bermudagrass stands greatly. In the humid tropics, hot weather tillage is not of much use in achieving bermudagrass control. In such areas one must depend (almost solely) upon herbicides cited earlier, to control this menace. The same is true of bermudagrass control projects in erosion-prone, semiarid regions of the world where excessive tillage would aggravate soil destruction.

An effective bermudagrass control programme should incorporate wide row crops in rotation to permit hard, row cultivations. In crop fields, the scattered clumps of bermudagrass can be spot-treated with dalapon, glyphosate, MSMA, DSMA, sethoxydim, and the like, depending upon the crop.

24.1.2 *Imperata cylindrica* (L.) Beauv. (lalang)

Biology and Habitat: *Imperata cylindrica* is a perennial grass, propagating extensively by rhizomes, which are located mainly in the top 20 cm of soil. Although it is widely used for thatching in many developing countries, at the same time it has become a serious menace in tea and other plantations, as well as in the deforested areas of the humid tropics, particularly in India, Indonesia, and Ceylon.

Control: *I. cylindrica* is found susceptible to flooding, frequent cultivations, competitive cropping, and herbicides *eg* dalapon, paraquat, and herbicidal oils. Initial clearance of the grass with herbicides, followed by frequent cultivations and competitive cropping can recover the land otherwise wasted in lalang. In Sri Lanka, slashing of lalang at intervals of 4-6 weeks resulted in suppression of its rhizome development which was comparable to the most effective chemical control methods using herbicides like dalapon (22.2 kg/ha) or dalapon with paraquat.

24.1.3 *Sorghum halepense* (L.) Pers. (johnsongrass, *baru*) (Fig. 24.1)

Biology and Habitat: *Sorghum halepense* is a perennial, robust grass with up to 2 m high culms. It reproduces from stout, deep rhizomes, and plentiful seeds. The rhizomes may be found as deep as 3 m in soil, though 35-37 cm depth is more common. A piece of Johnsongrass rhizome dragged to a new spot forms a new colony quickly. The food reserves in the rhizomes are lowest when the aerial shoots are 26-33 days old. At this time the Johnsongrass shoots are in boot stage and about 30-35 cm in height. Ripe seeds are produced in large numbers during the winter months and are disseminated extensively with wind. Thereafter, the old grass clumps undergo dormancy. The new seedlings appear in summer and these begin forming rhizomes within 3-4 weeks. The rhizome development is fast after the plants have formed the seed heads.

Johnsongrass is prolific in crops like maize, millets, sugarcane, and cotton, particularly on the heavy, moisture retentive soils. In many fields it becomes more dense than the crop itself, turning slowly a cultivable field into an unproductive land.

Control: In humid regions effective control of *S. halepense* has been obtained from the earlier cited tillage cum herbicide system. Cultivation should begin in hot weather when Johnsongrass is 30-40 cm tall. The weed should be allowed to regrow to the same height and then treated with two sprays of **dalapon** at 5-7.5 kg/ha each, using 0.5% of a suitable wetting agent, at an interval of 7-10 days. After two weeks, disc the treated field. Crops like cotton, maize, and soybean can be planted safely about two weeks after discing. To control Johnsongrass from seeds, the crops should be treated with a suitable soil active herbicide. Still if there is any stray emergence of Johnsongrass, it should be curbed with spot application of dalapon, MSMA, DSMA, or herbicidal oil. The organic arsenicals are selective to sugarcane and cotton, but unlike dalapon they do not translocate to the rhizomes of Johnsongrass.

In semiarid regions, the above tillage cum herbicide procedure of Johnsongrass control can be followed in rainy season.

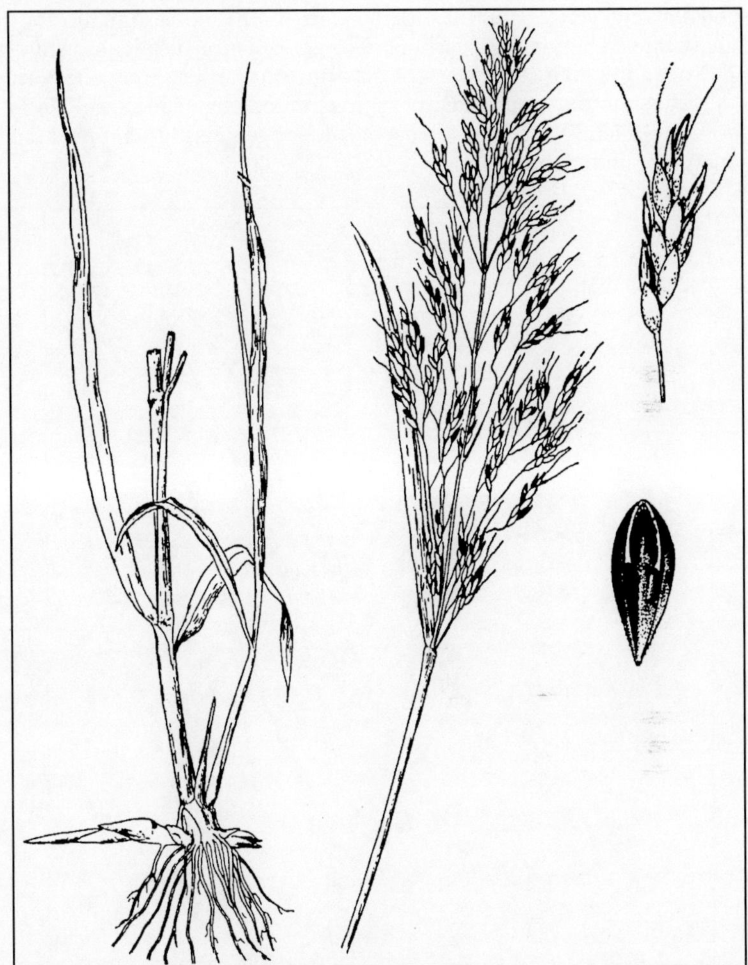

Fig. 24.1: *Sorghum halepense* (L.) Pers. (Johnsongrass)

It is important to control Johnsongrass not only within the fields but also that growing outside the crop fields to prevent it from setting and disseminating its highly viable seeds. This can be achieved with dalapon, diuron, bromacil, or sodium chlorate, applied at pre-arrowing stage of the weed. Fence rows and like places can be sterilized to prevent Johnsongrass (and other noxious plants) from establishing there.

24.1.4 *Saccharum spontaneum* L. and S. munja (tigergrass, kans) (Fig. 24.2)

Biology and Habitat: *S. spontaneum* is pernicious grass which reproduces rapidly by means of high viability seeds and rhizomes. Majority of rhizomes are found within 20-30 cm depth of soil, and only a few penetrate 90 cm or more deep. The culms produce prominent, silky white panicles that mature with numerous, air borne seeds during winter months before the grass undergoes dormancy for 3-4 months. Tigergrass tillers profusely and expands very fast to turn any neglected area into a miniature wasteland in relatively short time. The plant is particularly aggressive on heavy, moisture retentive, well drained soils, although it grows well also on sandy soils. From the uncared areas tigergrass migrates into the crop fields through its numerous viable seeds. In India about 3 million hectares of cultivable land are occupied by tigergrass in Madhya Pradesh, Uttar Pradesh, Rajasthan, and Maharashtra.

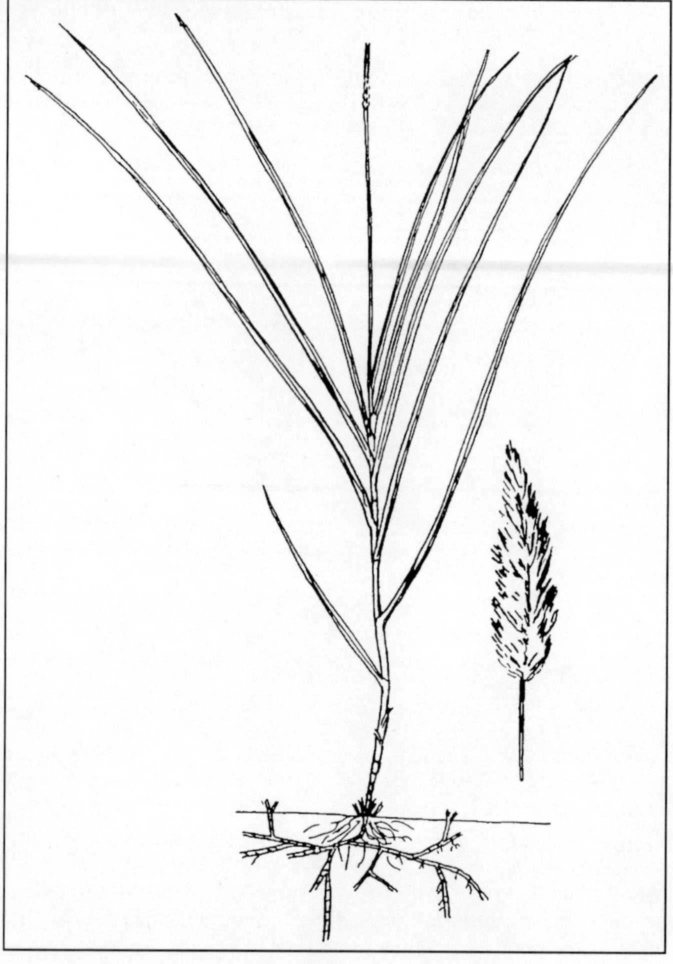

Fig. 24.2: *Saccharum spontaneum* L. (tigergrass)

Control: As early as in 1940's efforts were made in India to control *S. spontaneum* by physical methods under various systems named as Howard method, Indore Method, etc. All these methods had three common features, *viz* (i) deep summer cultivation, (ii) collection of rhizomes by hand, tooth-pegged wooden beams, or cultivators, and (iii) putting the land under a thick green manure crop of sunnhemp (*Crotolaria juncea*). In 1950's, the Government of India initiated about 30-35 cm deep ploughing with bulldozers in the tigergrass-infested areas in Madhya Pradesh and recovered about 5 lakh ha land. The wheat yields on the reclaimed land were increased about four-fold. In Gwalior, another method of tigergrass control was developed which was based on the fact that tigergrass is susceptible to waterlogging. In this method, after the summer tillage the fields were impounded with water, about 15-20 cm deep, for two days, in the rainy season. Then a tooth-pegged beam was run in wet fields to sweep out tigergrass rhizomes loosened by the flood. This was followed by transplanting of paddy in the flooded fields. The method was found highly successful in controlling tigergrass when the water supply was plentiful.

In modern times tigergrass has been brought under the banner of herbicidal control, but it requires a systematic approach and vigilant efforts to curb this weed. In the first place, seed production in *S. spontaneum* growing on the fence lines and waste places should be prevented by foliar application of **diuron** or **dalapon** (0.4-1%) at pre-arrowing stage of the weed, during the September and October months. The treatment will destroy tigergrass shoots, and maintain its soil binding benefits at the same time.

In non-crop areas, soil application of diuron at 10 kg/ha during summer months has proved very effective. In cropped areas, the new scattered patches of the weed can be treated likewise. Of late, tigergrass has been found very susceptible to **glyphosate** (1.5-2.0 kg/ha). It should be applied during the fallow period, with or without hot weather cultivations.

24.1.5 *Avena* spp. (wildoat. *jungli jai*) (Fig. 24.3 & 24.4)

Biology and Habitat: There are three common species of wildoat, namely, *Avena fatua* L., *A. ludoviciana* Dur, and *A. sterilis-macrocarpa* L. Of these, in India the first two species are of common occurrence. A. *sterilis* is the principal wildoat species in Africa.

Wildoat is a serious weed of mainly wheat and barley although it may infest other winter crops too. It is so because in small grains it survives by mimicry during its vegetative phase. Botanically it can be distinguished from wheat plants by its large ligule, absence of auricles, and anti-clockwise twist of its leaves. (The wheat leaves show clock-wise twist). But none of these characters can be used to identify wildoat while weeding it out from the wheat (and barley) fields.

Control: Adoption of crop rotation involving non-graminaceous winter crops, where wildoat shows itself distinctly, is a practical way of reducing the weed populations. From wheat and barley plots the weed can be pulled out only after it has shown its typical panicle. When large areas of wheat and barley are involved, herbicides are to be employed to reduce wildoat infestations. In these crops herbicides such as diallate, triallate, and barban were recommended for wildoat control in the past. In recent years, superior herbicides, *eg* clodinafop, fenoxaprop, mesosulfuron, and tralkoxydim, have replaced the older herbicides. The main advantage of **tralkoxydim** is that it can be applied at 3 to 5-leaf stage of wildoat whence most of its seeds have germinated. In variance with it, the other herbicides spare many late germinating wildoat plants because these are phytotoxic at only two-leaf stage of the weed (see Chaper 21).

Fig. 24.3: *Avena fatua* (wildoat)

Fig. 24.4: *Avena fatua* infesting wheat fields.

24.1.6 *Phalaris minor* Retz. (littleseed canarygrass, *gullidanda, vanri)* (Fig. 3.1)

Biology and Habitat: *Phalaris minor*, an annual, invasive alien, weed, has spread widely in many wheat growing areas of the world. Like wildoat, it mimics wheat and barley plants and sets seeds at almost the same height and time as the crop. Each plant of canarygrass produces about 300-460, shiny black, very small, flat seeds which readily contaminate the wheat seeds.

Control: Unlike wildoat, the seeds of canarygrass can be separated from wheat and barley seeds by sieving. Crop rotations involving broadleaf winter crops, and in certain areas winter maize, offer farmers chance to hoe out this grass at a very early crop stage. From winter grain crops the canarygrass plants can be pulled out only when they first show their foxtail- like spikes in February (in India), peeping through their flag leaves. Every effort should be made to adopt the labour-intensive uprooting of canarygrass at this stage, even though some herbicide was employed earlier to destroy the weed selectively. A few plants of canarygrass that escaped herbicide action are sufficient to produce and disperse their seeds (along with crop seeds or by shattering) to continue their future infestations. Uprooting of canarygrass should be continued into the non-crop areas.

Certain herbicides have exhibited adequate selectivity between *P. minor* and wheat (or barley). Some such herbicides are methibenzuron, metoxuron, **isoproturon**, and terbutryn, (Chapter 21).

24.2 PARASITIC WEEDS

24.2.1 *Striga* spp. (Striga, witchweed, *agia*) (Fig. 24.5)

Family - Scrophulariaceae.

Biology and Habitat: Striga is an annual, parasitic herb, propagating from seeds. A stimulus from a suitable host root exudate, continuously for 24-28 hours, is needed to trigger the germination process in striga seeds. Upon germination, striga produces 2-3 mm long radicles. The radicles then form haustoria on the nearby host roots and continue extending their growth involving the whole root system of the crop plant; sucking water, nutrients, and other food material from them. The affected crops look drought-stricken, despite the presence of adequate soil moisture. After about 20 days of subterranean life as a total parasite, striga emerges through the soil as green plant. At this stage it becomes a **partial parasite**, making its own carbohydrates. Each striga plant may produce over a million seeds, about 30 days after its emergence. The striga seeds are as fine as dust particles.

There are about 23 species of *Striga* on record in the world but, of these, only three are considered notorious. These are: *S. asiatica* (= *S. lutea*), *S. hermonthica*, and *S. densiflora*, attacking primarily sorghum and pearlmillet. While all the three species of *Striga* are found in Africa, in Asia only *S. asiatica* is common. Within each *Striga* species exist strains which are specific to either sorghum or pearlmillet, probably due to quite different stimulating substances they require to germinate. In West Africa, *S. gesnerioides* has become a serious pest of cowpea, and in other places of tobacco. Besides sorghum and pearlmillet, different species of *Striga* are known to attack a number of crops including ragi (*Eleusine corocana*), maize, sugarcane, rice, tobacco, groundnut, and sweet potato.

Striga causes a reduction of 15-75% in the yield of sorghum and pearlmillet in Asia and Africa. India, Sudan, South Africa, Rhodesia, Nigeria, and Egypt are particularly affected by striga menace. In West Africa, the striga invasion is so serious that it can force a millet farmer to move to a new land.

Control: It is generally agreed that for the subsistence farmers of the tropics, the development of resistant varieties of sorghum and pearlmillet will be the final answer to the striga menace. For instance, the new hybrids of pearlmillet seem free from striga.

Catch crops (striga susceptible, short duration crops to be planted and destroyed before planting the main crop) and *trap crops* (striga germination stimulating crops with inherent attachment barriers), are often suggested as possible means to reduce striga populations. However, in most sorghum and pearlmillet regions of the tropics, individual farmer is greatly limited in his choice of crops due to varied agroclimatic and socio-economic stresses. *Cotton*, sunflower, cowpea, groundnut, and castor are considered suitable trap crops of striga, but different strains of the parasite may defy the measure. Striga invasion is usually less in the wet season, in adequately N fertilised plots, and in densely sown crops. But again, the strains of striga persisting in irrigated agriculture may vary.

Techniques to reduce seed production in striga have been recommended. Even hand-pulling before striga plants putforth their flowers can be helpful in this respect, but it is impracticable in cases of severe infestations. Directed applications of 2,4-D is a practical alternative to this for breaking future populations of striga. Its amine salt is applied at 0.5-0.75 kg/ha, 2-3 times during the crop season to destroy flushes of striga in its vegetative phase. Dicamba and bentazon need be tried as more potent alternatives to 2,4-D for striga control in millets. In Nigeria, striga is spot-treated with ametryn. Preemergent granular atrazine is also reported effective against striga.

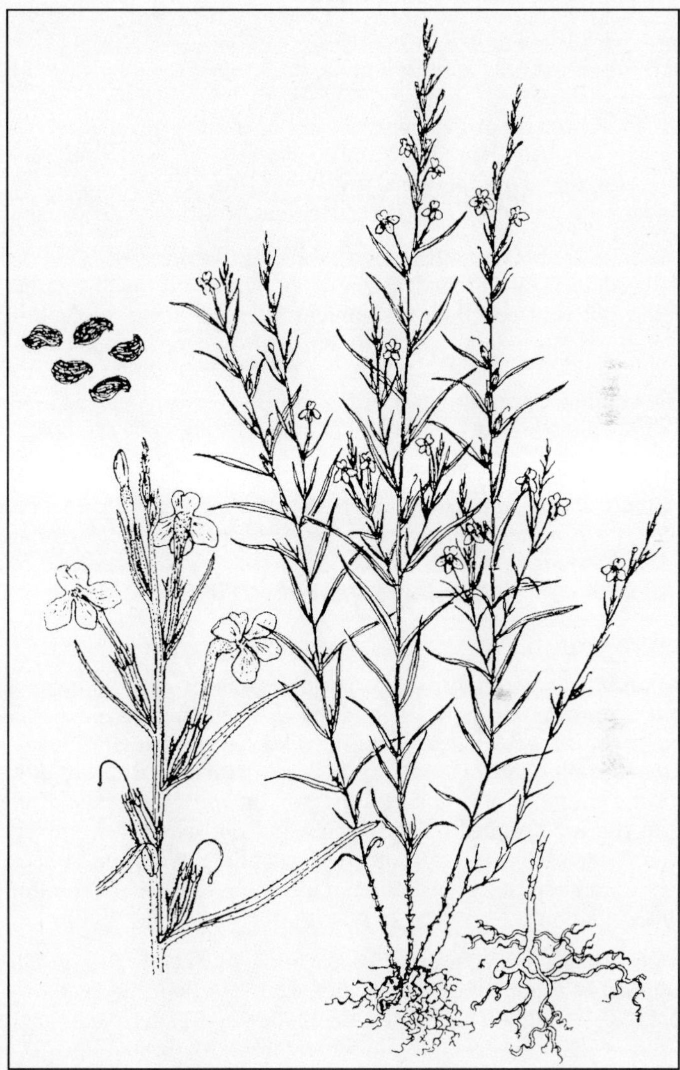

Fig. 24.5: *Striga lutea* Lour. (witchweed)

Extraction of a natural stimulant of striga germination from cotton roots, given the trivial name strigol, and later synthesis of several other similar compounds under a GR series (prominently GR 45 and GR 7), led to a new mechanism of striga eradication. These chemicals induce striga seeds to germinate, but the striga seedlings wither away in the absence of a suitable host plant, amounting to **suicidal germination**. The latest compound employed for causing the suicidal germination of striga on thousands of hectares of infested land each year in the USA is **ethylene (C_2H_4)**. Its common dose is 1.6 kg/ha (0.42-3.4 kg/ha). Ethylene is injected mechanically in the soil at 0.5 to 1 m spacings, and 10-30 cm deep before planting the crop. Probably, in irrigated farming ethylene could also be applied in the form of an ethylene releasing compound, such as Ethephon. For small farmers of the tropics, hand-operated ethylene injectors have been tried in Sudan. The ethylene treatment is most successful when the soil remains moist at least for 2-3 weeks after its application and when the temperature is about 20°C. A successful ethylene treatment achieves 90% reduction in striga seed population of the plough layer of the soil.

An important aspect of using synthetic germination stimulants against striga is that such chemicals should not continue their assignment after the striga susceptible crops have been planted. Thus, the timing of soil treatment with the stimulants and the planting of crops must be worked out properly. It may be ideal to use the chemical stimulants of striga seeds in combination with trap crops. Further researches to develop chemical stimulants of varied strains of striga are needed.

Isolated infestations of striga growing on some host weeds species, outside the field boundaries, should also be destroyed with any contact herbicide to prevent its seed production.

24.2.2 *Orobanche* spp. (broomrape, *haddda*) (Fig. 24.6)

Family Orobanchaceae

Biology and Habitat: There are four major parasitic species of broomrape. These are: *O. cernua* on tobacco and sunflower, *O. ramosa* and *O. aegyptiaca* on tomato and like crops, and *O. crenata* on broadbeans (*Vicia faba*). Besides, *O. ramosa* is a menace in *Brassica* crops. In India, losses due to *Orobanche* in tobacco alone are estimated at 30 to 35%. In this crop, *Orobanche* infests only the fibrous roots of tobacco plants. Therefore, it is a problem only in the transplanted tobacco fields and not in tobacco nurseries. It is first seen in tobacco fields about 45 days after transplanting. It flowers 4-5 days later and ripens its seeds in another 20-25 days. Broomrape has recently been found infesting also the potato fields.

Broomrape is an annual, parasitic herb propagating by seeds. The host root exudates induce germination of broomrape seeds within soil. The parasite seedlings then infect the nearby host roots forming haustoria on them. Soon thereafter the broomrape emerges through the soil as pale shoots, devoid of chlorophyll. Broomrape is thus a **total parasite**. Its clones are fleshy at the base, and they develop several tubercles which grow into separate flowering shoots. Each broomrape plant may produce over half a million seeds in a short period of about eight weeks. The broomrape seeds disseminate by wind, birds, and farm animals. They can remain dormant in soil for 2-12 years.

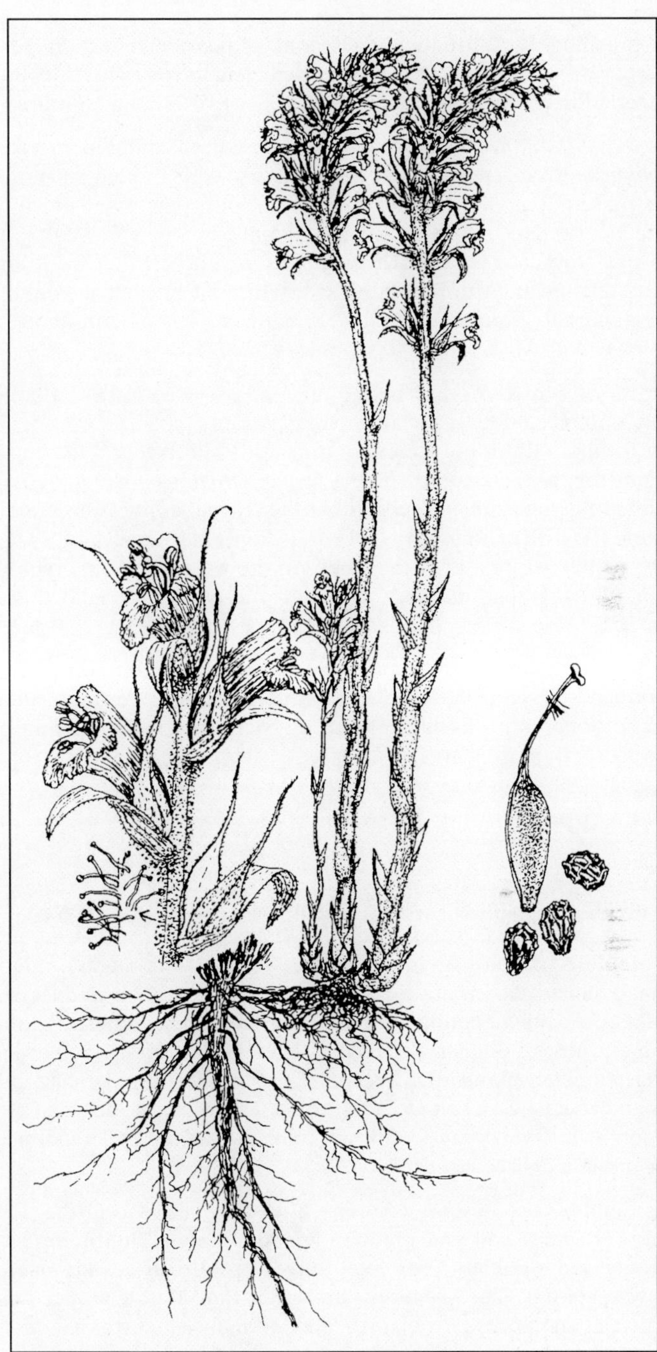

Fig. 24.6: *Orobanche minor* J.E. Smith. (Clover broomrape)

Control: Crop breeding for introducing *Orobanche* resistance has made only limited headway, thus far. In Israel, Ish (1993) reported genetic resistance to this parasite in certain sunflower cultivars and hybrids, *viz.*, SW-501, RW-637, and Sunbred-254.

Pepper (*Capsicum annum* L.) is generally regarded as a suitable trap crop for some species of *Orobanche*. Trap cropping, however, has a very limited scope for broomrape control in the present cropping systems in most countries. Hand-weeding at weekly intervals is effective in preventing its further spread, but it is too costly an operation. Ethylene does not stimulate *Orobanche* germination, but GR 7, GR 24 and GR 28 are found promising chemicals in this respect, at least under pot house conditions. Russian scientists have reported grounded sunflower plants to act as stimulant of *Orobanche* seeds.

Herbicidal control of *Orobanche* has been found possible with **allyl alcohol** applied at 0.1-3.2% spray, about 2-4 weeks after transplanting tobacco. Also, preplant soil treatment with dalapon, linuron, or metobromuron has been found to keep tobacco (and brinjal) free from this parasite to acceptable levels. *Orobanche* shoots have been further found susceptible to glyphosate and terbutol at their usual application rates, as well as to several vegetable oils (Krishnamurthy, 1992). Repeated applications of these were needed to destroy the new flushes of the weed. In the western world glyphosate resistant varieties of tobacco have been developed to control this parasite with this non-selective herbicide.

It may be pointed out here that broomrape can parasitise on roots of several weed species, even outside the crop fields and, thus, perpetuate by forming numerous seeds. Therefore, all efforts based on herbicidal and physical approaches should be adopted to destroy these weeds before the parasite sets seeds.

24.2.3. *Cuscuta* spp. (dodder, *akashbel*) (Fig. 24.7)

Family: Convolvulaceae.

Biology and Habitat: There are at least 170 species of *Cuscuta*, an invasive alien parasitic weed, in the world. Of these, *C. campestris, C. reflexa,* and *C. hyalina* are most common. *Cuscuta* is a **complete parasite**, twining, golden yellow, wiry stems, rudimentary scaly leaves, and small clusters of minute, bell-shaped flowers. The dodder stems contain carotenoid pigment capable of conducting only limited photosynthesis. Of the field crops, lucerne is the main host of dodder. Besides, it severely parasitises many species of trees, hedges, and ornamental plants. Of recent, *C. chinensis* Damk. has invaded Niger (*Guizotia abyssinica* (L.f.) Cass) in Orissa (India). Likewise, in M.P. and Orissa *Cuscuta* is reported on lentil. In Hyderabad (Andhra Pradesh) *C. chinesis* is reported to parasitise blackgram, besides some dicot weeds.

Germination of dodder seeds does not require any stimulation form the host crop. They germinate readily in moist soil and produce wiry plumules. The plumules try to strike nearby plant roots and stubbles. Then they travel upward in search of a suitable host shoot, as yellow seedlings. The seedlings survive if they find a proper host plant, else they perish. On the stems of a true host, dodder makes haustoria and multiplies its threads rapidly, ultimately forcing the host plant to perish. A single dodder seedling can grow 2 km or more in length.

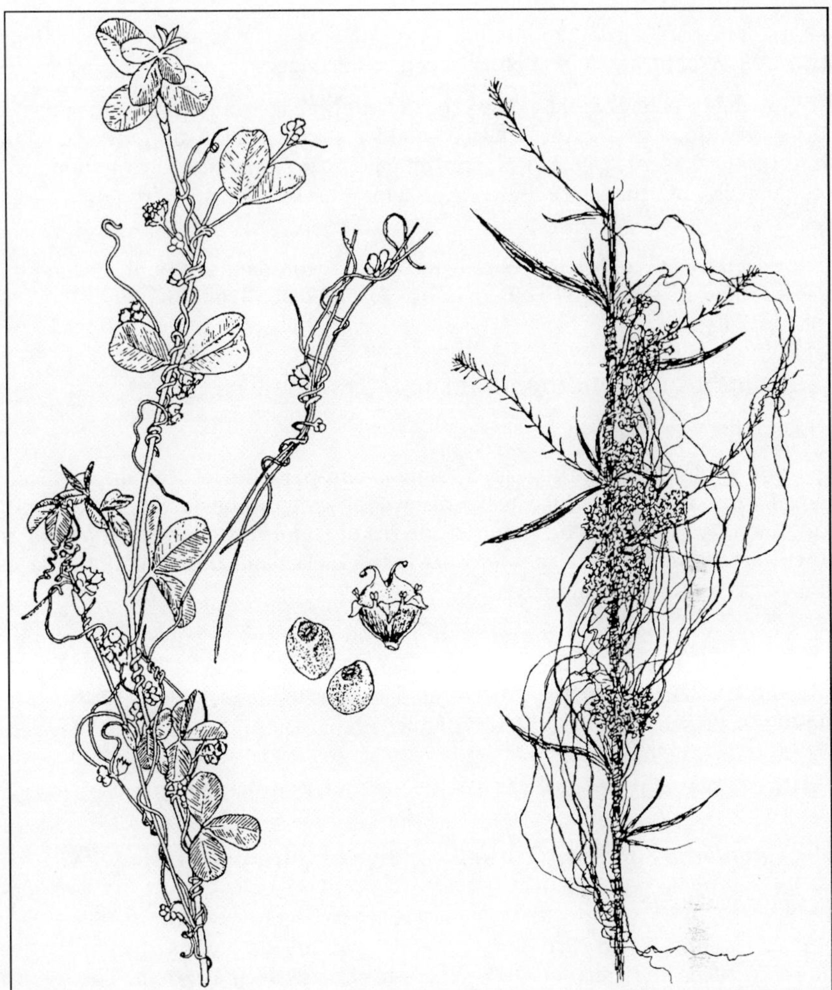

Fig. 24.7: *Cuscuta* sp. (dodder)

Dodder disseminates by seeds as well as through movement of its fragments with men and animals.

Control: *Cuscuta* is one of the very few weeds that can be controlled hand and foot by adopting **crop rotations**; replacing its host crop with a non-host crop for a couple of years. This is the most pragmatic approach to control this parasitic weed. Among the selective herbicides, dodder has been found susceptible to chlorpropham, pronamide, glyphosate, dichlobenil, fluchloralin, pendimethalin, imazaquin, and metolachlor. Choice amongst these shall depend upon their specific selectivity to the host crop in question. Pronamide has been reported particularly useful in killing *Cuscuta* growing on niger. It is applied at 2 kg/ha, about 20 d.a.s. of the crop. The treatment can also be tried in *Brassica* oilseed crops which too host this parasitic weed.

Dodder growing in perennial field crops (*eg* lucerne), hedges, and trees can be desiccated with 0.1% **paraquat** spray. Any left-over dodder shoots should be retreated with this herbicide before these had chance to spread. The host plants may also temporarily dry up in the process, but these usually recover soon after receiving 1-2 irrigations (see also Chapter 21).

In chickpea, linseed, and lentil, herbicides like pendimethalin and imazaquin are reported effective in causing selective control of cuscuta. Glyphosate could be used 30 d.a.s. in linseed.

24.2.4 *Loranthus* (= *Dendrophthoe*) spp. (Loranthus)

Family: Loranthaceae

Biology and Habitat: Loranthus is a **stem semi-parasite** of certain tropical and subtropical trees and bushes like teak, rosewood, sandalwood, mango, citrus, sapota, jackfruit, and tea. In India alone about 60 species of *Loranthus* (= *Dendrophthoe*) are on record. Of these *L. longiflorus var. falcatus* is the most damaging. Loranthus seeds are spread by birds to fresh tree branches.

Control: The only control measure of loranthus on record is to bore two rows of holes down the infected tree, reaching the sap wood. In each hole a mixture of 8 g copper sulphate and 1 g 2,4-D powder is pushed in. The treatment is supposed to free the trees from loranthus for a period of up to 4 years.

24.3 BROADLEAF WEEDS

24.3.1 *Convolvulus arvensis* L. (fieldbindweed, hirankhuri) (Fig. 24.8)

Family: Convolvulaceae

Biology and Habitat: *C. arvensis* is a vigorous, twining or trailing, perennial herb. It reproduces by seeds and creeping roots which may be as deep as 6-9 m. Though it is an evergreen plant, in excessive drought conditions it undergoes dormancy. Each root fragment of bindweed can grow into an infestation up to 3 m in diameter in one season. The seeds have long dormancy period. Bindweed is prominent in semiarid regions, infesting arable land, gardens, and uncultivated places. On crop lands it is troublesome in wheat, barley, grain oat, potato, and sugarcane. It binds the crop plants and makes their harvesting extremely cumbersome.

Control: In fallow fields summer tillage with overlapping sweeps every time the bindweed plants are 14-18 days old, followed by competitive cropping with fodder crops, forms good cultural method of its control. The cultivation should begin at early bud stage of the weed. Its last growth may be treated at the early bud stage with **2,4-D** at 0.5-1.0 kg/ha.

In winter grains **2,4-D** has been used for long to control bindweed sufficiently well to permit acceptable crop harvests. It is applied twice during the crop season, once each at the tillering and stiff dough stages of the crop. Besides, after crop harvest the left-over bindweed plants are recommended to be treated with 0.2-0.3% spray of mixture of 2,4-D and silvex (2:1). Bentazon (1 kg/ha) had sometimes proved superior to 2,4-D for bindweed control in wheat. In general, the ester formulations of these herbicides have been found more effective than their other formulations against this perennial weed.

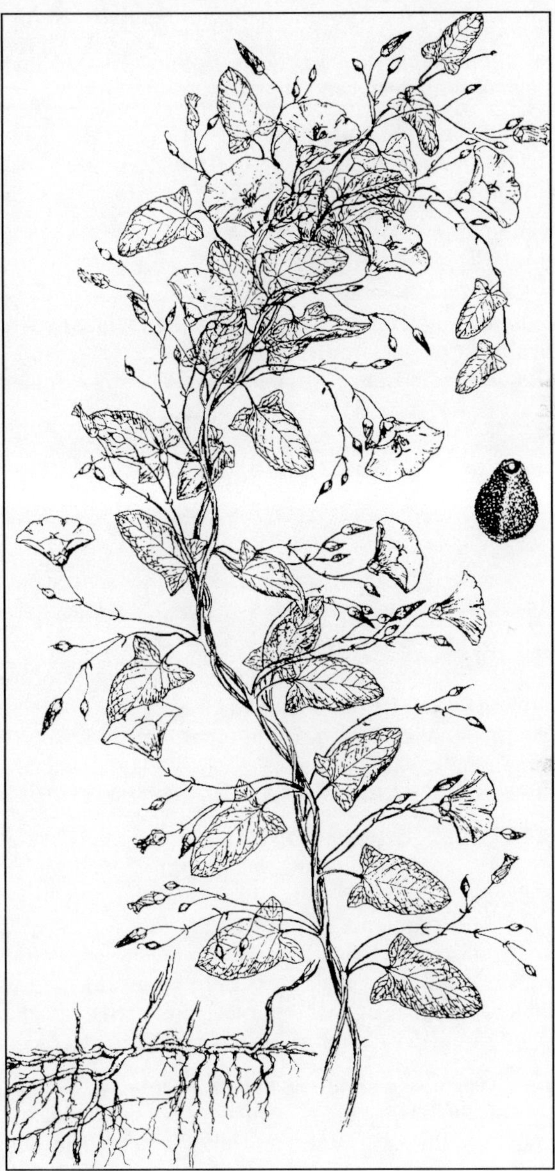

Fig. 24.8: *Convolvulus arvensis* L. (fieldbindweed)

Of recent, single foliage application of **carfentrazone** at 0.02-0.025 kg/ha, about 25 d.a.s. wheat has been found extremely effective in destroying bindweed shoots, almost hands down.

In *potato*, bindweed can be controlled with directed or spot treatment with either paraquat or a tank mixture of 2,4-D (0.5 kg/ha) and metoxuron (0.625 kg/ha).

Glyphosate (3-4 kg/ha) is good for controlling blooming bindweed in orchards.

In grasslands, repeat applications of 2,4-D with dicamba (0.5 kg/ha) or picloram (0.25 kg/ha) at the bud stage of bindweed can eventually eradicate it.

Sometimes bindweed may be a problem in summer season crops. Good results have been obtained with herbicides like trifluralin, nitralin, prometryn, and 2,4-D plus dicamba, in the respective tolerant crops.

A bindweed control programme should extend to non-crop areas which offer ready weed nurseries for the crop fields. In the open environment of non-crop areas, bindweed usually exhibits some degree of tolerance to 2,4-D, particularly in dry areas. Also, certain ecotypes of bindweed are completely resistant to this herbicide. As such, in the non-crop areas foliage applications of picloram, dicamba, 2,3,6-TBA, and silvex should be preferred over 2,4-D. Soil sterilisation is desirable in fence rows, under pipe lines, and in other like situations.

24.3.2 *Cirsium arvense* (L.) Scop (Canadathistle, *kateli*) (Fig. 3.6)

Family: Asteraceae

Biology and Habitat: *Cirsium arvense* is a perennial, dioceous rough herb, with somewhat spiny leaves. It grows up to 150 cm tall, in dense stands of as much as 45 shoots/sq m ground area. The weed has a worldwide distribution in the temperate regions. In India it is problematic in winter season crops in certain areas. It remains dormant during the late summer and rainy period. The thistle propagates through its extensive root system and seeds. Its roots may reach as much as 5 m deep, though about 50% of the root biomass is concentrated in the top 30 cm soil. Root segments, as small as 0.3 x 1.2 cm in length are capable of producing new plants and a 19 days old seedling can form adventitious root buds.

Control: Lucerne and berseem (Egyptianclover) form very good smother crops for the control of Canadathistle. Their multicuts weaken the thistle plants sufficiently to discourage their propagation. In open crops like chickpea and mustard, on the other hand, the farmers get sufficient opportunity to physically remove 2-3 flushes of the thistle. However, in the close row crops like the winter grains, Canadathistle control is difficult by such means and it is necessary here to resort to the use of selective herbicides. Some suitable herbicides for the purpose are, 2,4-D, MCPB, and sulfonylureas (see Chapter 21). MCPB can also be used in pea to control this weed.

Like other problematic weeds, Canadathistle should also be destroyed on fence lines and other non-crop areas of the farm, using non-selective herbicides like chlorsulfuron, paraquat, or glyphosate, as the case may be. This is essential to check the every year dissemination of the weed. Picloram is also a very effective herbicide against Canadathistle growing in grasslands and non-crop areas. The rates of picloram in the two situations are 0.5 and 1-3 kg/ha, respectively. Dicamba and TIBA (4-8 kg/ha) can be used in non-crop areas where 2,4-D usually fails to damage the thistle.

24.3.3 *Alhagi pseudalhagi* (M. Bieb) Desv. (camelthorn, *jawasa*)

Family: Leguminosae

Biology and Habitat: A. *pseudalhagi* is a semi-woody, perennial, thorny weed. Its roots are found as deep as 6 m in soil. Every spring the plant throws out new shoots from its crown buds. It remains vegetative all winter and early summer period whereafter it flowers and sets seeds. Usually the weed remains dormant during the rainy period. Camelthorn is largely a weed of light soils where it infests winter crops, particularly the small grains. The weed depletes the soil of its deep-seated moisture, and makes crop harvesting cumbersome because of its thorny nature.

Control: Glyphosate and dicamba form two very good translocated herbicides for controlling *A. pseudalhagi*. These herbicides are applied after the harvest of winter crops when the weed growth is usually prolific. The effective herbicide spray concentration is 0.1 to 0.4%. The spray should be applied to the plants to the point of liberal run off from their foliage. Regrowth of the weed must be treated likewise at its young stage. Two applications of any one of the above herbicides can provide about 92-95% control of camelthorn in single season, and in two to three years its complete eradication is possible.

It may be pointed out that in sandy soils, farmers often consider camelthorn as boon to prevent wind erosion during the fallow periods.

24.3.4 *Pluchea lanceolata* (DC.) C.B. clarke (arrowwood, *baisuri*) (Fig. 24.9)

Family: Asteraceae

Biology and Habitat: The biology of *P. lanceolata* is almost similar to *Alhagi pseudalhagi* described above. *Pluchea,* however, is not thorny.

Control: The control measures for *P. lanceolata* are similar to those described for the control of A. *pseudalhagi*.

24.3.5 *Opuntia dillenii* (Kev-Gawler) Haw (pricklypear, *nagphani*) (Fig. 24.10)

Family: Cactaceae

Biology and Habitat: *O. dillenii* is a perennial xerophyte. Its fleshy leaf-like pads are equipped with prickles and inconspicuous scaly leaves which usually drop off. Each pricklypear plant may constitute several storeys of such pads, which upon fragmentation give rise to new plants. Also, in the tropics many pricklypear types bear yellow flowers and berries that are edible by birds. The birds disseminate the seeds from these berries.

Fig. 24.9: *Pluchea lanceolata* (DC.) C.B. Clarke (arrowwood)

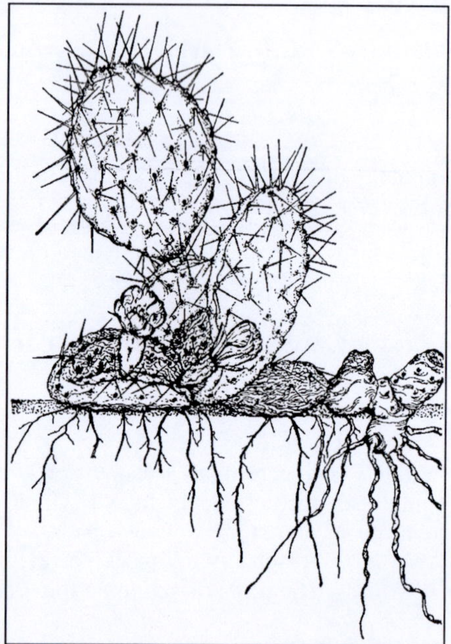

Fig. 24.10: *Opuntia* sp. (pricklypear, cactus)

Pricklypear is very aggressive in grasslands and non-crop lands. Drought, overgrazing, and mismanagement of grasslands enhance pricklypear infestations. Rangelands that have been root-ploughed for brush control also get very heavily infested with this weed because ploughing transplants numerous, broken pads (stems) of *Opuntia*.

Control: **Silvex** and **picloram** are possible choices to control *Opuntia* sp. The herbicides prove more effective against pricklypear when these are applied after mechanically briuising its pads with a bridge eyebeam or a railroad rail. The effective rate of either herbicide is 2 kg/ha. The treatment can destroy pricklypear stands within 2 years. Pads that escape initial herbicide treatment must be resprayed as soon as possible with either a 0.8% emulsion of 2,4,5-T, silvex, or straight diesel oil. (see also Chapter 9). In Australia, a harvesting machine has been devised for pricklypear control in grasslands and pastures. The machine has a side delivery rake, modified to uproot and windrow pricklypear, which is then de-spined for use as animal feed (Muller *et al.*, 1994). With each run of the machine, the native forage species tend to take-over the ground from pricklypear.

24.3.6 *Lantana camara* L. (lantana, putus, phul-lakri) (Fig. 24.11)

Family: *Vrbenaceae*

Biology and Habitat: *Lantana camara* is a perennial, evergreen, invasive alien shrub that spreads rapidly by its abundant seeds and shallow crown buds. The weed is native to Mexico. In India, it was initially introduced in 1809 from Sri Lanka as a hardy, ornamental hedge, bearing multicolour flowers. But then it escaped to open pastures, river beds, wastelands, cultivable lands, and forests where it easily displaced the indegenous vegetation, thereby adversely affecting the grazing grounds and other land utilities (Prakash, 1995). In deciduous forests, lantana is a source of fire hazard since it can catch fire even when green.

The seeds of lantana are spread by birds, chiefly Indian Myna and Chinese Turtledove. Also, it regenerates quickly from the crown buds after cutting, trampling, or burning, to form to dense, impenetrable thickets. Lantana leaves contain a toxic compound, Lantad - C, which causes hepatic lesions and changes in blood plasma of the animals compelled to graze upon it.

Control: Biological control of lantana has been widely practised in Australia and Hawaii, in particular (see Chapter 9), although it has not proved successful in India, thus far.

Herbicidal control of lantana, though possible, has not met with great acceptance. The plant is susceptible to the commonly known brush killers (Chapter 22). In India, a spray of glyphosate (0.75-1.0%) on the new growth of lantana occurring after burning or slashing its thickets has been found encouraging in extirpating the weed in Himachal Pradesh. The cleared land may be planted at the earliest with some fast growing fodder grasses and trees.

The Himalayan Environment Studies and Conservation Organisation (HESCO), Dehra Dun (Uttaranchal, India) has developed some novel technologies for utilizing lantana in a big way. Its twigs have been demonstrated to be fit for making low cost, termite resistant furniture and huts in replacement of bamboo sticks.

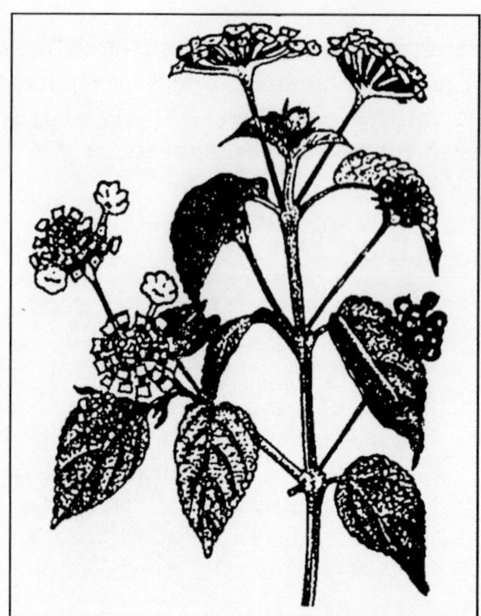

Fig. 24.11: *Lantan acamara* L. (lantana)

Other promising utilization venues of lantana are (i) for green leaf manuring in rice fields and (ii) mixing of partially decomposed lantana with cattle dung (4:1) for use in biogas plants. (See also Chapter-1, Sec. 1.8).

24.3.7 *Carthamus oxyacantha* Bieb. (wild safflower, *pohli*)

Family: Asteraceae

Biology and Habitat: *C. oxyacantha* is a persistent weed of chiefly winter grain crops. It germinates in large number late in the winter season and grows profusely during the spring and early summer. It flowers and sets seeds after the winter crops have been harvested. The strong hot winds in June uproots the wild safflower plants and roll them long distances, shattering their numerous seeds on route.

Wild safflower is spiny in nature. This makes harvesting of the infested winter crops very cumbersome.

Control: *C. oxyacantha* control should be a community venture; the individual efforts can be easily nullified by intrusion of its seeds from neighbourhood. Crop rotation with berseem, lucerne, potato, and like crops, is helpful in controlling wildsafflower. In wheat and barley fields, two applications of 2,4-D (at 1 kg/ha) can virtually eliminate this weed in a couple of years. Its first application should be made at 5 to 6-leaf crop stage and the second after all the winter crops have been harvested from the area. For the second spray, pre-bloom stage of the weed is most appropriate. In regions where wheat and barley are followed by cotton, paraquat should replace the *second* 2,4-D spray.

24.3.8 *Tribulus terrestris* L. (puncturevine, baragokhru) (Fig. 24.12)

Family: Zygophyllaceae.

Biology and Habitat: *T. terrestris* is a dryland weed of light soils. It is an annual herb reproducing from seeds. It has a tap root and prostrate stems that branch from the base to form dense mats on the soil surface. The seed pods carry 2-4, sharp, stout prickles, strong enough to penetrate wheel tyres and shoe soles. On village walk-ways and in grasslands and lawns this is the most objectionable feature of the weed. Puncturevine produces 2-3 flushes during the rainy season and matures its seeds in winter. Dryland crops grown on light soils, particularly pearlmillet, are plagued with puncturevine.

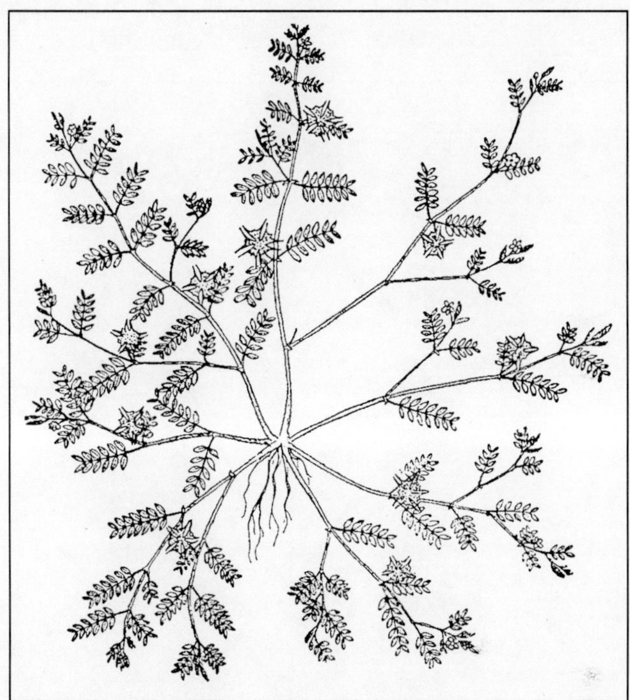

Fig. 24.12: *Tribulus terrestris* L. (puncturevine)

Control: *T. terrestris* is susceptible to several herbicides; the choice amongst these depends upon the habitat involved. In pearlmillet and grain sorghum, postemergent 2,4-D and atrazine have proved effective (Chapter 21). The effective spray liquid concentrations of the two compounds are 0.15% and 0.07%, respectively. In pastures, grasslands, ranges and lawns, spot sprays containing a weed killer like amitrole or glyphosate prove effective against puncturevine. These herbicides must be applied when puncturevine is in seedling stage. The more grown-up puncturevine plants must be destroyed by spot treatment with diesel oil or crankcase oil. The herbicidal oils destroy even the seeds of puncturevine contained in its pods. Other herbicides like picloram and dicamba need be tried for selective control of puncturevine in grasslands and turfs.

In non-crop situations, soil sterilants like monuron, fenac, sodium borate, and sodium chlorates may be used to eliminate puncturevine (Chapter 23).

24.3.9 *Eupatorium odoratum* L. (siamweed, croftonweed, *kali basuti*) (Fig. 24.13)

(= *Chromolaena odorata* (L.) King Robinson)

Family: Asteraceae

Biology and Habitat: *E. odoratum* is a serious invasive alien weed of particularly plantations (oilpalm, rubber, cocoa, tea, coffee, etc.) in the tropical countries, including India. It is already problematic in her citrus orchards in the N-E region and in rubber plantations in Kerala. Now it is spreading fast in the mid hills of Himachal Pradesh.

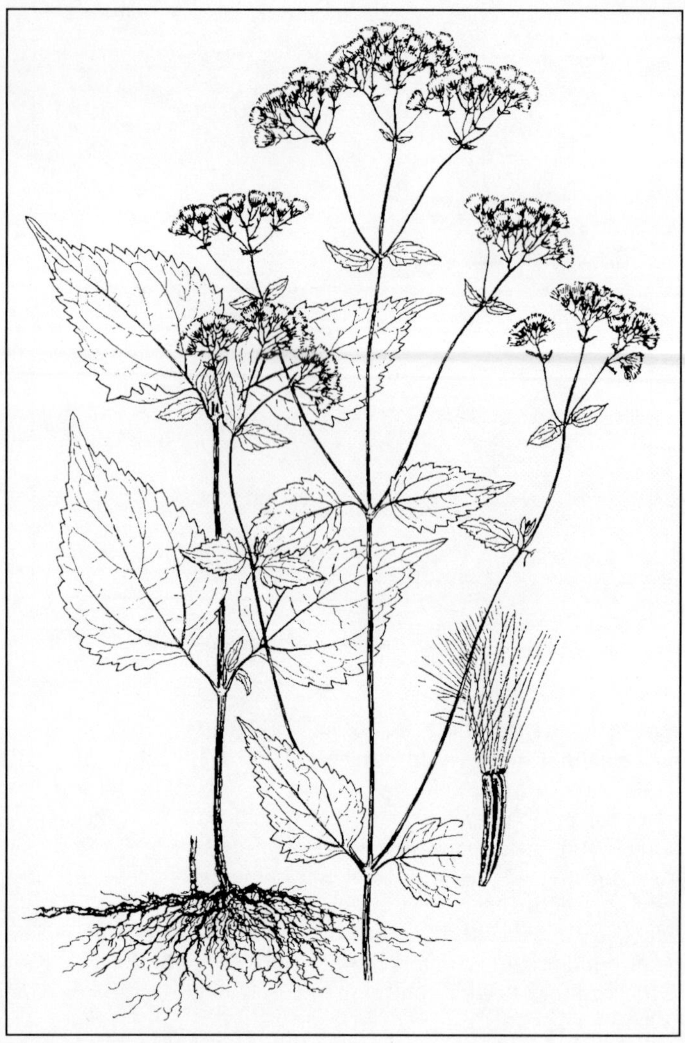

Fig. 24.13: *Eupatorium* sp. (siamweed)

Siamweed is a much branched, fast growing shrub, attaining height of 3-5 m. It emits a typical, aromatic odour. Its pale-blue flowers produce air-borne seeds, and the cut plants regenerate from the crown buds, making thickets in which few other plants can survive. It can replace even a hardy weed like *Imperata cylindrica*.

Control: Physical destruction of *Eupatorium* seedlings is helpful in eventually exhausting the soil of its seeds. Its foliage is susceptible to herbicides, *eg* 2,4-D, atrazine, diuron, glyphosate, paraquat, diquat, picloram, and Dowco-433. Dowco-433 (0.25 kg/ha) is best applied during May to November. Likewise, paraquat (1-2 kg/ha) and glyphosate (1-2 kg/ha) are found to act most effectively during September and October (Singh, *et al.* 1992). 2,4-D (4-6 kg/ha) will cause only temporary damage to the thickets of Siamweed, while its young growth is damaged almost completely. A mixture of picloram (0.4 kg/ha) and 2,4-D (1.6 kg/ha) has been found extremely effective in destroying the croftonweed thickets for up to six months. Several cover crops have been found effective in the containment of *Eupatorium* establishment.

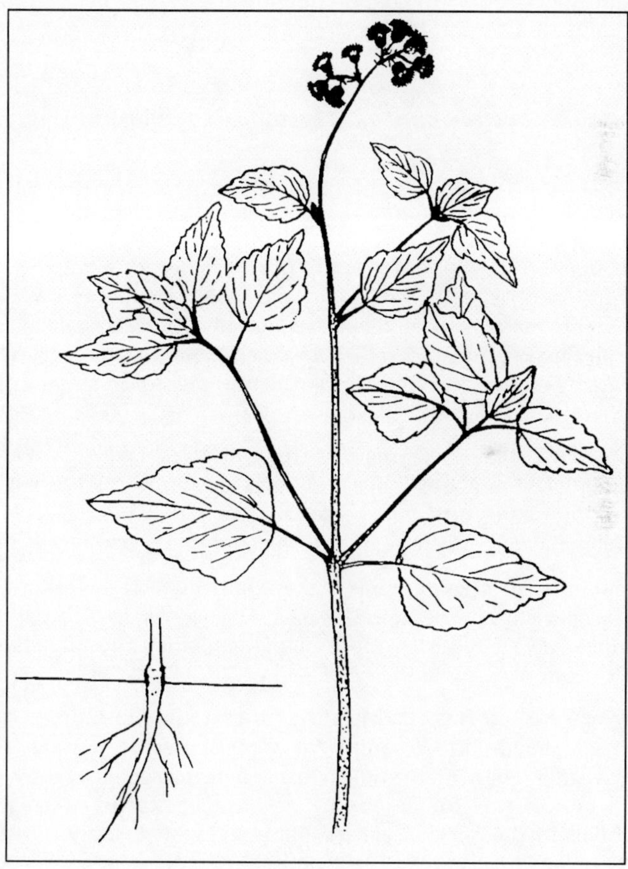

Fig. 24.14: *Ageratum conyzoides* (L.) (billgoat weed)

24.3.10 *Ageratum* spp. (billgoatweed, *neela phulnu, pudeni, ujaru, and ukhal buti*) (Fig. 24.14)

Family: Asteraceae

Biology and Habitat: *Ageratum*, is an invasive alien weed that is native to tropical America. Its two species, namely *A. conyzoides* (L.) and *A. houstonanium* (Mill.) are common in India. While *A. conyzoides* is an annual species invading both crop and non-crop lands, the latter is a common perennial species infesting largely undisturbed areas like the road sides, field boundries, pasture land, orchards, and water channels. *A. conyzoides* causes serious yield losses in *kharif* crops *eg* maize. It bears blue, attractive flowers which continue for considerable period before setting seeds in October. The perennial species of Ageratum (*A. hostonanium*) multiplies by stems and roots, besides numerous seeds, capable of remaining dormant in soil for up to three months.

Control: Ageratum is susceptible to common herbicides used in maize and other '*kharif*' crops, like atrazine and alachlor. In non-crop areas, it can be damaged severely with a non-selective herbicide like glyphosate.

24.3.11 *Parthenium hysterophorus* (carrotgrass, chandni) (Fig. 3.1)

Family: Asteraceae

Biology and Habitat: *P. hysterophorus* is an annual invasive alien plant, with wide amplitude of ecological adaptability; being both photo and thermo-insensitive. It reproduces itself freely from numerous seeds (5000-10000 per plant), besides its crown buds which put forth new shoots as and when the mother shoot is cut. Thus, the weed spreads by leaps and bounds in any new, neglected area. The weed is notorious for causing allergic dermatitis and mental depressions in human beings. The main toxin responsible for such effects of the weed is 'parthenin', present in a concentration as high as 0.33% (d.w.b.).

Parthenium is known to have its origin in tropical North and South America. It was introduced in India at Pune about 5 decades back and now it is estimated to infest an area of about 5 million ha throughout the country. In Madhya Pradesh, *P. hysterophorus* has become problematic even in crop fields; displacing some local weeds in the process.

In dry summer months *Parthenium* tends to stunt its growth and remain in rosette form. It shoots up new growth in the rainy season and grows fast through the winters, attaining a height of up to 90 cm, with profuse branching. The plant flowers and sets seeds throughout its growing period.

Control: Initially when carrotgrass had just started spreading in India in patches, almost half a century back, hand-pulling campaigns were started to pull-out the weed from below its crown region. As a precaution, gloves were provided to the volunteers. The practice can still be followed for destroying new patches of the weed around houses, gardens, and schools by the affected parties and individuals to ward off various kinds of allergies.

Currently the carrotgrass infestations have taken gigentic shapes in the country on her vast waste lands, roadsides, around buildings and, in fact, any where. Chemical control of such parthenium infestations is found scientifically possible with certain herbicides, particularly, 2,4-D esters (2-5 kg/ha), diquat (0.5-1.0%) glyphosate (0.5-1.0%), **metribuzin** (0.3-0.5%), chlorimuron (0.02-0.04 kg/ha), and metsulfuron (0.035-0.045 kg/ha). In each case, a wetting agent should be added in the spray tank, if not already present in the formulation, and the herbicide should be applied on the new active growth of the weed before it had chance to flower. Of these herbicides, metribuzin is the latest recommended one against *P. hysterophorus*.

Although the herbicidal controls is effective in controlling carrotgrass, the practice seems infeasible because of the non-ownership of the vast wasted lands infested with the weed. It is only in the personal property areas that this option can be considered feasible. Moreover, herbicidal control of carrotgrass is a 2-3 year's, or longer, venture till its all seeds stored in the soil were exhausted. But in places where *Parathenium* has invaded certain agricultural fields, several preemergence herbicides which are selective to the crop grown, can take care of the weed.

Finding that the major *P. hysterophorus* problem cannot be addressed to with the herbicides for economic and feasibility reasons, the scientists laid stress on its biological control. After testing different possible bioagents for several years, Mexican beetle ***Zygogramma bicolorata*** was finally accepted as the most effective bioagent for damaging the established carrotgrass infestations on the vast non-crop lands of the country. The bioagent was first test-released in the infested fields in 1984 in Banglore. After observing its success in controlling the weed and safety to our plants of economic importance for a number of years, it has now been registered by the GOI as an effective and safe biocontrol agent against *P. hysterophorus* for release throughout the country. The National Research Centre for Weed Science (of ICAR) at Jabalpur has demonstrated the efficacies of the bioagent on large scale at its release rates of 50-100 beetles/ plant. The bioagent multifield fast and cleared large areas of this menace. Earlier, similar successful experiences were also recorded in the states of Karnataka and Tamil Nadu. (Jayanath, 1993 and Yaduraju *et al.* 2005). (See also Chapter 9).

Presently, the management of *P. hysterophorus* through biocontrol may be considered as the most cost-effective and self-sustaining option. When possible, the land recovered from *Parthenium* should put to some fast growing plant species like *Cassia tora*, *Tephrosia purpurea*, and *Tagetu erecta*, depending upon the location.

24.3.12 *Mikania micrantha* H.B.K. (mile-a-minute weed)

Family: Asteraceae

Biology and Habitat: Mikania is an alien invasive, perennial weed introduced from South and Central America. It grows and spreads extremely fast as for its name. it has infested heavily the high rainfall areas of Western Ghats with humid tropical climate. It is a voracious climber; climbing even medium-sized trees, including banana, and all grasses and other vegetation on the way, choking these with its dense mat of leaves and twines. The weed is unpalable to animals. It poses threat to native flora in forests, tea and rubber plantations, grasslands, and some agricultural eco-systems in Assam and Kerala. Its seeds are air-borne with hairy parachutes (pappus).

Control: *Mikania* is susceptible to glyphosate, paraquat, and 2,4-D. Suitable combinations of these herbicides may curb the weed in 35 days and hold it back up to 80 days after the herbicide spray. But selectivity to plantation crops, forage grasses and other crop plants has to be kept in view. A rust species, *Puccinia spegazzinii* from Trindad has been identified in India as a potential biocontrol agent of the weed. Further research is under way.

24.3.13 *Mimosa* spp. (giant or creeping sensitive plant)

Family: Leguminosae

Biology and Habitat: *M. invisa* Mart. and *M. prainina* Gamble are the recently recognised troublesome, alien weeds, introduced in India from Tropical America as cover crop plants for plantations. But now these two plants are spreading fast, forming gregarious thickets on valuable pasture lands of Kerala and Assam, in particular. *M. invisa* occurs in throny as well as smooth biotypes. *Mimosa* is avoided by animals due to its toxic alkaloid 'mimosine' and in some cases, also due to its prickly nature. In many places the weed has become problematic in rice and sugarcane fields too.

Control: *Mimosa* is found susceptible to glyphosate, 2,4-D, paraquat, atrazine, diuron, hexazinone, and sodium arsenite. Physical weeding is difficult, labour intensive and expensive.

24.3.14 *Solanum elaeagnifolium* Cav. w.(wildbrinjal, silver leaf nightshade, white weed) (Fig. 24.15)

Family: Solanaceae

Biology and Habitat: Silverleaf nightshade is a deep rooted, perennial weed with erect and branched stems covered with fine hair and orange colour prickles. Its leaves are silvery white due to numerous white hairs. The flowers are purple to violet. The plant grows profusely during the rainy season, infesting roadsides, garden lands and neglected drylands. Its root pieces can give rise to new plants. In India, the weed is presently noxious in her southern states. The weed is native to S-W USA and Mexico. It is poisonous to livestock.

Control: The weed has been found susceptible to 2,4-D and glyphosate but it regrows after about 2 weeks of the treatment. Further research has shown that dicamba can translocate to the roots of this weed and, thus, it holds good promise against it (Velu and Kempuchetty, 1991). Hopefully in near future the scientists shall come out with some successful biocontrol alternative to combat this menace.

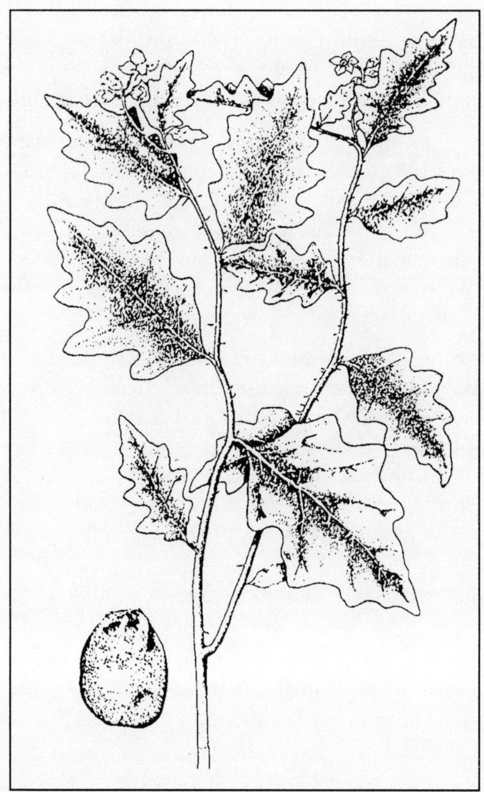

Fig. 24.15: *Solanum elaeagnifolium* (white horsenettle)

24.4 SEDGES

24.4.1 *Cyperus* spp. (nutsedge, *motha*) (Fig. 3.5)

Family: Cyperaceae

Biology and Habitat: There are two common species of nutsedge, namely, *Cyperus esculentus* L. (yellow nutsedge) and *C. rotundus* L. (purple nutsedge). A purple nutsedge plant possesses a prominent basal bulb just below the ground level. This basal bulb produces a chain of tubers which ramify as deep as 60 cm in soil. But in yellow nutsedge, instead of a basal bulb, there are crown buds a little below the soil surface which give rise to cluster of short rhizomes ending in small tubers. When mother shoots of yellow nutsedge are destroyed by tillage, new aerial shoots are borne by these crown buds. In purple untsedge, on the contrary, the new shoots arise from the tubers.

The chief mode of propagation of yellow nutsedge is from seeds (nuts), which are 90-95% viable. Its tubers are small and slow growing. In variance with this, the purple nutsedge seeds are of very low viability (2-10%) but its tubers are prominent and grow rapidly. During the first one month growth of purple nutsedge, a mother tuber can produce four daughter tubers, and in three months the tuber population may reach almost 100. This makes purple nutsedge much more problematic than yellow nutsedge.

Nutsedge is one of the most difficult perennial weeds of the world, particularly in the moisture retentive soils of the tropics and subtropics. Vegetable crops are worst affected by nutsedge, although it also infests many summer field crops like maize, sugarcane, and cotton. In winter season the weed usually remains dormant, but in mild season it can also pose problem in wheat and potato. In potato, nutsedge shoots have been found to penetrate through its tubers. Not only this, on roadsides the nutsedge can grow through even asphalt.

Control: Nutsedge is found susceptible to tillage. In summer fallows, hot weather cultivations can desiccate the tubers to death. Crowbar and overlapping sweeps are good for this purpose. A tuber exposed to summer sun in the arid and semi-arid tropics, is desiccated in about 14 days if the soil was completely dry. The nutsedge tuber desiccation can be greatly improved by supplementing tillage with 2,4-D (2-4 kg/ha) at the last cultivation before the onset of monsoon. In variance with the arid areas, in humid areas the fallow tillage should be shallow and repeated every time the nutsedge shoots are 18-20 days old. This is about the pre-flowering time of nutsedge when its food reserves in the tubers are low. The objective of tillage in this case is to destroy nutsedge tubers by starvation.

In high value vegetables and ornamentals, a 1000 gauge, black polythelene film lay in the interrows has been found useful in holding back the nutsedge. Nutsedge shoots can penetrate through thinner and transparent films.

Several herbicides like 2,4-D, amitrole-T, liquid atrazine, bentazon, salts of MAA, paraquat, propanil and linuron, are effective on nutsedge shoots but they seldom achieve extended control of the weed beyond 1-2 weeks. These herbicides are employed for postemergence treatment in specific crops (Chapters 13 & 20). **Glyphosate** is much more effective in this respect since it is translocated to its tubers to check its regeneration (Thakur *et al.*, 1993).

Thiocarbamates like EPTC, butylate, vernorate, and pebulate inflict strong inhibitory effects on the nutsedge tubers. Crops that are tolerant to these herbicides can be included in crop rotations. Nutsedge from seeds, particularly yellow nutsedge, is much easier to control. Many preemergence herbicides applied to different crops for the control of annual weeds are effective on nutsedge seedlings too. Atrazine is particularly good for the control of seedling nutsedge.

In orchards, fortified oils, dichlobenil, bromacil, and terbacil have proved highly effective as long residue herbicides against nutsedge, In turfs, two applications of bentazon (0.5-1.0 kg/ha) at 10 days' interval were found effective. Postemergent bentazon can also be used in soybean. Soil fumigation with metham or methyl bromide is satisfactory for treating nurseries and pot soils. The treatment, however, is found effective against only the non-dormant nutsedge tubers.

Certain growth substances like BA, Kinetin, and GA, have been successfully employed to force yellow nutsedge to produce its tubers near the ground to fall easy prey to the herbicides. But the field application of the technique is not proven.

SUMMARY

There are certain weeds which are dominant, but are not controlled by the "usual" cultural and herbicidal practices followed to curb the mixed growths of weed species in different crop and non-crop situations. These weeds require special treatment, many a time as a round the year programme for 3-4 years in a row. In this chapter such programmes for 22 weed species, most of them perennial and some parasitic, belonging to different families have been provided, along with their biologies.

SELECTED BIBLIOGRAPHY

1. Abraham, C.T., *et al.* 1991. Chemical control of *Parthenium*. Proc. Kerala Sci. Congress. Feb-March, 1991, 122-123.
2. Abraham, M. and C.T. Abraham. 2005. Biology of Mile- A Minute weed (*Mikania micrantha* H.B.K.), an alien invasive weed in Kerala. Ind. J. Weed Sci. 37 (1 & 2): 153-155.
3. Adagba, M.A. *et al.* 2002. Nitrogen effect on the incidence of *Striga hermonthica* (Del.) Benth in upland rice. Acta Agronomica Humgarica 50(2) : 145-150. (Nigeria)
4. Alam, M.K. 1986. A critical review on the biology and control of loranthaceae with a particular reference to Bangladesh. Bano Biggyan Patrika. 13 (1/2) 7-18
5. Anon. 2004-2005. Annual Report NRC for Weed Science, Jabalpur (India). 59 P.
6. Babu, V.S. and Muniyappa, T.V. 1994. The control of silverleaf nightshade (*Solanum elaeagnifolium* Cav.) Ind. J. Weed Sci. 26 (3-4) 22-27.
7. Banks, P.A. *et al.* 1979. Control of bindweed in winter wheat. Weed Sci. 27 (3) 332-335.
8. Barrentine, W.L. and McWhorter, C.G. 1988. Johnsongrass (*Sorghum halepense*) control with herbicides in oil diluents. Weed Sci. 36 (1) 102-110.
9. Bir, D., *et al.* 1993. Control of arrowwood (*Pluchea lanceolata*) in uncropped situations. Ind. J. Weed Sci. 25 (3-4) 86-87.
10. Buddhi, M. *et al.* 2002. Growth and development of *Cuscuta chinensis* Lam. and its impact on selected crops. Weed Biology and Management 2(2): 79-83. (Sri Lanka)
11. Chinnusamy, C. *et al.* 2003. Herbicidal management of invasive weed, *Solanum elaeagnifolium* -- an on farm research. Abst. National Sem. Alien Invasive Weeds in India, held at AAU, Jorhat (India), April 27-29, 2003: 62-63.
12. Cubero, J.I. 1986. Breeding for resistance to *Orobanche* and *Striga*– A review. (In) Biology and Control of *Orobanche* (Ed. Borg, S.J. ter), Wagenigen, Netherlands.
13. Dawson, J.H. 1990. *Dodder* control with dinitroaniline herbicides in alfalfa. Weed Technol. 4: 341-348.
14. Dawson, J.H. 1978. Control of dodder (*Cuscuta* spp.) with pronamide. Weed Sci. 26 (6) 660-664.
15. Dejongh, K. *et al.* 1993. Suicidal germination of striga seeds using several trap crop varieties. Weed Abs. 1994. 43 (12) 672.

16. Dixit, A. *et al.* 2003. Herbicidal control of problematic weeds, Parthenium and Ipomoea in non-crop situations. Abst. Bienn. Conf. ISWS held 12-14 March 2003 at G.B.P. Univ. Agr. & Technol. Pantnagar (India): 87.

17. Eizenberg, H. *et al.* 2002. First report of the parasitic plant *Orobanche aegyptica* infecting olive. Plant Disease 86(7) : 814. (USA)

18. Eplee, R.E. and Langson, M.A. 1976. Developments in the control of *Striga* in the USA. PANS 22 (1) 61-64.

19. Frans, R. *et al.* 1982. Chemical and cultural methods of bermudagrass control in cotton. Weed Sci. 30: 481-84.

20. Gupta, O.P. and Sharma, J.J. 1977. *Parthenium* menace in India and its possible control measures. FAO Plant Prot. Bull. 25 (3) 112-117.

21. Hodgson, J. 1974. Canadathistle. Weeds Today 5 (1) 10-11.

22. Holm, L.G. *et al.* 1977. The world's Worst Weeds: Distribution And Biology. An East-West Centre Book, Univ. Hawaii press. 609 pp.

23. Hosamani, M.M. 1978. Striga - A Noxious Root Parasitic Weed. Royal Printers; Bangalore, 165 pp.

24. Ish-Shalom-Gordon, N. *et al.* 1993. Inheritance of resistance to *Orobanche cumana* in sunflower. Phytopathology 83 (11) 1250-1252.

25. Ivens, G.S. 1979. The problem of *Eupatorium odoratum* L. in Nigeria. PANS, 20 (1) 76-82.

26. Jayanath, K.P. 1993. Ecological impact of insects introduced for biological control of weeds - conflicting interests. Current Science 65 901-904.

27. Kaneria, B.B. *et al.* 1993. Herbicidal control of Johnsongrass (*Sorghum halepense*). Ind. J. Agro. 38 (1) 158-160.

28. Kar, B.C. *et al.* 2003. Mikania: a new introducer to coastal Orissa and its control. Abst. Nat. Sem. Alien Invasive Weeds in India held April 27-29, 2003, Jorhat (India): 60.

29. Keeby, P.E. *et al.* 1987. Repeated annual applications of herbicides for control of rhizome Johnsongrass in cotton. Weed Sci. 35 (1) 75-80.

30. Khattri, G.B. *et al.* 2002. Identification of *Orobanche* species occurring in Nepal. Hautorium 41, 4-6. (Nepal)

31. Krishna Murty, G.V.G. 1992. Two new methods to control *Orobanche* on tobacco. Ind. Fmg. 426 (1) 7-8.

32. Kumar, S. 2002. Preliminary studies on the control of broomrape (*Orobanche aegyptica*) in mustard. Ind. J. Weed Sci. 34: 303-304.

33. Liolas, P.C. 1986. Control of broomrape (*Orobanche ramosa*) in tobacco (*Nicotiana tabaccum*). Weed Sci. 34 (3) 427-430.

34. Mahere, J. *et al.* 2000. Chemical weed control in linseed with special reference to *Cuscuta*. Ind. J. Weed Sci. 32: 216-217.

35. Maliwal, P.L. *et al.* 2002. Integrated management of camelthorn (*Alhagi camelorum*) in tank bank conditions. Ind. J. Weed Sci. 34: 331-332.

36. Mazaheri, A. *et al.* 1991. Studies on the chemical control of broomrape in tobacco. Weed Abst. 1993, 42 (9) 472 (item 3801).

37. McClelland, M.R. *et al.* 1978. Responese of six morningglory (*Ipomoea*) species to bentazon. Weed Sci. 26 (5) 459-464.

38. Mehta, H.M. 1991. Foliar application of herbicides for control of purple nutsedge. Ind. J. Weed Sci. 23 (3, 4) 96-97.

39. Miller, S.D. *et al.* 1978. Difenzoquat for wilodoat control. Weed Sci. 26 (6) 571-576.

40. Mishra, J.S. and Bhan, V.M. 1994. Efficacy of sulfonylurea herbicides against *Parthenium hysterophorus* L. Ind. J. Weed Sci. 26 (3-4) 104-108.

41. Moorthy, B. *et al.* 2003. Certain investigations on the parasite weed cuscuta in field crop. Ind. J. Weed Sci. 35: 214-216.

42. Mueller, D.M. *et al.* 1994. Mechanical harvesting of pricklypear for control and feeding. J. Range Mgmt. 47 (3) 251-254.

43. Okonkwo, C.A.C. and Garba, A. 1993. Selection of *Striga* resistant sorghum germplasm in the N. Guinea savanna. Plant Varieties & Seeds 6 (3) 197-205.

44. Om, H. *et al.* 2005. Dormancy and viability of *Phalaris minor* seed in a rice – wheat cropping system. Weed Res. 45(2): 140-148.

45. Pandey, D.K. 2004. Role of *exotic weeds* in ecosystem deterioration, loss of biodiversity and possible ways of ecosystem restoration. Int. J. Ecol. Environ. Sci. 30(3) : 209-222.

46. Parocheti, J.V. *et al.* 1975. Activity of glyphosate on Johnsongrass. Weed Sci. 23 395-400.

47. Patil, V.C. *et al.* 1993. Chemical control of *Cynodon dactylon* (L.) Pers. In. Proc. ISWS Int. Sump. held at Hisar (India), Nov. 1993. Vol. III, 238-239.

48. Pepperman, A.B. *et al.* 1982. Evaluation of precursors and analogs of strigol as witchweed seed germination stimulants. Weed Sci. 30: 561-566.

49. Pitt, J.L. 1992. Parthenium weed (*Parthenium hysterophorus*). Agnote (Darwin) No. 81/14 UPDT, 2 pp.

50. Poonia, B.L. *et al.* 2001. Weed management with special reference to *Asphodelus tenuifolius*. Ind. J. Weed Sci. 33: 100-103.

51. Prakash, R. 1995. Conservation of genetic resources. Everyman's Science, ISCA, XXX(1) 2-6.

52. Pratibha, N.C. *et al.* 1994. A preliminary evaluation of herbicides on the control of *Oxalis latifolia*. H.B. & K. Ind. J. Weed Sci. 26 (3-4) 135-138.

53. Punia, S.S. *et al.* 2006. Evaluation of carfentrazone-ethyl against *Convolvulus arvensis* L. and *Malva parviflora* L. in wheat. Ind. J. Weed. Sci. 38(1&2): 5-8.

54. Rajkhowa, D.J. *et al.* 2003. Agrobiology and management of *Mimosa* spp. Abst. National Sem. Alien Invasive Weeds in India held at Jorhat (India), April 27-29, 2003: 35-36.

55. Ramchandra, P.T.V. *et al.* 2003. Agro-biology and management of alien weed *Chromolaena odorata*, Abst. Nat. Seminar Alien Invasive Weeds, held April 27-29, 2003 at AAU, Jorhat (India): 42-43.

56. Sahir, A.R. 1986. Dormancy and germination of *Orobanche* seeds in relation to control methods. (IN) Biology and Control of *Orobanche* (Ed. Borg. S.J.), Wagenigen, Netherlands.

57. Sarvanane, P. and H.V. Nanjappa 2003. *Mikania micrantha* a growing menace in Western Ghats. Abst. National Sem. Alien Invasive Weeds in India, held at AAU, Jorhat (India), April 27-29, 2000: 61-62.

58. Seth, A. 1970. Chemical control of *Imperata cylindrica* (L.) Beauv. in Malasia. Weed Res. 10: 87-93.

59. Sharma, O.P. *et al.* 1992. Biological action of lantadana C from *Lantana camara* var. *aculeata*. J. Biochem. Toxicol. 7 (2) 73-79.

60. Shivakumar, H.R. *et al.* 2003. Effect of postemergence herbicides on the control of nutgrass (*Cyperus rotundus*). Abst. Bienn. Conf. ISWS held 12-14 March 2003 at G.B.P. Univ. of Agr. & Technol. Pantnagar (India): 81.

61. Shukla, A.K. and S.P. Singh 2001. Chemical and cultural control of thalctigrass (*Imperata cylindrica* L. Rauschel). Annals Plant Protection Sciences 9(2) : 364-366. (India)

62. Singh, C.M. *et al.* 1992. Biology and control of *Eupatorium adenophorum* in Himachal Pradesh. Ind. Soc. Weed Sci. 24 (1 & 2) 62-64.

63. Sukhadia, N.M. *et al.* 2000. Efficacy of herbicides in *Cynodon dactylon* and *Cyperus rotundus* on fallows and its after effects on succeeding summer greengram. Ind. J. Weed Sci. 32: 160-163.

64. Thakur, D.R. *et al.* 1993. Herbicidal control of purple nutsedge (*Cyperus rotundus* L.). Ind. J. Weed Sci. 25 (3 & 4) 22-26.

65. Tiwari, A.N. and Singh, R.D. 1991. Studies on *Cyperus rotundus* L. - Control through summer treatments in maize-potato cropping systems. Ind. J. Weed Sci. 23 (1 & 2) 6-11.

66. Trivedi, G.C. *et al.* 2000. Some problematic weeds and their management - a review. Agricultural Reviews 21(4): 238-243. (India)

67. Umarani, R. *et al.* 1994. Studies on dormancy and germination of *Trianthema portulacastrum*. Ind. J. Weed Sci. 26 (3-4) 82-88.

68. Varshney, J.G. and Saxena, A. 1994. Allelopathic activity of *Cyperus rotundus* on germination and growth of grain legumes. Ind. J. Weed Sci. 26 (3-4) 52-56.

69. Veeradhadraiah, G.P. *et al.* 1980. Increase of penetration and translocation of foliar applied 2,4-D into the underground part of nutsedge. Ind. J. Agri. Sci. 50: 352-356.

70. Velu, G. and Kempuchetty, N. 1991. Translocation of Dicamba (*Solanum elaeagnifolium*). Ind. J. Weed Sci. 23 (1 & 2) 58-60.

71. Wills, G.D. 1987. Description of purple and yellow nutsedge (*Cyperus rotundus* and *C. esculantus*). Weed Technol. 1: 2-9.

72. Yadav, A. *et al.* 2000. Regrowth of *Cynodon dactylon, Cyperus rotundus,* and *Echinochloa* spp. after spray of paraquat and glyphosate. Ind. J. Weed Sci. 32: 223-226.

73. Yaduraju, N.T. *et al.* 2005, Major Invasive Alien Weeds of India. Pub. National Res. Centre for Weed Sci., Jabalpur (India), 52 p.

Chapter 25

HERBICIDE RESIDUES IN FOOD AND WATER

Pesticides, especially herbicides, play a major role in maintaining agricultural production in the developed countries. In other countries too, their use is contributing increasingly to better the output of farming systems. However, unless used judiciously, there is always possibility of occurrence of their residues in our food and animal feed. This, together with great public concern about food safety, makes it necessary to monitor pesticide residues in food and feed and take necessary measures to minimise these to within permissible limits.

The pesticide monitoring programmes are operated by different countries all over the world. In general, an important percentage of food monitored has been found to contain measurable pesticide residues, chiefly of insecticides. In fact, the insecticide residues in food form over 89% of all the pesticide residues detected in various agricultural commodities. The residues of herbicides in food and feed have not been frequently reported in scientific literature, particularly in the current years, and most of the herbicide residue data are well below the officially accepted Tolerance Levels. Also, the evidences of ill effects of herbicide residues in food on man have been inconsistent, and far from conclusive.

25.1 PESTICIDE RESIDUES AND OUR CONCERN

Pesticide residue means any specified substances in food, agricultural commodity or animal feed resulting from the use of the pesticide. The term includes any derivatives of a pesticide, such as conversion products, metabolic products, reaction products, and impurities considered to be of toxicological significance. The pesticide residues may originate from both, known uses of the pesticide as well as from unknown or unavoidable sources *eg* environmental. Sometimes, the presence of a pesticide in food where its intentional use had not been made is differentiated from Pesticide Residue, as **Pesticide Contaminant.**

Despite the worldwide success in controlling crop pests and securing adequate food supplies, most synthetic, organic pesticides may adversely affect human welfare by leaving their residues in human food and animal feed. This generally happens when pesticides are used with disregard to the recommended Good Agricultural Practices (GAP). Further, the pesticide residues can be detected frequently not only locally at the site of their application but also in the distant ecosystems due to their easy mobility in air and water. Even rain water has been found to carry pesticides, including herbicides like alachlor, atrazine, metolachlor, prometryn, and molinate (Charizopoulos and Papadopoulou, 1999 and Scharf *et al.*, 1992).

The voluminous data available on pesticide residues in food clearly reveal that of different pesticides, the insecticide residues are most notorious in different kinds of food and feed (Gupta, 2006). The herbicide residues seem to have little contribution to the total pesticide residues of different kinds of pesticides. It may be because of the fact that selective herbicides are found to get metabolised fast to their non-phytotoxic products in crop plants, else it will make the crop plant sick in the first instance. However, when the mode of selective action of a herbicide is such that its intact molecule is saved by bonding or otherwise in the crop plants, there is some possibility of its continuing in plants till maturity. There could be other versions to explain the limited herbicide residues persisting in edible parts of the crop plants at maturity as reported by some residue analysts. However, in majority of the cases these residues have been well within the maximum residue levels (MRLs). Also, the disturbing health effects of herbicide residues on man remain controversial and inconclusive. Despite all this, we cannot be complacent about it and ignore further research on possible herbicide residues in varied foodstuffs. The status of herbicide residues in our food, however, need not be hyped beyond proportions.

25.2 SOURCES OF HERBICIDE RESIDUES IN AGRICULTURAL COMMODITIES AND FOODSTUFFS

1. The primary source of herbicide residues in agricultural commodities is the purposeful application of herbicides to agricultural fields for weed management, growth regulation, and desiccation, as the case may be. Besides, unintentionally the herbicides may move as spray and volatile drifts and cause local and long range contamination of the non-target crop fields. Some of the drift clouds may stay in the environment for considerable periods to cause future contamination of our agricultural commodities.

2. Leaching of herbicides and their movement with runoff from agricultural fields form the major sources of herbicide residues often detected in groundwater and varied surface water-bodies, both of which are the major sources of our drinking water supplies.

3. The herbicide contamination of milk has been traced back to the milch animals which were either allowed to graze in freshly herbicide-treated pastures and meadows or were fed with fodder from the herbicide treated fields.

4. The herbicide contamination of honey is caused when honeybees collect nectar from the herbicide treated orchards, gardens, and non-crop areas.

5. In the developed countries herbicides are major tools to control aquatic weeds in relevant water-bodies. From here these are easily absorbed by fish and other aquatic fauna. The pesticide factory discharges in water-bodies also contribute to herbicide contamination of our aquatic food.

25.3 STATUS OF HERBICIDE RESIDUES IN FOOD

The herbicide residues status in agricultural commodities and food is determind by the pesticide residues scientists in two major ways. *First*, through the Supervised Field Trials (SFTs) and *second* by Monitoring research. In the SFTs, the test herbicide is applied in the intended crops at the field recommended and double the recommended doses, and the pesticide residues are determined in plants at the fixed crop growth stages, using modern equipment like the GLC and HPLC. The data are used to know the dissipation rates and pattern of the herbicide in question. In the 'monitoring studies'[**], on the other hand, framgate and market samples of food material are collected and analysed for their herbicide residues. The details of conducting the 'SFTs' and 'Monitoring research' are provided by Gupta (2006).

Some research results obtained and reported from SFTs and Monitoring research on the herbicide residue status in various food commodities are presented here, as follows:

25.3.1 Food Grains

In Canada when *2,4-D* was applied to **wheat** fields in spring to control weeds, the mature grain did not contain significant levels of the herbicide residues. However, when it was applied at the soft-dough stage of the crop, the mature wheat grains, upon analysis, revealed the presence of 2,4-D residues in concentrations of 0.03-0.26 mg/kg, which were close to or exceeded the Canadian MRL of 0.1 mg/kg. In view of this, the late stage application of 2,4-D was not recommended in wheat (Anon., 1995), which is sometimes adopted to control the late appearing broadleaf weeds (Chapter-21). In another investigation, the persistence of postemergent *mecoprop* in wheat, **Oat**, and **barley** was looked into. The analysis revealed no detectable residues of the herbicide in mature seeds of any of these food crops. On these cereal leaves, the mecoprop residues were dissipated to 0.1-0.2 mg/kg within 6 weeks after its application (Anon, 1994).

Shioda *et al.* (1994) in Japan monitored 215 imported food crop samples. Of these, only in the wheat samples traces of 2,4-D residues (0.1-0.11 mg/kg) were detected. Sozeri and Alaziz (2003) in Turkey determined residues of field applied *chlorsulfuron* in wheat grains. The authors reported the residues in concentrations of 0.027-0.037 mg/kg, depending upon the time and rate of application of the herbicide. These residues were considered unacceptable as per Codex MRLs. In India, Saha, *et al.* (2003) reported results of analysis of wheat grain and straw from post-emergence application of *sulfosulfuron* in wheat fields. The herbicide was targetted to control *Phalaris minor*. The analysis revealed no harvest time residues of the herbicide in wheat grain. At IARI, New

---

[**] The operation of Monitoring of Pesticide Residues in Food Commodities has been recently allocated to the Department of Agriculture and cooperation of the Ministry of Agriculture, GOI, by the cabinet secretariat (see India, 2006, GOI).

Delhi, wheat grains and straw were found to contain residues of postemergence applied trisulfuron below detectable limit (BDL) of 0.01-0.002 mg kg^{-1} (Singh and Kulsrestha, 2006). The harvest time residues of postemergent clodinafop in wheat grain were found below delectable limits (BDL).

In a survey conducted in Denmark, the average concentration of *glyphosate* in 46 samples of cereals was found to be 0-0.8 mg/kg in 1998 and 0.11 mg/kg in 1999. Both these residue levels were below MRL and thus no violation of food laws was considered (Granby and Vahl, 2000).

One potential use of *diquat* in European countries is as a desiccant to rescue the lodged wheat, barley, and oat. In an investigation, of the 200 analytical results available on diquat cation residues in wheat grain, only four exceeded the national MRL of 2 mg/kg. The diquat residues were found located primarily in the outer layers of the grain. The overall residues of diquat in bran were approximately twice those found in the whole grain. The highest diquat residue in bran was 2.7 mg/kg. The herbicide residues in wheat flour were generally 20-25% of those present in the whole grains. The baking process did not materially affect the diquat residue levels. In barley, three of the 43 samples analysed were found to contain residues of diquat in excess of the set MRL of 5 mg/kg. In the lodged oat crop desiccated with diquat, the mean residue in its grain was determined at 1.3 mg/kg, with highest level of 3.8 mg/kg (Anon., 1994). In Japan, no herbicide residues were found by Hirahara *et al.* (1995) in 6 polished **rice** and 41 brown rice samples drawn from the grain imported from USA. In Canada, diquat applied as desiccant to laid-rice, was detected as residue in rice grain up to a maximum concentration of 0.16 mg/kg, with a mean level of 0.07 mg/kg. Most of these residues were located in the rice husk. The diquat residues were seldom detected in dehusked rice (Anon., 1994). In Italy, rice plants after field application of endothal to paddies, did not contain any algicide residues at the minimum detectable level of 0.01 mg/kg (Maini, 1992).

In *India*, in Tamil Nadu the analysis of winter rice grain and straw for possible residues of anilofos showed below MRL levels of the herbicide residues (Jayakumar and Sankaran, 1995). In Haryana, butachlor applied at 1-2 kg/ha at the time of transplanting rice was not found to persist in either grain or straw of the crop at harvest. The butachlor residues were below detectable limit of 0-03 mg/kg (Singh *et al.*, 1996). Guha *et al.* (1992) in West Bengal determined the harvest time residues of fluchloralin in rice grain and straw and reported these as 0.008 mg/kg and 0.015 mg/kg respectively. Both these residue concentrations were below the prescribed MRLs. In the Northern and Central highlands of India, the longtime use of butachlor and isoproturon for over 10 years for weed management in rice-wheat cropping system did not result in any herbicide residue in the either grain crop (Report NRCWS, Jabalpur). Krishnamurthi (2001) reported harvest time residues of anilophos and oxadiazon in transplanted rice below detectable limit (BDL).

In Japan, Hirahara *et al.* (1995) examined the residues of fenoxaprop-ethyl in six polished and 41 brown rice samples of imported food grains from USA and reported no contamination, at the detection limit of 0.01 mg/kg by HPLC.

In Canada, the radiolabelled residues of thifensulfuron in mature **soybean** seeds were found in extremely low concentrations of 0.4-1.6 ppb. (Anon., 1995). In India, Kumar *et* *al.* (2004) studied the residue levels of trifluralin applied as preplant incorporated treatment in **mungbean** (*Vigna aureus*) at 1 and 2 kg/ha for weed management. The scientists reported that in both the pulse and straw, the herbicide residues were below the official MRL of 0.05 mg/kg.

25.3.2 Vegetables and Fruits

The residues of *pendimethalin* applied at 1-2 kg/ha for weed management in **onion** were found below detectable limit (BDL) in its bulbs and below MRL in its leaves (0.1 ppm) (Sharma and Mehta, 1989). The residues of preemergent *pendimethalin, fluchloralin, and oxadiazon* applied at 0.5 - 1.0 kg/ha in onion fields in Gujarat were examined by Raj *et al.* (1999). The authors reported the presence of herbicide residues, respectively, in concentrations of 0.003 - 0.021 mg/kg, 0.004 - 0.03 mg/kg, and 0.8 - 0.104 mg/kg; all of which were below MRL of 0.1 mg/kg. Diwan, *et al.* (1999), also from Gujarat, found no detectable residues of *pendimethalin* and *fluchloralin* in onion bulbs. Frank *et al.* (1991) treated onion crop in field with oxyfluorfen at 60-240 g/ha and found that its residues were dissipated from the foliage within 10 days to BDL (0.05 mg/kg). At Jabalpur (India), the residues of early postemergent oxyfluorfen (150 to 300 g ha) in mature onion bulbs were found below detectable limit. Sondhia and Dubey (2006) in Madhya Pradesh (India) found residues of soil-applied butachlor and pendimehtalin in onion bulbs at crop harvest, well within the MRL of 0.0255 mg kg 1.

In Tokyo, Japan, Nagayama *et al.* (1988 and 1990) in their monitoring programme found no herbicide residues in the locally grown **vegetables and fruits**. Also, in the imported crop, of the 56 commodities examined, only 29 carried detectable but below MRL herbicide residues. Giza and Sztcoiertnia (2002) conducted pesticide residue monitoring on fruits and vegetables in Poland. They reported that of the 50 active pesticide ingredients detected, only 3.5% of these constituted herbicide residues and of these only dithiocarbamate herbicide residues were in above MRL quantities and that too in four samples alone. In **potato** tubers, CIPC residues were found limited almost solely to their skin, which is usually peeled off and discarded. These residues in the peels were 196-219 mg/kg when tubers were dipped in 1% CIPC solution (Anon., 1994). Whole tuber boiling reduced the peel residues to almost half.

Residues of glyphosate were examined in **strawberry** fruits by Cessna and Cain (1992) through a supervised field trial repeated for 3 years. The herbicide residues were found below the national MRL. Zhou *et al.* (1996) studied dissipation behaviour of pendimethalin, acetachlor, and metribuzin in strawberry and **tomato** in Shanghai. In fruits of both crops the herbicide residues were BDL.

In Taiwan, Shyu *et al.* (1995) analysed 70 **citrus fruit** samples and 45 **citrus juice** samples for possible *2,4-D* residues in these. The study revealed only two lemon fruit samples contained *2,4-D* residues below the national MRL. In Brazil, *diuron* is used frequently for weed management in **pineapple**. The residue analysis of its fruits at maturity revealed diuron residues below the MRL of 0.1 mg/kg and, thus, the pineapple from the diuron treated fields was considered fit for human consumption (Cabrera *et al.*, 1999).

25.3.3 Forages

Cessna and Waddington (1995) studied the dissipation of *glyphosate* and its major metabolite *AMPA* in fodder grass, ***Agropyron desertorum*** (crested wheatgrass), and reported that the herbicide residues decreased within two weeks to below Codex MRL of 50 mg/kg.

Field studies were conducted in Voke, Lithuania during 1994-96 to study degradation behaviour of *clopyralid* in **fodder beets** (*Beta valgaris*). The residues of the herbicide were detected in beets up to 6 weeks after application. However, by the harvest time, insignificant amount of clopyralid residues were detected in beet roots (Sakaliene, 1998).

Edwards *et al.* (1976) found no ill effects on meat and milk of animals fed with *diquat* desiccated forage in **pastures**. The available data on the fate of diquat and its photoproducts showed that these chemicals were rapidly eliminated by the ruminants up to 90% or more in their faeces. In Texas, in a Supervised Field Trial, *2,4,5-T (GBEE)* applied to pastures at 0.5 and 1.0 kg/ha was found degraded up to 98% in 6 weeks. After 26 weeks the herbicide residue levels in the grasses ranged from 0-0.5 mg/kg. In another trial with *picloram,* the herbicide content of mature grasses was highest immediately after spraying (28-113 mg/kg), which was degraded rapidly to harmless levels (Bovey and Baurl, 1972).

25.3.4 Honey

In Switzerland, in five out of six spring honeys collected from three apiaries, the residues of *asulam* and its break down product *sulphanilamide* were detected. The asulam contamination in honey ranged from 13 to 702 μg/kg, with an average of 244 μg/kg as against the Swiss MRL of 200 μg/kg. Likewise, the sulphanilamide contamination in honey was greater than its tolerance limit of 50 μg/kg. Kaufman and Kaenzig (2004) assigned the presence of asulam and its degrade in honey to the honeybees collecting nectar from meadows treated with this herbicide in Switzerland. As a result, the Swiss Federal Agricultural Office decided to ban the use of asulam on the blooming pastures (Bogdanov and Edder, 2005).

25.3.5 Fish

Lee *et al.* (1990) studied bioaccumulation of *cinmethylin* in bluegill sunfish in the USA. The results showed that over 99% of the herbicide residues in the tissues were eliminated from the exposed fish after 14 days of depuration period. The major metabolities of the herbicide isolated from the treated fish were of toxicological significance. *Ametryne* is frequently recommended as aquatic herbicide from where it can be absorbed by fish. A study in Egypt showed that the mean levels of ametryne residues in the three species of fish varied from 33 to 43 μg/kg in their flesh (Khalafalla *et al.*, 1994). *2,4-D* applied to aquatic environment dissipated to BDL within 42-60 days. Fish mortality was observed only during period of up to 35 days (Bhatt, *et al.*, 2004).

Hunter and Caroll (1982) monitored residues of *phenoxy herbicides* in fishes in lake in Texas, USA and reported these averaged 244 μg/kg wet weight for *2,4-D* and 1001 μg/kg for *2,4,5-T*. The lake sediments also contained the two contaminants. These herbicides were applied to the lake for aquatic weed control.

Dissipation studies with absorbed *2,4-D* in fish from surrounding water was detected chiefly in its kidney. Also, nearly 90% of the absorbed 2,4-D was excreted in urine of the fish within 24 hours. In edible portion of fish (*ie* muscles), little 2,4-D residues could be detected after 2 hours, and none after 8 hours of release of the herbicide in water (Anon., 1994).

25.3.6 Others

The residues of metamitron in **sugar beet** were not found to exceed the acceptable limits in Poland as per the country's standards (Kucharski, *et al.* 2004).

Residues from three uracil herbicides, *bromacil, lenacil,* and *terbacil,* applied at 2 kg/ha on *Melissia officinalis* were determined in its **essential oil** in Slovakia. At crop harvest (full flowering stage), the essential oil was detected to carry these herbicide residues below the accepted MRL of 0.1 mg/kg. Therefore, the use of uracil herbicides in this medicinal plant was permitted for weed control before the full flowering stage of the crop plant (Tekel, *et al.*, 1997).

Herbicide residue trials conducted in Gujrat by Patel *et al.* (1996) in **Chicory** (*Cichorium intybus*) showed that preplant incorporated *fluchloralin* (0.67-1.35 kg/ha) did not persist in its leaves and tubers at harvest time.

In **beer** made from diquat desiccated barley, the diquat residues were found to persist in mean concentration of 0.05 mg/kg, which is much below the European MRL set for this herbicide in beer. Further, it was noted that diquat residues in beer formed hardly 2-3% of its residues in the whole grain of barley (Anon., 1994).

Pensabene *et al.* (2000) reported from their chick feeding study that *atrazine* and two of its dealkyl metabolic products were present in **eggs**.

25.4 STATUS OF HERBICIDE RESIDUES IN WATER

A. ***Groundwater:*** The extent of contamination of groundwater with herbicides depends upon their relative mobility in soils which, in turn, is influenced by their water solubility and sorption behaviour, soil texture, layer change of different clay minerals, and hydraulic conductivity of the soil. The humic amendments often added to the agricultural lands are believed to reduce the herbicide leaching by promoting sorption and biodegradation of the herbicides. Soil temperature may also influence absorption and consequent leaching of the herbicides (Jenkins *et al.*, 2000). However, some authors opine that both adsorbed and non-adsorbed herbicides eventually are susceptible to leaching at least to the shallow groundwaters. For instance, although paraquat is strongly adsorbed by soil matrix, yet it has potential of polluting groundwater, depending upon the layer charge of different clay minerals. The Ca-montmorillonite adsorbent showed a higher adsorption capacity for paraquat then the Zn-montmorillonite absorbent (Gonzaler *et al.*, 2000). The leaching of *glyphosate* (also a non-selective herbicide), is subjected to very limited leaching in soils. Its phytotoxic degrade, AMPA, too exhibits restricted mobility in soils. There are reports that P-rich environment induced glyphosate leaching through soils since its molecules compete with PO_4 ions for the adsorption sites on the soil matrices.

Another non-selective herbicide *Glufosinate - ammonium* and its degrades have been detected in groundwater as contaminants, particularly in areas with coarse soils and high water tables. Some specific examples of leaching behaviour of herbicides in soils follow:

Atrazine is highly prone to leaching in soils, with liberal contamination of groundwater. It frequently happens in areas where the herbicide is used extensively, like in the maize belts and similar farming areas. In many of these areas, the groundwater contamination with atrazine may exceed the 'maximum contaminant level (MCL), Larger field irrigations (or rainfall) further promote the problem of atrazine leaching. In a study conducted in the USA during 1993-95, six herbicides *viz.*, atrazine, cyanazine, simazine, alachlor, acetachlor, and metolachlor were detected in groundwater in 20 major hydrological basins across the country. But, of all these herbicide contaminants in groundwater only atrazine was found to exceed the MCL criteria of 1 ppb (Barbash *et al.*, 2001). Forbidding the use of atrazine in these hydrological areas could result in decreasing, and eventually eliminating the undue contamination of groundwater with atrazine.

Pendimethalin, fluchloralin and oxadiazone have been found weakly leaching herbicides in soils. These are restricted primarily to the top 0-6cm soil layer (Raj *et al.*, 1999).

Groundwater samples from 15 wells in U.P. (India) showed the presence of very low concentrations of *2,4-D*, well below the accepted safe limits (Bansal and Gupta, 2000). In Hawaii (USA), monitoring of water of several wells revealed the presence of *bromacil* in three wells with concentrations of 0.82-2.45 ppb. *Hexazinone* was detected in eight wells in concentration of 0.13-0.099 ppb (Li, *et al.*, 2001). The low dose *sulfonylurea* herbicides are considered, in general, even more leachable in soils than the conventional herbicides that have been found to impact groundwater. On the contrary, the vertical movement of herbicides like *flufenacet* and *terbuthylazine* in soils is reported weak (James, *et al.*, 1998). Thus, these herbicides are unlikely to contaminate the groundwater.

The no-till farming system may often lead to lower herbicide leaching to groundwater. It is postulated that the enrichment of soils with crop residues in the no-till farming elevate the herbicide adsorption sites in soils which, in turn, prolongs the persistence of the herbicides in surface soil, unduly.

In quite some cases, the herbicide degradation products of toxicological importance have indicated higher propensity to leach in soils than their parent compounds. It all depends upon the specific herbicide molecules.

B. *Surface Water:* The herbicide pollution of surface water-bodies is closely related to the ability of the pesticide to be transported with runoff from agricultural fields. Many a time the contaminated surface water-bodies are located thousands of km away from the site of the current use of the herbicides. Often higher amounts of herbicides are transferred with water in the runoff than with the soil sediments. Most of these losses are found to occur in the first two rainfall events following the application of herbicides (Muller *et al.*, 2004).

In many western countries, the intensive use of two common maize herbicides, *atrazine* and *simazine*, has resulted in widespread contamination of surface water resources with these. Likewise, around paddy fields, the surface water-bodies are found frequently contaminated with *molinate* in concentrations of 2-46 ppm (Mattice 1999). In Japan, the presence of pesticides (including herbicides) in the river water was correlated with the time of pesticide application in the surrounding rice fields. The river water analysis showed 53 pesticides, of which 22 were herbicides (Tanabe *et al.*, 2001). Wood charcoal was found effective in adsorption and removal of atrazine residues (up to 75-80%) from water (Sharma *et al.*, 2006).

Diquat removal from surface water is primarily by its binding to the suspended sediment. The rate of its loss in runoff is, therefore, related to water turbidity and sediment settling rates. Photolysis can partially remove diquat from surface water. In California, well water was found contaminated with diquat to variable levels (DPR, FAO, 1999b).

Druzina and Erjavec (2001) analysed drinking water in Republic of Slovenia and concluded the presence of atrazine and alachlor, although in below 'maximum permissible intake (MPI) levels. The daily intake of the two herbicides through water by man was calculated as 0.06 - 0.24 μg. In Mauritius, of the nine herbicides used frequently in sugarcane fields, only residues of atrazine, *hexazinone*, and *diuron* could be detected in fresh water sources in very low quantities. (Kwong *et al.*, 1999) *The authors concluded that public fear and mistrust of herbicides were not justified since these did not, in general, posed a risk to human health.*

25.5 MINIMIZING HERBICIDE RESIDUES

Although, neither it is possible nor necessary to aim at our zero exposure to pesticides, including herbicides, yet it is better to be attentive to minimize their residues in our food and environment. Some recommendations in this regard are as follows:

1. While planning weed management on farms, think first of the adequately effective non-chemical options (Chapters 8 and 9).
2. Follow crop rotations and herbicide rotations.
3. Apply herbicides strictly as per official recommendations made available in the area.
4. When possible, prefer band application of herbicides over their usual broadcast application to reduce the per hectare input of the toxicants.
5. Herbicides should complement, and *not* substitute the alternative effective and economic tools of weed management.
6. Follow Good Crop Husbandry Practices (Chapter - 7) to raise healthy crops to reduce residues of the applied herbicides in them by dilution.
7. Research should be initiated on decontamination of herbicide residues in agricultural commodities, if any.

SUMMARY

When a herbicide is sprayed on vegetation, part of it is deposited on plant foliage, soil, and nearby objects. The remainder contributes to environment. Of the herbicide deposited on leaves, some is absorbed into their living tissues; often resulting in mortality of the plant. The residue remaining in the tissue of the dead plants is largely decomposed as the plant material rots; however, some is released in the soil. The herbicide remaining in the unhurt, surviving tolerant plants is broken down over a period of a few days to few weeks to its non-phytotoxic moieties.

The herbicide residues in food commodities, including in drinking water, are responsible for less than 5% of the residues of all categories of pesticides combined, in the world. And a large percentage of these seldom found herbicide residues are most of the time below the officially accepted, national or WHO/FAO, maximum residue limits. Direct application of herbicides in food crops, fodder, and pastures forms the main source of residues of a few, unmetabolised herbicides in agricultural commodities. Herbicide contamination of aquatic food (*eg* fish) is through the use of aquatic herbicides and that of honey through nectar collected by bees from the pesticide treated plants. In drinking water, leaching of herbicides through soil to groundwater and their runoff from agricultural fields to the surface water-bodies are the primary sources of herbicide contamination.

The prominant results of herbicide residue research available in literature, either from the 'monitoring' of agricultural commodities or from the 'supervised field trials' as harvest time residues, are incorporated in the text. These include residues of 2,4-D and diquat (used as desiccant) in winter grains; anilofos, butachlor, fenoxaprop-ethyl and fluchloralin in rice grains and straw; trifluralin in mungbean and thifensulfuron in soybean grains; pendimethalin, fluchloralin, oxadiazon, and oxyfluorfen in onion blubs; CIPC in potato tubers; glyphosate in strawberry; pendimethalin, acetachlor, and metribuzin in tomato and strawberry; 2,4-D and diuron in citrus fruits and juice; glyphosate, clopyralid, and 2, 4, 5-T in pasture grasses; asulam in honey; cinmethylin, ametryne, 2,4-D, and 2,4,5-T in fish, uracil herbicides in essential oils, fluchloralin in chicory leaves and tubers; diquat in beer; and atrazine in chick eggs.

In groundwater and surface water resources used for our drinking water supplies, herbicide contaminants reported include: atrazine, pendimethalin, fluchloralin, oxadiazon, hexazinone, sulfonylureas, flufenacet, alachlor, and diuron.

The judicious use of herbicides can minimize or even eliminate their residues in food and water. Research on decontamination of food commodities of their herbicide residues, if any, requires action from the scientists, the way it is being done for dealing with the insecticide residues in the country and outside.

SELECTED BIBLIOGRAPHY

1. Anon. 1994. Food Safety. Food Research Institute, University of Wisconsin, Madison, USA. 521 p.
2. Anon. 1995. Food Safety. Food Research Institute. University of Wisconsin, Madisan, USA., pp. 256-257.
3. Audo, C. *et al.* 2002. Residues of Forestry Herbicides in Plants of Interest to Native Americans in California National Forests. California EAP, Sacramento, California, USA.

4. Bansal, O.P. and R. Gupta. 2000. Groundwater quality of Aligarh district of U.P. Pesticide Res. J. 12(2): 188-194.
5. Barbash, J.E. *et al.* 2001. Major herbicides in groundwater : results from the national water quality assessment. J. Environ. Quality 30(3) : 831-845.
6. Barrett, M.R. and W.M. Williams. 1989. The occurrence of atrazine in groundwater as a result of agricultural use. Weed Abst. 1991, 40(7): item 2485.
7. Baur, J.R. *et al.* 1969. Herbicide concentrations in live oak treated with mixture of picloram and 2,4,5-T. Weed Sci. 17: 567-570.
8. Bennemann, N.B. 1992. Controlling pesticide residues : Communicating the importance to farmers. Tobacco Int. 194(17) : 32-38.
9. Bhatt, M.C. *et al.* 2004. Persistence of 2,4-D in water and its effect on aquatic life. Pesticide Res. J. 16(1): 58-61.
10. Bhatt, M.C. *et al.* 2004. Persistence of 2,4-D in water and its effect on aquatic life. Pesticide Res. J. 16(1) : 58-61.
11. Bogdanov, S. and P. Edder. 2005. Contamination of honey by a sulfonamide after the use of a herbicide in agriculture. Weed Abst. 54(6) : 410, item 2376.
12. Bovey, R.W. and J.R. Baurl. 1972. Persistence of 2,4,5-T in grasslands of Texas. Bull. Env. Contam. Toxicol, 8:229-233.
13. Brian, P.B. and M.B. Charlles. 2002. Pesticide Residues in Conventional, IPM- Grown and Oganic Foods : Insights from Three US Data Sets. (IN) Food Additives and Contaminants, 19(5). pp. 427-446.
14. Cabras, P. and E. Conte. 2000. Pesticide residues in grapes and wine in Italy. Third European Pesticide Residues Workshop (EPRW 2000), York, U.K. [W.A. 51(1): 25, item 158].
15. Cabrera, H.A.P. *et al.* 1999. Evaluation of the residual levels of diuron and methyl parathion in processed pineapple sub-products. Weed Abst. 49(4) : 224, item 1491.
16. Calderbank, A. and R.H. Mekenna. 1964. Bipyridylium herbicides : residues of diquat and paraquat in food crops from 1963 trials. ICI Plant Protection Ltd., Report No. PP/E/292.
17. Cepeck, J. 2004. Incedence of residue sof triaznie herbicides in infant formulae. Weed Abst. 54(1), 271 (UK).
18. Cessna, A.J. 1992. Residues of mecoprop in postemergence treated wheat and oat. Pesticide Science 36(1) : 31-33.
19. Cessna, A.J. and J. Waddington. 1995. Dissipation of glyphosate and its metabolite AMPA in established crested wheat-grass following spring application. Canad. J. Pl. Sci. 75(3) : 759-762.
20. Cessna, A.J. and N.P. Cain. 1992. Residues of glyphosate and its metabolite AMPA in strawberry fruit following spot and wiper applications. Canad. J. Plant Sci. 72(4) : 1359-1365.
21. Charizopoulos, E. and M. Papadoporilou. 1999. Occurrence of pesticides in rain of the Axios river basin, Greece. Environ. Sci. & Technol. 33(14): 2363-2368.
22. Deepa, S. and R. Jayakumar. 2006. Persistence of pretilachlor in water at different pH levels. Pesticide Res. J. (India) 18(2): 199-200.

23. Diwan, K. *et al.* 1999. Dissipation of pendimethalin and fluchloralin in soil and their residues in onion. Pesticide Res. J. 11(1) : 76-80.

24. Dourson ML, Stara JF. 1985. The conceptual basis of the acceptable daily intake. U.S. EPA Environmental Criteria and Assessment Office, Cincinnati, Ohio.

25. DPR. 1999b. Well Inventory Reports for 1996 and 1997, available online at http://www.cdpr.ca.gov. Department of Pesticide Regulation, Cal/EPA, Sacramento, California.

26. Druzina, B. and Erjavec 2001. Monitoring of atrazine, alachlor, and metabolites in drinking water and OP based pesticides in fruit processing in the republic of Slovenia. Fresenius Environmental Bull. 10(5): 484-489.

27. Dupont, S. and S.U. Khan, 1993. Bound and extractable ^{14}C residues in Canola (*Brassica napus*) plants treated with radiolabelled atrazine. Weed Res. 33(1) : 9-16.

28. Edwards, M.J. *et al.* 1976. Diquat residue in grain, flour, and bread - UK and German trials 1973-1975. ICI Plant Protection Division Report No. AR 2682 A.

29. FAO and WHO. 1996. Pesticide residues in food 1995. FAO Plant Prod. and Prot. paper No. 133, XXII + 237 pp.

30. FAO. 1971. 1970 Evaluations of Some Pesticide Residues in Food. United Nations Food and Agriculture Organization. Rome, Italy. DPR Vol. 226-002 #916123. (as cited in DPR, 1994)

31. FAO. 1993. Pesticide Residues in food - 1992. Part 2 - residues. Plant Production and Protection Paper No. 118, xiii + 836 pp.

32. Frank, R. *et al.* 1991. Disappearance of oxyfluorfen (Goal) from onions and organic soils. Bull. Environ. Contam. & Toxicol. 46(4): 485-491.

33. Ghauch, A. *et al.* 1999. Rapid treatment of water contaminated with atrazine and parathion with zero-valent iron. Chemosphere 39(8): 1309-1315.

34. Giza, I. and M. Sztwiertnia. 2002. Monitoring of pesticide residues in fruits and vegetables from South Poland. Results obtained in 1998-2001. Prog. in Pl. Prot. 42(2): 748-751.

35. Gonzaler, P.E. *et al.* 2000. Removal of paraquat and atrazine from water by montmorillonite (Ce or Zr) phosphate cross-linked compounds. Pest. Mgmt. Sci. 56(6): 565-570.

36. Granby, K. and M. Vahl. 2000. Investigation of glyphosate, chlormequat and mepiquat in cerceals produced in Denmark. Third Europ. Pesticide Residues Workshop, York, U.K., 3-5th July 2000 [WA 5(1):25, item 159].

37. Grover, R. 1998. Environmental Chemistry of Herbicides. CRC Press, Florida, USA.

38. Guha P.K. *et al.* 1992. Dissipation of fluchloralin in *kharif* paddy under West Bengal agroclimatic conditions. Pesticide Research J. 4(2) : 165-169.

39. Gupta, A. 2006. Pesticide Residues in Food Commodities. Agrobios (India), Jodhpur, 322 p.

40. Hafner, M. 1996. Drinking water quality as a reflected image of water production and pesticidal use in agriculture. Weed Abst. 45(11), 608, item 4332.

41. Hansen, N.C. *et al.* 2001. Herbicide banding and tillage system interactions on runoff losses of alachlor and cyanazine. J. Environ. Quality 30(6): 2120-2126.

42. Hirahara, Y. *et al.* 1995. Determination of fenoxaprop-ethyl in polished rice and brwon rice by HPLC. J. Food Hygienic Soc. Japan. 36(2) : 289-292. Weed Abst. 45(6): 312.

43. Hunter, R.G. and J.H. Carroll. 1982. Chlorophenoxy herbicide residues in fishes and sediments of lake Texoma. Proc. Okla Acad. Sci. 62 : 34-37.

44. James, T.K. *et al.* 1998. Degradation and movement of terbuthylazine in soil. Weed Abst. 51(3) : 127, item 797.

45. Jayakumar, R. and S. Sankaran. 1995. Evaluation of anilofos 50EC residues in transplanted rice. Madras Agri. J. 82(4): 296-298.

46. Jenkins, S.R. *et al.* 2000. Temperature effects on retention of atrazine and imazapyr on soils. Water, Air, and Soil Pollution 118(1/2) : 169-178.

47. Kaufmann, A. and A. Kaenzig. 2004. Contamination of honey by the herbicide asulam and its antibacterial active metabolite sulfanilamide. Food Additives and Contaminants. 200 21(6): 564-571.

48. Kello, D. 1989. WHO drinking water quality guidelines for selected herbicides. Food Additives and Contaminants 6 (Suppl.1) 579-585.

49. Khalafalla, F.A. *et al.* 1994. Ametryne residues in fresh water fishes. Vet. Medical J. Giza 42(2) : 25-7.

50. Kimbrough, R.A. and D.W. Litke, 1996. Pesticides in stream draining agricultural and urban areas in Calorado. Environ. Sci. & Technol. 30(3): 908-916.

51. Krishnamurthi, V.V. 2001. Evaluation of anilophos and oxadiazon residues in transplanted rice. Madras Agricultural J. 88 (1&3): 183.

52. Kucharski, M. *et al.* 2004. Influence of adjuvants on residues of metamitron in sugar beet. Weed Abs. 54(6), 2359 (UK).

53. Kumar, A. *et al.* 2004. Fate of trifluralin residues in mungbean. Pesticide Res. J. 16(2): 55-56.

54. Kwong K.F.N.K. *et al.* 1999. Ground and surface water contamination by herbicide residues used in sugarcane fields in Mauritius. Sugarcane (Mauritius Sugar Ind. Res. Instt., Reduit) 3 : 14-18.

55. Lee, P.W. *et al.* 1990. Bioaccumulation of cinmethylin in bluegill sunfish. J. Agri. & Food Chemistry 38(1): 323-327.

56. Leng, M.L. 1977. Residue in milk and meat and safety to livestock for the use of phenoxy herbicides in pastures and rangelands. Down to Earth 28(1) : 12-20.

57. Lewis, R.J. 1995. Food Additives Handbook. Springers, USA. 573 p.

58. Li, Q.X. *et al.* 2001. Occurrence of herbicides and their degradates in Hawaiis groundwater. Bull. Environ. Contam. & Toxicol. 66(5) : 653-659.

59. Liang, T. and X. Lou. 1990. Studies on the residues and degradation behaviour of the herbicide bentazon in rice. Chinese J. of Rice Sci. 4(2) : 84-88.

60. Maini, P. 1992. Residues of algicide endothal in water, soil, and rice, after paddy field applications. Pesticide Sci. 34(1): 45-52.

61. Mattice, J.D. 1999. Environmental implications of pesticides in rice production project report. Weed Abst. 49(2) : 40, item 257. (Res. Ser. Arkausas Agri. Expt. St. 468 : 97-102, (USA).

62. Meredith, P. 1991. Herbicide residues in foodstuffs. Weed Abst. 43(2) : 82; item 615.
63. Miles, C.J. and R.J. Pfeuffer, 1997. Pesticides in canals of south Florida. Archives of Environ. Contam. & Toxicol. 32(4): 337-345.
64. Montgomery JH. 1993. Agrochemicals Desk Reference, Environmental Data. Lewis Publishers, Boca Raton, FL, pp. 180-1.
65. Morton, H.L. *et al.* 1967. Persistence of 2,4-D and 2,4,5-T, and dicamba in range forage grasses. Weeds 15 : 268-271.
66. Muller, K. *et al.* 2004. Herbicide loss in runoff : effects of herbicide properties, slope, and rainfall intensity. Australian J. Soil Res. 42(1) : 12-27.
67. Nagayama, T. *et al.* 1988. Survey of pesticide residues in imported crops - Apr. 1988 to Mar. 1990. Annl. Report Tokyo Metropolitan Res. Lab. Public Health. 41 : 125-132.
68. Nagayama, T. *et al.* 1990. Survey of pesticide residues in vegetables and fruits - Apr. 1989 to Mar. 1990. Annl. Report Tokyo Metropolitran Res. Lab. Public Health. 41 : 119-124.
69. Nurizzo, C. *et al.* 1993. Removal of herbicides from groundwater. Environ. Management & Health. 4(2): 24-28.
70. Patel, R.B. *et al.* 1996. Dissipation of fluchloralin in soils and its residues in chicory. Pesticide Res. J. 8(2) : 182-185.
71. Pensabene, J.W. *et al.* 2000. SFE of atrazine and other triazine herbicides from fortified and incurred eggs. J. Agri. Food Chem, Washington DC, ACS, 48(5) : 1668-1672.
72. Prasad, H. *et al.* 2006. Dessipation kinetics of trifluralin in water at different pH levels under laboratory conditions. Pesticide Res. J. (India) 18(2): 208-210.
73. Pylypiw, H.M. Jr. and L. Hankin. 1991. Herbicides in pooled raw *milk* in Connecticut. J. Food Protection Chemistry, USA, 54(2) : 136-137.
74. Raj, M.F. *et al.* 1999. Pendimethalin, fluchloralin, and oxadiazon residue in/on onion. Pesticide Res. J. 11(1): 68-70.
75. Rani, S. *et al.* 2006. Effect of pH on the dissipation behavour of flufenacet in water. Pesticide Res. J. (India) 18(2): 201-204.
76. Rector, R.J. *et al.* 2003. Atrazine, metolachlor, and isoxaflutole in runoff as affected by rainfall and management. Weed Sci. 51(5) : 810-816.
77. Reeve, M. 1972. Diquat residue on wheat grain, white flour, and bran for New Zealand trials, 1971-72. ICI Plant Protection Ltd.
78. Roy, S. *et al.* 2006. Persistence of clodinafop in soil, wheat, and *Phalaris minor*. Pesticide Res. J. 18(1): 87-91.
79. Saha, S. *et al.* 2003. Residue studies and efficacy of sulfosulfuron in wheat crop. Pesticide Res. J. 15(2) : 173-175.
80. Sakaliene, O. 1998. Duration of persistence of herbicide clopyralid in fodder beet and soil. Weed Abst., 1999 48(5) item 1384.
81. Scharf, J. *et al.* 1992. Pesticides in the atmosphere. Fresenius J. Analytical Chem. 342(10): 813-816.
82. Schlett, C. and H. Ehlers. 1996. Herbicide contamination of surface water in a German catchment area. Pesticide Outlook 7(2): 11-14.

83. Sharma, R. and H.M. Mehta. 1989. Studies on pendimethalin and fluchloralin residues in soil and onion. Ind. J. of Agronomy 34(2) : 245-247.

84. Sharma, R. K. *et al.* 2006. Screening of low cost adsorbents for removal of atrazine from water. Pesticide Res. J. (India) 18(2): 205-207.

85. Shioda, H. *et al.* 1994. Survey of pesticide residues in imported crops. Annl. Rept. Tokyo Metropolitan Res. Lab. of Public Health No. 45, 98-104.

86. Shyu, J. *et al.* 1995. Levels of 2,4-D residues in marketed citrus fruits and juices collected from eastern Taiwan area. J. Food and Drug Analysis 3(2): 127-132.

87. Shyu, J.F. *et al.* 1995. Levels of 2,4-D residues in marketed citrus fruits and juices collected from Eastern Taiwan area. J. Food and Drug Analysis 3(2) : 127-132.

88. Silternen, H. and C. Rosenberg. 1978. Analysis of 2,4-D and 2,4,5-T in lingoberries, wild mushrooms. Bull. Env. Cont. & Toxical. 19, 177-182.

89. Singh, R. *et al.* 1996. Harvest time residues of butachlor, quinalphos, and triazophos on paddy and endosulfan on maize. Pesticide Res. J. 8(2) : 176-181.

90. Singh, S. B. *et al.* 2004. Residues of clodinafop propargyl in/on wheat crop. Ann. Pl. Prot. Sci. 12: 473-475.

91. Singh, S.B. and G. Kulshrestha. 2006. Persistence and harvest time residues of trisulfuron in soil and heat crop. Pesticide Res. J. (India) 18(2): 196-198.

92. Sondhia, S. and J. S. Mishra, 2005. Determination of terminal residue of clodinafop propargyl in soil, wheat, grains, and straw. Ind. J. Weed Sci. 37 (3&4): 296-297.

93. Sondhia, S. and R. P. Dubey. 2006. Terminal residues of butachlor and pendimethalin in onion. Pesticide Res. J. 18(1): 85-86.

94. Sozeri, S. and I.M.M.A. Alaziz. 2003. Determination of chlorsulfuron residue by HPLC in soil and wheat grain applied as postemergence at different times and rates. Turkiye Herboloji Dergisi 6(1): 60-72 (W.A. 54(1): 45, item 264).

95. Stevens MA, Walley JK. 1966. Tissue and milk residues arising from the ingestion of single doses of diquat and paraquat by cattle. J.Sci. Fd. Agric. 17: 472-5 (as cited in DPR, 1994).

96. Tanabe, A. *et al.* 2001. Seasonal and spatial studies on pesticide residues in surface waters of the Shinano river in Japan. J. Agri. & Food Chem. 48(8) : 3847-3852.

97. Tekel, J. *et al.* 1997. Determination of uracil herbicide residues and components in essential erl of *Melissa officinalis* L. in its main development phases. J. Essential Oil Res. (Slovakia) 9(1): 63-66.

98. Unger, P.W. 1994. Managing Agricultural Residues. CRC Press. Inc., USA. 234 p.

99. Wickramaratne GA. 1989. Diquat: teratogenicity study in the rat. ICI Study No. CTL/P/2331. DPR Vol. 226-089 #075531.

100. Winter, O.K. 1996. Pesticide residues in foods : recent events and emerging issues. Weed Technol. 10(4) : 969-973.

101. Zhou G. *et al.* 1996. The determination of residual herbicides in tomato and strawberry from fields covered with nonwovens sprayed with herbicides. Acta Agriculture Shanghai 12(3): 86-88. (WA 46(7): 386).

Chapter 26

IMPACT OF HERBICIDES ON AGRICULTURAL TECHNOLOGY

A partial or complete change-over from the physical methods of weed control to the herbicidal control of weeds on farmland, besides affecting a better overall weed control, enables the farmer to alter many of his conventional crop husbandry practices to his advantage. Some of these changes are optional while others are inevitable. The present chapter deals with the impact of herbicides on several crop husbandry practices from seedbed preparation to harvesting and farm management. Also, the indirect effects of herbicides on the quality of crops are discussed.

26.1 SEEDBED PREPARATION

Destruction of weeds is the chief objective of tillage employed in the preparation of seedbeds. Several kinds of tillage implements are used by farmers round the world to accomplish weedfree seedbeds. But the spirit of innovation and the creativity among scientists led to a new concept in this basic farming operation about 3-4 decades before. The concept, known as minimum tillage farming, employs herbicides to replace the ploughs and harrows, partially or completely. When such a change-over is total, the farming system is called **no-tillage farming** (Gupta, 1972). In this system, crops are planted directly in the soil amidst chemically killed weeds and stubbles. The concept of no-tillage farming is based on the premise that if nature could grow luxuriant vegetation leading to forests without tillage, it should be possible for man to grow food crops without plough or with its minimum use. No-tillage practice has been successfully employed in the U.S.A. and U.K. in the cultivation of maize, winter grains, soybean, sorghum, and rice, as well as in the renovation of pastures. Broadly speaking, the practice comprises application of suitable herbicides to destroy the existing weedy vegetation, followed by drilling of fertilizers and seeds at appropriate depths. As the weeds and grasses dry under the influence of herbicides, healthy crop seedlings emerge beautifully through the trash.

The success of no-tillage farming depends upon proper choice of the herbicides, besides availability of a good no-till planter and proper soil. The components of a herbicide mixture used in the no-till planting are: (a) a non-selective, non-residual herbicide *eg* paraquat, herbicidal oils, amitrole, MSMA, DSMA, or glyphosate and (b) a residual preplanting herbicide with adequate selectivity to the immediate and rotation crops. In the absence of a suitable residual, preplanting herbicide, postemergence weed control during the crop season may be practised. In soybean, for instance, suitable preplanting herbicides for its no-tillage farming are paraquat and chloramben (or linuron) (Wiles and Haywarde, 1981). In no-till maize and sorghum, mixtures containing paraquat and atrazine are common in the U.S.A. Likewise, in the no-till renovation of pastures, two common herbicide systems are: (a) pre-seeding spray of dalapon + paraquat and (b) paraquat followed by post-seeding application of EPTC granule. 2,4-D or dicamba can be included in the herbicide mixtures when the proportion of broadleaf weeds in the vegetation under destruction is high. Paraquat has also been successfully employed to desiccate weeds before puddling of paddies and in direct seeding of upland rice (Mukhopadhyay and Rooj, 1971; Misra and Lenka, 1973). No-tillage planting of pearlmillet after desiccation of weeds with paraquat has also been demonstrated. Glyphosate is a very good addition to the list of no-tillage farming herbicide where perennial weeds pose problem (Ndahi, 1982).

26.1.1 Advantages of No-Till Farming

1. *Depletion of weed seed bank*: Tillage influences the vertial distribution of weed seeds in soils as well as occurrence of the weed diversity on the ground. No-till cropping systems leave most seeds in the top about 1.0 cm of soil profiles. Here these germinate together in a flush and succumb easily to single herbicide treatment. The weed seeds lying deeper, in soil fail to put forth, unwanted weed populations latter. As such, gradually over years, in the absence of weeds reaching their seed formation stage, the weed seed bank in the soil is depleted to the advantage of the farmers

   In Haryana and U.P. (India), the scientists have demonstrated on large fields the utility of no tillage cultivation of wheat in reducing the *Phalaris minor* infestations, which is a burning weed problem in the country (Malik, 2000)

2. *Protection of Soil Against Erosion And Maintenance of Proper Soil Structure*: The dead weed and stubble mulches resulting on chemical seedbeds act as barrier to erosive forces of rainfall and wind and, thus, saves huge soil losses on otherwise erodable lands. In the semi-arid, dry farming areas the surface soil is usually found to possess more moisture under the stubble mulch than the stubble-free surfaces. Also, on many soils, no-tillage system may prevent the destruction of soil structure usually caused by excessive tillage.

   Extending minimum tillage to certain areas of rolling topography may prevent soil erosion sufficiently to justify conversion of pasture-lands to field croplands, if the need arises.

3. *Saving of Tractor Fuel*: With the growing scarcity of diesel in the world, reduced tractor trips over the fields are a notable advantage of no-tillage farming using herbicides.

4. *Rapid Seedbed Preparation*: It takes about one third to one fourth time in preparing no-tillage or chemical seedbeds in comparison to the conventional tillage seedbeds. Time saving in seedbed preparation is an important consideration in double and triple cropping systems where one must rush the agricultural operations to make use of favourable rain and temperatures at a particular time. For example, in certain southern and eastern states of India, two and three crops of rice can be grown on the same land each year, but there is not enough time for preparing satisfactory seedbeds the conventional way. The chemical or no-tillage seedbeds have wide scope in such areas. Likewise, in wheat-rice cropping systems, wheat can be sown timely after the harvest of rice by adopting no-till farming, which incidentally also reduces the weed infestations.

26.1.2 Limitations of No-Till Farming

1. No-tillage methods may lead to the perpetuation of *perennial* weeds because the present day selective herbicides are not as effective against them.
2. Many soil borne insect pests and disease organisms may multiply faster under the trash that accumulates on the soil surface in the no-till system. In fact, in some situations, in no-tillage system the stubble and weed trash may build up to unmanageable thickness.
3. Clay soils do not lend themselves to no-tillage farming, particularly when they form clods, and develop hard pans. So is true of sandy, crust forming soils.
4. Seeding rates used in chemical seedbeds are usually higher than in the conventional seedbeds to ensure adequate crop stands. This, however, may be of concern only in the case of some very costly seeds.

In view of the varied advantages and limitations of no-tillage farming and keeping in view the agricultural conditions in the developing tropical world, it is at present more appropriate to develop a reduced tillage programme in association with suitable herbicides, rather than eliminating tillage altogether. For instance, the **plough-plant system** eliminates the harrowing operation and it conducts the seedbed preparation and sowing in a single traffic. In the less mechanised regions, it can also be accomplished in two separate operations. It is only in specific situations that no-tillage seedbeds may be used to some distinct advantage, as earlier mentioned.

26.2 CHEMICAL FALLOWING

Chemical fallowing is the use of herbicides instead of tillage to kill volunteer vegetation on the fallow fields. It leaves the ground under a dry vegetation mulch which protects the soil against erosive agencies and paves the way to larger storage of rain in the soil. It may also guard against undue surface crusting and cracking of the soil. The scientists are not agreed on the role of chemical fallowing in reducing the loss of stored soil moisture in comparison to the ploughed fallows. Chemical fallows, of course, slow down the drying rate of soil surfaces which may be useful in the dry farming areas.

The herbicides found suitable for fallow land management are the same as mentioned for the no-tillage seedbed preparation. These herbicides are usually non-residual types, though sometimes the short residue ones can also be used. Both selective and non-relative herbicides are suitable for the purpose. The biggest limitation in the adoption of chemical fallows is their high maintenance costs since 2 to 3 applications of herbicides may be needed to keep the fallow land weedfree for full season. Perhaps, a more practical approach to maintain fallow lands weedfree would be to use herbicides against the deep-rooted weeds and follow it with tillage with sweeps, blade harrow, and like any other improved implements, aiming at minimum stubble incorporation.

26.3 DIRECT SEEDING OF CROPS

Conventionally, rice, tobacco, and vegetables like tomato, eggplant, and cole crops, are transplanted crops. Transplanting gives farmer opportunity to curb the weed growth with less labour than is required in the direct seeded crops. However, transplanting itself is a very labour intensive practice. Now, with the availability of suitable soil-active herbicides, it is possible to adopt direct seeding of rice, and many vegetables, in the main fields, thus eliminating the costly nursery raising and transplanting processes. Experimental evidences have accumulated to show that the direct-seeded rice yielded as much as the transplanted crop, if herbicides were used judiciously to control the weeds. Besides lowering the cultivation costs, the practice saved enormous quantities of water, usually applied to suppress the weeds by flooding the paddies (Mukhopadhyay and Rooj, 1971). In Japan, U.S.A., and some other countries direct seeding of rice is a common commercial practice. The direct seeding has made much headway also in the cultivation of tomato and certain cole crops, using modern herbicides to allow the crop seeds to germinate in a weedfree environment.

26.4 HILL-PLANTING OF CROPS

Crops like cotton and sugarbeet are planted thick, in continuous rows in order to provide competition to weeds at an early stage before they are thinned to a stand. With proper herbicidal control, these crops can be hill-planted straight away to a stand. Besides saving the labour used in thinning the crops, hill-planting will reduce considerably the seeding rates of crops. This may be very important in the case of costly seeds of new, high yielding varieties of crops. For many crops, including cotton and sugarbeet, suitable herbicides are available to curb early weed growth and make their hill-planting a great success.

26.5 SEEDING RATES AND ROW-SPACINGS

Often crops are seeded at excessive rates in an attempt to enable them to have a competitive advantage over the weeds. Also, many crops are planted in wide rows to ease their inter-cultivation. With herbicides to ensure adequate weed control, excessive seed rates and undue row widths can be reduced to achieve agronomic optima.

26.7 IRRIGATION

Introduction of chemical weed control on any farm demands better land levelling and irrigation control in order to achieve proper penetration of the preemergence herbicides in soils and thus ensure consistency in weed control. Also, the present system of irrigating crops to the brim of the field levels may have to be replaced by metered irrigation system to apply only a pre-determined quantity of water to avoid undue deep movement of the herbicide in fields. In rice, a herbicide like propanil may dictate the fields to be drained and flooded at particular times.

Preemergence herbicides prove effective only when seedbeds are kept adequately moist by irrigation (in the absence of rain). Sprinkler irrigation has proved a valuable tool to ensure good weed control with preemergence herbicides. Thus, irrigation practices may need to be altered in many cases in order to make the most effective use of herbicides.

In rice culture, flooding has been employed to control weeds since ages. In lowland rice it has been misconceived as a necessity, as if rice itself needed that much water for its proper growth. The discovery of effective rice herbicides made it possible for the scientists to show that when weeds were controlled with chemicals, all that rice needed was a constant water saturation condition of the soil, and not several centimeters of the flood. Based on such findings, rice cultivation was revolutionised in some advanced countries and considerable economy in irrigation water was affected. However, subsequent experience showed that without constant flooding of rice fields, the weeds, particularly the perennial ones, became very persistent despite the use of herbicides. So the farmers are now setting for a compromise with herbicides and flooding in rice cultivation to obtain economic crop production.

26.7 CHOICE OF CROP AND CROP VARIETIES

With inter-row cultivation as an option to control weeds, almost any wide row crop can be used in crop rotation. But herbicides are specific on weeds, and to control particular weeds only those crops and crop varieties that are tolerant to particular herbicide, can be grown in field under treatment. For example, it is easy to control *Cirsium arvense* 'Canadathistle' with herbicides in wheat and peas but not in gram (chickpea) or potato (Chapter 24). Herbicide usage may thus influence farm plans. Therefore, due consideration may be given to this point in the choice of crops and crop varieties. Herbicidal control in inter-cropping system is often not suitable; the herbicide-minded farmers, therefore, must stay most of the time with solid cropping systems.

26.8 DISEASES AND INSECT PESTS

Herbicides may either aggravate, suppress, or have no effect on the incidence of insect pests and diseases on the treated crops. But when they do influence these in some way, changes in farm pest control programme may become important. The herbicide-induced changes in crop pests may result from either (i) their direct effects on insect pests, plant pathogens, and crop plants or (ii) their indirect effects on these due to non-cultivation of the crop rows. This is illustrated by a marked reduction in the incidence of *Rhizoctonia* sp. and *Sclerotium* sp. in groundnut treated with dinoseb for weed control. The incidence of these two pathogens is aggravated by frequent row cultivation and the role of herbicides in suppressing their invasion may be only in as much as they avoid inter-row cultivations, in groundnut. Fungistatic effect of napropamide on *R. solani* are also known (Kurtz *et al.*, 1982). Likewise, dinitrophenol and dinitroaniline herbicides suppressed 'root rots' and other fungal pathogens in beans. Penner (1974) observed increased resistance of DCPA treated onion and beans to rootknot nematodes and diminished tolerance of trifluralin treated lucerne and tomato to these pests.

Trifluralin and pendimethalin (10 ppm) retarded the growth of 'damping off' of soybean, but not to the level of fungicides. Fluchloralin (1.2 kg/ha) caused 61% control of *Alternaria* blight (Saimbhi *et al.*, 1992). Maize root rot incidence was found increased in picloram treated soil. In tobacco, photosynthesis inhibiting herbicides increased tobacco 'mosaic virus (TMV)'. In potato, virus X and Y were suppressed by diallate and chloroxuron, but were activated by monolinuron and linuron treatments. In wheat, 2,4-D decreased the incidence of root rot. In sugarbeet, pebulate and pyrazon applied for weed control were found to increase *Rhizoctonia solani* incidence. EPTC, chloramben, and alachlor increased root rot development in beans. Trifluralin reduced incidence of clubroot on cabbage and stem rot in peas. 2,4-D could sometimes increase pea aphid population in fields.

Chlorsulfuron increased root rot in wheat and barley (Rovira and McDonald, 1986). Likewise, the effects of herbicides on onion diseases were reported by Pathak *et al.*, 1988.

Trifluralin is reported involved in enhancement of soil-borne disease organisms like *Fusarium* in beans and brinjal (eggplant) and *Rhizoctonia* in beets. Likewise, root rots caused by *Fusarium* were found aggravated with soil applied herbicides *viz.*, EPTC, alachlor and atrazine in certain crops. Also, residues of chlorsulfuron in soil are reported to increase the take-all and root-rot diseases in small grains. Cycloate and diallate enhanced the sugarbeet and powery mildew in winter grains.

In variance with the above undesirable herbicide crop-pathogen interactions, beneficial interactions have also been reported. For instance, soil applied diallate is found to suppress to some extent root rots in maize and wheat. Glyphosate, oxyfluorfen and paraquat proved effective in reducing intensity of pomergranate wilt. Azafenidin, flumioxazin, and sulfentrazone inhibited the *in vitro* growth of *Pythium* root rot of sugarcane (Daugrois *et al.*, 2005). Trifonova and Peneva (2003) reported lessened population of parasitic nematodes infesting beans (*Phaseolus vulgaris*), in pot soil treated with imazethapyr.

Oxadiazon, a common herbicide, has been reported to possess considerable insecticidal activity against leaf-folder larvae.

Table 26.1: Effect of Two Herbicides on Tikka Disease Index of Groundnut in Madhya Pradesh (India), During 1990 (After Sangar *et al.*, 1993).

Treatment	Disease Index (*Cercospora* sp.)
Unweeded check	6.00
Hand-weeded twice (20, 35 d.a.s.)	3.93
Fluchloralin (1.25 kg/ha)	4.07
Pendimethalin (1.5 kg/ha)	3.90
C.D. (at P = 0.05)	2.10

Comments: *Besides controlling weeds, the two nitralins helped in reducing the Tikka disease in groundnut, significantly.*

26.9 FARM EQUIPMENT

Herbicides may introduce marked changes in the kind of equipment needed on farms. Farms under herbicidal control possess sprayers instead of cultivators and hoes. The ploughs often become less used implements. On large farms, ridging of crops like potato and sugarcane may be mechanized when such crops are treated with herbicides. Machines may also be used for harvesting bumper crops more frequently after the introduction of chemicals to control weeds than before. Further, the herbicidal control often makes the weed seed cleaners as less important farm equipment.

26.10 FARM MANAGEMENT

An immediate impact of introducing herbicides on farms is rendition of considerable labour as surplus. Farm management must make provision for this radical change by utilizing the excess labour in more fruitful farm operations like fencing, timely application of fertilizers, insecticides, and fungicides, and in expediting sowing and harvesting of crops which are often delayed due to the shortage of farm labour.

These are few of the many influences of herbicides on crop husbandry that indicate the need of replanning farm operations when chemical weed control is introduced. As new, more efficient herbicides and their application methods are discovered in future, many other traditional cultural practices in crop production may have to be reevaluated and modified.

26.11 CROP QUALITY

In potato, the proportion of large tubers to small tubers was found increased when paraquat or EPTC were applied for weed control in comparison to the manually weedfree crop (Gupta, 1977). In sugarcane, late stage use of paraquat withheld arrowing to allow the cane growth for some additional period. In certain pulses and legume oilseed crops, herbicidal control of weeds has been reported to simultaneously influence the nodulation in plants (Prakash and Pahwa, 1985; Bertholet and Clark, 1985; Pahwa *et al.*, 1988; Durgesha, 1994; and Pahwa and Prakash, 1992). For instance, in groundnut nodulation and nitrogenase activity were found to increase with fluchloralin. But nitralin, benefin, and dinitramine decreased these parameters, while pendimethalin showed neither kind of influence.

SUMMARY

Introduction of herbicidal control of weeds in agriculture is accompanied by several direct and indirect effects on the cropping practices. To start with, this new technology has potential of reducing dependence on tillage of the land to the extent it is practised for weed destruction. In several advanced countries, this replacement led to no-tillage or zero-tillage farming system. The advantages and limitations of this major change in agriculture are enumerated in this chapter.

In other cases, direct seeding of vegetables and some other crops, instead of their conventional transplanting, has been found possible when herbicides were used for weed control. In transplanted, irrigated rice flooding of the field much above the water requirement of the crop, often practised to control weeds, could be avoided if herbicides were used to curb them. Likewise, crop geometries may be changed to accommodate optimum plant populations when herbicides are used, making very wide crop rows, recommended for conducting the tillage control of weeds, unnecessary. Also, the choice of crops, crop varieties, irrigation methods, etc. are influenced by the introduction of herbicides.

Certain herbicides may decrease or increase invasion of specific crop diseases to different levels. In other cases the different kinds of farm machinery needed on the farm and several farm management decisions may have to be altered by the introduction of herbicides.

Finally, it has been noted that certain herbicides often improve crop quality by their indirect effects; quite apart from their weed control effects.

In future, agriculture may see several other changes in the cropping systems when herbicides are adopted more extensively on the farms.

SELECTED BIBLIOGRAPHY

1. Ali, A.M. and Rao, R.S. 1987. Effect of sublethal rates of phenoxy and triazine herbicides and nitrogen on sorghum. Ind. J. Agro. 32 (1): 88-89.
2. Bertholet, J. and Clark, K.W. 1985. Effect of trifluralin and metribuzin on faba bean growth, development, and symbiotic N-fixation. Cand. J. Plant Sci. 65: 921.
3. Bhagat, P. *et al.* 1977. Effect of some herbicides on the chemical composition of carrot roots. J. Res. and Industry 13 (2): 202-205.
4. Dahiya, R.S. *et al.* 1988. Some new host records of *Meloidogyne javanica*. Int. Nematology Network News Letters 5 (3): 32-34.
5. Durgesha, M. 1994. Effects of dinitroaniline herbicides on rhizobia, nodulation, and N_2 (C_2H_2) fixation of four groundnut cultivars. Annals of Applied Biology 124 (1): 75-82.
6. Gupta, O.P. 1972. No-tillage farming. SPAN 13 (4): 20-23.
7. Gupta, O.P., *et al.* 1977. Evaluation of response of potato to chemical control of early weed infestation. IASS J. 1 (1): 139-143.
8. Hemphill, D.D. and Montgomery, M.L. 1981. Weed Sci. 29: 632-635.
9. Huffaker, R.C. *et al.*, 1967. Effect of field application of 2,4-D and iron supplements on yield and protein content of wheat and barley, and yield of beans. Crop Sci. 7: 17-19.
10. Kasera, P.K. and Sen, D.N. 1986. Weed seed inviability caused by postemergence herbicides. Current Sci. 55 (18): 937-938.
11. Kurtz, M.E. *et al.*, 1982. Some metabolic responses of *Rhizoctonia solani* to napropamide. Weed Sci. 30: 491-494.

12. Malik, R. K. (ed) 2000. Herbicide Resistance Management of Zero Tillage in Rice-Wheat Cropping System. Proc. International Workshop held 4-6 March 2000 at C.C.S. Haryana Agri. Univ., Hisar (India), 210 p.
13. Misra, P.K. and Lenka, D. 1973. A note on minimum tillage in rice cultivation. Ind. J. Weed Sci. 5 (1): 57-59.
14. Mukhopadhyay, S.K. and Rooj, S. 1971. Rice production with minimal cultivation using Gramoxone. Ind. J. Agron. 16 (3): 362-363.
15. Ndahi, W.B. 1982. Evaluation of glyphosate and paraquat as substitute for seedbed preparation by tillage in hoe farming system. Trop. Pest Management 28 (1) 10-13.
16. Pahwa, S.K. and Prakash, J. 1992. Effect of herbicides on growth, development, and nodulation in groundnut (*Arachis hypogea* L.). Ind. J. Weed Sci. 24 (1&2): 37-41.
17. Pahwa, S.K., *et al.* 1988. Effect of herbicides on growth, nodulation, and symbiotic N-fixation in pigeonpea (*Cajanus cajan* L. Willsp). Crop Res. 1 (2) : 131-140.
18. Pathak, A.K., *et al.*, 1988. Effect of herbicides on onion rhizosphere microflora. Ind. J. Weed Sci. 20: 58-62.
19. Penner, D. 1974. The effectiveness of pesticide interaction. Weeds Today 5 (3): 13-14.
20. Prakash, J. and Pahwa, S.K. 1985. Effect of some herbicides on growth, nodulation, and chlorophyll content of cowopea (*Vigna unguilata* (L.) Walp.) plants. Haryana J. Agro.
1: 39-41.
21. Randhawa, S.K. *et al.*, 1988. Effect of herbicides on protein content in grain of winter maize. J. Res. Punjab Agri. Univ. 25 (1): 35-36.
22. Rao, S. Padmaja and Venkateswarlu, 1985. An efficient pre-harvest desiccant for rice. Indian Fmg. 35 (8): 23-25.
23. Ries, S.K. 1971. Herbicides as growth boosters. Weeds Today 2 (1) 6-8.
24. Ries, S.K. *et al.*, 1970. Wheat seed protein: Chemical influence on and relationship to subsequent growth and yield in Michigan and Mekuo. Agron. J. 62: 646-748.
25. Rovira, A.D. and McDonald, H.J. 1986. Effects of the herbicide chlorsulfuron on *Rhizoctonia* bare patch and take all of barley and wheat. Plant Diseases 70 (9) 879-882.
26. Saimbhi, M.S. *et al.* 1992. Use of herbicide for weed and disease control in cabbages. Adv. Hort. Sci. 6 (3) 125-128.
27. Sangar, R.B.S. *et al.* 1993. Efficacy of weed control methods on Tikka disease of groundnut and their economics. Ind. J. Weed Sci. 25 (1&2) 100-102.
28. Thomas, T.H. (ed.). 1982. Plant Growth Regulator Potential and Practice. BCPC Publ. Croydon, 271 pp.
29. Wiedman, S.J. and Appleby, A.P. 1972. Plant growth stimulation by sublethal concentrations of herbicides. Weed Res. 12 (1) 65-74.
30. Wiles, T.L. and Hayward, D.M. 1981. The principles and practices of weed control for no-tillage soybean. Trop. Pest. Mgmt. 27 (3) 388-400.
31. Pandey, J. and Verma, A. K. 2005. Effect of low doses of herbicides on weeds, nutrient uptake and yield of transplanted rice. Ind. J. Agro. 50(3): 197-199.

32. Daugrois, J.H. *et al.* 2005. Protoporphyrinogen oxidate inhibitor herbicide effects on *Pythium* root rot of sugarcane. Phytopathology 93(3) : 220-226 (USA).

33. Trifonova, Z. and A. Peneva. 2003. Influence of imazethapyr on the population densities of plant parasitic nematodes on bean (*Phaseolus vulgaris* L.). Bulgarian J. Agric. Sci. 9(4) : 515-520 (Bulgaria).

34. Friedrich, T. 2005. Does no-till farming require more herbicides? Outlooks on Pest Mgmt. Aug. 2005 : 188-191.

Chapter 27

FIELD RESEARCH WITH HERBICIDES- A MATERIALS AND METHODS OUTLINE

Weed science research comprises a variety of projects to enable safe and economic use of herbicides for the benefit of mankind. These projects can be pooled into two main groups; viz., (1) the study of weeds in respect of their species composition, biology, ecology, anatomy, and harmful effects; and (2) the study of herbicides and their effects on target and non-target organisms. The latter include screening of herbicides for specific uses, determining their best time and rates of application, study of their mode of action on weeds and selectivity to the crops, measuring herbicide presistence in soils, crops, water-bodies, animals, and environment; herbicide effects on weed population dynamics, both inter and intra specific; developing crop protection measures against herbicides by chemical and breeding methods; making new herbicide application equipments to meet new situations; and above all, synthesising new herbicide structures to solve the unsolved weed problems.

It is beyond the scope of this book to go into the research methodology of all the above aspects of herbicides. Here only a very brief account shall be given of the procedures that can be followed for establishing a weed research centre to develop herbicide recommendations for crop fields at the University or Government Research Centres, particularly in the developing countries with limited resources.

27.1 EQUIPMENT FOR A WEED SCIENCE LABORATORY

To begin with, a weed science laboratory should procure open shelves with label strips for storing herbicides; steel almirahs with glass doors for storing weed herbarium; about six vasculums; two herbarium presses; some museum jars; two good physical balances, one or two tripple beam balances; two to four sensitive pan balances; two ovens; half a dozen steel quadrats of 0.25 sqm each; two, 100m plastic twines; two plumber tapes;

several wooden pegs; four plastic jerricans, each about 10 l capacity, mixing spoons; two suitable plot sprayers with plastic tanks and necessary accessories, spanners and screw drivers; gloves, gumboots, two face masks or respirators; first-aid kit; some enamel buckets; and usual glassware like measuring cylinders, automatic pipettes, beakers, bottle brushes, *etc.* The laboratory should be well ventilated and provided with exhaust fans, adequate light, and uninterrupted supply of fresh water.

After some years when the weed science research has made adequate headway at any centre, its lab facilities could be enriched in phases with more sophisticated equipment to go into deeper investigations in herbicide usages. These may include plant and soil analysis instruments, from simple pH meter and colorimeter to Gas Chromatograph (GC) to study herbicide residues in soils and crops. For instant killing of plant samples deep freezing equipment, and for concentrating leachates and extracts, a vacuum evaporator could be introduced. In fact, there is no limit to expanding weed research laboratories, provided there is adequate technical manpower and a real felt need to use them. *Collecting equipment without using it, however, will only decorate the laboratories, which is not very uncommon in India and elsewhere.*

27.2 PROCEDURE FOR FIELD EVALUATION OF HERBICIDES

- **Step-1.** Specify the geographical area that your research results are required to serve and list all important agronomic, horticultural, and plantation crops of the area. Select crops in which either the farmers admit they needed a herbicide to control weeds or where you feel introduction of a herbicide could further boost crop yield and/or quality within the means of the farmer. Set priorities amongst these crops, keeping in view their economic importance and the trained manpower available on hand to conduct the needed weed science research.

- **Step-2.** Select a suitable site for your experiments at the station. It should, as far as possible, have weed flora, weed intensity, and soil which represent the area where the research results are supposed to be implemented. The gross area needed for weed science research is about three times the area actually covered under the experiments in any one crop season. One third of the area should be kept under a uniform heavy crop cover, another one third under fallow to grow weeds, and the remainder one third to actually lay the experiments. Also if needed, weed seeds can be sown at the site of experimentation to simulate the farming situation of the area.

- **Step-3.** Initial couple of years should be devoted to studying weed flora and its biology on farmer fields and experiment station, as well as in conducting research on critical periods of weed-crop competition, using crops selected in Step-1.

- **Step-4.** Simultaneous to steps 1 to 3, procure all your laboratory needs, and get in touch with several herbicide companies, both within and outside country. Herbicide samples often begin pouring at the first correspondence. As soon as a herbicide turns in your office, give it an accession number and enter its code number, and common and trade names, as well as date received and source, in an edge punched paper file or computer. Spend considerable time in reading the past research results, if any, on the herbicides that will possibly be used by you.

- **Step-5.** Write down the objectives of each of your experiments. Correct these couple of times and also make someone read these. Rearrange, if needed. Choose the herbicides likely to meet your objectives. Decide their doses and methods of application for inclusion in your experiment.

- **Step-6.** If you are working with experimental herbicide compounds, you will do better if you first conduct some screening row trials. In these, several crops are planted in long rows and the test herbicides are sprayed across the rows in one metre wide strips. The crop tolerance and weed mortality ratings are recorded by visual, point scale method to earmark the promising herbicides. Such herbicides can further be screened by testing them again in microplot trials. About 1 sq m plots are adequate for these trials, and unweeded and hand-weeded plots are included in the trials for comparison with the herbicides. Numerical data on weed counts and crop yields usually form basis of selecting herbicides for the final field tests.

- **Step-7.** The more promising herbicides and herbicide mixtures from the above trials can now be tested for their agronomic suitability in regular, replicated field trials in 30 to 40 sq m plots. Depending upon the objectives, their optimum doses, interactions with row cultivation, *etc.* can be studied. There should be adequate replicates to provide at least 12 degrees of freedom (DF) for the statistical analysis of the data. The design of the experiment shall again depend upon the objectives of your experiment. You shall do better if you consult a good agricultural statistician for the purpose. Detailed observations on periodical dry weed yield, crop yield and yield attributes, and crop quality are gathered from these trials to evaluate each treatment. Too many observations on weeds are, however, unnecessary. There are two stages when it is most important to record weed yields. *First*, when the weeds began to grow enough to make it necessary to row cultivate the treated crop. *Second*, at most critical weed-crop competition stage as earlier determined from experiments in step-3 (or from literature). For example, in maize and soybean 40 days after sowing will be a good time to make the weed yield records. For sampling weeds, a quadrat 0.25 sqm in area is usually handy. The spots per plot should be selected by using random numbers and marked on a paper layout, a night before collecting the weed samples. All the weeds falling in a quadrat are cut close to ground, categorised, and quickly brought to lab in polythelene bags, and weighed immediately in a pan balance. A 100 g sub-sample is drawn from each sample of the weeds for oven drying at 80-100°C for 48 hrs and determining its dry matter content. Dry weed yield per plot or per ha can then be easily computed. The easiest way to categories the weeds is as grasses, broadleafs, and sedges. Someone may further consider these as annuals and perennials. But now there is a serious growing concern of development of herbicide – resistance in weed species and biotypes which create alarming weed management problems (Chapter – 17). As a result, today there is need to observe the effect of the test herbicides on individual weed specie, both dominant and otherwise. To what extent this can done, shall obviously depend upon the time and manpower available on hand, but a postgraduate research work should peep deep enough into this aspect.

- **Step-8.** Do not forget to study effects of possible field residues of herbicides on the common rotation crops of the area. For this, after harvesting the main crop, in each plot one or two common rotation crops can be planted in equal divisions. Data on the performance of these crops should be used to evaluate herbicide effects on the rotation crops.

27.3 EXPERIMENT LAYOUT AND APPLICATION OF HERBICIDES

Although a lot could be said about experiment layouts, here only a few important points are brought home.

1. Keep the plots narrow and long and square each replication. A replication with side ratio of over 1:2 should be discarded. Row crops should be planted along the width of each plot.
2. Lateral movement of the herbicides in a crop like rice should be minimised by proper bunds (levees) although in most other crops couple of guard rows are often adequate to discount for this effect.
3. Before applying herbicides to research plots, callibrate the sprayer with an amount of water equal to the spray liquid that you intend to use for each plot. Adjust the walking speed of the sprayman so as to empty the tank in single pass.
4. Needless to say, the herbicides must be applied evenly. Granular herbicides can be applied to research plots through a large table salt shaker, if a regular granulator was not available.
5. Weigh the dry herbicides in the lab for all replications of an experiment at one time and carry them in small, polythene bags, with prominent labels on them. Distribute the herbicide volumetrically over replications and doses. The liquid herbicides can be measured directly in the field with automatic pipettes, or by using 10 ml measuring cylinders.
6. Each time a herbicide is changed, wash and rinse the sprayer, buckets, measuring cylinder, *etc.*

Although all care to raise healthy crops in the research plots should be taken, but it should not be overdone. Else the results may not be reproduceable on the farmer fields. Also, the weed intensity in the experiment should be at least as much as in the farmer's field, if not more.

27.4 REPORTING RESULTS

1. Percentage increase in yield due to herbicide use is very misleading. One should report the absolute increase in yield over the farmer way of weeding as the base treatment. Also, the crop yield from the base plots should not be less than the yield often obtained by the progressive farmers of the area. Unless you can show in your herbicide recommendation plots a better crop standing than in the above average farmers fields, your recommendation is not likely to be accepted.
2. While reporting results from weed control field experiments, one must spell out the soil and climatic conditions, weed flora, past plot history, and adequate herbicide application details in the research report.

3. There are some well recognised ways the weed and crop responses to the weed control treatments are recorded. Initially, say within the first week of application of treatments, their effects on the weeds and crops can be recorded by visual scoring on 10 points scale, as summarised in Table 27.1. Later, the effects on the weeds could be recorded at 2-3 crop stages in terms of either weed population count or better as the dry weed biomass per unit area. Again, for a more detailed study one could record these data weed species-wise or weed category-wise, instead of on total weed basis alone, as the facilities will permit. But in any case at least the dominant weed flora composition should be documented in the report.

Table 27.1: An Outline of 10 Points Scale of Visual Scoring for Herbicide Effects on Weeds/Crops

	Level of injury	Rating in points	Effect grade
A:	**Weeds**		
	None	0	None
	Very poor to poor	1-3	Slight
	Low to moderate	4-6	Moderate
	Satisfactory to excellent	7-9	Severe
	Complete destruction	10	Complete
B:	**Crops**		
	None	0	None
	Slight discolouration, stunting; a few plants lost; injury more pronounced but effect temporary.	1-3	Slight
	Moderate injury, recovery possible; recovery doubtful; non recoverable injury.	4-6	Moderate
	Severe injury, with only few plants spared.	7-9	Severe
	Complete destruction	10	Complete

Note: *Within each class, three further sub-gradings are possible while allotting points.*

4. A sample model of reporting of the weed and crop data obtained from a field trial is provided in Table 27.2. In this table the results of one year field experiment on weed control in blackgram are reported, keeping all points so far discussed in view. This should be considered as one of the possible standard formats in which a satisfactory weed control experiment results can be reported. However, there is always a room for improvement, for instance, here column No. 2 of Table 27.3 could also be added for reasons already discussed.

   Since in agriculture some kind of crop rotation, of low or high intensity, is invariably followed, it is desirable to study and report not only the direct effect of herbicides, but also their residual effects on the follow-up crops. By combining the two effects by some statistical procedure, one can determine the cumulative effects of herbicides in a given crop sequence. Then it becomes more appropriate to call it a *weed management research in crop sequences*. Further, sometimes the base crop of the rotation is cultivated in different situations by different methods, like in case of rice culture. When weed management is tagged to any specific production system of the base crop of the crop sequence, the scientists prefer to call it *weed management in cropping systems*.

Table 27.2: Main Effects of Herbicides And Physical Methods of Weed Control on Weed Yield And Performance of Blackgram at Udaipur (India), During 1991 (From Gupta, O.P. and Choudhry, N.K., 1986. Trop. Pest Mngmt. 32 (2) 167-170.)

Treatment			Dry weed biomass (q/ha)			Crop yield attributes			Grain	Benefit:
Herbicide	Dose (kg *a.i.*/ha)	Application method	3 w.a.s.	6 w.a.s	At crop harvest	No. of pods/plant	No. of seeds/pod	Test weight (g)	yield (q/ha)	Cost ratio
Fluchloralin	0.75	PPI	1.95	4.06	9.67	23.1	5.5	38.0	7.50	3.85
Fluchloralin	1.50	PPI	1.14	2.95	6.45	26.8	6.0	38.8	11.08	4.11
Terbutryn	0.5	PE	1.72	3.61	8.04	25.7	5.7	38.6	10.75	13.90
Terbutryn	1.0	PE	1.56	3.45	7.62	21.3	5.4	37.5	7.30	-
Pendimethalin	0.5	PE	1.89	3.87	8.15	25.5	5.6	38.4	10.34	4.69
Pendimethalin	1.0	PE	1.78	3.58	7.86	20.6	5.1	37.5	5.25	-
Methabenzthia-zuron	0.5	PE	3.50	6.75	9.25	18.3	5.3	37.2	1.62	-
Methabenzthia-zuron	1.0	PE	3.06	5.34	8.36	17.3	4.9	37.1	2.16	-
Cyanazine	0.75	PE	2.65	4.55	8.56	15.5	4.9	37.3	2.05	-
Cyanazine	1.50	PE	2.06	3.76	8.23	14.3	4.6	37.4	1.48	-
Oxadiazon	1.0	PE	1.98	3.15	7.65	23.7	5.2	37.5	5.34	-
Oxadiazon	2.0	PE	1.46	2.98	6.21	17.5	4.8	37.2	4.01	-
Hand-weeded 4 times (4,5,6,7 w.a.s.)	-	-	-	4.48	4.73	23.3	5.6	38.7	7.67	1.67
Hoed twice (4&6 w.a.s.)	-	-	-	6.21	8.10	21.6	5.5	38.2	6.95	9.62
Hoed once (4 w.a.s.)	-	-	-	6.43	9.24	19.4	5.3	38.0	5.05	8.17
Unweeded check	-	-	5.50	12.54	22.40	16.7	4.6	35.4	3.65	-
SEm ±			0.25	0.35	0.35	0.75	0.29	0.36	0.27	
CD (at P = 0.05)			0.72	1.02	1.01	2.18	0.84	1.05	0.75	

Note: *PE = preemergence; PPI = preplant incorporation; w.a.s. = weeks after sowing*

Some scientists prefer to process the data on weeds in terms of certain indices. Several such indices in proposed are reproduced here as under:

a) **Weed Control Efficiency (WCE) or Weed Control Index (WCI),**

Or Weed Susceptibility Index (WSI) $= \dfrac{Wc - Wt}{Wc \times 100}$

Where Wc is the average weed count or weight per unit area in the unweeded check plot, and Wt is similar information obtained from the treated plots.

b) ***Weed Index (WI)*** $= \dfrac{YHW - Y}{YHW} \times 100,$

where YHW is the average crop yield in the hand-weeded plot, and Y = average crop yield in the treatment under study.

c) In experiments dealing with the determination of the efficacy of some inter-crop on the suppression of weeds *vis-a-vis* solo cropping, the WCE (or WCI) in the first formula is replaced by WSE. *ie.* Weed Smothering Efficiency. It is given as:

$$WSE = \frac{Mdw - Idw}{Mdw} \times 100,$$

where Mdw and Idw are the average dry weed biomasses obtained from respectively, the solo main crop plots and the intercropped plots.

d) **Relative Weed Density (RDe):** $\dfrac{NPw}{NPtw} \times 100,$

where NPw and NPtw are the per unit area population of the weed species in question and those of all the weed species combined present in the area, respectively.

e) **Relative Weed Frequency (RF):** $\dfrac{Fw}{Fsw} \times 100,$

where FW is the frequency of occurrence of the weed species in question in given samples (= spots) and Fsw the sum of frequencies of all individual weed species combined present in these samples.

f) **Relative Dry Weed Weight (RDW):** $\dfrac{DWw}{DWsw} \times 100,$

where DWw and DWsw are dry weed weights of species in question and that of all the weed species combined present in the unit area, respectively.

g) **Relative Weed Dominance (RDo):** $\dfrac{Dw}{Dsw} \times 100,$

where DW and Dsw are the frequencies of dominance of the weed in question and those of all species combined present in the test area or sample.

h) **Summed Dominence Ratio (SDR):** $\frac{\text{RDe} + \text{RDw}}{2}$

i) **Importance Value Index (IVI):** $\frac{\text{RDe} + \text{RF} + \text{RDo}}{3}$

j) **Weed Persistence Index (WPI):** $\frac{(\text{DWw})_t}{(\text{DWw})_c} \times \frac{W_t}{W_c}$

27.5 CALCULATING ECONOMICS OF THE TREATMENTS

Any new technology should be economically viable before it can be accepted by the consumer. In farming community in India and many other countries, besides the relative gains, the level of monetary input required to achieve that gain is equally important. The relative monetary gains can be calculated and presented in many ways. In weed management, as in most other agricultural research, it is most common to compare the economics of the treatments as Benefit-Cost ratio (B:C). In Table 27.3, columns required to arrive at B-C ratios are provided. In the final reporting, however, only column Nos. 2 and 6 may be recorded. The importance of column 2 in the final report lies in deciding the level of input a farmer could afford to make.

Table 27.3: An **Arbitray** Example of Steps in the Calculation of B:C in a Weed Management Experiment

(1)	(2)	(3)	(4)	(5)	(6)	(7)
Treatments	**Total cost of weed control** treatment, including herbicide, labour, etc. (Rs./ha)	**Value of the produce** including grain, straw, tuber, cane, oilseed, etc. (Rs./ha)	**Additional weeding cost** *over* control (Rs./ha)	**Additional value of produce** *over control* (Rs./ha)	**B/C*** **(5/4)**	**Net**** **B/C**
			BC	Y	Y/X	
Unweeded check	0	1547	-	-	-	
Hand weeded	540	3618	540	2071	3.84	2.84
Herbicide-I	233	2049	230	502	2.15	1.15
Herbicide-II	358	3174	358	1627	4.55	3.55
Herbicide-III	419	2349	419	802	1.91	0.91

**(1) B:C shows the benefit (Rs/ha) derived by spending additional 1 Rs/ha on the new technology.*

***(2) When B:C is further reduced by Rs 1, it is termed Net B:C.*

Comments: *It is very important to note that high output value (Col.3) does not necessarily mean a high B:C (Col.6). Same is true for input cost, where a higher monetary input may not be associated with a lower B:C.*

27.6 CHOOSING HERBICIDE RECOMMENDATIONS FROM FIELD EXPERIMENTS

Field experiments on weed control in different crops were initiated in India about five decades back. At that time the standard approach to select the best treatment was based on its significant superiority to handweeding or manually weedfree treatment in respect of crop yield. This was natural since in those days farm labour for handweeding of crops was cheap and easily available. But this situation did not last logn and rise in wages began. This made manual weeding costilier than the popular herbicides of the time, like say 2,4-D, simazine and atrazine. As a result, the herbicide treatments with capability of producing even as much crop yield as the handweeding treatments were also accepted for recommendation.

With further passage of time, there was sudden fillip given to industrial sector in the country, which was further enhanced by its globalization. This swelled the labour wages several folds while the herbicide costs remained much less elevated. This compelled the weed agronomists to compare different weed control treatments on the basis of Benefit, Cost ratios (B:C), instead of on crop productivity basis. Obviously, in this approach, depending upon the wages and herbicide costs, *there were chances that high B:C treatments with even lower crop productivity potential could get included among the recommendations.*

Further, in areas where farm labour for weeding was just not available at any cost during the period of critical weed-crop competition (or the soil condition was not sutiable for physical weeding), the experimenter was justified in comparing the herbicide treatments with unweeded control as a check in place of the usual practice of comparing these with the manually weedfree or some other conventional weeding methods.

Of late, choosing of herbicide recommendations from experiments has entered a new phase where, besides the crop yield and B, C ratios, **weed dynamics effects** are also taken into consideration; sometimes preferentially. This became necessary to deal with recent reports of alarming weed shifts caused by the continuous use of single herbicide recommendation based on highest B:C. (Chapter 17). Now **alternate herbicide treatments** even with lower B:C values but with capability of dealing with some specific weed species or biotypes, which were not controlled with some higher B:C treatment, can also be chosen for recommendation. The objective here is to minimise the possible weed shifts, while still obtaining sustainable crop productivity over period of 3-4 years by using different herbicides in rotation.

In summary, there are at least six aspects which a weed scientist must keep in view while choosing herbicide treatments for recommendation. These are:

1. Economic viability,
2. Feasibility,
3. Weed dynamics,
4. Logn-term crop productivity,
5. Residual and other effects of herbicides, and

6. Environmental concerns.

Depending upon the requirement of the operation area, one could subject the treatment effects to one or more of the above parameters and make best of the choice.

SUMMARY

The weed management research requires special techniques, equipments, and care. These aspects have been discussed in this chapter to the extent possible, both for laboratory and field experimentation.

Reporting of weed science research in the literature is frequently highly incomplete; many times not depicting even the parameters of experiment conditions. There is need to standardise the method of presenting the results. One such basic model is provided in the text but one could add any other information to it. Also the methods of reporting the treatment effects on weeds and calculation of the economic feasibility of the weed control treatments have been examplified. It is hoped that the young weed scientists will benefit from this chapter by adopting at least the minimum requirements of conducting and reporting the weed management research.

Above all, much emphasis has been given on the procedure that should be adopted in choosing the herbicide recommendations from the results obtained from the multi-location and multi-season field experiments. This is an extremely important aspect of conducting weed management research, which every student and young researcher should understand, analyse, and follow.

SELECTED BIBLIOGRAPHY

1. Camper, N.D. 1986. Research Methods in Weed Science. 3rd ed. SWSS, America
2. Diggle, P.J. 2003. Statistical Analysis of Spatial Point Patterns. Oxford University Press, Oxford (U.K.).
3. Johnson, R. A. and G. K. Bhattacharya. 2001. Statistics : Principles and Methods. John Wiley & Sons. Ind., N.Y. (USA), 733 p.
4. Luschei, E.C. and R.D. Jackson. 2005. Research methodologies and statistical approaches for multistatic systems. Weed Sci. 53(3) : 393-403.
5. Mishra, M. and A. Mishra. 1997. Estimation of integrated pest management index in jute - a new approach. Ind. J. Weed Sci. 29 (1,2) : 39-42.
6. Ripley, B.D. 1981. Spatial statistics. John Wiley & Sons. N.Y. (USA).
7. SAS. 1996. SAS System for Mixed Models. SAS Institute, Cary, MC (USA).

Appendix 1

COMMON TROPICAL AND SUBTROPICAL TERRESTRIAL WEEDS*

Key symbols: h = herbaceous; w = woody; a = annual; b = biennial; p = perennial; kh = summer season crops; r = winter season crops; dl = drylands; o = orchards; pl = plantations; nc = non-crop areas; gl = grasslands; l = lawns

Botanical name and family	English and *Hindi* names	Major habitat
ABUTILON (Malvaceae)		
indicum (L.) Sweet *theopharsti* medic.	velvetleaf, pilibuti, patata, kanghi	a/p, w, nc, gl, o
ACACIA (Papilionaceae) spp.	acacia	p, w, dl, gl, nc
ACALYPHA (Euphorbiaceae)		
indica L. *ciliata* Fors	Copper leaf, *kuppi*	a, h, kh, rice, o, nc
ACANTHOSPERMUM (Asteraceae)		
hispidum DC	bristly starbur, sandbur	a, sugarcane, h, nc, vegetables, o
ACHILLEA (Asteraceae)		
millefolium L.	yarrow, *chopandiga*	a, h, gl
ACHYRANTHUS (Amaranthaceae)		
aspera L.	Pricklychaffflower, *chirchit*	a, h, dl, nc, kh, rice
AEGILOPS (Poaceae).		
cylindrica	jointed goatgrass	a, h, r, o
AESCHYNOMENE (Leguminosae)		
aspera L. *indica* L.	*shola, phulan*	a, h, rice, jute

---

* *Limited aquatic weeds have also been included here since these often infest the lowland rice fields.*

** *Following equivalents of family names of plants have been used in this Appendix :- Gramineae = Poaceae; Cruciferеae = Asteraceae, Compositae = Brassicaceae*

*** *In some western countries, different weed species have been assigned computer codes. See Weed Science 32 (suppl. 2), 1994.*

Botanical name and family	English and *Hindi* names	Major habitat
AGERATUM (Asteraceae)		
conyzoides L.	ageratum, billgoat weed, *mahakaua*	a, h, kh, dl, gl, nc, l, pl, o
houstonianum Mill.		p, h, nc, gl, l, pl, o
AGROPYRON (Poaceae)		
repens (L.) Beauv.	quackgrass	p, h, kh, nc
AGROSTIS (Poaceae)		
palustris (Huds) Pers.	bentgrass	p, h, kh
semiverticulatus (F) Christ		
ALHAGI (Leguminosae)		
pseudalhagi (M.Bied) Desv.	camelthorn, *Jawasa*	a, w, dl, r, nc
ALISMA (Alismataceae)		
plantago-aquatica		p, rice, ph
ALLIUM (Liliaceae)		
vineale L.	wildgarlic, *gandhan, onion weed*	a, h, gl, l, r
canadense	wildonion	
ALLOTEROPSIS (Poaceae)		
cimicina Stapf.		p, kh
smi-alata Hitch		
ALTERNANTHERA (Amaranthaceae)		
pungens H. B. & K. (*= echinata or repens*)	*kantawali santhi,* alligatorweed	p, h, jute, rice
sessilis Br.	*garundiarak*	p, h, jute, rice
philoxeroides (Mart.) Griseb.		
ALYSCARPUS (Leguminosae)		
rugosus DC.	*shevra*	a, h, kh, cotton
vaginalis DC.		
ALYSUM (Brassicaceae)		a, h, gl, l
linifolium Stapf. Ex. Willed.		a, r, h
AMARANTHUS (Amaranthaceae)		
cruentus L.	smooth pigweed	a, h, kh, nc, o, r,
polygamus		
retroflexus L.	redwood pigweed	vegetables, l,
spinosus L.	spiny amaranthus, *kataili chaurai*	rice,
viridis L.	slender amaranthus, *janglichaulai*	
AMBROSIA (Asteraceae)		
artemisiifolia L.	common ragweed	a, h, gl, nc
AMISCHOPHACELUS (Commelinaceae)		
axillaris (L.) R. R. & K.		p, h, rice, kh, o,
cuculata (Roth) R. R. & K.		nc

Botanical name and family	English and *Hindi* names	Major habitat
AMMANNIA (Lythraceae)		
baccifera L. (= vesicatoria Roxb.)	*dadmari*, *jungli mehndi*, redstem	a, h, rice
AMSOMELES (Laminaceae)		
indica (L.). O. K.		a, h, jute, rice
ANAGALLIS (Primulaceae)		
arvensis L.	scarlet or blue pimpernel, *dhabbar*, *krishanneel*	a, h, r, wheat, chickpea, vegetables
ANDROGRAPHIS (Acanthaceae)		
echioides Nees	-	a, h/s
paniculata Nees		
ANDROPOGON (Poaceae)		
virginicus L.	broomsedge	p, nc, gl
ANEILEMA (Commelinaceae)		
dimorphum Daly.		
lenuginosum Wall.		
APIUM (Umbelliferae)		
nodiflorum Reichb. f.	wildcelery, *ajmod*, *karafsh*	a, h, r,
ARABIS (Brassicaceae)		
spp.		a/p, r, hills
ARENARIA (Caryophyllaceae)		
serpyllifolia L.	sandwort	a, h, kh, dl, r, vegetables
ARGEMONE (Papaveraceae)		
mexicana L.	Mexican poppy, *dhamoi. bharband*	a, h, r, nc, dl, vegetables, cl
ochroleuca		
ARISTIDA (Asteraceae)		
dichotoma Michx.	threeawn, *lamba*, *jandar*	a, h, dl, nc, gl, kh, o
ARTIMISIA (Asteraceae)		
indica Wild.		a, h, pl, gl, vegetables
ARUNDINELLA (Poaceae)		
bengalensis (Spreng) Druce		h, p, nc, paddy
ASPHODELUS (Liliaceae)		
tenuifolius Cavan	wild onion, *piazi*	a, h, r, vegetables
ASTER (Asteraceae)		
subulatus Michx.	*gulbas*	
trifolium L.		
ASTERACANTHA (See HYGROPHILA)		
ASTRAGALUS (Leguminosae)		
punjabicus	locoweed, *rutphuli*,	a, p, h, nc, gl, r

Botanical name and family	English and *Hindi* names	Major habitat
	milkvetch	
ATRIPLEX (Chenopodiaceae)		
tetarica Linn.	*surakka*	
ATYLOSIA (Leguminosae)		
elongata Benth.		a, h, jute, rice
AVENA (Poaceae)		
fatua L.	wild oat, *janglijai*	a, h, r, o, nc
ludocians		
AXONOPUS (Poaceae)		
compresus (SW) Beauv.		p, h, tea
BACOPA (Scrophuleriaceae)		
monnieria (L.) Wettstsin.		a, h, rice
BERBERIS (Berberidaceae)		
canadenses Mill.	barberry	w, o
Vulgaris, L.	*nunia-sak*	
BERGIA (Berberideae)		
ammannioides Roxb.	-	a, h/s
verticillata Willd.		
BIDENS (Asteraceae)		
pilosa L.	beggersticks	pl, kh, l, a, o
BIOPHYTUM (Geraniaceae)		
sensitivum DC.	*kajaria*	a, h, kh
BLUMEA (Asteraceae)	*ku-karonda*	a, h, kh, nc, hills
glomerata		sugarcame
mollis (D. Don) Merr. (= *wightiana* DC.)		
BOERHAVIA (Nyctaginaceae)		
diffusa L.	spiderling,	a, h, kh, rice, o,
(= *repens*)	*bish-khapra, helra*	nc
Errecta		cotton
BONNAYA (Scrophulariaceae)		
multiflora Bonati		a
veronicaefolia Urban		
BORRERIA (Rubiaceae)		
articulate		jute, kh, tea, o,
hispida (K) Sch.		dl, nc
Sirida		rice
BRACHIARIA (Poaceae)		
eruciformis		a, kh
ramosa (L.) Stapf.	signalgrass	a, h, kh, dl, nc
BRASSICA (Brassicaceae)		
kaber (DC.) Wheeler	wildmustard	a, h, r, nc
nigra (L.) Koch.		
communis Spann.		

Botanical name and family	English and *Hindi* names	Major habitat
BRIZA (Poaceae)		
minor		rice
BROMUS (Poaceae)		
tectorum L.	downybrome	a, h, gl, o
danthoniae (Desf. Trin.		
BULBOSTYLIS (See FIMBRISTYLIS)		
BUTOMUS (Alismataceae)		
umbellatus L.		p, kh, rice
BUPLEURUM (Umbelliferae)		
tenue Don		a, h, kh
CAESULIA (Asteraceae)		
axillaris Roxb.		h, a, kh, rice
CALOTROPIS (Asclepiadaceae)		
gigantea R. Br.	swallowwort, *aak, akra, madar, ankta*	a, h, dl, nc, o
CANNABIS (Cannabinaceae)		
sativa L.	hemp, *bhang, ganja, charas*	a, h, nc, r, o
CAPSELLA (Brassicaceae)		
bursa-pastoris (L.) Medic.	shepherds purse	a, h, l, r
CARDAMINE (Brassicaceae)		
impatiens L.	*todrisurkh*	a, h, r, hills
CARDUUS (Asteraceae)		
nutans L.	*kanchari*, nodding-thistle,	b, h, r
tenuiflorus Curt.	slenderthistle, *kanchari*	
CAREX (Cyperaceae)		
lasiocarpa Ehrh.	bullrush	p, gl, swamps.
CARTHAMUS (Astraceae)		
oxyacantha Bieb.	wild safflower, pohli	a, r, h, wheat, vegetables
pusillus		
CASSIA (Leguminosae)		
obtusifolia L. (or *tora* L.)	coffee weed, sicklepod, *Chakor-chakunda*	a, h, nc, dl, kh, rice, Jute, l
occidentalis L.	*bara-kasondi*	a, h, kh, nc,
pumila Lamk.		ah, kh, gl, nc
CAYRATIA (Vitaceae)		
carnosa Gagnep.	*amarlati*	p, h, sugarcane, l
CELOSIA (Amaranthaceae)		
argente L.	cock's comb, *safed murga, sarwali*	a, h, kh, nc, vegetables, o, rice

Botanical name and family	English and *Hindi* names	Major habitat
CENCHRUS (Poaceae)		
biflorus Roxb.	sandbur. *bhort*	a, h, gl, kh
ciliaris L.		
CENTELLA (Umbelliferae)		
asiatica (L.) Urban	pennywort	a, h, gl, o
CENTAUREA (Asteraceae)	Russian knapweed	p, h, nc, dl, gl, r, kh
repens L. (= *picris* Pall.)		
diffusa Lam.	diffuse knapweed	b, nc
CHARA (Characeae)		
vulgaris		p, aq, rice
CHENOPODIUM (Chenopodiaceae)		
album L.	*bathua*, common lambsquarters	a, h, r, vegetables, l
murale L.	*kerund*, goosefoot	a, h, r, salty soils
CHLORIS (Poaceae)		
barbata Sw.	fingergrass	p, h, kh, rice
virgata Sw.		
inflata		
CHROMOLAENA (Asteraceae) (=-EUPATORIUM)		
adenophorum Spreng.	croftonweed, Siamweed,	p, w, pl, nc, gl
odorata (L.) R.M. King & Robinson	*kali basuti*	vegetables, o, rice
CHROZOPHORA (Euphorbiaceae)	*souballi*	a
obliqua Vahl (Sprengel)		
plicata A. Juss.		
rottleria		
tinctoria L.		
verbascifolia (Willd.) A. Juss		
CHRYSANTHEMUM (Asteraceae)		
richilaria L.	*gendi, kalzang*	a, h, r,
CHRYSOPOGON (Poaceae)		
aciculatus Trin.	*shili ghas*	p, nc, kh
CICHORIUM (Asteraceae)		
intybus L.	chicory, *kasni*	b, h, s, p, berseem, lucerne, l
CIRSIUM (Asteraceae)		
arvense (L.) Scop.	canadathistle, *kateli* creepingthistle	p, h, r, nc, gl
CLEOME (Capparidaceae)		
cheledonii	spiderflower	a, h, dl, kh
gynandra L.		
pentaphylla	*kabarra*	a, h, kh, vegetables, dl, rice, jute
viscosa L.		

Botanical name and family	English and *Hindi* names	Major habitat
CLERODENDRON (Verbenaceae)		
viscosum (=infortunatum (L.) Gaertn.)	*kali basuti, dawai mubarik*	p, w, jute
COIX (Poaceae)		
lacryma-Jobi L.	job's tears	a, h, kh, rice
COLOCASIA (Araceae)		
esculenta (L.) Schott. (=*antiquorum* Schott.)	jangli, kachalu	p, damp, lands
COMMELINA (Commelinaceae)		
benghalensis L.	dayflower, *kanna*	a, h, kh, nc, vegetables, o, rice
communis		
diffusa Burm. f.		
(= *communis* Clarke)		
erecta L.		
hasskarlii Clarke		
forskelli		
kurzia		
CONVOLVULUS (Convolvulaceae)		
arvensis L.	fieldbindweed, deer's foot, *lehli hirankhuri, hiran podi*	p, h, r, kh, dl, o, vegetables, l, nc
CONYZA (Asteraceae)		
aegyptica Dryand.	horseweed, marestail	a, h, o, nc, kh, tea
sonariensis	bitterweed	
CORCHORUS (Tilliaceae)		
aestuans Linn.		
(=*acutangulus* Lamk.)	wildjute, *junglipat*	a, h, kh, rice, jute, vegetables, nc
capsularis L.		
olitorius L.		
tridens		
trilocularis		
CORONOPUS (Brassicaceae)		
didymus (L.) Sm.	swinecress, *janglibaloon*	a, h, r, egyptianclover, lucerne. o
CORYDALIS (Papaveraceae)		
vaginans Roxle		a, h, r
COUSINIA (Asteraceae)		
spp.		p, h, r
CROTALARIA (Leguminosae)		
medicaginea Lamak.	*gulali, jhojhru*	a, h, kh, nc
prostrata Roxb.	*nanha jhunka,* crotalaria	p. h, nc
CROTON (Euphorbiaceae)		
bonplandianus Baill.	croton, *harimirch*	a, h, r, nc, kh

Botanical name and family	English and *Hindi* names	Major habitat
(=*sparsiflorus* Morung)		
CREPIS (See YOUNGIA)		
CUCUMIS (Cucurbitaceae)		
callosus (Rottler) Cogn.		
(= *trigosus* Roxb.)	wild cucumber, *indryan, gomuk*	a, h, kh, vegetables l, dl, rice
CUSCUTA (Convolvulaceae)		
campestris L.	dodder, *swaranlata, amarbel*	p, h, parasitic, trees, lucerne, greengram, blackgram (see Chapter 23)
chinensis Lamk.		
hyalina Roth		
reflexa Roxb.		
CYNODON (Poaceae)		
dactylon (L.) Pers.	bermudagrass, *dab, doob, khobbal,* devilgrass	p, h, kh, o, vegetables, pl, nc, rice
CYANOTIS (See Amischophacelus)		Kh
CYPERUS (Cyperaceae)		
articulatus L.		a, h, kh, rice, jute
compactus Retz.		a, h, rice
compressus L.		a, h, kh, jute
corymbosus L.		a, h, kh, rice, jute
cuspidatus H. B. K.		p, h, kh, pl
cyperoides (L.) O. Kuntz.		
difformis L.		a, h, kh, rice, jute
digitatus L.		a, h, kh, rice, jute
distans L. F.		p, h, rice, nc
esculentus L.	yellow nutsedge, *motha*	p, h, kh, l, o
flavidus Retz.		
iria L.		a, h, rice, jute
kalpan L.		
kyllingia Endl.		a, h, kh, rice, jute
pilosus Vahl.		p, h, rice
platystylis		
rotundus L.	purple nutsedge, *motha, deda*	p, h, kh, l, o, r, vegetables
serotinus Rottb.	waternutsedge	p, rice
CYROTOCOCCUM (Poaceae) sp.		p, gl
DACTYLIS (Poaceae)		
glomerata L.		a, h, r

Botanical name and family	English and *Hindi* names	Major habitat
DACTYLOCTENIUM (Poaceae)		
aegyptium (L.) P. Beauv.	crowfoot grass, *makraghas*	a, h, kh, vegetables, o, rice
DATURA (Solanaceae)		
stramonium L. (=*alba* Nees.)	thornapple, *Hindu datura*, jimsonweed	a, h, kh, dl, nc
DENDROPHTHOE (Loranthaceae)		
falcata (L. f.) Etting	loranthus	parasitic, pl, o
DENTELLA (Rubiaceae)		
repens Forst.		a, h, kh, jute
DESMODIUM (Leguminosae)	*tinpatia*, beggerweed	p, h, l, nc, gl, kh
triflorum (L.) DC.		
DESMOSTACHYA (Poaceae)		
bipinnata (L.) Stapf.		a, h, p, nc, kh
DIGERA (Amaranthaceae)		
alternifolia (L.) Aschers. (=*arvensis* Forsk.)	*kundra, kali gandhari, jhur, kuna,* digera	a, h, kh, vegetables, o, l, dl, rice
DIGITARIA (Poaceae)		
ciliaris (Retz.) Koelar	crabgrasses	a, h, rice, l, kh,
ischaemum (S) Muhl.		vegetables, o, l, dl,
marginata		
sanguinalis (L.) Scop.	large crabgrass	pl
setigeria Roth		
DINBRA (Poaceae)		
arabica Jacq.		p, h, kh, nc, gl, o
retraflexa		
DIOSCOREA (Dioscoreaceae)		
wallichii H. f. (=*aculeata* L.)	*pitaalu*	p, w, jute, rice
DRYMARIA (Caryophyllaceae)		
cordata (L.) Willd.	heartleaf drymary	p, h, tea
pachyphylla Woot & Standl.	inkweed drymary	
ECHINOCHLOA (Poaceae)		
colonum (L.) Link (= *colona*)	jungle rice, *samaghas*	a, h, rice, kh, vegetables
crusgalli (L.) Beauv.	barnyardgrass, *dhidanghas*	a, h, rice, kh
aegypticum		
glabrascens		
oryzoides		
ECLIPTA (Asteraceae)		a, h, rice, o, kh, c, nc
alba (L.) Hassk.	*mukand, bhangra*	
Prostrate		

Botanical name and family	English and *Hindi* names	Major habitat
EICHHORNIA (Pontederiaceae)		
crassipes	waterhyacinth, *jalkumbhi*	p, h, rice
ELEOCHARIS (cyperaceae)		
dulcis (Burm. f.) Trin.	spikerush	p, h, rice, kh
ELEUSINE (Poaceae)		
acutangula (Roxb.) Schlt		
indica (L.) Gaerth.	*kodra, kodon,* goosegrass, *silver crabgrass, yardgrass*	a, h, kh, l, dl, o, rice
EMILA (Compositae)		
sonchifolia (L.) DC.	red tasselflower	tea, h
EQUISETUM (Equisetaceae)		
debile Roxb.	*buki, trotak,* horsetail	a/p, h, nc, gl
ERAGROSTIS (Poaceae)		
cilianesis All.	stinkgrass, lovegrass, *kusaghas*	a, h, kh, o, rice l, dl, vegetables, nc
namaquenses		
ERIGERON (Asteraceae)		
bonariensis L.	horseweed	a, h, kh, nc, gl, l
canadensis L.		
ERIOCAULON (Cyperaceae)		
cinereum R. Br.	piperwort	a, h, kh, rice
nepalense		
EUPATORIUM (See Chromolaena)		
EUPHORBIA (Euphorbiaceae)		
dracunculoides Lamk.	spurge, *dudhia*	a, h, ph, o, vegetables, damp, nc
geniculata Orteg.		-do-
hirta L.	*bari dudhi*	-do-
hypericifolia L.	*dudhia*	-do-
microphylla Heyne	*choti dudhi*	-do-
EVOLVULUS (Convolvulaceae)		
alisnoides L.	*sankh pushpi, shyamakrantha*	p, h, jute, gl, dl, l
nummularius (L.) L.		a, h, sugarcane, nc
FAGOPYRUM (Polygonaceae)		
esculentum (see *Poloygonum fagopyrum*)		
FISCUS (Moraceae)		
hispida L.f.		p, pl, gl, vegetables,
FISSENDOCARPA (Onagraceae)		
linifolia Bennet	-	h, rice, semi-squatic
FIMBRISTYLIS (Cyperaceae)		
barbata (Rottb.) Benth.	*Choti booin*	p, h, rice, kh, o,

Botanical name and family	English and *Hindi* names	Major habitat
dichotoma (Linn.) Vahl.		a, h, jute, rice, kh, vegetables
littoralis		
miliacea		
FUMARIA (Fumariaceae)		
indica (Haussk.) Pugsley (=*Parviflora* Lamk.)	fumitory, *pitpapra, bansoya*	h, a, r, vegetables
GALIUM (Rubiaceae)		
aparine L.	bedstraw, cleavers	a, h, r
GALINSOGA (Asteraceae)		
parviflora Cav.	smallflower galinsoga	a, h, r, kh, veg, o, l, damp, nc
GERANIUM (Geraniaceae)		
nodosum L. (= *neplanese Sweet*)	wild geranium, *bhand*	a/b, h, l, nc, rb
GIRARDINIA (Urticaceae)		
zeylanica Decaisne (=*heterophylla* F. B. I.)	neetle	a, h, kh
GLECHOMA (Labiatae)		
hederercea L.	groundivy, creeping charlie	p, h, l, gl, o, damp grounds
GNAPHALIUM (Asteraceae)		
indicum		
obtusifolium	cudweed	b, h, s, r, kh, veg, o, rice
purpureum L.		
GOMPHRENA (Amaranthaceae)		
decumbens Jacq.		a, h, nc, ditches, r, kh, l
procumbens L.		
GYNANDROPSIS (See CLEOME)		
HALOGETON (Chenopodiaceae)		
glomeratus C.A. Mey	halogeton	a, h, dl, gl, nc
HEDYOTIS (Rubiaceae)		
aurialaria (L.) Mudl.		p, pl, gl, vegetables, cotton, rice
biflorus		
corymbosa (L.) Lam.		
HELENIUM (Asteraceae)		
spp.	sneezeweed	a, p, h, nc, gl
HELIANTHUS (Asteraceae)		
argyrophyllus Torr. & Gr.	*safed surajmukhi*, rain's sunflower	a, h, nc, kh
HELIOTROPIUM (Boraginaceae)		
ellipticum Ledebour (=*eichwaldi* Steud.)	heliotrope, *oontchara*	a, h, kh, dl
strigosum Willd.	heliolrope, *hathisura*	p, h, gl, sugarcane

Botanical name and family	English and *Hindi* names	Major habitat
HETEROPOGON		
contortus	Speargrass	pl
HYDROLEA (Hydrophyllaceae)		
uniflora Raf.	one flover hydrolea	aquatic, rice
HYGROPHILA (Acanthaceae)		
auriculata (K. Schum) Heine	*tal makhana*	a, h, rice
HYPERICUM (Guttferae)		
perforatum L.	St. Johnswort	p, h, nc, gl
HYPTIS (Lamiaceae)		
suvaveolens Poit.	*ganga tulsi*	a, h, jute, nc
ILYSANTHES (Scropuleriaceae)		
ciliata Spreng		jute
IMPATIENS (Poaceae)		
thomsoni Hook. f.		a, h, kh
IMPERATA (Poaceae)		
cylindrica (L.) Beauv.	congograss, *lalang*	a, h, pl, l, nc
INDIGOFERA (Leguminosae)		
cordifolia Hyene ex Roth	wildindigo, *neel.*	a, h, l, nc, kh
glandulosa		
linifolia Retz.	*neel, leel, sankhahuli, torki*	a, h, l, gl
IPOMOEA (Convolvulaceae)		
carnea		
eriocarpa R. Br.		
(=*hispida* Roem & Sch.)	*boota, ghiabato,* morningglory	p, h, kh, sugarcane, pigeonpea, nc
reptans (L.) Poir.	*nali, sarnali,*	a, h (aquatic)
(=*aquatica* Forsk.)	*karmi-sag*	rice, jute
nil (L.) Roth	*nilkamli*, ivyleaf	p, w, sugarcane
(=*hederacea* Cl.)	morningglory, *ratti, kaladana*	p, w, sugarcane
ISCHAEMUM (Poaceae)		
pilosum Hack		a, h, nc, kh, o, l, rice
rugosum Salis		
JUSSIAEA (See LUDWIGIA)		
JUSTICIA (Acanthaceae)		
quinqueangularis Koen. ex Roxb.	*darhua*	a, h, kh, dl
diffusa Willd.		a, h, kh
KYLLINGA (Cyperaceae)		
brevifolius Rottb.		a, h, rice, nc
LACTUCA (Asteraceae)		
dissecta L.	*kahi*	o
LAGASCA (Asteraceae)		

Botanical name and family	English and *Hindi* names	Major habitat
mollis Cav.		a, r, vegetables, o
LAMIUM (Labiatae)		
amplexicaule L.		p, h, r
LANTANA (Verbenaceae)		
camara L.	lantana, *putus*,	w, nc, p, gl,
indica	*phulkakri*	riverbeds, forests, pl
LATHYRUS (Leguminosae)		
aphaca L.	*matri, pipari, rawari*	a, h, r, veg, l
sphaericus Retz.		
sativus L.	*khesari, chatra-matra*	a, h, r
LAUNAEA (Asteraceae)		
asplenifolia		a, r, gl
nudicaulis L.		p, h, l, ph, nc
LEERSIA (Poaceae)		
hexandra sw		p, pl, gl, vegetables
LEMNA (Lemnaceae)		
minor		p, aq, rice
LEPIDIUM (Brassicaceae) (=CARDUS)		
sativum L.		a, h, r, kh
LEPTOCHLOA (Poaceae)		
apnicea		a, h, kh, damp nc
chinensis (L.) Nees.		
LEERSIA (Poaceae)		
hexandra sw		p, pl, gl, vegetables
LEUCAS (Labiatae)		
aspera (Willd.) Spreng.	*maldoda, chatra, gumma*	a, h, l, r, kh, veg, o, rice
cephalotes (Roth) Spreng.	*dhurpisag*	a, h, kh
LIMNOPHYLLA (Scrophulariaceae)		
halerophylla (Roxb.) Benta	figurt	aq
LINDERNIA (Scrophulariaceae)		
ciliata (Colsm.) Pennel		a, h, sugarcane, rice
LIPPIA (=PHYLA) (Verbenaceae)		
nodiflora Rich.	*makana, jalpapili*	p, h, jute, l, kl, dl
LOLIUM (Poaceae)		
multiflorum	darnel	a, h, r
rigidum		
temulentum L.		
LORANTHUS (See DENDROPHTHOE)		
LUDWIGIA (Onagraceae)		
octovalvis (Jacq.) Raven.	winter primose	a, h, kh, rice
Parirflora		

Botanical name and family	English and *Hindi* names	Major habitat
LUFFA (Cucurbitaceae)		
graveolens Roxb.		a, h, sugarcane
LUPINUS (Leguminosae)		
sericeus Pursh	silky lupine	a, h, gl
MALVA (Malvaceae)		
neglecta Wallr.	mallow, *gogi sag*	a, h, o, l
parviflora L.		
rotundifolia L.		
MALVASTRUM (Malvaceae)		
coromandelianum (L.) Garcke (=*tricuspidatum* A. Gray)	*kakri, kharenti*	a, h, kh, nc, o
MARSILEA (Marsilaceae)		
minuta L.	*chaupatti*	p, h, (aquatic), kh
qadrifoliata		rice
MARTYNIA (Martyniaceae)		
annua L. (=*diandra* Glox.)	devil's law, *makoe*	a, h, ph
MEDICAGO (Leguminosae)		
denticulata L.	black medick, yellow trefoil, *miana, chandausi*	a, h, r, l, veg.
hispida	burclover	
lupulina L.	burclover, *maina, maruaini*	a, h, r
MELASTOMA (Melastomataceae)		
malabathriscum L.	banks melastoma	b, w, gl, pl, vegetables
MELILOTUS (Leguminosae)		
alba Desr. (=*leucantha* Koch.)	sweetclover, *safed senji, khandai, senji*	a, h, r, nc
indica (L.) All. (=parviflora L.)	*senjimethi, metha*	a, h, r, nc
MELOCHIA (Sterculiaceae)		
corchorifolia L.	redweed, *banputhia*	a, h, kh, nc, sugarcane, rice
MERREMIA (Convolvulaceae)		
gangetica (L.) Cvf.		p, sorghum, dl, sugarcane, kh
emarginata		
MIKANIA (Asteraceae)		
micrantha H.B.K.	mile-a-minute weed	tea, o, pl, nc
MIMOSA (Leguminosae)		
invisa Mart.		
prainiana Gamble		
pudica L.	sensitive plant	p, h, kh, jute, o,

Botanical name and family	English and *Hindi* names	Major habitat
rubcaulis sub. sp. *himalayana* (Gamble) Ohashi		forests, pl, gl
MITRACARPUS (Rubiaceae)		
villosus (Sw.) DC.	girdlepod	h, tea
MOLLUGO (Aizoaceae)		
lotoides Kuntz.	carpetweed, *gokhula*	a, h, kh, dl, l, o, rice, sugarcane
pentaphylla L.		
MOMORDICA (Cucurbitaceae)		
charantia		p, h, kh, sugarcane
dioica Roxb. ex. Willd.		
MONOCHORIA (Ponteriaceae)		
hactata L. Solm.		p, kh, rice
vaginalis (Burm)		
MUCUNA (Leguminosae)		
pruriens (Linn.) DL.	cowage	a, h, sugarcane
MURDANNIA (Commeliniceae)	marshdayflower	
spirata (L.) Bruckn.	doveweed	a, h
keisak	Asian dayflower	
nudiflora (L.) Brenam		
NICOTIANA (Solanaceae)		
pllumbaginifolia Vw.	wild tobacco, *ban-tambaku*	a, h, tobacco, kh
NITELLA (Characeae)		
spp.		
NYMPHAEA (Nymphaeaceae)		
spp.	waterlillies,	aquatic, rice
OENOTHERA (Onagraceae)		
drimmondii Hook f.		a, h, kh
rosea Ait.		
OLDENLANDIA (Rubiaceae)		
aspera DC.	*gobi, parpata*	a, h, r, dl, kh, l, rice
corymbosa L.		
umbellata		
OLIGOCHAETA (Asteraceae)		
ramosa (Roxb.) Wagenitz.		a, h, dl, kh
OPLISMENUS (Poaceae)		
burmannii (Retz.) P.Beauv.		p, pl, gl, vegetables
OPUNTIA (Cactaceae)		
dillenii (Kev-Gawler) Haw	pricklypear, *nagphani,*	p, fleshy shrub, nc, gl
monacantha Haw.	cactus	

Botanical name and family	English and *Hindi* names	Major habitat
OROBANCHE (Orobanchaceae)		
aegyptiaca Pars.	broomrape, hadda, *thokra, sarson-banda*	a, h, parasitic, several crops (See Chap. 23)
cernua Loefl.		
ramosa Linn.		
ORYZA (Poaceae)		
rufipogon	wildrice	a, kh, rice
OXALIS (Oxalidaceae)		
acetosella L.	woodsorrel, *khatmithi*	p, h, kh, r, l, gl, o, pl, rice
corniculata L.	*bohi*	
debilis ABK var. *carymbosa* (DC) lour	*champa methi, nonki*	
latifolia H. B. & K.	*teepativa, khat-mithi*	
	khat-mithi, khat-mandari	
PANICUM (Poaceae)		
dichotomiflorum Michx.	fall panicum,	a, h, kh, o, nc, rice
maximum	spreading	
repens L.	panicgrass, torpedograss, gingergrass	
PAPAVER (Papaveraceae)		
dubium L.		a, h, r,
hybridum L.		
PARTHENIUM (Asteraceae)		
hysterophorus L.	parthenium, carrotgrass, *chandni*	a, gl, h, o, nc
PASPALUM (Poaceae)		
commersonii Lamk.	knotgrass, *naru*	p, h, kh, rice, jute, pl, nc
conjugatum Berg.		
corgitolium		
dilatatum Poir.	dallis grass	
distichum L.	knotgrass	
longifolium		
scorbicularis L.		
PENNISETUM (Poaceae)		
clandestinum Hoehst ex. Chiov.		a, h, pl, tea, cotton
hohenackeri		
PHALARIS (Poaceae)		
minor Retz.	littleseed canarygrass, *gullidanda, vanri*	a, h, nc, r, wheat, vegetables
PHASEOLUS (Leguminosae)		
trilobus Ait.	*ban-moong*	a, h, kh, nc

Botanical name and family	English and *Hindi* names	Major habitat
PHRAGMITES (Poaceae)		
karka Retz. Trin. ex. Steud.	reed	h, p, nc
communis Trin.		
PHYLLANTHUS (Euphorbiaceae)		
fraternus Webster	*hazardana, bhuin*	a, h, kh, dl, veg, nc,
(=*niruri* Hook. f.)	*anwla*	flowerbeds, rice
medraspatensis		
PHYSALIS (Solanaceae)		
minima L.	ground cherry, *banmakoya, papotan*	a, h, kh, rice
PLANTAGO (Plantaginaceae)		
lanceolata L.	plantains, isafghol	p, h, l, kh
media L.	buckhorn	
PLUCHEA (Asteraceae)		
lanceolata (D.C.) C.B.	arrowwod, *baisuri, rukhri*	p, w, dl, r, nc
Clarke		
POA (Poaceae)		
annua L.	annual bluegrass	a, h, l, o, nc, r, wheat,
pratensis		
POLANISIO (See CLEOME)		
POLYGONUM (Polygonaceae)		
aviculare L.	postrate, knotweed	a, h, l, gl, nc
fagoprym Linn.	buckwheat	a, h, r,
glabrum Willd.	*pankheri*	a, h, rice, l, o, sugarcane, veg, pl
orientale		
pensylvanicum		
persicaria		
pumila Willd.	*jiri*	cumin
plebejum R. Br.	Indian knotgrass, *raniphul, noni*	a, h, gl, nc, ditchbanks, kh.
hydropiper L.		p, rice, ditches
POLYPOGON (Poaceae)		
annua		
monspeliensis (L.) Desf.		a, h, r, wheat, l
PORTULACA (Portulacaceae)		
oleracea L.	purslane, *kulfasag, nunka*	a, h, kh, veg, o, rice, l
quadrifida L.		
POTENTILLA (Rosaceae)		
fulgens Wall	cinquefoil	p, h, kh
nepalensis Hook, f.		

Botanical name and family	English and *Hindi* names	Major habitat
POUZOLZIA (Urticaceae)		
zeylanica (L.) Benn.		
PROSOPIS (Leguminosae)		
chilensis (Molina) Stuntze	*khar, jhand,* mesquite	p, h, nc, w, gl
PTERIDIUM (Pteridaceae)		
aquilinum (L.) kuhn ex Decken	bracken	p, gl
PYCERUS (Cyperaceae)		
polystachys Beauv.		
(=*Cyperus strigosus* Wt.)		p, kh, rice
RANUNCULUS (Ranunculaceae)		
sceleratus Linn.	crowfoot, buttercup	a, h, gl, moist nc, wheat
RHODODENDRON (Ericaceae)		a, w, gl, nc
spp.		
RHUS (Anacardiaceae)		
radicans L.	poison ivy	p, w, gl, nc
ROSA (Rosaceae)		
indica		p, pl, gl, o
eqlantaria		
moschala		
ROTALA (Lythraceae)		
densiflora (Roem & Sch.) Koehne		a, h, rice
indica		
verticularia		
ROTTBOELLIA (Poaceae)		
exaltata L.f,		h, p, nc,
RUBUS (Rosaceae)		
spp.	blackberry, dewberry, rasberry,	w, orchards
RUMEX (Polypogonaceae)		
acetosella L.	*jangli palak*	p, h, r, l, o, nc
crispus L.	curleydock,	
dentatus	sourdock	
obtusifolius L.	broadleafdock	
spinosus	*kantiali palak*	a
RUNGIA (Acanthaceae)		
repens		*aq, rice*
parviflora		
SACCHARUM (Poaceae)		
munja L.		p, h, kh, dl, nc, gl
spontaneum L.	tigergrass, *kans*	p, h, kh, dl, nc, gl
SACCIOLEPIS (Poaceae)		
interrupta (Willd.)	*palla*	p, rice

Botanical name and family	English and *Hindi* names	Major habitat
SAGITTARIA (Alismataceae)		
guaynensis	*chiri-napay*, arrowhead	p, rice, marshlands
trifolia L.		
SALSOLA (Chenopodiaceae)		
kali L. *var, tenuifolia* T.	Russian thistle	a, h, r, nc
SAPONARIA (Caryophyllaceae)		
vaccaria L.	*takla*	a, h, r, wheat
SCIRPUS (Cyperaceae)		
mucronatus L.	*murak*	p, rice, l
maritimus		
roylei		
SCOPARIA (Scrophulariaceae)		
dulcis Linn.		a, h, kh, nc
SEHIMA (Poaceae)		
nervosum		p, h, kh
SENECIO (Asteraceae)		
jacobaea L.	ragwort, groundsel	b, h
vulgaris L.		
gallicus Chaix		
SESBANIA (Leguminosae)		
bispinosa (Jacq.) W.F.Weight.	sesbania, *dhedhan*	a, w, kh, l
(=*aculeata* Pers.)		
(=*Aeschynomene bipinosa* or *spinulosa*)		
SETARIA (Poaceae)		
glauca (L.) Beauv.	foxtails	a, h, kh, gl, nc, l, o, rice, veg.
pumila		
viridis (L.) Beauv.		
SIDA (Malvaceae)		
rhombifolia L.		
spinosa L.		p, w, nc, banks
veronicifolia Lamk.	sida, *bariar*	p, h, gl, nc, o, pl
SILYBUM (Asteraceae)		
marianum (L.) Gaertn.		p, h, r, nc
SILENE (Caryophyllaceae)		
gallica L.		a, h, r,
SINAPIS (Brassicaceae)		
alba L.		a, h, r
arvensis L.		
SIMLAX (Liliaceae)		
zeylanica L.		p, w, jute, o, gl
SISYMBRIUM (Brassicaceae)		
irio Linn.		

Botanical name and family	English and *Hindi* names	Major habitat
strictum Hook. f. & t.	tumble mustard	a, h, r, l, nc
SOLANUM (Solanaceae)		
elaeagnifolium cav. w	white horse neetle, wildbrinjal, silverleaf nightshade	p/a, h, nc, gl, kh, pl
nigrum L.	black nightshade	a, h, kh, vegetables, rice, nc
surrattense Burm. f.	*berkateli, rengni*	p, h, r, nc
(=*Xanthocarpum* Schrad.)		
SONCHUS (Asteraceae)		
biochyotus DC.	perennial sowthistile, *sonchus*	p, h, r, nc, gl
(=*arvensis* L.)		
oleraceous L.		
SORGHUM (Poaceae)		
halepense (L.) Pers.	Johnsongrass, baru	p, h, kh, nc, vegetables
SPERGULA (Caryophyllaceae)		
arvensis L.	corn spurry, *ban-dhania*	a, h, r, vegetables
SPHAERANTHUS (Asteraceae)		
indicus L.	*mundi*	a, h, rice
(=*hirsuta* Willd.)		
SPHENOCLEA (Campanulaceae)		
zeylanica Gaertn.	gooseweed, *mirchbooti*	a, h, rice
SPILANTHES (Asteraceae)		
acmella Murr. var. *oleracea paniculata*		a, kh, rice, nc, alien
SPIRODELA (Lemnaceae)		
sp.	grand duckweed	aq, rice
SPOROBOLUS (Poaceae)		
diander	smutgrass	p, l, rice, nc
indicus auct. non (Linn.) R.Br.		
STACHYTARPHETA (Verbenaceae)		
indica Vahl.		a, h, o, pl
STELLARIA (Caryophyllaceae)		
media (L.) Will	chickweed	a, h, r, o
crispata		
STEMODIA (Scrophulariaceae)		
viscosa Roxb.	-	h/w
STEPHANIA (Menispermaceae)		
japonica (Th.) Miers		

Botanical name and family	English and *Hindi* names	Major habitat
STRIGA (Scrophullariaceae)		
asiatica (L.) Kuntze	witchweed, *agia*, *kher*	a, h, parasitic, chiefly millets (See Chap. 23)
(=*lutea*)		
densiflora Benth.		
hermonthica Benth.		
TARAXACUM (Asteraceae)		
officinale Wiggers	dandelion	p, h, r,
TEPHROSIA (Leguminosae))		
purpurea (L.) Pers.	*sarphuka*, wild indigo, *ban-neel*	p, w, nc, kh
THALASPI (Brassicaceae)		
arvense L.	field pennycress	a, h, gl, nc
THEMEDA (Poaceae)		
quadrifolia		p, o, gl
THYSANOLAENA (Poaceae)		
maxima (Roxb.) O.K.		p, pl, gl, vegetables
TRIANTHEMA (Aizoaceae)		
portulacastrum L. (=*monogyna* L.) *Thigueta*	horsepurslane, carpetweed, *patharchatta*, *itsit*	a, h, kh, vegetables, o, l, rice
pentandra L.		
(=*govindia*)		
TRIBULUS (Zygophyllaceae)		
terrestris L.	puncturevine, *desi gokhru*, *goksura*	a, h, dl, o, kh, nc, gl, vegetables
TRICHODESMA (Boraginaceae)		
indicum R. Br.	*hetamundia*	a, h, kh, nc
TRIDAX (Asteraceae)		
procumbens L.		p, h, l, o, nc
TRIGONELLA (Leguminosae)		
indica		a, h, r, l, veg.
polycerata L.	*jangli methi*	a, h, r, l, veg.
TRIUMFETTA (Tiliaceae)		
rhomboidea Jacq. (=*angulata* Lam.)	parraqueet burr, *chikti*, *lapta*	a, h, w, jute, sugarcane, damp, nc
TYPHA (Typhaceae)		
spp.		p, aq, rice
ULEX (Leguminosae)		
europaeus L.	gorse	a, w, gl, nc
URTICA (Urticaceae)		
urens L.	neetles, *bhabar*	a, p, h, nc
pilulifera L.		

Botanical name and family	English and *Hindi* names	Major habitat
VACCARIA (Caryophyllaceae)		
pyramidata Medik		a, h, r, (grains)
VERBESINA (Asteraceae)		
encelioides Benth, & Hk. f. ex A. Gray	golden crown	p, h, gl, nc, kh
VERONICA (Scrophulariaceae)		
agrestis L.	speedwell	a, h, kh, dl, r
persica		
cinerea Boiss & Bal.	fleambane	gl, nc, veg., l
persica		
VERNONIA (Asteraceae)		
baldwini Torr.	iron wheel	p, o, nc
persica		
VICIA (Leguminosae)		
hirsuta (Linn.) S. F. Gray	hairy tare, *misia*	a, h, r, veg.
sativa L.	commonvetch, *ankta chatri-matri, matra*	a, h, r,
VITIS (See CAYRATILA)		
VOLUTARELLA (See OLIGOCHAETA)		
WEDELLIA (Compositae)		
calendulacea	bhringa-raj kesha-raj	
WITHANIA (Solanaceae)		
somnifera Dun.	*asgand*	a, h, kh, o, nc
XANTHIUM (Asteraceae)		
strumarium L.	cocklebur, *gokhru*	a, h, nc, dl, kh
YOUNGIA (=CREPIS) (Asteraceae)		
japonica (L.) Benth.		a, h, r, damp nc
ZIZYPHUS (Rhamnaceae)		
nummularia (Burm. f.) w. & A.	*kantaberi, jharberi, simli*	p, w, nc, dl, gl
ZORINA (Leguminosae)		
diphylla Pers.		a, h, gl, o
gibbosa Span		

Appendix 2

CONVERSION FACTORS OF MEASUREMENTS COMMONLY NEEDED IN HERBICIDE USE AND WEED CONTROL RESEARCH WORK

To convert from:	To convert to:	Multiply (1) by:
(1)	(2)	(3)
Ac	ha	0.405
	Sq m	4046.8
Cu ft (water)	Cu m	0.028
	1	28.4
ft	cm	30.48
	m	0.305
Gal	1	4.546
Gal ac^{-1}	1 ha^{-1}	9.35
g l^{-1}(of water)	ppm	1000
g m^{-2}	Kg ha^{-1}	10
ha	ac	2.471
in	cm	2.540
Kg	g	1000
Kg ha^{-1}	g 10 m-2	1.0
Kg 1000 l^{-1} water	% solution	0.1
Kg $10m^{-2}$	q ha^{-1}	10
Kg m^{-2}	q/ha^{-1}	100
ppb	ppm	0.001
ppm	g l^{-1}	0.001
	mg l^{-1}	1.00
	%	0.0001
m	Km	0.001
mile	Km	1.6
% Solution	ml (or $g)^{-1}$ water	10
	1 (or kg)/1000 l water	10
lb	Kg	0.453
lb ac^{-1}	Kg ha^{-1}	1.121
(q)	Kg	100

To convert from:	To convert to:	Multiply (1) by:
(1)	(2)	(3)
Sq ft	Sq m	0.093
tonne (t)	Kg	1000
Table spoon	g	15

Note: *Ac = acre; ha = hectare; Sq = Square; m = meter; ft = feet; Gal = gallon; l = liter; g = gram; in = inch; ppm = parts per million; lb = pound; mg = milligram; q = quintal*

Appendix 3

ANSWERS TO THE UNSOLVED PROBLEMS OF CHAPTER 10

Ex. 1.	3.75 litres
Ex. 2.	333 g (or 0.333 kg)
Ex. 3.	5.68 l/ha
Ex. 4.	About 384 ml
Ex. 5.	12.5 litre
Ex. 6.	240 g (or 0.24 kg)
Ex. 7.	105 g or 115 ml
Ex. 8.	0.65 ha
Ex. 9.	B, C, A, D
Ex. 10.	20 Kg

Appendix 4

ANSWERS TO THE UNSOLVED EXERCISES OF CHAPTER 11

Ex. 1	About 600 l/ha	Ex. 9	6 l
Ex. 2	0.66 l/mt	Ex. 10	9 km/hr
Ex. 3	257.1 l/ha	Ex. 11	6.5 m
Ex. 4	0.666 l/mt	Ex. 12	9.6 l/m
Ex. 5	450 l/ha	Ex. 13	a = 93.75 l/ha
Ex. 6	0.675 l/mt		b = 46.87 l/ha
Ex. 7	3.8 km/hr		a = 62.5 mt
Ex. 8	6 m		b = 62.5 mt
	0.066 ha	Ex. 14	4.6 kg/ha
	682 l/ha	Ex. 15	70 mt
	0.648 ha		

Note: mt = minute

Appendix 5

HERBICIDES REGISTERED UNDER SECTION 9(3) OF THE INSECTICIDES ACT-1968, AS ON 28-12-2006 IN INDIA ALONG WITH THEIR COMMON NAMES, TRADE NAMES, AND MANUFACTURERS

Common name*	Trade name(s)	% a.i.	Manufacturer
2, 4-D	Agrodex	variable	Bayer
	Agrodar		Zeneca-ICI
	Agrdone-48		Agromore
	Combi		Dhanuka
	Erbitox		Rallis
	Tafacide		Atul
	Weedmar		Bharat Pulverizers
Alachlor	Lasso	50 EC	Monsanto
		10 G	
Anilophos (Anilofos)	Aniloguard	30 EC	Bayer
	Anilodhan		Gharda
	Arozin		Dhanuka
	Sumo		Dupont
			AIMCO
			Shaw Wallace
(Anilophos + 2, 4-DEE)	Shot One	45 EC (24:32)	Bayer
(Anilophos + Ethoxysulfuron)	Rice Guard	26 WP (25+1)	Bayer
Atrazine	Atrataf	50 WP	Bayer
	Dhanuzine		Dhanuka
	Solaro		Pesticide India
Butachlor	Bilchlor	50 EC	Monsanto
	Dhanuchlor	5 G	Dhanuka
	Machete		Coromandal Indag
	Teer		Hindustan Insecticides
	Trapp		Montari
	Weedkill		Searle
	Arochlor		Siris
	Hiltachlor		Sundanshan Chemicals
	Lambast		Isagro

* After Pesticide Res. J. 18(2): 241-242, 2006, and some other sources.

Common name*	Trade name(s)	% a.i.	Manufacturer
	Rasayanchlor		Bayer
(Butachlor+ Propanil)	Butanil	28+ 28 EC	Monsanto
Chlorimuron-ethyl	Kloben	25 WP	DuPont
(Chlorimuron-ethyl + metsulfuron-methyl)	Almix	20 WP	DuPont
Cinmethylene		10 EC	
Clodinafop-propargyl	Topik	15 WP	Syngenta
Clomazone	Command	50 EC	Rallis
Cyhalofop-butyl	Clincher	10 EC	De-Nocil
Dalapon	Dalapon	85 WP	De-Nocil
	Dowpon		BASF
Dazomet			
Diclofop-methyl	Illoxan	28 EC	Bayer
Diuron	Agromex	80 WP	Aventis
	Karmex		Cyanamid
	Klass		Rhone-Poulenc
	True		Atul
			Agromore
Ethoxysulfuron	Sunrise	15 WDG	Bayer
Fenoxaprop-p-ethyl	Puma Super	10 EC	Bayer
	Power, Whip	5 EC	Aventis
Fluchloralin	Basalin	45 EC	BASF
Flufenacet			
Glufosinate ammonium	Basta	15 SL	Bayer
	Liberty		
Glyphosate	Comet	41 EC	Monsanto
	Glycel		Excel
	Glytaf		Rallis
	Noweed		Dhanuka
	Roundup		Pesticide India
	Weed All		
Imazethapyr	Pursuit	10 SL	BASF
(Imazethapyr+pendimethalin)	Valour	32 EC (2+32)	BASF
Isoproturon	Alon	50 WP	Bayer
	Arelon	75 WP	Gharda
	Carelon		Bayer
	Ciluron		Nocil
	Delron		Rallis
	Dhanulon		Dhanuka
	Dhar		Montari
	Graminon		IFFCO
	Greniran		Hexamar
	Hilproturon		DeNocil
	Isocin		
	Isoguard		
	Isohit		
	Isolon		
	Isoptoturon		

Common name*	Trade name(s)	% a.i.	Manufacturer
	Isotox		
	Jaiproturon		
	Kanak		
	Marklon		
	Milron		
	Monolon		
	Nocilon		
	Norlon		
	Pestolon		
	Phulon		
	Prow		
	Rahshak		
	Ranak		
	Shivron		
	Sonaron		
	Sulron		
	Taurus		
	Tolkan		
	Totalon		
	Tritilon		
	Wonder		
Linuron	Afalon	50 WP	Bayer
MCPA		40 SL	
		40 AS	
Methabenzthiazuron	Ambonil	70 WP	Bayer
	Perch		
	Tribunil		
	Yield		
Metolachlor	Dual	50 EC	Syngenta
Metribuzin	Barrier	70 WP	Bayer
	Lexone		Rallis
	Sencor		Dhanuka
	Tata Metri		United Phosphorus
Metsulfuron-methyl	Algrip	20 WP	DuPont
(Metsulfuron-methyl+ Chlorimuron-ethyl)	Almix	20 WP (10+10)	DuPont
Mextoxuron	Dosanex	80 WP	
	Hilnex		
	Hexanor		
	Invest		
Oxadiargyl	Raft	6 EC	Bayer
	Topstar	80 WP	Rallis India
Oxadiazon	Ronstar	25 EC	Rhone-Poulenc
Oxyfluorfen	Alto	23.5 EC	Indofil
	Goal		Bayer
	Oxygold		Fungicides India
Paraquat dichloride	Garamaxone	24 SL	Syngenta
Pendimethalin	Dhanutop	30 EC	Bayer

Common name*	Trade name(s)	% a.i.	Manufacturer
	Dost		Dhanuka
	Mop up		Rallis
	Panida		BASF
	Pendiherb		UPL Cheminova
	Pendigold		Crop Health
	Pendilin		Syngenta
	Prowl		
	Stomp		Meghmani Organics
Pretilachlor	Refit	50 EC	Syngenta, Nagarjuna
	Eraze		
(Pretilachlor+safener)	Sofit	50 EC	Syngenta
Propanil	Stam F-34	34 EC	Cyanamid
			Bayer
Quizalofop-ethyl	Targa Super	5 EC	Dhanuka
		10 EC	
Sirmate			
Simazine	Sathi	50 WP	Gharda Chemicals
Sulfosulfuron	Leader	75 WP	Monsanto, Gharda Chem, United Phosphorus
Thiobencarb (=ben thiocarb)	Saturn	50 EC	Pesticide India
Triallate	Avadex BW	50 EC	Monsanto
Trifluralin	Flora	48 EC	De Nocil
	Rampage		Zeneca-ICI
	Tip Top		EID
	Treflan		Fungicides India
	Trinetra		Gharda
	Trilex		Isagro
	Trofan		Herbicides India
			UPL

Footnote: *Presently of the 186 pesticides of different kinds registered in India, 42 are herbicides (22.5%). This number is only next to insecticides (82).

**There are about 10 other herbicide molecules which are under very advance stages of testing in India, but are not registered so far. These are included in Appendix-6.

Appendix 6

COMMERCIAL HERBICIDE PRODUCTS IN INDIA WITH THEIR COMMON NAMES, AT VARIOUS STAGES OF TESTING AND FIELD USE

Trade Name	Common Name
1. Afalon	Linuron
2. Affinity	Carfentrazone ethyl
3. Agrgold	Cinanethylin
4. Agrodar (32, 96)	2, 4-D (dimethylamine)
5. Agrodex G	2, 4-D (ellylester)
6. Agrodone (48 EC, 18 WP)	2, 4-D (ethyester)
7. Agrosodium	2, 4-D (Na salt)
8. Aim	Carfentrazone ethyl
9. Algrip	Metsulfuron methyl
10. Alkombo	Chlorimuron ethyl + metsulfuron methyl + anilophos
11. Allie	Metsulfuron-methyl
12. Ally	Metsulfuron-methyl
13. Almix (20 WP)	Chlorimuron+metsulfuron
14. Alto	Oxyfluorfen
15. Amber	Triasulfuron
16. Ambinil (70 WP)	Methabenzthiazuron
17. Amiben	Chloramben
18. Ammate	AMS
19. Aniloguard (30 EC)	Anilofos (or Anilophos)
20. Aniloguard plus	Anilophos+2, 4-DEE
21. Ansar	MAA
22. Ansar-529D	DSMA
23. Aqualin	Acrolein
24. Arelon (50 WP & 75 WP)	Isoproturon
25. Argold Plus	Cinmethylin + 2, 4-DEE
26. Arochlor	Butachlor
27. Arozin (30 EC)	Anilophos
28. Assault	Imazapyr
29. Assert	Imazamethabenz-methyl

Trade Name	Common Name
30. Atlantis	Mesosulfuron + iodosulfuron
31. Atrataf (50 WP)	Atrazine
32. Avadex BW	Diallate
33. Avenge	Difenzoquat
34. Banvel-D	Dicamba
35. Barnon	Flamprop (IP salt)
36. Basagran	Bentazon
37. Basagram (40 EC)	Anilophos
38. Basalin (45 EC, 48 EC)	Fluchloralin
39. Basamaize	Prynachlor
40. Basta	Glufosinate-aommonium
41. Bengran	Isoproturon
42. Betasan	Bensulide
43. BGE	Anilophos+ triclopyr
44. Bladex	Cyanazine
45. Brominal	Bromoxynil
46. Brushoff	Metsulfuron-methyl
47. Buctril	Bromoxynil
48. Butanex	Butachlor
49. Butanil	Butachlor+ Propanil
50. Butoxone	2, 4-DB
51. Casoron	Dichlobenil
52. Cattch (50 EC)	Alachlor
53. CGA-184927	Clodinafop with safener
54. Chemshoe	Propham
55. Cinch	Cinmethylin
56. Classic	Chlorimuron-ethyl
57. Clincher	Cyhalofop-butyl
58. Cobex	Lactofen
59. Command	Clomazone
60. Cotoran	Fluometuron
61. Curtail	Clopyralid + 2,4-D
62. Delchlor (50 EC, 5G)	Butachlor
63. Delron (75 WP)	Isoproturon
64. Devrinol	Napropamide
65. Dicuron	Chlortoluron
66. Dimension	Dithiopyr
67. DMC	Metsulfuron
68. Dow Weed Millor	Dinoseb
69. Dowco-233	Triclopyr
70. Dowco-443	Haloxyfop-methyl
71. Dowpon	Dalapon
72. Doxanex (80 WP)	Metoxuron
73. Dual (500 EC, 720 EC)	Metolachlor

Trade Name	Common Name
74. Enfield	Trifloxysulfuron sodium
75. Eraze	Pretilachlor 50 EC
76. Escort	Metsulfuron
77. Evolus	Azafenidin
78. Express	Tribenuron (methyl)
79. Falcon	Propaquizafop
80. Fenoxurone WP	2, 4-D (ammine)
81. Focus	Haloxyfop-butyl
82. FOE-5043	Flufenacet
83. Fusilade (12.5 EC)	Fluazifop-p-butyl
84. Galaxy	Bentazon + Blazer
85. Gallant	Haloxyfop
86. Garlon	Triclopyr
87. Gemini	Linuron+Chlorimuron ethyl (12:1)
88. Gesagard	Prometryn
89. Gesatopso	Simazine
90. Glean	Chlorsulfuron
91. Glycel	Glyphosate
92. Goal (23.5 EC, 0.35 G)	Oxyfluorfen
93. Gramoxone (20 EC)	Paraquat
94. Gramoxone-S	Paraquat (without surfactant)
95. Gramuron	Paraquat
96. Gropper	Metsulfuron
97. Hammer	Imazathapyr
98. Haproturon	Isoproturon
99. Harmony	Thifensulfuron
100. Heolon	Dichlofop methyl
101. Hexanil	Propanil
102. Hexapon	Dalapon
103. Hexazine	Simazine
104. Hexuron	Diuron
105. Hiltachlor	Butachlor
106. Hoe-404	Sulfonylurea
107. Hydrothol	Endothall
108. Hytane	Isoproturon
109. Hyvar-X	Bromacil
110. Illoxan	Diclofop methyl
111. Image	Imazaquin
112. Isoguard	Isoproturon
113. Isoguard plus	Isoproturon+ 2, 4-D
114. Jaguar	Bromoxynil
115. JV-485	Isopropagyl
116. Karmax	Diuron
117. Key-D	2, 4-D

Trade Name	Common Name
118. Klass	Diuron
119. Kloben	Chlorimuron-ethyl
120. Knockweed	2, 4-D (sodium)
121. Knockweed (4G, 18EC & 36EC)	2, 4-D (ethylester)
122. Knockweed 72	2, 4-D (dimethyl amine)
123. Koban	Pethoxamid
124. Krenite	Fosamine
125. Krilin	Trifluralin
126. Lambast	Butachlor
127. Lanex	Fluometuron
128. Lasso (50 EC)	Alachlor
129. Leader	Sulfosulfuron 75 WG
130. Lexus (50 DF)	Flupyrsulfuron-methyl
131. Liberty	Glufosinate ammonium
132. Logran 20WG, 75WG	Triasulfuron
133. Londax 60 DF	Bensulfuron-methyl
134. Lorox	Linuron
135. Lorox plus	Linuron+Chlorimuron-ethyl
136. Machete (5G, 50EC)	Butachlor
137. Mataven	Flamprop-methyl
138. Mesox maxx	Mesosulfuron-methyl
139. Milogard	Propazine
140. Milzine	Atrazine
141. MON 29870	Alachlor+atrazine
142. Mowdown	Difenoxuron
143. Mylone	Dazomet
144. Nocilon (50 WP)	Isoproturon
145. Norex	Choroxuron
146. Ordram	Molinate
147. Oxygold	Oxyfuorfen
148. Pandia	Pendimethalin
149. Parlan	Isoproturon
150. Patoran	Metobromuron
151. Pillarset	Butachlor
152. Pivot	Imazethapyr
153. Planvin	Nitralin
154. Poast	Sethoxydim
155. Preforan	Fluordifen
156. Premerge	Dinoseb
157. Preview	Metribuzin+chlorimuron ethyl
158. Princep	Simazine
159. Probe	Methazole
160. Prometrex	Prometryn
161. Puma	Fenpxaprop-p-ethyl

Trade Name	Common Name
162. Puma super (=Puma Power)	Fenoxaprop-p-ethyl
163. Pursuit	Imazethapyr
164. Pursuit plus	Imazethapyr+pendimethalin
165. Pyramin	Pyrazon
166. Avirosan-rilof	Piperphos
167. Radapon	Dalapon
168. Raft	Oxadiagryl
169. Rallis 10 wp	Pyrazosulfuron – ethyl (10 wp)
170. Ramrod	Propachlor
171. Randip	Glyphosate
172. Rasayanochlor	Butachlor
173. Ready mix	Pretilachlor+2, 4-D Glyphosate + 2, 4-D (IPA salts)
174. Redeem	Triclopyr + clopyralid
175. Refit (50 EC)	Pretilachlor
176. Rice 30EC	Anilophos
177. Rice guard	Anilophos+ethoxysulfuron
178. Rice star	Fenoxaprop-p-ethyl
179. Rico	Anilophos
180. Ronak	Isoproturon
181. Ronstar	Oxadiazon
182. Roundup	Glyphosate
183. Saathi	Pyrazosulfuron-ethyl (10 wp)
184. Saturn (10 G)	Thiobencarp
185. Saturn (50 EC)	Benthiocarb
186. Sencor	Metribuzin
187. Sector	Imazaquin
188. Sethoxydim	Cyclocydim
189. Setoff	Cinosulfuron
190. Sinbar	Terbacil
191. Sirmate	Dichlormate
192. Sofit	Pretilachlor (with safener)
193. Solaro	Atrazine
194. Squadran	Imazaquin+pendimethalin
195. Stam F-34	Propanil
196. Starane	Fluroxypyr
197. Starane plus	Fluroxypur+2, 4-D
198. Stomp (20 EC)	Pendimethalin
199. Successor-600	Pethoxamid
200. Suffex plus	Benzoylprop-methyl
201. Suffix super	Flamprop (methyl)
202. Sunrise	Ethoxysulfuron
203. Surflan	Oryzalin

Trade Name	Common Name
204. Sweep	Paraquat
205. Tafade	2, 4-D (DMA)
206. Tafapon	Dalapon
207. Tafazine (50 WP)	Simazine
208. Taguard 30 EC	Anilophos
209. Takeoff	Imazosulfuron
210. Targa Super	Quizaiofop ethyl
211. Tata Metri	Metribuzin
212. Taurus	Isoproturon
213. Teer	Butachlor
214. Tenoran	Chloroxuron
215. Tetrapion	Flupropanate
216. Tillam	Pebulate
217. Tok E-25	Nitrofen
218. Tolkan	Isoproturon
219. Tone-up	Imazaquin
220. Topik	Clodinafop-propargyl
221. Topstar	Oxadiargyl
222. Tordon	Picloram
223. Traga Super	Quizalofop ethyl
224. Trapp 50 EC	Butachlor
225. Tribunil	Methabenzthiazuron
226. Traflan	Triflaralin
227. Valan	Molinate
228. Valour	Imazethapyr+pendimethalin
229. Vapam	Metham
230. Vegfru taurus	Isoproturon
231. Velpar	Hexazinone
232. Venzar	Lenacil
233. Verdict	Haloxyfop-butyl
234. Visor (2E)	Thiazopyr
235. Weedar	2, 4-D (amine)
236. Weedazol	Amitrole
237. Weedazol-TL	Amitrole + ammonium thiocyanate
238. Weedhoe-108	MSMA
239. Weedoff	Glyphosate
240. Weedol	Paraquat-dichloride
241. Whip Super (EW & EC)	Fenoxaprop-p-ethyl
242. Yield	Methabenzthiazuron
243. Zeneca-ICI	Acetachlor

Appendix 7

HERBICIDES NO MORE ALLOWED FOR USE IN AGRICULTURE IN INDIA UNDER INSECTICIDES ACT, 1968 OF G.O.I. [FROM: PESTICIDES RES. J. 18(2): 243, 2006

Herbicide		Status
Nitrofen	:	Banned
Paraquat dimethyl sulfate	:	Banned
PCP (Pentachlorophenol)	:	Banned
PMA (Phenyl mercuric acetate)	:	Banned
MH (Maleic hydrazide)	:	Banned
TCA (Trichloroaceticacid)	:	Registration withdrawn
Dalapon	:	Registration withdrawn
Sumazine	:	Registration withdrawn
2,4,5-T	:	Registration refused

Appendix-8

STATUS OF HERBICIDE PRODUCTION IN INDIA IN TERMS OF ACTIVE INGREDIENTS DURING 2004

	Herbicide	Installed Capacity (t)	Actual production (t)
1.	2, 4-D	1300	186
2.	Atrazine/simazine	500	61
3.	Butachlor	500	333
4.	Diuron	100	64
5.	Fluchloralin	200	157
6.	Glyphosate	3540	308
7.	Isoproturon	5388	4409
	Total herbicides	11528	5518

Appendix 9

PRODUCTION AND CONSUMPTION OF HERBICIDES IN INDIA OVER YEARS

Year	Production (`000 m t)	Consumption (`000 m t)
1965	0.06	-
1975	0.240	0.98
1985	1.80	3.67
1989	2.86	4.73
1994	NA	7.6
2004	11.0	NA

Appendix 10

RELATIVE CONSUMPTION OF DIFFERENT KINDS OF PESTICIDES IN INDIA *VIS-A-VIS* WORLD (1998)

Sl. No.	Pesticide group	India	World
1.	Herbicides	8%	43.6%
2.	Insecticides	77%	29.7%
3.	Fungicides	12%	20.6%
4.	Others	3%	6.1%
	Total	100%	100.0%

Footnote: (1) The average pesticide consumption in India is about 400 g/ha. Of the herbicide share is only about 35 g/ha.

(2) The major herbicide consumption in India is in crops like rice, wheat, soybean, groundnut, seed spices, and tea and coffee.

Appendix 11

ADDRESSES OF SOME FIRMS DEALING WITH HERBICIDES IN INDIA

1. AGROMORE (P) LTD., P.O. Box-2602, Mysore Road, Bangalore-560026
2. ATUL LTD, (Agrochemical Division), Valsad (Gujarat)
3. AVENTIS AGR. EVO. INDIA LTD., Hoechst House, 54-A, Andheri Kurla Road, Andheri (E), Mumbai - 400 093 (or B-3/86, Safdarganj Enclave, New Delhi-110029)
4. BASF INDIA LTD., Crop Protection Division, P.B. 19108, SK Ahire Marg, Worli, Mumbai - 400 125
5. BAYER INDIA LTD., Bayer House, Central Avenue, Hiranandani Gardens, Powal Mumbai - 400 076 (or 1-2, Community Centre, Aram Bagh, Panchkuian Road, New Delhi-110055)
6. CHEMINOVA INDIA LTD., Keshava, 7th Flora, Bandra, Kurla Complex, Mumbai – 400 051
7. CREATIVE INDUSTRIES, 102, Creative Industrial Building, Sundarnagar, Road No. 2, Kalina, Santacruz (E), Mumbai - 400 098
8. CYANAMID INDIA LTD., Nyloc House, 254-D2, Dr. A.B. Road, Worli, Mumbai-400025
9. DE NOCIL CROP PROTECTION. PVT. LTD., 706-707, Tolstoy House, Tolstoy Marg, New Delhi - 110 001 (Also 10th Floor, Viedocon Tower, E-1, Jhandewalan Extension, New Delhi - 110 055) and 1st Floor Adm. Building, Pirojsha Nagar, Eartern Express Highway, Vikhroli (E), Mumbai - 400 079
10. DHANUKA GROUP, 861-862, Joshi Road, Karol Bagh, New Delhi - 110 005
11. E.I. DU PONT INDIA LTD., DLF Plaza Tower, 7th & 8th Floors, Arjun Marg, DLF Qutab Enclave, Phase-I, Gurgaon - 122 002 (Haryana)
12. EXCEL CROP CARE LTD., 184-187, Swami Vivekanand Road, Jaeshwari (W), Mumbai-400102.
13. FMC-RALLIS INDIA LTD., 17/2, Palace Road, High Grounds, Bangalore - 560 052
14. GHARDA CHEMICALS LTD., 5/6 JER Mansion, W.P. Varde Road, Bandra (W) Mumbai - 400 050
15. GODREJ AGRO. VET. LTD., Pirojshnagar, Eastern Express High Way, Vikhroli (East), Mumbai - 400 079
16. HOECHST SCHERING AGR. EVO., Hoechst House, 4th Floor, 3/1, Asaf Ali Road, New Delhi - 110 002

17. HYDERBAD CHEMICAL PRODUCTS LTD., A-24/25, APIE, Bangalore, Hyderabad – 500 037
18. INDOFIL CHEMICALS LTD., Nirlon House, Dr. Annie Besant Road, Worli, Mumbai - 400 025
19. INSECTICIDES (INDIA) LTD., 401-402, Lusa Tower, Azadpur, Commercial Complex, Delhi – 110 033
20. MONSANTO INDIA LTD., Ahura Centre, 5th Floor, 96, Mahakali Caves Road, Andheri (E), Mumbai - 400 093
21. NAGARJUNA AGRICHEM LTD., P.No. 61, Nagarjuna Hills, Panjagudda, Hyderabad (A.P.)
22. NOVARTIS INDIA LTD., 201, Palika Bhavan, Sector XIII, RK Puram, New Delhi - 110 066
23. PESTICIDES INDIA INDUSTRIES, PB No. 20, Udaisagar Road, Udaipur – 313 001
24. RALLIS INDIA LTD., Plot No.21 & 22, Phase-II, Peenya Industrial Area, P.B. 5813, Bangalore, 560058
25. RPG LIFE SCIENCES, Ceat House, Annie Besant Road, Worli, Mumbai - 400 018
26. SEARLE (INDIA) LTD., 21. D. Sukhadvala Marg, Mumbai-400001
27. SUMITOMO CHEMICAL PVT. LTD., 145-14th Floor, Market Chamber VI, 220, Narsiman Pount, Mumbai-400021.
28. SYNGENTA INDIA LTD., House No.10-A, D-Block (Executive), Suncity Extn., Bareilly- 243 122 (or 347/7, UE, Karnal-132001 (Haryana) (or Royal Insurance Building, 14 J Tata Road, Church Gate, Mumbai - 400020).
29. T. STANES & COMPANY LTD., 8/23-24, Race Course Road, Coimbatore - 641 018 (T.N.)
30. UNITED PHOSPHORUS LTD., Uniphos House, Madhu Park, 11th Road, Mumbai – 400 052

Other Useful Addresses

1. Directorate of Plant Protection,, Quarantine and Storage N.H. IV, Faridabad-121001
2. Crop Care Federation of India, Uniphos House, Madhupark, Khar (W), Mumbai – 400 052

Appendix 12

SIGNIFICANCE OF SYMBOLS GIVEN ON HERBICIDE LABELS

Sl. No.	Toxicity category	Toxicity values in LD 50 (mg pesticide per kg body weight of test animal)		Colour of triangle	Signal word on label	Warning symbol on label
		Oral	Dermal			
1.	Extremely toxic	up to 50	up to 200	Bright Red	Poison	Skull and cross bones
2.	Highly toxic	51-500	201-2000	Bright Yellow	Poison	-
3.	Moderately toxic	501-5000	2001-20000	Bright Blue	Danger	-
4.	Slightly toxic	Over 5000	Over 20000	Bright Green	Caution	-

Appendix 13

MAXIMUM RESIDUE LIMITS (MRLS) OF HERBICIDES (UPDATED UP TO 2005)

Herbicide	Commodity	MRL mg/kg	Authority
(1)	(2)	(3)	(4)
Alachlor	Cotton seed	0.05	PFA* (India)
	Groundnut	0.05	PFA
	Maize	0.10	PFA
	Soybean	0.50	PFA
Anilophos	Rice	0.10	PFA
Atrazine	Maize	Nil	PFA
	Sugarcane	0.25	PFA
Butachlor	Rice	0.05	PFA
Chlorimiron-ethyl	Wheat	0.05	PFA
Clodinafop-propargyl	Wheat	0.10	PFA
Cyhalfop-butyl	Rice	0.50	PFA
Diclofop-methyl	Wheat	0.10	PFA
Diuron	Cotton seed	1.00	PFA
	Banana	0.10	PFA
	Sweet orange	1.00	PFA
	Grapes	1.00	PFA
	Maize	0.50	PFA
Diquat	Soy bean (dry)	0.20	CAC** (FAO/WHO)
	Rice, polished	0.20	CAC
	Potato	0.05	CAC
	Beans (dry)	0.20	CAC
	Lentil (dry)	0.20	CAC
	Peas (dry)	0.20	CAC
	Soybean	0.20	CAC
	Wheat flour	0.50	CAC

* PFA (India) = Prevention of Food Adulteration Act, 1954 and Rules, 1955, U/R-65(2), Ministry of Health and Family Welfare, New Delhi.

** CAC = Codex Alimentarius Commission, Joint FAO/WHO Food Standards Programme, Rome

Herbicide	Commodity	MRL mg/kg	Authority
(1)	(2)	(3)	(4)
	Wheat wholemeal	2.00	CAC
	Maize	0.05	CAC
	Eggs	0.05	CAC
2,4-D	Eggs	0.05	CAC
Ethoxysulfuron	Rice	0.01	PFA
Fenoxaprop	Wheat	0.02	PFA
	Soybean seed	0.02	PFA
Fluchloralin	Cotton seed	0.05	PFA
	Soybean	0.05	PFA
Glufosinate-ammonium	Tea	0.01	PFA
	Sugarbeet	0.05	CAC
	Soyabean (dry)	0.10	CAC
	Rape seed	5.00	CAC
	Rape seed oil (Crude)	0.05	CAC
	Potato	0.50	CAC
	Peas (dry)	3.00	CAC
	Sunflower seed	5.00	CAC
	Carrot	0.05	CAC
	Maize	0.10	CAC
	Corn salad	0.05	CAC
	Broad bean (dry)	2.00	CAC
	Common bean (dry)	2.00	CAC
	Peas (dry)	3.00	CAC
Glyphosate	Tea	1.00	PFA
	Wheat four	0.50	CAC
	Peas (dry)	5.00	CAC
	Cotton seed	10.0	CAC
	Rape seed	10.0	CAC
	Eggs	0.10	CAC
	Sweet corn (corn-on-the cob)	0.10	CAC
	Wheat wholemeal	5.00	CAC
	Cotton seed oil (edible)	0.05	CAC
	Soybean (dry)	20.00	CAC
	Beans (dry)	2.00	CAC
Imazethapyr	Soybean oil	0.10	PFA
	Groundnut oil	0.10	PFA
Isoproturon	Wheat	0.10	PFA
Linuron	Pea	0.05	PFA
Methabenzthiazuron	Wheat	0.50	PFA
Metolachlor	Soybean oil	0.05	PFA
Metribuzin	Soybean oil	0.10	PFA

Herbicide	Commodity	MRL mg/kg	Authority
(1)	(2)	(3)	(4)
Metsulfuron-methyl	Wheat	0.10	PFA
MH	Onion	15.0	PFA
	Potato	50.0	PFA/CAC
Oxadiazon	Rice	0.03	PFA
Oxyfluorfen	Rice	0.05	PFA
	Groundnut oil	0.05	PFA
Paraquat – dichloride (determined as paraquat cation)	Food grains	0.10	PFA
	Milled food grains	0.025	PFA
	Potatos	0.20	PFA
	Other vegetables	0.05	PFA
	Cotton seed	0.20	PFA
	Cotton seed oil (edible, refined)	0.05	PFA/CAC
	Milk (whole)	0.01	PFA/CAC
	Fruits	0.05	PFA
	Sunflower seed oil (edible)	0.05	CAC
	Soybean (dry)	0.10	CAC
	Rice, polished	0.50	CAC
	Eggs	0.01	CAC
	Potato	0.20	CAC
	Maize	0.10	CAC
Pendimethalin	Wheat	0.05	PFA
	Rice	0.05	PFA
	Soybean oil	0.05	PFA
	Cotton seed oil	0.05	PFA
Pretilachlor	Rice	0.05	PFA
Simazine	Maize	Nil	PFA
	Sugarcane	0.25	PFA
Sulfosulfuron	Wheat	0.02	PFA
Thiobencarb	Cotton seed oil	0.02	PFA
Triallate	Wheat	0.05	PFA
Trifluralin	Wheat	0.05	PFA

Appendix 14

ORAL LD_{50} OF SOME COMMON HERBICIDES

Herbicide	Oral LD_{50} (rat)* (mg/kg)	Herbicide	Oral LD_{50} (rat)* (mg/kg)
Alachlor	930	Paraquat dichloride	150
Atrazine	1869-3080	Pendimethalin	1050 – 1250
Butachlor	1740-3000	Pretilachlor	6099
2,4-D	375	Profenofos	358
Dalapon	7570-9300	Propanil	1285 – 1483
Diuron	3400	Simazine	Over 5000
Fluchloralin	Over 6400	TCA	3200 – 5000
Glyphosate	5600	Triallate	1675 – 2165
Isoproturon	1800 – 3600	Trifluralin	Over 10000
MH	Over 5000	DNOC	40
MCPA	700 – 800	PCP	280
Metolachlor	2780	2,4,5-T	300
Metoxuron	3200-2000	Methabenzthiazuron	1000
Metribuzin	2200-2345	Thiobencarb	1903
Oxadiazon	Over 8000	Nitrofen	2630
Oxyfluorfen	Over 5000		

According to the LD50 data included in this table, trifluralin is least toxic and DNOC the most, to the test mammals. Paraquat, 2,4-D, profenphos, PCP, and 2,4,5-T are other high mammalian toxicity herbicides.

According to the LD50 data included in this table, trifluralin is least toxic and DNOC the most, to the test mammals. Paraquat, 2,4-D, profenphos, PCP, and 2,4,5-T are other high mammalian toxicity herbicides.

Appendix 15

SOME OTHER BOOKS ON WEED SCIENCE

1. Anon, 1992. Weed Control Manual, Meister Publishing Co. USA, 442 pp.
2. Ashton, F.M. 1991. Weed Science. John Wiley and Sons Inc., New York.
3. Cavellor, R. 1988. Weed Control in Vegetable Production. A.A. Balkema Pub.
4. Chandra, K. L. *et al.* 1997. Weed Management in Horticulture and Plantation Crops, Malhotra Publications, New Delhi, 218 pp.
5. Crafts, A.S. 1975. Modern Weed Control. Univ. California Press, California, 440 pp.
6. Gupta, A. 2006. Pesticide Residues in Food Commodities. Agrobios (India), Jodhpur, 323 p.
7. Gupta, O.P. 2001. Weedy Aquatic Plants: Their Utility, Menace, and Management, Agrobios (India), Jodhpur, 273 pp.
8. Gupta, O.P. 2007. Fundamentals of Weed Science, Agrobios (India) Jodhpur (India), 379 pp.
9. Hance, R.J. 1989. Weed Control Handbook: Principles, 8th edition, Blackwell Scientific Pub., Oxford.
10. Joshi, N.C. 1984. Manual of Weed Control (revised and enlarged edition). Researchco Publications, Delhi, India
11. Khuspe, V.S. *et al.* 1982. A compedium of Indian Weed Science Research (Vol. I and II), Metropolitan Book Co., N. Delhi.
12. Klingman, G.C. 2002. Weed Science: Principles and Practices (2nd ed.), John Wiley and Sons Inc., N. York, 688 pp.
13. Kondap, S. and Upadhyay, U.C. 1985. A Practical Manual on Weed Control. Oxford and IBH Publishing Co., N. Delhi, India, 55 pp.
14. Lewis, R. J. 1995. Food Additives Handbook. Springers, USA. 573.
15. Liebman, M. *et al.* (eds.). 2001. Ecological Management of Agricultural Weeds. Cambridge University Press, Cambridge (U.K.).
16. Mandal, R.C. 1990. Weeds, Weedicides, and Weed Control: Principles and Practices. Agro Botanical Pub. (India), Bikaner, India, 350 pp.
17. Martin, H. 2005. Integrated Weed Management. Ministry of Agri., Food, and Rural Affairs, Ontario, Canada. 112 p.
18. Moody, K. 1986. Weed Control in Tropical Crops. Vol. II, Los Banos, Phillipines, Weed Sci. Soc., Phillipines, 293 pp.

19. Parsons, W. T. and Cuthbertson, L. E. G. 2001. Noxious Weeds of Australia. CSIRO Publishing, Australia. 712 p.
20. Petroski, R.J. *et al.* (eds) 2005. Semiochemicals in Pest and Weed Control. Amer. Chem. Soc. Symposium Series No. 906. 184 p.
21. Rao, V.S. 2000. Principles of Weed Science. Oxford and IBH Pub. Co., New Delhi, 555 pp.
22. Singh, H.P. *et al.* 2006. Handbook of Sustaniable Weed Management. Food Products Press, N.H., London, Oxford. 855 p.
23. Somani, L.L. 1992. Dictionary of Weed Science. Agrotech Pub. Academy, Udaipur, 200 pp.
24. Stephens, R.J. 1982. Theory and Practice of Weed Control. McMillan, London, 215 pp.
25. Subramanian, S. *et al.*, 1991. All About Weed Control. Kalyani Publishers, Ludhiana, India, 315 pp.
26. Thakur, C. 1993. Scientific Weed Management. Syndicate Publication (India) xv + 345 pp.
27. Torrey, S. (ed). 1982. Preemergence Herbicides- Recent Advances. Noyes Data Corporation, 334 pp.
28. Unger, P. W. 1994. Managing Agricultural Residues, CRC Press Inc., USA. 234 p.
29. Withamson, D.R. 1989. Use of Herbicides in the Forest. 3rd ed. Her Magesty Office, London.
30. Zimdahal, R. 1993. Fundamentals of Weed Science. Academic Press, USA.

Appendix 16

SELECTED JOURNALS, PERIODICALS, HANDBOOKS, AND MONOGRAPHS RELATING TO WEED SCIENCE

1. Advances in Pest Control Research:, Inter Science Publishers, N.Y., USA.
2. Australian Weed Control Handbook: Plant Press, Toowoomba, Queensland.
3. Australian Weeds: Journal of the Council of Australian Weed Science Societies. Inkata Press Pvt. Ltd., Victoria 3168, Australia.
4. Bulletin of Environment Contamination and toxicology, Springer verlag, N.Y. USA.
5. Herbicide Handbook: Weed Science Society of America, Illinois, USA; an annual monograph.
6. Indian Journal of Weed Science: Indian Society of Weed Science, Department of Agronomy, PAU Ludhiana-141004
7. International Pest Control, Rhodes Industrial Magazine Ltd., 54-55, Wilton R6, London.
8. Journal of Agriculture and Food Chemistry (American Chemical Society, Washington DC, USA).
9. Pest management Science (earlier Pesticide Science (John Wiley Sons Ltd.).
10. Pesticide Hand Book: College Science Publishers, Pennsylvania, USA.
11. Pesticide Research Journal (Pesticide Assoc. of India, IARI, New Delhi).
12. Plant Protection Bulletin: F.A.O., Rome (Italy).
13. The World Weeds: Int. Book Distributors, Dehradoon (India)
14. Tropical Pest Management (formerly PANS): Centre for Overseas Pest Research, College House, Wrights Lane, London W8 5S.J., U.K.
15. Weed Abstracts: CAB, Fornhan Royal, Slough SL 23 BN, U.K.
16. Weed Control Hand Book: An yearly monograph series of Blackwells Scientific Pub., Oxford, U.K.
17. Weed Research: Blackwells Scientific Pub., Oxford, London, U.K.
18. Weed Research: Weed Science Society Japan, 1-26 Nishigahora, Kitaku, Tokyo, Japan.
19. Weed Science (Formerly Weeds): Weed Science Society of America (WSSA), 113 North Neil Street, Champaign, Illinois 61820, USA.

20. Weed Technology: Weed Science Society of America (WSSA), 113, North Neil Street, Champaign, Illinois 61820, USA.
21. Weed Trees, and Turf: USA
22. Weeds Today: Weed Science Society of America (WSSA), 113, North Neil Street, Champaign, Illinois 61820, USA.

Appendix 17

IMPORTANT WEED SCIENCE SOCIETIES IN CERTAIN COUNTRIES

1. Argentina- Association Argentina para *et* Control de Malezas (ASAM), Casilla de Correo N. 37, Sucursal 34, Buenos Aires.
2. Australia- The Weed Science Society of New South Wales, Australia, Amalgamated Chemicals, Northarm Ave., P.O. Box 59, BaSkston, N.S.W. 2000.
3. Brazil- Brazilian Weed Conference, Instituto Agronomico, Caxia Postal 28, Campinas Sao Paulo.
4. Chile- Chilean Weed Control Society, Casilla 5427, Santiago.
5. Columbia- Sociedad Columbiana de Control de Malezas, y Fisiologia Vegetal, COMALFI, Apartado Aereo 29688 Bogota DE.
6. India- Weed Science Society of India, National Research Centre Weed Science (ICAR) Jabalpur, M.P.
7. Indonesia- Weed Science Society of Indonesia, Jalan IR H. Juanda 1, P.O. Box 17, Bogor.
8. Israel- Weed Science Society of Israel, 1 Hayessod Str., Tel Aviv.
9. Japan- Weed Science Society of Japan, Natl. Inst. of Agricultural Sciences, Konosu, Saitama.
10. Latin America- Association Latino Americana de la Ciencia de Malezas (ALAM), Instituto Agronomico, Caixa Postal 28, Campinas, Sao Paulo, Brazil.
11. Peru- Peruvian Weed Society, 555 Zoila Amoretti, Lima 21, Peru.
12. Philippines- Weed Science Society of the Philippines. Dept. of Agricultural Botany, College of Agriculture, College, Laguna.
13. Tanzania- East African Community Weed Conference. P.O. Box 3024, Arusha.
14. U.S.A.-1 Asian Pacific Weed Science Society, College of Tropical Agriculture, Kauai Branch Station, P.O. Box 154, Kapaa, Hawaii, USA.

    2. Weed Science Society of America, 2028 Forest Hill Driver, Silver Spring, MD 20903, USA.

Appendix 18

MAXIMUM PERMISSIBLE NUMBER OF TOTAL WEED SEEDS PER KG OF FOUNDATION AND CERTIFIED SEEDS OF SOME CROPS AS PER APPROVAL OF THE GOI, NEW DELHI

Crop	Number of Total Weed Seeds (Maximum) Per Kg:	
	Foundation seed	Certified seed
A. Grain Crops		
1. Paddy, Wheat, Barley, Triticale, Pearlmillet	10	20
2. Sorghum	5	10
3. Maize	None	None
B. Pulses		
1. Blackgram, Greengram, Pigeonpea, Mothbeary	5	10
2. Chickpea, Pea	None	None
3. Frenchbean, Cowpea	None	10
4. Lentil	10	20
C. Oilseeds		
1. Castor, Peanut	None	None
2. Rape & Mustard, Sesame, Niger, Taramera	10	20
3. Linseed, Sunflower, Safflower, Soyabean	5	10
D. Fibre Crops		
1. Cotton	5	10
2. jute	10	20
E. Forages		
1. Egyptian clover, Lucerne, Oat	10	20
2. Clusterbean	None	None
3. Sesbania*	5	10
F. Vegetables etc		
1. Gourds, Cucumber, Melons, Squashes, Pumpkin, Brinjal, Okra, Tomato	None	None
2. potato (True seeds – TPS)	NA	10
3. Fennel, Radish, Cumin	10	20
4. Spinach, Cabbage, Cauliflower, Pepper, Onion, Carrot, Sugarbeet, Turnip	5	10
5. Fenugreek	10	10

* ***Footnote:*** 1. *After Tunwar and Singh, 1988.*
2. See also Chapter – 5.

Appendix 19

MAXIMUM PERMISSIBLE LIMITS OF OBJECTIONABLE WEEDS IN *CERTIFIED SEEDS* OF CERTAIN CROPS AS APPROVED BY THE GOI, NEW DELHI*

Crop	Objectionable Weed	Permissible Limit	
		% weed plants (by number)	No. of weed seeds/kg crop seeds
1. Oat (forage)	Wildoat (*Avena* spp.)	0.02	5
2. Safflower	Wild safflower (*Carthamus oxycantha*)	None	None
3. Sunflower	Wild sunflower (*Helianthus* spp.)	None	None
4. Triticale	Wild morningglory (*Convolvulus arvensis*) & Canarygrass (*Phalaris minor*)	0.01	5
5. Vegetables (many)	Wild relatives	None	None
6. Cumin	Jiri (*Polygonum pumila*)	-	10

* ***Footnote:*** 1. *After Tunwar and Singh, 1988.*
2. See Also Table 5.2 of Chapter 5 for Data for some more crops.

Appendix 20

HELP TO CHAPTER-11

Table 1: Concentration Produced by Adding 1 Kg or 1 lb of Herbicide in Variable Volumes of Water

Volume of water in spray tank in litre									
5	10	25	50	100	200	250	333	500	1000
% concentration in water by adding *1 Kg* herbicide									
20	10	4	2	1	0.5	0.4	0.3	0.2	0.1

Table 2: Herbicide Required for 30 Cm (12") Wide Band Spray at Blanket Rate of 1 Kg/ha in Crops of Variable Row Spacings.

Crop row spacing					
Cm (inch)	45(18)	60 (25)	75 (30)	90 (36)	100 (40)
Herbicide required					
Kg	0.666	0.5	0.40	0.333	0.30

Table 3: Time Required for Tractor Mounted Sprayer to Travel 500 ft (or 152.4m) at Various Field Speeds

Required Speed (mph)	Time for 500 ft (152.4m)	
	Minutes plus	Seconds
1.00	5	41
1.50	3	47
2.00	2	50
2.50	2	16
3.00	1	53
3.50	1	37
4.00	1	25
4.50	1	16
5.00	1	8
6.00	0	56
7.00	0	49
8.00	0	43
9.00	0	38
10.00	0	34

(Note: mph = 1.609 kmph)

Table 4: Nozzle Spray Output Required for Different Rates of Application of Herbicide at Four Speeds

Broadcast rate gal. per acre	Nozzle output at 4 speeds			
	3 mph	4 mph	5 mph	6 mph
	oz. per minute			
10	8.4	11.2	14.0	16.8
15	12.6	16.8	21.0	25.2
20	16.8	22.4	28.0	33.6
25	21.0	28.0	35.0	42.0
30	25.2	33.6	42.0	50.4
35	29.4	39.2	49.0	58.8
40	33.6	44.8	56.0	67.2

(Note: mph = 1.609 kmph; gal/ac = 9.35 l/ha; 1 oz = 29.57 ml)

Table 5: Calibration Table for Band-Spraying of Liquid Herbicides

Volume of spray (oz) delivered by 1 nozzle in 300 ft	Gallons per acre applied at band width of:			
	9"	12"	15"	18"
8	12.1	--	--	--
10	15.1	11.3	--	--
12	18.1	13.6	10.9	--
14	21.2	15.9	12.7	10.6
16	24.2	18.2	14.5	12.1
18	27.2	20.5	16.3	13.6
20	30.2	22.7	18.2	15.1
22	33.3	25.0	20.0	16.6
24	36.3	27.2	21.8	18.2
26	39.3	29.5	23.6	19.7
28	--	31.8	25.4	21.2
30	--	34.0	27.2	22.7
32	--	36.3	29.0	24.2

(Note: 1 oz = 29 57ml; Gl/ac = 9.35 l/ha; 1"=2.54cm)

Table 6: Acres Sprayed Per Tankful of Herbicide Spray Liquid

Gallons per acre	Acres per tankful for various tank capacities, gallons									
	30	50	55	60	75	100	110	150	200	500
5	6.0	10	11	12	15	20	22	30	40	100
6	5.0	8.3	9.2	10	12.5	16.7	18.3	25	33.3	83.3
7	4.3	7.1	7.9	8.6	10.7	14.3	15.7	21.4	28.6	71.4
8	3.8	6.3	6.9	7.5	9.4	12.5	13.7	18.8	25.0	62.5
9	3.3	5.6	6.1	6.7	8.3	11.1	12.2	16.7	22.2	55.6
10	3.0	5.0	5.5	6.0	7.5	10.0	11.0	15.0	20.0	50.0
15	2.0	3.3	3.7	4.0	5.0	6.7	7.3	10.0	13.3	33.3
20	1.5	2.5	2.8	3.0	3.8	5.0	5.5	7.5	10.0	25.0

(Note: 1 gal/ac = 9.35 1/ha; 1 ac=0.405 ha; 1 gal = 4.546 l)

Table 7: Number of Rows Per Acre for Various Row Spacings and Lengths

Length of row in ft	Rows per acre when row spacing is:			
	36 inches	38 inches	40 inches	42 inches
330	44.0	41.8	39.6	37.8
660	22.0	20.9	19.8	18.9
990	14.6	13.9	13.2	12.6
1,320	11.0	10.4	9.9	9.5
1,650	8.8	8.3	7.9	7.6
1,980	7.3	7.0	6.6	6.3
2,310	6.3	6.0	5.6	5.4
2,640	5.5	5.2	4.9	4.7

(Note: 1 ft = 0.3 m; 1 inch = 2.54 cm)

Appendix 21

HELP TO CHAPTER-12

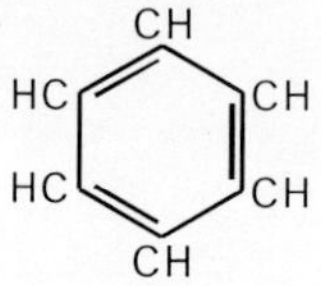 CH, HC, CH, HC, CH, CH Benzene	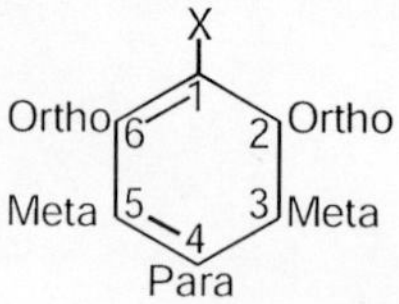 X, Ortho 6, 1, 2 Ortho, Meta 5, 3 Meta, 4, Para Mode of numbring of carbon atoms of a mono substituted Benzene ring ($C_6H_5.X$)	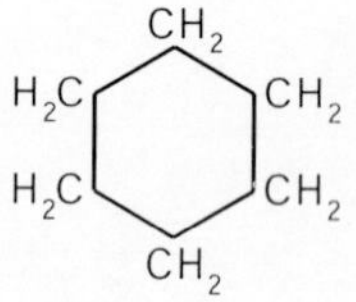 CH_2, H_2C, CH_2, H_2C, CH_2, CH_2 Cyclohexane (C_6H_{12})
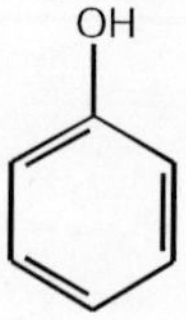 OH Phenol	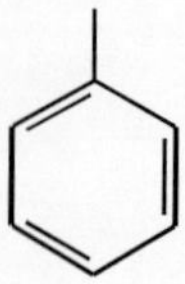 Phenyl	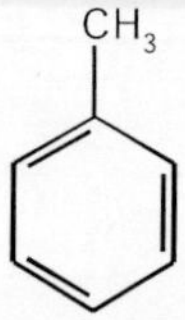 CH_3 Toluene
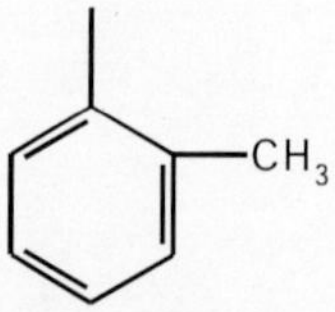 CH_3 Tolyl	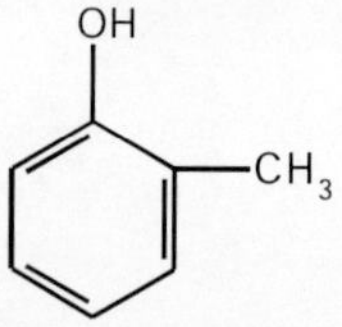 OH, CH_3 *O*- cresol	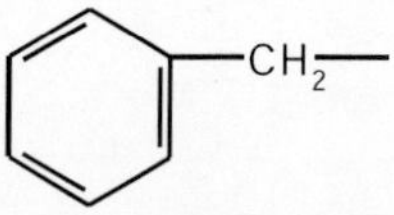 CH_2 Benzyl
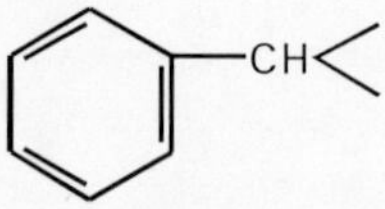 CH Benzal	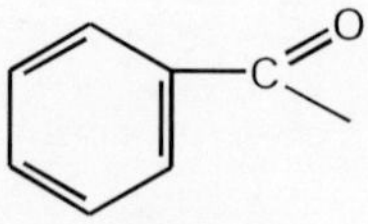 C, O Benzoyl	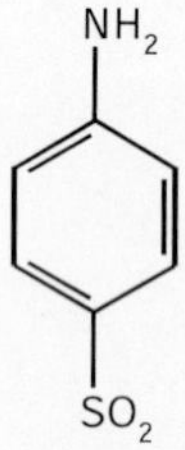 NH_2, SO_2 Sulphanyl

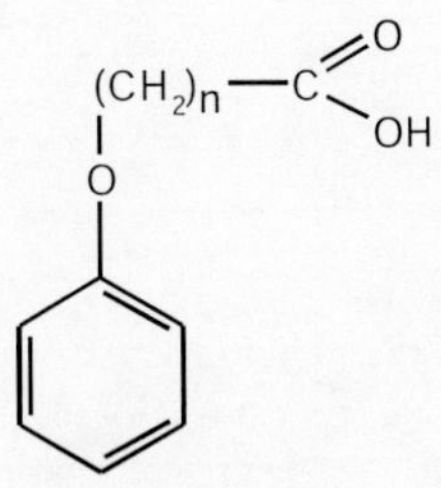

$(CH_2)_n$—COOH, O, benzene ring Phenoxyalkaonic acid	$(CH_2)_n$—COOH, O, CH_3 Tolyl oxy-alkanoic acid	C(=O)—OH, C(=O)—OH Phathalic acid
C(=O)—OH Benzoic acid	C(=O)—OH, O-CH_3 *O* - anisic acid	C(=O)—NH_2, C(=O)—OH Phthalamic acid
X, C, N, N, H, H, N—C, C—N, N, H, H Symmetrical amini triazine ring	N Pyridine ring	OH, N Pyridinol ring
N, C(=O)OH Picolinic acid		
H, N, HC, C=O, HC, NH, C, O A uracil molecule	O, H, H, HN—C—NH, (3) (2) (1) Urea	NH_2, CH_3 *P* - toluidine

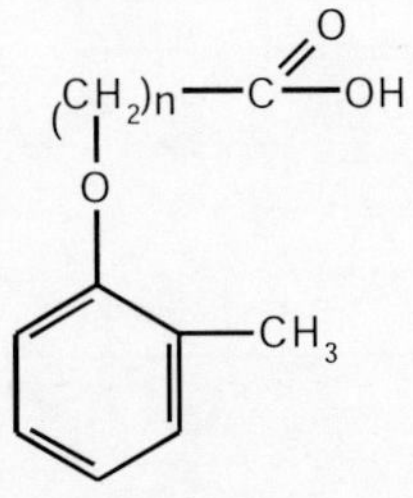

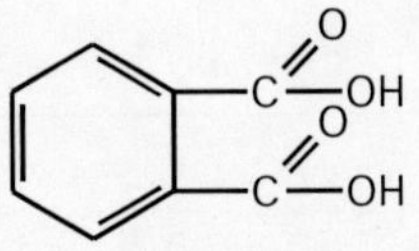

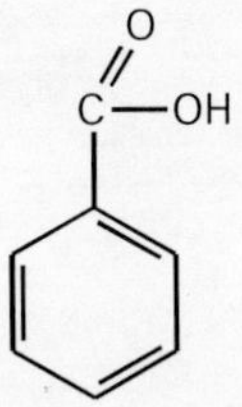

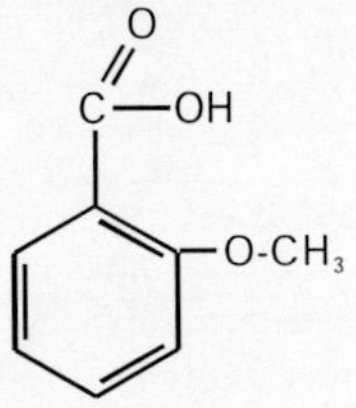

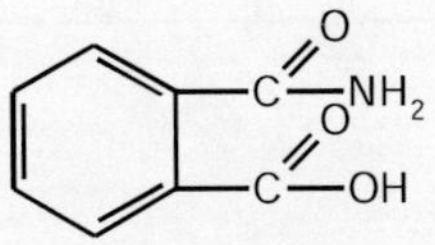

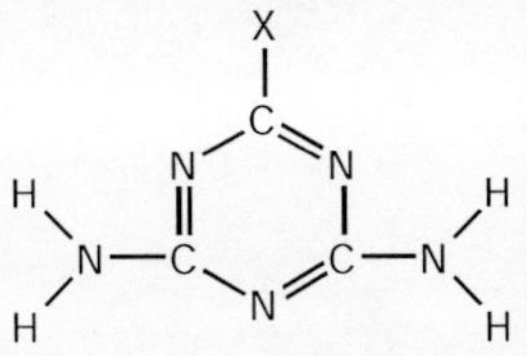

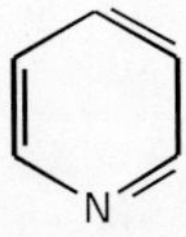

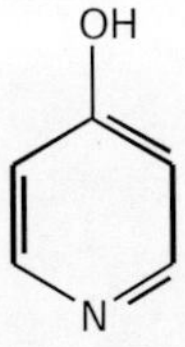

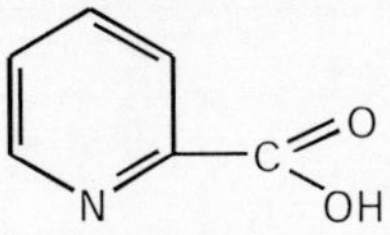

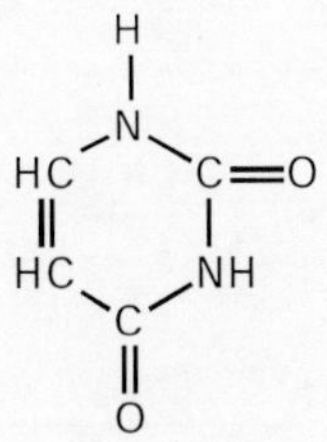

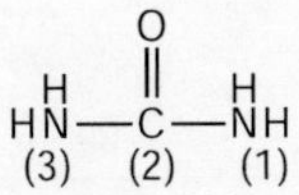

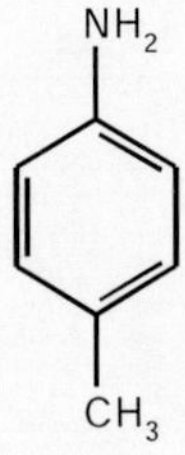

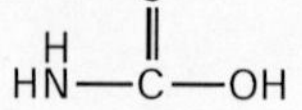

C ‖ HN(H)—C—OH Carbamic acid	O ‖ (phenyl)—N(H)—C—OH Carbanilic acid	C | HN(H)—C—S.H Thiocarbamic acid
S ‖ HN(H)—C—S.H Dithiocarbamic acid	O ‖ CH_3—C—NH_2 Acetamide	O ‖ CH_3—C—N(H)—(phenyl) Anilide
O ‖ CH_2═CH—C—NH_2 Acrylamide		
R (aryl) ¦ $SO_2NHCONH$ ¦ (pyrimidine: N, N; X, Y) Aryl Bridge Heterocycle Sulfonylurea		
—C_4—C_3—C_2—C(═O)OH α β ∝ An aliphatic chain depicting mode of numbring of carbon atoms	H H H H H H H—C—C—C—C—C—C—H H H H H H H n-Hexane (C_6H_{14})	CH_2═CH—CH_2— Allyl
—CH(CH_3)(C≡CH) 1-butynl	—CH(CH_3)(CH_3) Isopropyl	—CH(CH_2)(CH_2) Cyclopropyl

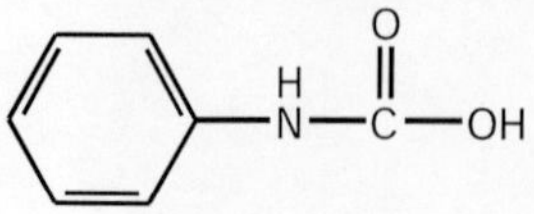

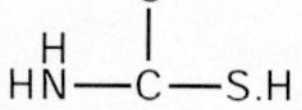

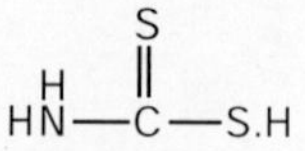

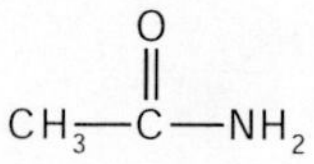

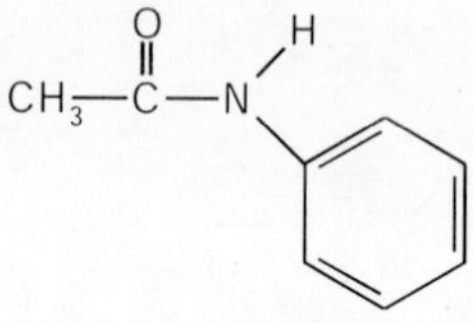

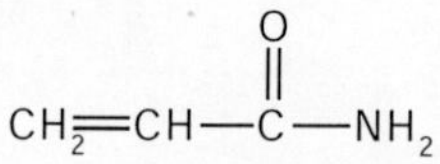

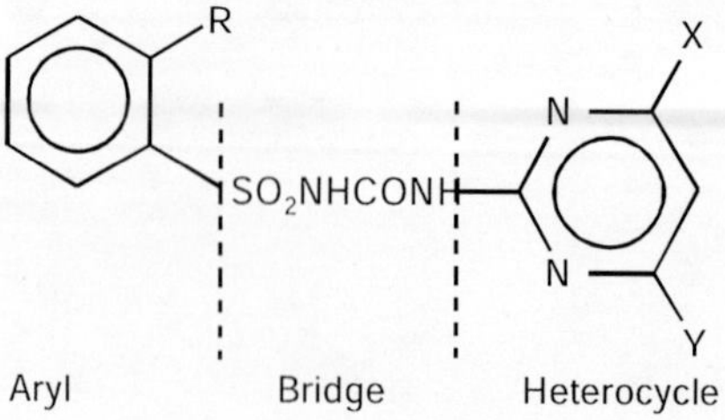

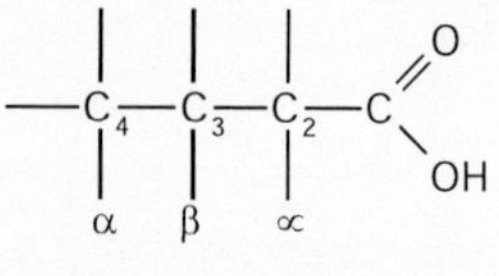

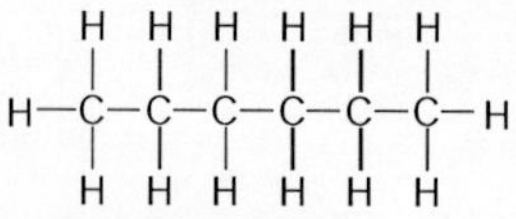

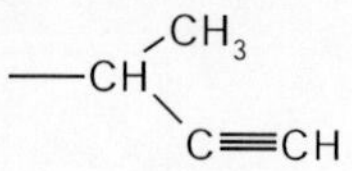

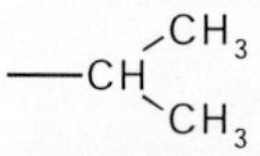

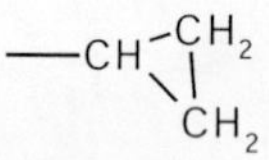

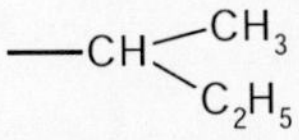

$-CH(CH_3)(C_2H_5)$ Secondary butyl	$-C(CH_3)_3$ Tert. butyl	$CH_2{=}CH{-}C({=}O)OH$ Acrylic acid
$CH_2{=}CH{-}C({=}O)NH_2$ Acrylamide	$CH_3{-}CH_2{-}CH_2{-}CH_2{-}C({=}O)NH_2$ Valeric acid or (Pentanoic acid)	$CH_3{-}CH_2{-}CH_2{-}CH_2{-}C({=}O)NH_2$ Valeramide

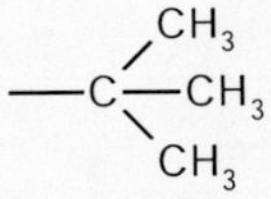

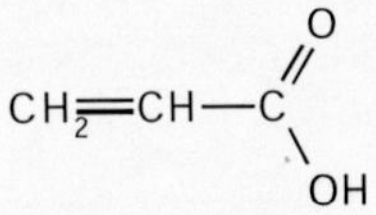

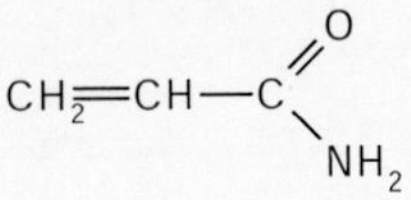

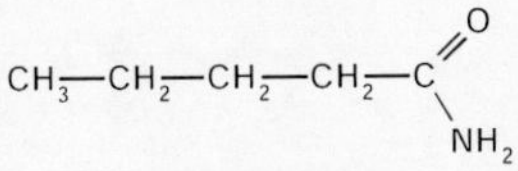

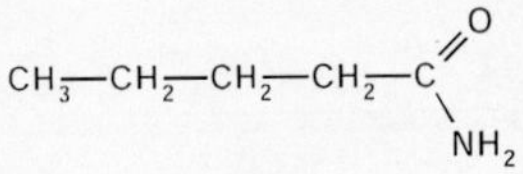

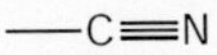

$-C{\equiv}N$ Cyano	$-N{=}N$ (ring with N) Azido	$-N{=}N-$ Diazonium	$O{=}S{=}O$ Sulfonyl

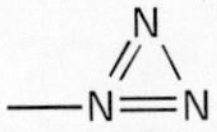

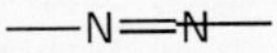

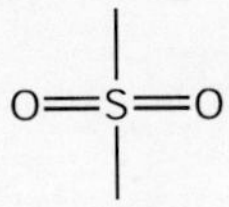

GLOSSARY

Absorption (of herbicide) = Entry of herbicide from treated plant surface into localised zone of that plant organ.

Acceptable Daily Intake (ADI) = It is the daily intake which, during the entire lifetime of human being appears to be without appreciable risk to the health of the consumer on the basis of all known facts at the time of the evaluation of the chemical by the joint FAO/WHO Meeting on Pesticide Residues (or by an appropriate national authority).

Acid = A molecular species having a tendency to lose a proton (to a base).

Acid Equivalent = The theoretical yield of parent acid from an active ingredient.

Active Ingredient = The chemical in a product responsible for the herbicidal effects.

Adjuvant (*additive*) = Chemical capable of improving the herbicidal effect in some way.

Adsorption = Physical gathering of toxicant molecules or ions at specific colloid-water interfaces.

Adsorption Coefficient (equilibrium coefficient) = Relative adsorption capacity of a soil for a given herbicide.

Agricultural Ecotype = An ecotype adapted to certain agricultural practice/s.

Algaecide = Chemical used to destroy algal growth.

Alien Weed = An alien weed species is one that occurs outside its normal distribution, usually a country. It is also called 'exotic weed (*cf* Invasive Alien Weed).

Aliphatic compounds = Organic compounds which have carbon atoms arranged in straight or branched chains *eg* n-butane, butyl alcohol, isopentane, isopropyl alcohol, CDEC, EPTC. CDAA *etc.* The aliphatic compounds also include those cyclic compounds which resemble open chain compounds such as cyclopropane, cyclohexane cycloate, molinate, *etc.*

Allelopathy = Detrimental effects of a plant on the germination, growth, or development of its neighbouring plant through its toxic exudates; usually the root exudates released in the soil.

Annual = A plant that completes its seed to seed life cycle in one year.

Antagonism = Negative action of chemicals used in combination so that the total action is inferior to their independent effects. (*Opp.* synergism).

Anthrophyte = See Alien Weed

Antidote = See safener.

Apophyte = See Facultative Weed

Apoplast = A non-living continuum in plants through intercellular spaces and cell walls.

Arboricide = Chemical used to kill trees. (see also Silivicide).

Aromatic compounds = A class of cyclic organic compounds having a characteristic stability despite having unsaturation. These may have one or more benzene rings (benzenoid) or may not have benizonal ring (non-benzenoid). These compounds emit typical fragnence.

Asexual Reproduction = Growth of detached reproductive cells into new individuals by fission or spore formation.

Band Application = An application to a continuous restricted band along a crop row rather than over the entire area. (*cf*. broadcast application).

Basal Treatment = Herbicide application to the stem of woody plants, at or just above the ground.

Below Detectable Limit (BDL) = Any concentration of a pesticide residing in the matrix that is below the limit of detection of the instrument is reported as a BDL (*cf* LOD).

Bidirectional Translocation = Simultaneous two way mobility of a herbicide (or other solvent) in opposite directions in the phloem tissues of plants.

Biennial = A plant that completes its life cycle in two years. The first year it produces leaves and stores food while, in the second year it produces flowers and seeds.

Bioagent = A living organism employed to control a pest.

Bioassay = Measurement of the potency of and stimulus induced by a chemical (herbicide) by means of reaction which it produces in living matter.

Biocontrol = Pest control with living organisms, like the plant insects, plant pathogens, herbivorous fish, etc.

Bioherbicide = Sprayable bioagent, presently the fungal spores or their extracts, applied like herbicides to kill the existing growth of weed/s.

Biostatic Effect = Reduced microbial decomposition of a pesticide in the presence of some chemical, called extender.

Blind Cultivation = Cultivating before the crop is emerged.

Break Crop = A crop grown in rotation to break continuity of some crop-bound or crop associated weed.

Broadcast Application = An application of a chemical (herbicide) over an entire area.

Brush Control = Control of woody plants.

Carrier = The liquid or solid material added to a chemical compound to facilitate its application.

Catch Crop = A crop employed to stimulate germination and growth of some specific, parasitic weed which is then destroyed before planting the main crop.

Chaining = Bruising of rooted aquatic weeds with a heavy chain in ditches filled with water.

Common Name (of pesticide) = Technically accepted abbreviation of a chemical name (of any pesticide).

Compatibility Agent = Chemical used as aid to keep two or more kinds of toxicant molecules together.

Compatible = compounds or formulations which can be mixed and applied together without undesirably altering their separate effects.

Competition = An action of endeavouring to gain what another endeavours to gain at the same time.

Concentration = The amount of active ingredient or acid equivalent in a given volume of liquid or in a given weight of dry material.

Conjugation = Coupling of herbicide molecules to some plant constituent, with consequent herbicide deactivation.

Contact Herbicide = A herbicide that kills a plant primarily by contact with its tissue rather than as a result of translocation.

Co-solvent = Secondary substance aiding a solvent.

Coupling Agent = Solvent used to solublise parent herbicide compound to form either its soluble concentrate (SC) or emulsifiable concentrate (EC).

Critical Period = The shortest time span in the ontogeny of plant growth when a treatment will result in maximum effect.

Crop Oil = Petroleum oil with 14-25% aromatic content; used for selective weed control.

Crop-Associated Weed = Non-parasitic weed associated with specific crop.

Crop-Bound Weed = See Parasitic Weed.

Cross Resistance = When an individual of a weed biotype is resistant to more than one herbicide, all of which possess a single resistance mechanism, the phenomenon is termed 'cross resistance'. (*cf* Multiple Resistance).

Cuticle = An uneven, lipoidal covering on plant shoot, comprising chiefly cutin lamella impregnated with waxes. Cutin is both lipophilic and hydrophilic.

Cut-Stump Treatment = Application of a brush-killing chemical to freshly cut stump of unwanted tree.

Decomposition = Alteration of the toxicant molecular structure in soil.

Defoliant (or defoliator) = A compound which causes the leaves or foliage to drop from the plant.

Degradation = Alteration of herbicide molecule structure in plant or soil, leading to its inactivation.

Deposit Builder = Chemical that aids the toxicant to stick to the target surface. (same as Sticker and Filming Agent).

Desiccant = A compound that promotes dehydration of plant tissue.

Dicot weed = Weed producing two cotyledon seeds.

Diffusion = Net movement of a substance due to random, kinetic motion of its molecules, atoms, or ions.

Diluent = Any liquid or solid material serving to dilute an active ingredient in the preparation of a formulation.

Dioecious = Plants bearing male and female flowers on separate individuals.

Directed Application = An application to a restricted area, such as a row or bed at the base of the crop plants.

Dispersal (of plants) = Movement of seeds and other plant propagules to short or long distance, away from the mother plant.

Dispersal Agent = Physical source that provides energy for dispersal (of plants).

Dormancy

Dredging = Mechanical pulling of rooted aquatic weeds alongwith their shallow roots and rhizomes, covered in mud.

Early Postemergence = After emergence of the weeds but before crop emergence.

Ecophene = Non-hereditable, morphological adaptation to prevalent environmental stresses.

Ecotype = Hereditable adoption to prevalent environmental stresses.

ED_{50} *(Effective dose 50)* = Dose of a pesticide that would prove lethal to 50% of the population of a test, pest species. (*cf.* LD_{50})

Emulsifying Agent = A surface active material which facilitates the suspension of one liquid in another.

Emulsion = The suspension of one liquid as minute globules in another liquid, *eg.*, oil dispersed in water.

Epinasty = Increased growth on the upper surface of a plant organ or part (especially leaves) causing it to bend downwards.

Extender = See Biostatic Effect.

Facultative Weed = Weed of a wild community origin, escaping sometimes to the crop field.

Fate of Herbicide (in soil) = The dilution of the herbicide in soil by its transfer or decomposition.

First Order Reaction = A reaction in which the rate of loss of chemical is proportional to its concentration in the medium.

Flaming = Killing green plants by momentary exposure to very high temperature from a flame thrower (*cf.* burning, which is setting dry vegetation to fire).

Free Radical = High reactive atom or group of atoms containing an unpaired electron, which would damage any biological system it contacts.

Good Agricultural Practices, In the Use of Pesticides (GAP) = GAP includes the nationally authorised safe uses of pesticides under actual conditions necessary for effective and reliable pest control.

Growth Substance = An organic substance effective in minute amount in modifying specific plant processes.

Half Life = Time needed for half the pesticide to disappear from the scene; usually soil.

Half Reaction = Reaction involving a cation accepting electron to form an atomic species (*eg.* $Cu^{2+} + 2e = Cu$).

Herbaceous plant = A vascular plant that does not develop woody tissue.

Herbicide = A chemical used for killing or inhibiting the growth of plants.

Herbicide Mulch = Loosely woven cloth or other like material, impregnated with herbicide to fit the crop inter-rows for controlling young, germinating weeds there.

Herbicide Resistance = When some biotypes of a normally susceptible weed population remain unhurt even at double, or more than the field recommended doses of the herbicide, the phenomenon is termed 'herbicide resistance'. (*cf* Herbicide Tolerance).

Herbicide Rotation = System of using different kinds of herbicides in recurrent succession on same land.

Herbicide Therapeutics = Herbicide molecules possessing certain plant disease suppression effects.

Herbicide Tolerance = It is the inheritable ability or aptitude of a plant population to survive and reproduce after treatment at the *field recommended doses*. (*cf* Herbicide Resistance).

Humicant (Hygroscopic Agent) = Chemical employed to keep a herbicide moist longer on the leaf surface.

Interference (within plants) = combined effect of competition and allelopathy among plants.

Invasive Alien Weed (IAW) = An invasive alien weed refers to an alien plant species which becomes established in natural or semi-natural ecosystems or habitat; is an agent for change in native flora; and threatens natural biological diversity, *eg Lantana* and *Eichhornia* spp. in India. (*cf* Alien Weed). The IAWs are categorised under 'black lists'.

Invert Emulsion (water-in-oil emulsion) = An emulsion with carrier water globules surrounded by oil, embodying the toxicant in continuous phase.

Laser Herbicide = A herbicide that kills the target plant by way of inducing excessive production of singlet oxygen in its green tissue cells.

LD_{50} (Lethal Dose 50) = Dose of a pesticide that would prove lethal when ingested by a specified **test animal**, usually the rat or rabbit, by 50%. Its unit is mg of pesticide/1000g body weight. Besides this oral LD_{50}, inhalation LD_{50} and Dermal LD_{50} values are also sometimes reported. (*cf*. ED50)

Limit of Determination (LOD) = It is the lowest concentration of a pesticide residue or contaminant that can be identified and quantitatively measured in a specific food, agricultural commodity, or animal feed with an acceptable degree of certainty by a regulatory method of analysis (*cf* BDL).

Lipophilic (hydrophobic) = Molecules or surfaces attracted by oil-like surfaces and molecules but repelled by water.

Lipophobic (hydrophilic) = Molecules or surfaces attracted towards water but repelled by oil- like surfaces or substances.

Maximum Residue Limit (MRL) = MRL is the maximum concentration of a pesticide residue (expressed as mg/kg or ppm), recommended by the Codex Alimentarius Commission (CAC) (or an appropriate national authority) to be legally permitted in or on food commodities and animal feeds.

Microbial Adaptation = It is the build up of relevant microbial population responsible for biodegradation of the herbicide in response to its repeat application at the same site in the soil.

Miscible Liquids = Two or more liquids capable of being mixed and remaining so under normal conditions.

Monocot Weed = Weed producing single cotyledon seeds.

Monoecious = plant bearing male and female flowers on the same individual.

Movement (of herbicide) = Advancement of absorbed herbicide across the thickness of a root or shoot.

Mulch (for weed control) = Any material employed to cut light to the young, germinating weeds.

Multiple Resistance = When an individual plant biotype possess more than one mechanism of resistance to one or more herbicides it is a case of 'multiple resistance'. (*cf* Cross resistance).

Non-Residual herbicide = Herbicide subjected to its inactivation immediately or within a short period of its reaching the soil. (It is active on plants through shoots only).

Non-Selective Herbicide = A herbicide that can be used to kill plants generally with disregard to species.

No-Till Crop = Crop grown without any tillage to prepare seedbed or row weeding, depending grossly on the use of herbicides.

Noxious Weed = A plant arbitrarily defined by law as being especially undesirable, troublesome, and difficult-to-control. The definition of the term will vary according to legal interpretation.

Objectionable Weed = Troublesome weed whose seeds once mixed with crop seeds are extremely difficult to separate.

Obligate Weed = Weed of cropland incapable of surviving in a wild community.

Parasitic Weed = A weed that partially or fully depends for its growth on some nutrients drawn from its host plant.

Particulate Matter = Soil colloids.

Particulating Agent = A kind of spray drift control chemical agent.

Perennial = A plant that lives for more than two years.

Persistence = Ability to withstand extremes of climatic, edaphic, and biotic stresses in nature.

Pest = Organism that competes with man for his food supply, damages his possession, and attacks his person.

Pest Control = A continuous warfare against man's competitors.

Pesticide Residue = Pesticide residue means any specified substances in food, agricultural commodity, animal feed, water, soil or in any other element of environment, resulting from the use of pesticide. The term includes any derivatives of a pesticide, such as conversion products, metabolic products, reaction products, and impurities considered to be of toxicological significance.

Photolysis = Decomposition of toxicant molecule under the influence of light from a surface.

Phytobland oil (crop oil) = Non-phytotoxic oil used to aid herbicide penetration in plant.

Phytotoxic = Poisonous to plant.

Polar molecule = Molecule with clear electropositive and electronegative regions. (*Opp.*, apolar or non-polar).

Postemergence = After emergence of specified weed or crop.

Preemergence = Prior to emergence of specified weed or crop.

Preplanting = Any time before crop is planted.

Rate (or dose) = The amount of active ingredient or acid per unit area.

Redox potential = The tendency of a compound to undergo redox reaction. The redox potential is measured with potentiometer and the unit of reporting is volt (v) or millivolt (mv).

Redox Reaction = Reaction involving transfer of one or more electrons from one chemical (donor) species to another (acceptor).

Reverse metabolism = Molecular change in pesticide within plant, leading to its activation (*eg.* 2,4-DB).

Reverse Xylem Mobility = Movement of herbicide or other solvent from shoot to root through xylem in plant.

Rouging Glove = A hand-glove fitted with mechanism to release some drops of a herbicide each time the wearer grips a plant.

Safener = Substance capable of antagonising specific herbicide phytotoxicity to plant. (also called Antidote).

Satellite Weed = Weed that has become an integral part of a crop ecosystem.

Seed Analysis = Number of weed seeds present per unit weight of initial test seed sample.

Seed Content (purity) = Weed seed admixture in agricultural seeds as percentage by weight of the initial test sample.

Selective Herbicide = A herbicide that will kill some plant species when applied to a mixed population without serious injury to the other species.

Selectivity Index = Ratio of ED_{50} of test crop to ED_{50} of associated weeds.

Sexual Reproduction = Conjugation and fertilization of gametes resulting in spore and seed formation, respectively.

Silvicide = Chemical used to kill tree. (see also Arboricide).

Sink = Final destination of a pesticide in the plant.

Smother Crop (competitive crop) = Crop plants with early vigour and capable of smothering the later weed seedlings.

Soil Application = Application of chemical made primarily to the soil surface rather than to the vegetation.

Soil Fumigant = A soil sterilant acting through its toxic vapours on weeds and other soil life.

Soil Incorporation = Mechanical or otherwise mixing of the herbicide with soil.

Soil Injection = Mechanical placement of herbicide beneath the soil surface with minimum of soil disturbance.

Soil Sterilant = A herbicide that prevents the growth of plant when present in soil. The soil sterilization effects may be temporary or relatively permanent.

Solution = A physically homogenous mixture of solute and the solvent.

Source = The point of entry of pesticide in plant.

Spot Treatment = Application of herbicide to small patches of weeds, leaving the weed-free gaps untreated.

Spray Drift = The movement of airborne spray particles from the intended area of application to non-target area.

Spray Volume = Total quantity of liquid applied as spray per unit area.

Stabiliser = chemical for obtaining stable emulsion and suspension in the spray tank, individually known as emulsifier and dispersant, respectively.

Stale Seed-Bed = A seed-bed left unsown to let a heavy flush of weeds appear and be destroyed with herbicide before seeding the crop, without any further tillage.

State of suspended growth of seed or other plant organ due to internal causes.

Sub-Surface Application (of herbicide) = Application of herbicide in a concentrated band, about 7-10 cm wide, below the soil surface, usually under the future rows of the crop.

Surfactant = A material which facilitates and accentuates the emulsifying, dispersing, spreading, wetting, and other surface modifying properties of herbicide formulation.

Suspension = A system consisting of very finely divided solid particles dispersed in a solid, liquid, or gas medium.

Symplast = The living continuum in plants through interconnecting protoplasm.

Synergism = Cooperative action of different chemicals such that the total effect is greater than the sum of their independent effects. (*Opp.*, antagonism).

Synergist = Substance boosting herbicidal phytotoxicity (also called activator).

Teratogenic = A toxicity effect leading to the production of monstrosities-an abnormally formed growth in animals.

Total Weed Content = Per cent of weed seeds by weight in the test seed sample.

Transfer (of pesticide) = Division of pesticide into parts among different phases of the soil.

Transgenic crop (TCP) = Pest or Pesticide resistant crop varieties produced by genetic engineering technique.

Translocated Herbicide = A herbicide which moves within plant from the point of entry to other plant parts (sinks).

Trap Crop = A crop employed to induce germination of specific parasitic weed without succumbing to it.

Unsaturated Compound = Organic compound containing at least one pair of adjacent carbon atoms linked by a double or multiple bond.

Vapour Drift = The movement of herbicide vapours from the treated surface to non-target area.

Vegetative Reproduction = Growth of specific, detached vegetative organs of plants into new individuals.

VMD (=Volume Mean Diameter) = The droplet diameter in a spray where 50% of the droplets are above and another 50% below this size. VMD is used in the classification of fineness of a spray.

Voilure Coefficient = Ratio of surface area of a seed (or fruit) to its weight.

Volatile = A compound is volatile when it vapourizes at ordinary temperature on exposure to air.

Weed = A plant growing where it is not desired.

Weed and Feed = Mixed application of some herbicide and fertilizer.

Weed Competition index = Gain in crop yield due to weeding as percentage of yield of the weed-free crop.

Weed Content = Percentage of weeds by weight of the initial seed test sample.

Weed Control = The process of limiting weed infestation so that crops could be grown profitably or other operations could be conducted efficiently.

Weed Eradication = The complete elimination of all live plants, plant parts, and seeds of a weed infestation from an area.

Weed Oil = Petroleum oil over 25% aromatic content; used for non-selective weed control.

Weed Population Dynamics = Study of stages in the weed species shifts.

Weed Prevention = Any measure to deny the entry or establishment of new weed in an area.

Weed Wiper = A tool or machine devised to smear herbicide on to weeds.

Wettable Powder = Active ingredient carried on fine, solid particles capable of forming a suspension in a suitable carrier.

Wetting Agent = A compound which when added to a spray solution causes it to contact plant surfaces more thoroughly.

SUBJECT INDEX

-A-

-B-

-C-

-E-

-F-

-G-

-H-

-I-

-J-

-K-

-L-

-M-

-N-

-O-

-Q-

-T-

-U-